The Parliament Buildings, Ottawa, Canada, at the changing of the guard. In the left wing is the House of Commons; in the right wing, the Senate. The central Peace Tower contains a war memorial. Paolo Koch–Photo Researchers, Inc.

Funk & Wagnalls New Encyclopedia

VOLUME 5

BUILDING ACTS to CHAETOGNATHA

LEON L. BRAM
Vice-President and Editorial Director

NORMA H. DICKEY
Editor-in-Chief

Funk & Wagnalls L.P.
Publishers since 1876

Steven G. Weinfeld,
Vice-President, Manufacturing

Volumes are published subsequent
to copyright dates to contain
the latest updated information

ISBN 0-8343-0091-5
Library of Congress Catalog
Card Number 72–170933

MANUFACTURED IN THE UNITED STATES OF AMERICA
PRINTED AND BOUND BY R. R. DONNELLEY & SONS COMPANY

bij 10 9 8 7 6 5 4 3 2 1

Funk & Wagnalls New Encyclopedia is liberally provided with **finding devices** that aid in the search for information. The brief descriptions and suggestions that follow are intended to encourage the proper use of these devices so that full use is made of the information resources within these pages.

The **index** in volume 29 should be the starting point in a search for information. If a search is made *without* the use of the index, the following suggestions should be kept in mind:

- If the search is *unsuccessful,* the index should be used to search again. The topic may be discussed in an article that was overlooked. Only after use of the index can a search be considered thorough or completed.

- If the search is initially *successful,* the index should be used to find additional information. A topic may be discussed in several articles; the index can locate the less-obvious ones.

The use and structure of the index is explained in the Guide to the Index, volume 29, pages 6–8.

Cross-references of several types are used frequently within most articles in Funk & Wagnalls New Encyclopedia. Each cross-reference directs the search for information to other articles that contain additional or related information. The types of cross-references and their specific uses are explained in the Guide to Funk & Wagnalls New Encyclopedia, volume 1, pages 10–13, under the subhead, Cross-references.

Bibliography cross-references follow all the major articles in Funk & Wagnalls New Encyclopedia. They direct the search for further information from the articles to appropriate **reading lists** of books and periodicals in the **bibliography** in volume 28. The reading lists may also be used for independent study. A full description of bibliography cross-references and reading lists is found in the Preface and Guide to the Bibliography, volume 28, pages 186–87.

SELECTED ABBREVIATIONS USED IN TEXT*

AC alternating current
AD *anno Domini* (Lat., "in the year of the Lord")
alt. altitude
AM *ante meridiem* (Lat., "before noon")
AM amplitude modulation
amu atomic mass unit(s)
Arab. Arabic
Arm. Armenian
A.S. Anglo-Saxon
ASSR Autonomous Soviet Socialist Republic
atm. atmosphere
at.no. atomic number
at.wt. atomic weight
b. born
BC before Christ
b.p. boiling point
Btu British Thermal Unit
bu bushel(s)
Bulg. Bulgarian
C Celsius
c. *circa* (Lat., "about")
cent. century
Chin. Chinese
cm centimeter(s)
Co. Company, County
cu cubic
Czech. Czechoslovakian
d. died
Dan. Danish
DC direct current
Du. Dutch
E east; eastern
ed. edited, edition, editors
e.g. *exempli gratia* (Lat., "for example")
Egypt. Egyptian
Eng. English
est. established; estimated
et al. *et alii* (Lat., "and others")
EV electron volt(s)
F Fahrenheit
Finn. Finnish
fl. flourished
FM frequency modulation
Fr. French
ft foot, feet
g gram(s)
gal gallon(s)
Ger. German
GeV billion electron volts
Gr. Greek
ha hectare(s)
Heb. Hebrew
hp horsepower
hr hour
Hung. Hungarian
Hz hertz or cycle(s) per second
Icel. Icelandic
i.e. *id est* (Lat., "that is")
in inch(es)
inc. incorporated
Ital. Italian
Jap. Japanese
K Kelvin
kg kilogram(s)
km kilometer(s)
kw kilowatt(s)
kwh kilowatt hour(s)
Lat. Latin
lat latitude
lb pound(s)
long longitude
m meter(s)
mass no. mass number
MeV million electron volts
mg milligram(s)
mi mile(s)
min minute(s)
ml milliliter(s)
mm millimeter(s)
m.p. melting point
mph miles per hour
Mt(s). Mount, Mountain(s)
N north; northern
Nor. Norwegian
O.E. Old English
O.Fr. Old French
O.H.G. Old High German
O.N. Old Norse
Op. *Opus* (Lat., "work")
oz ounce(s)
Pers. Persian
PM *post meridiem* (Lat., "after noon")
Pol. Polish
pop. population
Port. Portuguese
q.v. *quod vide* (Lat., "which see")
r. reigned
R. River
repr. reprinted
rev. revised
Rom. Romanian
Rus. Russian
S south; southern
sec. second(s); secant
SFSR Soviet Federated Socialist Republic
Skt. Sanskrit
Span. Spanish
sp.gr. specific gravity
sq square
sq km square kilometer(s)
sq mi square mile(s)
SSR Soviet Socialist Republic
St. Saint, Street
Sum. Sumerian
Swed. Swedish
trans. translated, translation, translator(s)
Turk. Turkish
Ukr. Ukrainian
UN United Nations
U.S. United States
USSR Union of Soviet Socialist Republics
v. versus; verse
Ved. Vedic
vol. Volume(s)
W west; western
yd yard(s)

* For a more extensive listing, see ABBREVIATIONS AND ACRONYMS. Charts of pertinent abbreviations also accompany the articles DEGREE, ACADEMIC; ELEMENTS, CHEMICAL; MATHEMATICAL SYMBOLS; and WEIGHTS AND MEASURES.

FUNK & WAGNALLS NEW ENCYCLOPEDIA

BUILDING ACTS, also building codes, municipal and state laws regulating the construction of buildings and prescribing minimum requirements for fire protection, sanitation, and safety. Such laws are intended primarily to set standards for new construction but also to prevent the continued use of buildings deficient in these respects. These laws, often attacked as confiscatory, have been held by the courts to be within the police power (q.v.) of the state.

Various American colonies enacted building laws to prevent the spread of fires as early as the 17th century. No general action was taken, however, until late in the 19th century, when numerous conflagrations, notably the Chicago fire of 1871, led to a more general adoption of requirements for fire-retarding and fireproof construction. Improved standards for multiple dwellings were drafted at the beginning of the present century, with the enactment of tenement housing laws, first by New York and later by other states. About the same time, associations of fire insurance underwriters formulated building codes, and although these had no force as law, compliance was obtained by setting prohibitive insurance rates on buildings of unsatisfactory construction. These codes served as guides in the enactment of local building laws, which now contain most of their important provisions. The trend toward unification of such building codes has increased, leading to the development of regional codes, which serve groups of municipalities, and state building codes, which have been established throughout the U.S.

Manufacturers of building materials have recently been experimenting with their products to allow for relatively rapid and inexpensive construction. In 1968 New York City passed legislation permitting building with prestressed concrete, structured plywood, and reinforced brick, but most other communities retain laws requiring the use of traditional materials only.

As distinct from zoning laws, which regulate the location, use, and size of various types of buildings (*see* CITY PLANNING), modern building laws set standards for planning and layout and for providing adequate passages and exits, daylight, and ventilation; establish requirements for construction and materials, ensuring proper strength of materials and safety; and set standards for such equipment as elevators, fire escapes, and plumbing, heating, and electrical installations. Many of these building laws are of the specification type; that is, they establish exact specifications for all materials and methods of construction. A newer type, known as a performance code, allows for the continuing presentation of improved materials and techniques to a board of building standards. Such a code has been used to some extent in Cleveland, Ohio, and in New York City. J.L.W.

BUILDING CONSTRUCTION, procedures involved in the erection of various types of structures. The major trend in present-day construction continues away from handcrafting at the building site and toward on-site assembly of ever larger, more integrated subassemblies manufactured away from the site. Another characteristic of contemporary building, related to the latter trend, is the greater amount of dimensional coordination; that is, buildings are designed and components manufactured in multiples of a standard module (10 cm/4 in being standard in the U.S.), which drastically reduces the amount of cutting and fitting required on the building site. A third trend is the production or redevelopment of such large structural complexes as shopping centers, entire campuses, and whole towns or sections of cities.

Construction Industry. Building construction in the U.S. is the product of a diverse group of subindustries, with many individuals and organizations involved in the construction of a single structure, from the manufacture of necessary components to final assembly. As a general rule, except for buildings that are built and occupied by the owner and that do not involve public use or occupancy, state laws require a registered architect or engineer, or both, to execute the design and to make sure that the design complies with public health, zoning, and building-code requirements. The design must at the same time conform to the requirements of the owner. The architect or engineer converts these requirements into a set of drawings and written specifications that usually are sent to interested general contractors for bids. The successful bidder or bidders in turn subcontract plumbing, painting, electrical wiring, structural frame construction and erection, and other jobs to firms specializing in these crafts.

Contractors ordinarily carry out their work under the supervision of the architect, who acts as agent of the owner. State and local inspectors ensure that the work is accomplished according to the standards of the local building code. The immediate responsibility of the contractor and architect ends when the local authorities approve the building for occupancy and the owner accepts the building. However, the contractor and architect are usually legally responsible for any defects or deficiencies in the construction for a period of a year or more after acceptance, the time depending on the terms of the contract and on local requirements.

ELEMENTS OF A BUILDING

The major elements of a building include the following: (1) the foundation, which supports the building and provides stability; (2) the structure, which supports all the imposed loads and transmits them to the foundation; (3) the exterior walls, which may or may not be part of the primary supporting structure; (4) the interior partitions, which also may or may not be part of the primary structure; (5) the environmental-control systems, including the heating, ventilating, air-conditioning, lighting, and acoustical systems; (6) the vertical transportation systems, including elevators, escalators, and stairways; (7) communications, which may include such subsystems as intercommunications, public address, and closed-circuit television, as well as the more usual telephone-wiring systems; and (8) the power, water supply, and waste disposal systems.

Building Loads. The loads imposed on a building are classified as either dead (static) or live (dynamic). Dead loads include the weight of the building itself and all the major items of fixed equipment. Dead loads always act directly downward, act constantly, and are additive from the top of the building down. Live loads include wind pressure, earth motion, vibrations caused by machinery, movable furniture, stored goods and equipment, occupants, and stresses caused by temperature changes. Live loads are temporary and produce pulsing, vibratory, impact, or distorting stresses.

In general, the design of a building must accommodate all possible dead and live loads to prevent the building from settling or collapsing and to prevent any permanent distortion, excessive motion, or rupture at any point.

Foundations. The structural design of a building depends greatly on the nature of the soil and underlying geologic conditions and modification by man of either of these factors.

Ground conditions. If a building is to be constructed in an area that has a history of earthquake activity, the earth must be investigated to a considerable depth. Faults in the crust of the earth beneath the soil must obviously be avoided. Some soils, under vibratory motion, may liquefy and become much like quicksand; in such a case construction must either be avoided or the foundation made deep enough to reach solid material below the unstable soil. Certain clay soils have been found to expand 23 cm (9 in) or more if subjected to long cycles of drying and wetting, producing powerful forces that can lift light buildings and shear foundations. Some soils have a high organic content and may, over a period of time, decrease in volume through decay, allowing the structure above to settle. Other soils have a tendency to slide under loads.

Soils that have been modified in some way often perform differently, especially when fill has been added or mixed with existing soil, or the soil has been made wetter or drier than normal, or chemicals such as lime have been added. Sometimes the soil under a proposed building varies so greatly in characteristics over the entire site that a building simply cannot be constructed safely or economically.

Soil and geologic analyses are necessary, therefore, to determine whether a proposed building can be supported adequately and what would be the most effective and economical method of support.

If sound bedrock is below the construction site, the area over which the building loads must be distributed may be quite small because of the strength of the rock. As progressively weaker soils are encountered, the area over which the loads are to be distributed must be increased.

Types of foundations. The most common types of foundations include spread footings, piles, caissons, and rafts (Fig. 1). The foundation chosen for any particular building depends on the

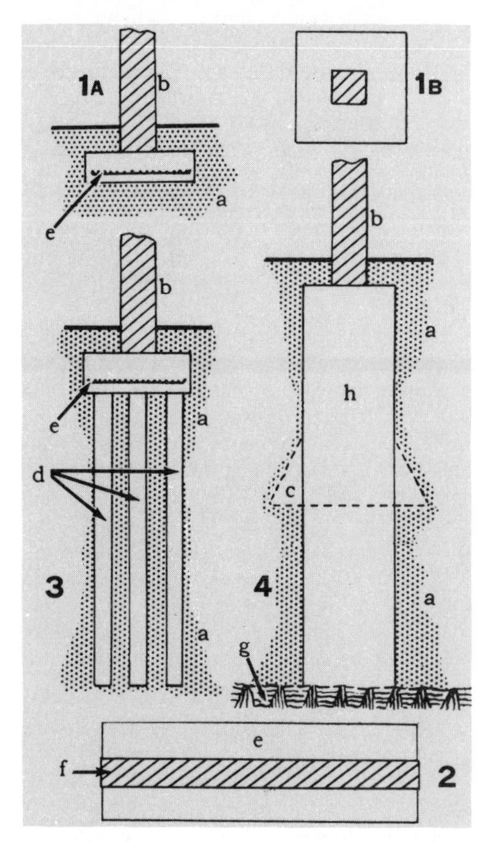

Fig. 1
Various types of foundations used in building construction. (1) Spread footing under structural column. (1A) Side view of soil (a); column (b); and reinforced concrete footing (e). (1B) Top view. (2) Continuous spread footing under wall: top view of reinforced-concrete slab (e) with wall (f) at its center. (3) Pile foundation: soil (a); structural column (b); piles (d); reinforced-concrete cap (e). (4) Caisson foundation: soil (a); structural column (b); cone-shaped shaft when bearing level is not at bedrock (c); bedrock (g); concrete shaft (h).

strength of the soil, the magnitude of the structural loads, and the depth of the groundwater level.

The most economical foundation is the spread reinforced-concrete footing, which is used for moderate-sized buildings in areas where the surface conditions present no unusual difficulties. The foundation consists of concrete slabs placed under each structural column or a continuous slab under the load-bearing walls.

Piles are used primarily in areas where soil conditions are poor. They are made of timber, concrete, or steel, and are placed in clusters. The piles are driven to a predetermined depth, and each cluster is then covered by a cap of reinforced concrete. A pile may support its load either at the lower end or by skin friction along its entire length. The number of piles in each cluster is determined by the average load-carrying capacity of each pile in the cluster.

Timber piles are usually cut off and capped with concrete at the groundwater level to prevent decay, as most kinds of timber deteriorate quickly when exposed to dampness and air unless chemically treated. A timber pile is simply the trunk of a tree stripped of its branches and is thus limited in height. A concrete pile, on the other hand, may be of any reasonable length and may extend below groundwater level as well. For extremely heavy or tall buildings, steel piles, known as H-piles because of their shape, are used. H-piles are driven through to bedrock, often as far as 30 m (100 ft) below the surface. H-piles can be driven to great depths more easily than piles made of wood or concrete; although they are more expensive, the cost is usually justified for large buildings, which represent a substantial financial investment.

Caisson foundations are used when soil of adequate bearing strength is found below surface layers of weak materials such as fill or peat. A caisson foundation consists of concrete shafts placed in excavation wells under the projected structural columns. The caisson foundation is excavated within a series of concentric shells, the diameters of which decrease with increasing depth. The concrete shafts carry the building loads at their lower ends, which are often cone or bell shaped.

Raft foundations are used whenever the building loads are so extensive and the soil so weak that individual footings would cover more than half of the building area. A raft is a flat concrete slab heavily reinforced with steel, which carries as a unit the downward loads of the individual columns or walls. The raft load per unit area that is transmitted to the underlying soil is small in magnitude and is distributed over the entire area. For very large rafts supporting heavy buildings, the loads are distributed more evenly by using supplementary foundations and cross walls, which stiffen the raft.

Groundwater level. Foundation problems are complicated by groundwater flowing above the bottom of the proposed foundation. In such cases the sides of the excavation may be undermined and may cave in. Lowering the groundwater level by pumping the water out of the excavation usually requires the installation of braced sheathing to retain the sides of the excavation. When the amount of water within the excavation is excessive, ordinary pumping methods, which bring to the surface loose soil mixed

Precast in a horizontal position, concrete wall panels are hoisted upright during construction.

Portland Cement Assn.

with the water, can undermine the foundations of buildings on adjoining property. To prevent damage caused by soil resettlement, dewatering is often used. Small pipes that have a perforated screen on one end are driven into the ground. The screens prevent soil from flowing in with the water. The pipes are connected to a common manifold, which is in turn connected to a water pump. In this way the groundwater is removed from below the excavation without damage to the surrounding property. Dewatering may also eliminate the necessity for sheathing the sides of the excavation, unless the soil may slide because of its composition or because of vibrations caused by nearby heavy traffic or machinery.

Structure. The basic elements of any ordinary structure are the floors and roof (including horizontal supporting members), columns and walls (vertical members), and bracing (diagonal members) or rigid connections used to give the structure stability.

One- to three-story buildings. With low buildings the variety of possible shapes is much greater than with taller buildings. In addition to the familiar box shape, which is also used in very tall buildings, low buildings may use cathedral-like forms, vaults, or domes. A simple single-story structure might consist of a reinforced-concrete slab laid directly on the ground, exterior masonry walls supported by the slab (or by a spread footing cast continuously around the perimeter of the building), and a roof. For low buildings, the use of interior columns between masonry load-bearing walls is still the most common construction method. Spaced columns supported by the slab or by individual spread footings may be used, however; in that case the exterior walls can be supported by or hung between the columns. If the roof span is short, abutting planking made of wood, steel, concrete, or other material can be used to form the roof structure.

Each structural material has a particular weight-to-strength ratio, cost, and durability. As a general rule, the greater the roof span, the more complicated the structure supporting the roof becomes and the narrower the range of suitable materials. Depending on the length of the span, the roof may have one-way framing (beams, Fig. 2a and 2b) or two-way framing (beams supported on larger girders spanning the longest dimension). Trusses can be substituted for either method. Trusses, which can be less than 30 cm (12 in) or more than 9 m (30 ft) deep, are formed by assembling tension and compression members in various triangular patterns. They are usually made of timber or steel, but reinforced concrete, aluminum, or even reinforced plastic may be used.

Sections of stainless steel 4.6 sq m (48 sq ft) in size are used to sheathe entire skyscrapers. The panels can be positioned by three workers in 1.5 min.

Stainless Steel News Bureau

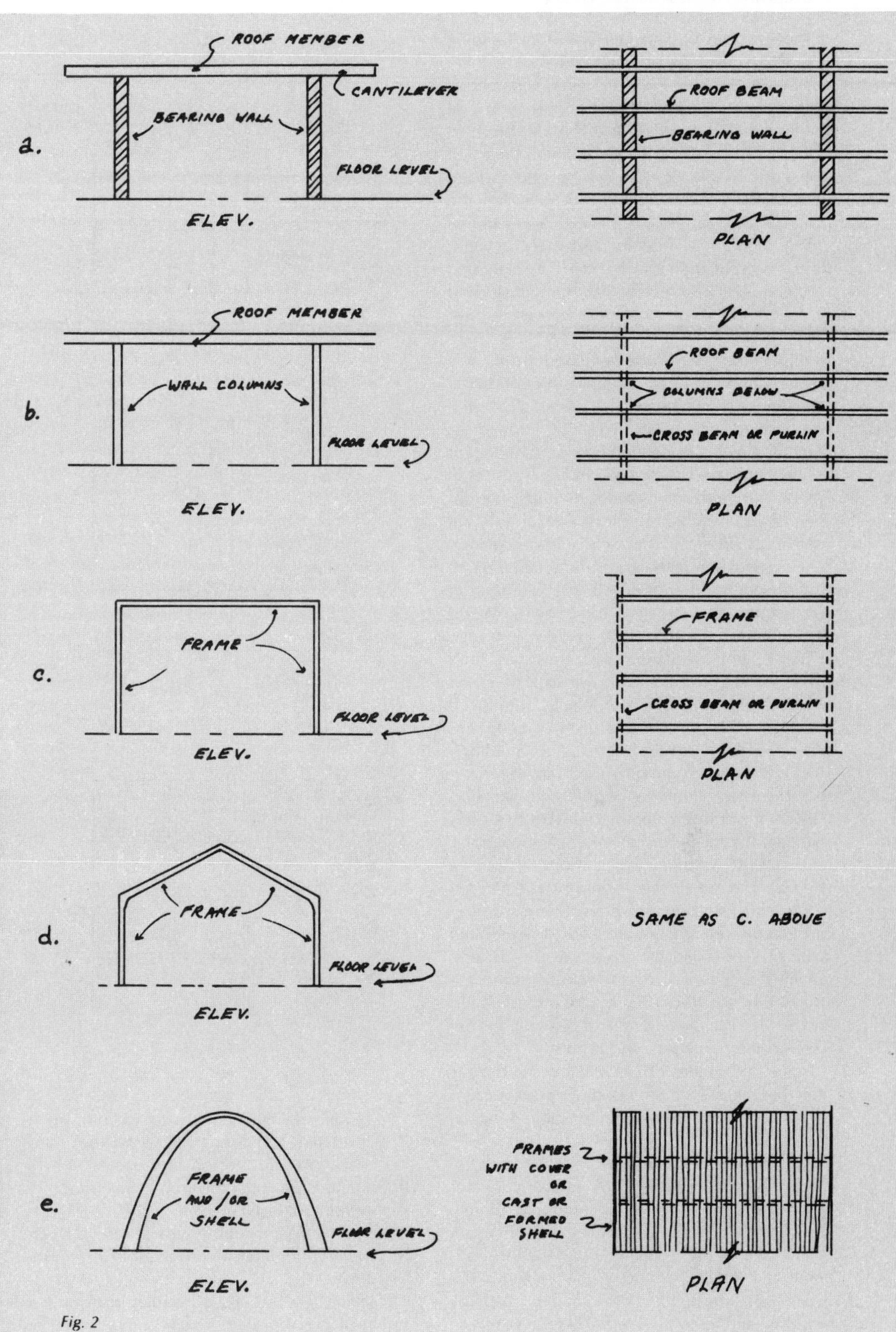
a.
ROOF MEMBER
CANTILEVER
BEARING WALL
FLOOR LEVEL
ELEV.
ROOF BEAM
BEARING WALL
PLAN
b.
ROOF MEMBER
WALL COLUMNS
FLOOR LEVEL
ELEV.
ROOF BEAM
COLUMNS BELOW
CROSS BEAM OR PURLIN
PLAN
c.
FRAME
FLOOR LEVEL
ELEV.
FRAME
CROSS BEAM OR PURLIN
PLAN
d.
FRAME
FLOOR LEVEL
ELEV.
SAME AS C. ABOVE
e.
FRAME AND / OR SHELL
FLOOR LEVEL
ELEV.
FRAMES WITH COVER OR CAST OR FORMED SHELL
PLAN

Fig. 2

The structure of a simple one-story building may also consist of the wall and roof framing combined by being either fastened together or shaped in one piece. The possible structural shapes are almost infinite and include the three sides of a rectangle fastened together into a unit called a bent (Fig. 2c), the familiar church form of vertical sides and sloping roof (Fig. 2d), the parabola (Fig. 2e), and the semicircle or dome.

The supporting structure and exterior walls, floor, and roof may also be made as a unified whole, much like a rectangular pipe with closed or open ends. These forms may be cast in reinforced plastic.

Multibay and Multistory buildings. By far the most common form of building structure is the skeleton frame, which consists essentially of the vertical members shown in Fig. 2a, 2b, and 2c, combined with a horizontal framing pattern. For tall buildings, the use of load-bearing walls (as in Fig. 2a) with horizontal framing members has declined steadily; nonload-bearing curtain walls are used most often. In the early 1960s, however, new construction techniques using load-bearing wall masonry were introduced and were used in construction of such tall buildings as the World Trade Center (411 m/1350 ft) in New York City.

The skeleton frame most often consists of multiples of the construction shown in Fig. 2c. For structures up to 20 stories in height, reinforced concrete, steel, or composite-reinforced concrete and steel are used. For higher buildings, steel is the most commonly used framing material. The basic elements of the steel skeleton frame are vertical columns, horizontal girders spanning the longer distance between columns, and beams spanning the shorter distance (Fig. 3a). The skeleton frame must be reinforced to prevent distortion and possible collapse because of uneven or vibratory loads. The required stability is provided by connecting the beams, columns, and girders; by the support given the structure by the floors and by the interior walls; and by diagonal bracing or rigid connections between columns, girders, and beams.

Newer techniques of constructing moderately high buildings include inserting prefabricated units within the skeleton frame; cable hanging; and stacking.

For the insertion technique, a stable skeleton frame may be constructed with a utility core that includes fire stairs, elevators, plumbing, piping, and wiring. Prefabricated boxlike units then can be inserted in the openings between the horizontal and vertical framing. Major changes in the future use of the building could then be made by removing and replacing the boxlike units.

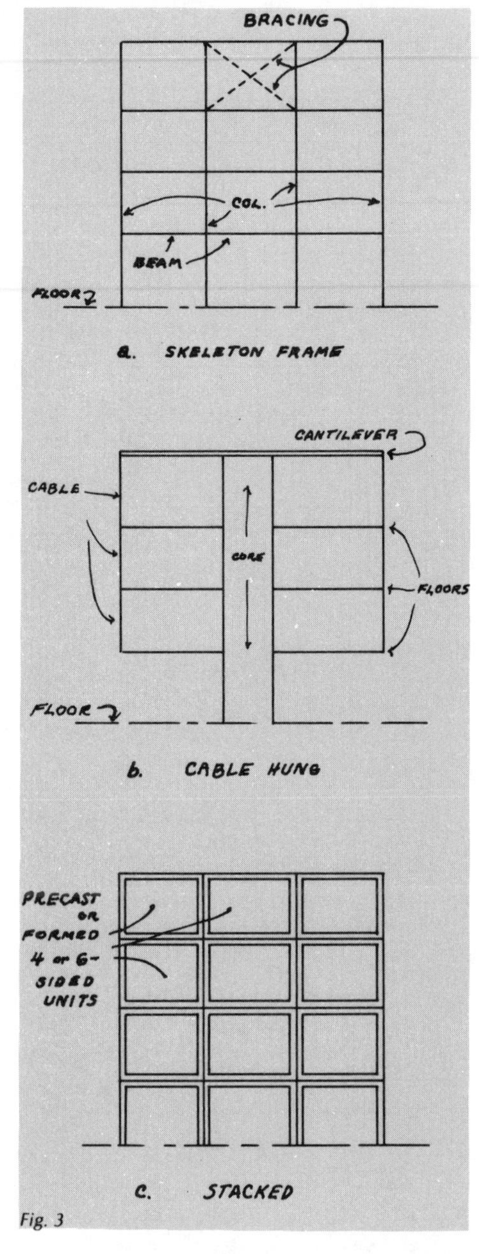

Fig. 3

In cable hanging (Fig. 3b), a vertical utility core is constructed, and strong horizontal roof framing is anchored to the top of the core. All the floors below, except at the ground level, are then supported by attaching them to the core and to cables hung from the roof framing. After the core is completed the floors are constructed from the top down.

Stacking (Fig. 3c) is a construction technique in which prefabricated, boxlike units are raised

View of construction of an elementary school shows extensive use of precast structural members.

by cranes and placed on top of and alongside each other and then are fastened together.

The "lift-slab" construction technique has been used to a limited extent for a number of years. In this procedure, concrete floors are cast one on top of the other at ground level on a hydraulic jack over a supporting structure. After the floors have cured they are jacked, or lifted, one at a time into the air and connected to previously erected columns; or supports are placed under each successive floor and the next lower floor is built. Both floors are then jacked up to make room for the next lower floor, and so on, until the entire structure has been completed. The advantages of this technique are that all the heavy construction labor is accomplished at or near ground level and, as the floors are completed, electricians, painters, plumbers, and other craftsmen can complete the interior with greater convenience and at less expense. By the time the last floor has been raised, the building is almost ready for occupancy.

Exterior Walls and Roof. The curtain wall, the most common type of nonload-bearing wall, may be assembled either on or off the site. It consists of an exterior skin backed with insulation; a vapor barrier; sound-deadening materials; and an interior skin that may be part of the curtain wall or may be attached separately. The exterior skin may be made of metal (stainless steel, aluminum, bronze), masonry (concrete, brick, tile), glass, or reinforced plastics.

The traditional method of constructing a roof is to lay down, over a steel or concrete deck spanning the framing members, rolls of roofing felt laminated with tar and topped with gravel. Synthetic materials are also being used increasingly in place of felt and tar. New grasslike and ruglike materials made of plastic enable recreation areas to be built on top of roofs at little expense.

Interior Partitions. Traditional methods of partitioning a building interior include the use of masonry walls 10 to 15 cm (4 to 6 in) thick made of concrete, gypsum, or pumice block, painted or plastered; or wood or metal frames covered with lath over which plaster is spread. Plasterboard and wallboard are increasingly used.

To provide for greater flexibility within buildings, movable or easily disassembled partitioning systems are used, the only restriction to their placement being the spacing of the interior columns. Such partitions may be metal, prefabricated plasterboard components, accordionlike rolling curtains, or, if sound transmission is a problem, leaded curtains that move either horizontally or vertically. Lightweight materials usually mean an increase in transmitted sound and a loss of privacy. Nevertheless, the trend is toward lighter partitions and increased use of sound-absorbing materials. In many buildings, the only walls still made of masonry are fire walls, which enclose elevator shafts, stairs, and main corridors.

Environmental Control. Perhaps the greatest improvements in building construction have been in the control of light, heat, sound, and ventilation. In most large buildings, complete, year-round air conditioning is now standard. Buildings may be partially cooled and partially heated even in summer, depending on the distance from exterior walls and on the heat radiated from people, lighting fixtures, and office equipment. The level and quality of lighting have improved greatly. Largely as a consequence of these changes, the cost of the mechanical and electrical systems in buildings is increasing at a greater rate than overall building costs; in the late 1960s it amounted to more than one-third of all construction costs. The environmental controls of many buildings constructed since the early 1970s are monitored and actuated by computers in order to minimize power costs.

Communications and Power Systems. The growing use of closed-circuit television and computer systems, in addition to conventional telephone, telegraph, and intercommunication systems, has increased the amount of wiring that must be installed in buildings. Main cables are generally carried in the utility core or along columns, and power is distributed to each of the stories through conduits embedded in reinforced-concrete floors.

The power required in buildings has increased with the use of more complicated environmental control and communications systems. Emergency power generators are being installed in an increasing number of buildings to ensure continuity of service in the event of a public utility power failure. Some buildings, particularly in remote locations, now install their own primary electrical generating systems, using diesel and gas-turbine generators.

Vertical Transportation. Elevators, especially high-speed, automatically controlled, cable-operated elevators, are the major form of vertical transportation in high-rise structures (*see* ELEVATOR). Low-rise buildings and the lower floors of commercial buildings may also have escalators. For fire protection, it is necessary to provide at least two means of egress from every major space in a building. Therefore, in addition to elevators and escalators, all buildings, even the tallest, have two enclosed and protected stairways for their entire height.

Water Supply and Waste Disposal. Buildings must have a piped-in water supply for a variety of purposes: for drinking, washing, and sanitary waste removal; for internal firefighting standpipes; and for the service of air-cleaning equipment, boilers, and heat exchangers.

Disposal of wet and dry wastes in buildings is accomplished by a variety of means, including incinerators, garbage grinders, shredders, compressors, and other devices to alleviate waste-pickup and -disposal problems. The usual method of carrying away waterborne waste is the use of piping systems; however, efforts are being made to use water-recycling systems to reduce waste and pollution.

See also CONCRETE; HOUSE.

For further information on this topic, see the Bibliography in volume 28, sections 638–41, 661, 679.

BUILDING AND LOAN ASSOCIATIONS. *See* SAVINGS INSTITUTIONS.

BUITENZORG. *See* BOGOR.

BUJUMBURA, formerly USUMBURA, city, capital of Burundi and of Bujumbura Province, W Burundi, at the NE end of Lake Tanganyika. Bujumbura is a trade center, with ferry service to Kigoma-Ujiji, Tanzania; from the latter city goods are shipped by rail to Dar es-Salaam. Bujumbura is in a cotton-growing region; in addition to cotton products, handicrafts, fishing equipment, hides, beer, cement, and pharmaceuticals are produced here. Lake fishing is an important occupation, and the city has fish- and coffee-processing plants. It is the seat of the University of Burundi (1960).

The settlement was visited by David Livingstone and Henry Morton Stanley in 1871. It was an important army camp in German East Africa. In 1923 the city became the capital of the Belgian mandate (after 1946 the trust territory) of Ruanda-Urundi. It became the capital of Burundi in 1962, and the name of the city was changed from Usumbura to Bujumbura. Pop. (1986) 272,600.

BUKA. *See* SOLOMON ISLANDS.

BUKAVU, city, E Zaire, capital of Kivu Region, on the SW shore of Lake Kivu. A trade and communications center for an area producing coffee, citrus fruits, and vegetables, the city has industries producing pharmaceuticals and insecticides, breweries, and food-processing and printing plants. The city is the site of two junior colleges and serves as a base for tourists to the lake districts and nearby national parks. Called Costermanville under Belgian rule, Bukavu succeeded Rutshuru as province capital in the 1920s and became a center of European settlement before independence. Pop. (est.) 209,100.

BUKHARA, also Bokhara, city, capital of Bukhara Oblast, Uzbek SSR, in S Central Asian USSR, located in an oasis on the Zeravshan R. Situated in a region producing natural gas, cotton, fruit, and silk, the city has industries manufacturing textiles, processed karakul pelts, carpets, and clothing. Among Bukhara's many architectural monuments, some dating from the 9th century, are several mosques, the Ark Fortress (now a museum), and the mausoleum of Ismail Samani (9th–10th cent.). A teachers college is here.

Founded by the 1st century AD, Bukhara was an important trade and cultural center when it was captured (early 8th cent.) by the Arabs. It was a leading center of Islamic learning under the Arabs and the Persian Samanid dynasty, which held the city in the 9th and 10th centuries. It later was captured successively by the Qarakhanids and Tatars, and in 1555 it became the capital of an Uzbek emirate. The emirate was conquered in 1866 by Russia, which held it as a protectorate from 1868 to 1920; then the emir was removed and the city made the capital of the Bukhara People's Soviet Republic. In 1924 the republic was dissolved, and the city incorporated into the Uzbek SSR. Pop. (1983 est.) 200,000.

BUKHARI, al-, full name MUHAMMAD IBN-ISMAIL AL-BUKHARI (810–70), Arab scholar, born in Bukhara (now in Uzbek SSR). As a youth he began traveling throughout the Muslim world collecting the oral traditions of the prophet Muhammad. Of the more than 600,000 traditions he collected, he compiled 7275 of them in *al-Sahih* (The Genuine). *Al-Sahih* is regarded by orthodox Muslims, the Sunnites, as being surpassed in importance only by the Koran. Following a theological dispute, al-Bukhari was banished to Kartank, near Samarkand (now in Uzbek SSR), where he died. His tomb has been the destination of many pilgrimages.

BUKHARIN, Nikolay Ivanovich (1888–1938), Russian Communist leader, born in Moscow, and educated at the University of Moscow. As a youth he participated in revolutionary activities against the czarist government and was soon identified as a Bolshevik. He was frequently imprisoned, and in 1911 he was exiled. By 1916 he was in New York City, where he edited *Novy Mir* (New World), a radical newspaper. After the Russian Revolution began in March 1917, he returned to Moscow; he was elected to an influential Bolshevik committee, was editor (1917–29) of the official Communist party newspaper *Pravda* (Truth), and was a member (1924–29) of the Politburo. During the struggle for control of the party, he allied himself with Joseph Stalin against Leon Trotsky, Grigory Zinovyev (1883–1936), and Lev Kamenev (1883–1936); in 1926 he replaced Zinovyev as head of the Third International. Three years later, having fallen out of favor with Stalin, he was stripped of all his positions. He briefly regained some of his prestige when he became editor of *Izvestia* (News), the official government newspaper, in 1934. Arrested on charges of Trotskyist activities in 1937, he was convicted during one of the Stalin purge trials. In February 1988, fifty years after Bukharin's execution as a traitor, the verdict was reversed and his name cleared by the Soviet supreme court.

BUKOVINA, former province of Romania, adjoining Bessarabia, in the foothills of the eastern Carpathian Mountains. A part of the principality of Moldavia, Bukovina was ruled by the Ottoman Turks until 1769, when it was occupied by Russia. Taken by Austria in 1775, Bukovina formed part of Galicia until 1849, and was then made a separate crown land, or province. When the Austro-Hungarian Empire was dissolved at the end of World War I, Bukovina became independent and joined Romania as a province. During World War II, Bukovina and Bessarabia were ceded to the Soviet Union (1940), in compliance with a Soviet ultimatum, but were occupied by German and Romanian forces from 1941 to 1944. By the terms of an armistice signed in September 1944, northern Bukovina and Bessarabia became part of the Soviet Union and southern Bukovina remained in Romania. Area of the former province: 10,440 sq km (4031 sq mi). *See also* CHERNOVTSY.

BULAWAYO, city, SW Zimbabwe, on the Matsheumlope R., at an elevation of about 1340 m (about 4400 ft). It is the second largest city of Zimbabwe and a major industrial center; it is also a vital national distribution point and railroad junction. Industries include printing and publishing, brewing, and the manufacture of clothing, tires, radios, metal products, and construction materials. The city is also the processing center for produce of the ranches and farms of its hinterland. Located here are Bulawayo Technical College (1927) and the National Museum (1901), with exhibits of wildlife and geology. Nearby are Government House, built by the British statesman Cecil John Rhodes, and the African ruins of Khami (17th–18th cent.). The community was founded in 1893 after the defeat of the Ndebele king Lobengula, on the site of his village, Gubulawayo. It was moved S to its present site in 1894. A railroad was constructed to the town in 1897. Pop. (1982) 413,800.

BULB, mass of overlapping leaves on a short stem, enclosing, protecting, and serving as a source of food for at least one bud that may develop into a new plant. The bulb, usually developed underground, has roots growing down from the stem. The truncated bulb, as in the onion, has tightly overlapping leaves; the scaly bulb, as in garlic, is looser. In common usage the term *bulb* also refers to bulblike stems, such as the corm of the crocus or the tuber of the dahlia, and even to rhizomes, masses of roots, and some underground stems.

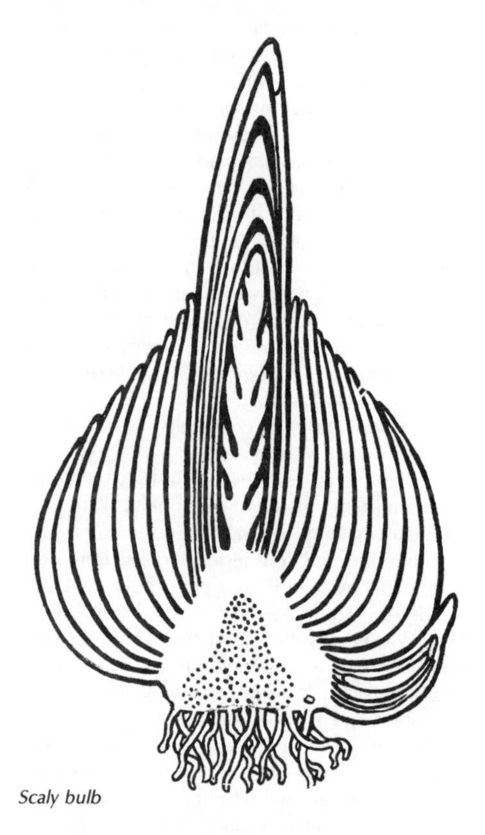

Scaly bulb

BULBUL, songbird, probably a Persian nightingale, that is often mentioned in poetry, and more than 100 species of singing birds of the family Pycnonotidae native to Africa, and southern Asia. They are small, gregarious, arboreal birds, often of brilliant blue and green plumage. They feed on fruit, berries, and insects. In the Orient, the crested males are often caged.

BULFINCH, Charles (1763–1844), American architect, who worked in the Federal style. Born in Boston and educated at Harvard University, he traveled (1785–87) in Europe, where he was influenced by the classical architecture in Italy and the neoclassical buildings of Sir Christopher Wren, Robert Adam, and others in England. From these elements he evolved the distinctive Federal style, with its classical domes, columns, and precise ornament, that dominated early 19th-century American architecture. In 1793 Bulfinch designed the Federal Street Theater in Boston; the Meeting House in Taunton; the Bulfinch Church in Pittsfield; and the State House in Boston (completed 1798). He also drew plans for the Old State House (1796) in Hartford, Conn., and the State House (1829–32) in Augusta, Maine. In 1813 he designed University Hall at Harvard, and in 1818 he planned the Bulfinch Building of Massachusetts General Hospital in Boston.

Bulfinch also designed houses, notably the Harrison Gray Otis House (1796) and the town houses facing Boston Common. On the Boston Board of Selectmen (1791–1818), Bulfinch was responsible for the design of the Common, the remodeling of Faneuil Hall, and the construction of India Wharf. In 1818 he succeeded Benjamin Henry Latrobe as architect of the U.S. Capitol, completing it in 1830. Bulfinch was the first native American professional architect.

BULGANIN, Nikolay Aleksandrovich (1895–1975), Soviet statesman, born in Nizhny Novgorod (now Gorkiy). He joined the Bolshevik party in 1917, was a secret police officer from 1918 to 1922, and then transferred to the Supreme Economic Council. From 1931 to 1937 he served as chairman (mayor) of the Moscow city soviet. He became a full member of the Central Committee of the Communist party of the Soviet Union in 1939 and of the Politburo in 1948. After the death of Joseph Stalin in 1953, Bulganin was appointed deputy premier and minister of defense under Georgy M. Malenkov, and two years later he replaced Malenkov as premier. Together with Nikita S. Khrushchev, first secretary of the Soviet Communist party, he traveled widely in an attempt to establish détente with the West. In 1958, having cast his lot with the losing side in the preceding party struggle, Bulganin was replaced by Khrushchev, who appointed him chairman of the Stavropol Economic Council. In 1960 he retired from public life.

BULGARIA, in full, People's Republic of Bulgaria, nation of Europe, situated in the Balkan Peninsula, and bounded on the N by Romania, on the E by the Black Sea, on the S by Turkey and Greece, and on the W by Yugoslavia. Formerly an independent kingdom, Bulgaria became a Communist-dominated republic in 1946. Since then

Young people from around the world vacation each year at the International Youth Resort at Primorsko, Bulgaria, on the Black Sea. Bulgarian Tourist Office

the country has experienced considerable economic growth, and by the early 1980s the once-dominant agricultural sector had been overtaken by manufacturing. The capital and largest city is Sofia. The area of Bulgaria is 110,912 sq km (42,823 sq mi).

LAND AND RESOURCES

More than half of Bulgaria is hilly or mountainous; the average elevation is about 480 m (about 1575 ft). The Balkan Mts. cross the country from the NW corner to the Black Sea and form the watershed between the Danube R. and the Aegean Sea. The N side of the Balkan Mts. slopes gradually to form the N Bulgarian plateau, which ends at the Danube R. The central portion of the S side of the range is fringed by a series of narrow plains, notably the Thracian Plain. In the S part of the country are the broad and irregular Rhodope Mts., which delineate the boundary with Greece. At the W end of these mountains, in SW Bulgaria, are the Rila Mts., which culminate in Musala Peak (2925 m/9597 ft), the highest point in the Balkans. Several smaller ranges lie along the Bulgarian-Yugoslav boundary.

The principal river draining Bulgaria is the Danube, which has among its Bulgarian tributaries the Iskŭr (about 370 km/about 230 mi long) and the Yantra (about 290 km/about 180 mi long). Other important rivers are the Kamchiya (about 180 km/ about 110 mi long), which empties into the Black Sea, and in the SW, the Struma and Mesta, which flow S to the Aegean Sea.

Climate. Most of Bulgaria has a continental climate, with cold winters and hot summers. The climate in general is more severe than in other European areas of the same latitudes, and the average annual temperature range is greater than that of neighboring countries. Severe droughts, frosts, wind, and hail frequently damage crops. A Mediterranean climate, with dry summers and mild, humid winters, prevails in the valley of the SW Rhodope Mts.; the N limit of the climatic zone is the Balkan Mts.

The average annual temperature is about 12.8° C (about 55° F). The average rainfall is about 635 mm (about 25 in) per year, ranging from a low of 193 mm (7.6 in), in the NE, to a high of 1905 mm (75 in), in the Rila Mts. The wettest period is early summer in most of the country and autumn or winter in the S valleys.

Natural Resources. The main resources of Bulgaria are agricultural. The country also has a wealth of metallic and nonmetallic minerals, mainly iron ore and coal. Other mineral reserves are small, but some deposits, particularly those of manganese and petroleum, are valuable.

Plants and Animals. Approximately one-third of Bulgaria is forested, and half this area supports tall trees suitable for timber. About 30% of the timber trees are conifers. The Balkan Mts. and their foothills support forests of various trees. In the timber zone of the Rhodope Mts. and their W extensions are found conifers, beech, and oak. Wild animal life is confined to the mountainous SW portion of the country, where bear, wolf, elk, fox, and wildcat are found.

Soils. Soil types vary considerably. In some tablelands are fertile black and gray soils, high in humus content and well suited for growing grain. The Thracian Plain contains brown, loamy soils that are fertile and adapted to diversified cultivation. Deforestation and inadequate soil-conservation practices have caused gradual deterioration of several fertile areas.

POPULATION

About 85% of the population is classified as ethnic Bulgarian and about 9% is Turkish. Small groups of Armenians, Gypsies, Greeks, and Macedonians also inhabit the country. The population of Bulgaria became increasingly urbanized after 1945, and in the mid-1980s about 65% of the people were defined as urban.

Population Characteristics. The population of Bulgaria (1985 official est.) was 8,948,000. The overall population density was about 81 per sq km (about 209 per sq mi).

Political Divisions and Principal Cities. Bulgaria's principal political divisions include 8 administrative regions, the city of Sofia (with 12 districts), and more than 4000 village communes (*obshtinas*). The capital and largest city in Bulgaria is Sofia (pop., 1982 est., 1.07 million). Other major cities are Plovdiv (358,200), a center for light industry, and Varna (294,000), the main seaport.

Language and Religion. The official language is Bulgarian, spoken by about 90% of the population. *See* BULGARIAN LANGUAGE; BULGARIAN LITERATURE.

The Bulgarian government promotes atheism, to which an estimated 65% of the population subscribed in the early 1980s. The Bulgarian Orthodox church, a branch of the Eastern Orthodox church, was attended by about 27% of the population. Other religious groups include Muslims, Roman Catholics, Protestants, and Jews.

Education. All schools in Bulgaria are free and state controlled and are modeled after those in the Soviet Union. A major aim of the Bulgarian educational system is to supply technical and skilled workers to meet the growing demands of industry. Education is compulsory for all children between the ages of 7 and 16.

In the mid-1980s approximately 1.1 million pupils attended elementary schools in Bulgaria, and about 356,000 students were enrolled in secondary, vocational, and teacher-training schools.

The country has about 33 institutions of higher learning, including the University of Sofia and various specialized professional institutes. Total yearly enrollment in the mid-1980s amounted to approximately 102,500 students.

CULTURE

In the Middle Ages (especially in the 10th and 11th cent.), Bulgaria was the center of Slavic culture. Over the centuries, Bulgarian culture has been influenced successively by Byzantine, Greek, Russian, and Western cultures.

Libraries and Museums. Large libraries in Sofia include the Central Library of the Bulgarian Academy of Sciences, the library of the University of Sofia, and the Cyril and Methodius National Library. The Ivan Vazov National Library is located in Plovdiv. In addition, the people of Bulgaria are served by many smaller public libraries.

The country has over 200 museums. In Sofia are botanical and zoological museums and gardens; the National Archaeological Museum, with a collection of old coins and finds from many ancient burial mounds; and the National Ethnographical Museum. Other museums in the coun-

Rose pickers work in traditional peasant costume in the Valley of the Roses, central Bulgaria. The damask rose is cultivated as a source of attar of roses and rose water, used in perfume. Bulgarian Tourist Office

The Krustyu Sarafov National Theater, in Sofia, renamed to honor a noted Bulgarian actor who died in 1952. State supported, the theater presents a wide variety of works for a small admission charge. Bulgarian Tourist Office

try are devoted to history, science, and the revolutionary movement.

Art. The chief architectural monuments of Bulgaria are medieval churches and monasteries. The oldest is the circular Church of Saint George in Sofia, originally a pagan temple. The Rila Monastery, founded in the 9th century, is striking in its mountainous setting. An important monument of the 11th century is Bachkovo Monastery, S of Plovdiv. A major modern structure is the large, ornate Cathedral of Saint Alexander Nevski in Sofia.

The 13th-century frescoes of the Boyana Church near Sofia are outstanding examples of the painting of that period. Bulgarian handicrafts include rich folk embroideries and ornaments. Some of the best sculpture, wood carving, etchings, and painting are based on traditional culture and native subjects. Outstanding Bulgarian artists include the following: the etcher Peter Morozov (1881–1951), the painter Vladimir Dimitrov (1882–1960), and the sculptors Ivan Lazarov (1889–1952) and Christo. The last-named, an avant-garde artist noted for his technique of wrapping objects and landscape features, now lives in the U.S.

Music. Traditional Bulgarian music includes folk songs and choral plain chants in the Greek mode for church services. The chief native musical instruments are the bagpipe and the kaval, a wooden shepherd's flute. The characteristic folk dances are variations of the hora, a round chain dance, and the ruchenitsa, a lively dance of two couples. Modern Bulgarian orchestral and operatic compositions have occasionally gained recognition in other countries. Among leading composers are Petko Stainov (1896–1977) and Pancho Vladigerov (1899–   ).

ECONOMY

The economic system of Bulgaria resembles closely that of the Soviet Union. Until 1947 Bulgaria was predominantly agricultural, with virtually no heavy industry. The government is presently emphasizing the development of heavy industry. All industrial enterprises are nationalized and operate under a series of five-year economic plans, with financial aid from the USSR. Since the mid-1950s new resorts have been developed along the Black Sea, partly by private individuals, in an attempt to attract foreign visitors and their currencies. In the mid-1980s the national budget was approximately balanced, with about $19.5 billion for revenue and for expenditure.

Agriculture. Collectivization of agriculture in Bulgaria was begun in the early 1950s, and by the mid-1980s most farmland was part of the country's collective and state farms. Private holdings were limited to a small size, but accounted for more than one-quarter of total agricultural output. The chief crops are wheat, rye, corn, barley, oats, cotton, tobacco, grapes, tomatoes, sugarbeets, potatoes, and cabbage. In the mid-1980s some 3.6 million metric tons of wheat, 3 million metric tons of corn, and 125,200 metric tons of tobacco were harvested each year.

The livestock sector of farming has also been socialized. In the mid-1980s the livestock population included some 10.5 million sheep, 3.7 million pigs, 1.8 million cattle, and 43 million poultry.

Forestry and Fishing. The principal Bulgarian timber areas are in the vicinity of the Rila, Rhodope,

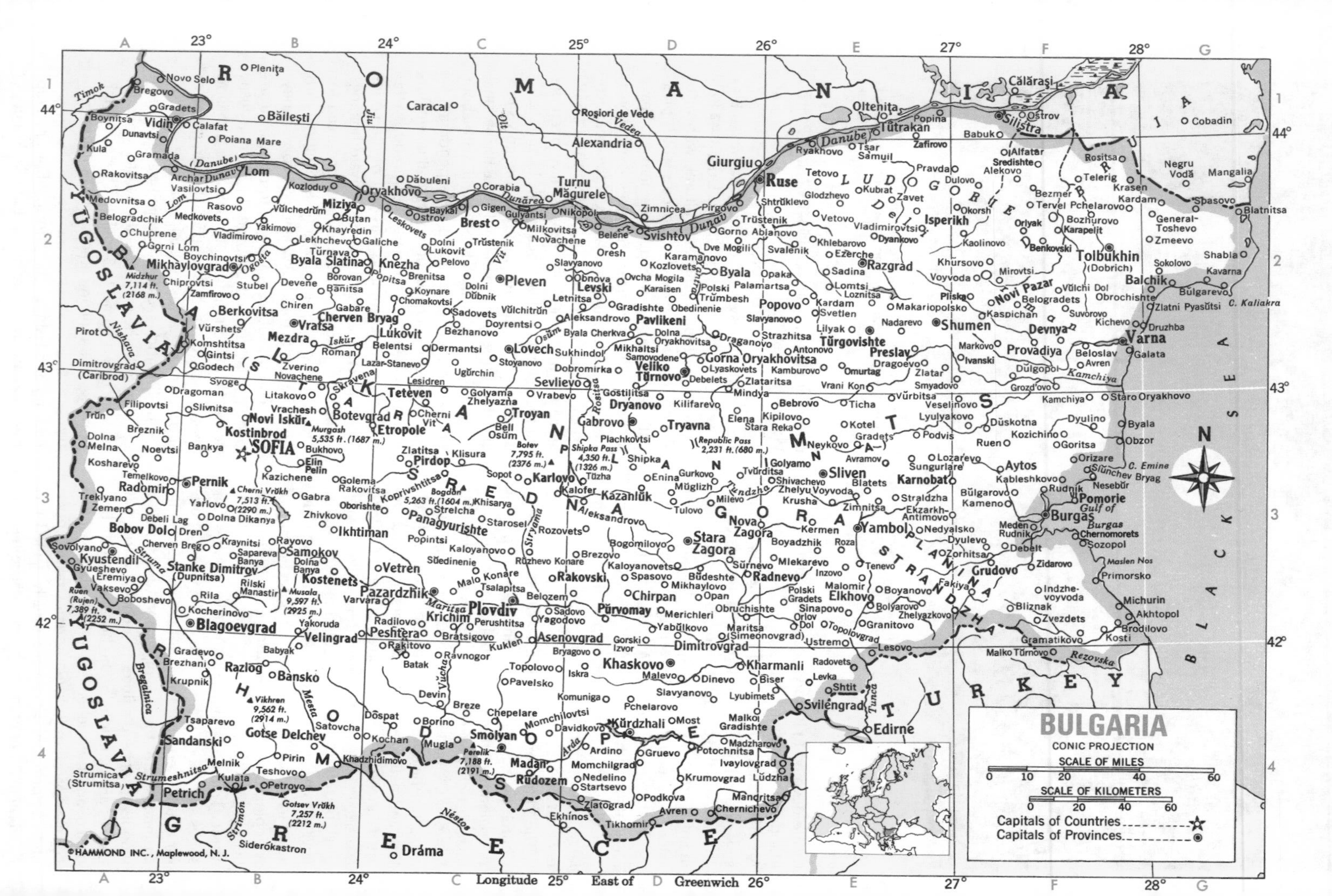

BULGARIA
CONIC PROJECTION
SCALE OF MILES
0 10 20 40 60
SCALE OF KILOMETERS
0 20 40 60
Capitals of Countries
Capitals of Provinces
ROMANIA
YUGOSLAVIA
GREECE
TURKEY
BLACK SEA
Danube
SOFIA
Plovdiv
Varna
Burgas
Ruse
Stara Zagora
Pleven
Shumen
Tolbukhin (Dobrich)
Sliven
Khaskovo
Yambol
Pernik
Vidin
Mikhaylovgrad
Vratsa
Lovech
Gabrovo
Veliko Tŭrnovo
Tŭrgovishte
Razgrad
Silistra
Kŭrdzhali
Smolyan
Pazardzhik
Kyustendil
Blagoevgrad
Sandanski
Petrich
Edirne
Dráma
STARA PLANINA
SREDNA GORA
RHODOPE
LUDOGORIE
STRANDZHA PLANINA
Longitude 25° East of Greenwich 26°
©HAMMOND INC., Maplewood, N. J.

INDEX TO MAP OF BULGARIA

Cities and Towns

Aleksandrovo D 2
Aleksandrovo D 3
Alfatar F 2
Antonovo E 2
Archar A 2
Ardino D 4
Asenovgrad C 3
Avren F 2
Aytos F 3
Balchik G 2
Bansko B 4
Batak C 4
Belene D 2
Belogradchik A 2
Belogradets F 2
Beloslav F 2
Belozem C 3
Berkovitsa B 2
Bezhanovo C 2
Blagoevgrad B 3
Boboshevo A 3
Bobov Dol A 3
Bolyarovo E 3
Borovan B 2
Botevgrad B 3
Boynitsa A 2
Bratsigovo C 3
Bregovo A 1
Brenitsa C 2
Brest C 2
Brezhani B 4
Breznik A 3
Brezovo D 3
Bŭlgarovo F 3
Bukhovo B 3
Burgas F 3
Butan B 2
Byala D 2
Byala Cherkva D 2
Byala Slatina B 2
Chepelare C 4
Cherven Breg A 3
Cherven Bryag B 2
Chiprovtsi A 2
Chirpan D 3
Dermantsi C 2
Devin C 4
Devnya F 2
Dimitrovgrad D 4
Dobrich (Tolbukhin) F 2
Dobromirka D 2
Dolna Banya B 3
Dolna Dikanya B 3
Dolna Oryakhovitsa D 2
Dolni Dŭbnik C 2
Dolni Lukovit C 2
Doyrentsi C 2
Draganovo D 2
Dren B 3
Dryanovo D 3
Dŭlgopol F 2
Dulovo F 2
Dunavtsi A 2
Dupnitsa (Stanke Dimitrov) B 3
Dve Mogili D 2
Elena D 3
Elkhovo E 3
Enina D 3
Etropole C 3
Ezerche E 2
Gabare B 2
Gabrovo D 3
Galiche B 2
General-Toshevo G 2
Gigen C 2
Glodzhevo E 2
Godech B 2
Golyamo Shivachevo E 3
Gorna Oryakhovitsa D 2
Gorno Ablanovo D 2
Gorski Izvor D 3
Gotse Delchev B 4
Gradets A 1
Gradishte D 2
Gramada A 2
Grozd'ovo F 2
Grudovo F 3
Gruevo D 4
Gulyantsi C 2
Gurkovo D 3
Ikhtiman B 3
Inzovo E 3
Iskra D 4
Isperikh E 2
Ivaylovgrad D 4
Kalofer D 3
Kalovo C 3
Kaloyanovo C 3
Kamchiya F 3
Kameno F 3
Kaolinovo F 2
Karaisen D 2
Karamanovo D 2
Kardam E 2
Karlovo C 3
Karnobat E 3
Kaspichan F 2
Kavarna G 2
Kazanlŭk D 3
Kermen E 3
Khadzhidimovo B 4
Kharmanli E 4
Khaskovo D 4
Khayredin B 2
Khisarya C 3
Kilifarevo D 3
Klisura C 3
Knezha C 2
Kocherinovo B 3
Koprivshtitsa C 3
Kostenets B 3
Kotel E 3
Koynare C 2
Kozloduy B 2
Kozlovets D 2
Kraynitsi B 3
Krichim C 3
Krumovgrad D 4
Kubrat E 2
Kuklen C 4
Kula A 2
Kŭrdzhali D 4
Kyustendil A 3
Lazar-Stanevo C 2
Lekhchevo B 2
Leskovets C 2
Lesovo E 4
Letnitsa C 2
Levski D 2
Litakovo B 3
Lom B 2
Lovech C 2
Loznitsa E 2
Lukovit C 2
Lyaskovets D 2
Lyubimets D 4
Madan C 4
Madzharovo D 4
Malko Tŭrnovo F 4
Malo Konare C 3
Malomir E 3
Maritsa D 3
Meden Rudnik F 3
Medkovets D 2
Merichleri D 3
Mezdra B 2
Michurin F 3
Mikhaltsi D 2
Mikhaylovgrad A 2
Milevo D 3
Milkovitsa C 2
Miziya B 2
Momchilgrad D 4
Mŭglizh D 3
Nedelino D 4
Nesebŭr F 3
Nikopol D 2
Novachene B 2
Novachene C 2
Nova Zagora D 3
Novi Iskŭr B 3
Novi Pazar F 2
Novo Selo A 1
Obedinenie D 2
Obnova D 2
Obruchishte D 3
Omurtag E 2
Opaka E 2
Oresh D 2
Oryakhovo B 2
Ostrov C 2
Ovcha Mogila D 2
Palamartsa D 2
Panagyurishte C 3
Pavlikeni D 2
Pazardzhik C 3
Pelovo C 2
Pernik B 3
Perushtitsa C 3
Peshtera C 3
Petrich B 4
Pirdop C 3
Pirgovo D 2
Pleven C 2
Plovdiv C 3
Polski Trŭmbesh D 2
Pomorie F 3
Popina E 1
Popintsi C 3
Popitsa C 2
Popovo E 2
Preslav E 2
Provadiya F 2
Pŭrvomay D 3
Radilovo C 3
Radnevo D 3
Radomir A 3
Rakhman Ashiklar F 2
Rakitovo C 4
Rakovski D 3
Rasovo B 2
Razgrad E 2
Razlog B 4
Rila B 3
Rudozem C 4
Ruse E 2
Rúzhevo Konare C 3
Sadina E 2
Sadovets C 2
Sadovo C 3
Samokov B 3
Sandanski B 4
Sapareva Banya B 3
Sevlievo C 2
Shtrŭklevo E 2
Shumen F 2
Silistra F 1
Simeonovgrad (Maritsa) D 3
Slavyanovo D 2
Sliven E 3
Slivnitsa B 3
Smedovo E 2
Smolyan C 4
Sofia (cap.) B 3
Sopot C 3
Sozopol F 3
Stanke Dimitrov B 3
Stara Zagora D 3
Stoyanovo C 2
Straldzha E 3
Strazhitsa E 2
Strelcha C 3
Sŭedinenie C 3
Sukhindol D 2
Sungurlare E 3
Suvorovo F 2
Svetlen E 2
Svilengrad E 4
Svishtov D 2
Svoge B 3
Temelkovo A 3
Tenevo E 3
Tervel F 2
Teteven C 3
Tetovo E 2
Tolbukhin F 2
Topolovgrad E 3
Topolovo C 4
Troyan C 3
Trŭn A 3
Trŭstenik C 2
Trŭstenik D 2
Tryavna D 3
Tsalapitsa C 3
Tsar Kaloyan E 2
Tsar Samuil E 2
Tulovo D 3
Tŭrgovishte E 2
Tŭrnava B 2
Tutrakan E 1
Tvŭrditsa D 3
Ugŭrchin C 2
Ustrem E 3
Varna F 2
Varvara B 3
Vasilovtsi A 2
Veliko Tŭrnovo D 2
Velingrad B 4
Vetovo E 2
Vetren C 3
Vidin A 2
Vladimirovo B 2
Vladimirovtsi E 2
Vrachesh B 3
Vrani Kon E 2
Vratsa B 2
Vŭlchedrŭm B 2
Vŭlchi dol F 2
Vŭlchitrŭn C 2
Vŭrbitsa E 3
Vŭrshets B 2
Yabŭlkovo D 3
Yagodovo C 3
Yakimovo B 2
Yakoruda B 3
Yambol E 3
Zamfirovo B 2
Zavet E 2
Zhelyu voyvoda E 3
Zimnitsa E 3
Zlatar E 2
Zlataritsa E 2
Zlatitsa C 3
Zlatograd D 4
Zlokuchen F 2

Other Features

Anti-Balkans (mts.) D 3
Arda (river) D 4
Balkan (mts.) C 3
Black (sea) G 3
Bogdan (mt.) C 3
Botev (mt.) C 3
Burgas (gulf) F 3
Cherni Vrŭkh (mt.) B 3
Danube (Dunav) (river) E 2
Dobruja (reg.) F 2
Iskŭr (river) B 2
Kaliakra (cape) G 2
Kamchiya (river) F 2
Lom (river) A 2
Ludogorie (region) E 2
Maritsa (river) C 3
Mesta (river) B 4
Midzhur (mt.) A 2
Murgash (mt.) B 3
Musala (mt.) B 3
Ogosta (river) B 2
Osŭm (river) C 2
Perelik (mt.) C 4
Republic (pass) D 3
Rezovska (river) F 4
Rhodope (mts.) C 4
Rosita (river) D 3
Ruen (Rujen) (mt.) A 3
Shipka (pass) D 3
Sredna Gora (Anti-Balkans) (mts.) D 3
Stara Planina (Balkan) (mts.) C 3
Strandzha, Planina (mts.) E 3
Struma (river) A 3
Strumeshnitsa (river) B 4
Stryama (river) C 3
Tundzha (river) D 3
Vit (river) C 2
Vŭcha (river) C 4
Yantra (river) D 2

and Balkan mountains. Forest reserves have deteriorated, however, because of exploitation and negligence. The government, consequently, instituted a 20-year afforestation plan (1961–80); some 6 million saplings were produced annually for afforestation. In the mid-1980s about 4.84 million cu m (about 171 million cu ft) of timber were produced annually.

The fishing industry, which began to expand in the 1960s and '70s, produced a catch of about 142,000 metric tons annually in the mid-1980s. Mackerel typically makes up about 65% of the total catch. Canning and processing plants are located at Varna and Burgas, on the Black Sea coast.

Mining. Coal furnishes the bulk of Bulgaria's mineral production. More than half the total coal production goes to industry, and the annual output (32.5 million metric tons in the mid-1980s) no longer meets domestic demand. Petroleum was discovered in 1951; in the mid-1980s about 2.2 million barrels of crude oil were produced each year. Annual production of iron ore was about 2.1 million metric tons. Copper, zinc, lead, and natural gas also are commercially exploited.

Manufacturing. Since the nationalization of the Bulgarian manufacturing industry, many sectors have substantially increased their total output. In 1939 manufacturing and construction together represented about one-fourth of total production; by the mid-1980s the two sectors accounted for more than 60% of the country's net material product (a Marxist gauge of national output that excludes public administration, professional services, and other activities not contributing directly to material production). The metalworking and chemical industries, as well as the food-processing, tobacco-processing, and machinery-manufacturing enterprises, are among the newer, more productive areas. Textiles are the oldest manufacture of Bulgaria and, except for cotton goods, largely utilize domestic raw materials. The manufacture of building materials, including cement, brick, and glass, is well developed. Leather goods and leather and rubber footwear are well-established manufactures but are not yet equal to demand. Metallurgical and metalwork industries are largely dependent on imports of raw materials. The ores mined domestically, however, are refined and fabricated into manufactures in Bulgaria. Machine building and engineering are being expanded, especially for light electric equipment. The most famous product of Bulgaria is attar of roses, which is used as a perfume base.

Energy. In the mid-1980s about 60% of Bulgaria's electricity production was generated in thermal plants fired by coal, lignite, and petroleum products. The country's first nuclear power station was opened at Kozloduy in 1974, and within ten years nuclear facilities accounted for almost one-third of electricity output. In the mid-1980s Bulgaria had an installed electricity-generating capacity of about 10.2 million kw, and annual electricity production was some 44.6 billion kwh.

Currency and Banking. The unit of currency in Bulgaria is the lev (0.87 lev equals U.S. $1; 1987). All banks were nationalized in 1947. The National Bank of Bulgaria is the bank of issue and handles government funds and nationalized enterprises. The State Savings Bank has numerous agencies and branches throughout the country.

Commerce and Trade. Most Bulgarian foreign trade is with the Soviet Union, East Germany, and other Soviet-bloc countries. In the West, Italy and West Germany are the main trade partners. Trade with the U.S. is negligible.

Annual exports in the mid-1980s were valued at about $12.2 billion. The chief exports were machinery, food products, tobacco, nonferrous metals, cast iron, leather products, and textiles. Yearly imports in the same period were valued at about $12 billion. The principal imports were petroleum, natural gas, machinery, transportation equipment, steel, cellulose, and timber.

Transportation. Bulgaria is largely dependent for transport on railroads, with about 4280 km (2660 mi) of track in use. The country is also served by about 37,630 km (23,380 mi) of roads. A major event in the development of communications was the opening of the Ruse-Giurgiu rail-and-road bridge over the Danube R. in 1954; it is the chief bridge of that type connecting Bulgaria and Romania.

The Danube R. is a major artery of commerce. Of the dozen Danube ports, Ruse, Svishtov, Lom, and Vidin have the greatest importance. Much of the Bulgarian freight and passenger traffic with the countries of the Soviet bloc utilizes the Danube and the Black Sea.

The Bulgarian state airline, Balkan, serves the major cities of the country as well as several European capitals and other major cities.

Communications. In the mid-1980s about 1.8 million telephones were in operation in Bulgaria, and some 2 million radios were in use. Television started on an experimental basis in 1954 and was officially inaugurated in 1959. By the mid-1980s, some 20 television stations were in operation, and more than 1.7 million television receivers were in use.

All Bulgarian periodicals are published either by the government or by government-approved organizations, and reflect government policy. In the mid-1980s about 14 dailies, with a combined circulation of 2.3 million, were being published. The leading dailies included *Workers' Cause* (the organ of the Communist party), *Fatherland Front,* and *Labor,* all published in Sofia.

Labor. The chief labor organization in Bulgaria is the federated Central Council of Trade Unions, which includes the great majority of nonagricultural workers and government employees; membership was about 4 million in the mid-1980s. Strikes are not permitted, and various types of voluntary and forced labor are employed, together with production quotas and bonuses that are intended to increase output.

GOVERNMENT

Bulgaria is governed under a constitution adopted in 1971, as amended. As in other Soviet-bloc nations, the Communist party plays a leading role in the government, and its first secretary is the most powerful person in the country.

Central Government. According to the 1971 constitution, the State Council, chosen by the legislature (National Assembly), is the supreme organ of state power; its president serves as Bulgaria's head of state. The Council of Ministers, also selected by the legislature, is defined as the chief executive and administrative body; it is headed by a chairman (similar to the premier in Western nations).

Health and Welfare. Matters of health and medicine in Bulgaria are under the overall control of the ministry of public health. Health services are provided free to all, although physicians are permitted part-time private practice. In the mid-1980s Bulgarians were served by more than 23,000 physicians and 5200 dentists.

A program providing pensions, recreational facilities, and welfare benefits was established in 1958. Funds are contributed by employers, and payments are provided for in the national budget. The state provides monthly allowances to parents with children under the age of 16.

Legislature. The legislative body of Bulgaria is the unicameral National Assembly, made up of 400 members elected to 5-year terms. The legislature meets for only a few days each year, and the State Council administers all legislative functions of the government when the assembly is not in session. In theory the Council of Ministers is responsible to the National Assembly, but in practice the assembly automatically approves measures taken by the Council of Ministers.

Political Parties. The Bulgarian Communist party controls all political life and dominates and controls the government. The party is ruled by the Political Bureau, or Politburo, which in the mid-1980s included 11 full members and 6 candidate members. The Politburo is elected by and from the Central Committee of the party. The Central Committee, comprising some 195 members and 145 candidate members, meets four times a year; its main function is the administration of party work. The Communist party dominates its mass organization, the Fatherland Front. The Front was formed in 1943 as a coalition of Communists, Socialists, and other factions. The Bulgarian Agrarian People's Union, a remnant of what was formerly the largest political party in Bulgaria, is now a subordinate part of the Fatherland Front. Membership in the Front was about 4.4 million in the early 1980s; the Communist party had some 826,000 regular and candidate members.

Local Government. All *okrŭgs* and *obshtinas* in Bulgaria are administered by popularly elected people's councils. Council members are elected to terms of two and one-half years. The councils are responsible for all economic, cultural, and social problems within the area and supervise all government-owned enterprises.

Judiciary. The chief judicial body in Bulgaria is the supreme court, which sits in Sofia. Its members are elected to 5-year terms by the National Assembly. Lower tribunals include provincial courts, regional courts, and military courts.

Defense. The regular Bulgarian army has up-to-date Soviet equipment; total strength numbered some 105,000 persons in the mid-1980s. The air force, numbering some 35,000 in strength, is equipped with about 275 Soviet-built combat planes. The navy is small, with a force of about 8500. Other branches of the military include the internal-security force, the people's territorial militia, and the frontier army.

HISTORY

The region now called Bulgaria was once part of the Roman Empire and comprised parts of the provinces of Thrace and Moesia. It was inhabited by the Thraco-Illyrians, a little-known people. Beginning in the 6th century AD Slavic tribes migrated into the region and either absorbed or drove out the original inhabitants. During the latter part of the 7th century a tribe of Bulgars migrated from their domain on the east side of the Black Sea, crossed the lower reaches of the Danube River, and subjugated Lower Moesia, then a province of the Byzantine Empire. Imperial armies failed repeatedly to dislodge the invaders during the 8th century. Fewer in number than the Slavonic population of Lower Moesia, the Bulgars gradually became Slavicized during this period. By the end of the century they had annexed considerable additional territory and laid the foundations for a strong state under Khan Krum (r. 803–14). The Krum armies inflicted (811)

Courtyard of the venerable Rila Monastery, a 1000-year-old Byzantine structure, in the Rila Mts. of eastern Bulgaria. W. H. Hodge–Peter Arnold, Inc.

a devastating defeat on an invading Byzantine force and, assuming the offensive, nearly succeeded (813) in taking Constantinople. Bulgarian-Byzantine relations were thereafter relatively peaceful and continued to be so during the first half of the 9th century. The immediate successors of Krum enlarged their dominions, mainly in the region of Serbia and Macedonia. In 860, however, during the reign (852-89) of Boris I, Bulgaria suffered a severe military setback at the hands of the Serbs. Four years later Boris, responding to pressure from the Byzantine emperor Michael III (842-67), made Christianity the official religion of the khanate. Boris accepted the primacy of the papacy in 866, but in 870, following the refusal of Pope Adrian II (r. 867-72) to make Bulgaria an archbishopric, he shifted his allegiance to the Eastern Orthodox church.

The First Bulgarian Empire. Bulgaria became the strongest nation of Eastern Europe during the reign (893-927) of Boris's son Simeon (d. 927). A brilliant administrator and military leader, Simeon introduced Byzantine culture into his realm, encouraged education, obtained new territories, defeated the Magyars, and conducted a series of successful wars against the Byzantine Empire. In 925 Simeon proclaimed himself czar (emperor) of the Greeks and Bulgars. He conquered Serbia in 926 and became the most powerful monarch in contemporary Eastern Europe. Simeon's reign was marked by great cultural advances led by the followers of St. Cyril and his brother St. Methodius, the "apostles to the Slavs." During this period Old Church Slavonic, the first written Slavic language, and the Cyrillic alphabet were adopted.

Weakened by domestic strife and successive Magyar raids, Bulgarian power declined steadily during the following half century. In 969 invading Russians seized the capital and captured the royal family. The Byzantine emperor John I Tzimisces, alarmed over the Russian advance into southeastern Europe, intervened (970) in the Russo-Bulgarian conflict. The Russians were compelled to withdraw from Bulgaria in 972, and the eastern part of the country was annexed to the Byzantine Empire. In 976 Samuel (980-1014), the son of a Bulgarian provincial governor, became ruler of western Bulgaria. Samuel's armies were annihilated (1014) by the Byzantine emperor Basil II, who incorporated the short-lived state into his empire in 1018.

The Second Empire and Turkish Rule. Led by the nobles Ivan Asen (d. 1196) and Peter Asen (d. 1197), the Bulgarians revolted against Byzantine rule in 1185 and established a second empire. It consisted initially of the region between the Balkan Mountains and the Danube; by the early 13th century it included extensive neighboring territories, notably sections of Serbia and all of western Macedonia. In 1204, following the Latin occupation of Constantinople, Ivan and Peter's brother, Kaloyan (r. 1197-1207) temporarily broke with the Eastern Orthodox church and accepted the primacy of the pope (renouncing it again in 1234). Ivan Asen II (d. 1241), the fifth ruler of the Asen dynasty, added (1230) western Thrace, the remainder of Macedonia, and part of Albania to the empire.

Feudal strife and involvement in foreign wars caused gradual disintegration of the empire after the death of Ivan Asen II. The Bulgarian armies were decisively defeated by the Serbs in 1330, and for the next quarter century the second empire was little more than a dependency of Serbia. Shortly after 1360 the Ottoman Turks began to ravage the Maritsa Valley, completing the subjugation of Bulgaria in 1396. During the next five centuries the political and cultural existence of Bulgaria was almost obliterated. After a century of terrorism and persecution, Turkish administration improved, and the economic condition of the remaining Bulgarians rose to a level higher than it had been under the kingdom, although unsuccessful revolts against Turkish rule occurred from time to time.

With the revival of a Bulgarian literature glorifying the history of the country, in the latter half of the 18th century and the early part of the 19th century, Bulgarian nationalism became a powerful movement. In 1876 the Bulgarians revolted against the Turks, but were quelled; in reprisal, the Turks massacred some 15,000 Bulgarian men, women, and children. In 1877, prompted by the desire to expand toward the Mediterranean Sea and by Pan-Slavic sentiment, Russia declared war on Turkey. As a result of the Russo-Turkish War, in which Turkey was defeated, a part of Bulgaria became an autonomous principality; another part, Eastern Rumelia, was made an autonomous Turkish province.

Modern Bulgaria. Elected by a Bulgarian assembly in 1879, the first prince of the new Bulgaria was a German, Alexander of Battenberg (1857-93), also a prince and a nephew of Emperor Alexander II of Russia. Eastern Rumelia revolted against Turkey in 1885 and was united with Bulgaria. Russia, however, considered the action inopportune and withdrew all officers who had been detailed to train the Bulgarian army. Thereupon, Serbia declared war on Bulgaria but was quickly defeated. In 1886 a group of Russian and Bulgarian conspirators abducted Prince Alexander and established a Russian-dominated government. Within a few days the government was overthrown by the Bulgarian statesman Stepan Stambolov (1855-95), but the Russians compelled Prince Alexander to abdicate. The new ruler, chosen in 1887, was Prince Ferdinand of Saxe-Coburg-Gotha. Taking advantage of a revolution in Turkey, in 1908 Ferdinand declared Bulgaria independent and assumed the title of King, or Czar, Ferdinand I.

The Balkan wars and World War I. In the First Balkan War (1912-13), Bulgaria, allied with Serbia, Montenegro, and Greece, defeated Turkey. Division of the reconquered Balkan territories, however, resulted in the Second Balkan War, which Bulgaria lost to Serbia, Montenegro, Greece, Turkey, and Romania; as a consequence, Bulgaria lost considerable territory. Bulgaria entered World War I in 1915 on the side of the Central Powers, but was forced to agree on an armistice with the Allies in September 1918. Czar Ferdinand abdicated in October and was succeeded by his son, Boris III. By the Treaty of Neuilly on Nov. 27, 1919, Bulgaria lost most of what it had gained in the Balkan Wars and all of its conquests in World War I. It was also required to abandon conscription, reduce armaments, and pay large reparations.

The interwar period and World War II. The Agrarian party government under Aleksandr Stambolisky (1879-1923), who became premier in 1919, attempted to improve the condition of the large peasant class and maintain friendly relations with the other Balkan countries. Stambolisky's dictatorial regime, unpopular with the army and the urban middle class, was overthrown by a coup d'etat in 1923; he himself was captured and killed while seeking to escape. Internal dissension continued under the new government, which represented all political parties except the Agrarians, Communists, and Liberals. Bulgaria and Greece again came into conflict in 1925, and the Greek army invaded Bulgaria. The Council of the League of Nations brought the conflict to an end and penalized Greece. In 1934, Czar Boris staged a coup of his own and established a royal dictatorship. In September 1940, Germany compelled Romania to cede southern Dobruja to Bulgaria. In March 1941, under German pressure, Bulgaria joined the Axis powers, agreeing to immediate occupation by German forces. Bulgaria declared war on Greece and Yugoslavia in April, shortly afterward occupying all of Yugoslav Macedonia, Grecian Thrace, eastern Macedonia, and the districts of Florina and Castoria. Bulgaria signed the Anti-Comintern Pact in November and the following month declared war on the

U.S. and Great Britain. Although allied with Nazi Germany, Czar Boris and his government resisted German demands for the persecution of Bulgarian Jews, most of whom survived the Holocaust.

When the tide of war turned against the Germans in 1943, Hitler attempted to force Bulgaria to declare war on the USSR. In August 1943, after returning from a meeting with the German dictator, Czar Boris died under mysterious circumstances and was succeeded by his six-year-old son, Simeon II (1937-), and a pro-German government under Dobri Bozhilov (1884–1945). An anti-German resistance movement organized by the Communists and the Agrarians opposed the Bozhilov regime, which fell in May 1944. The succeeding government severed its ties with Germany, but it was too late. The USSR formally declared war on Bulgaria on September 5. No fighting occurred, and the Bulgarian government subsequently asked the USSR for an armistice; Bulgaria, moreover, declared war on Germany on September 7. The armistice was agreed to by the USSR on September 9, and under the protection of Soviet forces a government subservient to the USSR was immediately established. The armistice, signed by the USSR, the U.S., and Great Britain in October 1944, provided for the control of Bulgaria, until the signing of final peace treaties, by the Allied Control Commission under the chairmanship of the Soviet representative, who was also the commander of the Soviet occupation forces. The armistice provided also that the Bulgarians evacuate Yugoslav Macedonia and territories they had taken from Greece.

Soviet pressure in the Bulgarian election engaged the attention of Great Britain and the U.S. in the fall of 1945. National elections originally scheduled for August were postponed because of U.S. protests concerning the nature of Soviet political maneuvers within Bulgaria. The opposition parties boycotted the elections held on November 18, and a single list of candidates of the Communist-dominated Fatherland Front won 85 percent of the vote.

The Communist regime. By a plebiscite in September 1946, the Bulgarians ousted Czar Simeon and ended the monarchy; a week later Bulgaria was proclaimed a people's republic. The constitution drawn up by the Fatherland Front, which won an overwhelming victory in the elections to the National Assembly, held in October, provided for freedom of the press, assembly, and speech. The National Assembly, which gained full control of state affairs, then elected the premier and also the president. The first president was Vasil Kolarov (1877–1950), a Communist party leader. Georgi Dimitrov, a former key figure in the Communist International, was elected premier in November 1946.

In February 1947, the peace treaty formally ending Bulgarian participation in World War II was signed in Paris. It provided for reparations to be paid to Greece in the amount of $45 million and to Yugoslavia in the amount of $25 million; severe limitation of military strength, with partial demilitarization along the Greek frontier; and the retention of southern Dobruja. (The borders with Greece were returned to their status as of 1941.) In December 1947 the National Assembly adopted a new constitution modeled on that of the USSR; this document replaced the presidency with the presidium. That September, Nikola Dimitrov Petkov (1891–1947), leader of the opposition to the Fatherland Front, had been executed

Premier Todor Zhivkov addresses the opening session of the Bulgarian Communist party Congress in 1971. Behind him, center, Soviet leader Leonid Brezhnev. UPI

after being convicted of conspiring to overthrow the government.

In its campaign against religion, which began in 1949, the government seized the property of foreign church organizations and imprisoned Protestant ministers. The patriarchate of the Bulgarian church, nonexistent for 600 years, was reestablished in 1951, and a patriarch was elected in 1953; nonetheless, Communist party organizations are expected to fight religious groups, which are still quite strong within the country.

Under pressure from the USSR, Bulgaria renounced its treaty of friendship with Yugoslavia after the Soviet-Yugoslavian rift in 1948; relations with the country have since continued to fluctuate, as have those with neighboring Greece and Turkey. Diplomatic ties with the U.S., broken in 1950 but restored in 1959, have frequently been marred by Bulgarian accusations of U.S. espionage activities. The U.S. ministry was raised to the status of an embassy in 1966.

Leadership, both of the Communist party and of the government, has changed less in Bulgaria than in other satellite countries. Since 1954, the country has been ruled by Todor Zhivkov, who at that time became secretary of the Communist party. Zhivkov held the premiership as well from 1964 to 1971, when Stanko Todorov (1920–) assumed the office; Zhivkov then became head of state, but retained his position as party chief.

Bulgaria is a member of the Council for Mutual Economic Assistance, Warsaw Pact, and of the UN. During the 1970s the country received extensive financial aid from the USSR, which was used for industrialization. At the same time, economic ties with the West were cautiously strengthened. Todorov relinquished the premiership in 1981. Bulgaria remained, in the late 1980s, one of the most restrictive societies of Eastern Europe. A five-year government campaign to assimilate members of Bulgaria's Turkish minority by forcing them to take Slavic names, prohibiting them from speaking Turkish in public, and subjecting them to other forms of harassment led more than 300,000 Bulgarian Turks to cross the border into Turkey in 1989.

For further information on this topic, see the Bibliography in volume 28, section 1007.

BULGARIAN LANGUAGE, the national language of Bulgaria. Bulgarian and the closely related Macedonian language form the eastern group in the southern branch of the modern Slavic languages (q.v.). They are outstanding among Slavic languages in having eliminated nearly all noun inflections, often using prepositional phrases instead. They have also taken on several regional non-Slavic traits, notably the use of a definite article and its placement after the noun (*see* YUGOSLAV LANGUAGES) and the use of a clause where other Slavic languages use an infinitive. Old Bulgarian (10th–11th cent.) is believed to be essentially the same as the earliest form of Old Church Slavonic (10th–11th cent.), the medieval Macedonian dialect that became the liturgical language of the Eastern Orthodox church and for which the Cyrillic alphabet (q.v.) was devised. Middle Bulgarian dates from the 12th century and Modern Bulgarian after the 15th century. The local form of Church Slavonic remained the Bulgarian literary language until a literary language based on modern speech was adopted in the 19th century. Bulgarian has absorbed loanwords mainly from Russian, Church Slavonic, Greek, and Turkish. It has two principal dialect groups, eastern (the basis of the literary language) and western. *See also* BULGARIAN LITERATURE.

BULGARIAN LITERATURE, literature written in the language of Bulgaria. It began in the second half of the 9th century AD with the translations by St. Cyril and St. Methodius of religious works from Greek into the vernacular, now known as Old Church Slavonic. From this period until the Turkish conquest of Bulgaria (1396), Bulgarian literature consisted mainly of ecclesiastical writings; historical chronicles were also written. During the Turkish rule and Greek ecclesiastical domination (1396–1878), Bulgarian literature virtually ceased to exist.

The 19th century marked a revival of Bulgarian literature. It had its origin in historical works such as *Istoria Slaveno-Bolgarska* (History of the Slavic-Bulgarians), written in a form of ecclesiastical Slavonic mixed with popular language by a monk, Paisij (b. 1720?), about 1762. After 1830, a movement in Bulgaria for freedom from Turkish rule and Greek church domination, the establishment of Bulgarian schools and printing establishments, and the publication of Bulgarian grammars and other educational works all played a part in producing a new Bulgarian literature.

Before 1878 writers were concerned with social and political questions, above all with national independence, rather than with literary style or the problems of the inner life of the individual. The most important writer of this preliberation period was the revolutionary poet Christo Botev (1848–76). The principal writer of the next period was Ivan Vazov (1850–1921), one of the most prolific as well as one of the most popular of Bulgarian writers and the one who scored a success in English translation, with his novel *Under the Yoke* (1893; trans. 1912). Other important writers of this period were Stoyan Mikhaylovski (1856–1927) and Aleko Konstantinov

(1863–97). The former was a pessimistic philosopher, disillusioned with politics; the latter was a satirist who characterized the Bulgarian peasant in *Bai Ganyu* (Uncle John, 1895).

In the postliberation period, the writers increasingly emphasized technique and form and harmony and rhythm of language. Important writers of this third period are the short-story writers Dimiter Ivanov (1878–1951), who wrote under the pen name of Elin-Pelin, and Yordan Yovkov (1884–1938); both are noted for their interest in peasant life and the countryside.

Bulgarian literature after 1944 adhered closely to the requirements of Soviet socialist realism. The work of some talented current writers, including the poets Blaga Dimitrova (1922–), Lubomir Levchev (1936–), and Pavel Matev (1924–), nevertheless reveals a fresher point of view and may signal a movement toward greater artistic freedom. The prose of Jordan Radichkov (1929–) is especially interesting. He handles historical themes, always a Bulgarian favorite, with unusual finesse, and his short novel *Khradriatyat chovek* (A Brave Man, 1967) has earned wide popularity.

Elias Canetti (1905–) won the 1981 Nobel Prize for literature for his novels and plays about individuals at odds with society. Born in Bulgaria, Canetti has lived in England since 1938 and writes in German. S.S. & I.S.

BULGE, BATTLE OF THE (December 1944–January 1945), last German offensive in the west during World War II. Following the Normandy invasion (June 1944), Allied forces swept rapidly through France but became stalled along the German border in September. On December 16, taking advantage of weather that kept Allied aircraft on the ground, the Germans launched a counteroffensive through the hilly and wooded Ardennes country and advanced 50 km (31 mi) into Belgium and Luxembourg. Their aim was to divide the Americans and the British and retake the vital seaport of Antwerp. They created a "bulge" in the Allied lines, but their advance was halted near the Meuse in late December. Managing to avoid being cut off by an Allied pincer movement, the Germans withdrew to their own lines in January, but heavy losses, including some 220,000 casualties, contributed to their final collapse in the following spring.

BULIMIA, an eating disorder in which persistent overconcern with body weight and shape leads to repeated episodes of binging (consuming large amounts of food in a short time) associated with induced vomiting, use of laxatives, fasting, and/or excessive exercise to control weight. Bulimia was classified as a distinct disorder by the American Psychiatric Association in 1980; the name was changed to bulimia nervosa in 1987.

Sometimes bulimic behavior is observed in cases of anorexia nervosa (q.v.), or abnormal dieting, but bulimia in itself does not result in severe weight loss. It can, however, cause gastrointestinal problems and serious potassium depletion, and teeth may be damaged due to the acid nature of the regurgitated food. Bulimia usually develops during adolescence (most commonly among females) as a result of various psychological pressures, the most obvious one being the social emphasis on the desirability of slimness. Various modes of group and behavioral therapy are used in treating the disorder. Because patients with bulimia often suffer from depression as well, antidepressant drugs may be effective.

BULL, GOLDEN. *See* GOLDEN BULL.

BULL, PAPAL, special letter or document bearing the pope's own seal. The word *bull* originally meant "seal" in the Middle Ages; it was applied also to the document to which the seal was affixed. Application of the word exclusively to papal documents, as opposed to documents of state bearing the seal of a sovereign, is a relatively modern development.

The papal seal affixed to most bulls is made of lead and is inscribed with the name of the reigning pope on one side and representations of the heads of St. Peter and St. Paul on the other side. A golden seal, or *bulla aurea,* is attached to papal documents of special gravity. A decree of Pope Leo XIII in 1878 made it permissible to use red stamps in place of seals for ease in mailing. Another of Leo XIII's innovations was the substitution of Roman script for the archaic Gothic script used by previous popes. Until the 11th century papal bulls were written on papyrus; thereafter they were written on parchment.

BULLBAITING, barbarous sport, once popular in England. A bull was tethered to a stake and attacked by specially trained bulldogs. In a similar sport, bullrunning, men and women maddened the bull with hideous noises and then pursued and beat the animal to death. Bullbaiting, bearbaiting, cockfighting, and similar practices were outlawed by the British Parliament in 1835.

BULLDOG, breed of dog developed in England in the 13th century for courage and ferocity needed in the sport of bullbaiting. After bullbaiting became illegal in 1835, the dog was bred to eliminate viciousness. The bulldog has a heavy, thickset, low-slung body; a massive head; wide shoulders; short, stout, and straight forelegs; long hind legs; and a fine-textured coat of short, straight hair. It is also characterized by small, thin ears, located high on the head; a large, broad nose; and a deep, broad, and full chest. The lower jaw projects, enabling the dog to take a grip that is difficult to break. The tail is short, straight, or screw, but not curled, and is hung low. The color of the dog may be red brindle, other brindles, solid white, or piebald. Mature male dogs weigh about 23 kg (about 50 lb); females, about 18 kg (about 40 lb).

BULLDOZER. *See* EARTH-MOVING MACHINES.

BULLFIGHTING, sports spectacle involving conflict between a bull and one or more contestants, fought in an outdoor arena according to certain rules and procedures. Traditionally, the bullfight is a combination of ritual and mortal combat, with an attempt, at the risk of the principal contestant's life, to maneuver a bull gracefully and kill it in a manner both courageous and aesthetically unrepugnant. Although bullfighting is confined largely to Spain and to the Spanish-speaking countries of the western hemisphere (especially Mexico), such contests take place also in southern France and in Portugal.

In Spanish-speaking countries the bullfight is known as *la fiesta brava* ("the brave festival") or *la corrida de toros* ("the running of the bulls"). The corrida, as it is popularly known, takes place before crowds of enthusiasts, often numbering many thousands.

History. Often termed "indefensible but irresistible," the spectacle of bullfighting has existed in one form or another since ancient days. For example, a contest of some sort is depicted in a wall painting unearthed at Knossos in Crete, dating from about 2000 BC. It shows male and female acrobats confronting a bull, grabbing its horns as it charges, and vaulting over its back.

Bullfights were popular spectacles in ancient Rome, but it was in the Iberian Peninsula that these contests were fully developed. The Moors from North Africa who overran Andalusia in AD 711 changed bullfighting significantly from the brutish, formless spectacle practiced by the conquered Visigoths to a ritualistic occasion observed in connection with feast days, on which the conquering Moors, mounted on highly trained horses, confronted and killed the bulls.

As bullfighting developed, the men on foot, who by their capework aided the horsemen in positioning the bulls, began to draw more attention from the crowd, and the modern corrida began to take form. Today the bullfight is much the same as it has been since about 1726, when Francisco Romero (1698–1763) of Ronda, Spain, introduced the estoque (the sword) and the muleta (the small, more easily wielded worsted cape used in the last part of the fight).

The Spectacle and Its Principals. Six bulls, to be killed by three matadors, are usually required for one afternoon's corrida, and each encounter lasts about 15 minutes. At the appointed time, generally five o'clock, the three matadors, each followed by their assistants, the banderilleros and

The procession opening a corrida in Pamplona, Spain.
Walter S. Clark

A rejoneador, *a mounted picador, lances the bull, weakening its strong neck muscles, during a bullfight in Pamplona, Spain.* Vance Henry–Taurus Photos

the picadors, march into the ring to the accompaniment of traditional paso doble ("march rhythm") music. The matadors (the term *toreador,* popularized by the French opera *Carmen,* is erroneous usage) are the stars of the show and can be paid as high as the equivalent of $25,000 per corrida. They wear a distinctive costume, consisting of a silk jacket heavily embroidered in gold, skintight pants, and a montera (a bicorne hat). A *traje de luces* ("suit of lights"), as it is known, can cost several thousand dollars; a top matador must have at least six of them a season.

When a bull first comes into the arena out of the toril, or bull pen gate, the matador greets it with a series of maneuvers, or passes, with a large cape; these passes are usually verónicas, the basic cape maneuver (named for the woman who held out a cloth to Christ on his way to the crucifixion).

The amount of applause the matador receives is based on his proximity to the horns of the bull, his tranquillity in the face of danger, and his grace in swinging the cape in front of an infuriated animal weighing more than 460 kg (more than 1000 lb). The bull instinctively goes for the cloth because it is a large, moving target, not because of its color; bulls are color-blind and charge just as readily at the inside of the cape, which is yellow.

Fighting bulls charge instantly at anything that moves because of their natural instinct and centuries of special breeding. Unlike domestic bulls, they do not have to be trained to charge, nor are they starved or tortured to make them savage. Those animals selected for the corrida are allowed to live a year longer than those assigned to the slaughter house. Bulls to be fought by *novilleros* ("beginners") are supposed to be three years old and those fought by full matadors are supposed to be at least four.

The second part of the corrida consists of the work of the picadors, bearing lances and mounted on horses (padded in compliance with a ruling passed in 1930 and therefore rarely injured). The picadors wear flat-brimmed, beige felt hats called *castoreños,* silver-embroidered jackets, chamois trousers, and steel leg armor. After three lancings or less, depending on the judgment of the president of the corrida for that day, a trumpet blows, and the banderilleros, working on foot, advance to place their banderillas (brightly adorned, barbed sticks) in the bull's shoulders in order to lower its head for the eventual kill. They wear costumes similar to those of their matadors but their jackets and pants are embroidered in silver.

After the placing of the banderillas, a trumpet sounds signaling the last phase of the fight. Although the bull has been weakened and slowed, it has also become warier during the course of the fight, sensing that behind the cape is its true enemy; most gorings occur at this time. The serge cloth of the muleta is draped over the estoque, and the matador begins what is called the faena, the last act of the bullfight. The aficionados (ardent fans) study the matador's every move, the balletlike passes practiced since childhood. (Most matadors come from bullfighting families and learn their art when very young.) As with every maneuver in the ring, the emphasis is on the ability to increase but control the personal danger, maintaining the balance between suicide and mere survival. In other words, the real contest is not between the matador and an animal; it is the matador's internal struggle.

The basic muleta passes are the *trincherazo,* generally done with one knee on the ground and at the beginning of the faena; the *pase de la firma,* simply moving the cloth in front of the bull's nose while the fighter remains motionless; the *manoletina,* a pass invented by the great Spanish matador Manolete (Manuel Laureano Rodríguez Sánchez, 1917–47), where the muleta is held behind the body; and the *natural,* a pass in which danger to the matador is increased by taking the sword out of the muleta, thereby reducing the target size and tempting the bull to charge to larger object—the bullfighter.

After several minutes spent in making these passes, wherein the matador tries to stimulate the excitement of the crowd by working closer and closer to the horns, the fighter takes the sword and lines up the bull for the kill. The blade must go between the shoulder blades; because the space between them is very small, it is imperative that the front feet of the bull be together as the matador hurtles over the horns. The kill, properly done by aiming straight over the bull's horns and plunging the sword between its withers into the aorta region, requires discipline, training, and raw courage; for this reason it is known as the "moment of truth."

Realities Behind the Spectacle. Bullfighting today is big business for the successful few who make it to the top. Such immortals as the Spanish fighters Juan Belmonte (1892–1962) and El Cordobés (Manuel Benítez Pérez, 1936?–) were multimillionaires, but paid for their fame with many severe horn wounds; Joselito (José Gómez, 1895–1920), Manolete, and dozens of others paid with their lives. Bullfighters generally expect to receive at least one goring a season. A star matador will fight as many as 100 corridas a year. The great Mexican matador Carlos Arruza (Carlos Ruiz Camino, 1920–66) once fought 33 times in a single month.

The Great Matadors. Ranking the great matadors is highly subjective. Most aficionados would agree, however, that the following names must be included in any list of the modern greats: Rodolfo Gaona (1888–1978), Armillita (Fermín Espinosa, 1911–80), and Arruza, of Mexico; and Belmonte, Manolete, and Antonio Ordoñez (1932–), of Spain. Few South Americans have

In the bullring at Madrid, a member of the bullfight team exits hastily at the barrier, as the bull halts his charge to avoid crashing. The barrier permits a person to leave the arena, but not the bull.
Harvey Lloyd–Peter Arnold, Inc.

The matador makes a pass, and the bull thunders by with only centimeters to spare.
Klaus D. Francke–Peter Arnold, Inc.

made an impact on the international bullfighting world. Although several North Americans have attempted careers as matadors, only Sidney Franklin (1903-76) and John Fulton Short (1933-) managed to "take the alternative," that is, to pass the requirements for professional status and to be accepted as full matadors in a special ceremony.

Many women also have been bullfighters, including the American Patricia McCormick (1934-); the greatest, however, was Conchita Cintrón (1921-), who fought in Spain and Latin America during the 1940s with great success. The most successful matadora at present is Spain's Maribel Atienzar (1959?-).

Bullfighting Outside Spain. Although Spain's bullfighting season is in the spring and summer, Mexico's main season is in the winter, and Peru's is in the fall. Bullfights can also be seen in Venezuela, Colombia, and southern France at various times of the year, usually on Sundays and feast days. In Portugal the costume and ceremony are the same as in Spain, with the important difference that the bull is not killed in the arena in front of the spectators but afterward, in the slaughterhouse. Another feature of the Portuguese version is *el rejoneo* (in effect, a matador on horseback), a skilled rider astride a highly trained horse, who avoids the bull's charges while placing the banderillas in the bull's withers. This spectacle is appreciated by tourists because the horses, often valued at the equivalent of about $40,000 each, are rarely injured.

The Corrida in Art and Literature. Artists have always been attracted to *la fiesta brava.* The Spanish artist Francisco Goya did dozens of etchings of bullfight scenes in his *La tauromaquia* series, and both the French painter Édouard Manet and Pablo Picasso were fascinated by the personages and ritual of the corrida.

The descriptions of bullfighting in the novel *Blood and Sand* (1908; trans. 1913), by the Spanish writer Vicente Blasco Ibáñez, and in the documentary study *Death in the Afternoon* (1932), by the American novelist Ernest Hemingway, have had the greatest impact on the non-Latin world. B.Co.

For further information on this topic, see the Bibliography in volume 28, section 750.

BULLFINCH, common name for birds of the genus *Pyrrhula,* family Fringil, particularly the common European bullfinch, *P. pyrrhula.* The bird is so named because of the short, thick, rounded bill, bulging at the sides, which suggests the head of a bull. The plumage of the male is grayish-brown above and pinkish-brown below. The head and most of the wings and tail are black; the wings are crossed with a conspicuous white bar. The birds are good mimics, and individuals can be caged and taught to whistle several tunes.

BULLFROG, common name for various large frogs of the genus *Rana,* especially *R. catesbeiana,* a species native to the eastern part of North America from Canada to Mexico. It has been introduced to western states. The solitary male is characterized by a deep resonant croak, commonly heard at night during the spring. A mature frog is dull green, with a yellowish or white belly, and dark, barred legs. Its body is up to 20 cm (8 in) long with 25-cm (10-in) hindlegs. The large "ears," or tympani, behind the eyes are specifically receptive to the mating calls of its species. Bullfrogs live in or near quiet lakes and ponds. They eat fish, crustaceans, mice, snakes, and small frogs. During the mating season the males float in the water at night, giving their mating calls. They are very aggressive in defending their calling territories and attack intruders violently. Females, distinguishing the call of their species, are attracted to a calling bullfrog. Often another male near the territory does not call but tries to intercept females as they approach the caller. After breeding, the female lays as many as 10,000 eggs in quiet water. The eggs hatch into dark spotted tadpoles that mature into adult frogs in one year in a warm climate and in two or three years if the climate is cool. Other bullfrog species are *R. adspersa* in Africa and *R. tigrina* in India and Malaysia.

BULLHEAD, any of several small catfish of the U.S., especially the species *Ameiurus nebulosus,* found in many streams in the east. The fish is brownish, reaches a length of 46 cm (18 in), and has a large head (hence its name). The black bullhead, *A. melas,* is smaller. The bullhead is also called bullpout and hornpout. In England the miller's-thumb, a small edible fish found also in North America, is called bullhead.

BULLINGER, Heinrich (1504–75), Swiss religious reformer, born in Bremgarten, in the canton of Aargau, and educated at the University of Cologne. There he became acquainted with the writings of Martin Luther and became a Protestant before he took his degree in 1520. In 1529 he married Anna Adlischwyler (1504?–64), formerly a nun, who bore him 11 children. In the same year, he succeeded his father as pastor at Bremgarten. In a powerful sermon, he induced his congregation to burn the images in the church and to pass reform laws.

Succeeding Huldreich Zwingli as head of the Swiss Reformed congregation in Zürich in 1531, Bullinger exerted great influence on the Church of England by giving shelter and counsel to the English Protestants exiled during the reign of Mary I, queen of England. In the controversy about the Eucharist and the affairs of the Anabaptists, Bullinger distinguished himself by his integrity and moderation, and in his house in Zürich he gave refuge to several German theologians. He shared in the First Helvetic Confession (1536) and was the sole author of the Second Helvetic Confession (1566). His writings are numerous but largely uncollected and unreprinted.

BULLMASTIFF, a breed of working guard dog, the result of a 19th-century cross between the mastiff and the bulldog. The bullmastiff was originally bred and trained to protect large English estates from poachers. For this work a less visible coat of a dark brindle color was preferred; light fawn coloring is now acceptable. The hair is short and dense, enabling the breed to live in warm climates and out in the open in rough weather. Possessing great strength and endurance, it is fearless but docile. The skull is square, with V-shaped ears close to the cheeks. The compact body has a wide, deep chest and muscular neck and hindquarters. Bullmastiffs stand 61 to 68 cm (24 to 27 in) and weigh 45 to 59 kg (100 to 130 lb).

BULL MOOSE PARTY. *See* PROGRESSIVE PARTY.

BULL RUN, BATTLE OF, also called the Battle of Manassas, two battles of the American Civil War fought in Virginia near Bull Run, a small stream about 48 km (about 30 mi) southwest of Washington, D.C.

The First Battle of Bull Run, the earliest important engagement of the war, was fought on July 21, 1861, between a Union army of about 28,000 under the command of Gen. Irvin McDowell (1818–85) and a Confederate army of about 33,000 commanded by Gen. Pierre Gustave Toutant Beauregard. Both sides were ill-trained for war, but a Union order to blockade the South and public pressure in the North led to a march, accompanied by many spectators, toward the Confederate capital at Richmond. At Bull Run the Union troops encountered the Confederate forces coming from their base at Manassas, about 4.8 km (about 3 mi) south of the stream. The 5-hour battle began with a Union assault resulting in a Confederate retreat to Henry House Hill. There, a part of a brigade commanded by Gen. Thomas Jonathan Jackson held back the Union troops until 9000 reinforcements under Gen. Joseph Eggleston Johnston arrived. The Union general Robert Patterson (1792–1881) had earlier failed to retain Johnston, and the combined Confederate force easily routed the Union army. The stubbornness of his defense earned for Jackson the nickname Stonewall. Although the flight of the Union army did not end until the troops reached Washington, the Confederate forces were too disorganized to pursue. The Union army lost about 2900 men killed, wounded, captured, or missing; the Confederates, about 2000. The Confederate victory encouraged the South and spurred the North to greater effort. The battle, demonstrating as it did the effectiveness of the Confederate army, changed the status of the conflict from a rebellion to a civil war.

The Second Battle of Bull Run was fought on two days, Aug. 29 and 30, 1862, near Bull Run. After failing to capture Richmond during the Peninsular Campaign, the North planned to unite the armies of Gen. George Brinton McClellan and Gen. John Pope (1822–92) for an assault on the city. By August 29, Pope, with about 35,000 men, had been driven north by a Confederate army of some 50,000 under Gen. Robert E. Lee. Pope was facing Lee, whose forces were to the south, when Stonewall Jackson, with 23,000 troops, came eastward through Thoroughfare Gap and approached Pope's forces from the rear. The Union troops turned and, with Bull Run on their rear, faced Jackson's army. Jackson was speedily reinforced by Lee's troops and by a corps under Gen. James Longstreet. Although the first day of the battle was inconclusive, on the second day Longstreet drove the Union army from the field. Pope retreated northward, was finally joined by McClellan, and then entered Washington. The Union loss was about 14,500; that of the Confederates about 9500. Lee, maintaining his offensive, then invaded Maryland. This ended with the Battle of Antietam. The site of both Bull Run battles is preserved in the Manassas National Battlefield Park.

For further information on this topic, see the Bibliography in volume 28, section 1155.

BULL SNAKE, common name for any of several species of harmless snakes constituting the genus *Pituophis,* of the family Colubridae, found in the U.S. The bull snake varies in length from 1.5 to 2.4 m (5 to 8 ft) and in color from whitish to pale brown with dark blotches. It lives in agricultural areas and preys on rodents that are destructive to crops. Three common species are the gopher snake, *P. sayi,* of the central U.S.; the western bull snake, *P. catenifer,* of the West Coast; and the pine snake, *P. melanoleucus,* of the East and Gulf coasts. The unique hissing mechanism of the bull snake consists of an erectile filament in front of the windpipe that vibrates as air is exhaled, producing an extremely loud and sharp hiss.

BULL TERRIER, breed of terrier developed more than 100 years ago by crossing the English bulldog with the now extinct white English terrier, and the resulting type with the Spanish pointer. Formerly bred for the sport of dogfighting, the bull terrier is unusually agile and courageous. The dog has a long head with a flat skull; very small, black, oblique, close-set eyes; a broad, black nose; a broad, deep chest; a short, muscular back; big-boned legs; and a short, straight tail. The coat, generally pure white in color, is dense, with short, glossy hair. Bull terriers weigh between 5 and 27 kg (12 and 60 lb); the standard weight is about 23 kg (about 50 lb) for the male and 20 kg (45 lb) for the female.

BÜLOW, Bernhard, Fürst von (1849–1929), German statesman, born in Flottbek (now Kleinflottbek), and educated at the universities of Leipzig, Berlin, and Lausanne. Bülow entered the diplomatic service in 1874, and after several promotions he was made secretary of state for foreign affairs in 1897. In 1900 he became chancellor of the German Empire, and in 1905 he was made a prince. As chancellor, Bülow's foreign policies antagonized the British, French, and Russians. In the so-called Morocco crisis of 1905, Bülow alienated the French by forcing the resignation of the French minister of foreign affairs, Théophile Delcassé (1852–1923).

In 1908, when Austria-Hungary annexed Bosnia and Herzegovina, Bülow supported the annexation despite opposition from Russia and Great Britain. Bülow's policies helped to strengthen the Triple Alliance and the Triple Entente, resulting in the increase of European tensions that eventually led to World War I. Opposition from William II, emperor of Germany, and from members of the Reichstag in 1909 led to his resignation and retirement. During World War I the German government sent him to Rome in a vain attempt to persuade Italy not to enter the war on the side of the Allies.

BÜLOW, Hans Guido von (1830–94), German composer, celebrated pianist, and the first virtuoso conductor. Born in Dresden, Bülow studied

Prince von Bülow at his desk at the German embassy in Rome, 1915. UPI

law in Leipzig and Berlin, but turned to a musical career. After studying conducting with the German composer Richard Wagner and piano with the Hungarian pianist Franz Liszt, he became an outstanding concert pianist. In 1857 he married Liszt's daughter Cosima (1837–1930); she left Bülow in 1869 and became the wife of Richard Wagner. In 1864 Bülow became conductor of the royal opera in Munich, where he conducted the first performance of Wagner's *Tristan und Isolde* (1865) and *Die Meistersinger* (1868). From 1880 to 1885 he was conductor at the court ducal at Meiningen; his orchestra became one of the finest in Europe.

Bülow was a prolific composer, but he is better known for his editions, especially of the piano sonatas of Ludwig van Beethoven, and for his transcriptions of Wagnerian works.

BULRUSH. *See* SEDGE.

BULTMANN, Rudolf Karl (1884–1976), German Lutheran New Testament scholar, who pioneered the form critical method of studying the synoptic Gospels.

Born in Wiefelstede, Oldenburg, on Aug. 20, 1884, Bultmann studied at the universities of Marburg, Tübingen, and Berlin. He taught at Breslau and Giessen before becoming professor of New Testament at Marburg in 1921, a post he held until his retirement in 1951. A world-renowned theologian, Bultmann continued to lecture and to write until his death in Marburg on July 30, 1976.

Bultmann, a skeptic in regard to the historical elements of the Bible, believed that the Scriptures, and especially the Gospels, must undergo a demythologization, or reinterpretation, of those mythical elements that have no application or relevance to contemporary concerns. His theology was strongly influenced by the writings of the existentialist philosopher Martin Heidegger (*see* EXISTENTIALISM).

Bultmann became known as a radical critic when, in his *History of the Synoptic Tradition* (1921; trans. 1963), he concluded that the Gospels are not biographies of Jesus Christ (although he did not deny that Jesus was a historical figure). He asserted that the Gospels are, rather, devotional and apologetic materials of the early church that were more or less strung together and are capable of being classified according to their literary forms. In *Jesus and the Word* (1926; trans. 1934) he scandalized many by claiming that little can be known of the life and personality of Jesus and that what is important to Christians is Jesus' call for believers to make a decision to accept the gospel message (which Bultmann called the kerygma, or proclamation) and to obey its commands. His major work is *Theology of the New Testament* (1948–53; trans. 1952–55).

See also BIBLICAL SCHOLARSHIP. J.D.G.

BULWER-LYTTON, Edward George Earle Lytton, 1st Baron Lytton (1803–73), English novelist, dramatist, and politician, born in London, and educated at the University of Cambridge. After graduation in 1826, he figured prominently in British and Continental social circles, which were intimately described in *Pelham* (1828), his first popular novel. From 1831 to 1841 he was a Liberal party member of Parliament, where he supported the Reform Bill of 1832. He broke with the Liberal party and in 1852 returned to Parliament as a Conservative. Lytton was appointed colonial secretary in 1858 and was created a baron in 1866. He displayed remarkable versatility as a writer, and he is remembered chiefly for his historical novels. Among the more notable of these are *The Last Days of Pompeii* (1834) and *Rienzi* (1835). Lytton was also the author of several successful plays, including *The Lady of Lyons* (1838) and *Richelieu* (1839). Among his other works are the novels *Falkland* (1827), *Eugene Aram* (1832), and *The Caxtons* (1849).

BUMBLEBEE, common name for any of the large, hairy, usually black and gold social insects constituting the tribe Bombini, of the family Apidae, order Hymenoptera, which also includes wasps and ants. Bumblebees are also sometimes placed in a separate family, Bombidae. Almost worldwide in distribution, they range farther poleward and higher up on the mountains than other bee species. This is made possible by special body adaptations to cooler weather that keep the flight muscles sufficiently warm, as well as protecting the developing larvae within a colony. Bumblebees also forage for longer hours than do other bees.

Bumblebee colonies are less complex than those of honeybees and are populated by three castes: queens, sterile female workers, and male drones. The workers vary in size, each becoming habituated to visiting flowers suited to the length of its tongue, and both queens and workers bear pollen baskets on their hind legs. Pregnant young queens leave their parent colony to found new ones, building nests of vegetable material in abandoned holes such as mouse burrows. No complex language has been developed by bumblebees comparable to that observed in honeybee hives.

The bumblebee nest consists of a spherical chamber with a single exit. The queen builds a small dome of pollen paste in the middle of the nest, lays a batch of eggs in it, and seals it with a small dome of wax. She also constructs a hemispherical wax cup in the entranceway floor and fills it with honey. The queen then sits on the eggs until they hatch, feeding on the honey in the cup. The hatched larvae partially consume the paste in their cell but are later fed through a small opening by the queen. Eventually they spin cocoons, which ultimately harden and become rigid. The queen then clears away the remains of the cell and broods her offspring.

Some species of bumblebee are parasitic on the nests of nonparasitic bumblebees. The parasitic bumblebees lack pollen baskets and therefore invade the nests of allied species; they often kill the resident queen and force the workers to raise the young parasitic bees along with the rightful brood of the nest. Occasionally the invaders permit only their own young to be cared for, and the brood of the resident bees dies.

See also BEE.

For further information on this topic, see the Bibliography in volume 28, section 466.

BUNAU-VARILLA, Philippe Jean (1859–1940), French engineer, born in Paris, and educated at the École Polytechnique. He was associated with the French company that in 1881 attempted to build the first canal across the isthmus of Panama. After the company failed (1889), he organized (1894) the New Panama Canal Co. and became chief engineer for the project. Still lacking funds, in 1902 he persuaded President Theodore Roosevelt to acquire the rights and assets of the French company for the U.S. The following year, Bunau-Varilla helped to instigate the revolt against Colombia that resulted in the establishment of the Republic of Panama. In 1903, as minister of Panama to the U.S., he negotiated the Hay-Bunau-Varilla Treaty, by the terms of which the U.S. acquired the Panama Canal Zone. The following year, he returned to Europe and directed engineering projects in both Europe and Africa, including the Congo railway in Africa and the first subway system in France.

BUNCHE, Ralph Johnson (1904–71), American diplomat and Nobel laureate, known for his work in the UN. Born in Detroit, Mich., Bunche taught political science at Howard University in Washington, D.C., between 1928 and 1941. From 1938 until 1940 he worked with the Swedish sociologist Gunnar Myrdal on a classical study of American blacks that resulted in Myrdal's book *An American Dilemma* (1944). During World War II Bunche served (1941–44) in the Office of Strategic Services and later joined (1944) the U.S. Department of State; in 1945 he became the first black to head a departmental division. An expert on trusteeship matters, Bunche participated in the writing of the UN Charter, and in 1946 he became director of the trusteeship division of the UN. As a senior member of the staff of the UN commission on Palestine, beginning in 1947, he participated in the mediation efforts that resulted in recognition of the state of Israel. International esteem for his skill as a mediator culminated in the award to Bunche of the 1950 Nobel Peace Prize for negotiating the four armistice agreements that halted the 1948–49 war in the Middle East. Continuing to work at the UN, he became undersecretary without portfolio in 1955 and undersecretary for political affairs in 1958. In 1967 he was promoted to undersecretary-general of the UN.

Ralph J. Bunche accepting the 1950 Nobel Peace Prize from Gunnar Jahn, president of the Nobel Peace Prize Committee from 1942 to 1969. UPI

For further information on this person, see the section Biographies in the Bibliography in volume 28.

BUNDELKHAND, region, central India, in Madhya Pradesh State. Before the termination (1947) of British rule in India, the region consisted mainly of nine small princely states, grouped for administrative purposes in the Bundelkhand Division of the Central India Agency. Generally hilly, with elevations up to 608 m (about 2000 ft), the region is traversed by numerous tributaries of the Jumna R. Dense jungles cover large sections of Bundelkhand. Wildlife, including leopards, tigers, and antelopes, is abundant. Agriculture is the chief industry, and the cultivated areas are irrigated by water drawn from artificial lakes. Diamonds are mined in various parts of the region, but the output is small.

Nowgong is the former administrative center. The British acquired control of the region through the Treaty of Poona, an agreement concluded with the ruling Marathas in 1817. British influence grew as Maratha power waned.

BUNIN, Ivan Alekseyevich (1870–1953), Russian poet and novelist and Nobel laureate, born in Voronezh, and educated at the University of Moscow. In 1903 he received the Pushkin Prize of the Russian Academy for his translations of the American poet Henry Wadsworth Longfellow and the English poets Lord Byron and Alfred, Lord Tennyson. Bunin's literary reputation rests mainly on his realistic tales, short stories, and novels, in which his principal theme is the bleakness of life in provincial Russia. Bunin was considerably influenced by the works of the Russian writers Anton Chekhov and Ivan Turgenev. After the Bolshevik Revolution of 1917, Bunin made his home in Paris. In 1933 he became the first Russian to be awarded the Nobel Prize in literature. His works include *The Gentleman from San Francisco and Other Stories* (1916) and the novels *The Village* (1910) and *Mitya's Love* (1925).

BUNION, inflamed bursa, or sac, that forms over a protruding bone in the first joint of the great toe, accompanied by distortion of the joint. Bunions are usually the result of poorly fitted shoes. The part gradually becomes enlarged as fluid fills the bursa or sac. If the bones thicken, it may result in permanent deformity. Treatment sometimes includes surgical removal of the bunion.

BUNKER HILL, BATTLE OF, first large-scale engagement of the American Revolution, fought on June 17, 1775, in Charlestown (now part of Boston), Mass. At issue in the battle was possession of Bunker Hill (34 m/110 ft) and Breed's Hill (23 m/75 ft), adjoining heights dominating Boston Harbor. About 1200 American troops, led by Col. William Prescott (1726–95), occupied and fortified Breed's Hill during the night of June 16 as part of a strategic plan to compel the British to evacuate Boston. After daybreak on June 17 the British commander in chief Thomas Gage began preparations for an attack on the American position. Naval units were brought within shelling range of Breed's Hill and about 2400 troops under the command of Gen. William Howe were dispatched from Boston. Meanwhile, about 300 additional volunteers, including Gen. Joseph Warren, had joined the American force.

The British troops, heavily supported by cannonading from naval guns, launched their initial assault on the American earthworks on Breed's Hill about 3 PM. Col. Prescott issued the famous order: "Don't one of you fire until you see the whites of their eyes." The Americans allowed the British to advance almost to the base of the earthworks and then opened fire. Sustaining severe losses, the British retreated in confusion to the base of the hill. Gage ordered a second charge, which was similarly repulsed. During the third British assault the American troops, having exhausted their ammunition, were forced to withdraw. The British then attacked and captured both hills. American losses in the battle totaled about 440 killed (including Warren), wounded, or taken prisoner. In the course of the engagement Charlestown was set on fire by British shells and burned to the ground. The British suffered more than 1050 killed and wounded, many of them officers. Although Howe's victory enabled the British to retain their hold on Boston, the American defense action demonstrated that hastily organized militiamen could trade blow for blow with British regulars and thereby strengthened morale and the spirit of resistance throughout the rebelling colonies. An obelisk, the Bunker Hill Monument, stands on Breed's Hill in commemoration of the battle.

For further information on this topic, see the Bibliography in volume 28, sections 1149–50.

BUNSEN, Robert Wilhelm (1811–99), German chemist, who, with the German physicist Gustav Robert Kirchhoff, invented the spectroscope and discovered spectrum analysis (*see* SPECTRUM), which led to their joint discovery of the elements cesium and rubidium (qq.v.).

Bunsen was born in Göttingen on March 31, 1811, and was educated at the University of Göttingen. Between 1836 and 1852 he taught successively at the Polytechnic Institute in Kassel and at the universities of Marburg and Breslau; thereafter he was professor at the University of Heidelberg until his retirement in 1889. Considered one of the greatest chemists in the world, Bunsen discovered (1834) the antidote that is still used today for arsenic poisoning: hydrated iron oxide. His research on the double cyanides confirmed the principle in organic chemistry that the nature of a compound depends on the radicals composing it. Contrary to popular belief, he had little to do with the invention of the Bunsen burner, a gas burner used in scientific laboratories. Although Bunsen popularized the device, credit for its design should go to the British chemist and physicist Michael Faraday. Among Bunsen's inventions are the ice calorimeter, a filter pump, and the zinc-carbon electric cell. He used the cell to produce an electric-arc light and invented a photometer to measure its luminosity. The cell was used also in his development of an electrolytic method of producing metallic magnesium. Results of his research on waste gases of blast furnaces were published in the classic *Gasometric Methods* (1857). Bunsen died in Heidelberg on Aug. 16, 1899.

BUNSEN BURNER, heating device widely used in laboratories because it provides a hot, steady, smokeless flame. It is named for the German chemist Robert Wilhelm Bunsen, who adapted the concept of a gas-air burner in 1855 and popularized its use. The burner is a short, vertical tube of metal connected to a gas source and perforated at the bottom to admit air. The flow of air is controlled by an adjustable collar on the tube.

BUNSHAFT, Gordon (1909-), American architect, born in Buffalo, N.Y., and educated at the Massachusetts Institute of Technology. A partner in the New York City office of the architectural firm of Skidmore, Owings, & Merrill, he is best known for Lever House (1952), the first curtain-wall skyscraper in New York City. This building inaugurated a new concept in urban design, in which a building occupied only a portion of its site, the rest of which formed a pedestrian plaza. Bunshaft's later work, such as the Beinecke Rare Book and Manuscript Library at Yale University (1963), shows an increased use of concrete and a movement away from the severe style of the 1950s. He was also in charge of design for the Hirshhorn Museum and Sculpture Garden in Washington, D.C. (1974), and the Haj Terminal at the airport in Jiddah, Saudi Arabia (1981).

BUNT. *See* SMUT.

BUNTING, common name of a number of birds forming the subfamily Emberizinae of the family Fringillidae (*see* FINCH). Restricted to the Old World, the true buntings include the yellowhammer (q.v.) and ortolan and the corn bunting, cirl bunting, and reed bunting; they form a distinct genus, *Emberiza.* The chief distinguishing characteristics are a downward-turning angle of the gape, or corner of the bill, and a hard knob on the palate, used for husking seeds, the chief food of the bunting. Among the New World finches, no such sharp distinctions can be drawn. The shewink and dickcissel are much like the buntings, the snow bunting less so, and the lark bunting and the indigo bunting (q.v.) are not true buntings at all.

The corn bunting, *E. calandra,* is brown, considerably larger than a house sparrow, and has a slightly forked tail. Common in low cultivated round in Europe and many parts of Asia, corn buntings live in pairs during spring and summer and in flocks during winter. The reed bunting, *E. schoeniclus,* with a black head and throat and a white nape, is common in marshy places. The cirl bunting, *E. cirlus,* has an olive-green head, with black streaks and patches of lemon yellow on the cheeks and over the eyes; it is found in southern Europe and northern Africa.

BUÑUEL, Luis (1900-83), Spanish film director, born in Calanda, and educated at the University of Madrid, where he met the surrealist artist Salvador Dalí, with whom he coauthored his first two films, *Un Chien Andalou* (1928) and *L'Age d'Or* (1930), which introduced the bizarre, disjunctive imagery that characterized the more than 30 films that followed. These two films are masterpieces of avant-garde cinema. Buñuel next made a documentary about impoverished peasants, *Land Without Bread* (1932). He then worked in various aspects of film in Europe and the U.S. before he resumed directing in 1947, working in Mexico and in Spain, where his films were banned by the Franco regime. Buñuel's vision of human impulses warped and paralyzed by religious and political repression is conveyed through disturbing but often absurdly humorous images. A classic example of his black humor, *The Discreet Charm of the Bourgeoisie* (1972), won the Academy Award for best foreign-language film and has been cited by many critics as one of the outstanding films of the 1970s. Other notable Buñuel films include the following: *Los Olvidados* (1950), *Viridiana* (1961), *The Exterminating Angel* (1962), and *That Obscure Object of Desire* (1977).

BUNYAN, John (1628-88), English writer and Puritan minister, author of *The Pilgrim's Progress,* one of the most famous religious allegories in the English language.

Bunyan was born in November 1628 at Elstow, near Bedford, the son of a tinker. He served an apprenticeship at his father's trade, and at about the age of 17, during the civil war, fought in the Parliamentary army. About 1648 he married Margaret Bentley (1603-55), a member of one of the Puritan sects of the day; Bunyan experienced a religious conversion and joined her church.

In 1655 Bunyan became one of the leaders of a congregation of Nonconformists in Bedford, giving sermons as a lay preacher. After his wife died, Bunyan remarried and became a popular preacher, speaking to large audiences. After the restoration of Charles II in 1660, Puritans lost the privilege of freedom of worship, and it was declared illegal to conduct divine service except in accordance with the forms of the Church of England. Bunyan, who persisted in his unlicensed preaching, was confined to Bedford county jail in 1660-72, although during a part of this time he was allowed a degree of freedom and was able to support his family by making shoelaces.

While Bunyan was in prison his library consisted of the Bible and the *Book of Martyrs* by the theologian John Foxe. Studying the content and literary style of these works, Bunyan began to write religious tracts and pamphlets. Before his release he wrote the first of his major works, the spiritual autobiography *Grace Abounding to the Chief of Sinners* (1666).

In 1675 Bunyan was imprisoned for six months, and during that time he probably wrote the major part of his masterpiece, *The Pilgrim's Progress from This World to That Which Is to Come,* a prose allegory of the pilgrimage of a soul in search of salvation (1st part published 1678; 2d part, 1684). Ten editions of this great work were printed during Bunyan's lifetime, and it eventually became the most widely read book in English after the Bible. It exerted great influence on later English writers. Noted for its simple, biblical style, *The Pilgrim's Progress* is now generally considered one of the finest allegories in English literature, and it has been translated into many languages.

During his last years Bunyan was universally recognized as the leading Puritan clergyman and author. He died of pneumonia on Aug. 31, 1688, in London. His other writings include *The Life and Death of Mr. Badman* (1680), a description of the life of a reprobate, and *The Holy War* (1682), a religious and political allegory.

BUNYAN, Paul, legendary hero of lumber camps of the American Northwest. Endowed with prodigious strength, vision, speed, humor, and cunning, Paul Bunyan has become since the 1830s the basis of a saga suited to the vastness of the North American continent. Some authorities find a French-Canadian origin for this modern folklore; others consider it a European import, elements of which were later magnified; but all agree that this fusion of bigness with the "tall story" is a legend peculiarly American. The origin of this legend was probably in the logging camps of Michigan, Wisconsin, and Minnesota, where the rugged loggers first heard and then retold the Paul Bunyan fables, adding local or personal or ancestral embellishments. The stories have been rewritten by many popular writers for readers of all ages.

BUNYORO, former kingdom east of Lake Albert, in present Uganda. It was founded in the 15th century by Nilotic invaders from the north, cattle breeders who established their dominance over the indigenous Bantu farming population. Bunyoro was ruled by a divine monarch (the omukama) who had the right to appoint local chiefs; he had no fixed abode, but traveled regularly from one part of the kingdom to another. It was the leading state in the region in the 17th and 18th centuries; after 1800 it was eclipsed by the kingdom of Buganda to the south. Reduced in size, Bunyoro was annexed by the British in the 1890s. From 1962 until it was abolished in 1967, it was part of the federation of Uganda.

BUONAPARTE. *See* BONAPARTE.

BUOY, metal or wooden floating object usually anchored or moored on a dangerous rock or shoal at the entrance of a harbor, or at the edge of a channel, as a guide to navigators. Mooring buoys are also used as anchorages to secure vessels in specified positions. Buoys are often named according to shape, as the can buoy, which is a metal cylinder; the nun buoy, which has the shape of a truncated cone; and the spar buoy, which is an upright post, or spar, anchored at one end. The bell buoy is surmounted by a bell that is sounded by the action of the waves; the gong buoy, similarly operated, produces several distinctive, bell-like tones; and the whistle or horn buoy is fitted with a device by which air, compressed by the action of the waves, is led to escape through a whistle. Lighted buoys are extremely important aids to navigation at night; they are battery powered and emit light signals of different color and duration. *See* LIGHTHOUSE.

Each nation has a buoyage system of shapes, colors, numbers, and markings to indicate dangers to navigation. In the U.S. buoyage system, red, even-numbered buoys mark the starboard

A Coast Guard buoy marking the entrance to Pollack Rip channel off the coast of Massachusetts is equipped with a foghorn and battery-operated light.

U.S. Coast Guard

(right-hand) side of a channel, when coming from seaward, and black odd-numbered buoys indicate the port (left-hand) side. Buoys with red and black horizontal stripes mark channel junctions and isolated dangers.

BUOYANCY. *See* FLUID MECHANICS.

BURBAGE, Richard (c. 1567–1619), English actor, considered the first great performer in the English theater. Born probably in Stratford-on-Avon, he was the son of the actor James Burbage (1530?–97), who built (1576?) the Theatre, the first permanent building in England for dramatic performances, and founded (1596?) the Blackfriars Theatre. After his father's death, Richard, in association with his elder brother Cuthbert (1566?–1636), moved (1598) the Theatre building to another London site and renamed it the Globe. He performed at the Globe and at Blackfriars (in which he also had a major share) as leading man in the theatrical company founded in 1594 as the Chamberlain's Men (known after 1603 as the King's Men). William Shakespeare wrote plays for the company and also acted in them. Excelling in tragedy, Burbage created many leading Shakespearean roles, including Richard III, Hamlet, Lear, and Othello. He also appeared in the plays of other leading dramatists of the period—Ben Jonson, Thomas Kyd, John Webster, and the collaborators Francis Beaumont and John Fletcher. When Shakespeare died, he left a ring to Burbage as a token of friendship.

BURBANK, city, Los Angeles Co., SW California, a N suburb of Los Angeles, in the San Fernando Valley; inc. 1911. It is noted for its prominent aircraft, movie, and television industries. Manufactures include electrical and agricultural equipment and cosmetics. The community was platted (1887) on land that had been part of a sheep ranch belonging to David Burbank (1821–95), after whom it is named. Pop. (1970) 88,871; (1980) 84,625.

BURBANK, Luther (1849–1926), American horticulturist, botanist, and pioneer plant breeder.

Burbank was born in Lancaster, Mass., on March 7, 1849, and was educated at local schools and at Lancaster Academy. His boyhood was spent on a farm, and at the age of 21 he purchased a plot of land near Lunenburg, Mass., and began his lifework of plant breeding. In 1873 he developed the so-called Burbank potato, a large, hardy variety much superior to the small, easily spoiled type then grown. In 1875 he moved to Santa Rosa, Calif., and established a nursery garden and a greenhouse that were the site of his plant-breeding experiments for the next 50 years. There he originated the edible, thornless Opuntia cactus; several improved varieties of fruits and vegetables; several new strains of roses and many other ornamental and decorative flowers and plants; and a new fruit, the plumcot, a cross between the plum and the apricot. At the time of his death he had more than 3000 experiments under way and was growing more than 5000 distinct botanical species native to many other parts of the world. His experiments stimulated worldwide interest in plant breeding.

Burbank's primary concern was the development of new varieties of plants. In the realm of

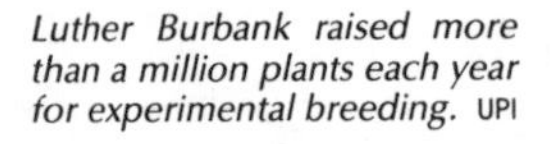

Luther Burbank raised more than a million plants each year for experimental breeding. UPI

theory he was influenced by the principle of heredity set forth in Mendel's laws and by Lamarckism, a formerly accepted theory of the inheritance of acquired characteristics. He died in Santa Rosa on April 11, 1926. Among his writings are *Luther Burbank. His Methods and Discoveries* (12 vol., 1914-15) and *How Plants Are Trained to Work for Man* (8 vol., 1921).

BURCHFIELD, Charles Ephraim (1893-1967), American painter, born in Ashtabula, Ohio, and educated at the Cleveland School of Art. At one time a wallpaper designer, Burchfield devoted himself entirely to painting after 1929. His specialty was depicting scenes of American small-town and country life. From 1943 Burchfield concentrated on landscapes in watercolor. His work ranges from the moody, semiabstract canvases of his early period, represented by *Night Wind* (1918, Museum of Modern Art, New York City), to the intensely realistic genre painting of midcareer, such as *November Evening* (1931-34, Metropolitan Museum, New York City) and *Freight Car Under a Bridge* (Detroit Institute of Art), and the highly romantic landscapes, with anthropomorphized natural features, of his later years.

BURCKHARDT, Jakob (1818-97), Swiss historian of art and culture, who to a great extent molded the modern concept of the European Renaissance. He was born in Basel and educated at the universities of Basel and Berlin. With the exception of three years (1855-58), during which he taught at the Zürich Polytechnic Institute, he spent the following half century (1843-93) as professor of the history of art and civilization at the University of Basel.

Burckhardt's first important work was *The Age of Constantine the Great* (1852; trans. 1949), a study of the Roman Empire in the 4th century AD, in which he analyzed the decay of classical civilization and the triumph of Christianity. He followed it with *The Cicerone: A Guide to the Works of Art in Italy* (1855; trans. 1873), which became extremely popular. His most famous work, however, is *The Civilization of the Renaissance in Italy* (1860; trans. 1878), on which his reputation rests. In it, he traced the cultural patterns of transition from the medieval period to the awakening of the modern spirit and creativity of the Renaissance. He saw the transition as one from a society in which people were primarily members of a class or community to a society that idealized the self-conscious individual. This work remains one of the most important on the subject.

BURDETT-COUTTS, Angela Georgina, Baroness (1814-1906), British philanthropist, born in London. A member of a wealthy and prominent family, she used much of her inherited wealth to promote charitable works. She endowed schools, churches, and housing throughout the British Empire, founded an establishment in Australia to aid the aborigines, and began a relief fund for refugees of the 1877 Russo-Turkish War. In 1871 she became the first woman to be honored with a peerage for public achievement. She is buried in Westminster Abbey.

BURDOCK, common name for coarse biennial weeds of the genus *Arctium* of the family of composite flowers (q.v.); the genus is characterized by bristly burrs. Two species—the great burdock, *A. lappa,* and the common burdock, *A. minus*—were native to Europe, and are now common throughout the U.S.

BUREAUCRACY, personnel and administrative structure of an organization. Business, labor, religious, educational, and governmental organizations depend on a large work force arranged in hierarchical fashion to carry out specialized tasks and guided by internal rules and procedures. The term *bureaucracy* is used most frequently in referring to government administration, especially with regard to officials in the federal government and civil service. It is often used derogatorily to insinuate waste, inefficiency, and red tape.

In a more important sense, the growth of governmental systems depends on bureaucracy, without which no modern government can function. A major hindrance to development in some nations has been the lack of large-scale organizational techniques.

The U.S. federal bureaucracy is the result of almost two centuries of tinkering and compromise. During the early days of the nation executive officials were recruited mainly from an educated class that had an interest in a long-term career in government. In 1820 Congress imposed a 4-year term for federal administrators, leading to rapid turnover and the beginning of a spoils system (q.v.) that allocated federal jobs to political supporters of the party in power.

The Pendleton Act of 1883 created a competitive civil service (q.v.), dedicated to professionalism and nonpartisanship. During the 20th century, as these attributes of political independence took hold, the civil service came under fire for being insufficiently responsive to Congress and the president. At the same time, critics complained about its bureaucratic aspects. In 1978 Congress passed the Civil Service Reform Act, which replaced the Civil Service Commission with the Office of Personnel Management, under closer control of the president. The act also established the Senior Executive Service to provide presidents with greater discretion in reassigning top officials to various departments and agencies.

The generalization that government bureaucracy is anonymous and unaccountable does not always accord with facts. Federal officials in field offices around the nation operate close to the public. Various statutes require broad representation within the executive branch of different social and economic interests, geographical units, political parties, and minority groups. The administrative process of the federal government is purposely designed to encourage participation by the public, private interest groups, and local officials. Bureaucracy then need not be viewed as an impediment to efficient government operation. A responsible and an effective bureaucracy is a very important part of any democratic system. L.F.

BURGAS, city and seaport, E Bulgaria, capital of Burgas Province, on the Gulf of Burgas (an inlet of the Black Sea). The surrounding region is chiefly agricultural. The city has a good harbor and is connected by rail, through Sofia, with the general European railroad system. The major part of Bulgaria's Black Sea grain trade passes through Burgas, and trade in other agricultural products is second only to that of Varna. The city also has flour and sugar mills. Pop. (1979 est.) 165,994.

BURGENLAND, province, E Austria, lying S of the Danube R. It is bounded on the N by Lower Austria Province, on the E by Hungary, on the S by Yugoslavia, and on the W by Styria and Lower Austria provinces. The low-lying plains of the N section contain large tracts of pastureland and arable farmland. Elsewhere, the terrain is hilly and thickly forested. About two-thirds of Lake Neusiedler lies within Burgenland; the main river is the Raab. Temperate climatic conditions prevail throughout most of the province; and the mean annual temperature is about 10° C (50° F). Livestock farming, especially the raising of cattle, hogs, and poultry, and lumbering are leading industries. The principal crops include grains, fruits, wine grapes, legumes, sugar beets, hemp, and flax. Deposits of bituminous coal, limestone, and sulfur are worked. Manufacturing consists largely of small-scale food processing. The population of Burgenland is mostly rural. The larger communities are Eisenstadt (the capital), Oberwart, and Deutschkreutz.

After the 8th century AD the region occupied by present-day Burgenland was settled by German, Slavic, and Magyar colonists. Becoming an Austrian possession in 1491, it remained under Austrian control until 1647, when Holy Roman Emperor Ferdinand III (1608–57) ceded it to Hungary. Under the terms of the Allied peace agreements with Austria and Hungary after World War I, Hungary was required to return Burgenland to Austria. The Hungarian government rejected this decision, and the ensuing controversy was settled (December 1921) by a plebiscite on the future of Sopron, then the capital of Burgenland, and adjacent areas. A majority of the voters cast ballots in favor of Hungary. The disputed city and its immediate locality were returned to Hungary in February 1922. Soviet troops occupied the province in April 1945, and it was assigned to the Soviet Zone of Occupation until 1955. Area, 3966 sq km (1531 sq mi); pop. (1981) 272,274.

BÜRGER, Gottfried August (1747–94), German poet, born near Halberstadt. He taught philosophy and aesthetics at the University of Göttingen. His greatest work, the folk ballad *Lenore* (1773), recounts the macabre tale of a dead soldier who marries his sweetheart. *Lenore* and his other poems strongly influenced the poets of his time and generally inspired a long-lasting revival of the ballad. Bürger wrote several other ballads and lyric poems, most of which were well received. In addition he translated some of the works of Homer and Shakespeare.

BURGER, Warren Earl (1907–), American jurist and the 15th chief justice of the U.S.

Burger was born on Sept. 17, 1907, in Saint Paul, Minn., and educated at the University of Minnesota and St. Paul College of Law (now William Mitchell College of Law). After graduating from law school in 1931, he began private practice in St. Paul, handling both criminal and civil cases. During the next 22 years, he practiced law, taught at his law school, and was active in Republican party politics.

In 1953 Burger joined the U.S. Department of Justice, serving as assistant attorney general in charge of the civil division under Attorney General Herbert Brownell (1904–). In 1956, President Dwight D. Eisenhower appointed Burger to the U.S. Court of Appeals for the District of Columbia. He soon acquired a reputation as the most conservative judge in the appellate court. His conservative views brought him to the attention of President Richard M. Nixon, and in 1969 Nixon appointed Burger to succeed Earl Warren as chief justice of the U.S. On the Court, Burger did not hold the strong leadership position of his predecessor, partly because of the division between liberals and conservatives on the bench. Burger resigned in 1986 and was replaced by William H. Rehnquist.

See also SUPREME COURT OF THE UNITED STATES.

BURGESS, John William (1844–1931), American educator and political scientist, born in Giles Co., Tenn., and educated at Cumberland University, Amherst College, and German universities. During the American Civil War he went north and served in the Union army. He thereafter taught at Knox College and Amherst until 1876, when he became professor of political science and constitutional law at Columbia College (now Columbia University). He was instrumental in forming the Columbia graduate school of political science, the first such school in the U.S. He became the first dean of the school in 1890 and founded the periodical *Political Science Quarterly*. Burgess was an authority on American constitutional law, with special reference to the periods of the Civil War and Reconstruction.

BURGH, Hubert de (d. 1243), English statesman. He was in the service of King Richard I, and by 1201 he had become chamberlain to King John. According to Ralph of Coggeshall (d. after 1227), a contemporary English chronicler, after the English subjugated Normandy, Burgh, as jailer, refused to obey a royal order to mutilate his prisoner Arthur, duke of Brittany (1187–1203). Burgh also is said to have urged John to grant the Magna Charta. In 1215 the king appointed Burgh chief justiciar, or justice, of England, an office he held for 17 years. In 1217, after Louis VIII of France had invaded England, Burgh won a naval victory that forced Louis to withdraw and renounce his claims to the English crown. From 1219 until 1227 Burgh was virtual ruler of England as regent for John's successor, Henry III. When Henry attained his majority in 1227, he made Burgh earl of Kent. Later the two men quarreled about a military expedition to France and royal subservience to the papacy. Charged in 1232 with treason, Burgh was jailed and stripped of his title and estates. These were restored in 1234, when he received a full pardon.

William Cecil, 1st Baron Burghley

National Portrait Gallery, London

BURGHLEY, William Cecil, 1st Baron (1520–98), English statesman, who was chief adviser to Queen Elizabeth I.

Cecil was born on Sept. 13, 1520, in Bourne, and educated at Saint John's College, University of Cambridge. He first served in the Court of Common Pleas and then as a member of Parliament; eventually, through patronage, he became a secretary to King Edward VI. During the reign of Mary I, invited to participate in the government, he chose to withdraw from court.

On the accession in 1558 of Elizabeth I, whose favor he had carefully cultivated, Cecil became principal secretary to the queen. Together with her, he set about improving the economic footing of England, among other measures adopting a new coinage in 1561. To heal the religious division of the country, they prepared a compromise settlement, acceptable to a majority of the English, that resulted in the establishment of the Anglican church (1559). He also ended the costly war with France.

Their most immediate problems solved, at least temporarily, Cecil and Elizabeth began to develop the long-term policies of moderation and compromise that were to guide England for the next 40 years: measures aimed at building up prosperity at home and dealing prudently with threats from foreign powers. Cecil strengthened the army and navy, and, because the government periodically was menaced by subversion, he organized an efficient secret service. His chief rival was the queen's favorite, Robert Dudley, earl of Leicester, with whom he carried on a lengthy power struggle. Cecil managed, however, to survive the many challenges to his relationship with the queen, and his triumph over all his enemies was manifest when he was made 1st Baron Burghley in 1571 and lord high treasurer in 1572.

During the 1570s and '80s, Burghley's vigilance protected England and its sovereign against the many plots and invasion schemes hatched by Roman Catholic nations to unseat the Protestant queen. His close scrutiny of the machinations of Elizabeth's cousin, Mary Stuart of Scotland, led ultimately to her trial for treason and her execution. His insight into the intentions of Spain and his preparations for resistance, especially by sea, culminated in the defeat of the Spanish Armada in 1588, bringing relative security at last.

Burghley's enormous contribution to his country was perhaps best recognized by Elizabeth herself, who said of him: "No prince in Europe hath such a counselor as I have in mine."

BURGKMAIR, Hans, the Elder (1473-1531), German Renaissance painter and engraver. A pupil of the artist Martin Schongauer and possibly also of Albrecht Dürer, he combined northern Germanic tradition with Italian Renaissance motifs derived from several visits to Italy. His altarpieces and other religious works were a major contribution to the spread of the Renaissance style in Germany. He made nearly 700 wood engravings and was one of the first masters of the color woodcut.

BURGLARY, in law, the crime of breaking into and entering the dwelling of another with felonious intent, whether or not the felony is actually perpetrated. English common law defined burglary as housebreaking at night only; in the U.S., however, statutes vary from state to state. Some retain the common-law definition; others include housebreaking by day. To constitute burglary, breaking and entering must be inferred as, for example, gaining admission through a trick or threat or by raising a window and putting the hand inside with intent to steal, without bodily entrance.

In the U.S. other variables that affect the nature of the crime and influence the punishment include the type of structure involved (for example, whether it is a home, a store, or an office), whether the structure is occupied at the time of entry, the means used to obtain entry, the presence or absence of a weapon on the intruder, and the crime committed or intended after entry. In most of the U.S., entry into a movable structure, such as a train or boat or an airplane, with intent to commit a felony also constitutes burglary. Although burglary is usually committed for the purpose of robbery, it may be charged against other offenders, including murderers, rapists, and kidnappers.

BURGOS, city, N Spain, capital of Burgos Province, on the Arlanzón R. Burgos consists of the old town, on the W bank of the Arlanzón, and a modern district on the E bank, connected by several bridges. The Cathedral of Burgos, begun in 1221 and completed in 1567, is the best example of Gothic architecture in Spain. Built of white limestone in the form of a Latin cross, it contains the tombs of Fernán González (910-70) and El Cid, national heroes of the period of the Moorish invasion. Wool and farm products are the principal commercial commodities in Burgos. Chief industries include the manufacture of woolen and leather goods, candy, paper, and chemicals.

Founded in the 9th century, Burgos was the capital of the kingdom of Castile and León from 1035 until 1560, when Madrid became the capital of all Spain. It became an episcopal see in 1074 and an archiepiscopal see in 1574. The city was the commercial center of Castile during the 15th century, but thereafter its prosperity declined. In 1833 it became the capital of the province. During the Spanish civil war (1936-39), Burgos was

A view of Burgos. In the foreground is its most celebrated building, the Cathedral of the Assumption, built in the 13th century. Dick Huffmann–Monkmeyer Press

the seat of the Nationalist government of Francisco Franco until the capture of Madrid at the end of the war. Pop. (1981 est.) 148,112.

BURGOYNE, John (1722–92), British general, best known for his role in the American Revolution.

Burgoyne was born in Sutton, England, and was educated at Westminster School. He first entered the army in 1740 but sold his commission in 1746. He rejoined at the outbreak of the Seven Years' War in 1756 and saw his first action in France. In 1761, while the war was still going on, he was elected to Parliament. The following year he served with distinction in the campaign along the Spanish-Portuguese frontier, where, as brigadier general, he captured Valencia de Alcántara. After the war he became a critic of the colonial policies of the British government.

At the start of the American Revolution, in 1775, Burgoyne served under Gen. Thomas Gage in Boston, and in 1776 he was second in command to Sir Guy Carleton, commander of the British forces in Canada. Dissatisfied with the conduct of the war, he won official approval of his own campaign strategy to invade New York from Canada and combine his troops at Albany with the army of the British commander in chief Sir William Howe. In May 1777, Burgoyne replaced Carleton in command and in the early summer moved southward with 10,000 men. He captured Fort Ticonderoga on July 6, but thereafter his advance toward Albany was slowed. He reached Saratoga in September, fought an indecisive battle with the Americans, and retreated. On October 7 he again made contact with the Americans at Saratoga but, lacking reinforcements and supplies, surrendered ten days later to Gen. Horatio Gates. The American victory is generally regarded as the turning point of the war.

When Burgoyne returned to England, he was subjected to severe criticism in Parliament for his failure at Saratoga. In 1782 he served briefly as commander in chief in Ireland, but thereafter devoted most of his time to writing. He had a measure of success as a dramatist. Burgoyne died in London on Aug. 4, 1792.

BURGUNDY (Fr. *Bourgogne*), several historic kingdoms, counties, duchies, and a province situated within France. During the 5th century AD, the Burgundians, a Germanic tribe, invaded and established the first kingdom of Burgundy in France. The kingdom expanded until it included most of what is now southeastern France and part of present-day Switzerland. The Burgundians were conquered in 534 by the Merovingian rulers of the Franks and were later absorbed into the Carolingian Empire. In 843 Burgundy was divided between Charles I of France (later Charles II, Holy Roman emperor) and his brother, Emperor Lothair I. In 879 the kingdom of Provence, or Cisjurane Burgundy, was organized in the south, and in 888 the kingdom of Trans-Jurane Burgundy was created in the north. Two other divisions, the duchy of Burgundy and the Free County of Burgundy, or Franche Comté, were also established in the 9th century. In 933 the two kingdoms were united as the second kingdom of Burgundy, with the capital at Arles. In 1033 the kingdom was annexed by Conrad II, Holy Roman emperor. Also known as the kingdom of Arles, Burgundy was ceded to France in 1378, and the kingdom ceased to exist as a separate state.

Franche Comté, in northern Cisjurane Burgundy, was part of the territory ruled by Lothair I. It passed to the Holy Roman Empire in 1033, but control was thereafter contested by other European powers. From 1295 to 1477 the region was influenced by France; after 1477 it passed to the Spanish line of the Habsburg family, and in 1678 it was permanently joined to France.

The duchy of Burgundy was a part of the first kingdom of Burgundy and was a possession of France after 1015. Until 1361 it was ruled by the house of Capet, and after 1363 by Philip the Bold of France and his successors, the dukes of Burgundy. The duchy was expanded to the English Channel and included several provinces in the Low Countries. By the middle of the 15th century the duchy dominated French affairs. The antagonism between the dukes of Burgundy and the kings of France reached a climax in 1465, when Charles the Bold, the last duke, attempted to restore the kingdom of Burgundy. The struggle ended in 1477 during a battle near Nancy in which Charles was killed. A dispute over possession of the ducal territories developed subsequently, and a large portion of the territory known as the Circle of Burgundy became part of the Holy Roman Empire. The rest of the duchy was a province of France from 1678 until the French Revolution (1789). Subsequently the province was divided into the departments of Ain, Côte-d'Or, Saône-et-Loire, and part of Yonne. The region is well known for its Burgundy wines.

BURHANPUR, city, central India, in Madhya Pradesh State, on the Tapti R. The town has many mosques and tombs and a palace built by the Mughal emperor Akbar. Silver and gold brocades, gold wire, and a variety of other high-quality products are produced in Burhanpur. Founded by Muslims about AD 1400, the town was the capital of an independent principality until the reign of Akbar, who made it one of his provincial administrative centers. During the 17th and 18th centuries, the town was the center of much of the internecine strife then current in India. Burhanpur was under British control from 1861 to 1947. Pop. (1981 prelim.) 141,142.

BURIAL, entombment of a corpse. Under U.S. law, burial is a civil matter and is regulated by statute. Although the law varies from state to state, it always provides that burial may not take place without a certificate attesting the cause of death from the last physician attending the deceased, or an order from an official, such as the coroner or medical examiner. Court decisions have established that a corpse has no commercial value and is legally the property of the nearest surviving relatives (in order of inheritance), who may dispose of it with or without respect for the wishes of the deceased. In some states neglect on the part of those legally responsible for and financially able to bury the corpse of a relative is a criminal offense. Unclaimed corpses and those that cannot be identified may, at the option of the authorities, be buried in municipal or other cemeteries at government expense or be given to scientific institutions for their use.

See also CATACOMBS; CREMATION; EMBALMING; FUNERAL RITES AND CUSTOMS; TOMB.

BURIDAN, Jean (1300–58), French Scholastic philosopher, who held a theory of determinism, contending that the will must choose the greater good. Born in Bethune, he was educated at the University of Paris, where he studied with the English Scholastic philosopher William of Ockham. After his studies were completed, he was appointed professor of philosophy, and later rector, at the same university. Buridan is traditionally but probably incorrectly associated with a philosophical dilemma of moral choice called "Buridan's ass." In the problem an ass starves to death between two alluring bundles of hay because it does not have the will to decide which one to eat.

BURKE, Edmund (1729–97), British statesman and orator, who championed many human rights causes and brought attention to them through his eloquent speeches.

Burke was born in Dublin and educated at Trinity College. He studied law briefly in London before embarking on a literary career. His first important work was *Vindication of Natural Society* (1756), a satire ridiculing the reasoning of the British statesman Henry Bolingbroke. This work, published anonymously, attracted considerable attention. Soon afterward he published an essay, *The Philosophical Inquiry into the Origin of Our Ideas on the Sublime and Beautiful* (1756). The following year he began a 30-year association with *The Annual Register,* a British yearbook.

Edmund Burke (after a painting by Sir Joshua Reynolds).

After 1761, when he became private secretary to the British chief secretary for Ireland, William Hamilton (1729–96), he demonstrated his aptitude for political service. Four years later he became private secretary to the new British prime minister Charles Watson-Wentworth, 2d marquis of Rockingham, and in 1766 Burke was elected as a Whig to Parliament. Almost immediately Burke sought repeal of the Stamp Act. In a pamphlet, *Thoughts on the Cause of the Present Discontents* (1770), and in two speeches, "On American Taxation" (1774) and "Conciliation with America (1775), he urged justice and conciliation toward the American colonies. Burke took a deep interest in India and advocated a reversal of the British policy that allowed the East India Co. to exploit the population of that country. On Feb. 15, 1788, Burke began a four-day-long opening speech in Westminster Hall in the unsuccessful impeachment proceedings against the statesman and colonial administrator Warren Hastings for high crimes and misdemeanors committed in India. Although Hastings was acquitted after a trial that lasted seven years, Burke had made the English aware of the oppression in India.

Burke later appeared as the champion of the feudal order in Europe, with the publication of *Reflections on the Revolution in France* (1790). The text, which was read throughout Europe, encouraged European rulers in their hostility to the French Revolution. Burke became more and more vehement in his denunciation of the French Revolution as time went on.

Burke retired from Parliament in 1794, after a career remarkable for its laborious, earnest, and brilliant discharge of duties.

BURKINA FASO. *See* UPPER VOLTA.

BURLESQUE (Ital. *burla,* "mockery"), form of comic art characterized by ridiculous exaggeration. Burlesque, a satiric method (*see* SATIRE), appears in two forms: the mock epic in which a trivial subject is treated grandly, as in "The Nun's Priest's Tale" of *The Canterbury Tales,* and the travesty, in which a serious subject is regarded frivolously, as in *Don Quixote.* Burlesque is often confused with two other related forms of satire, farce and parody. Parody is a mocking imitation of a particular work or of the style of a particular author; farce is a dramatic piece written only to excite laughter.

One of the earliest uses of the burlesque form in literature was in the ancient Greek mock epic poem "The Battle of the Frogs and the Mice." Burlesque in drama first appeared in the plays of the Greek dramatists Aristophanes and Euripides and the Roman playwright Plautus. In England burlesque developed about the beginning of the Renaissance; the foremost author of burlesque was Geoffrey Chaucer. The works of Chaucer, the Spanish writer Miguel de Cervantes, and the French writer Alain Le Sage effectively ridiculed the medieval romance. Two French comic playwrights, Paul Scarron and Molière, and the English playwright John Gay all excelled in dramatic burlesque. The English poet Samuel Butler achieved a similar excellence in his mock epic poem *Hudibras.* Of modern writings, the *Nonsense Novels* (1911) of the Canadian author Stephen Leacock is one of the best examples of light burlesque. A rich vein of travesty runs through most of the operettas of Sir William Gilbert and Sir Arthur Sullivan.

In the U.S. the word *burlesque* is applied to a form of theatrical production especially popular between World Wars I and II. Although American burlesque began in the late 1860s as a combination of the minstrel show and vaudeville (qq.v.), by the first quarter of the 20th century emphasis was already being placed upon broad, ribald comedy and scantily clad girls. The striptease, a feature of American burlesque in the 1930s, is a routine in which a female performer gradually divests herself of her clothing as she moves about the stage to music. Of the many strippers who achieved fame, Gypsy Rose Lee (1914-70) was the most prominent. As films and radio became increasingly popular and audiences became more sophisticated, interest in burlesque declined; also, the producers often ran afoul of local blue laws. The major importance of burlesque was as a training ground for comics; these included such performers as Fanny Brice, Bobby Clark (1888-1960), Bert Lahr (1895-1967), Red Skelton (1913-   ), and Phil Silvers (1912-85).

BURLINGAME, city, San Mateo Co., W California, on the W shore of San Francisco Bay; inc. 1908. It is chiefly a residential community, but manufactures include industrial burners, beverages, and foodstuffs. An influx of refugees following the 1906 San Francisco earthquake and fire provided the impetus for the community's early residential growth. The city is named for the American statesman Anson Burlingame, who acquired the land in 1866. Pop. (1970) 27,320; (1980) 26,173.

BURLINGAME, Anson (1820-70), American statesman, born in New Berlin, N.Y., and educated at the University of Michigan and Harvard University. He practiced law in Boston and was elected to the Massachusetts Senate in 1853. He served in the U.S. House of Representatives from 1855 to 1861, when he was defeated for reelection. He was U.S. minister to China from 1861 to 1867 and after 1867 special envoy of Prince Kung (1833-98), then coregent of China, to the U.S. and the European nations. In 1863 he negotiated the Burlingame Treaty, by which China accepted the principles of international law. The treaty also opened the U.S. to unlimited Chinese immigration until the passage of the first Chinese Exclusion Act in 1882.

BURLINGTON, city, seat of Des Moines Co., SE Iowa, a port of the Mississippi R., opposite Illinois; inc. 1836. It is a regional transportation, manufacturing, and financial center. Among its many products are earth-moving equipment, engine parts, electronic equipment, processed food, and furniture. A community college is in the city. Here Zebulon Pike raised the U.S. flag in 1805, and a trading post operated from 1808 to 1812. The community was founded in 1833, after the Black Hawk Treaty opened the area to white settlement. Burlington was the temporary capital of Wisconsin Territory in 1837 and Iowa Territory during 1838-41. It is named after Burlington, Vt. Pop. (1970) 32,366; (1980) 29,529.

BURLINGTON, town, Middlesex Co., E Massachusetts, near Boston; settled 1641, inc. 1799. Manufactures include microwave equipment, information-processing systems, measuring and optical instruments, and particle accelerators. Originally a part of Woburn, the community became a separate town in 1799. Its main growth as a manufacturing center began in the 1950s. Pop. (1970) 21,980; (1980) 23,486.

BURLINGTON, city, Burlington Co., central New Jersey, on the Delaware R.; inc. as a city 1784. Manufactures here include cast-iron products, clothing, and footwear. Among the city's many historic buildings is a house dating from 1685. The community was settled in 1677 by English

Quakers and named for Burlington, England. It was capital of the Province of West Jersey from 1681 to 1702, and of the United East and West Jersey alternately with Perth Amboy from 1702 to 1790. In 1726 Benjamin Franklin printed the first colonial money in Burlington. The state's first constitution was signed here in July 1776. Pop. (1970) 12,010; (1980) 10,246.

BURLINGTON, city, Alamance Co., N North Carolina, on the Haw R., near Greensboro; settled 1837, inc. 1866. It is an important textile and hosiery manufacturing center located in a fertile agricultural region. Nearby are Elon College (1889) and Alamance Battleground, where in 1771 the Regulators, an armed group seeking governmental reform, were defeated by a British force. The city, which grew around railroad shops established in 1855, was known as Company Shops until 1893, when the name Burlington was selected at random from a postal guide. Pop. (1970) 35,930; (1980) 37,266.

BURLINGTON, city, Halton Regional Municipality, SE Ontario, Canada, on Burlington Bay (an arm of Lake Ontario), opposite Hamilton; inc. as a city 1974. Manufactures include steel products, processed food, plastic goods, and electrical equipment. An Indian museum and the Bronte Creek Provincial Park are here. The community, named for the bay, was laid out in 1810 on lands awarded Joseph Brant, a Mohawk Indian chief. It became an important industrial center in the mid-20th century. Pop. (1981) 114,853; (1986) 116,675.

BURLINGTON, city, seat of Chittenden Co., NW Vermont, on Lake Champlain; inc. 1865. The largest city in Vermont, it is a port of entry and a manufacturing, commercial, and tourist center. Major products include electronic equipment, steel and wood items, maple syrup, business machinery, and textiles. The University of Vermont and State Agricultural College (1791), Trinity College (1925), Burlington College (1972), and a junior college are here. Burlington was the home of Ethan Allen, a hero of the American Revolution, from 1787 to 1789, and it also is the birthplace of the American philosopher and educator John Dewey. Settled in 1773, the community is named for the Burling family, early settlers of the area. During the War of 1812, Burlington served as a U.S. military base and was the scene of several skirmishes. Pop. (1970) 38,633; (1980) 37,712.

BURLINGTON, Richard Boyle, 3d Earl of (1694–1753), English architect and arbiter of taste, whose advocacy of the Palladian style was the dominant influence on English architecture from the 1720s to the '50s. As a student, he traveled to Italy to see Andrea Palladio's classically inspired buildings. Burlington designed houses and public buildings in England during the 1720s; his own villa at Chiswick (c. 1725) was the single most influential Palladian building of its time in England. Retiring from public life in the 1730s, Burlington supported the work of other architects. He also attempted to foster a neoclassical renaissance in painting and sculpture.

BURMA, officially known as the Union of Myanmar, republic of Southeast Asia, bounded on the N by Tibet Autonomous Region of China; on the E by China, Laos, and Thailand; on the S by the Andaman Sea and the Bay of Bengal; and on the W by the Bay of Bengal, Bangladesh, and India. The coastal region is known as Lower Burma, while the interior region is known as Upper Burma. The total area of the country is 676,552 sq km (261,218 sq mi).

LAND AND RESOURCES

A horseshoe-shaped mountain complex and the valley of the Irrawaddy R. system are the dominant topographical features of Burma. The mountains of the N margin rise to 5881 m (19,296 ft) atop Hkakabo Razi, the highest peak in Burma. The two other mountain systems have N to S axes. The Arakan Yoma range, with peaks reaching more than 2740 m (more than 9000 ft), forms a barrier between Burma and the subcontinent of India. The Bilauktaung range, the S extension of the Shan Plateau, lies along the boundary between SW Thailand and SE Lower Burma. The Shan Plateau, originating in China, has an average elevation of about 910 m (about 3000 ft).

Generally narrow and elongated in the interior, the central lowlands attain a width of about 320 km (about 200 mi) across the Irrawaddy-Sittang delta. The deltaic plains, extremely fertile and economically the most important section of the country, cover an area of about 46,620 sq km (18,000 sq mi). Both the Arakan (in the NW) and the Tenasserim (in the SW) coasts of Burma are rocky and fringed with islands. The country has a number of excellent natural harbors.

Climate. Most of Burma lies within the Tropic Zone. The hot season extends from March through October; and the cool season, the period of the Northeast Monsoon, from November through February. Temperatures from the cool to hot seasons range from 15.6° to 37.8° C (60° to 100° F) in Lower Burma and from less than 15.6° C (60° F) to more than 37.8° C (100° F) in Upper Burma. Temperatures are generally lower in mountainous regions. The country receives practically all its rainfall between mid-May and October, the period of the Southwest Monsoon. Annual precipitation in most of Upper Burma av-

Buddhist shrines in Mandalay, Burma. The large building on Mandalay Hill in the rear is a Buddhist monastery. George Holton–Photo Researchers, Inc.

erages about 890 mm (about 35 in) and in Lower Burma about 5080 mm (about 200 in).

Natural Resources. The most important resources of Burma are agricultural. Approximately 250 commercially useful kinds of trees abound, 50 of which have been exploited. Important mineral deposits, such as lead, zinc, tin, tungsten, coal, iron ore, natural gas, and petroleum, also exist, as do deposits of precious stones such as rubies and lapis lazuli.

Plants and Animals. Forests and woodland cover about half of Burma. In the regions of maximum precipitation, the dense tropical forests contain extensive stands of timber and oil-bearing trees, including commercially valuable teak forests. Other trees include rubber, cinchona, acacia, bamboo, ironwood, mangrove, coconut, betel palm, and, chiefly in the N highlands, oak, pine, and many species of rhododendron. Tropical fruits, such as citrus, bananas, mangoes, and guavas, grow extensively in the coastal regions. Vegetation in the arid regions is sparse and stunted.

Jungle animals, such as the tiger and leopard, are common in Burma. Among the larger native quadrupeds, found mainly in the highlands of Upper Burma, are the elephant, rhinoceros, wild buffalo, wild boar, and several species of deer and antelope. Elephants, tamed or bred in captivity, are used as work animals, particularly in the lumbering industry. Smaller quadrupeds include the gibbon, several species of monkey, the wildcat, the flying fox, and the tapir. Burma has over 1200 known varieties of birds, including parrots, peafowl, pheasants, crows, herons, and paddybirds. Among typical reptiles are crocodiles, geckos, cobras, pythons, and turtles. Many edible species of freshwater fish are plentiful in Burmese waters.

Soils. The richest soils are found in a narrow alluvial strip along the Bay of Bengal, where mountain streams irrigate the land; in the wide river valleys; and in the alluvial deposits of the Irrawaddy delta. These deep deposits form a vast, fertile belt especially suitable for rice cultivation by virtue of the abundant moisture.

POPULATION

The indigenous population of Burma is essentially Mongoloid. More than two-thirds of the people are Burman, racially akin to the Tibetans and the Chinese. In addition, several indigenous minorities with their own languages and cultures also inhabit the country. The most important of these groups are the Karen (q.v.), Shan, Mon, Chin, and Kachin. The Karen have their own state in Lower Burma. The Shan, a people related to the Thai, live mainly in the hills along the Thai border. The Mon, or Mon-Khmer, the first major ethnic group known to have migrated to Burma, live mainly in the delta region and are becoming assimilated with the Burman ethnic majority.

The Chin, who are related to ethnic groups of neighboring Assam State of India, live in the NW mountainous region. The Chin live primarily by

A typical village of thatched roofs on a canal near Lake Inle, in Shan State of east-central Burma. The Shan are closely linked to the people of nearby Laos and Thailand in language and customs. George Holton–Photo Researchers, Inc.

hunting and fishing. In Chin society, absolute leaders, who are usually also head priests of the traditional religion, rule the groups. The Kachin, a hill people, are concentrated in the far N of Burma, along the Chinese border. They are related ethnically to the Chinese. The Kachin are ruled by hereditary leaders. The Burmese population also includes large immigrant minorities, notably from India and China.

Population Characteristics. The population of Burma (1983 census) was 35,313,905. The overall population density was 52 per sq km (135 per sq mi), one of the lowest in the Far East. The population is more than 75% rural; most of the urban areas are actually agricultural villages.

Political Divisions. The Socialist Republic of the Union of Burma comprises Burma proper and the seven states of Arakan, Chin, Kachin, Karen, Kayah, Mon, and Shan. Burma proper consists of the seven divisions of Irrawaddy, Magwe, Mandalay, Pegu, Rangoon, Sagaing, and Tenasserim.

The capital, largest city, and principal seaport is Rangoon, or Yangon (pop., 1983 prelim., 2,458,712). Mandalay (532,895), in central Burma, is an important trade center. Other important cities are Moulmein (219,991), on the Gulf of Martaban, and Sittwe (107,607), a major seaport on the Bay of Bengal.

Religion and Language. About 85% of all Burmese are Buddhists, most of whom adhere to the Theravada school of Buddhism. Small groups of Hindus, Muslims, and Christians also live here.

Most of the linguistic groups of the Union of Burma are monosyllabic and polytonal, similar to those of Tibet and China (*see* SINO-TIBETAN LANGUAGES). Burmese, the principal language, is spoken by about 60% of the people. The Burmese alphabet is based on Sanskrit and a form of the alphabet of Pali, which is the sacred tongue of Buddhism.

About 15% of the population speaks the Shan and Karen languages, and the remainder speaks Mon. English is spoken among the educated, and the country contains a sizable number of Chinese speakers.

Education. Education is free, and is compulsory in primary schools. Instruction is in Burmese; English is the second language in many secondary schools. In the mid-1980s some 4,856,000 pupils attended about 27,500 primary schools, and about 1,251,500 students attended some 2240 high schools and middle schools.

The chief universities of Burma are the University of Rangoon (1920) and the University of Mandalay (1964). Other institutions of higher education include state schools of fine arts and of music and drama, in Rangoon and in Mandalay, and the Defense Services Academy (1955), in Maymyo. Burmese universities and colleges enrolled more than 174,000 students each year in the mid-1980s.

CULTURE

Burmese civilization is largely an outgrowth of Indian influences. The Burmese have shunned such Indian institutions as the caste system, however, and have retained an indigenous language and literature. Burma is one of the strongest enclaves of Buddhist culture in all of Asia; the numerous temples have led Burma to become widely known as the Land of Golden Pagodas.

Libraries and Museums. Formal libraries and museums, as such, are limited in number and facilities in Burma. The thousands of Buddhist temples, however, serve as repositories for books and religious artifacts. A particularly noted pagoda is Shwe Dagon, in Rangoon. The National Museum of Art and Archaeology (1952) is in Rangoon, and state museums are in Kyaukpyu, Mandalay, and Moulmein.

Literature. The first examples of Burmese literature are found on stone carvings dating from AD 1113. By the 15th century a rich tradition of historical and religious poetry had developed. Prose works did not become important until the late 19th century, when the proliferation of novels and plays received impetus from a revival of Burmese nationalism.

Theater. A popular form of entertainment in Burma is the *pwe.* A type of folk opera, it combines generally light story lines with music and dance.

Art. Secular art is almost unknown in Burma; the large body of sculpture and painting is confined to a Buddhist context. Architecture, as well as other art forms, displays a dominant Indian influence. Burmese artisans are known for their lacquer ware and woven silks.

ECONOMY

Burma is primarily an agricultural country, and more than half the working population is engaged in growing or processing crops. Industrial development, however, which was almost nonexistent before World War II, accelerated in the 1960s and '70s. A major aim of the socialist government is to modernize and diversify the economy; consequently, all private enterprises are being nationalized. The estimated annual national budget in the mid-1980s included about $827 million in revenue and about $954 million in expenditure.

Agriculture. About 15% of the total land surface of Burma is suitable for farming; in the mid-1980s, however, only a small portion of the arable land was under cultivation. Burma is one of the leading rice producers in the world; about 14.5 million metric tons of rice were harvested annually in the mid-1980s. Much rice is produced in the Irrawaddy delta. Other important crops, grown mainly on small farms in the central lowlands, are corn, cotton, peanuts, legumes, millet, nuts, sesame, sugarcane, and tobacco.

Forestry and Fishing. The Burmese forests are an important source of wealth, especially in teak and natural rubber. In the mid-1980s, timber production amounted to about 19.5 million cu m (about 689 million cu ft) annually. Important tree products, in addition to rubber, are quinine

In experiments conducted to improve and standardize the nutritional quality of fish paste, a UN research officer tests samples in the food technology laboratory of the Applied Research Institute in Rangoon, Burma. Fish paste is a basic foodstuff of the Burmese people and, in some regions, one of their major sources of protein.
United Nations

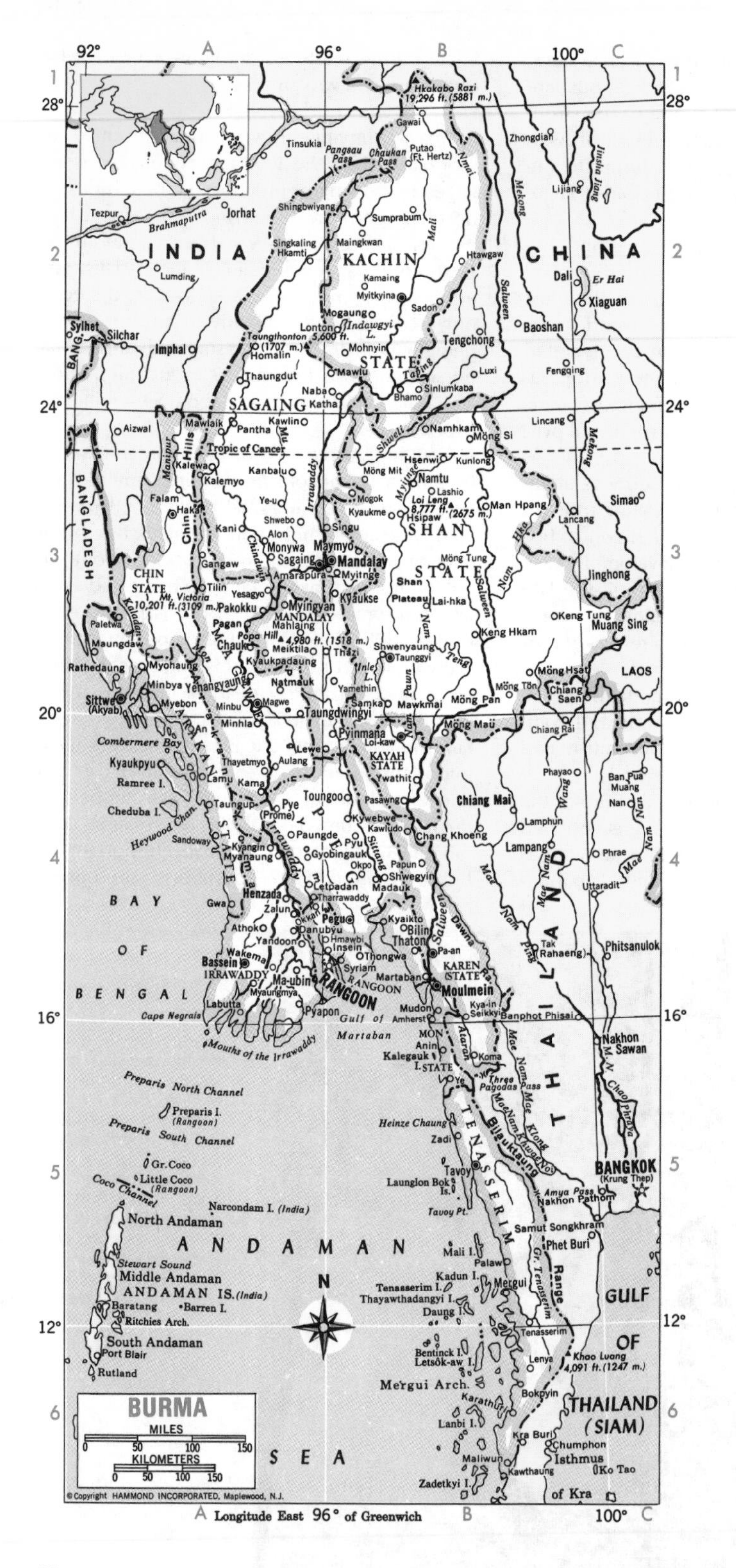

INDEX TO MAP OF BURMA

Internal Divisions

Cities and Towns

Möng Pan	B 3
Möng Ton	B 3
Möng Tung	B 3
Monywa	A 3
Moulmein	B 4
Mudon	B 4
Myanaung	A 4
Myaungmya	A 4
Myebon	A 3
Myingyan	A 3
Myitkyina	B 2
Myitnge	B 3
Myohaung	A 3
Namhkam	B 3
Namtu	B 3
Natmauk	A 3
Okkan	A 4
Okpo	B 4
Pa-an	B 4
Pagan	A 3
Pakokku	A 3
Palaw	B 5
Pantha	A 3
Pasawng	B 4
Paungde	A 4
Pegu	B 4
Prome (Pye)	A 4
Pyapon	A 4
Pye	A 4
Pyinmana	B 4
Pyu	B 4
Rangoon (cap.)	B 4
Rathedaung	A 3
Sadon	B 2
Sagaing	A 3
Sandoway	A 4
Shwebo	A 3
Shwegyin	B 4
Shywenyaung	B 3
Singu	B 3
Sinlumkaba	B 2
Sittwe	A 3
Sumprabum	B 2
Syriam	B 4
Taungdwingyi	B 3
Taunggyi	B 3
Taungup	A 4
Tavoy	B 5
Tenasserim	B 6
Tharrawaddy	B 4
Thaton	B 4
Thaungdut	A 2
Thayetmyo	A 4
Thazi	B 3
Thongwa	B 4
Toungoo	A 4
Victoria Point	B 6
Wakema	A 4
Yamethin	B 3
Yandoon	A 4
Ye	B 5
Yenangyaung	A 3
Yesagyo	A 3

Other Features

Amya (pass)	B 5
Andaman (sea)	A 5
Arakan Yoma (mts.)	A 4
Ataran (river)	B 5
Bengal (bay)	A 4
Bentinck (island)	B 6
Bilauktaung (range)	B 5
Cheduba (island)	A 4
Chin (hills)	A 3
Chindwin (river)	A 3
Coco (chan.)	A 5
Combermere (bay)	A 4
Daung (island)	B 5
Dawna (range)	B 4
Diphu (pass)	B 1
Great Coco (island)	A 5
Great Tenasserim (river)	B 5
Heinze Chaung (bay)	B 5
Heywood (chan.)	A 4
Hka, Nam (river)	B 3
Hkakabo Razi (mt.)	B 1
Indawgyi (lake)	B 2
Irrawaddy (river)	A 4
Irrawaddy, Mouths of the	A 5
Kadan (island)	B 5
Kaladan (river)	A 3
Kalegauk (island)	B 5
Khao Luang (mt.)	B 6
Kumjawng (pass)	B 2
Lanbi (island)	B 6
Launglon Bok (islands)	B 5
Letsôk-aw (island)	B 6
Mali (island)	B 5
Manipur (river)	A 3
Martaban (gulf)	B 5
Mekong (river)	C 3
Mergui (arch.)	B 6
Mon (river)	A 3
Mu (river)	A 3
Naga (hills)	A 2
Negrais (cape)	A 4
Nmai Hka (river)	B 2
Patkai (range)	A 2
Pegu Yoma (mts.)	A 4
Popa Hill (mt.)	A 3
Preparis (island)	A 5
Preparis North (chan.)	A 5
Preparis South (chan.)	A 5
Ramree (island)	A 4
Salween (river)	B 4
Shan (plat.)	B 3
Shweli (river)	B 3
Sittang (river)	B 4
Taungthonton (mt.)	A 2
Tavoy (point)	B 5
Tenasserim (island)	B 5
Teng, Nam (river)	B 3
Thayawthadangyi (island)	B 5
Three Pagodas (pass)	B 5
Tu, Nam (river)	B 3
Victoria (mt.)	A 3
Zadetkyi (island)	B 6

and catechu, or cutch, the source of a dye.

Fish are caught for local consumption and are a main source of protein in the Burmese diet. Freshwater fish are traditionally preferred, but the government now is encouraging saltwater fishing. In the early 1980s the total catch was estimated at about 585,800 metric tons; about 75% of the catch was made up of marine fish.

Mining. Burma has a rich and varied supply of minerals. Most of the mines are located in the mountainous areas in the W and along the Tenasserim coast. Such precious stones as jade, rubies, and sapphires are mined, as are copper, nickel, silver, lead, and zinc. In the mid-1980s, about 11.8 million barrels of crude petroleum were produced each year. Annual mineral production in the mid-1980s included silver (576,000 troy oz), lead (21,900 metric tons), zinc concentrates (5320 metric tons), and tin concentrates (745 metric tons). Large deposits of natural gas and iron ore have also been found.

Manufacturing. Rice milling and the processing of agricultural products are the chief Burmese manufacturing enterprises. In order to spur the industrial sector of the economy, the government has started a steel mill, a jute mill, a brick and tile factory, and other plants. Lumber mills, petroleum refineries, sugar refineries, plants for extracting vegetable oils, flour mills, and cotton mills also are in operation. In the mid-1980s annual manufacturing output included 62,000 metric tons of sugar, 328,000 metric tons of cement, and 14,100 metric tons of cotton yarn.

Energy. Burma has great potential for producing hydroelectricity, and in the mid-1980s about 49% of its electricity was produced by hydroelectric facilities. Most of the rest was generated by thermal plants using coal or refined petroleum. In the mid-1980s the country had an electricity-generating capacity of about 818,000 kw, and annual output was some 1.7 billion kwh.

Currency and Banking. The unit of currency is the kyat (6.7255 kyats equal U.S.$1; 1987). All banks were nationalized in 1963. In 1969 the banks were amalgamated to form the Union of Burma Bank. The bank regulates banking operations, controls the currency, and acts as banking agent for the government.

Commerce and Trade. All foreign trade is handled by the government. The principal exports are rice (about 41% of the export total), teak (about 25%), cotton, ores and metals, and rubber. The chief imports are machinery, transportation equipment, chemicals, textiles, and foodstuffs. In the mid-1980s yearly exports earned about $311 million, and annual imports cost some $513 million. Burma's main trade partners are Japan, Singapore, Indonesia, West Germany, Great Britain, and the U.S.

Transportation and Communications. The Burmese railroad system, owned and operated by the government, has about 3135 km (about 1950 mi) of track. The railroad links all the important cities of the country but does not connect with railroads outside Burma. Inland waterways, totaling about 5800 km (about 3600 mi) of navigable rivers and canals, are far more important as transportation arteries than the railroad system; most large towns are river ports. The Irrawaddy R. is the chief artery, and sections of the Chindwin

An elephant follows its handler's bidding in moving a heavy length of lumber. Elephants are highly valued in Burma, which lacks the machinery of more industrialized nations.
Herbert Lanks–Monkmeyer Press

and Salween rivers also are navigable. The highway system aggregates about 23,065 km (about 14,330 mi), of which about one-sixth is paved. Several roads cross the border, notably the Burma Road (q.v.), to China. A government-owned airline, Burma Airways Corp., provides both domestic and international service.

All postal, telegraph, telephone, and broadcasting systems in Burma are controlled by the government. About 52,600 telephones (most of them in Rangoon), 725,000 radios, and 35,000 television sets are in use.

Labor. In the mid-1980s the Burmese labor force numbered about 14,792,000 persons, of whom nearly 50% were engaged in agriculture and related activities. Few workers are organized into labor unions, and labor disputes are settled by government labor committees.

GOVERNMENT

Burma was governed according to the provisions of the constitution of 1948 until the coup d'état of 1962, after which the existing form of government was wiped out. In 1974 a new constitution was adopted. This document served as the basis of governmental organization until its suspension after the military coup of September 1988.

Central Government. Under the 1974 constitution, the country's chief executive official is the president, who is chairman of the 29-member State Council. The State Council and the Council of Ministers (headed by the prime minister) are chosen by the unicameral People's Assembly, Burma's principal legislative body, which is made up of 489 members elected to 4-year terms.

Health and Welfare. In 1956 the government inaugurated a social security program that provides accident and illness insurance, free medical care, and survivor's benefits. Funds are collected from employers, employees, and the government.

The health services in the country have been greatly extended, and since 1964 the number rural health stations, dispensaries, and hospitals have steadily increased. In the early 1980s the country had more than 600 hospitals with a total of 31,500 beds. Since the 1940s Burma has been faced with leprosy, tuberculosis, and venereal diseases. The number of malaria cases has sharply declined, however, as a result of the aid provided by the World Health Organization.

Political Parties. Following the Burmese coup d'état in 1962, the Revolutionary Council urged that all existing parties unite within a single party, the Burma Socialist Program party (BSPP). Under the 1974 constitution, the BSPP is recognized as the only legal political party.

Local Government. Burma proper is administered centrally from Rangoon. The country as a whole is divided into seven divisions inhabited by Burman people and seven states populated by national minorities. People's councils, headed by executive committees, are elected at all levels of local and regional or state government.

Judiciary. The Burmese judiciary system is highly centralized. The highest court in the land is the Council of People's Justices, which is elected by the People's Assembly. Lesser courts include state, divisional, and township courts.

Defense. In the mid-1980s the armed forces of Burma included about 186,000 persons. The army had 170,000 members, the navy had 7000, and the air force had 9000. The personnel was used primarily for internal-security purposes.

HISTORY

Burma's history has been made by a succession of peoples who migrated down along the Irrawaddy River from Tibet and China, and who were influenced by social and political institutions that had been carried across the sea from India. First came the Mon, perhaps as early as 3000 BC. They established economic centers in central Burma, in the Irrawaddy delta, and farther down the eastern coast of the Bay of Bengal. They constructed irrigation systems and developed commercial and cultural contacts with India while maintaining loose ties with other Mon civilizations in the Chao Phraya River valley of Siam (now Thailand). The Pyu followed much later, moving down the western side of the Irrawaddy and founding a capital near present-day Prome in AD 628. The Burmans entered the Irrawaddy River valley in the mid-9th century, absorbing the nearby Pyu and Mon communities. Later waves brought in the Shan and Kachin, who, along with the indigenous Karen, have all played a part in the country's development.

The Pagan Kingdom. The first unified Burmese state was founded by King Anawratha (r. 1044–77) at Pagan in Upper Burma and was brought to full flower by his able son, Kyanzittha (r. 1084–1112). Their domain advanced from the dry zone to incorporate the delta Mon centers at Pegu and Thaton; they extended political and religious ties overseas to Ceylon (now Sri Lanka) and fought off a Chinese invasion from the north. The internal structure of the state was that of a Hinduized kingdom, with a court at the capital supported by direct household taxes or service obligations drawn from villages, which in turn were under the guidance of hereditary myothugis ("township headmen"). As time passed, an increasing proportion of the land was donated to Buddhist monasteries in the form of slave villages for the maintenance of the sangha ("monkhood"). Kingship was legitimated by both Hindu ideology and the king's role as defender of the Buddhist faith. During 250 years of relative peace the devout rulers built the many pagodas for which Pagan is so well known today.

The fall of Pagan to the Mongols under Kublai Khan in 1287 was the beginning of a turbulent period during which Upper Burma led an uncertain existence between Shan domination and tributary relations with China, while Lower Burma reverted to Mon rule based at Pegu.

The Toungoo Dynasty. In the second quarter of the 16th century a new Burmese dynasty emerged from the sleepy principality of Toungoo in central Burma. With the aid of Portuguese adventurers, the Toungoo dynasty established what became under its third king, Bayinnaung (r. 1551–81), a reunified and precariously prosperous state. After his death, succession squabbles and encroachment by the Portuguese along the coast, by the Siamese on the east, and by Manipuri horsemen from the west brought on the decline of the dynasty, although the system itself endured until the mid-18th century. Its survival was made possible by a stable administrative and legal system at the central and local levels. It was finally toppled by a Mon rebellion in 1752.

The Konbaung Dynasty and the Anglo-Burmese Wars. Increasing European commercial and political pressure set the context for the rise and demise of the last Burmese dynasty. During the 1600s and early 1700s competing British, Dutch, and French interests had established commercial ventures at Syriam, near present Rangoon, and elsewhere on the coast. In 1752 Alaungpaya (d. 1760) founded the Konbaung dynasty by restoring Burmese rule first at Ava and later in the delta. He moved against the British at the Negrais trading post and then initiated another attack on the Thais, whose capital at Ayutthaya was later destroyed by his son King Hsinbyushin(r. 1763–76). Another son, Bodawpaya (r. 1781–1819), lost control of Siam but captured the Arakan, a rich coastal province bordering on Bengal. By the early 19th century, political friction over an Arakanese independence movement based in Bengal was compounded by the military successes of the Burmese general Maha Bandula (d. 1825) in Assam. The British responded by sea in the First Anglo-Burmese War (1824–26). The ensuing Treaty of Yandabo left the British in control of Arakan to the west and Tenasserim to the east of the Irrawaddy delta. The production of rice and timber flourished in these two areas under British administration, while their relative political stability induced massive population growth, a general pattern that was repeated after the remainder of the delta was annexed in the Second Anglo-Burmese War (1852). Commercial ambition and political pretext, heightened by Anglo-French regional rivalry, precipitated the final annexation, when Mandalay fell after a brief battle

The stark outline of the Independence Monument in Rangoon, Burma, contrasts sharply with the traditional architecture of the pagoda in the background.
United Nations

in 1885. These extensions of British rule were progressively less popular with the resident population, and each in turn required a period of pacification. In the longer run, British rule brought widespread administrative and social modernization to a land that, except for the benign efforts of King Mindon (r. 1853-78), the builder of Mandalay, had been swamped in reclusive policies and wracked by court intrigues.

British Rule. The Burmese culture, now submerged under a colonial overlay, had three main aspects: the Burmese language, with some accretions from Mon and Pali; Theravada Buddhism, which had come from Ceylon and mixed with local *nat* ("animist") rituals; and the small society of rice-growing peasant villages. Under colonial rule the linkage of government and religion was lost, the monastic orders fell into disarray, and the monastic schools, which had given Burma a higher rate of male literacy than the England of that day, declined as English became the language of social advancement. The indigenous culture nevertheless persisted: in the magical world of the *pwe* ("theater"), in the practice of everyday Buddhism and *nat* worship, and in the language of the peasantry.

The British moved the capital from royal Mandalay to the port city of Rangoon in 1886, developing it as a substation of the British Empire in India. Rangoon thus became the hub of a "steel frame" of administration spreading out into the hinterland, where district officers maintained law and order, collected revenue, and administered justice. As the country was opened up to the world market, it became the world's major exporter of rice—from 0.5 million metric tons before the fall of Mandalay, to 2 million at the turn of the century, and 3 million before World War II. British rule and economic penetration gradually engendered social disintegration and provoked a nationalist movement in the capital. This movement used modern institutions, such as the Young Men's Buddhist Association, student strikes, and political participation in partial self-government, to agitate for immediate reforms, including separation from India, and later for independence. In the countryside, the antimodern Saya San Rebellion of 1930-32 drew widespread support.

The political leaders who eventually linked capital and countryside into a truly independent Burma had their start as student leaders who flaunted the title Thakin (master), a term that had previously been applied to the British. The Thakin movement formed a Burma Independence Army (BIA), which supported the successful Japanese invasion of Burma in World War II. This political movement then took advantage of the strains of wartime occupation and the weakness of the Japanese-installed government to stage resistance to Japanese rule under the name of the Anti-Fascist People's Freedom League (AFPFL).

The Modern Nation. After the war the returning British discovered that the AFPFL, led by former student leader and BIA head U Aung San, had monopolized indigenous political power. The AFPFL forced Britain to grant independence to Burma in 1948. It also compelled the inclusion into a "federal" republic of such peripheral groups as the Shan and Karen, who had thought they had special British protection.

Constitutional democracy. The new independence confronted the AFPFL government of U Nu (Aung San had been assassinated by a prewar politician) with a series of political and ethnic insurrections, which continued over the next three decades. During the 1950s a major threat created by the Karen revolt was blunted, and the Communist insurgents were forced to retreat into the hills. Burma then established a rigorously nonaligned foreign policy. Economic reconstruction was accomplished and some new growth undertaken with multilateral foreign aid. AFPFL rule was validated in national elections in 1951-52 and 1956. By 1958, however, a party split required the constitutional intervention of a caretaker army government for 18 months. Gen. Ne Win's government tightened administrative discipline to promote modernization and curbed separatist tendencies in the Shan states. The 1960 election gave a resounding victory to U Nu's faction, based largely on respect for his personal piety. His promotion of Buddhism as the state religion and his tolerance for ethnic separatism precipitated a bloodless army coup that returned Ne Win to power in March 1962.

The Ne Win regime. During the 1960s and '70s Ne Win attempted to build an effective, totalitarian government, establish legitimacy with the Burmese people, and maintain autonomy on the world scene. Socialization of the economy during the first dozen years cut agricultural production and exports, which recovered following liberalization in the late 1970s. A new constitution was promulgated in 1974, transferring power by referendum and single-party election from the military Revolutionary Council to a People's Assembly, with commanding positions held by Ne Win and other former military leaders. Student strikes still erupted at intervals, as when U Thant, a political figure of the constitutional democracy period and UN secretary-general, died and was returned to Burma for burial in 1974. Ethnic insurrections, which broke out in the Kachin and Shan states after the army coup, continued to deny major areas to government control, including Burma's part of the Golden Triangle (a major supplier of the world opium market). The Burma Communist party insurrection retained official support from China. At one stage, U Nu escaped to Thailand and attempted to rally an overthrow of Ne Win's government. In 1980 he was permitted to return to Burma as a private citizen.

Burma's singular success in the post-World War II period was its ability to keep free of major political involvements, such as the Indochina wars. U Nu was, along with India's Nehru, China's Zhou Enlai, and Yugoslavia's Tito, a founder of the Conference of Nonaligned Nations. While maintaining relations with the People's Republic of China, the government pushed autonomy even further, reducing foreign aid and delaying membership in the Asian Development Bank. At the Havana meeting in 1980, Burma withdrew from the Nonaligned Conference in protest at its slide toward the Soviet bloc. In 1981 Ne Win relinquished the presidency to San Yu (1919-), a retired general, but he stayed on as chairman of the country's ruling Burma Socialist Program party. Antigovernment riots in March and June 1988 led Ne Win to resign the party chairmanship in July, ushering in a period of political instability. In September Gen. Saw Maung (1928-), chief of staff under Ne Win, emerged from a power struggle to head a military government. In June 1989 the country's name was officially changed in English to the Union of Myanmar, and the name of the capital from Rangoon to Yangon. J.F.G.

For further information on this topic, see the Bibliography in volume 28, sections 120, 668, 1092–93.

BURMA ROAD, vehicular highway about 1125 km (about 700 mi) long, extending from the railhead of Lashio, Burma, to Kunming, capital of Yunnan Province, China. Built by the Chinese as a military supply route in 1937–38, it was used by the Allies to send arms and other supplies to China during the early months of World War II. The supplies were landed in Rangoon and shipped by rail to Lashio; from there they were carried by truck over the serpentine road across rugged mountainous terrain, with elevations ranging from 975 to 2590 m (3200 to 8500 ft).

In April 1942, the Japanese captured Lashio and gained control of the road, which was not reopened until Jan. 20, 1945. The Allies in the meantime had constructed an alternate supply route from Ledo, a railhead in Assam, India, to the Chinese portion of the original route. The name of this route was changed to Stilwell Road in honor of the American general Joseph W. Stilwell. After the war the value of the road decreased substantially, and it fell into disuse.

BURMESE, breed of short-hair cat, probably the result of crossing several breeds native to Asia with the Siamese. In the U.S. only the Brown Burmese, with a lustrous, rich seal-brown coat, is recognized; elsewhere, red, cream, blue, lilac, chocolate, and several tortoiseshell varieties are permitted. The distinctive "Burmese look" is dif-

A village farmer on his way home with a wagonload of rice harvested from his fields. Burma is one of the world's chief producers of rice. United Nations

One of the short-haired breeds, the Burmese cat is known for its rich, warm sable-brown coat, muscular body, and expressive face. Creszentia

ficult to define. In general, however, the cat is medium-sized, muscular, and surprisingly heavy for its size. The head is rounded and in profile displays a noticeable break at the nose. Eyes are various shades of yellow. The tail is straight and fairly long and thin. The Burmese was first shown in the U.S. in 1936.

BURMESE LANGUAGE. *See* SINO-TIBETAN LANGUAGES.

BURN, injury to the skin and deeper tissues caused by hot liquids, flames, radiant heat, direct contact with hot solids, caustic chemicals, electricity, or electromagnetic (nuclear) radiation. Skin exposed to temperatures as low as 120° F is burned after about 5 minutes.

Incidence. Approximately 2 million persons suffer serious burns in the U.S. each year; of these 115,000 are hospitalized and 12,000 die.

Classification. The severity of a burn depends on its depth, its extent, and the age of the victim. Burns are classified by depth as first, second, and third degree. First-degree burns cause redness and pain (e.g., sunburn). Second-degree burns are marked by blisters (e.g., scald by hot liquid). In third-degree burns, both the epidermis and dermis are destroyed, and underlying tissue may also be damaged (*see* SKIN). The extent of a burn is expressed as the percent of total skin surface which is injured. Persons under 1 year and over 40 years old have a higher mortality rate than those between 2 and 39 for burns of similar depth and extent. Inhalation of smoke from a fire significantly increases mortality.

Pathology. Thermal destruction of the skin permits infection, which is the most common cause of death for extensively burned persons. Body fluids and minerals are lost through the wound. The lungs, heart, liver, and kidneys are affected by the infection and fluid loss.

Treatment. First aid for most burns is cool water applied soon after the burn. Application of home remedies should be avoided. Burns of 15 percent of the body surface or less are usually treated in hospital emergency rooms by removing dead tissue (debridement), dressing with antibiotic cream (often silver sulfadiazine), and administering oral pain medication. Burns of 15 to 25 percent often require hospitalization to provide intravenous fluids and avoid complications. Burns of more than 25 percent of the body surface are usually treated in specialized burn centers where aggressive surgical management is directed toward early skin grafting and avoidance of such complications as dehydration, pneumonia, kidney failure, and infection. Pain control with intravenous narcotics is frequently required. The markedly increased metabolic rate of severely burned patients requires high-protein nutritional supplements given by mouth and intravenously. Extensive scarring of deep burns may cause disfigurement and limitation of joint motion. Plastic surgery is often required to reduce the effects of the scars. Psychological problems often follow burn injuries with scarring.

Research. Investigations are under way to improve nutritional support, enhance the immune response to infection, and grow skin in tissue culture to cover large wounds from small donor sites.

Prevention. Since over 50 percent of all burns are preventable, safety programs can significantly reduce the incidence of burn injuries.

See also FIRST AID; PLASTIC SURGERY. J.M.S.

For further information on this topic, see the Bibliography in volume 28, section 498.

BURNE-JONES, Sir Edward Coley, professional name of EDWARD COLEY JONES (1833-98), English painter and designer, born in Birmingham, and educated at the University of Oxford. Trained by the Pre-Raphaelite painter Dante Gabriel Rossetti, Burne-Jones shared the Pre-Raphaelites' concern with restoring to art what they considered the purity of form, stylization, and high moral tone of medieval painting and design. His paintings, inspired by medieval, classical, and biblical themes, are noted for their sentimentality and dreamlike romanticized style; they are generally considered among the finest works of the Pre-Raphaelite school. They include *King Cophetua and the Beggar Maid* (1884, Tate Gallery,

London) and *Pygmalion and the Image* (1868-78, Birmingham City Museum and Art Gallery).

Burne-Jones was also prominent in the revival of medieval applied arts led by his Oxford friend the poet and artist William Morris. For Morris's firm he designed stained-glass windows, mosaics, and tapestries. His windows may be seen in many English churches, including Christ Church, Oxford, and Birmingham Cathedral. He also illustrated books of Morris's Kelmscott Press, notably *Chaucer* (1896). Burne-Jones was knighted in 1894.

BURNETT, Frances Eliza Hodgson (1849-1924), American novelist, born in Manchester, England. She immigrated to the U.S. at the close of the American Civil War. She was the author of the well-known children's books *Little Lord Fauntleroy* (1886) and *The Secret Garden* (1911). The latter, which she considered her best novel, is still popular today. Burnett's plays include *Esmeralda* (1881), which she wrote with the American playwright William H. Gillette.

BURNEY, Fanny (1752-1840), English novelist and diarist, daughter of the musical historian Charles Burney (1726-1814). She was born in King's Lynn and was self-educated. Her first novel. *Evelina,* was published anonymously in 1778. After she acknowledged herself as author of the book, she became a favorite of the leading literary figures of the day, particularly Samuel Johnson and members of his famous Literary Club. From 1786 to 1791 Burney was Keeper of the Robes for Queen Charlotte. In 1793 she married a French Royalist refugee, Gen. Alexandre d'Arblay. Madame d'Arblay's fame rests principally on her diary, which she began on May 30, 1768, and kept for 17 years. It was published posthumously in two sections, *Diary and Letters of Madame d'Arblay* (1842-46) and *The Early Diary of Frances Burney* (1889). These volumes are valuable for the excellent picture they gave of contemporary people, customs, and court life. Her other novels are, like *Evelina,* sentimental but witty descriptions of innocent young women entering society; they include *Cecilia* (1782), *Camilla* (1796), and *The Wanderer* (1814).

BURNHAM, Daniel H(udson) (1846-1912), American architect and urban planner, born in Henderson, N.Y. At the age of 26 he formed a partnership with the architect John W. Root in Chicago. Burnham was administrator while Root was designer. Together these leaders of the Chicago school built the first steel-frame structures, such as the Montauk Block (1882), that were forerunners of modern skyscrapers. Their many commissions in Chicago included the Masonic Temple (1890s), which was then the tallest building in the world. They also helped to plan the 1893 World's Columbian Exposition in Chicago, but Root died before the project was completed. In Burnham's later buildings, such as the towering Flatiron Building (1902) in New York City, the steel skeleton is concealed by an eclectic Beaux-Arts skin. A member of the commission to enhance Washington, D.C., Burnham also designed notable city plans for Cleveland, Ohio; San Francisco; Manila; and the famous Burnham Plan for Chicago.

BURNHAM, (Linden) Forbes Sampson (1923-85), longtime prime minister (1964-80) and president (1980-85) of Guyana. A British-educated lawyer, he was the cofounder with Cheddi Jagan (1918-) of the People's Progressive party in 1950. In 1955 he broke with Jagan and founded the more moderate People's National Congress. In 1964 he won the prime ministry from Jagan, whom the British considered too radical, by forming a coalition government acceptable to the British. Burnham led the nation to independence in 1966. He was prime minister until 1980, when he became president under a constitution that concentrates most executive, legislative, and military powers in the office of the president. Burnham held the presidency until his death.

BURNLEY, borough, Lancashire, N England, at the junction of the Burn and Calder rivers. Burnley is located in a coal-mining region and is known for its textile industry, especially the production of coarser cotton fabrics. Other manufactures include electrical equipment and machinery. Burnley had an active wool industry by the late 13th century. Its modern industrial growth dates from the early 19th century, when the Leeds and Liverpool Canal was constructed through the town. Pop. (1981) 93,779.

BURNS, Anthony (1834-62), American slave, born in Stafford Co., Va. Burns escaped from slavery in February 1854 and was arrested in Boston on May 24, on a charge of theft. He was detained for violation of the Fugitive Slave Law of 1850 (*see* FUGITIVE SLAVE LAWS). A protest meeting, in which the abolitionist leaders Theodore Parker and Wendell Phillips took part, was held in Faneuil Hall. On May 26 the abolitionists stormed the courthouse but failed to rescue Burns; during the ensuing riot a deputy was killed. The court decided that Burns should be returned to his master. Burns was later resold to a friendly master and resold to friends in Boston who set him free. With their help he studied at Oberlin College in Ohio and became a minister in the city of Saint Catherines, Ont., Canada.

BURNS, George (1896-), American comedian, who began his career in vaudeville as a child and whose career spanned more than 50 years, including appearances in films, on radio, and on television. Orginally a vaudeville dancer, Burns soon specialized in comedy acts. He met the American actor Gracie Allen (1906–64) in the early 1920s; they formed a comedy team in 1923 and performed together for 35 years. Married in 1926, Burns and Allen made more than a dozen films before 1944. In 1932 they made their radio debut, starring in a popular show that moved to television in 1950. Allen retired in 1958, although Burns continued in television. After a 30-year hiatus, Burns returned to the screen in the 1975 film *The Sunshine Boys,* for which he received an Academy Award for best supporting actor.

BURNS, Robert (1759–96), Scottish poet, whose works are known and loved wherever the English language is read.

Early Poverty. Burns was born in Alloway, Ayreshire, Jan. 25, 1759. He was the eldest of seven children born to William Burness, a struggling tenant farmer, and his wife, Agnes Broun. Although poverty limited his formal education, Burns read widely in English literature and the Bible and learned to read French. He was encouraged in his self-education by his father, and his mother acquainted him with Scottish folk songs, legends, and proverbs. Arduous farm work in his youth, combined with an inadequate diet, permanently injured his health, leading to the rheumatic heart disease from which he eventually died. He went in 1781 to Irvine to learn flax dressing, but when the shop burned down, he returned home, jobless and penniless. He had, meanwhile, composed his first poems. The poet's father died in 1784, leaving him as head of the family. He and his brother Gilbert rented Mossgiel Farm, near Mauchline, but the new venture proved a failure.

First Vernacular Poems. In 1784 Burns read the works of the Edinburgh poet Robert Fergusson. Under his influence and that of Scottish folk tradition and older Scottish poetry, he became aware of the literary possibilities of the Scottish regional dialects. During the next two years he produced most of his best-known poems, including "The Cotter's Saturday Night," "Hallowe'en," "To a Daisy," and "To a Mouse." In addition, he wrote "The Jolly Beggars," a cantata chiefly in standard English, which is considered one of his masterpieces. Several of his early poems, notably "Holy Willie's Prayer," satirized local ecclesiastical squabbles and attacked Calvinist theology, bringing him into conflict with the church.

Social Notoriety. Burns further angered church authorities by having several indiscreet love affairs. In 1785 he fell in love with Jean Armour (1767–1834), the daughter of a Mauchline building contractor. Jean soon became pregnant, and although Burns offered to make her his wife, her father forbade their marriage. Thereupon (1786) he prepared to immigrate to the West Indies. Before departing he arranged to issue by subscription a collection of his poetry. Published on July 31 in Kilmarnock in an edition of 600 copies, *Poems, Chiefly in the Scottish Dialect* was an immediate success. In September Burns abandoned the West Indies plan; the same month Jean became the mother of twins. He moved in the fall of 1786 to Edinburgh, where he was lionized by fashionable society. Charmed by Burns, the Edinburgh literati mistakenly believed him to be an untutored bard, a "Heavens-taught Plowman." He resented their condescension, and his bristling independence, blunt manner of speech, and occasional social awkwardness alienated many admirers.

Robert Burns (from a contemporary engraving).

While Burns was in Edinburgh, he successfully published a second, 3000-copy edition of *Poems* (1787), which earned him a considerable sum. From the proceeds he was able to tour (1787) the English border region and the Highlands and finance another winter in Edinburgh. In the meantime he had resumed his relationship with Jean Armour. The next spring she bore him another set of twins, both of whom died, and in April Burns and Armour were married.

In June 1788, Burns leased a poorly equipped

farm in Ellisland, but the land proved unproductive. Within a year he was appointed to a position in the Excise Service, and in November 1791 he relinquished the farm.

Later Songs and Ballads. Burns's later literary output consisted almost entirely of songs, both original compositions and adaptations of traditional Scottish ballads and folk songs. He contributed some 200 songs to *Scots Musical Museum* (6 vol., 1783-1803), a project initiated by the engraver and music publisher James Johnson (1750?-1811). Beginning in 1792 Burns wrote about 100 songs and some humorous verse for *Select Collection of Original Scottish Airs,* compiled by George Thomson (1757-1851). Among his original songs in this collection are such universal favorites as "Auld Lang Syne," "Comin' Thro' the Rye," "Scots Wha Hae," "A Red, Red Rose," "The Banks o' Doon," and "John Anderson, My Jo."

After the outbreak of the French Revolution, Burns became an outspoken champion of the Republican cause. His enthusiasm for liberty and social justice dismayed many of his admirers; some shunned or reviled him. After Franco-British relations began to deteriorate, he curbed his radical sympathies, and in 1794, for patriotic reasons, he joined the Dumfriesshire Volunteers. Burns died in Dumfries, July 21, 1796.

A memorial edition of Burn's poems was published for the benefit of his wife and children. Its editor, the physician James Currie (1756-1805), a man of narrow sympathies, represented the poet as a drunkard and a reprobate, and his biased judgment did much to perpetuate an unjustly harsh and distorted conception of the poet.

Burns touched with his own genius the traditional folk songs of Scotland, transmuting them into great poetry, and he immortalized its countryside and humble farm life. He was a keen and discerning satirist who reserved his sharpest barbs for sham, hypocrisy, and cruelty. His satirical verse, once little appreciated, has in recent decades been recognized widely as his finest work. He was also a master of the verse-narrative technique, as exemplified in "Tam o'Shanter." Finally, his love songs, perfectly fitted to the tunes for which he wrote them, are, at their best, unsurpassed. D.D.

For further information on this person, see the section Biographies in the Bibliography in volume 28.

BURNS, William John (1861-1932), American detective, born in Baltimore, Md., and raised in Ohio, where his father was police commissioner in Columbus. Burns became interested in detective work and joined the U.S. Secret Service in 1889. He distinguished himself in several important criminal cases. In 1909 he founded the William J. Burns International Detective Agency, which he made one of the largest and most important agencies in the country. From 1921 to 1924 he served as director of the Investigation Section of the U.S. Department of Justice (now the Federal Bureau of Investigation).

BURNSIDE, Ambrose Everett (1824-81), American general and politician, born in Liberty, Ind., and educated at the U.S. Military Academy. He served in the Mexican War and in several Indian campaigns; at the outbreak of the American Civil War he accepted command of a Union regiment, which he led in the First Battle of Bull Run. Promoted to brigadier general in August 1861, he took part in the capture of Roanoke Island and Fort Macon in North Carolina. In September 1862, by now a major general, he fought in the Battle of Antietam under Gen. George B. McClellan, whom he succeeded in November as a commander of the Army of the Potomac; a month later his forces were decisively defeated by Confederate Gen. Robert E. Lee. Burnside was subsequently transferred to the Army of Ohio and successfully resisted the Confederate siege (1863) of Knoxville, Tenn. He served under Generals George G. Meade and Ulysses S. Grant at Petersburg (1864), but was held responsible for heavy Union losses and relieved of command. After the war Burnside was governor of Rhode Island (1866-69) and a U.S. senator (1875-81).

Ambrose Everett Burnside

BURNSVILLE, city, Dakota Co., E Minnesota, on the Minnesota R. A residential and industrial suburb near the Minneapolis-Saint Paul International Airport, the community originally developed as part of an agricultural region. The name Burnsville is derived from that of William Byrnes, an early (1850s) settler here. The community was incorporated as a village in 1964. Pop. (1970) 19,940; (1980) 35,674.

BURR, Aaron (1756–1836), third vice-president of the U.S. (1801–05).

Burr was born in Newark, N.J., on Feb. 6, 1756, and educated at the College of New Jersey (now Princeton University), of which his father had been president. He joined the Continental army in 1775 and rose to the rank of lieutenant colonel. Retiring in 1779 because of ill health, he was admitted to the bar in New York City in 1782 and achieved a reputation as one of the foremost lawyers of that city. Burr was appointed attorney general of New York in 1789 and served as U.S. senator from 1791 to 1797. He was a leader of the Democratic-Republican party, the forerunner of the present-day Democratic party, a position that brought Burr into conflict with his professional rival, the Federalist leader Alexander Hamilton.

In the presidential election of 1800 Burr ran with the Democratic-Republican candidate Thomas Jefferson. Each received the same number of votes in the electoral college, and, according to Article II, Section 2, of the U.S. Constitution, the election was decided by the House of Representatives, which chose Jefferson as president and Burr vice-president. In 1804 Burr failed to win renomination as vice-president and also failed to win the governorship of New York State because of the forceful opposition of Hamilton. Hamilton for years had attacked Burr publicly and privately, and Burr eventually challenged him to a duel. They fought in Weehawken, N.J., on July 11, 1804. Hamilton was killed, and Burr was discredited. He then became involved in a scheme that made his political recovery hopeless. The so-called Burr conspiracy still remains a mystery, because no one knows what Burr's intentions were. He purchased land in the newly acquired Louisiana Territory and apparently planned to invade Spanish territory if, as expected, war developed between Spain and the U.S. His plan, allegedly, was either to establish a separate republic in the Southwest or to seize land in Spanish America. The American soldier James Wilkinson, one of Burr's close associates in the project, denounced him to Jefferson, who had Burr arrested. Burr was indicted for treason, but after a six-month trial in Richmond, Va., he was acquitted on Sept. 1, 1807.

Aaron Burr Brown Brothers

Burr went to Europe and tried to enlist European assistance for his schemes. He spent some years there, often in great financial distress, and returned to New York City in 1812 to practice law. His daughter Theodosia (1783–1813), who had remained loyal to her father throughout his career, was lost at sea while on her way to meet him. In 1833 he married a wealthy widow, Eliza Brown Jumel (1775–1865); within a year she divorced him because of his financial demands. Burr died on Sept. 14, 1836, in Port Richmond, Staten Island, N.Y.

For further information on this person, see the section Biographies in the Bibliography in volume 28.

BURRO. *See* ASS.

BURROUGHS, Edgar Rice (1875–1950), American novelist, born in Chicago. Burroughs was a soldier, business executive, gold miner, cowboy, storekeeper, and policeman before turning to writing as a career. He is known chiefly as the creator of Tarzan, who first appeared in *Tarzan of the Apes* (1914); more than 20 novels depicting the adventures of Tarzan achieved widespread popularity. Many of them served as the basis of films, and they have been translated into over 50 languages.

BURROUGHS, John (1837–1921), American naturalist and essayist, born in Roxbury, N.Y., and educated at Cooperstown Seminary. Beginning his career as a teacher, Burroughs later was a clerk (1864–73) in the U.S. Treasury Department in Washington, D.C. He published poetry and

John Burroughs UPI

nature essays during this period and also entered a close friendship with the American poet Walt Whitman. Burroughs's first book, *Notes on Walt Whitman, Poet and Person* (1867), was the earliest serious public recognition that Whitman received. From 1873 to 1884 Burroughs was a federal bank examiner for New York State; he moved to a fruit farm near Esopus, N.Y., and devoted his spare time to writing, studying nature, and raising fruit. He enjoyed the friendship of many of the important people of his day who also were nature lovers, and he traveled to many parts of the world recording his observations of the beauties of nature. His writings did much to promote popular interest in nature study. Among his best-known works are *Wake Robin* (1871), *Locusts and Wild Honey* (1879), *Breath of Life* (1915), and *Bird and Bough* (1906), his one volume of poetry.

BURSA, formerly BRUSA *or* BRUSSA (anc. *Prusa*), city, NW Turkey, capital of Bursa Province. The city is near Mudanya, a port on the Sea of Marmara, with which it is connected by rail. Bursa is divided into three parts by a series of ravines, which are spanned by a number of bridges. A ruined castle on a rocky eminence in the central section marks the site of ancient Prusa. The city is noted for its mosques, some of which show the influence of Byzantine, Persian, and Arab architecture; for its hot sulfur springs and baths; and for its tombs, containing the remains of several early Ottoman sultans. Silk spinning and the manufacture of towels and rugs are among the principal industries of the city.

Founded in the 3d century BC by Prusias I, king of Bithynia (r. 237–192 BC), and made the royal capital, Bursa later was included in the Roman and Byzantine empires. Orhan (1288–1360), son of the second sultan of Turkey, captured the city in 1326 during the Turkish conquest of the Byzantine Empire and made it the capital of the Turkish Empire; in 1361 Arhan's son, Murad I, moved the royal residence to Adrianople (modern Edirne). Sacked by the Tatars in 1402, Bursa was burned by mutinous Janissaries in 1607. Between 1921 and 1922, during the Greco-Turkish War, considerable fighting took place in and around Bursa. Pop. (1985) 614,133.

BURSITIS. *See* JOINTS.

BURSTER, in astronomy, deep-space source of abrupt surges of energy in the X-ray region of the electromagnetic spectrum. A research satellite first detected a burster in 1975. Since then, several other bursters have been detected, mainly in the disk of the Milky Way galaxy. The bursts last a few seconds and amount to about a tenfold increase in X-ray energy. The mechanisms involved are under investigation. Comparable gamma-ray outbursts may also be called bursters.

BURT, Sir Cyril Ludowic (1883–1971), British educational psychologist, noted for his contributions to the use of statistical analysis in psychology and for his studies of child development. Appointed to the London City Council in 1913—the first such appointment of a psychologist to an education authority—Burt later served as professor of psychology at University College, London (1931–50) and was knighted in 1946. After his death, Burt became a figure of controversy. It was determined that his famed studies of the importance of heredity in the determination of intelligence, involving the testing of many sets of twins, among others, contained significant amounts of fraudulent data slanted to emphasize the role of heredity. Much of Burt's earlier work is still valued, however, particularly his contributions to factor analysis, a method of analyzing sets of interrelated performances into independently varying factors to a degree that is computationally useful. Among Burt's most noted writings are *The Young Delinquent* (1925) and *The Backward Child* (1937).

BURTON, city, Genesee Co., E Michigan. It is a suburb of Flint, situated on the Thread R. Pop. (1980) 29,976.

BURTON, Harold Hitz (1888–1964), American, associate justice of the U.S. Supreme Court, born in Jamaica Plain (now part of Boston), Mass., on June 22, 1888, and educated at Bowdoin College and the Harvard Law School. Burton practiced law in Ohio and later became an instructor in corporation law at Western Reserve University. Between 1929 and 1932, he served as a member of the Ohio state legislature and as director of law for the city of Cleveland. He was elected mayor of Cleveland in 1935 and went on to the U.S. Senate in 1941. In 1945 President Harry S. Truman appointed him to the U.S. Supreme Court. On the bench Burton supported the desegregation of public schools and transportation. Burton retired from the Court in October 1958 because of failing health. He died in Washington, D.C., on Oct. 28, 1964.

BURTON, Richard, professional name of RICHARD WALTER JENKINS (1925-84), British actor, born in Pontrhydyfen, Wales. He attended the University of Oxford and served in the Royal Air Force. Burton had great success on the stage and in films. He is particularly noted for his stage performances in such Shakespearean plays as *Hamlet, Twelfth Night, The Tempest,* and *Othello.* His films include *Look Back in Anger* (1959), *Becket* (1964), and *Night of the Iguana* (1964). He was married five times, twice (1964-74, 1975-76) to the American actor Elizabeth Taylor, with whom he appeared in such films as *Cleopatra* (1963), *The Taming of the Shrew* (1967), and *Who's Afraid of Virginia Woolf?* (1966). In 1983 Burton made his final appearance on the New York stage in a revival of *Private Lives,* costarring with Taylor.

BURTON, Sir Richard Francis (1821-90), English explorer, Orientalist, and author, born in Torquay, Devonshire, and educated at the University of Oxford. In 1842 Burton joined the army maintained by the East India Co., serving in Sind, India, for seven years. During this period he mastered a number of Eastern languages in preparation for a series of journeys and explorations. In 1853, disguised as an Afghan pilgrim, he made the pilgrimage to Medina and Mecca, being one of the first Europeans to enter those cities. His next journey was into Somaliland, a region that few Europeans had penetrated. In 1854 he explored Somaliland with the English explorer John Hanning Speke. After service in the Crimean War, Burton returned to Africa in 1858 with Speke. Together they discovered Lake Tanganyika; Speke alone discovered Lake Victoria. After 1861 Burton was a member of the British diplomatic service, stationed in Fernando Po, Brazil; Damascus; and Trieste. He was knighted in 1886.

Burton is best known for his definitive translation (16 vol., 1885-88) of the collection of Oriental tales known as the *Arabian Nights.* Among his other works are *Personal Narrative of a Pilgrimage to El Medina and Mecca* (1855), *First Footsteps in East Africa* (1856), *The Lake Regions of Central Africa* (1860), *Wanderings in West Africa* (1863), and studies of Brazil, Paraguay, Syria, Zanzibar, Etruscan Bologna, and the Gold Coast.

BURTON, Robert (1577-1640), English writer and clergyman, born in Lindley, Leicestershire, and educated at the University of Oxford. He became vicar of Saint Thomas Church at Oxford in 1616 and a rector in Seagrave, Leicestershire, in 1630, holding both positions until his death. Burton's masterpiece, *The Anatomy of Melancholy,* was published under the pseudonym Democritus Junior in 1621; he enlarged it several times. This ambitious book, characterized by wide learning and a quaint and penetrating style, ranks among the most important prose works in English literature. The work analyzes the medical, historical, and social causes and cures of melancholy, covering a vast scope of scholarship in numerous fields, such as classical studies, theology, philosophy, science, and politics. Burton's work influenced other writers in England, including John Milton in the 17th century and Charles Lamb in the 19th century. Among Burton's other writings is the Latin comedy *Philosophaster* (1606).

BURU, island of E Indonesia. It is one of the Moluccas in the Malay Archipelago (q.v.), located between the Ceram Sea and Banda Sea. Generally oval-shaped, Buru is about 145 km (about 90 mi) long and about 80 km (about 50 mi) wide. The terrain is mountainous, with the chief uplifts located in the NW section. Mt. Tomahu (about 2050 m/6726 ft) is the highest summit. Dense forests cover most of the island, and such trees as ebony, teak, and sago and coconut palm are plentiful. Nimlea is an important town of the island. Occupied by the Dutch in 1683, Buru was part of Moluccas Residency, Netherlands Indies, before the termination (1949) of Dutch supremacy in Indonesia. The island was a center of rebel resistance during the abortive Moluccan revolt (1950) against the Indonesian republic. Area, about 8805 sq km (about 3400 sq mi); pop. (est.) 37,700.

BURUNDI, landlocked republic, E Africa, bounded on the N by Rwanda, on the E and S by Tanzania, and on the W by Lake Tanganyika and Zaire. With an area of 27,834 sq km (10,747 sq mi), it is one of the smallest countries on the African continent.

THE LAND

Burundi is mostly a hilly plateau region, with an average elevation of about 1520 m (about 5000 ft). Elevations decrease gradually to the E and SE. The narrow W margin of the country, bordering the

Ruzizi R. and Lake Tanganyika, lies in the trough of the Rift Valley (q.v.). The main rivers are the Ruzizi, the Maiagarasi, and the Ruvuvu.

Climate. The climate is tropical, moderated in most places by altitude. The average annual temperature is 21.1° C (70° F) on the plateau and 24.4° C (76° F) in the Rift Valley. A dry season lasts from May to August, and the country is subject to droughts.

Plants and Animals. Savanna vegetation, a grassland interspersed with trees, predominates in most of the country. Eucalyptus, acacia, and oil palm are the most common trees. Wildlife is diverse. Elephant, hippopotamus, crocodile, wild boar, leopard, antelope, and flying lemur are common, as are the guinea hen, partridge, duck, goose, quail, and snipe.

POPULATION

The population is more than 95% rural; most of the people live in family groupings dispersed throughout the mountainous regions, and villages are uncommon. The chief ethnic groups are the Hutu, a Bantu-speaking people making up about 85% of the population, and the Tutsi, a Nilotic-speaking people forming nearly 15% of the total. The Twa, a pygmy group, account for less than 1% of the total. The official languages are Kirundi and French. Swahili is also widely spoken. About 80% of the population is Christian, chiefly Roman Catholic. The remainder adheres to Islam or traditional religions. The population (1986 census) of Burundi was 4,782,406. The overall population density of about 172 per sq km (about 445 per sq mi) is one of the highest in Africa.

Principal Cities. The country's only important city is Bujumbura, the capital, with a population (1986) of 272,600. The town of Gitega, with a population of 95,300, is the former royal residence.

Education. Schooling is free but not compulsory for children aged 7 to 16. Only about one-third of the population is literate, however. In the mid-1980s about 337,000 students annually attended primary schools, and about 9760 attended sec-

The Royal Drum Band celebrates the independence of Burundi in July 1962. UPI

ondary schools. The Université du Burundi, located in Bujumbura, is the leading institution of higher education; it had an enrollment of about 1900. Some 12,300 students were enrolled in vocational and teacher-training programs.

THE ECONOMY

The economy of Burundi is dependent on agriculture. Export earnings are dominated by a single crop—coffee. National budget figures for the mid-1980s showed about $160 million in revenue and $156 million in expenditures.

Agriculture. Subsistence agriculture is the main means of livelihood in Burundi. Chief food crops are cassava, sweet potatoes, bananas, beans, peas, and grain sorghum. The most important cash crop is arabica coffee. Cotton and, increasingly, tea are also grown for export. In the mid-1980s the livestock population numbered about 565,000 cattle, 315,000 sheep, and 770,000 goats. Social and cultural importance is attached to the ownership of large cattle herds. They are, however, economically underutilized and have been responsible for overgrazing that has contributed to extensive soil erosion.

Manufacturing and Mining. Manufacturing in Burundi is largely limited to the processing of agricultural products. Other manufactures include textiles, cement, and insecticides. Mining is based on the exploitation of small amounts of gold, bastnaesite, and cassiterite (a tin ore). Important reserves of uranium, nickel, and peat remain to be exploited.

Currency, Commerce, and Trade. The unit of currency is the Burundi franc (97 francs equal U.S.$1; 1987). Coffee accounts for more than 80% of the value of exports. Cotton, hides, and tea are the only other important exports. Textiles, motor vehicles, flour, and petroleum products are imported, principally from Western Europe.

Communications. Burundi has no railroads but possesses a road network of about 5140 km (about 3190 mi), of which about 7% is paved. Most of the country's trade is shipped via Tanzania, Zambia, and Zaire through the port of Bujumbura at the head of Lake Tanganyika. Bujumbura has the country's lone international airport. The country has a government radio station and one daily and two weekly newspapers. Some 180,000 radio receivers and 6000 telephones are in use.

GOVERNMENT

A constitution adopted by national referendum in 1981 establishes as head of state a president elected to a 5-year term by universal adult suffrage. The president also heads the nation's sole legal political party, Unity for National Progress (Union pour le Progrès National, or UPRONA).

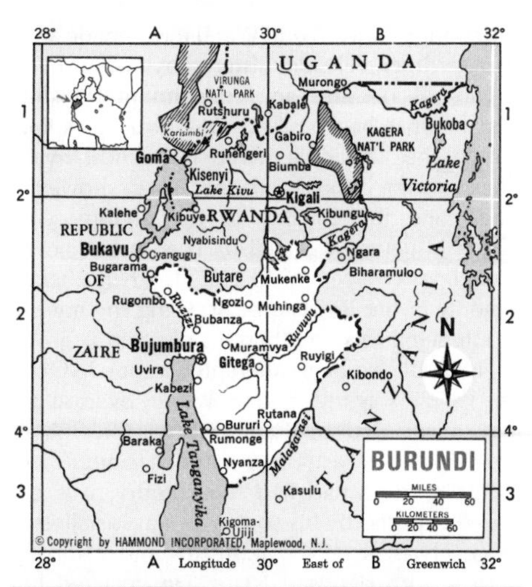

INDEX TO MAP OF BURUNDI

Cities and Towns

Bubanza	A 2
Bujumbura (cap.)	A 2
Bururi	A 2
Gitega	A 2
Kabezi	A 2
Muhinga	B 2
Mukenke	B 2
Ngozi	A 2
Nyanza	A 3
Rugombo	A 2
Rumonge	A 3
Rutana	B 2
Ruyigi	B 2

Other Features

Kagera (river)	B 2
Malagarasi (river)	B 3
Ruvuvu (river)	B 2
Ruzizi (river)	A 2

The National Assembly has 65 members, 52 elected and 13 appointed to 5-year terms. A local government reorganization in 1982 divided Burundi into 15 provinces; each province is subdivided into arrondissements and communes.

HISTORY

The Twa are believed to be the original inhabitants of Burundi; they were there when the Hutu arrived in the early 14th century, imposing their language and customs. The development of an organized kingdom began in the 15th century, when migrating Tutsi established themselves as feudal rulers over the Hutu. After the caste system was organized, power was concentrated in the hands of a monarch, the *mwami*. Burundi, however, never maintained the rigid political and social structures that characterized neighboring Rwanda. The power of the mwami was not absolute, and various royal clans, known as *ganwa*, frequently vied for the throne. Intermarriage between the Hutu and Tutsi was common, and the Hutu enjoyed greater economic independence than in Rwanda.

Burundi was occupied by Germany in the 1880s and subsequently became a part of German East Africa. Following World War I, the League of Nations gave Belgium a mandate over the country. After World War II it was made a UN trust territory, still administered by Belgium.

Burundi became an independent constitutional monarchy on July 1, 1962, and was admitted to the UN in September. Political rivalry between the Hutu and the Tutsi, however, threatened the stability of the country. The power structure was still in Tutsi hands, even though, after elections in 1965, the Hutu held a majority in the legislature. Accusing the mwami of intriguing to strengthen his position, a group of Hutu police officers attempted a coup in October 1965. It was thwarted, however, by loyal police officers led by Capt. Michel Micombero (1940–83). In July 1966, Mwami Mwambutsa IV (1913–78), who had fled the country, was declared deposed by his son, who was installed as Mwami Ntare V (1947–72). In November Micombero in turn deposed Ntare. He declared Burundi a republic, appointed himself president, and established a National Revolutionary Committee to help stabilize his regime and develop the economy. In April 1972, a Hutu uprising led to widespread massacres, in which Ntare, who was under house arrest, was killed. The uprising was quelled, but unrest continued; thousands of Hutu refugees found haven in nearby countries.

President Micombero was overthrown in a bloodless army coup in November 1976. A Supreme Revolutionary Council subsequently named Jean Baptiste Bagaza (1946–) to the presidency. Peace between the ruling Tutsi and the majority Hutu, however, remained precarious. A new constitution in 1981 confirmed Burundi as a one-party state. Reelected without opposition in 1984, Bagaza was ousted by a military coup in September 1987. Maj. Pierre Buyoya (1949?–) became president, ruling as head of the Military Committee for National Redemption. A resurgence of ethnic violence in August 1988 left an estimated 5000 dead.

For further information on this topic, see the Bibliography in volume 28, sections 1009, 1012.

BURY, borough, in the metropolitan county of Greater Manchester, N England, on the Irwell R. Bury has diversified industry with spinning and weaving factories, dye works, and manufactures that include paper and metal products. It is connected by canal to Bolton and Manchester to the S. Bury was long known as a wool-weaving center, the industry having been introduced here in the 14th century by Flemish immigrants. The manufacture of cotton cloth became dominant in the early 18th century. Pop. (1981) 176,568.

BURY SAINT EDMUNDS, town, in the borough of Saint Edmundsbury, Suffolk, E England, on the Lark R. It is the trading and processing center of a farming region. In about AD 630 the town, known as Beodricsweorthe, was made the seat of a monastery. Its present name honors the memory of St. Edmund, the East Anglian king who was interred here in the early 10th century. In 1020 the Danish king of England, Canute II, established a Benedictine abbey here that became one of the most important abbeys in England. In 1214 the English barons met in the abbey and took a vow to force King John to accept their demands. This action led to the signing of the Magna Charta. Until 1974, Bury St. Edmunds was the county town of the former county of West Suffolk. Pop. of St. Edmundsbury Borough (1981) 86,054.

George Bush David Valdez–The White House

BUS. *See* PUBLIC TRANSPORTATION.

BUSH, George Herbert Walker (1924–), 41st president of the U.S. (1989–).

Bush was born on June 12, 1924, in Milton, Mass., and grew up in Greenwich, Conn. A carrier pilot in the Pacific theater during World War II, he was discharged in 1945 with a Distinguished Flying Cross. Three years later he was graduated from Yale University with a degree in economics. He then moved to Texas, where he became wealthy in the oil business.

Turning to politics, Bush ran unsuccessfully for the U.S. Senate in 1964 but won a seat in the U.S. House of Representatives two years later. Reelected in 1968, he gave up his seat in 1970 to run for the Senate—again unsuccessfully. President Richard M. Nixon then appointed him U.S. ambassador to the UN (1971–72), and he subsequently held a series of appointive posts that familiarized him with both the internal and external politics of the U.S.: national chairman of the Republican party (1973–74); chief U.S. liaison officer in Peking (1974–75); and director of the Central Intelligence Agency (1976–77). Bush ran a vigorous campaign for the Republican nomination for the U.S. presidency in 1980. Having lost to Ronald Reagan, however, he subsequently agreed to be Reagan's running mate, and he became vice-president in 1981.

After winning reelection on the Reagan ticket in 1984, Bush competed successfully for the 1988 Republican presidential nomination; as his running mate in the general election he chose a young and relatively unknown U.S. senator from Indiana, Dan Quayle. Emphasizing his own government experience and branding his Democratic opponent, Massachusetts governor Michael Dukakis (1933–), a far-left liberal on social, economic, and defense issues, Bush became the first incumbent vice-president since 1836 to win election to the U.S. presidency.

For further information on this person, see the section Biographies in the Bibliography in volume 28.

BUSH, Vannevar (1890–1974), American scientist, educator, and administrator, born in Everett, Mass., and educated at Tufts College, Harvard University, and Massachusetts Institute of Technology (MIT). During World War I he served with the U.S. Navy as a research engineer. From 1919 to 1971 Bush served in various teaching and administrative positions at MIT and the Carnegie Institution of Washington.

Vannevar Bush adjusts the controls of his invention, the differential analyzer. UPI

While at MIT Bush invented the differential analyzer, a device for rapidly and automatically solving complex mathematical problems and a forerunner of the modern computer (q.v.). Bush is best known for his federal scientific work with the national Defense Research Committee, of which he was chairman; the Office of Scientific Research and Development, which he directed throughout World War II; and the Research and Development Board of the Army and Navy.

BUSH BABY. *See* GALAGO.

BUSHIDO (Jap., "the way of the warrior"), unwritten code of ethics observed by the warrior noblemen, or samurai (q.v.), of feudal Japan. Like the rules of chivalry that prevailed in medieval Europe, Bushido was based on such virtues as rectitude, endurance, frugality, courage, politeness, veracity, and, especially, loyalty to ruler and country. Only through the exercise of these virtues could a knight maintain his honor, and one who had forfeited honor was compelled to commit suicide by hara-kiri (q.v.). By the late 12th century, when feudal practices were established in Japan, the code was fully developed. It became a written code in the 16th century. When feudalism was abolished about the middle of the 19th century, the code was abandoned, but it continued to exert an influence on Japanese culture, particularly on the armed forces.

BUSHIRE, also Abu Shehr, city and seaport, SW Iran, in Fars Province, on the Persian Gulf. Bushire was once a terminal of one important caravan route. Raw cotton, silk, tobacco, carpets, and hides are exported; cotton goods, tea, metals, sugar, and spices are imported. Pop. (est.) 57,700.

BUSHMASTER, common name for a poisonous snake, *Lachesis mutus,* of the pit viper family Crotalidae (*see* PIT VIPER). It is found in tropical South America and as far north as Nicaragua. An average adult is about 2.6 m (about 8.5 ft) long, but an occasional specimen reaches 3.6 m (12 ft). It is the largest venomous serpent in the Americas. Pale brown in color, it has dark brown blotches that form a regular pattern along the back and sides. When angered, it vibrates its tail rapidly. Unlike the closely related rattlesnake, it does not have a rattle on the tail. Unlike other pit vipers, the bushmaster is an egg-laying snake, usually laying about a dozen at a time.

BUSHMEN. *See* SAN.

Bushpig, Potamochoerus porcus.
John Marinus–National Audubon Society

BUSHNELL, David (1742–1824), U.S. inventor, born in Saybrook, Conn., who in 1775 built the first military submarine (q.v.). Called "Bushnell's turtle," the one-passenger craft was a tarred, oaken sphere banded with iron and powered by hand-operated propellers and pumps. Attached outside was a gunpowder bomb with a time fuse. Bushnell failed, however, to blow up British ships during the American Revolution.

BUSHNELL, Horace (1802–76), American theologian, born in Bantam, Conn., and educated at Yale College (now Yale University). In 1833 he became pastor of the North Congregational Church in Hartford, Conn., which he served for 26 years. He was strongly evangelical in belief but denied the Calvinistic theory of the atonement. For this and other deviations from orthodoxy he was accused of heresy, but he was never brought to trial. Bushnell was a voluminous writer, an inspiring preacher, and a bold and original thinker on theological subjects. His influence extended to almost all Protestant denominations in the U.S., profoundly modifying 19th-century religious thought. His works include *Christian Nurture* (1847), *God in Christ* (1849), *Nature and the Supernatural* (1858), and *The Vicarious Sacrifice* (1866).

BUSHPIG, common name for an African wild pig, *Potamochoerus porcus,* also known as the African water hog, of the family Suidae (*see* HOG). It is closely related to the genus *Sus,* which includes the domestic pig and the European wild boar. The bushpig lives in forested regions or dense bush areas south of the Sahara. The pigs are distinguished by red coats that turn gray with age, long ears tipped with long tufts of hair, elongated snouts, general hairiness, and two pairs of horny growths on the face. The animal is about 61 cm (about 2 ft) high and weighs about 91 kg (about 200 lb). A related species is found in Madagascar. Bushpigs avoid people and are usually active only at night.

BUSHRANGERS, Australian highwaymen or robbers who during the late 18th and early 19th centuries, terrorized settlers in the New South Wales and Victoria regions. Made up almost exclusively of escaped convicts from the British penal colonies, they were named for their places of refuge in the wooded areas of the Australian frontier. By 1815 their depredations had become so serious that martial law was proclaimed. Despite this measure and the enactment in 1830 in New South Wales of the Bushranging Act, which provided severe penalties for their crimes, the bushrangers continued for nearly a century. After the discovery of gold in 1851, they preyed upon gold shipments and robbed banks. The last of the notorious chieftains, Ned Kelly (1855–80), was caught and executed at Melbourne in 1880.

BUSHTIT, common name for any of the diminutive North American birds of the genus *Psaltriparus* in the family Paridae (*see* TITMOUSE). They are closely related to the chickadees and about the same size. They are brownish or olive-gray above and lighter or whitish below. Several varieties are part of a common species, *P. minimus,* found in the western U.S., Mexico, and Guatemala. The nests of the bushtit, long and gourd-shaped, with entrance in the side, are woven of vegetable fibers and attached to the tips of tree branches.

BUSINESS, pattern of complex operations in the lives of people concerning all those functions that govern the production, distribution, and sale of goods and services for the benefit of the buyer and the profit of the seller. Control of production in the modern world is largely in the hands of individual businesspeople or entrepreneurs, who organize and direct industry, induced to do so by the expectation of private gain in the form of business profits. Since the beginning of that extraordinary era of economic progress ushered in by the Industrial Revolution, old ways of conducting business have been modified, and new forms of business organization have been introduced. This modification has enabled the various branches of industry to adapt to changing conditions and to function more easily, efficiently, and profitably. The main forms of business organization are described below.

Individual Proprietorship. In this form of organization the owner is in sole charge of the business and is responsible for its success or failure. Unless an activity is specifically prohibited by law, no line of business is closed to an owner.

Although advantages for the small business exist in this form, certain drawbacks make it undesirable for larger concerns. In the first place the single owner is seldom able to invest as much capital as can be secured by a partnership or a corporation. If single owners are able to invest large amounts of capital, they run great risk of losing it all because they are personally liable for all the debts of their businesses. This is called unlimited liability. Only in agriculture is the individual owner still a predominant figure.

Partnership. A business association of two or more persons who have agreed to combine their financial assets, labor, property, and skill or some or all of these things. The agreement to form an association of this nature is called a partnership contract and may include general policies, distribution of profits, fiscal responsibilities, and a specific length of time during which the partnership is in effect.

Unless a limited partnership has been established, in which one of the partners assumes complete financial responsibility for losses, all parties equally share the burden of loss and debts. *See* PARTNERSHIP.

The Corporation. It was to provide a financing device that did not have the weaknesses of the single ownership and the partnership that the corporation came into existence. According to the classic definition given by Chief Justice of the U.S. John Marshall in the *Dartmouth College* case in 1819, "A corporation is an artificial being, invisible, intangible, and existing only in contemplation of law." In general, the corporation laws of each state set forth the requirements for the persons who may incorporate. The granting of a charter usually follows when the requirements for incorporation have been met.

Business combinations may be classified in several ways. The major simple forms of integration are as follows. A vertical integration characterizes companies that engage in the different steps in manufacturing or marketing a product. A horizontal combination brings under one control companies engaged in the sale of the same or similar products. A complimentary combination takes place when companies selling allied, but not competitive, products combine. A conglomerate combination involves firms in widely diverse industries, such as an automobile company owning a food manufacturer or book publisher.

After the corporation became the accepted method of carrying on business in the U.S., means were sought to control production and prices by combination. One of the early methods was pooling. A pool was a federation of independent units sometimes used to limit production, to control prices, or to accomplish both purposes. The one major disadvantage of pooling was that the arrangement was temporary.

The corporate structure then sought a more permanent combination, and the trust seemed to meet the need. In a trust the stockholders of the corporation deposited their stock certificates with one or more trustees and received in exchange trust certificates. Many abuses of this practice developed, and the resulting demands for reform caused the breakup of the trusts. The business community then turned to the holding company, which is a corporation that holds the common stock of other corporations.

As business became more competitive, new and more complex corporate combinations came on the scene. A merger is the absorption of one or more companies by another. In an amalgamation, the corporations involved form a new corporation, exchange their stock for that of the new corporation, and all give up their individual charters. An interlocking directorate exists when two or more corporations have officials who serve on the board of directors of each company. A community of interests, with respect to the control of corporations, exists when a small number of persons having other interests in common hold the stocks of two or more corporations. In the 1960s and 1970s a speedup occurred in the merger movement, particularly in connection with takeovers by conglomerates that brought under one management scores of companies belonging to unrelated industries. The number of mergers increased further in the mid-1980s.

A corporate combination that is contrary to the letter and spirit of American antitrust laws is the cartel, a voluntary association of private business concerns for the purpose of coordinating marketing practices. It may engage in price fixing, limitation of production, the division of marketing territories, and the pooling of profits.

Of great economic importance is the multinational corporation. Such companies maintain extensive business activities and large-scale production facilities throughout the world, and their revenues sometimes exceed the total revenues of some countries in which they operate.

Levels of Business Operation. The operation of large business firms is characterized by great complexity of organization and administration. The highest level of management is concerned with the overall planning and evaluation of production and distribution, and various administrative departments carry on the functions of research, production, finance, and marketing. Business management is a specialized field of study that investigates the requirements of efficiency in the context of technological expansion.

Regulation of Business by Government. Public interest requires that the organization and operation of business be subject to governmental regulation, and many laws have been enacted for the purpose of ensuring a competitive pluralism with regard to production and trade. Trusts and monopolistic practices are outlawed by the Sherman Antitrust Act (1890) and the Clayton Antitrust Act (1914); stock and bond issues are under the control of the Securities and Exchange Commission.

Profit and Responsibility. In a free enterprise economy, business is governed by the theory that businesses profit to the extent that they serve their communities. Responsibility to consumers has become an established principle, and measures such as guarantees benefit the customer while enhancing the seller's reputation. Business ethics are determined by the competitive system, which makes it profitable to satisfy the consumer. J.J.F.; REV. BY W.P.C.

For further information on this topic, see the Bibliography in volume 28, sections 228, 242–43, 613, 617–19.

BUSINESS CYCLE, term used in economics to designate changes in the economy. Ever since the Industrial Revolution (q.v.), the level of business activity in industrialized capitalist countries has veered from high to low, taking the economy with it.

Phases of the Business Cycle. The timing of a cycle is not predictable, but its phases seem to be. Many economists cite four phases—prosperity, liquidation, depression, and recovery—using the terms originally developed by the American economist Wesley Mitchell (1874-1948), who devoted his career to studying business cycles.

During a period of prosperity a rise in production becomes evident. Employment, wages, and profits increase correspondingly. Business executives express their optimism by investing to expand production. As the upswing continues, however, obstacles begin to occur that impede further expansion. For example, production costs increase; shortages of raw materials may further hamper production; interest rates rise; prices rise; and consumers react to increased prices by buying less. As consumption starts to lag behind production, inventories accumulate, causing a price decline. Manufacturers begin to retrench; workers are laid off. Such factors lead to a period of liquidation. Business executives become pessimistic as prices and profits drop. Money is hoarded, not invested. Production cutbacks and factory shutdowns occur. Unemployment becomes widespread. A depression is in progress.

Recovery from a depression may be initiated by several factors, including a resurgence in consumer demand, the exhaustion of inventories, or government action to stimulate the economy. Although generally slow and uneven at the start, recovery soon gathers momentum. Prices rise more rapidly than costs. Employment increases, providing some additional purchasing power. Investment in capital-goods industries expands. As optimism pervades the economy, the desire to speculate on new business ventures returns. A new cycle is under way.

In fact, business cycles do not always behave as neatly as the model just given, and no two cycles are alike. Business cycles vary considerably in severity and duration. In the U.S. the major cycles have lasted slightly longer than eight years, on the average. Minor cycles have a shorter span, generally from two to four years. The American economist Alvin Hansen (1887–1975) accounted for 10 major and 23 minor cycles in the U.S. between 1857 and 1937.

The most severe and widespread of all economic depressions occurred in the 1930s. The Great Depression affected the U.S. first but quickly spread to Western Europe. The American economy, however, suffered the most. From 1933 to 1937 the U.S. began to recover from the depression, but the economy declined again from 1937 to 1938, before regaining its normal level. This decline was called a *recession,* a term that is now used in preference to liquidation. Real economic recovery was not evident until early 1941.

Since then, the U.S. has been spared another severe depression. Recessions have, however, occurred repeatedly. In addition, the general pace of economic growth has slowed.

Special Cycles. Apart from the traditional business cycle, specialized cycles sometimes occur in particular industries. The building construction trade, for example, is believed to have cycles ranging from 16 to 20 years in length. Prolonged building slumps made two of the most severe American depressions worse (in 1872–73 and in the 1930s). On the other hand, an upswing in building construction has often helped to stimulate recovery from a depression.

Some economists believe that a long-range cycle, lasting for about half a century, also occurs. It has been shown that a periodic shift in wholesale prices recurred in the U.S. throughout the 19th and early part of the 20th centuries. The pattern went as follows: From about 1790 to the early 1800s, wholesale prices rose; about 1815 this trend was reversed, and prices declined until the middle of the century; after another rise, prices again declined following the American Civil War and continued into the 1890s; a rising-price trend took over until 1920; thereafter prices fell until 1933. These rise-and-fall cycles averaged about 50 years each.

Studies of economic trends during the same period were made by the Russian economist Nikolai Kondratieff (1892–c. 1956). He examined the behavior of wages, raw materials, production and consumption, exports, imports, and other economic quantities in Great Britain and France. The data he collected and analyzed seemed to establish the existence of long-range cycles similar to those just described for wholesale prices. His "waves" of expansion and contraction fell into three periods averaging 50 years each: 1792–1850, 1850–96, and 1896–1940. Such studies, however, are not conclusive.

Causes of Cycles. Economists did not try to determine the causes of business cycles until the increasing severity of economic depressions became a major concern in the late 19th and early 20th centuries. Two external factors that have been suggested as possible causes are sunspots and psychological trends. The sunspot theory of the British economist William Jevons was once widely accepted. According to Jevons, sunspots affect meteorological conditions. That is, during periods of sunspots, weather conditions are often more severe. Jevons felt that sunspots affected the quantity and quality of harvested crops; thus, they affected the economy.

A psychological theory of business cycles, formulated by the British economist Arthur Pigou (1877–1959), states that the optimism or pessimism of business leaders may influence an economic trend. Some politicians have clearly subscribed to this theory. During the early years of the Great Depression, for instance, President Herbert Hoover tried to appear publicly optimistic about the inherent vigor of the American economy, thus hoping to stimulate an upsurge.

Several economic theories of the causes of business cycles have been developed. According to the underconsumption theory, identified particularly with the British economist John Hobson (1858–1940), inequality of income causes economic declines. The market becomes glutted with goods because the poor cannot afford to buy, and the rich cannot consume all they can afford. Consequently, the rich accumulate savings that are not reinvested in production, because of insufficient demand for goods. This savings accumulation disrupts economic equilibrium and begins a cycle of production cutbacks.

The economist Joseph Schumpeter was a proponent of the innovation theory. He related the upswings of the business cycle to new inventions, which stimulate investment in capital-goods industries. Because new inventions are developed unevenly, business conditions must alternately be expansive and recessive.

The Austrian-born economists Friedrich von Hayek and Ludwig von Mises (1881–1973) subscribed to the overinvestment theory. They suggested that instability is the logical consequence of expanding production to the point where less efficient resources are drawn upon. Production costs then rise, and, if these costs cannot be passed on the consumer, the producer cuts back production and lays off workers.

A monetary theory of business cycles stresses the importance of the supply of money in the economic system. Since many businesses must borrow money to operate or expand production, the availability and cost of money influence their decisions. Sir Ralph George Hawtrey (1879–1975) suggested that changes in interest rates determine whether executives decrease or increase their capital investments, thus affecting the cycle.

Accelerator and Multiplier Effects. Basic to all theories of business-cycle fluctuations and their causes is the relationship between investment and consumption. New investments have what is called a multiplier effect: that is, investment money paid to wage earners and suppliers becomes income to them and then, in turn, becomes income to others as the wage earners or suppliers spend most of their earnings. An expanding ripple effect is thus set into motion.

Similarly, an increasing level of income spent by consumers has an accelerating influence on investment. Higher demand creates greater incentive to increase investment in production, in order to meet that demand. Both of these factors also can work in a negative way, with reduced investment greatly diminishing aggregate income, and reduced consumer demand decelerating the amount of investment spending.

Regulating the Cycle. Since the Great Depression, devices have been built into the U.S. economy to help prevent severe business declines. For instance, unemployment insurance provides most workers with some income when they are laid off. Social security, together with the pensions given by many companies, furnishes some livelihood to the increasing number of retired people. Trade unions are a powerful obstacle to the cumulative wage drop that aggravated previous depressions. Government support of farm prices shields the farmer from disastrous loss of income. The stock market is now regulated by the Securities and Exchange Commission and the Federal Reserve System in order to prevent a recurrence of the 1929 financial collapse.

The government can also attempt direct intervention to counter a recession. There are three major techniques available: monetary policy, fiscal policy, and incomes policy. Economists differ sharply in their choice of technique.

Monetary policy is preferred by the American economist Milton Friedman and followed by conservative governments such as that of Prime Minister Margaret Thatcher in Great Britain. Monetary policy involves controlling, via the central Federal Reserve Bank, the money supply and interest rates. These determine the availability and costs of loans to businesses. Tightening the money supply theoretically helps to counteract inflation; loosening the supply helps recovery from a recession. Unfortunately, inflation and recession occurred simultaneously in economic downturns during the 1970s (a phenomenon sometimes called stagflation); this made it difficult to know which monetary policy to apply.

Considered more effective by American economist John Kenneth Galbraith are fiscal measures, such as increased taxation of the wealthy, and an incomes policy, which seeks to hold wages and prices down to a level that reflects productivity growth. This policy has not had much success in the post-World War II period.

The U.S. has escaped a serious depression since 1933 at least in part because of the federal government's exercise of anticyclical measures, including wage and price controls, and deficit spending. Inflation and unemployment, which increased greatly in the late 1970s and early 1980s, were controlled, in part, by an expansionary monetary policy and by tax cuts that augmented consumers' buying power while greatly increasing the Federal budget deficit. An important concern in attempting to deal with these problems is the fear that inappropriate or drastic measures might precipitate a severe recession or even a major depression.

See also FINANCE; INFLATION AND DEFLATION; UNEMPLOYMENT. REV. BY W.C.P.

For further information on this topic, see the Bibliography in volume 28, section 237.

BUSINESS EDUCATION, field of training in business practices and in specific skills such as accounting, information processing, keyboarding/typewriting, recordkeeping, and shorthand. Business education in the U.S. is conducted on two distinct levels: education for administrative support personnel in business and industry and collegiate education for business administration and for business teacher preparation.

Vocational Education. Business education for administrative support personnel is included in the programs of almost every high school and community college, as well as in independent business colleges. Included in such curricula are courses in secretarial skills; bookkeeping and accounting; data processing; business communication, mathematics, and law; computer programming; and business management. These courses are important to the U.S. economy because they provide a steady flow of office workers who are in great demand.

Professional Education. Colleges and universities provide professional education for persons who function at the administrative and management levels and also for those who teach business at the secondary and collegiate levels. The first business school at the collegiate level was the Wharton School of Finance and Commerce, founded in 1881 at the University of Pennsylvania. Today about 1200 colleges offer bachelor's degree programs in business administration; more than 600 schools have master's degree programs; and about 100 have doctoral programs.

The typical college of business administration offers concentrations in accounting, finance, marketing, manufacturing, management information systems, operations management, and international business. Many business schools now offer education in areas not usually classified as business, such as governmental or public administration and institutional management. Enrollment in undergraduate schools of business administration is now more than 2.5 million students, and graduate enrollment is about 200,000.

Organizations and Journals. The largest professional organization in the U.S. devoted exclusively to serving business education is the national Business Education Association. Professional associations also exist in each specialized field of business. The professional association serving college business programs is the American Assembly of Collegiate Schools of Business. While no single publication covers all fields, *Business Education Forum* and the *Journal of Education for Business* deal with a variety of areas included in education for business. Individual fields are served by such journals as the *Journal of Accountancy* and the *Journal of Marketing.*

Modern Trends. The development of the computer has effected many changes in business education. At the vocational level the emphasis has been on training programs for computer operators and programmers, and at the collegiate level on utilization of more efficient management information systems to provide data for making business decisions. G.B.C.

BUSINESS MACHINES. *See* OFFICE SYSTEMS.

BUSONI, Ferruccio Benvenuto (1866–1924), Italian composer, pianist, conductor, and author, born in Empoli. He received his first musical instruction from his parents, both musicians, and later studied composition at Graz, Austria, and Leipzig, Germany. He taught piano and composition in various European cities, as well as at the New England Conservatory, Boston (1891-93). His tours of Europe and America established Busoni as one of the great concert pianists of the early 20th century. Devoted to the progress of modern music, Busoni invented several new scales; as a conductor he emphasized the works of his contemporaries. He wrote several books on musical theory and criticism. Much of his critical writing was collected in English translation in *The Essence of Music* (1965). Although he composed an enormous amount of music, his most important contributions were in fostering modern music; in teaching; and in transcribing, arranging, and annotating much of the keyboard music of Johann Sebastian Bach. His monumental unfinished opera *Doktor Faust* (1916-24), for which Busoni wrote his own libretto, was completed after his death by his pupil the Spanish-German composer Philipp Jarnach (1892-1982).

BUSTAMANTE, Sir Alexander (1884-1977), first prime minister of Jamaica (1962-67), born in Blenheim. As a young man he served in the Spanish army and then worked in various capacities in Cuba, Panama, and New York City; he returned to Jamaica in 1932. Although shrewd investments had made him a rich man, Bustamante's concern for Jamaican sugar plantation workers led him to organize the Bustamante Industrial Trade Union in 1938. He was jailed by the British for his union and political activities in 1941-42. In 1943 he formed the Jamaica Labor party, and he later served as mayor of Kingston (1947-48) and chief minister of Jamaica (1953-55). When the country gained independence in 1962, Sir Alexander (he had been knighted in 1955) became its first prime minister. Conservative in his politics, he closely aligned the country with the U.S.

BUSTARD, any of 23 species of birds constituting the family Otididae, or Otidae, of the order Gruiformes, which also includes cranes and gallinules. Bustards are found in Europe, Africa, Asia, and Australia. They are stocky birds with long necks, heavy bills, and long, powerful legs with the rear toe absent. The plumage is brown to gray, often with darker bars or spots. A large pouch that opens under the tongue and extends down the front of the neck may be for courtship display. The female lays one to five eggs and tends the young alone. The birds are omnivorous.

The great bustard, *Otis tarda,* is one of the largest flying birds, with a wingspread of up to 2.4 m (8 ft), and it weighs as much as 14.5 kg (32 lb). Formerly it ranged over a large part of Europe, but it has been overhunted and is becoming rare. A powerful but slow flyer, it rarely takes wing and prefers to run from danger. The little bustard, *O. tetrax,* is found on the shores of the Mediterranean Sea. Other species include the Kori bustard of southern Africa and the florican of India.

Kori bustard, Choriotis kori
Arthur W. Ambler–National Audubon Society

BUS TRANSPORTATION. *See* PUBLIC TRANSPORTATION.

BUTADIENE, synthetic chemical compound, used principally in the manufacture of synthetic rubber, nylon, and latex paints.

Most commercial butadiene is made by dehydrogenation of butene or of mixtures of butene and butane. Because butadiene has high reactivity, it is useful in synthesis, particularly in polymerization reactions. A large percentage of automobile tires are made from Buna rubber, a copolymer of butadiene and styrene.

Butadiene is a colorless, gaseous hydrocarbon with the formula C_4H_6. It is liquefied by cooling to −4.4° C (24.1° F) or by compression to 2.8 atmospheres at 25° C (77° F).

BUTANE, either of two saturated hydrocarbons, or alkanes, with the chemical formula C_4H_{10}. In both compounds the carbon atoms are joined in an open chain. In *n*-butane (normal), the chain is continuous and unbranched, whereas in *i*-butane (iso) one of the carbon atoms forms a side branch. This difference in structure results in small but distinct differences in properties. Thus, *n*-butane melts at −138.3° C (−216.9° F) and boils at −0.5° C (31.1° F), and *i*-butane melts at −145° C (−229° F) and boils at −10.2° C (13.6° F).

Both butanes occur in natural gas, petroleum, and refinery gases. They show little chemical reactivity at ordinary temperatures but burn readily when ignited in air or oxygen. They make up the most volatile portion of gasoline and are sometimes added to propane (q.v.) to be marketed as bottled gas. Most *n*-butane is converted to butadiene (q.v.), which is used to make synthetic rubber and latex paints.

BUTCHER-BIRD. *See* SHRIKE.

BUTE, island in the Firth of Clyde, SW Scotland, separated from the mainland by a narrow, winding strait called the Kyles of Bute. The terrain in the N section is high, rugged, and barren, attaining an elevation of about 277 m (about 909 ft); in the center and S it is low and undulating and comparatively fertile. More than half the island is under cultivation, producing barley, oats, and potatoes. Fishing and tourism are the leading industries. Points of interest include the ruins of Rothesay Castle, built in the 14th century. Area, about 119 sq km (about 46 sq mi).

BUTENANDT, Adolf Friedrich Johann (1903–), German chemist, born in Bremerhaven (now in West Germany) and educated at the universities of Göttingen and Marburg. He isolated and studied the sex hormones estrone (1929), androsterone (1931), and progesterone and testosterone (1934), determining their relationships to other sterols (*see* STEROIDS). For this work he shared the 1939 Nobel Prize in chemistry with the Yugoslav-Swiss scientist Leopold Ružička. From 1936 to 1972 he was director of the Kaiser Wilhelm Institute for Biochemistry (since 1945, the Max Planck Institute), and served as president (1960–72) of the Max Planck Society for the Advancement of Science. Butenandt also studied insect hormones (*see* PHEROMONE) and viruses.

BUTEO, name for any of the more than 30 hawks of the widely distributed genus *Buteo,* or for hawks of related genera. In Great Britain the word buzzard is commonly used for the buteos; in the U.S. buzzard usually refers to the vulture (q.v.), especially the turkey vulture, *Cathartes aura.* Buteos are of medium or large size, heavy-bodied, and of strong but measured flight. They live largely on the smaller mammals and on insects, but they also capture birds. The wings, long and rounded, exceed the tail; the feet are robust, with tarsi (ankles) partially feathered.

The type species is the common buteo of Europe, *B. buteo,* which measures about 1 m (about 4 ft) across the wings and is prevailingly brown, with a mixture of black on the upper parts and of white or grayish-white on the underparts.

The most common North American buteo is the red-tailed hawk, *B. jamaicensis.* The tail of the adult bird is a rich rufous, tipped with white and with a narrow black band near the tip. The nest, of sticks, is built high up in medium to tall trees. Three or four eggs are usually laid early in spring; they are dull white and somewhat marked with brown.

BUTESHIRE, former county, W Scotland; Rothesay was the county town. The county comprised Arran, Bute, the Cumbraes, and several smaller islands, all lying in the Firth of Clyde. On the islands are the remains of prehistoric structures and many early Christian (6th cent.) churches. In 1975 Buteshire became part of the newly created Strathclyde Region (*see* STRATHCLYDE).

BUTLER, Alban (1710–73), British priest and hagiographer, born in Appletree, Northampton, England, and educated for the priesthood at the English Roman Catholic College in Douai, France. For a number of years he served there as professor of philosophy and of divinity. Subsequently he became chaplain in an English ducal house. From 1768 until his death, he was president of the English College of Saint-Omer. His great work, *The Lives of the Fathers, Martyrs, and Other Principal Saints* (4 vol., 1756–59) has been reissued in many editions and translations.

BUTLER, Benjamin Franklin (1818–93), American general and politician, born in Deerfield, N.H. He was educated at Waterville College (now Colby College), Maine, and admitted to the bar in 1840. After a career as a criminal lawyer and a Massachusetts state legislator (as a member of the Democratic party), he became brigadier general of the Massachusetts militia and major general of volunteers in the American Civil War. He commanded the land forces that captured New Orleans and for seven months (May–December 1862) was military governor of the city. His arbitrary rule provoked charges of corruption, earned him the name Beast Butler, and caused his dismissal as governor. He later commanded the Army of the James in Virginia. Butler, having become a member of the Republican party, served in the U.S. House of Representatives from 1867 to 1875. From 1877 to 1879 he served another term in Congress, as a member of the Greenback party. He rejoined the Democratic party and was elected governor of Massachusetts in 1882, serving until 1884, the year he became the unsuccessful presidential candidate of the Anti-Monopoly party and the Greenback party.

BUTLER, John (1728–96), Tory leader in the American Revolution, born in New London, Conn. During the French and Indian War he participated in several campaigns as captain in command of pro-British Indian auxiliaries. He fled to Canada after the outbreak of the American Revolution; there he organized Butler's Rangers, a force consisting of several hundred Indians and a number of Loyalists, whom he led in an invasion of the Wyoming Valley of Pennsylvania in 1778.

The successful expedition climaxed in a massacre conducted by Butler's Indian rangers. In 1779 American troops under Gen. John Sullivan and Gen. James Clinton (1733-1812) defeated Butler's Rangers in a battle fought near present-day Elmira, N.Y. In 1780 Butler engaged in a British raid of the Mohawk Valley. At the close of the war he was appointed British commissioner of Indian affairs at Niagara, Upper Canada (now Niagara-on-the-Lake, Ont.).

BUTLER, Nicholas Murray (1862-1947), American educator, born in Elizabeth, N.J., and educated at Columbia College (now Columbia University). In 1885 Butler became an assistant professor of philosophy at Columbia College. He organized the New York College for Training Teachers (now Teachers College of Columbia University) and served from 1886 to 1891 as its first president. He was president of Columbia College from 1902 to 1912 and of the newly created Columbia University from 1912 to 1945. Butler was largely responsible for the expansion and original organization of Columbia University.

In addition to his work as an educator, Butler was active in American politics, particularly between 1904 and 1936, when he served as a delegate to seven national conventions of the Republican party. Butler received the votes of the Republican party electors for vice-president in the presidential election of 1912; the original candidate, James S. Sherman, had died during the campaign.

His interest in world peace, disarmament, and international understanding led Butler to serve as president of the Carnegie Endowment for International Peace from 1925 until 1945 and to advocate U.S. participation in the League of Nations. He shared the Nobel Peace Prize for 1931 with the American social worker Jane Addams.

Butler wrote a score of books on education and world affairs. Among them are *The Meaning of Education* (1898; rev. ed., 1915), *The World Today* (1946), and his autobiography, *Across the Busy Years* (2 vol., 1939-40).

BUTLER, Samuel (1612-80), English poet, born near Pershore, Worcestershire. He wrote the mock-heroic poem *Hudibras,* a satire on Puritanism, in octosyllabic couplets, and inspired by the 17th-century Spanish novel *Don Quixote.* The first part of *Hudibras* was published in 1663, the second part in 1664, and the third part in 1678. Although the poem was a popular success and met with the favor of Charles II, Butler lived in poverty. Nearly a century after his death two volumes of his satirical works were published as *Genuine Remains in Verse and Prose of Mr. Samuel Butler* (1759).

BUTLER, Samuel (1835-1902), English novelist, born at Langar-cum-Barnstone, Nottinghamshire, and educated at the University of Cambridge. Rather than becoming a clergyman, as his father wished, Butler immigrated to New Zealand, where he was a successful sheep rancher from 1860 to 1864, when he returned to England.

Butler is best known for his satirical works. In *Erewhon* (1872), the story of an imaginary land, he criticized the customs and manners of contemporary England. His most important work is the novel *The Way of All Flesh,* published posthumously in 1903. It is a satirical autobiographical study of mid-Victorian family life. His works include studies in Darwinism, such as *Life and Habit* (1878); several works on the Homeric legends, including *The Authoress of the Odyssey* (1897); and *Erewhon Revisited* (1901).

BUTON. *See* BUTUNG.

BUTTE, in full, Butte-Silver Bow, Silver Bow Co., SW Montana; inc. as a city 1879. Consolidated in 1977 with Silver Bow Co., the city is situated in a mineral-rich region on the W slope of the Rocky Mts. at an altitude of about 1740 m (about 5700 ft). Until copper-mining operations declined in the early 1980s, the mines here supplied an important share of the nation's copper; silver, lead, zinc, and manganese are also produced. The city is the seat of the Montana College of Mineral Science and Technology (1893) and headquarters of adjoining Deerlodge National Forest. Settled by prospectors in the 1860s, it was originally a gold-mining and later a silver-mining center. During the 1880s, copper mining was begun and the city was reached by railroad. The city is named for a nearby butte. Pop. (1970) 23,368; (1980) 37,205.

BUTTER, solidified milk fat, especially cow's milk, used principally as a food item. In the manufacture of butter, the cream is skimmed from the milk or separated mechanically. It is then placed in a churn, and the butter is coagulated by agitation. The crude butter is then worked (or kneaded) and is washed with water to remove as much of the milk curd and other nonfatty components of the cream as possible. Sometimes butter color and vitamin A are added. In the U.S., federal regulations require that the finished butter contain not more than 16 percent water and not less than 82.5 percent butter fat. Annual production of butter in the U.S. in the years just before World War II exceeded 908 million kg (2 billion lb), of which less than one-fourth was produced on farms, the balance being made in factories. Per capita consumption of butter declined after World War II, largely because of competition from the lower-priced margarine. As part of the federal price-support program for dairy products, the government accumulated large stocks of surplus butter in the postwar period, but disposed of them in the mid-1980s. Butter production in the U.S. in the mid-1980s was about 566,000 metric tons annually.

BUTTERCUP, common name for the order Ranunculales, one of the largest groups of flowering plants (with 10 families and about 3000 species), and for its representative genus *Ranunculus.* Plants in the order are almost all herbaceous (nonwoody) or climbers and are most abundant in temperate areas of the world. Many species are of ornamental value, a few are common weeds, and some are poisonous to mammals, including humans.

The Ranunculales are a diverse order of plants, but several features are shared by many members of the group. Vegetatively, these include the herbaceous trait, alternately arranged leaves that lack stipules (small leaflike appendages at the leaf bases), and the production of alkaloids. Flower parts are usually numerous, spirally arranged, and not fused. Members of the order occupy a wide range of habitats, deserts being the only areas in which they are not well represented. In general, however, the Ranunculales are adapted to moist-to-wet habitats.

The brightly colored flowers found in most of the order function to attract insects for pollination. The order has two flower types: pollen flowers, such as those of the *Clematis* genus, and nectar flowers, such as those of columbines (genus *Aquilegia*).

Seven of the ten families included in the order contain only a few species each and have restricted distributions. The Menispermaceae is a family of about 400 species of climbers found throughout the Tropics. A kind of curare used as a muscle relaxant is obtained from one of its members. The Berberidaceae (*see* BARBERRY), with about 650 species, mostly North Temperate, includes the mayapple (q.v.) and several useful ornamentals such as Oregon grape (genus *Mahonia*) and barberry (*Berberis*). The largest family is Ranunculaceae, the buttercup or crowfoot family, with about 2000 species. It contains many ornamentals, including clematis, anemone, larkspur, and columbine (qq.v.).

Buttercups of the genus *Ranunculus* possess shiny, conspicuous, lemon-yellow, cup-shaped flowers. Common species include the tall buttercup (*R. acris*) and the bulbous buttercup (*R. bulbosus*), both widely distributed in pastures and meadows, although the latter is restricted to the eastern U.S. Cursed crowfoot (*R. sceleratus*) and small-flowered buttercup (*R. abortivus*) have

Tall buttercup, Ranunculus acris

smaller petals and are less conspicuous. Buttercups, marsh marigold (q.v.), and some other members of the buttercup family produce a harmless glycoside in their tissues. This compound, however, breaks down spontaneously to form an oily substance, protoanemonin, which is a strong irritant. Buttercups are usually avoided by livestock, but, if eaten, may produce severe irritation of the mouth and digestive system. Drying of the plant causes further spontaneous change, and hay containing buttercups cannot harm grazing livestock.

Plants of the order Ranunculales are dicots (q.v.) in the class Angiospermae (*see* ANGIOSPERM). M.R.C.

BUTTERFISH, silver-blue, toothed saltwater fish, *Porontus triacanthus,* inhabiting the Atlantic Coast of North America from Nova Scotia to Florida. Flat with a deeply forked tail, it is sometimes called the dollarfish because of its round, silvery appearance. It is distinguished from the similar pompano (q.v.) by the absence of ventral fins. The butterfish ranges in length from 20 to 30 cm (8 to 12 in); it is valued for its fine taste. It lays its eggs, which are buoyant, between late June and August in deep water. The young often remain under large jellyfish for protection and feed on small crustaceans close to shore. Adults feed on small fish and squid.

BUTTERFLIES AND MOTHS, members of the second largest insect order, Lepidoptera. They are outnumbered only by the beetles. The Latin name refers to the scale-covered, membranous wings common to all species. Most adult Lepidoptera are additionally characterized by a pair of well-developed compound eyes; mouthparts consisting of a long, coiled sucking tube, or proboscis; and prominent antennae.

Life Cycle. Lepidoptera undergo complete metamorphosis (*see* INSECT). Four stages make up the full life cycle: egg, larva (caterpillar), pupa (cocoon or chrysalis), and adult. After mating, the adult females of most Lepidoptera usually lay eggs on a plant that serves as the food source for the larvae when they hatch. In a few species, however, the larvae are predators. Some butterfly caterpillars, for example, eat aphids; some form complex associations with ants, live in their nests, and eat ant larvae. Some larvae eat stored cereals or even woolen clothes. Larvae have rather elastic cylindrical bodies, simple eyes, chewing mouthparts, small legs on the thorax, and legs on the abdomen as well. They eat continuously, periodically shedding their skin as they grow to hundreds of times their original size, and finally reach the stage where they spin cocoons and become pupae. During pupation the structures of the larvae totally transform; internal systems are reorganized and adult external structures develop.

Adult butterflies and moths feed on a wide variety of substances: nectar, pollen, rotting fruit, carrion, dung, urine, and other plant and animal exudates. Most Lepidoptera actively seek nectar from flowering plants, effectively carrying pollen from plant to plant and thus aiding in plant reproduction. In many species, such as sulfur butterflies (*Colias*), egg production is impossible without nectar meals. In others, such as the checkerspot butterflies (*Euphydryas*), unfed females lay about half as many eggs as those provided nectar. A few adult moths do not have functional mouthparts and lay all their eggs without obtaining nourishment.

Habitats and Range. Larvae of butterflies and moths are usually found feeding on a single species or a few related species of plants. This close relationship results in many Lepidoptera species being isolated in colonies in particular habitats. Other species may be more wide-ranging, especially those that lay eggs on widely distributed or weedy plants. A few butterflies, including the well-known monarch, *Danaus plexippus* (*see* MONARCH BUTTERFLY), may migrate thousands of kilometers to spend the winter in large aggregations at select sites. In some Lepidoptera, competition between larvae for host plants produces population cycles; large populations may build and then "crash," with most individuals dying. In other Lepidoptera, changes in population size are primarily due to climatic conditions.

Skipper butterfly, Bibasis gomata. *Skipper butterflies have many mothlike characteristics, including short, furry bodies and a chrysalis that resembles a cocoon.*
S. C. Bisserot–Bruce Coleman, Inc.

Butterflies and moths are found in a wide variety of habitats, from tundra to rain forest and from below sea level to nearly 6000 m (nearly 20,000 ft) in elevation. In tropical areas, where the Lepidoptera reach their greatest diversity, many butterflies may fly throughout the year. Continual good weather and ample resources allow for rapid larval development and long adult life, and as many as 15 generations may occur in one year. In temperate habitats, however, Lepidoptera enter an inactive stage, or diapause, during their development, to avoid severe weather conditions. Diapause may occur in the egg, larval, pupal, or adult stage. In snowy climates, win-

A swallowtail butterfly, family Papilionidae, after emerging from its chrysalis. The wings have stiffened and dried in preparation for flight.
E. R. Degginger–Bruce Coleman, Inc.

ter hibernation is common; in areas with hot, dry seasons, summer diapause (estivation) is the rule. Larval development is generally slower in temperate areas, and an adult's life span is often only a few days or weeks. In alpine or arctic habitats, growing seasons may be so short that many species require two years for development.

Characteristics. No absolutely consistent characteristics exist for separating butterflies and moths. Butterflies generally have scaleless, threadlike antennae with a club on the end. Wings are often brightly colored, and the wing color and pattern play a key role in mate recognition and courtship. Nearly all butterflies fly during daylight, but some tropical species fly at dawn or dusk, and a few are nocturnal. About 15,000 species are known worldwide. The largest butterflies (bird wings of Melanesia) have wingspans of up to 25 cm (10 in); the smallest (pygmy blues) may barely exceed 1 cm (0.4 in).

Moths have a wide variety of antennae forms, often feathery in appearance. Although many moths, especially day-flying ones, are brightly colored, most are dull shades of brown. Males are often attracted to females by a powerful chemical signal (*see* PHEROMONE) that the females release from special glands. Most moths fly at night, although many also fly during the day, especially in colder climates where evening temperatures often drop to freezing. (Their apparent attraction to a light source at night is a reflex; wing motion on the side struck by the light is reduced, causing them to turn in that direction.) About 250,000 moth species have been named, and many more probably exist. The largest moths (*Attacus* of Asia) may exceed 30 cm (12 in) in wingspan; the wings of the smallest (Microlepidoptera) may span only a number of millimeters.

A cecropia moth, Hyaloplora cecropia, *recently emerged from its cocoon. Cocoons, protective cases that surround the chrysalis, are spun mainly by moths.*
Robert L. Dunne–Bruce Coleman, Inc.

Coloration and Mimicry. The colors and patterns of the wings of butterflies and moths help to protect the organisms against predators. Some species possess eyespots or other markings that draw the attention of enemies away from vital body parts to the wings. In many species, cryptic coloration—wings looking like the natural background of soil, bark, and leaves—provides camouflage, protecting Lepidoptera from visually hunting predators.

The most intricate evolution is exhibited by butterflies with particularly bright or warning coloration. Some of these species deposit in their own tissues toxic chemicals from larval host plants that make them distasteful or poisonous to vertebrates. Butterflies of this sort are often marked with yellow, orange, or red on a dark background to warn predators of their unpalatability. In many locations, especially in tropical areas, edible butterflies and moths have evolved wing patterns mimicking inedible species and thus gaining protection themselves. This has been called Batesian mimicry, after its discoverer, the English naturalist and explorer Henry Bates (1825–92). Another type of association, Müllerian mimicry, occurs where several distasteful species fly together, sharing a similar warning coloration and presumably reducing predation on each individual species by giving predators fewer patterns to remember. *See* MIMICRY.

Importance. Moth species are among the most destructive pests of crops and stored products; very few butterfly species, however, attack economically important plants. Long studied by amateurs who have produced a large body of biological and distributional information, butterflies have become a key test group for ecological and evolutionary research. They are particularly amenable to laboratory analysis of a genetic nature, are easily monitored in the field, and are thought to be representative of most herbivorous insects, humanity's most important competitors for food. They also serve as key indicator species of environmental disruption.

Evolution. Few fossil Lepidoptera are known. Two records of primitive moths, more than 70 million years old, were found in Cretaceous amber. The earliest known butterfly fossils are those

Some common moths of North America. Top, left to right: Hummingbird moth, Hemaris thysbe; *brown-tail moth,* Nygmia phaeorrhoea; *Polyphemus moth,* Antheraea polyphemus. *Bottom, left to right: Promethea moth,* Callosamia promethea; *five-spotted hawkmoth,* Phlegethontius quinquemaculatus; *underwing moth,* Catocala cara.

from Green River Shale in Colorado, about 48 million years old. Today the order Lepidoptera consists of four suborders. More than 98 percent of the species are in one, the Ditrysia, which includes all the butterflies and higher moths.

D.D.M. & P.R.E.

For further information on this topic, see the Bibliography in volume 28, sections 466–67.

BUTTERFLY BUSH, common name for the genus *Buddleia,* comprising about 100 species of flowering shrubs and small trees widespread in subtropical and tropical areas. The genus is placed with several others in the family Buddleiaceae, a member of the order Scrophulariales (*see* FIGWORT). Some species have been used medicinally and as poisons, and several are grown for their scented, lilaclike flowers, which attract butterflies. Some of these plants grow up to 4.5 m (15 ft) high, and have arching, pendulous branches with profuse white, orange, or lavender flowers. *B. davidii,* also called summer lilac, is the hardiest and most widely grown species.

BUTTERFLY FISH, any fish of a tropical marine family, Chaetodontidae, named for the fish's bristlelike teeth. This gaily colored fish, found in coastal waters around coral reefs, is wide from top to bottom and narrow from side to side. Several species are known also as four-eyed fish because of a pair of eyelike spots on the back.

BUTTERFLY WEED, common name for a perennial plant, *Asclepias tuberosa,* found in open, dry ground in most of the U.S. east of the Rocky Mountains. The plant is 60 to 90 cm (24 to 36 in) high, with rough, lance-shaped leaves 5 to 15 cm (2 to 6 in) long; it bears brilliant orange flowers in summer. It belongs to the same genus as the milkweed (q.v.), but has little or no milky sap. It was used by the Indians for lung and throat ailments and is sometimes called pleurisy root.

BUTTERNUT, common name for a large, spreading American tree, *Juglans cinerla,* of the family Juglandaceae (*see* WALNUT), and for the fruit of the tree. The trees, found in eastern and central North America, grow to 18 m (60 ft) tall; they have large compound leaves with 11 to 17 leaflets. They are hardy from New Brunswick to Arkansas. The edible nuts are picked when green or dried after ripening. The wood of the tree, also known as white walnut, is hard and is valued for furniture and cabinetwork.

BUTTON (Fr. *bouton,* "bud" or "knob"), small knob or disk used for fastening or ornamenting clothing. Buttons are usually attached by sewing through holes in the disk or through a shank attached to the back. When used as fastening, they are pushed through loops or slits, called buttonholes. Precious metals, gems, and ivory have been used for buttons, but most buttons are made of such materials as wood, glass, mother-of-pearl, bone, horn, brass, pewter, and plastics. Worn as ornaments since the Bronze Age, buttons were sometimes used as fasteners by the Greeks and Romans. They became popular in Europe in the 13th and 14th centuries when form-fitted clothing came into fashion. In the 16th century, wearing buttons became a means of displaying wealth, and many buttons were set with diamonds and other gems. In the 18th century fine, handcrafted buttons were made of painted porcelain, tortoiseshell inlay, ivory, and engraved gems. Embroidered and brass buttons were also popular. Buttons in the late 20th century are primarily mass-produced in plastic. The collecting of fine buttons or of modern campaign or advertising buttons furnished with pins is a popular hobby.

BUTTONWOOD. *See* PLANE TREE.

BUTTRESS, pile of masonry built up against a wall to strengthen it, especially against lateral pressure, or thrust, from an arch or vault. Buttresses were used in ancient Mesopotamia and by the Romans, who built them against outside walls as piles of stone or against inside walls of vaulted buildings to serve as partitions. Vaulted Romanesque cathedrals in early medieval Europe had buttresses in the form of shallow projecting piers. Beginning in the 12th century, as Gothic cathedrals developed thinner walls and higher vaulted ceilings, with greater lateral thrust, additional support was needed. As buttresses projected farther from the walls, flying buttresses were devised, consisting of a wall buttress and a parallel detached buttress connected to it by an arc. The detached buttress was topped with a pinnacle or finial for added weight. Rows of carved pinnacled flying buttresses gave a delicate silhouette to such Gothic masterpieces as Notre Dame de Paris, Amiens, and Beauvais.

BUTUAN, municipality, S Philippines, capital of Agusan del Norte Province, near the mouth of the Agusan R., on the N coast of Mindanao. The city is a trade center for the Agusan R. valley, where gold, abaca, and copra are produced. Butuan is the site at which the Portuguese navigator Ferdinand Magellan proclaimed Spanish sovereignty over the Philippine Archipelago in 1521. Pop. (1980 prelim.) 172,404.

BUTUNG, also Buton or Boeton, island of Indonesia, part of the Malay Archipelago (q.v.), in the Banda Sea, lying SE of Celebes (Sulawesi). About 145 km (about 90 mi) long and 64 km (40 mi) wide, Butung is densely wooded and mountainous, with elevations higher than 1067 m (3500 ft). Asphalt mining, farming, fishing, and lumbering are the chief occupations. The major town is Baubau, at the SW extremity of the island. Area, 4556 sq km (1759 sq mi); pop. (est.) 188,200.

Flying buttresses in Reims Cathedral, France.
Marbury Art Reference Bureau

BUTYL ALCOHOL, organic chemical with the general formula C_4H_9OH. Three different forms exist, depending on the arrangement of the carbon atoms (*see* BUTANE); all are industrially important, being used in the production of solvents, plastics, detergents, and paint removers, and as bases for perfumes and fixatives. One form, tertiary butyl alcohol, is also used in denaturing ethyl alcohol (*see* ALCOHOL).

BUTZER, Martin *See* BUCER, MARTIN.

BUXTEHUDE, Dietrich (c. 1637–1707), Danish-born German organist and composer, a leader of the influential 17th-century North German school of organist-composers. Born probably in Oldesloe, he was the son of a church organist. In 1668 he became organist of the Marienkirche in Lübeck, Germany, where he instituted his annual *Abendmusiken,* or pre-Christmas evening concerts (a custom that continued into the 19th cent.). His toccatas, preludes and fugues had a profound impact on the music of other composers, including Johann Sebastian Bach, who in 1705 walked more than 320 km (198 mi) to hear the *Abendmusiken* concerts. Buxtehude also composed more than 100 church cantatas, suites for keyboard, and sonatas for strings.

BUXTON, town, in High Peak Borough, Derbyshire, central England. Buxton is a year-round resort and spa with numerous mineral baths; it is also the site of an annual arts festival. The town is encircled by Peak District National Park. The mineral waters here are used by the Romans, who called the place Aquae Armenetiae. The spa's modern revival dates from the 18th century. Pop. of High Peak Borough (1981) 82,142.

BUYS BALLOT, Christoph Hendrik Diederik (1817–90), Dutch scientist who helped lay the foundations of modern meteorology (q.v.), including the development of an internationally recognized system of weather observations. He was born in Kloetinge and studied at the University of Utrecht. He founded (1854) the Royal Netherlands Meteorological Institute, serving thereafter as its director. His name is attached to the observation, called Buys Ballot's law, that the direction of winds around a pressure center depends on whether the center is north or south of the equator.

BUZZARD, common Old World name for birds of prey of the subfamily Accipitridae. In the U.S.

the term *buzzard* is often used for New World vultures (Cathartidae). The Accipitridae and most other diurnal birds of prey of the phylum Falconiformes are called hawks. *See* BUTEO.

BUZZARDS BAY, inlet of the Atlantic Ocean, SE Massachusetts. About 48 km (about 30 mi) long by 8 to 16 km (5 to 10 mi) wide, it is sheltered from the ocean and partly separated from Vineyard Sound by the Elizabeth Islands. Buzzards Bay is the center of a popular resort region. Among the communities bordering its shores are South Dartmouth, Fairhaven, Wareham, Onset, Buzzards Bay, Monument Beach, and Falmouth. The W entrance of the Cape Cod Canal (q.v.) lies at the NE extremity of the bay.

BYBLOS, ancient city of Phoenicia, on the Mediterranean Sea, near present-day Beirut, Lebanon. Extensive archaeological investigations, begun in 1921, indicate that Byblos is one of the oldest continuously inhabited cities in the world, with remains of civilizations dating from about 5000 BC. The city was the principal city of Phoenicia and an important seaport during the 2d millennium BC, when it exported cedar and other woods to Egypt. The name Byblos, applied by the Greeks to papyrus, which they imported from Byblos, is the source of the word Bible. Gebal was the biblical name for the city; the Book of Ezekiel (see 27:9) mentions the maritime pursuits of its inhabitants. The city of Byblos is now occupied by a Lebanese village called Jubayl.

BYDGOSZCZ (Ger. *Bromberg*), city, central Poland, capital of Bydgoszcz Province, on the Brda R. Bydgoszcz is situated in a low-lying region, which is largely agricultural; the principal crops are grain, potatoes, and sugar beets. The city, an important industrial and commercial center, is served by a network of railways and inland water carriers, and lies at the E end of the Bydgoszcz Canal, which connects the Brda and Noteć (Netze) rivers. The chief manufactures include chemicals, electrical equipment, nonelectrical machinery, and precision instruments.

The city, captured in the 13th century by Teutonic Knights, was subsequently incorporated into Poland. It became a part of Prussia in 1772 and, except for a brief period, remained under Prussian rule until 1919. It was badly damaged during World War II. In the early 1980s Bydgoszcz was the scene of political and social unrest. Pop. (1985 est.) 366,400.

BYELORUSSIAN SOVIET SOCIALIST REPUBLIC. *See* BELORUSSIAN SOVIET SOCIALIST REPUBLIC.

BYRD, Harry Flood (1887–1966), legislator, born in Martinsburg, W.Va. He left school at the age of 16 to work for the *Winchester* (Va.) *Evening Star,* a newspaper that he subsequently bought. Later he also engaged in farming, specializing in the cultivation of apples. A member of the Democratic party, he served in the Virginia Senate (1915–25) and was later governor of the state (1926–30). Appointed to the U.S. Senate to fill a vacancy in 1933, he remained a senator until his retirement in 1965, serving for ten years as chairman of the finance committee. His son, Harry Flood Byrd, Jr. (1914–   ), was appointed to succeed him in 1965 and was returned in 1970, the first independent candidate in 34 years to be elected U.S. senator. He was reelected in 1976 but declined to run again in 1982.

BYRD, Richard Evelyn (1888–1957), American explorer, author, aviator, and naval officer, known for leading several expeditions, by air and land, to the Antarctic and for discoveries there.

Byrd was born in Winchester, Va. He attended the Virginia Military Institute and the University of Virginia and graduated from the U.S. Naval Academy in 1912. Designated a naval aviator in 1918, he was promoted to the rank of lieutenant commander. In 1925 he commanded the naval air unit of the expedition to Greenland, led by the American explorer Donald Baxter MacMillan.

With the American aviator Floyd Bennett as copilot, he made the first flight over the North Pole in 1926. For this achievement Byrd received the Medal of Honor. In 1927 he flew the first transatlantic airmail from New York to France with the Norwegian-American Bernt Balchen (1899–1973) and the Americans Bertrand B. Acosta (1895–1954) and George O. Noville (b. 1890).

During his first expedition (1928–30) to Antarctica, Byrd established a base, Little America, on the Bay of Whales. In the course of mapping 388,300 sq km (150,000 sq mi) of Antarctica, members of the expedition discovered the Edsel Ford Range and Marie Byrd Land. In 1929 Byrd made the first flight over the South Pole, together with Balchen and the American pilots Harold I. June (1895–1962) and Ashley C. McKinley (1897–1940). Byrd was promoted in 1930 to the rank of rear admiral, retired.

During his second expedition (1933–35) to the Antarctic, for five months Byrd conducted meteorological and auroral researches alone in a shack 196 km (121.7 mi) south of Little America. The expedition party surveyed 1,165,000 sq km (450,000 sq mi) of territory and undertook research in many branches of science.

Byrd organized a third expedition (1939–40) to Little America. Four exploratory flights were made during the expedition, resulting in many discoveries, including several new mountain ranges and extensive new coastline.

The fourth Byrd Antarctic expedition (1946–47)

was mainly explorational, although meteorological research and tests of military equipment were carried out. Approximately 323,500 sq km (845,000 sq mi) of territory, about one-third of it newly discovered, was mapped. Included among the discoveries were a new mountain range and a large ice-free region in the interior. Byrd made his second flight over the South Pole before returning to the U.S. In 1955 Byrd was appointed head of "Operation Deep-Freeze," an Antarctic expedition organized by the U.S. in connection with the International Geophysical Year (1957–58). Early in 1956 Byrd made his third flight over the South Pole. He left the expedition shortly thereafter. Byrd wrote *Skyward* (1928), *Little America* (1930), *Discovery* (1935), *Exploring with Byrd* (1938), and *Alone* (1938).

BYRD, William (1543?–1623), greatest English composer of the Elizabethan age. Born probably at Lincoln, he was organist at the Lincoln Cathedral from 1563 to 1572, when he became organist for the Chapel Royal. In 1575 Queen Elizabeth I granted Byrd and his former teacher Thomas Tallis a monopoly in the printing and selling of music and music paper; it became Byrd's property upon Tallis's death in 1585. Although a Roman Catholic working in England under the Protestant Elizabeth, Byrd was nationally venerated, and his loyalty was never questioned. He died July 4, 1623, in Stondon, Essex.

Byrd composed 6 Anglican services and about 60 anthems, but his Latin church music is considered his most glorious work; its breadth and intensity are unmatched in English music. His major Latin works are his three masses, the 1589 and 1591 volumes of *Cantiones Sacrae,* and the two-volume *Gradualia* (1605, 1607), a year's cycle of settings of the changeable parts of the mass. Byrd was among the first to compose fantasias for viol consort. His more than 140 virginal (harpsichord) pieces helped establish the English school of virginal composition; they appear in his manuscript *My Ladye Nevells Booke* (1591) and in anthologies such as the manuscript *Fitzwilliam Virginal Book* (c. 1612–19). His secular vocal music includes songs for solo voice and viol consort.

BYRD, William (1674–1744), political leader in colonial Virginia, ancestor of the influential Byrd family. He was born in Virginia but educated in England and frequently represented the colony's interests there. A member of Virginia's Council of State, he played a leading role in the council's power struggle with Gov. Alexander Spotswood (1676–1740), and he also founded the city of Richmond. Byrd's diaries give an interesting picture of life at Westover, his plantation on the James River.

BYRNES, James Francis (1879–1972), American statesman, born in Charleston, S.C. At the age of 14 he went to work in a law office; ten years later he was admitted to the South Carolina bar. Byrnes represented South Carolina in the U.S. House of Representatives (1911–25) and in the U.S. Senate (1931–41). He was appointed (1941) an associate justice of the U.S. Supreme Court but resigned from the Court to serve as head of federal agencies established to achieve economic stabilization (1942–43) and economic mobilization (1943–45) during World War II. Appointed secretary of state (1945) by President Harry S. Truman, he represented the U.S. at the peace talks after the war. In 1947 he resigned because of ill health. Later he served as governor of South Carolina (1951–55). He was the author of two books, *Speaking Frankly* (1947) and *All in One Lifetime* (1958).

BYRON, George Gordon Noel, 6th Baron Byron (1788–1824), English poet, who was one of the most important and versatile writers of the romantic movement. His short life, filled with romance and adventure, was regarded as a model of that of the romantic hero.

Byron was born in London, Jan. 22, 1788, and educated at Harrow School and the University of Cambridge. He succeeded to the title and estates of his granduncle William, 5th Baron Byron, upon the death of the latter in 1798. Lord Byron adopted the name Noel as his third given name in 1822, in order to receive an inheritance from his mother-in-law.

In 1807 a volume of Byron's poems, *Hours of Idleness,* was published. An adverse review of this work in the *Edinburgh Review* prompted a satirical reply from Byron in heroic couplets, entitled *English Bards and Scotch Reviewers* (1809). In 1809 Byron took his seat in the House of Lords. Also in 1809 he began two years of travels in Portugal, Spain, and Greece.

George Gordon Byron, Lord Byron (from an oil painting by Thomas Phillips). Granger Collection

Fame and Marriage. The publication in 1812 of the first two cantos of *Childe Harold's Pilgrimage,* a poem narrating travels in Europe, brought Byron fame. The hero of the poem, Childe Harold, was the first example of what came to be known as the Byronic hero, the young man of stormy emotions who shuns humanity and wanders through life weighed down by a sense of guilt for mysterious sins of his past. The Byronic hero is, to some extent, modeled on the life and personality of Byron himself. The type recurs in his narrative poems of the following two years, which include *The Giaour* (1813), *The Bride of Abydos* (1813), *The Corsair* (1814), and *Lara* (1814). In 1815 his *Hebrew Melodies* was published, and in the same year Byron was married to Anna Isabella Milbanke (1792–1860). After giving birth to a daughter, named Ada (1815–52), Byron's only legitimate child, Lady Byron left her husband. In 1816, after agreeing to a legal separation from his wife and having been ostracized by society, Byron left England never to return.

Exile. In Geneva, Byron wrote the third canto of *Childe Harold* and the narrative poem *The Prisoner of Chillon.* He next established residence in Venice, where in the three years from 1816 to 1819 he produced, among other works, the verse drama *Manfred* (1817), the first two cantos of *Don Juan* (1818–19), and the fourth and final canto of *Childe Harold* (1818). For two years Byron traveled around Italy, settling in Pisa in 1821. He wrote the verse dramas *Cain* and *Sardanapalus* and the narrative poems *Mazeppa* and *The Island* during these years. In 1822, with the poets Percy Bysshe Shelley and Leigh Hunt, he started at Pisa a journal called *The Liberal,* but Shelley's death that year and a quarrel with Hunt put an end to this venture after only four numbers had been printed. *Don Juan,* a mock epic in 16 cantos, encompasses a brilliant satire on contemporary English society. Often regarded as Byron's greatest work, it was completed in 1823. At the news of the revolt of the Greeks against the Turks Byron, disregarding his weakened physical condition, in July 1823 joined the Greek insurgents at Missolonghi. He not only recruited a regiment for the cause of Greek independence but contributed large sums of money to it. The Greeks made him commander in chief of their forces in January 1824. The poet died at Missolonghi three months later on April 19, 1824.

For further information on this person, see the section Biographies in the Bibliography in volume 28.

BYTOM (Ger. *Beuthen*), city, SW Poland, in Katowice Province. Lying in a rich coal-mining and metal-mining region, the city is an important industrial center, with plants producing furniture and metal products. Bytom was part of the Prussian province of Upper Silesia until 1945. After World War II, under the terms of a decision of the Potsdam Conference, it was incorporated into Poland. Pop. (1985 est.) 238,900.

BYZANTINE ART AND ARCHITECTURE, the art of the Byzantine, or Eastern Roman, Empire. It originated chiefly in Constantinople, the ancient Greek town by Byzantium, which the Roman emperor Constantine chose in AD 330 as his new capital and named for himself. The Byzantine Empire continued for almost 1000 years after the collapse of the Western Empire in 476. Byzantine art eventually spread throughout most of the Mediterranean world and eastward to Armenia. Although the conquering Turks in the 15th century destroyed much in Constantinople itself, sufficient material survives elsewhere to permit an appreciative understanding of Byzantine art.

Byzantine art and architecture arose in part as a response to the needs of the Eastern, or Orthodox, church. Unlike the Western church, in which the popular veneration of the relics of the saints continued unabated from early Christian times throughout the later Middle Ages, the Eastern church preferred a more contemplative form of popular worship focused on the veneration of icons (*see* ICON). These were portraits of sacred personages, often rendered in a strictly frontal view and in a highly conceptual and stylized manner. Although any type of pictorial representation—a wall painting or a mosaic, for instance—could serve as an icon, it generally took the form of a small painted panel.

Something of the abstract quality of the icons entered into much of Byzantine art. The artistic antecedents of the iconic mode can be traced back to Mesopotamia and the hinterlands of Syria and Egypt, where, since the 3d century AD, the rigid and hieratic (strictly ritualized) art of the ancient Orient was revived in the Jewish and pagan murals of the remote Roman outpost of Dura Europos on the Euphrates and in the Christian frescoes of the early monasteries in Upper Egypt. In the two major cities of these regions, Antioch and Alexandria, however, the more naturalistic (Hellenistic) phase of Greek art also survived right through the reign of Constantine. In Italy, Roman painting, as practiced at Pompeii and in Rome itself, was also imbued with the Hellenistic spirit.

The Hellenistic heritage was never entirely lost to Byzantine art but continued to be a source of inspiration and renewal. In this process, however, the classical idiom was drastically modified in order to express the transcendental character of the Orthodox faith. Early Christian art of the 3d and 4th centuries had simply taken over the style and forms of classical paganism. The most typical form of classical art was the freestanding statue, which emphasized a tangible physical presence. With the triumph of Christianity, artists sought to evoke the spiritual character of sacred figures rather than their bodily substance. Painters and mosaicists often avoided any modeling of the figures whatsoever in order to eliminate any suggestion of a tangible human form, and the production of statuary was almost completely abandoned after the 5th century. Sculpture was largely confined to ivory plaques (called diptychs) in low relief, which minimized sculpturesque effects.

Mosaics (q.v.) were the favored medium for the interior adornment of Byzantine churches. The small cubes, or tesserae, that composed mosaics were made of colored glass or enamels or were overlaid with gold leaf. The luminous effects of the mosaics, spread over the walls and vaults of the interior, were well adapted to express the mystic character of Orthodox Christianity. At the same time their rich, jewellike surfaces were also in keeping with the magnificence of the imperial court, presided over by the emperor, the de facto head of the Orthodox church.

Early Period. Although the 5th-century art of the empire is sometimes referred to as early Byzantine, it should be more aptly called late Antique. It is a transitional phase between the classical antiquity of Early Christian art and the emergence of a truly Byzantine style shortly after 500, when the portraits of the Byzantine consuls on their ivory diptychs assume the hieratic, depersonalized character of the icons. The golden age of early Byzantine art and architecture falls within the reign (527–65) of the emperor Justinian, a prolific builder and a patron of the arts.

Mosaics. The still formative stage of Byzantine art in the age of Justinian is reflected in the variety of mosaic styles. They range from the austere grandeur of the *Transfiguration of Christ* (c. 540) in the apse of the monastery church of Saint Catherine at Mount Sinai to the mid-6th-century processions of the martyrs in Sant' Apollinare Nuovo in Ravenna, Italy, which recall the endless rhythmic sequences of marching figures in the art of the ancient Near East.

The facade of the palace of Theodoric, detail from the 6th-century mosaic frieze in the central nave of the Church of Sant' Apollinare Nuovo, built in Ravenna by the king, who made the town his capital at the end of the 5th century.

Hagia Sophia, in İstanbul. The historic Byzantine edifice was built in the 6th century as a Christian church and was converted in 1453 into a mosque. It currently serves as a museum.

The most extensive series of mosaics of the Justinian age, and the finest, are those (finished in 547) in the Church of San Vitale, Ravenna. Rather than a mere expression of stylistic diversity, the different pictorial modes of these mosaics were each adapted to its subject matter. The Old Testament scenes in the choir exemplify the narrative mode, in which the action takes place in picturesque settings of rocks and flowers against a background of rose-tinted clouds, all reminiscent of the illusionistic landscapes of Pompeian painting.

Beyond, on the curving wall of the apse, the emperor Justinian, surrounded by members of his court, confronts the empress Theodora in the midst of her attendant ladies; both rulers are sumptuously arrayed in diadems and imperial purple mantles. The emperor, venerated as Christ's representative on earth, and the revered empress are depicted, along with their retinues, in the uncompromising frontality and with the fixed gaze of the dematerialized figures of icons.

The classical heritage is visible in the beardless Christ, who, like a youthful Apollo, sits on the globe of the universe in the gold semidome of the apse—a Western type of the seated Christ derived from Early Christian sarcophagi. All three modes—the narrative, the iconic, and the classically inspired—are encountered again and again in all major periods of Byzantine art.

Architecture. As in art, a wide diversity characterizes the ecclesiastical architecture of the early Byzantine period. Two major types of churches, however, can be distinguished: the basilica type, with a long colonnaded nave covered by a wooden roof and terminating in a semicircular apse; and the vaulted centralized church, with its separate components gathered under a central dome. The second type was dominant throughout the Byzantine period.

Hagia Sophia, or the Church of the Holy Wisdom, in Constantinople, built in five years by Justinian and consecrated in 537, is the supreme example of the centralized type. Although the unadorned exterior masses of Hagia Sophia build up to an imposing pyramidal complex, as in all Byzantine churches it is the interior that counts. In Hagia Sophia the architects Anthemius of Tralles (d. 534) and Isidorus of Miletus created one of the great interior spaces in the history of architecture. The vast central dome, which rises some 56 m (185 ft) from the pavement, is dramatically poised over a circle of light radiating from the cornea of windows at its base. Four curved or spherical triangles, called pendentives, support its rim and are in turn locked into the corners of a square formed by four huge arches. The transition between the circular dome and its square base, achieved through the use of pendentives, was a major contribution of Byzantine builders to the development of architecture. To the east a vast semidome surmounts the three large vaulted niches of the sanctuary below. Arcades that recall the arcaded naves of the basilica churches occupy the ground story on the north and south sides of the central square. To the west is another huge semidome preceding a barrel-vaulted narthex.

The ethereal quality of this "hanging architecture," in which the supports—visible on the exterior as four immense buttress towers—of the dome, pendentives, and semidomes are effectively disguised, is reinforced by the shimmering mosaics and sheets of polished marble that sheathe the interior walls and arches.

Iconoclastic Period. Along with an appreciation of religious works of art, a strong bias had always existed among some members of the Eastern church against any depiction whatsoever of sacred scenes and personages. This antiiconic movement resulted in 726 in the order of Emperor Leo III for the destruction throughout the empire (Italy resisted) not only of icons, but of all representatives of the human figure in religious art of any kind (*see* ICONOCLASM).

During the ensuing iconoclastic period, however, the decorative arts flourished. Some idea of their character may be gained from the work of indigenous Byzantine mosaicists who created rich acanthus scrolls in the Dome of the Rock (685–705) at Jerusalem and delightful landscapes with feathery trees in the Great Mosque at Damascus (706–15). From the iconoclastic period date the oldest surviving examples of Byzantine silk textiles, some with motifs inspired by earlier Persian designs. Imported from the East, these Byzantine textiles were used in Western churches as altar hangings and as shrouds in the tombs of rulers and saints.

Mid-Byzantine Period: Macedonian Renaissance. In 843 the ban against icons was finally lifted, and a second golden age of Byzantine art, the mid-Byzantine period, was inaugurated with the advent of the new Macedonian dynasty (867–1056). During this appropriately named Macedonian Renaissance, Byzantine art was reanimated by an important classical revival, exemplified by a few illuminated manuscripts that have survived from the 9th and 10th centuries. As models for the full-page illustrations, the artists chose

St. Mark's Cathedral in Venice is considered one of the most magnificent Byzantine structures in existence. Originally a Romanesque church built in the 9th century as a shrine for the bones of St. Mark, it was reconstructed during the next two centuries with the help of Byzantine architects. It is decorated with spoils from the sack of Constantinople in 1204.

A wall mosaic in St. Mark's Cathedral, Venice, shows the Virgin, Christ, and St. Mark. Wall mosaics are major contributions of Byzantine art. Scala Fine Arts

manuscripts (now lost) from the late Antique period that were illustrated in a fully developed Hellenistic style.

Painting. In studying their prototypes the Byzantine artists learned anew the classical conventions for depicting the clothed figure, in which the drapery clings to the body, thus revealing the forms beneath—the so-called damp-fold style. They also wanted to include modeling in light and shade, which not only produces the illusion of three-dimensionality but also lends animation to the painted surfaces. Religious images, however, were only acceptable as long as the human figure was not represented as an actual bodily presence. The artists solved the problem by abstraction, that is, by rendering the darks, halftones, and lights as clearly differentiated patterns or as a network of lines on a flat surface, thus preserving the visual interest of the figure while avoiding any actual modeling and with it the semblance of corporeality. Thus were established those conventions for representing the human figure that endured for the remaining centuries of Byzantine art.

Architecture. In contrast to the artistic experimentations in the Justinian age, the mid-Byzantine period was one of consolidation. Recurring types of the centralized church were established, and the program of their mosaic decoration was systematized in order to conform to Orthodox beliefs and practices.

A common type of the mid-Byzantine centralized church was the cross-in-the-square. As at Hagia Sophia, its most prominent feature was the central dome over a square area, from which now radiated the four equal arms of a cross. The dome was usually supported, however, not by pendentives but by squinches (small arches) set diagonally in the corners of the square. The lowest portions of the interior were confined to the small areas that lay between the arms of the cross and the large square within which the whole church was contained.

Mosaic and enamel. From the fragmentary mosaic cycles in Hosios Lukas, Daphni, and several other 11th-century churches in Greece, the typical decorative program of the cross-in-the-square church can be readily reconstructed. The program was based on the hierarchical importance of the subjects disposed in an ascending scale. The lesser saints were relegated to the lowest and least conspicuous areas of the interior. The more important saints were placed on the more essential structural elements. On the larger wall surfaces and on the higher levels beneath the dome were scenes from the Gospels and from the life of the Virgin Mary. The heavenly themes, such as the ascension, were depicted on the vaults. Pentecost, represented by energizing rays descending on the heads of the apostles, occupied the vault over the eastern arm.

Beyond, in the center of the golden conch

St. Theodore's Church, Mistra, near Sparta, Greece. Constructed in the form of a square Greek cross surmounted by a dome, it is a good example of the architecture of the final phase of the 14th-century Palaeologan Late Byzantine style.
Spios Tselentis–Shostal Associates

(semidome) of the apse, the Virgin bearing the Christ Child reigned in isolated splendor. From the lofty center of the dome a huge bust of the bearded Christ, the Pantocrator, the awesome ruler of the universe, gazed down upon the created world below. The church thus became a symbol of the cosmos, and the whole interior, with its hierarchy of sacred images, was transformed into a vast three-dimensional icon.

On a smaller scale were works in cloisonné enamel, a technique in which Byzantine artisans were highly skilled (*see* ENAMEL). Surviving examples include a few Byzantine crowns (among them the famous crown of St. Stephen of Hungary) and a number of sumptuous reliquaries. The Byzantines also fashioned other magnificent liturgical objects of silver and gold.

Mid-Byzantine Period: Comnenian Art. The second major phase of the mid-Byzantine period coincided with the rule of the Comneni dynasty (1081–1185) of emperors. Comnenian art inaugurated new artistic trends that continued into the succeeding centuries. A humanistic approach alien to earlier Byzantine art informs the icon *Virgin of Vladimir* (c. 1125, Tretyakov Gallery, Moscow). Instead of showing her customary aloofness, the Virgin Mary here presses her cheek against that of her child in an embrace. Comnenian humanism is again encountered in the new theme of the *Threnos,* the lamentation over the dead body of Christ, rendered with intense pathos in a fresco of 1164 in the church of Nerezi in Yugoslavia. Like the *Virgin of Vladimir,* the fresco was the work of a Constantinople painter.

The most extensive series of Comnenian mosaics are those created by Byzantine artists in the large church at Monreale in Sicily, begun in 1174. The mosaic program, however, had to be readapted to the basilica form of the interior. Following a Western precedent, scenes from the Book of Genesis occupy the areas between and above the arches of the long nave arcade. The *Sacrifice of Isaac, Rebecca at the Well,* and *Jacob Wrestling with the Angel,* all masterpieces of a new dynamic narrative style, are skillfully adapted to the format of the undulating frieze that continues around and above the arches. Above, in the vast semidome of the apse, looms a gigantic bust of the Pantocrator.

The Sicilian mosaics are but one example among many of the exportation of mid-Byzantine art to regions beyond the much-reduced confines of the empire. Some Byzantine influence can also be detected in the domed churches of western France. During the 11th and 12th centuries Byzantine art and architecture were the norm in the Venetian Republic. The five-domed Church of Saint Mark's (begun c. 1063) was modeled in part on Justinian's cruciform Church of the Apostles in Constantinople. In the Cathedral of Torcello the great panorama of the *Last Judgment* on the western wall and the lovely standing figure of the Virgin in the apsidal conch are genuine Byzantine creations. The Byzantine style was introduced into Russia in the Cathedral of Hagia Sophia at Kiev, founded in 1037. The pervasive influence of Byzantine art on Western Europe continued into the 13th century. In the East, however, the mid-Byzantine period came to an abrupt, shocking end in 1204 with the sack of Constantinople by the Crusaders.

Palaeologue Period. A brief interlude of Western rulers in Constantinople was succeeded in 1261 by the last Byzantine dynasty, that of the Palaeologan emperors (1258–1453). The final flowering of Byzantine art occurred during the Palaeologue period, and its vitality and creativeness remained undiminished.

Architecture. The new architectural features had already been foreshadowed under the Comneni.

In general, the vertical lines of the churches were emphasized, and the five-domed church became the norm. The drums, or circular rings on which the domes rest, often assumed octagonal form and grew taller. The domes themselves were sometimes reduced to small cupolas. Special attention was also given to exterior embellishment.

Painting and mosaic. More profound were the changes in the pictorial arts. With few exceptions, notably the splendid mosaics of the Church of the Chora (1310–20) in Constantinople, fresco painting everywhere replaced the more costly medium of mosaic decoration. The rules governing the hierarchical program of the mid-Byzantine churches were also largely abandoned. Narrative scenes sometimes occupied the vaults, and the figures tended to diminish in size, resulting in a new emphasis on the landscapes and architectural backgrounds. In the mosaics of the Church of the Chora fantastic architectural forms reminiscent of modern cubism were carefully coordinated with the figures. In a contemporary fresco of the nativity in the Greek Church of the Peribleptos at Mistra, a vast rocky wasteland poignantly emphasizes the isolation of the small figures of the Virgin Mary and her child. In the background of the *Raising of Lazarus* in the Church of the Pantanassa at Mistra (1428), a wide V-shaped cleft between two tall peaks is eloquent of the chasm of death that separates the mummified corpse of Lazarus from the living Savior. In emphasizing the settings, however, the artists were careful to avoid any sense of actual space that might destroy the spiritual character of the scenes.

Although the basic compositions of the more traditional images were retained, they were reinterpreted with exceptional vitality. In a fresco in the mortuary chapel adjoining the Church of the Chora the time-honored theme of the *Anastasis,* the descent of Christ into limbo, was infused with extraordinary energy: The resurrected Christ strides victoriously across the shattered gates of hell to liberate Adam and Eve from the infernal

A Byzantine icon depicting the biblical scene of the presentation in the Temple. With its long, delicate lines and flattened two-dimensional surface, it is a good example of the style of the 12th-century school of Novgorod.

Scala–Editorial Photocolor Archives

A Byzantine silver dish (early 7th cent.), depicting the anointing of David by the prophet Samuel.
Metropolitan Museum of Art

regions. The *Koimesis,* the death and assumption of the Virgin Mary, was traditionally depicted in terms of a simple but effective arrangement: The horizontal corpse of the Virgin on her deathbed is counterbalanced by the central upright figure of Christ holding aloft the small image of her soul. In the Serbian church at Sopoćani (c. 1265) this basic composition of the Virgin and Christ is greatly amplified to include a whole cohort of angels who are arranged in a semicircle around the figure of Christ.

These are but a few highlights of a vigorous and creative art that continued in the Balkans right into the middle of the 15th century. By that time, however, the days of Constantinople's glory were long past. Harassed by the Turks, the impoverished empire was reduced to little more than the city itself. In 1453 the end came with the taking of Constantinople by Muhammad II. Nevertheless, a long afterlife was granted the art and architecture of the vanished empire. Hagia Sophia provided the model for the new mosques of Constantinople. In Russia the churches continued to be built in an exotic Slavic version of the Byzantine style. The age-old traditions of icon painting (later somewhat Westernized) were handed down for generations in Russia and other parts of the Orthodox world.

See also BYZANTINE EMPIRE; CHURCH; EARLY CHRISTIAN ART AND ARCHITECTURE; ISLAMIC ART AND ARCHITECTURE; İSTANBUL; ORTHODOX CHURCH.

W.M.H.

For further information on this topic, see the Bibliography in volume 28, section 651.

EMPERORS OF THE BYZANTINE EMPIRE

Constantinian Dynasty
Constantine I, 324–37
Constantius I, 337–61
Julian, 361–63
*Jovian, 363–64
*Valens, 364–78

Theodosian Dynasty
Theodosius I, 379–95
Arcadius, 395–408
Theodosius II, 408–50
*Marcian, 450–57
*Leo I, 457–74
*Leo II (associated with Leo I), 473–74
*Zeno, 474–91
*Anastasius I, 491–518

Justinianic Dynasty
Justin I, 518–27
Justinian I, 527–65
Justin II, 565–78
Tiberius II Constantinus, 578–82
Mauricius, 582–602
*Phocas, 602–10

Heraclian Dynasty
Heraclius, 610–41
Constantine III, 641
Heracleonas, 641
Constans II, 641–68
Constantine IV, 668–85
Justinian II, 685–95
*Leontius, 695–98
*Tiberius III Apsimar, 698–705
Justinian II (again), 705–11
*Philippicus, 711–13
*Anastasius II, 713–16
*Theodosius III, 716–17

Isaurian Dynasty
Leo III, 717–41
Constantine V, 741–75
Leo IV, 775–80
Constantine VI, 780–97
Irene (empress), 797–802
*Nicephorus I, 802–11
*Stauracius, 811
*Michael I Rhangabe, 811–13
*Leo V, 813–20

Amorian Dynasty
Michael II, 820–29
Theophilus, 829–42
Michael III, 842–67

Macedonian Dynasty
Basil I, 867–86
Leo VI, 886–912
Alexander, 912–13
Constantine VII, 913–59
*Romanus I Lecapenus (coemperor), 919–44
Romanus II, 959–63
*Nicephorus II Phocas, 963–69
*John I Tzimisces, 969–76
Basil II, 976–1025
Constantine VIII, 1025–28
Romanus III Argyrus, 1028–34
*Michael IV, 1034–41
*Michael V Calaphates, 1041–42
Zoë and Theodora, 1042
*Constantine IX, 1042–55
Theodora (again), 1055–56

Macedonian Dynasty (cont.)
*Michael VI Stratioticus, 1056–57
*Isaac I Comnenus, 1057–59
*Constantine X Ducas, 1059–67
*Romanus IV Diogenes, 1067–71
*Michael VII Ducas, 1071–78
*Nicephorus III Botaniates, 1078–81

Comnenian Dynasty
Alexius I Comnenus, 1081–1118
John II Comnenus, 1118–43
Manuel I Comnenus, 1143–80
Alexius II Comnenus, 1180–83
Andronicus I Comnenus, 1183–85

Angelian Dynasty
Isaac II Angelus, 1185–95
Alexius III Angelus, 1195–1203
Isaac II (again) and Alexis IV Angelus, 1203–04
*Alexis V, 1204

Latin Empire of Constantinople
Baldwin I, 1204–05
Henry of Flanders, 1205–16
Peter of Courtenay, 1216–17
Yolande, 1217–19
Robert of Courtenay, 1221–28
John of Brienne, 1228–37
Baldwin II, 1237–61

Palaeologan Dynasty
Michael VIII Palaeologus, 1261–82
Andronicus II Palaeologus, 1282–1328
Michael IX Palaeologus (coruler), 1295–1320
Andronicus III Palaeologus, 1328–41
John V Palaeologus, 1341–91
*John VI Cantacuzene (nominal coruler), 1347–54
Andronicus IV (coruler), 1376–79
John VII Palaeologus (coruler), 1390
Manuel II Palaeologus, 1391–1425
John VIII Palaeologus. 1425–48
Constantine XI Palaeologus, 1449–53

* Not a member of the dynasty.

BYZANTINE EMPIRE, eastern part of the Roman Empire, which survived after the breakup of the Western Empire in the 5th century AD. Its capital was Constantinople (now İstanbul, Turkey).

Constantinople became a capital of the Roman Empire in 330 after Constantine the Great, the first Christian emperor, refounded the city of Byzantium and named it after himself. Only gradually did it develop into the true capital of the eastern Roman provinces—those areas of the empire in southeastern Europe, western Asia, and the northeast corner of Africa (what is today much of Yugoslavia, as well as Bulgaria, Greece, southern Romania, Turkey, Syria, Jordan, Israel, Lebanon, Cyprus, Egypt, and the eastern part of Libya). Scholars have called the empire Byzantine after the ancient name of its capital, Byzantium, or the Eastern Roman Empire, but to contemporaries and in official terminology of the time, it was simply Roman, and its subjects were Romans (*Rhomaioi*). Its predominant language was Greek, although some of its subjects spoke Latin, Coptic, Syriac, Armenian, and other local languages during its long (330–1453) history. Its emperors and their advisers regarded their appropriate geographical sphere to be the onetime limits of the Roman Empire, and they looked to Roman precedents for their traditions, symbols, and institutions. The empire, ruled by an emperor (*basileus*) without any formal constitution, slowly formed a synthesis of late Roman institutions, orthodox Christianity, and Greek language and culture.

Early Period. Constantine established precedents for the harmony of church and imperial authorities that persisted throughout the history of the empire. These included his creation of a successful new monetary system based on the gold solidus, or nomisma, which lasted into the middle of the 11th century. The commercial prosperity of the 4th through the 6th century enabled many ancient cities to flourish. Large estates domi-

A mosaic portrait of Alexius I Comnenus, emperor of the Byzantine Empire from 1081 to 1118 and founder of the Comnenian dynasty. His reign marked a resurgence of the empire as frontiers were extended in Asia Minor and the Balkans. Dumbarton Oaks

THE BYZANTINE EMPIRE
ABOUT 1000
© Copyright HAMMOND INCORPORATED, Maplewood, N. J.
SCALE OF MILES
0 50 100 200 300 400
Byzantine Empire
Kdm.=Kingdom D.=Duchy Th.=Theme
KDM. OF GERMANY
D. of Bavaria
KDM. OF BURGUNDY
RHAETIA
VERONA
D. of Carinthia
FRIULI
CARNIOLA
D. OF VENICE
Kdm. of Lombardy
KINGDOM OF ITALY
D. of Tuscany
D. of Spoleto
PATRIMONY OF ST. PETER
D. OF BENEVENTO
D. OF SALERNO
KINGDOM OF HUNGARY
PRINCIPALITY OF TRANSYLVANIA
KDM. OF CROATIA
KDM. OF SERBIA
KINGDOM OF BULGARIA
Vlachs
Uzes
Pechenegs
PRINCIPALITY OF TMUTARAKAN
Cherkess (Adygey)
Alans
Caucasus
ABKHASIA
KDM. OF GEORGIA
GAFARIDS
VANAND
BAGRATID ARMENIA
TARON
HASAN-WAIHIDS
MARWANIDS
OKAILIDS
BUWAIHIDS
HAMDANIDS
ARABIA
Karmathians
FATIMID CALIPHATE
ZEIRIDS (Tributary to Fatimids)
BYZANTINE EMPIRE
BLACK SEA
ADRIATIC SEA
TYRRHENIAN SEA
IONIAN SEA
AEGEAN SEA
MEDITERRANEAN SEA
CASPIAN SEA
Th. of Cherson
Paristrian Theme
Th. of Strymon
Th. of Macedonia
Th. of Constantinople
Thrace
Thessalian Th.
Th. of Nicopolis
Th. of Dyrrhachium
Th. of Longibardia
Th. of Calabria
Th. of Cephallenia
Th. of Hellas
Th. of Peloponnesus
Aegean Theme
Th. of Crete
Th. of Samos
Thracesian Th.
Opsician Theme
Th. of Optimaton
Bucellarian Th.
Th. of Paphlagonia
Th. of Armenia
Charsianan Theme
Th. of Sebasteia
Th. of Colonea
Th. of Chaldea
Th. of Theodosiopolis
Th. of Mesopotamia
Th. of Lycandos
Th. of Cappadocia
Th. of Anatolia
Cibyrrhaeot Theme
Th. of Seleucia
Th. of Cilicia
Th. of Antioch
Th. of Cyprus
Dalmatia
Sardinia
Sicily
Malta
Rhodes
Mt. Athos
Danube R.
Tisza
Drava R.
Prut R.
Dnestr R.
Dnepr R.
Tigris R.
Euphrates
Nile R.
Ivrea
Bergamo
Milan
Pavia
Genoa
Pisa
Verona
Villach
Venice
Ravenna
Ancona
Spoleto
Rome
Gaeta
Naples
Amalfi
Salerno
Benevento
Bari
Otranto
Reggio
Messina
Palermo
Mazara
Syracuse
Aleria
Bonifacio
Cagliari
Esztergom
Fehervar
Pecs
Turda
Alba Iulia
Zengg
Siscia
Zara (Ven.)
Belgrad
Trau (Ven.)
Spalato (Byz.)
Soli
Ragusa (Ven.)
Dekatera (Byz.)
Belgrade
Bdin
Raska
Sredets
Ochrida
Dyrrhachium
Valona
Corfu
Larissa
Thessalonica
Philippopolis
Adrianople
Peristhlaba
Dorystolon
Mesembria
Constantinople
Nicomedia
Nicaea
Athens
Chalcis
Corinth
Chandax
Phocaea
Smyrna
Ephesus
Amorion
Ancyra
Iconium
Adalia
Heraclea Pontica
Sinope
Amasia
Cerasus
Trapezus (Trebizond)
Caesarea
Melitene
Tarsus
Antioch
Amida
Edessa
Aleppo
Theodosiopolis
Manzikert
Mush
Kars
Ani
Kutaisi
Tiflis
Nisibis
Mosul
Homs
Damascus
Tripoli
Sidon
Tyre
Acre
Jerusalem
Gaza
Petra
Ayla
Alexandria
Cairo
Cyrene
Barca
Tunis
Kairwan
Mahedia
Sfax
Cherson (to Kiev)
Sudak
Tmutarakan
Oleshye
10°
20°
30°
40°

A 6th-century mosaic showing the Empress Theodora with her attendants. Said to have been an actress and a courtesan, she later married Justinian I, who made her joint ruler. The mosaic is in the church of San Vitale in Ravenna, Italy. Scala Fine Arts

nated agriculture, and while heavy taxation resulted in much abandonment of land, agriculture continued to be productive. The church acquired vast landed estates and, along with the emperor himself, was the largest landholder during most of the empire's history. Rigorous imperial regulation of the purity and supply of precious metals, as well as the organization of commerce and artisanship, characterized economic life.

Emperor Justinian I (r. 527–65) and his wife, Theodora, attempted to restore the former majesty, intellectual quality, and geographic limits of the Roman Empire. At great cost, they reconquered North Africa, Italy, Sicily, Sardinia, and parts of Spain. This effort, however, together with substantial expenses incurred in erecting public buildings and churches—in particular, Hagia Sophia (Church of the Holy Wisdom) in Constantinople—overstrained the empire's resources, while plagues reduced its population.

The Empire Besieged. The empire had survived Germanic and Hunnic tribal migrations and raids in the 5th and 6th centuries and had stabilized a reasonably secure eastern frontier against the Sassanid Persian Empire, but it could not recover, hold, and govern the entire Mediterranean world. During the second half of the 6th century the Lombards invaded and gradually occupied much of former Byzantine Italy—except for Rome, Ravenna, Naples, and the far south—while Turkic Avar cavalry raided and depopulated much of the Byzantine Balkans.

Many features of the empire and its culture changed during the 7th century. Most of the Balkans were lost to the Avars and to Slavic tribes, who resettled abandoned sites. Meanwhile, the first assassination of a Byzantine emperor, Mauricius (c. 539-602), led to civil and external war. Emperor Heraclius (r. 610-41) finally terminated a long series of wars with the Persians by a decisive victory in 628. He recovered Syrian, Palestinian, and Egyptian areas and restored the wood of the True Cross to Jerusalem. Exhaustion from this struggle and bitter religious disputes between rival Christian sects weakened Byzantine defenses and morale, leaving the empire unprepared to face another danger in the decade that followed. Between 634 and 642, Arabs, inspired by a new religion, Islam, conquered Palestine, Syria, Mesopotamia, and Egypt. Constantinople weathered major Arab sieges in the 670s and in 717-18, and Byzantine Asia Minor survived almost annual Arab raids. Byzantium, by a process that remains controversial among historians, transformed its armies into an elite expeditionary guard named *tagmata* and into army corps called themes (*themata*). Each was commanded by a strategos, or general, who acquired civil and military authority over his army district; thematic armies became army corps districts, and their soldiers, who acquired tax-exempt lands, preserved the core of the empire while avoiding the ruinous drain of cash that had overstrained the salaried armies of the period before the Arab invasions. Urban life and commerce declined except in Thessaloníki and Constantinople. Warfare and resulting insecurity inhibited agriculture and education.

Age of Reconquest. Beginning in the 9th century, Byzantium experienced a major recovery that took several forms. The Muslim offensive halted on the eastern frontier, both because of the decline of the caliphate and because of the ingenuity of Byzantine strategy. Byzantium began to regain territory in southeastern Asia Minor in the early 10th century. Lands lost to the Slavs in Greece, Macedonia, and Thrace also were reconquered and reorganized. The recovery reached its maturity under the long-reigning Macedonian dynasty, which began in 867 under its founder, Emperor Basil I, and lasted until 1042. Intellectual life revived in many dimensions: Ancient manuscripts were recopied and summarized; encyclopedias and other reference works were compiled; and mathematics, astronomy, and literature received new attention. The revival of learning was accompanied by a conscious return to classical models in art and literature, called the Macedonian Renaissance. External trade also intensified in the Mediterranean and Black seas.

The recovery of territory took an uneven pace. Bulgaria declined and was occupied by Byzantine armies in the 970s, while these armies also reconquered land southeast of the Taurus Mountains from the Muslims, including parts of northern Mesopotamia, northern Syria, and the northern Syrian coast.

The greatest Macedonian emperor was Basil II (r. 976-1025), who sternly repressed a lengthy Bulgarian rebellion and expanded his control of formerly independent Armenian and Georgian principalities. His efforts, like those of his predecessors, ultimately failed to reverse the growing concentration of land in the hands of a few wealthy individuals and the church. This failure damaged the revenues, authority, personnel, and other military resources of the state, which depended on the free peasantry of Asia Minor.

After the death of Basil II, the empire suffered from a series of mediocre emperors who allowed the army and the purity of the gold solidus to decline. The Seljuk Turks, after making some devastating raids into Byzantium's eastern territories, crushed an imperial army at the Battle of Manzikert (1071) and quickly overran most of Byzantine Asia Minor. The old thematic armies had decayed. Meanwhile, the Byzantines lost their last foothold in Italy and were alienated from the Christian West by a schism (1054) between the Orthodox church and the papacy.

Decline and Fall. The new emperor, Alexius I (r. 1081-1118), founder of the Comnenian dynasty, nevertheless appealed to the pope for aid against the Turks. Western Europe responded with the First Crusade (1096-99).

Although Byzantium initially benefited from the Crusades, recovering some land in Asia Minor, in the long run they hastened the empire's decline. Italian merchant cities won special trading privileges in Byzantine territory and gained control of much of the empire's commerce and wealth. The Byzantines experienced a superficial prosperity in the 12th century, but their political and military power waned. Crusaders allied with Venice, then took advantage of internal Byzantine strife to seize and plunder Constantinople in 1204, establishing their own Latin Empire of Constantinople. Byzantine resistance sprang up in Epirus, Trebizond, and especially in the city and region of Nicaea, in Asia Minor. Emperor Michael VIII Palaeologus (r. 1261-82) recaptured Constantinople from the Latins in 1261 and founded the Palaeologan dynasty, which ruled the empire until 1453. The Palaeologan Empire's resources, however, were very limited in terms of finances, land, and central authority. Agricultural conditions worsened for the rural population. The emergent Ottoman Turks conquered the remnants of Byzantine Asia Minor early in the 14th century. After 1354 they overran the Balkans and finally took Constantinople, bringing the empire to an end in 1453.

The Imperial Office. The Byzantine Empire was ruled by autocratic emperors who were the source of governmental authority. Emperors were responsible for upholding correct religious doctrine by placing the full force of imperial power behind doctrinal uniformity. Emperors strove for religious unanimity, in part to cultivate favor from church officials, but also because they believed that the survival and welfare of the empire depended on divine favor. The emperor embodied living law, issued legislation, and was the final interpreter of secular law. Ultimate responsibility for all political and military appointments rested with him, and he had a decisive role in selecting and removing the patriarch of Constantinople and other church officials. The emperor was at the summit of a splendid formal etiquette, and byzantine society was characterized by rank consciousness and minute attention to protocol.

The Byzantine Legacy. This conception of imperial authority, together with the creation of the Cyrillic alphabet for the Slavs by Byzantine missionaries, and the preservation of ancient Greek manuscripts and culture by Byzantine scholars, were the most important contributions of Byzantium to posterity. The Byzantine intellectual tradition did not die in 1453: Byzantine scholars who visited Italy as individuals or imperial envoys in the 14th and 15th centuries exerted a strong influence on the italian Renaissance. The Palaeologan revival of elements of Greek classicism, especially in literature, philosophy, mathematics, and astronomy, was transmitted to a rarefied audience of Italian scholars and Greek residents of Italy, and in this fashion Byzantine scholarship long survived the disappearance of the Byzantine Empire. Byzantine traditions and procedures also survived among the Greek and Slavic peoples. Conversion of the rulers of the Bulgars, Serbs, and Russians to Orthodox Christianity in the 9th and 10th centuries drew these peoples into the Byzantine cultural and ecclesiastical sphere and greatly influenced their development in medieval and early modern times.

See BYZANTINE ART AND ARCHITECTURE; ICONOCLASM; and biographies of individual emperors.

W.E.K.

For further information on this topic, see the Bibliography in volume 28, sections 651, 875, 1045.

BYZANTINE MUSIC. *See* CHANT.

BYZANTIUM, city of antiquity, founded about 660 BC by Greek colonists. It was situated on the European side of the Bosporus and occupied part of the site of present-day İstanbul. With an excellent harbor, later called the Golden Horn, a strategic location between the Black and Mediterranean seas, and abundant fisheries, Byzantium soon became a leading port and distribution center, especially noted for its grain trade. Troops of the Persian ruler Darius I destroyed Byzantium early in the 5th century BC. In 479 BC it was rebuilt by the Spartans. During the next 100 years Athens repeatedly disputed Spartan control of the city. The Athenian general Alcibiades captured it in 409 BC. Four years later the Athenians were expelled by an expedition under the Spartan general Lysander. Byzantium fell to Athens again in 390 BC, but, in alliance (357 BC) with the Greek islands of Khíos, Rhodes, and Kos, as well as Kariá, a Persian satrapy, the city waged a successful struggle for freedom. In 341–340 BC Athens rallied to the defense of the city, then under siege by Philip II of Macedonia. During the reign (336–323 BC) of Philip's son Alexander the Great, Byzantium was forced to recognize Macedonian suzerainty; under his successors the Byzantines regained independence. The city was subsequently attacked by the Scythians, and in 279 BC the Celts, having overrun the neighboring Thrace, imposed tribute on the city. In order to secure funds, the Byzantines levied a toll on ships passing through the Bosporus, provoking war with Rhodes.

The Byzantines supported Rome in the war (191–188 BC) against the Syrian king Antiochus III. In appreciation of this help and additional aid extended during the Mithridatic Wars (88–65 BC), the Romans recognized Byzantium as a free confederate city. It was subsequently subjected to Roman imperial control, however, and required to pay tribute until the reign (AD 41–54) of Emperor Claudius I. In the civil war (194) between the Emperor Lucius Septimus Severus and the military leader Pescennius Niger (d. 194), Byzantium sided with Niger. Severus captured Byzantium in 196, revoked its privileges, and razed its walls. The emperor of the West, Constantine the Great, defeated the Roman emperor Licinius (AD 270?–325) near Byzantium in 324 and soon thereafter began rebuilding the city as his new capital; it was subsequently renamed Constantinople. A population of approximately 1 million inhabitants made Byzantium by far the largest and richest city in Christendom during the Middle Ages.

See BYZANTINE EMPIRE; İSTANBUL.

For further information on this topic, see the Bibliography in volume 28, section 1045.

Cc

C, third letter in the English- and Romance-language alphabets. The symbol is derived from Latin *C,* a rounding of the Greek Γ, gamma, which was derived from a Phoenician symbol called gimel or camel, which was in turn developed from an Egyptian symbol.

Latin *c* had both a *g* and a *k* sound. In Anglo-Saxon, *c* had at first only the *k* sound, the modern word *child* having been spelled *cild.* By the 12th century *c* had the sound of *s* in a number of words. From this arose the modern rule that *c* has the *s* or *sh* sound before *e, i, y ae,* and *oe,* and the *k* sound in all other cases.

CAABA. *See* KAABA.

CABALA (Heb., "received tradition"), generically, Jewish mysticism in all its forms; specifically, the esoteric theosophy that crystallized in 13th-century Spain and Provence, France, around *Sefer ha-zohar* (The Book of Splendor), referred to as the *Zohar,* and generated all later mystical movements in Judaism. *See* MYSTICISM; THEOSOPHY.

The earliest known form of Jewish mysticism dates from the first centuries AD and is a variant on the prevailing Hellenistic astral mysticism, in which the adept, through meditation and the use of magic formulas, journeys ecstatically through and beyond the seven astral spheres. In the Jewish version, the adept seeks an ecstatic version of God's throne, the chariot (*merkava*) beheld by Ezekiel (see Ezek. 1).

The Medieval Period. Medieval Spanish Cabala, the most important form of Jewish mysticism, is less concerned with ecstatic experience than with esoteric knowledge about the nature of the divine world and its hidden connections with the world of creation. Medieval Cabala is a theosophical system that draws on Neoplatonism and Gnosticism (qq.v.) and is expressed in symbolic language. The system is most fully articulated in the *Zohar,* written between 1280 and 1286 by the Spanish Cabalist Moses de León (1250–1305), but attributed to the 2d-century rabbi Simeon bar Yohai. The *Zohar* depicts the Godhead as a dynamic flow of force composed of numerous aspects. Above and beyond all human contemplation is God as he is in himself, the unknowable, immutable *En Sof* (Infinite). Other aspects or attributes, knowable through God's relation to the created world, emanate (*see* EMANATION) from *En Sof* in a configuration of ten *sefirot* (realms or planes), through which the divine power further radiates to create the cosmos. Zoharic theosophy concentrates on the nature and interaction of the ten *sefirot* as symbols of the inner life and processes of the Godhead. Because the *sefirot* are also archetypes for everything in the world of creation, an understanding of their workings can illuminate the inner workings of the cosmos and of history. The *Zohar* thereby provides a cosmic-symbolic interpretation of Judaism and of the history of Israel in which the Torah and commandments, as well as Israel's life in exile, become symbols for events and processes in the inner life of God. Thus interpreted, the proper observance of the commandments assumes a cosmic significance.

Lurianic Cabala. This cosmic aspect of the *Zohar* is developed dramatically and with great consequence in 16th-century Lurianic Cabala (named for its formulator, Isaac ben Solomon Luria). The Lurianic system represents a response to the cataclysmic experience of Jewish exiles expelled from Iberia in the 1490s; it projects this experience onto the divine world. In this system, the *En Sof* withdraws into itself (*tzimtzum*) at the outset of creation, making room for the world, but also for evil. A cosmic catastrophe occurs during emanation when vessels of the divine light shatter and the sparks are imprisoned in the world in shards of evil (*qelippot*). The human task, through prayer and proper observance of the commandments, becomes nothing less than the redemption (*tiqqun*) of the world and the reunification of the Godhead. The Cabala was thus transformed into a popular messianic movement, which later generated Sabbatian messianism and 18th-century Polish Hasidism (*see* HASIDIM; SABBATAI ZEVI). R.S.S.

For further information on this topic, see the Bibliography in volume 28, section 130.

CABALLERO, Fernán, pseudonym of CECILIA FRANCISCA JOSEFA DE ARROM (1796–1877), Spanish novelist, born in Morges, Switzerland, and educated in Germany. She moved to Spain about 1813 and spent the rest of her life in the Andalusia region, which was the setting for her works. In *The Sea Gull* (1849; trans. 1867), a sentimental book that is often regarded as the first modern Spanish novel, she introduced *costumbrismo,* the 19th-century Spanish and Latin American literary movement that emphasized regional color. She also compiled several volumes of folktales.

CABANATUAN, city, N Philippines, in Nueva Ecija Province, on Luzon, on the Pampanga R. It is near Manila, with which it is connected by railroad. Cabanatuan is one of the chief centers of trade in the province, and rice milling is the principal industry. During World War II a Japanese prison camp for Americans and Filipinos captured at Bataan and Corregidor was located in Cabanatuan. Pop. (1980 prelim.) 138,297.

CABBAGE, common name for a biennial herb, *Brassica oleracea* var. *capitata,* of the family Cruciferae (*see* MUSTARD), widely cultivated in temperate regions for food and fodder. The common cabbage and related varieties, including brussels sprouts, broccoli, cauliflower, kale, kohlrabi, and Chinese cabbage, were probably all developed from a wild cabbage (*B. oleracea*) native to the coasts of Europe. The common cabbage (Fr. *caboche,* "big head") has a dense head of leaves, a short stem, and additional edible leaves. The leaves, depending on the type of cabbage, are oblong, oval, or nearly circular; about 30 cm (about 12 in) wide; green, purple, or red; and may be wrinkled, as in the savoy cabbage, or smooth. In the U.S., many kinds of common cabbage are cultivated.

CABBAGE BUTTERFLY, common name applied to several species of white butterflies of the family Pieridae, of which the larvae, known as cabbageworms, feed on the leaves of plants of the Cruciferae family, especially the cabbage. The cabbage and other related plants secrete a chemical to which the butterfly is attracted. The butterfly deposits eggs on the leaves on which the larvae feed and grow to maturity. The infested foliage is toxic upon consumption by animals. About a dozen species are found in North America, the most destructive of which is *Pieris,* a European species introduced from Canada about the middle of the 19th century and now common throughout the U.S. The larva, or caterpillar, is about 4 cm (about 1.5 in) long and green with a lemon-yellow dorsal band. It not only eats the leaves before heading time of the plants but also burrows through the heads. The butterfly, also called the small white, has a wingspan of about 3 cm ($1\frac{1}{4}$ in). It is white and pale yellow; the fore wings are tipped with black. The female has two additional dots, the male, one. The other species are the *P. brassicae,* or large white, a European variety, and *P. protodice,* or southern cabbage butterfly, a common American variety.

CABELL, James Branch (1879–1958), American writer, born in Richmond, Va., and educated at the College of William and Mary. Before embarking on a literary career, he worked as a college teacher and newspaper reporter. In 1904 he published his first novel, *The Eagle's Shadow,* the first volume of the 18-volume series entitled *The Biography of Manuel.* The series related the fantasies of a swineherd, Manuel, in Poictesme, an imaginary medieval land. Two of the best-known books of the series are *The Cream of the Jest* (1917) and *Jurgen, a Comedy of Justice* (1919). *Jurgen,* temporarily suppressed as immoral, became very popular in the 1920s. Cabell, a member of a distinguished Virginia family, also wrote several genealogical studies of his and other families. In addition to his more than 50 novels, he wrote two collections of autobiographical essays, *Let Me Lie* (1947) and *Quiet Please* (1952).

CABET, Étienne (1788–1856), French social reformer and writer, born in Dijon, and educated as a lawyer. Following active participation in the July Revolution of 1830, he was elected to the Chamber of Deputies. In 1834 Cabet was exiled for his attacks on the government. He went to London, where, influenced by the works of the 16th-century English humanist Sir Thomas More and the social reform movement of the British Socialist Robert Owen, he adopted a Communist philosophy. In 1839 Cabet was permitted to return to France, where he published *Histoire populaire de la révolution française de 1789 à 1830* (Popular History of the French Revolution from 1789 to 1830, 4 vol., 1839–40) and the novel *Voyage en Icarie* (Voyage to Icaria, 1840). The latter book, which enjoyed great popularity, depicted an ideal society in which social and economic life is supervised by an elected government. Cabet's philosophy attracted many followers, who came to be known as Icarians (q.v.).

In 1849 Cabet and 280 of his adherents immigrated to the U.S. and founded an Icarian community at Nauvoo, Ill. The population never numbered more than 1800, and only some of Cabet's ideas were put into effect. In 1856, because of internal dissent, he left with 180 disciples to found a new colony; he died the same year in Saint Louis, Mo., but the movement he founded lasted in the U.S. until 1895.

CABEZA DE VACA, Álvar Núñez (1490?-1557?), Spanish explorer, born in Jerez de la Frontera. In 1527 he was appointed treasurer of a royal expedition of about 300 men led by the Spanish soldier Pánfilo de Narváez to conquer and colonize Florida. The expedition sailed into Tampa Bay about April 1528, began an overland march to Apalachee Bay, and then attempted to reach Mexico. During the next two years more than half the men died, and Cabeza de Vaca emerged as the leader. He led a small band of survivors to an island, possibly Galveston Island, off the southwestern coast of what is now Texas, where the band was captured by Indians. Early in 1535, Cabeza de Vaca and the three other survivors of the expedition escaped and began a trek through what are now the southwestern U.S. and northern Mexico. In 1536 the four men reached a Spanish settlement on the Sinalo River in Mexico. Cabeza de Vaca returned to Spain in 1537 and was rewarded with an appointment as governor of Río de la Plata (now largely Paraguay).

In 1541-42 Cabeza de Vaca led an expedition 1609 km (1000 mi) through the south of present-day Brazil to Asunción, the capital of Río de la Plata. He took office as governor of the province in 1542 but was ousted two years later as the result of a revolt. Recalled to Spain under arrest in 1554, he was later banished to Africa. In 1556 he obtained a pardon and a pension. His account of the Narváez expedition, *Relación* (1542), and his tales of the Zuñi Indians and their villages, the legendary Seven Cities of Cíbola, encouraged other expeditions to America, notably those of the explorers Hernando de Soto and Francisco Vásquez de Coronado.

CABIMAS, city, NW Venezuela, in Zulia State, on Lake Maracaibo, near the city of Maracaibo. Cabimas is an oil-producing center, surrounded by large refineries; it is linked by pipeline with the port of Ciudad Ojeda. Pop. (1977) 163,000.

CABINDA, exclave of Angola, central Africa, bounded on the W by the Atlantic Ocean, on the N by the Congo, and on the E and S by Zaire. It constitutes an administrative district of Angola. The capital and chief town is Cabinda, which has a small port on the Bele R. The district has extensive tropical rain forests; its products include timber and phosphates. Offshore petroleum production has been important since the late 1960s. In the 1970s Malembo was developed as the exclave's deepwater port. Pop. (est.) 81,300.

CABINET, name applied to the collective body of advisers to the executive head of a parliamentary government. The composition and functions of the cabinet vary in different countries.

The cabinet originated early in the 15th century as a council advising the king of England. As part of the Privy Council, the king's most important group of advisers, it met in the royal chamber or cabinet and was therefore called the cabinet council. At first this group had no special authority or legal standing; it was comparable to what was later known as a cabal or junta. In the 18th century, however, when the center of governmental power shifted from monarch to Parliament, the cabinet became the council of the most important minister in the government, the prime minister. Since about 1780 the composition of the British cabinet has been restricted to a limited number of important ministers, who are (with few exceptions) also department heads. From this organization developed the modern British cabinet, with the prime minister at the head, collectively responsible to Parliament.

In the U.S. the cabinet consists of the president's advisers, each of whom is a department head. The legal status of the cabinet is not defined except in federal statutes concerning the salaries and the method of appointing members.

Other parliamentary governments have adopted the cabinet as an institution. The cabinets of Latin America usually follow the U.S. type, whereas most European countries have adopted the British model.

European Cabinets. The principal characteristics of European cabinets are the responsibility of the

George Washington (extreme right) and his first cabinet, 1789.

cabinet to the legislature, and the identification of the cabinet with the government. The cabinet is formed by the prime minister or premier, and together they administer the country as long as they have the confidence of the legislature. If a cabinet lacks either legislative or popular support, the government is said to fall, and the executive must form a new cabinet capable of winning the required support.

Cabinets are usually composed of ministers, most of whom are department chiefs, but ministers are not necessarily cabinet members. Specific ministries are sometimes designated "of cabinet rank." Important individuals may be added to the cabinet without specific portfolio, that is, without ministerial responsibility. In emergencies special inner cabinets may be formed from the regular cabinet.

A cabinet of the British type typically comprises members of the party that has a decisive majority in the legislature. When no clear-cut majority exists, cabinets are sometimes formed by parties who together control a majority in the parliament. The prime minister charged with forming such a cabinet usually attempts to assign the posts in accordance with the proportional parliamentary strength of the groups composing the coalition. Inasmuch as this proportion tends to fluctuate, coalition cabinets are frequently unstable. Most European governments after World War II were administered by coalition cabinets.

British Cabinet. Members of the cabinet of the British government constitute the supreme executive authority of the government, and are the sole advisers to the Crown. They are members of Parliament, usually of the same political party as the prime minister, and thus combine executive and legislative duties. Members of the cabinet are individually responsible to the prime minister who appoints them, with approval of the Crown. The prime minister also may remove any of them. Collectively the cabinet is responsible to Parliament for its policies and actions.

The number of members of the British cabinet varies. The tendency is for the number to increase in normal times with the growth of governmental functions and to decrease in national emergencies when the executive power is concentrated in fewer hands. The cabinet meets at 10 Downing Street in London, in the house that the British statesman Robert Walpole presented to the nation. This house is the official residence of the prime ministers of Great Britain.

Canadian Cabinet. The cabinet in Canada is of the British type. It is formed, on the request of the governor-general, by a prime minister who is a member of the House of Commons and usually the leader of the strongest party in the house. Normally, a cabinet is formed as the result of a general election, but if a cabinet resigns, the governor-general may ask the opposition leader in the House of Commons to form a government from the opposition. The prime minister chooses cabinet ministers from members of parliament, largely from the House of Commons. Most ministers serve as heads of the executive departments of the federal government. Provincial cabinets are similarly formed and organized.

U.S. Cabinet. The cabinet of the U.S. government is made up of the administrative heads of the executive departments of the federal government, under the president. At present, the cabinet consists of the secretary of state, the secretary of the treasury, the secretary of defense, the attorney general, the secretary of the interior, the secretary of agriculture, the secretary of commerce, the secretary of labor, the secretary of health and human services, the secretary of housing and urban development, the secretary of transportation, the secretary of energy, and the secretary of education, and the secretary of veterans affairs. The vice president also participates, and the president may accord cabinet rank to other executive-branch officials.

Cabinet members are appointed by the president with the approval of the Senate and may be removed by the president either at will or as a result of censure or impeachment by Congress. Unless they resign or are removed, cabinet members serve for the duration of the term or terms of the president who appoints them. The salaries of cabinet officers are fixed by Congress.

The cabinet as a governmental institution is not provided for in the U.S. Constitution. It developed as an advisory body out of the president's need to consult the heads of the executive departments on matters of federal policy and on problems of administration. Aside from its role as a consultative and advisory body, the cabinet has no function and wields no executive authority. The president may or may not consult the cabinet and is not bound by the advice of the cabinet. Furthermore, the president may seek advice outside the cabinet; a group of such informal advisers is known in American history as a kitchen cabinet. The formal cabinet meets at times set by the president, usually once a week.

According to the constitutional provision barring persons holding federal office from being members of the legislative branches of the federal government, cabinet officers may not be members of Congress. Cabinet members in the U.S., therefore, unlike their counterparts in other countries, have no direct legislative function, but are consulted by or give testimony before congressional committees. A cabinet officer may speak in Congress by a special vote of the branch of the legislature desiring to hear him or her.

Because the executive departments of the federal government are equally subordinate to the president, cabinet officers are of equal rank, but ever since the administration of George Washington, the secretary of state, who administers foreign policy, has been regarded as the chief cabinet officer. In 1886 Congress enacted legislation stipulating the order of succession of cabinet officers to the presidency "in case of [the] removal, death, resignation, or inability of both the President and Vice-President." The secretary of state headed the list. In 1947 Congress, in order to give prior eligibility to elected members of the government in the order of succession to the presidency, modified the act of 1886, placing the Speaker of the House of Representatives and the president pro tempore of the Senate, in that order, before any cabinet members.

The cabinet of George Washington consisted of the secretaries of state, the treasury, and war, and the attorney general. In 1798, following the creation of a separate navy department, the secretary of the navy became a member. The postmaster general was added in 1829. As Congress created new executive departments, further additions to the cabinet were made as follows: the secretary of the interior in 1849, the secretary of agriculture in 1889, and the secretary of commerce and labor in 1903. After the division of the department of commerce and labor into two separate departments in 1913, the secretary of labor became a cabinet officer. In accordance with legislation unifying the armed forces, in 1949 the secretary of defense, previously a coordinator of the three military departments, received cabinet rank. The secretary of health, education, and welfare (now known as health and human services) became a cabinet officer in 1953 when the department was created, as did the secretary of housing and urban development in 1965, the secretary of transportation in 1966, the secretary of energy in 1977, the secretary of education in 1980, and the secretary of veterans affairs in 1989, when those departments were established. See articles under the names of the individual departments. REV. BY R.P.

For further information on this topic, see the Bibliography in volume 28, sections 259, 266.

CABINETMAKING. *See* WOODWORKING.

CABLE, ELECTRIC, cable composed of one or more electric conductors, covered by insulation (q.v.) and sometimes a protective sheath, often used for transmitting electric power or the impulses of an electric communications system.

For electric-power transmission, three-wire cables sheathed with lead and filled with oil under pressure are employed for high-voltage circuits; secondary distribution lines usually employ insulated single-conductor cables. In residential electric wiring, B-X cable is often used. This type of cable contains two insulated conductors, which are wound with additional layers of insulation and covered with a helically wound strip of metal for protection. The ignition cable used to carry high-voltage current to the spark plugs of an internal-combustion engine is a single-conductor cable; it is covered with cloth impregnated with shellac for insulation.

In communications systems, cables commonly consist of numerous pairs of paper-insulated wire, encased in a lead sheath; the individual pairs of wire are intertwined to minimize induced interference (q.v.) with other circuits in the same cable. To avoid electrical interference from external circuits, cables used in radio broadcasting are often shielded with a winding of metal braid, which is grounded. The coaxial cable, an important development in the communications field, consists of several copper tubes; each tube contains a wire conductor that extends along its center. The entire cable is sheathed in lead and is generally filled with nitrogen under pressure to prevent corrosion. Because the coaxial cable has a broad frequency range, it is valuable in the transmission of carrier-current telephony (*see* TELEPHONE) and television (q.v.).

See also FIBER OPTICS; WIRE.

CABLE, George W(ashington) (1844–1925), American writer and social reformer, born in New Orleans, La. After serving in the Confederate army during the American Civil War, he began to write for the *New Orleans Picayune.* His sketches of Creole life, published in *Scribner's Monthly,* made him well known in the U.S. and Great Britain. Among his books are *Old Creole Days* (1879), *The Creoles of Louisiana* (1884), *The Silent South* (1885), *The Cavalier* (1901), and *The Flower of the Chapdelaines* (1918). In his writings and lectures he sought reforms in the convict labor system in the southern U.S.

CABOT, George (1752–1823), American businessman and statesman, born in Salem, Mass., and educated at Harvard College (now Harvard University). He was a successful shipowner. About 1778 he entered politics as leader of the Essex Junto, the dominant faction of the Federalist party. He was a member of the Massachusetts Constitutional Convention (1779–80) and of the state convention that ratified the U.S. Constitution. As a U.S. senator (1791–96), he introduced

John Cabot sets forth from Bristol, England, in 1497, on his voyage to America. Bettmann Archive

the first of the fugitive slave laws in 1793. He declined a post as the first secretary of the navy in the cabinet of President John Adams in 1798. Cabot continued to be a leader of the Federalist party, and he was instrumental in calling the Hartford Convention (1814–15), over which he presided.

CABOT, John (c. 1450–99), English navigator and explorer, who attempted to find a direct route to Asia. Although Cabot was probably born in Genoa, as a youth he moved to Venice, where his seafaring career probably began. He became a naturalized Venetian in 1476, but about eight years later settled in Bristol, England. Cabot had developed a theory that Asia might be reached by sailing westward. This theory appealed to several wealthy merchants of Bristol, who agreed to give him financial support. In 1493, when reports reached England that Christopher Columbus had made the westward passage to Asia, Cabot and his supporters began to make plans for a more direct crossing to the Orient. The proposed expedition was authorized on March 5, 1496, by King Henry VII of England.

With a crew of 18 men, Cabot sailed from Bristol on May 2, 1497, on the *Matthew*. He steered a generally northwestward course, and on June 24, after a rough voyage, he landed, perhaps on present-day Cape Breton Island; he subsequently sailed along the Labrador, Newfoundland, and New England coasts. Believing that he had reached northeastern Asia, he formally claimed the region for Henry VII. Cabot returned to England in August and was granted a pension. Assured of royal support, he immediately planned a second exploratory voyage that he hoped would bring him to Cipangu (Japan). The expedition, consisting of four or five ships and 300 men, left Bristol in May 1498. The fate of this expedition is uncertain. It is believed that in June, Cabot reached the eastern coast of Greenland and sailed northward along the coast until his crews mutinied because of the severe cold and forced him to turn southward. He may have cruised along the coast of North America to Chesapeake Bay at lat 38° N. He was forced to return to England because of a lack of supplies, and he died soon afterward.

CABOT, Sebastian (1476?–1557), Italian navigator and cartographer, best known for his expeditions for Spain and England to South and North America during the 16th century.

Cabot was probably born in Venice. Although Sebastian Cabot claimed to have accompanied his father, John Cabot, to North America, it is unlikely he made a voyage to America until about 1508. In that year it is believed he reached the coast of present-day Labrador and cruised northward as far as Hudson Bay. Subsequently engaged as a cartographer by Henry VIII, king of England, he prepared maps of southwestern France for an invasion by Henry and his ally Ferdinand V, king of Spain. In 1512, while abroad with the invasion force, Cabot entered the service of Spain. After Ferdinand died, Cabot was retained by Charles I, king of Spain (later Charles V, Holy Roman emperor). About 1518 Charles promoted Cabot to the rank of pilot major.

In 1525 Cabot received command of an exploring expedition to the Pacific Ocean, and in 1526 he reached the coast of what is now Brazil, near the estuary of the river he named the Río de la Plata (Silver River). Believing reports that the La Plata region contained vast amounts of gold and silver, he abandoned his mission and began exploring the area, conducting a fruitless search for wealth. When he returned to Spain in 1530, he was arrested, found guilty of mismanagement, and banished to Africa for four years. Charles pardoned him in 1533, however, and restored him to his post of pilot major. In 1544, his last year in the service of Spain, Cabot completed an engraved map of the world. He later settled in England, and through the influence of friends and admirers in English court circles, about 1549, he received a pension from King Edward VI of England, who also named him grand pilot of England. In 1551 Cabot founded and became governor of the Muscovy Co. of Merchant Adventurers, an English trading organization. On his initiative the company financed expeditions to search for the Northwest Passage, a sea route from Europe to Asia. Richard Chancellor (d. 1556), a navigator employed by Cabot, reached the Russian port of Arkhangelsk by way of the White Sea, laying the foundation for commercial relations between England and Russia.

CABOT STRAIT, channel of SE Canada, between Cape Breton Island and Newfoundland, about 100 km (about 62 mi) wide. Named for the English navigator John Cabot, the waterway links the Gulf of Saint Lawrence with the Atlantic Ocean and is an important shipping route.

CABRAL, Pedro Álvares (1460?-1526?), Portuguese navigator, born probably in Belmonte. In 1500 Emanuel, king of Portugal, appointed him commander of a trading expedition to India. With 13 vessels and more than 1000 men, Cabral left Lisbon under orders to proceed along the Cape of Good Hope route discovered in 1497-98 by the Portuguese navigator Vasco da Gama. To avoid storms and calms, Cabral set a more westerly course than that followed by da Gama, but winds and currents drove his vessels still farther westward.

On April 22, 1500, about three months after the arrival of the Spanish explorer Vincente Yáñez Pinzón, Cabral reached the present-day Bahia State of Brazil. After claiming possession of the region for Emanuel, he sent a vessel to Portugal with news of his discovery. He then resumed his voyage, sailing eastward, but four of his vessels were lost in a storm off the Cape of Good Hope. The remainder of his expedition succeeded in reaching Calicut (now Kozhikode), India. There he negotiated a commercial treaty with the native ruler and established a trading post. Little is known of Cabral after his return to Portugal in 1501.

CABRERA, Ramón, Conde de Morella (1806-77), Spanish Carlist general, born in Tortosa. At the onset of the civil war in Spain known as the Carlist War (1834-39), he supported the claim of Don Carlos, pretender to the Spanish throne, against that of the young Queen Isabella II. Cabrera defeated the royalist forces in Aragón, Valencia, and Catalonia. After Cabrera's victory at Morella, Valencia, in 1839, Don Carlos gave him the title conde de Morella. Cabrera was known for his cruelty toward those he conquered, especially after the royalists executed his mother in 1836. He continued fighting even after the Carlists formally admitted defeat on Aug. 31, 1839. In 1840 he was driven out of Spain. He spent several years in France and England, returned to Spain in 1848, and led an unsuccessful Carlist uprising in Catalonia and again fled Spain. In 1875, when Alfonso XII succeeded Isabella II on the throne, Cabrera finally relented and called upon all Carlists to do likewise. He spent his last years in England.

CABRILLO, Juan Rodríguez (d. 1543), Portuguese explorer and soldier. He entered the service of Spain and in 1520 accompanied the Spanish soldier Pańfilo de Narváez to Mexico. There Cabrillo joined the conquistador Hernán Cortés and helped him to complete the conquest of Mexico. Cabrillo served in Guatemala and in 1540 became chief lieutenant of an expedition exploring the western coast of Mexico. Succeeding to the command of the expedition after the death in 1541 of the leader, Pedro de Alvarado, Cabrillo sailed northward and on Sept. 28, 1542, discovered San Diego Bay. His subsequent discoveries during the voyage include Santa Catalina Island,

Santa Barbara Channel, Monterey Bay, and San Miguel Island, where he died.

CABRILLO NATIONAL MONUMENT. *See* NATIONAL PARK SERVICE (table).

CABRINI, Saint Frances Xavier (1850–1917), Italian-American Roman Catholic nun, born in Lombardy. In 1880 she founded the Order of the Missionary Sisters of the Sacred Heart. She went to the U.S. in 1889, at the request of Pope Leo XIII, to organize charitable and religious work among Italian immigrants. Under her direction, schools, hospitals, orphanages, and convents were established in many of the principal cities of the U.S. and in Latin America. Mother Cabrini became a U.S. citizen in 1909. She was canonized in 1946, becoming the first U.S. citizen to be declared a saint. Her feast day is December 22.

For further information on this person, see the section Biographies in the Bibliography in volume 28.

CACAO, common name of *Theobroma cacao,* of the seed of that tree, and of other trees in the *Theobroma* genus of the family Sterculiaceae, which also contains the cola. *T. cacao* is a perennial tree that yields several harvests annually. First cultivated in South America, it was introduced into Europe during the 16th century. Today it is grown chiefly in western Africa. The average *T. cacao* attains a height of about 6 m (about 20 ft) and has shiny leaves, as long as 30 cm (12 in), and small pink flowers on the trunk and older branches. Only about 30 of the 6000 annual blossoms eventually bear seeds. Commonly called cocoa beans, the seeds are surrounded by a yellow or reddish-brown pod about 28 cm (about 11 in) long. Cocoa beans are either purple or off-white and resemble almonds. The high proportion of fat in the bean kernels (cocoa butter) is used in medications, cosmetics, and soaps. The pulverized residue, called cocoa, is used in beverages and as a flavoring. Chocolate is also derived from cocoa beans. The Sterculiaceae are in the order Malvales (*see* MALLOW).

CÁCERES, city, W Spain, capital of Cáceres Province. The city is on the slopes of a steep ridge, the upper heights of which are the site of the original town. In addition to ancient walls and ruins, the upper section contains several medieval castles and the Church of San Mateo, a Gothic edifice with a high tower. The principal industries include the packing of bacon and the manufacture of leather goods, cork products, hats, pottery, woolen goods, and soap. The surrounding region is impoverished and lacks highways and industrial development, but it has many large plantations. Pop. (1981 est.) 67,400.

CACHALOT. *See* WHALE.

CACOMISTLE, common name for a small nocturnal mammal, *Bassariscus astutus,* of the family Procyonidae (*see* RACCOON). The cacomistle (Span., "half mountain lion") is common to wooded and rocky areas from Oregon to Mexico. The animal, also called bassarisk, weighs about 1 kg (about 2.5 lb) and has a slender body about 41 cm (about 16 in) long and a 38-cm-long (15-in) tail. The face is foxlike, the ears are erect, and the large, bright eyes are surrounded by light patches of fur. The coat is long and soft, light brown above and darker along the back, and the long, bushy tail has six or eight broad white rings; the underparts are white. The cacomistle feeds on rodents and fruit.

CACTUS, common name for the order Cactales comprising a peculiar group of spiny, fleshy plants native to the New World. The order contins a single family, the Cactaceae, with about 90 genera and 2000 species, most of which are adapted to arid climates. The fruits of cacti are important sources of food and drink in many areas to which they are native. Because cacti require little care and exhibit bizarre forms, they are popular for home cultivation and are coming under increasing pressure as a result. More than 17 kinds of cacti now face extinction (*see* ENDANGERED SPECIES) because of plundering by avid collectors and professional poachers, especially in the southwestern U.S.

A spiny cactus shelters a desert dove's nest in Australia. Heavily armored cacti are the principal habitat for many of the small desert birds, rodents, and insects.
John Alcock

The prickly pear, Opuntia phaeacantha, *is one of the most common varieties of cactus, growing in most of the dry regions of the U.S. and northern Mexico.*
Gary R. Zahm—Bruce Coleman, Inc.

Cactus plants usually consist of spiny stems and roots. Leaves are greatly reduced or entirely absent. Only in two genera, *Pereskia* and *Pereskiopsis,* are fully formed leaves present. The stems of cacti are usually swollen and fleshy, adapted to water storage, and many are shaped in ways that cause rain to flow directly to the root system for absorption. The roots form extensive systems near the soil surface, assuring that a given plant will absorb the maximum amount of water from a wide area; plants in deserts are usually widely spaced.

The most distinctive vegetative feature of cacti is the areoles, specialized areas on the stems on which stiff, sharp spines usually grow. Some cacti lack spines but have hairs or sharp, barbed structures called glocids on the areoles. Areoles develop from lateral buds on the stems and appear to represent highly specialized branches.

The flowers of cacti are often large and showy and occur singly rather than in clusters of several flowers. The perianth (floral tube) does not consist of sharply differentiated sepals and petals, but rather of a series of bracts (modified leaves), which gradually grade into sepals and finally into showy petals. The flowers have many stamens; the ovary is inferior and fused to the perianth. The fruits are often brightly colored and fleshy.

Most of the 90 or so genera of cacti are found in cultivation, the small, slow-growing species being most popular because of their variety in shapes, colors, and spines. One of the best-known groups is the cereus (q.v.) containing beautiful night-blooming flowers and the familiar saguaro plant. Still more widely grown is the Christmas cactus group. These species, which naturally occur as epiphytes (air plants) in tropical rain forests, do not fit the popular idea of cacti as squat, fleshy plants of desert regions. Examination of their stems, however, reveals the presence of the cactus family's unique areoles; their flowers have the typical cactus features.

Many groups of plants that are unrelated to cacti have also adapted to survive in arid regions and often resemble cacti in appearance. These offer examples of parallel evolution: Unrelated organisms subjected to similar environmental stresses often evolve similar anatomical and functional characteristics. For example, many spurges that grow in dry parts of Africa, where cacti are not found, exhibit leafless, spiny, fleshy stems (*see* SPURGE).

Plants of the order Cactales are dicots (q.v.) in the class Angiospermae (*see* ANGIOSPERM).

M.R.C.

For further information on this topic, see the Bibliography in volume 28, sections 427, 452.

CADDIS FLY *or* **CADDICE FLY,** common name for insects of the order Trichoptera. Twelve families and some 150 species are known in North America. The adults are 2.5 to 5 cm (1 to 2 in) long. They resemble small moths and have a habit of nocturnal flight. Most species live near fresh water; a few are marine. Their eggs are deposited in green, gelatinous masses and are usually attached to water plants. The larvae, called caddis worms, caseworms, or cadbait (from their wide use for bait by anglers), are aquatic. The caddis worm is long and slender and has a small, hard head and thorax and a soft abdomen. For protection the larva lives in a characteristic tubular, silk case covered with sand grains, bits of shell, twigs, or leaves. Most caddis worms are herbivorous; several species, however, also eat water fleas and small aquatic larvae, which they catch in nets spun from secreted silk and anchored in running water. After several months in the larval stage, the caddis worm closes the mouth of the case and pupates. At the end of the pupal stage the pupa rises to the water's surface, and the adult quickly emerges and flies away.

CADDO, North American Indian tribe and confederacy of tribes of the Caddoan family, originally dwelling along the Red River area of Louisiana and Arkansas. The Caddo were a sedentary agricultural people. They lived in cone-shaped dwellings of thatched grass over poles. Groups of the dwellings surrounded temple mounds. A matrilineal society, the Caddo were class conscious, with a hereditary upper class. They were settled on an Indian reservation in Oklahoma during the 19th century. In 1901 the reservation was opened to white settlement, however, the Caddo were allowed to remain on allotments of land within the region. Traditional Caddo tribal life dissolved. From a population of 8000 in the late 17th century, the number of Caddo dropped to about 500 in the late 19th century. Today more than 1000 Caddo live on a reservation in Oklahoma. *See also* AMERICAN INDIANS.

CADDOAN LANGUAGE. *See* AMERICAN INDIAN LANGUAGES.

CADE, Jack (d. 1450), English leader of a revolt in Kent, England, against King Henry VI. According to some accounts, Cade was of Irish birth, called himself John Mortimer, and fought for France against England during the Hundred Years' War. The so-called Jack Cade's Rebellion began in late May 1450 as a protest by peasants and small landowners against the seizure of land by nobles, corruption in the courts, heavy taxation, and enforced labor imposed by the Statute of Labourers of 1351. About June 18 Cade defeated a government force at Sevenoaks, Kent, and on July 2 or July 3 entered London, where he was favorably received by the municipality. The rebels forced the London authorities to condemn and execute the sheriff of Kent and his father-in-law, the lord chamberlain under Henry VI. Cade soon thereafter lost his support in London when he resorted to further violence. Most of his men accepted pardons and concessions offered by the king and dispersed. Cade himself received an invalid pardon in the name Mortimer. On July 12 he was hunted down and mortally wounded by the new sheriff of Kent near Heathfield, Sussex.

Jack Cade proclaims himself lord of London in 1450 (from an 18th-cent. copper engraving). Granger Collection

CADENCE, musical formula that conveys a feeling of repose at the end of a phrase or a composition. Such formulas not only sound complete in a purely musical sense but also, because of their familiarity, lead the listener to expect a temporary or permanent stopping point. In Western music from the beginnings of multipart music (polyphony), certain chord sequences became standard at cadences. These sequences slowly became modified as musical styles changed. With the evolution of traditional tonal harmony (early 18th century), cadential formulas that are still recognized became common. The most widely used formula, called an authentic cadence, is a V–I progression, that is, a dominant chord (one built on the fifth note of the scale) followed by a tonic chord (one built on the first note, that is, the tonic or key note). A cadence that moves from the subdominant chord (built on the fourth note of the scale) to the tonic, that is, IV–I, as in the "Amen" cadence at the end of hymns, is called a plagal cadence. Many other kinds of cadential progressions exist as well. Their diversity allows composers to create different degrees of repose, from slight pauses at the end of a phrase to complete cessation of motion at the end of a piece. *See also* HARMONY.

In music consisting of unharmonized melody, such as plainchant or folk song, certain turns of melody may signal a cadence. Rhythm or the recurrence of certain instruments may also indicate a cadence, especially in some non-Western and 20th-century music.

CADENZA, virtuosic solo passage, either improvised or precomposed in the spontaneous, free-sounding style of an improvisation, inserted near the end of a musical composition or section. Cadenzas provide a soloist with opportunities not only to demonstrate technical brilliancy but also to show musical ability at elaborating on the basic materials of a composition. Cadenzas first flourished in 17th- and 18th-century opera, when singers improvised florid decorations immediately before the final cadence of an aria. Cadenzas are most familiar to modern listeners in instrumental concertos, where they occur near the end of some or all movements. Since about 1800, composers have generally written out cadenzas, which are rarely improvised today.

CADILLAC, Antoine de La Mothe, Sieur de (1658–1730), French military officer and colonial administrator, born in Gascony. He was stationed for a period in Acadia (now Nova Scotia) as a captain in the French army, and in 1694 he was appointed commander of the French post at Mackinac (now part of Mackinac Co., Mich.). In 1697 he presented to King Louis XIV of France a plan for a permanent trading post in the American Northwest. With royal approval, he founded Pontchartrain d'Étroit (now Detroit) in 1701. He was governor of French Louisiana from 1712 to 1717, when he returned to France.

CÁDIZ (anc. *Gadir;* later *Gades*), city and seaport, S Spain, capital of Cádiz Province, on the Gulf of Cádiz (an inlet of the Atlantic Ocean), near Gibraltar. It lies at the tip of a narrow isthmus that forms the W boundary of Cádiz Bay. The large harbor is divided into an outer bay and a nearly landlocked inner harbor.

Shipping, shipbuilding, and fishing are the principal industries, and a Spanish military base is located in the city. A large part of Spain's trade with the countries of South and North America moves through Cádiz. Exports consist largely of sherry wine, cork, olives, figs, salted fish, and salt. Machinery, iron, coal, timber, coffee, cereals, and other foodstuffs are the major imports.

Cádiz is a picturesque city, with white buildings in the Moorish architectural style, and with beautiful promenades. It has a cathedral dating from the middle of the 13th century. In the Church of Santa Catalina is the unfinished painting *Marriage of St. Catherine,* by the Spanish artist Bartolomé Esteban Murillo, who fell and died while working on the painting. The medical school of the University of Seville, a navigation school, and a theological school are here. Valuable Roman and Carthaginian antiquities are on exhibit in the Cádiz Archaeological Museum.

Cádiz, one of the oldest cities in Europe, was founded about 1000 BC by the Phoenicians. By 700-600 BC it was a flourishing market for amber and tin. The Carthaginians captured the city about 501 BC and lost it to the Romans at the end (201 BC) of the Second Punic War. The city was destroyed by the Visigoths in the 5th century AD. In 711 it was taken by the Moors, who rebuilt it. Alfonso X, king of Castile and Léon, captured the city in 1262.

After the discovery of America in 1492, Spanish fleets carrying treasure from the New World used Cádiz as a base, and it became one of the wealthiest cities of Europe. After the other maritime powers of Europe began to challenge Spanish naval supremacy, Cádiz was subjected to frequent attacks. An English naval force under the navigator Sir Francis Drake raided the port in 1587, destroying many vessels, and in 1596 the city was plundered by an English fleet commanded by Robert Devereux, earl of Essex.

During the next 100 years British naval forces attacked Cádiz on three occasions. It was blockaded by a British fleet for nearly 15 months in 1797-98. During the Napoleonic Wars, Cádiz was besieged by French naval forces from February 1810 to August 1812. Following the loss of the Spanish colonies in the New World in the 19th century the prosperity of the city declined. During the Spanish civil war (1936-39) Cádiz was used as a base by the Nationalist forces under Gen. Francisco Franco. Pop. (1981 est.) 145,400.

CADMIUM, metallic element, symbol Cd, in group IIb of the periodic table (*see* PERIODIC LAW); at.no. 48, at.wt. 112.40.

Properties. Cadmium was discovered in 1817 by the German chemist Friedrich Stromeyer (1776-1835), who found it in incrustations in zinc furnaces. Cadmium is a grayish-white metal, ductile and malleable. When heated, it burns in air with a bright light, forming the oxide CdO. Cadmium melts at 321° C (610° F), boils at 765° C (1409° F), and has a sp.gr. of 8.65.

Production and Uses. Cadmium occurs as the principal constituent of a mineral only in the rare greenockite. Almost the entire cadmium output of the U.S. is obtained as a by-product in the refining of zinc ores, chiefly from Missouri and Montana. It is also obtained from the zinc ores of Silesia. Fractional distillation or electrolysis is used to separate the cadmium and zinc.

Cadmium may be electrolytically deposited as a coating on metals, chiefly iron or steel, on which it forms a chemically resistant coating. Cadmium lowers the melting point of metals with which it is alloyed; it is used with lead, tin, and bismuth in the manufacture of fusible metals for automatic sprinkler systems, fire alarms, and electric fuses. An alloy of cadmium with lead and zinc is used as a solder for iron. The cliché metal used in stereotype plates contains 22.5 percent cadmium or bismuth. Cadmium salts are used in photography and in the manufacture of fireworks, rubber, fluorescent paints, glass, and porcelain. In recent years cadmium has been used as a control or shielding material in atomic energy plants because of its high absorption of low-energy neutrons. Cadmium sulfide is employed in a type of photovoltaic cell (*see* SOLAR ENERGY), and nickel-cadmium batteries are in common use for specialized purposes (*see* BATTERY).

Cadmium sulfate, $3CdSO_4 \cdot 8H_2O$, is used as an astringent. Cadmium sulfide, CdS, formed as a bright yellow precipitate when hydrogen sulfide is passed through a solution of cadmium salt, is an important pigment known as cadmium yellow. The selenide CdSe is also used as a pigment. Cadmium and solutions of its compounds are highly toxic, with cumulative effects similar to those of mercury poisoning.

CADMUS, in Greek mythology, Phoenician prince who founded the city of Thebes in

Greece. When his sister Europa was kidnapped by the god Zeus, Cadmus was ordered by his father, the king of Phoenicia, to find her or not to return home. Unable to locate his sister, he consulted the oracle at Delphi and was instructed to abandon his search and instead to found a city. Upon leaving Delphi, the oracle advised, Cadmus would come upon a heifer, follow her, and build the city where she lay down to rest.

Near the site of the new city Cadmus and his companions found a sacred grove guarded by a dragon. After the beast killed his companions, Cadmus slew the dragon and, on the advice of the goddess Athena, planted its teeth in the ground. Armed men sprang from the teeth and fought each other until all but five were killed. Cadmus enlisted the help of the victors in founding the citadel of the new city of Thebes, and they became the heads of its noble families. However, Cadmus had to do penance for killing the dragon, which was sacred to Ares, god of war. After eight years of servitude, Cadmus was made king of Thebes and was given Harmonia, the daughter of Ares and of Aphrodite, the goddess of love, as his wife.

Although Thebes prospered under Cadmus's rule, misfortune overcame his descendants. In his old age, after two of his daughters and two of his grandsons had suffered violent deaths, Cadmus fled with his wife to Illyria, where at his death he and Harmonia were changed into serpents. According to tradition, Cadmus introduced the alphabet into Greece.

CADUCEUS, symbolic staff surmounted by two wings and entwined with two snakes. Among the ancient Greeks the caduceus was carried by heralds and ambassadors as a badge of office and a mark of personal inviolability, because it was the symbol of Hermes, the messenger of the gods. According to Book IV of Virgil's *Aeneid,* the Greek god Apollo gave the staff to Hermes in return for the lyre. In Roman mythology the symbol is associated with the god Mercury. The staff of Asclepius, the Greek god of healing, which is entwined by a single snake, is also called a caduceus. It has been adopted as a symbol by the medical profession; it is also the emblem of the medical branches of the U.S. Army and Navy.

CAEDMON (c. 650–80), considered the earliest of the Anglo-Saxon Christian poets. The only information concerning Caedmon is in the *Ecclesiastical History of the English Nation* (731), by the English theologian St. Bede. According to Bede, Caedmon was an illiterate herdsmen who had a vision one night and heard a voice commanding him to sing of "the beginning of created things." Later Caedmon wrote the poem about the creation known as *Caedmon's Hymn,* which Bede recorded in prose. Bede further states that St. Hilda, the abbess of a nearby monastery (now called Whitby), recognized Caedmon's poetic ability and invited him to enter the monastery as a lay brother. Caedmon spent the rest of his life at the monastery writing poetry on biblical themes. In the Bodleian Library at the University of Oxford is a manuscript containing the so-called Caedmon poems. It is now agreed that many of them were probably written later than Caedmon's poetry. The hymn Caedmon composed is of philological interest because it is in the Northumbrian dialect of Old English.

CAEN, city, N France, capital of Calvados Department, on the Orne R., and linked by canal with the nearby English Channel, in Normandy. It is a seaport, a farm-trade center, and a manufacturing city; products include iron and steel, textiles, lace, electronic equipment, and processed food. Much iron ore is mined nearby.

The city retains several fine buildings despite suffering heavy damage in World War II. Especially noteworthy are two examples of 11th-century Norman Romanesque architecture—the Abbaye-aux-Hommes (Men's Abbey), founded by William the Conqueror, and the Abbaye-aux-Dames (Women's Abbey), founded by William's wife, Matilda (1031?–83). Both structures were later restored and altered and no longer house abbeys. Other landmarks in Caen include the Church of Saint Pierre, a chiefly Gothic structure with Renaissance embellishments; an 11th-century castle; and a 16th-century mansion. The city is the site of the University of Caen, founded in 1432 by Henry VI of England.

Caen became important in the early 10th century with the establishment of the duchy of Normandy. It was a favored city of William the Conqueror in the 11th century. Caen was captured and held for a time in 1346 by troops under Edward III of England, claimant to the French crown. Seized by Henry V of England in 1417, the city remained under English rule until 1450, when it was retaken by the French. Caen was a Protestant stronghold during the Reformation, and it declined after the revocation (1685) of the Edict of Nantes, which had assured French Protestants of many rights. During the French Revolution the city was a center of the moderate Girondist faction. In World War II the Germans made Caen a major point of resistance following the Allied invasion of Normandy in 1944, and much of the city was destroyed in the ensuing heavy fighting. Pop. (1982) 117,119.

CAERLEON, village, Newport Borough, Gwent, SE Wales, on the Usk R., near Newport. Caerleon is known as the site of the important Roman legionary fortress of Isca, founded here about AD 75 and occupied until the 4th century. Extensive remains are present, including those of an amphitheater, baths, and barracks, and there is a museum containing archaeological relics. Caerleon is also identified in legend as King Arthur's capital. Pop. of Newport Borough (1981) 133,698.

CAERNARVONSHIRE, also Carnarvonshire or Caernarfonshire, former county, NW Wales; Caernarvon (Caernarfon) was the county town. Caernarvonshire comprised an area dominated by the Snowdon Mts. Relics of prehistoric habitation and of the Roman occupation have been found in the area. Caernarvonshire was made a county in 1284 by Edward I. In 1974 it became part of the new county of Gwynedd (q.v.).

CAESAR, name of a patrician Roman family and an imperial title. The family of the Julian *gens* (clan) called Caesar was active in Roman public life from the time of the Punic Wars. The most renowned member of this family was Julius Caesar. His adopted son, Gaius Octavius, assumed the name Gaius Julius Caesar Octavianus in accordance with Roman custom, later adding the title Augustus (Lat., "majestic"), by which he is generally known. The four Roman emperors of the Julio-Claudian line—Tiberius, Caligula, Claudius I, and Nero—were also adopted into this family and thus properly called Caesar. After the dynasty ended with the death of Nero in 68, the name Caesar was retained to designate the imperial rulers. Emperor Hadrian adopted the imperial title Augustus; Caesar then became the title of the heir apparent to the Roman throne. In 285 Emperor Diocletian appointed a colleague, Maximian, to share the throne. Maximian was called Caesar until 286, when he was given the imperial title Augustus; two assistants, intended to be successors to the Augustuses, were selected and given the title Caesar. Each Augustus and each Caesar was assigned a portion of the Roman Empire to administer. Although this complex system did not survive, the title continued to be used for emperors-designate. The imperial significance of the title Caesar is preserved in medieval and modern derivations, including the German kaiser and the Russian czar.

CAESAR, Gaius Julius (100–44 BC), Roman general and statesman, who laid the foundations of the Roman imperial system.

Early Life. Born in Rome on July 12 or 13, 100 BC, Caesar belonged to the prestigious Julian clan; yet from early childhood he knew controversy. His uncle by marriage was Gaius Marius, leader of the Populares. This party supported agrarian reform and was opposed by the reactionary

Gaius Julius Caesar Bettmann Archive

Optimates, a senatorial faction. Marius was seven times consul (chief magistrate), and the last year he held office, just before his death in 86 BC, he exacted a terrifying toll on the Optimates. At the same time he saw to it that young Caesar was appointed flamen dialis, one of an archaic priesthood with no power. This identified him with his uncle's extremist politics, and his marriage in 84 BC to Cornelia (d. 68 BC), the daughter of Marius's associate, Cinna, further confirmed him as a radical. When Lucius Cornelius Sulla, Marius's enemy and leader of the Optimates, was made dictator in 82 BC, he issued a list of enemies to be executed. Although Caesar was not harmed, he was ordered by Sulla to divorce Cornelia. Refusing that order, he found it prudent to leave Rome. He did not return to the city until 78 BC, after Sulla's resignation.

Caesar was now 22 years old. Unable to gain office, he left Rome again and went to Rhodes, where he studied rhetoric; he returned to Rome in 73 BC, a very persuasive speaker. The year before, while still absent, he had been elected to the pontificate, an important college of Roman priests.

Triumvirate. In 71 BC Pompey the Great, who had earned his epithet in service under Sulla, returned to Rome, having defeated the rebellious Populares general Sertorius in Spain. At the same time Marcus Licinius Crassus, a rich patrician, suppressed in Italy the slave revolt led by Spartacus. Pompey and Crassus borh ran for the consulship—an office held by two men—in 70 BC. Pompey, who by this time had changed sides, was technically ineligible, but with Caesar's help he won the office. Crassus became the other consul. In 69 BC, Caesar was elected quaestor and in 65 BC curule aedile, gaining great popularity for his lavish gladiatorial games. To pay for these, he borrowed money from Crassus. This united the two men, who also found common cause with Pompey. When Caesar returned to Rome in 60 BC after a year as governor of Spain, he joined forces with Crassus and Pompey in a three-way alliance known as the First Triumvirate; to cement their relationship further, Caesar gave his daughter Julia to Pompey in marriage. Thus backed, Caesar was elected consul for 59 BC despite Optimate hostility, and the year after (58 BC) he was appointed governor of Roman Gaul.

Gallic wars. At that time Celtic Gaul, to the north, was still independent, but the Aedui, a tribe of Roman allies, appealed to Caesar for help against another Gallic people, the Helvetii, during the first year of his governorship. Caesar marched into Celtic Gaul with six legions, defeated the Helvetii, and forced them to return to their home area. Next, he crushed Germanic forces under Ariovistus (fl. about 71–58 BC). By 57 BC, following the defeat of the Nervii, Rome was in control of northern Gaul. (A last revolt of the Gauls, led by Vercingetorix, was suppressed in 52 BC.)

Power play. While Caesar was in Gaul, his agents attempted to dominate politics in Rome. This, however, threatened Pompey's position, and it became necessary for the triumvirs to arrange a meeting at Luca in 56 BC, which brought about a temporary reconciliation. It was decided that Caesar would continue in Gaul for another five years, while Pompey and Crassus would both be consuls for 55 BC; after that, each would have proconsular control of provinces. Caesar then went off to raid Britain and put down a revolt in Gaul. Crassus, ever eager for military glory, went to his post in Syria. Provoking a war with the Parthian Empire, he was defeated and killed at Carrhae in 53 BC. This removed the last buffer between Caesar and Pompey; their family ties had been broken by the death of Julia in 54 BC.

Civil War. In 52 BC, with Crassus out of the way, Pompey was made sole consul. Combined with his other powers, this gave him a formidable position. Jealous of his younger rival, he determined to break Caesar's power, an objective that could not be achieved without first depriving him of his command in Gaul. In order to protect himself, Caesar suggested that he and Pompey both lay down their commands simultaneously, but this was rejected; goaded by Pompey, the Senate summarily called upon Caesar to resign his command and disband his army, or else be considered a public enemy. The tribunes, who were Caesar's agents, vetoed this motion, but they were driven out of the Senate chamber. The Senate then entrusted Pompey with providing for the safety of the state. His forces far outnumbered Caesar's, but they were scattered throughout the provinces, and his troops in Italy were not prepared for war. Early in 49 BC Caesar crossed the Rubicon, a small stream separating his province from Italy, and moved swiftly southward. Pompey fled to Brundisium and from there to Greece. In three months Caesar was master of all Italy; his forces then took Spain and the key port of Massilia (Marseille).

In Rome Caesar became dictator until elected consul for 48 BC. At the beginning of that year he landed in Greece and smashed Pompey's forces at Pharsalus. Pompey escaped to Egypt, where he was assassinated. When Caesar arrived there, he installed Cleopatra, daughter of the late King Ptolemy XI (c. 112–51 BC) as queen. In 47 BC he pacified Asia Minor and returned to Rome to become dictator again. By the following year all Optimate forces had been defeated and the Mediterranean world pacified.

Dictatorship and Assassination. The basic prop for Caesar's continuation in power was the dictatorship for life. According to the traditional Republican constitution, this office was only to be held for six months during a dire emergency. That rule, however, had been broken before. Sulla had ruled as dictator for several years, and Caesar now followed suit. In addition, he was made consul for ten years in 45 BC and received the sanctity of tribunes, making it illegal to harm him. Caesar also obtained honors to increase his prestige: He wore the robe, crown, and scepter of a triumphant general and used the title *imperator.* Furthermore, as Pontifex Maximus, he was head of the state religion. Above all, however, he was in total command of the armies, and this remained the backbone of his power.

As a ruler Caesar instituted various reforms. In the provinces he eliminated the highly corrupt tax system, sponsored colonies of veterans, and extended Roman citizenship. At home he reconstituted the courts and increased the number of senators. His reform of the calendar gave Rome a rational means of recording time.

A number of senatorial families, however, felt that Caesar threatened their position, and his honors and powers made them fear that he would become a *rex* (king), a title they, as Republicans, hated. Accordingly, in 44 BC, an assassination plot was hatched by a group of senators, including Gaius Cassius and Marcus Junius Brutus. On March 15 of that year, when Caesar entered the Senate house, the group killed him.

Personal Life. After Caesar's first wife, Cornelia, died in 68 BC, he married Pompeia, a granddaughter of Sulla. When the mysteries of the Bona Dea, over which she presided, were violated, she was maligned by gossips, and Caesar then divorced her, telling the Senate that Caesar's wife must be above suspicion. His next marriage (59 BC) was to Calpurnia and was politically motivated. Since Caesar had no male heirs, he stipulated in his will that his grandnephew, Octavius, become his successor. It was Octavius who became Rome's first emperor under the name of Augustus.

Caesar was a gifted writer, with a clear and simple style. His *Commentaries,* in which he described Gaul and his Gallic campaigns, is a major source of information about the early Celtic and Germanic tribes.

Achievements. Scholarly opinion of Caesar's accomplishments is divided. Some regard him as an unscrupulous tyrant, with an insatiable lust for power, and blame him for the demise of the Roman Republic. Others, admitting that he could be ruthless, insist that the Republic had already been destroyed. They maintain that to save the Roman world from chaos a new type of government had to be created. In fact, Caesar's reforms did stabilize the Mediterranean world. Among ancient military commanders, he may be second only to Alexander the Great.

See also ROME, HISTORY OF. For additional information on historical figures, see biographies of those whose names are not followed by dates.

M.S.C.

For further information on this person, see the section Biographies in the Bibliography in volume 28.

CAESAREA, seaport of ancient Palestine, on the coast of Samaria, north of Joppa (modern Tel Aviv-Jaffa). Founded about 22 BC by the Judean king Herod the Great, it was named in honor of the Roman emperor Augustus. Herod provided the city with an amphitheater, a number of imposing temples and public buildings, excellent water-supply and drainage systems, and a magnificent harbor, protected by a breakwater. Ruins of some of these structures, including the breakwater, are extant. According to the New Testament (see Acts 10), it was at Caesarea that the disciple Peter converted Cornelius, the first Gentile to accept Christianity. In AD 66, on the outbreak of the Jewish revolt against Roman rule, the citizens of Caesarea vigorously supported the revolutionary cause. Most of the Jewish inhabitants were massacred after the Romans reestablished their authority in the city, and there the Roman general Vespasian made his headquarters

An ancient Roman aqueduct in Caesarea.
Stanley Newfield–Editorial Photocolor Archives, Inc.

during the subsequent fighting. In July 69, while at Caesarea, Vespasian was proclaimed emperor of the Roman Empire by his troops. Following the fall of Jerusalem in 70, Caesarea was made capital of Roman Palestine. Later, as an episcopal see, the city figured significantly in the early history of the church. About 232 the Christian teacher and theologian Origen founded a school there. After 638, when Caesarea fell to the Muslims, the city declined steadily. It was captured and plundered (1102) by troops under Baldwin I, ruler of the Latin kingdom of Jerusalem and a leader of the First Crusade. Caesarea was razed (1265) by the Mameluke sultan of Egypt Baybars I. The site of the ancient city is occupied by modern Sedot Yam, Israel.

CAESAREAN SECTION. *See* CESAREAN SECTION.

CAESAREA PHILIPPI, ancient city of the Golan Heights section of Syria (now occupied by Israel), southwest of Damascus. The city was originally called Paneas because it was a center for the worship of the Greek god Pan. In the 1st century BC, Emperor Augustus of Rome gave the region to Herod the Great, king of Judea. The city was subsequently enlarged by Herod's son, Philip the Tetrarch (20 BC–AD 34), who named it Caesarea in honor of the emperor (Caesar), adding Philippi (Lat., "of Philip") to distinguish the town from Caesarea Palestinae, a seaport to the south. According to Matt. 16:13–20, it was near Caesarea Philippi that Jesus commanded the apostle Peter to care for Jesus' followers. The site is now occupied by the village of Baniyas.

CAESARION. *See* PTOLEMAIC DYNASTY.

CAFFEINE, an alkaloid ($C_8H_{10}O_2N_4 \cdot H_2O$) found in coffee, tea, cacao, and some other plants. It is also present in most cola beverages. Caffeine was discovered in coffee in 1820. In 1838 it was established that theine, discovered in tea in 1827, is identical to caffeine. The drug increases the blood pressure, stimulates the central nervous system, promotes urine formation, and stimulates the action of the heart and lungs. Caffeine is used in treating migraine because it constricts the dilated blood vessels and thereby reduces the pain. It also increases the potency of analgesics such as aspirin, and it can somewhat relieve asthma attacks by widening the bronchial airways. Caffeine is produced commercially chiefly as a by-product in making caffeine-free coffee (see COFFEE).

Caffeine has been suggested as a possible cause of cancer or of birth defects. No studies, however, have yet confirmed any of these charges. Persons who stop drinking coffee do sometimes experience withdrawal headaches. The U.S. Food and Drug Administration does not include caffeine on its "generally recognized as safe" (GRAS) list, but acknowledges no clear evidence of hazard at normal levels of use.

CAGAYAN DE ORO, municipality and port, S Philippines, capital of Misamis Oriental Province, on the N coast of Mindanao. It lies at the mouth of the Cagayan R. on Macajalar Bay, Mindanao Sea. The city is a trade center for the agricultural Cagayan Valley. Xavier University (1933) is here. Pop. (1980 prelim.) 228,409.

CAGE, John (1912–), American composer of profound influence on avant-garde music and dance. Born Sept. 5, 1912, in Los Angeles, he studied with the American composers Henry Cowell and Adolph Weiss (1891–1971) and the Austrian-born composer Arnold Schoenberg. In 1942 he settled in New York City. Influenced by Zen Buddhism, Cage often used silence as a musical element, with sounds as entities hanging in time, and he sought to achieve randomness in his music. In *Music of Changes* (1951), for piano, tone combinations occur in a sequence determined by casting lots. In *4′33″* (1954), the performers sit silently before any instruments; the unconnected sounds of the environment are the music. Like *Theatre Piece* (1960), in which musicians, dancers, and mimes perform randomly selected tasks, *4′33″* dissolves the borders separating music, sound, and nonmusical phenomena. In Cage's exquisite pieces for prepared piano, such as *Amores* (1943), foreign objects modify the sounds of the piano strings. Cage wrote dance works for the American choreographer Merce Cunningham. His books include *Silence* (1961), *Empty Words* (1979), and *X* (1983).

John Cage Gerhard Gscheidle–Peter Arnold, Inc.

CAGLIARI, city and seaport in Italy, and S Sardinia, capital of Cagliari Province and Sardinia Region, on the Gulf of Cagliari. It is the principal port as well as the leading commercial and industrial city of Sardinia. Surrounded by salt lagoons, it has a large salt-producing industry. Other important industries are wine making, flour milling, and the manufacture of cement, steel, and chemicals. In the city are a Roman amphitheater and the Cathedral of Santa Cecilia (13th cent.). Cagliari is also the site of the University of Cagliari (1606) and the National Archaeological Museum.

Cagliari was probably founded by the Phoenicians and was later occupied by the Carthaginians. In 238 BC it was conquered by the Romans and was subsequently held by various peoples, including Vandals, Byzantines, Saracens, Pisans, Spanish, Austrians, and Savoyans. In 1861, Cagliari, along with the rest of Sardinia, became part of the kingdom of Italy. Pop. (1980 est.) 241,500.

CAGLIOSTRO, Alessandro, Conte di, real name GIUSEPPE BALSAMO (1743–95), Italian adventurer, born in Palermo, Sicily. During his youth he worked as an assistant to an apothecary, acquiring a superficial knowledge of chemistry and medicine. Subsequently he became one of the most infamous charlatans of his time. He excelled in swindles that ranged from forgery to fortune-telling, posing at various times as a physician, hypnotist, and founder of a religious order of Freemasons. Accompanied by his wife, a woman of great beauty, he traveled extensively throughout Europe, peddling his services and his wares, notably an "elixir of immortal youth." He became a well-known figure at the court of King Louis XVI of France; Cagliostro's dupes included members of the nobility, who patronized him even though he was frequently exposed. In 1789 he returned to Italy and was seized in Rome by members of the Inquisition, who condemned him to death as a heretic. His sentence, however, was commuted to life imprisonment, and he died in prison. The French novelist Alexandre Dumas *père* described Cagliostro's adventures in his *Mémoires d'un médecin: Joseph Balsamo* (Memoirs of a Physician: Joseph Balsamo, 1846–48).

CAGNEY, James Francis (1904–86), American actor, born in New York City. He attended Columbia University and made his Broadway debut in the chorus of the musical revue *Pitter Patter* (1920). He continued singing and dancing in vaudeville and musical revues until 1930, when he appeared in his first film, *Sinner's Holiday.* His performance in *The Public Enemy* (1931) established Cagney as a screen "tough guy," a role he played in many subsequent films, including *The Crowd Roars* (1932) and *Angels with Dirty Faces* (1938). He received an Academy Award for his portrayal of the dramatist and actor George M. Cohan in *Yankee Doodle Dandy* (1942). Cagney's versatility as an actor also extended to film comedy. He played Bottom in Shakespeare's *Midsummer Night's Dream* (1935), the lead role in *One, Two, Three* (1961), and the police chief in *Ragtime* (1981). Cagney was given the 1974 Life Achievement Award of the American Film Institute.

CAGUAS, town, in Caguas Municipality, E Puerto Rico, near Lake Carraízo; founded 1775. It is situated in an agricultural region; local industries manufacture processed food, tobacco products, and clothing. Pop. (1970) 63,215; (1980) 87,214.

CAHAN, Abraham (1860–1951), American editor and author, born in Vilna, Lithuania (now Lithuanian SSR). Arriving in the U.S. in 1882, Cahan joined the Socialist Labor party led by Daniel De Leon and became editor of the party publications. In 1897 Cahan became one of the founders and the editor of the *Jewish Daily Forward.* Under his direction the *Forward* became the leading Yiddish newspaper in the U.S. Cahan later became a leader of the Socialist party. Cahan wrote in both English and Yiddish. His many works include *Yekl, A Tale of the New York Ghetto* (Eng., 1899), *The Rise of David Levinsky* (Eng., 1917), and an autobiography, *Leaves from My Life* (Yiddish, 5 vol., 1926–31).

CAHOKIA, village, Saint Clair Co., SW Illinois, on the Mississippi R., a residential suburb of East Saint Louis; inc. 1927. Parks College (1927), a division of St. Louis University, is here, and Cahokia Mounds State Park, with prehistoric Indian mounds, is nearby. Founded in 1699 by French missionaries and named for a tribe of Illinois Indians, the village is the oldest permanent white settlement in Illinois. Pop. (1970) 20,649; (1980) 18,904.

CAHORS, town, S France, capital of Lot Department, on a rocky peninsula formed by a bend in the Lot R., in Quercy. It is a farm-trade and manufacturing center; products include processed food, liquor, and leather. Truffles, nuts, and fruit are produced nearby. Points of interest in the city include the Cathedral of Saint Étienne (founded 12th cent., altered 13th–16th cent.), notable for its cupolas; Roman and medieval ruins; and the Pont Valentré, an old fortified stone bridge spanning the Lot R.

Before the Romans conquered the area in the 1st century BC, the town was a capital of the Cadurci. Under the Romans it was known as Divona and later (3d cent. AD) as Cadurcum. It subsequently was captured by the Visigoths and by Muslim invaders of Europe. In the 13th century Cahors became an important financial center. Pope John XXII, who was born here, founded the University of Cahors in the early 14th century; it was merged into the University of Toulouse in 1751. Pop. (1982) 20,774.

CAIAPHAS (fl. AD 18–37), Jewish high priest, who presided at the trial of Jesus Christ. According to Christian sources, in a general council summoned to take action on the preachings of Jesus, Caiaphas favored putting Jesus to death as a matter of expediency (see John 11:47–53). When asked if he was indeed the Christ, the Son of God, Jesus replied, "I am" (Mark 14:60–64). Caiaphas is said to have been grieved at what he considered blasphemy. The council then determined that Jesus deserved death, and the sentence was ratified at a formal meeting of the Sanhedrin (q.v.; see Matt. 27:1). The high priest did not have the power of final condemnation, and Jesus accordingly was handed over to the Roman authorities for sentencing.

CAICOS ISLANDS. *See* Turks and Caicos Islands.

CAILLAUX, Joseph (1863–1944), controversial French political leader, born in Le Mans. Elected to the Chamber of Deputies in 1898, Caillaux joined the Radical Socialist party, serving as finance minister three times between 1899 and 1911. As prime minister (1911–12), he won Germany's agreement to a French protectorate over Morocco. As finance minister again (1913–14), he sponsored passage of France's first income tax law. In 1914 his wife (d. 1943) shot and killed *Le Figaro* editor Gaston Calmette (1858–1914) for having published personal letters written by Caillaux. He resigned from the government to defend her at her trial, and he won an acquittal. During World War I Caillaux was known to favor a negotiated peace with Germany; in 1917 he was accused by Premier Georges Clemenceau of treasonable correspondence with the enemy. He was imprisoned from 1918 to 1920. Caillaux served as finance minister again in 1925, 1926, and 1935.

CAIMAN *or* **CAYMAN,** common name for three genera of alligator-like reptiles in the order Crocodilia (see Crocodile). All are found in the New World tropics. The largest is the black caiman, *Melanosuchus niger,* of the Orinoco and Amazon Rivers; it may exceed 4.5 m (15 ft) in length and is the only species large enough to be a threat to humans. The smallest are the armored caimans, *Paleosuchus,* of mountain streams, which reach only about 2.1 m (7 ft). The spectacled and broad-nosed caimans, genus *Caiman,* are the most numerous and familiar. The black caiman is practically extinct.

Cain murdering Abel (from a 13th-cent. psalter manuscript). Pierpont Morgan Library

CAIN, in the Old Testament (see Gen. 4:1–16), elder son of Adam and Eve and the brother of Abel. When Abel's sacrificial offering was accepted in preference to his own, Cain slew Abel and became the first murderer. Cain was cursed and condemned to a life of wandering. A divine mark was placed upon him lest anyone meeting him should slay him. Sevenfold vengeance was to be visited upon anyone who disregarded the mark and killed Cain. For his wicked deed he is recalled in the New Testament (see 1 John 3:12; Jude 11). The story is interpreted by historians and biblical scholars as a symbolic account of an ancient nomadic tribe named Cain; of its distinguishing tattoo mark; and of its reputation for ferocious vengeance against other tribes who slew members of the tribe of Cain. The name Cain has become synonymous with murderer; the mark that was affixed to Cain has become known as the mark or brand of Cain and is used figuratively to denote a murderer.

CAIRNGORM. *See* Quartz.

CAIRN TERRIER, breed of terrier that originated on the Isle of Skye, perhaps as early as the 16th century. The breed is named for its ability to bolt vermin from cairns, or rock heaps. The dog has a broad, short head, with erect ears set wide apart and an alert, inquisitive gaze. The outer coat—usually gray or wheaten and darker at the ears, muzzle, feet, and tail tip—is wiry; the undercoat is soft and furry. The average male cairn weighs about 6 kg (about 14 lb) and measures about 25 cm (about 10 in) at the shoulders; females are slightly smaller.

CAIRO (Arab. *al-Qahirah*), city, capital of Egypt and its Cairo Governorate, a port on the Nile R. near the head of the Nile delta. The largest city of Africa and of the Middle East, Cairo has been a cultural center of Islam for 1000 years.

The Cairo region is the chief industrial area of the most populous Arab nation. The city's major manufactures include textiles, foodstuffs, construction supplies, motor vehicles, aircraft, printed materials, and chemical fertilizers. In addition, a big iron and steel mill is at the nearby suburb of Hulwan. The Cairo area also has a major tourist industry.

Cairo is a mass-media center; its newspapers, such as the semiofficial *al-Ahram,* exert wide influence in the Islamic world, as does Radio Cairo. Institutions of higher education in the city include al-Azhar University, one of the oldest universities in the world. Founded in 970, this religious school specializes in Islamic law and jurisprudence. The University of Cairo (1908), in nearby Giza, and Ain Shams University (1950) each enroll more than 60,000 students annually.

City Description. Almost all Cairo is situated on the E bank of the Nile. The modern city is centered at Tahrir Square, the site of a Western-style business district and government ministries. On Corniche Drive, along the Nile, are luxury hotels and foreign embassies. To the E of the business district is the extensive medieval city, where residences and small-scale industries are intermingled with mosques and minarets. Along with Buluq and Old Cairo (Misr al-Qadimah), the former to the N and the latter to the S of the business district, these are the poorest neighborhoods, in which densities of about 100,000 persons per sq km (about 259,000 per sq mi) occur. The suqs (bazaars) and narrow alleyways of medieval Cairo impart visions of another era. Most popular for tourists is Khan al-Khalili suq, where traditional gold, silver, and wooden handicrafts can be purchased.

Two islands in the Nile also are part of Cairo. Az-Zamalik (Gezira) Island encompasses prestigious residential neighborhoods, extensive gardens, and the tall Cairo Tower; and ar-Rawdah (Roda) Island is the site of the University of Cairo Hospital, one of the city's many excellent medical facilities.

The Cairo area dazzles the visitor interested in the civilizations of ancient Egypt and the heritage of Islam. The Sphinx and pyramids keep their silent vigil at Giza, a suburb on the W bank of the Nile, and beautiful treasures from the tomb of the ancient king Tutankhamen are displayed in the Egyptian Museum in Cairo. Art from the Islamic period is exhibited in the city's Museum of Islamic Art. A great number of magnificent minarets, carved masonry domes, mausoleums, and mosques have been preserved in Cairo, principally in the old medieval city. Especially notable are the Mameluke tombs and the mosques of Ahmad ibn-Tulun, al-Azhar, Sultan Hasan, and Muhammad Ali.

A view of the handsomely landscaped Tahrir Square, the hub of modern Cairo. Ed Drews–Photo Researchers

History. The ancient Egyptian capital of Memphis was located south of present-day Cairo, and the Romans later established the town of Babylon on the site of the modern city. In AD 641 Arabs from southwestern Asia founded the military encampment of Fustat on the site of Babylon. In 969 a dissident branch of Muslims, the Fatimids, conquered Egypt, establishing a fortified city northeast of Fustat. It was called al-Qahirah ("the victorious"), and the name has been corrupted in English to the name Cairo.

In the 12th century, Crusaders attacked Cairo, but they were defeated by a Muslim army from Syria led by Saladin, who then founded the Ayyubid dynasty in the city. Saladin built a great citadel (still standing) in Cairo. In the 13th century the city became the capital of the Mameluke dynasty. By the next century Cairo had 500,000 inhabitants, and no city in Europe or the Middle East could rival it in size or prestige. Cairo's population was decimated by the Black Death plague in the mid-14th century, however, and the city subsequently declined.

Cairo was captured (1517) by the Ottoman Turks. Napoleon conquered Egypt in 1798, and the ensuing 3-year French occupation of Cairo resulted in parts of the city being destroyed to widen and straighten major streets, of which many still exist. The Ottomans returned in 1801.

Important additions to Cairo occurred during the reign (1863–79) of Ismail Pasha. These included a European-style community, Ismailiyah, west of the medieval city. By the beginning of the 20th century the British, who now controlled Egypt, had developed a modern urban center in Ismailiyah and expanded it westward to the Nile. Az-Zamalik Island and parts of the west bank of the Nile were also built up by the British.

Following World War I the foreign presence in Cairo began to diminish. New residential areas were founded to house the city's growing number of Egyptian workers, many of whom were migrants from rural areas of the country. By 1927 Cairo had 1 million inhabitants, a number that had doubled by 1947. The population grew even more rapidly thereafter, especially in the 1960s and '70s. President Anwar al-Sadat of Egypt was assassinated in Cairo in 1981 while reviewing a military parade. Pop. (1983 est.) 5,881,000. M.E.Bo.

For further information on this topic, see the Bibliography in volume 28, section 1016.

CAIRO, city, seat of Alexander Co., extreme S Illinois, at the convergence of the Ohio and Mississippi rivers; inc. 1837. It is an agricultural center with flour mills and lumber- and soybean-processing plants. The community was founded in 1837. It was reached by railroad in 1855 and was a major Union supply base during the American Civil War. It is named for its supposed similarity to the geographic setting of Cairo, Egypt. Pop. (1970) 6277; (1980) 5931.

CAIRO CONFERENCE, meeting held Nov. 22–26, 1943, during World War II, in Cairo, to define the war aims of the Allied governments with respect to Japan. The major participants were President Franklin D. Roosevelt of the U.S., Prime Minister Winston Churchill of Great Britain, and Generalissimo Chiang Kai-shek of China, with their highest-ranking advisers. Because the Soviet Union was not then at war with Japan, it was not represented at the Cairo Conference.

On Dec. 1, 1943, the U.S. government released a joint communiqué, drafted in Cairo and signed by Roosevelt, Churchill, and Chiang Kai-shek, in which they declared the determination of their governments to prosecute the war until Japan surrendered unconditionally. The signatories stated that their governments sought neither territorial aggrandizement nor other gain. They also declared the intention of their governments to strip Japan of all the territory that country had gained since the beginning of World War I; to restore to China all territories taken by Japan, such as Manchuria and Taiwan; and to help Korea achieve independence "in due course."

CAISSON, term generally applied in architecture to several types of concrete, steel, and wooden shells for building foundations under water, below groundwater level, or in regions where soil of adequate strength is covered by surface layers of quicksand or peat.

In civil engineering, the caisson is a watertight chamber used in excavation or construction to accommodate workers under water and to facilitate the removal of excavated material.

In military language, a caisson is a two-wheeled ammunition vehicle that was formerly used attached to a battery of artillery.

CAITHNESS, former county, NE Scotland; Wick was the county town. The area is rich in relics of prehistoric habitation, including subterranean dwellings, forts, and cairns (memorial stone piles), as well as the later brochs (Pictish stone towers) and Christian chapels. Because of its vulnerable location at the tip of the N extremity of the Scottish mainland, Caithness was for many centuries dominated by Scandinavian raiders. In 1975 Caithness became part of the newly created Highland Region (*see* HIGHLAND).

CAJETAN (c. 1469–1534), Italian theologian, prelate, and diplomat. Originally named Giacomo de Vio, he was born in Gaeta. At the age of 16 he entered the Dominican order, and after study at the universities of Naples and Bologna, he taught theology at the University of Padua. He was appointed vicar-general of the Dominicans in 1507. Made a cardinal in 1517, he became bishop of Gaeta in 1519. He defended papal supremacy and ecclesiastical reform at the Fifth Lateran Council and disputed the stand of Martin Luther at Augsburg in 1518. Cajetan (from the Latin form of the name of his birthplace) was a formidable diplomat, serving as papal legate on many occasions. He was a biblical scholar and an influential commentator on the theology of St. Thomas Aquinas, and to him is attributed a major role in the revival of Thomism in the 16th century. He wrote widely on many aspects of theology, and his commentaries on some portions of the Bible anticipated modern criticism, raising contemporary opposition.

CAJUN, name applied to the descendants of French-Canadians who now reside mainly in southern Louisiana. The name Cajun is the corrupt form of Acadian, a pastoral people who originally lived in Acadia (now Nova Scotia), Canada. Acadia was a French colony until 1713, when it was acquired by Great Britain. In the mid-18th century the British expelled those settlers who would not swear allegiance to the Crown. About 4000 Acadians eventually moved to the fertile bayou lands of Louisiana.

Today the Cajuns live in small, self-contained communities along the Gulf of Mexico. They raise cattle and cultivate various crops, including sweet potatoes, sugarcane, corn, and cotton. Home crafts are important, and the people do much of their own spinning and weaving.

The Cajuns have a mixed white, black, and Indian ancestry, which helps set them apart from their neighbors. French-Canadian folk customs and traditions are preserved among this group. In addition to English, they speak their own distinctive dialect, a combination of archaic French and words taken from Spanish, English, German, black, and Indian peoples. Most Cajuns practice the Roman Catholic religion.

CAKEWALK, improvised, highly syncopated dance for couples strutting around a square. Named for the cake won by the most inventive dancers, it originated by the 1840s among American slaves as a satire on the social dances of plantation owners. It reached great popularity in the late 1800s in minstrel shows and stage revues, becoming a ballroom craze about 1900. The first of the black-influenced popular social dances, the cakewalk was danced to music that influenced ragtime music.

CALABAR, city and seaport, SE Nigeria, capital of Cross River State, on an estuary of the Gulf of Guinea. The city is the market center for the surrounding area in which cacao, palm oil, piassava, rubber, and timber are produced. Pop. (est.) 103,000.

CALABASH TREE, common name for a tree, *Crescentia cujete,* of the family Bignoniaceae (*see* BIGNONIA), common in tropical America, especially in the West Indies. The tree grows to an average height of 9 m (30 ft). Although the wood of the tree is tough and flexible, by far the most useful part is the gourd, or hard shell of the fruit, from which numerous articles, including domestic utensils and pipes for smoking tobacco, are made. Many articles made from the calabash gourd are given the name calabash.

CALABRIA, region, S Italy, comprising the so-called toe of the Italian Peninsula. It consists of the provinces of Catanzaro, Cosenza, and Reggio di Calabria. The city of Catanzaro is the capital. The southernmost tip is separated from Sicily by the Strait of Messina. The Apennines mountain range extends the full length of Calabria, providing a generally rugged terrain except for lowland marshes and a fertile coastal strip. Wheat, citrus fruits, figs, potatoes, and olives are grown, and livestock raising, lumbering, and fishing are important economic activities. The chief minerals mined are rock salt and sulfur. Until the 20th century, when social and economic reforms were introduced, Calabria was a generally backward area. Several hydroelectric plants and chemical and zinc works are in the region.

In ancient times Calabria was called Bruttium (q.v.). The modern name of Calabria, which in antiquity was applied to present-day Apulia, was not given to the region until the Middle Ages. Greeks settled the coast at an early date and several of their settlements, including Sybaris, Crotona, and Locri, were numbered among the leading cities of Magna Graecia during the 6th and 5th centuries BC. Conquered by the Romans in the 3d century BC, the region never regained its former prosperity. The inhabitants were in large part driven inland by the spread of malaria and during the early Middle Ages by pirate raids. Conquered by the Normans in the 11th century, Calabria thereafter shared the history of the kingdom of the Two Sicilies.

Area, 15,080 sq km (5822 sq mi); pop. (1983 est.) 2,078,400.

CALADIUM, plants of the genera *Caladium* and *Xanthosoma* of the family Araceae (*see* ARUM). Caladiums are commonly grown as houseplants and garden plants for their showy foliage. Wide variation is found in the colors and markings of the attractive, large, single-bladed leaves, which rise on long stalks from fleshy, underground bulblike corms. Under some circumstances, the

Caladium, Caladium bicolor

corms and other parts of the plant may contain crystals of calcium oxalate, which causes an intense, burning irritation if eaten.

CALAIS, city, N France, in Pas-de-Calais Department, on the Strait of Dover, opposite Dover, England. It is a seaport (notably for traffic with England) and a fishing and manufacturing center; products include lace, embroideries, processed food, lumber, and cables. Points of interest include the Church of Notre Dame; the Tour du Guet (13th cent.), a watchtower that served as a lighthouse until 1848; and the new city hall.

Because of the importance of its harbor and its position controlling communications between England and France, Calais was often the victim of military conquest. In 997 Baldwin IV, count of Flanders, improved its harbor, and it was fortified in 1224 by the count of Boulogne. In 1347 it was captured by the English after a long siege and held until 1558. From 1596 to 1598 it was in possession of the Spaniards, but was returned to France by the Treaty of Vervins. During World War I it was the principal debarkation port for British forces. In World War II, Calais was the scene of fierce fighting (1940, 1944) and suffered much damage. Pop. (1982) 76,935.

CALAMIAN GROUP *or* **CALAMIANES,** group of islands, W Philippines, part of Palawan Province, in the South China Sea. They extend in a southwesterly direction toward Palawan Island from Mindoro Island, from which they are separated by Mindoro Strait. Busuanga, Culion, Coron, and Linapacan are the most important of the 98 islands constituting the group. Of volcanic origin, the Calamianes are largely mountainous and forested, but have fertile areas yielding rice, sugarcane, tobacco, and tropical fruits. Important industries are cattle raising and fishing. Area, 1753 sq km (677 sq mi).

CALAMITY JANE, real name MARTHA JANE CANARY (1852?–1903), American frontierswoman. Born in Princeton, Mo., she grew up in mining towns of the West, where she became known as a sharpshooter and horsewoman and acquired a reputation for contempt of convention; she claimed she was the equal of any man and dressed in male attire. By her own account she served as a scout with the U.S. Cavalry and carried the mail between Custer, Mont., and Deadwood, S.D. She also performed in a company that toured the West. In 1891 she married a cab driver, Clinton Burke. The origin of her nickname is said to have been her threats that calamity would befall any man who offended her.

CALBAYOG, city and port, E Philippines, in Samar Province, on the W coast of the island of Samar, at the mouth of the Calbayog R. The city is the center of an agricultural area producing rice, corn, copra, abaca, and timber. Hot springs are nearby. Pop. (1980 prelim.) 110,938.

CALCEOLARIA (Lat. *Calceolarius,* "shoemaker"), genus of plants of the family Scrophulariaceae (*see* FIGWORT). They are natives of South America; most grow in the Andes at altitudes of more than 2736 m (more than 9000 ft). The calyx has four parts and the corolla has two lips, of which the lower in some species resembles a slipper; hence its name. It is also known as pouch flower. The flowers are most frequently yellow; purple ones are also fairly common. Calceolaria were introduced into floriculture about 1830 and have produced many hybrids and varieties. The plant is a perennial and is treated as a semihardy or greenhouse plant in the U.S. Its size ranges between 30 and 152 cm (between 12 and 60 in).

CALCHAS, in Greek mythology, the most famous soothsayer among the Greeks at the time of the Trojan War. When the Greek fleet was stranded at Aulis because of a lack of favorable wind, Calchas revealed that the goddess Artemis was offended and that King Agamemnon must sacrifice his virgin daughter Iphigenia before the winds would rise. Calchas predicted the 10-year siege of Troy, and shortly before the conclusion of the war, when the Greeks were stricken with a plague, explained that the god Apollo was angry because Agamemnon had taken as his mistress the daughter of one of Apollo's priests. Calchas was highly respected because of the accuracy of his prophecies, and at his suggestion the Greek commanders built the Trojan horse by which the Greek forces gained access to the city.

CALCINATION, chemical and manufacturing process in which a material is heated, without melting, in order to drive off the material's volatile components. Calcination is industrially important in the production of lime from limestone and in the manufacture of portland cement (q.v.) and plaster of Paris (*see* GYPSUM), and also as a first step in the extraction of metal from ores.

CALCITE, mineral consisting largely of calcium carbonate ($CaCO_3$). Next to quartz, it is the most abundant of the earth's minerals. Crystallizing in the hexagonal system (*see* CRYSTAL), calcite is noted for its wide variety of crystalline forms. It also occurs in massive or cryptocrystalline formations. Examples of the crystalline varieties are corn spar, hog-tooth spar, nailhead spar, dogtooth spar, satin spar, and Iceland spar (q.v.). The last named is the only pure form of calcite found in nature. Limestone, chalk, travertine, Oriental alabaster, and marble are among the most common of the massive forms of the mineral. Calcite is also found as stalactites (*see* STALACTITE AND STALAGMITE) and calcareous tufas, forms deposited by mineral waters.

Colorless, with a hardness (q.v.) of 3 and a sp.gr. of 2.72, pure calcite is readily identified by the ease with which it is cut or cleaved and by the rapidity with which it reacts with dilute acids. Such contaminants as magnesium, ferrous iron, manganese, and zinc will alter the properties of the mineral in varying degrees, depending on the amounts present.

CALCIUM, metallic element, symbol Ca, a member of the alkaline earth metals (q.v.) in group IIa of the periodic table (*see* PERIODIC LAW); at.no. 20, at.wt. 40.08.

Occurrence and Properties. Calcium has six stable and several radioactive isotopes. A malleable and ductile metal, calcium is silvery-white when pure, but it rapidly tarnishes to yellow on exposure to air. The British chemist Sir Humphry Davy isolated calcium in 1808 by means of electrolysis. Calcium is fifth in abundance among the elements in the earth's crust, but it is not found uncombined in nature. It occurs in numerous highly useful compounds, such as calcium carbonate, $CaCO_3$, which composes calcite, marble, limestone, and chalk; calcium sulfate, $CaSO_4$, in aiabaster or gypsum; calcium fluoride, CaF_2, in fluorite or fluorspar; calcium phosphate, $Ca_3(PO_4)_2$, in rock phosphate; and in many silicates. In cold, dry air, calcium is not readily attacked by oxygen, but when heated it unites vigorously with oxygen, the halogens, sulfur, phosphorus, hydrogen, and nitrogen. Calcium unites violently with water, forming the hydroxide $Ca(OH)_2$ and releasing hydrogen.

Calcium melts at 850° C (1562° F), boils at 1440° C (2624° F), and has a sp.gr. of 1.54.

Uses. The metal is obtained mainly by electrolysis of fused calcium chloride, a costly process. Until recently the pure metal had little use in industry. It is being used to an increasing extent, however, as a deoxidizer for copper, nickel, and stainless steel. Because calcium hardens lead when alloyed with it, lead-calcium alloys are excellent for bearings, superior to ordinary lead antimony for grids in storage batteries, and more durable as sheathing for lead-covered cable. Calcium is present in the chemically combined state in lime (calcium hydroxide), cement and mortar (as calcium hydroxide or a variety of silicates of calcium), teeth and bones (as a calcium hydroxyphosphate), and in many body fluids (as complex proteinaceous compounds) essential to muscle contraction, the transmission of nerve impulses, and the clotting of blood.

CALCIUM CARBONATE. *See* CALCITE; LIMESTONE.

CALCULATOR. *See* COMPUTER; OFFICE SYSTEMS.

CALCULUS, also the calculus, branch of mathematics concerned with the study of such concepts as the rate of change of one variable quantity with respect to another, the slope of a curve at a prescribed point, the computation of the maximum and minimum values of functions, and the calculation of the area bounded by curves. Evolved from algebra, arithmetic, and geometry (qq.v.) it is the basis of that part of mathematics (q.v.) called analysis.

Calculus is widely employed in the physical, biological, and social sciences. It is used, for example, in the physical sciences to study the speed of a falling body, the rates of change in a chemical reaction, or the rate of decay of a radioactive material. In the biological sciences a problem such as the rate of growth of a colony of bacteria as a function of time is easily solved using the calculus. In the social sciences calculus is widely used in the study of statistics and probability (qq.v.).

Calculus can be applied to many problems involving the notion of extreme amounts, such as the fastest, the most, the slowest, or the least. These maximum or minimum amounts may be described as values for which a certain rate of change (increase or decrease) is zero. By using the calculus it is possible to determine how high a projectile will go by finding the point at which its change of altitude with respect to time, that is, its velocity, is equal to zero. Many general principles governing the behavior of physical processes are formulated almost invariably in terms of rates of change. It is also possible, through the insights provided by the methods of the calculus, to resolve such problems in logic as the famous paradoxes posed by the Greek philosopher Zeno.

The fundamental concept of calculus, which distinguishes it from other branches of mathematics and is the source from which all its theory and applications are developed, is the theory of limits of functions of variables (*see* FUNCTION).

Let f be a function of the real variable x, which is denoted $f(x)$, defined on some set of real numbers containing the number x_0. It is not required that the function be defined at the point x_0 itself. Let L be a real number. The expression

$$\lim_{x \to x_0} f(x) = L$$

is read: "The limit of the function $f(x)$, as x approaches x_0, is equal to the number L." The notation is designed to convey the idea that $f(x)$ can be made as "close" to L as desired simply by choosing an x sufficiently close to x_0. For example, if the function $f(x)$ is defined as $f(x) = x^2 + 3x + 2$, and if $x_0 = 3$, then from the definition above it is true that $\lim_{x \to 3} f(x) = 20$. This is because, as x approaches 3 in value, x^2 approaches 9, $3x$ approaches 9, and 2 does not change, so the sum of all of these approaches is $9 + 9 + 2$, or 20. The concept of limit can be understood intuitively, but the logical foundations of calculus were completed only two centuries later.

Another type of limit important in the study of calculus can be illustrated as follows. Let the domain of a function $f(x)$ include all of the numbers greater than some fixed number m. L is said to be the limit of the function $f(x)$ as x becomes positively infinite, if, corresponding to a given positive number ε there exists a number M such that the numerical difference between $f(x)$ and L (the absolute value $|f(x) - L|$) is less than ε whenever x is greater than M. In this case the limit is written as

$$\lim_{x \to \infty} f(x) = L$$

For example, the function $f(x) = 1/x$ approaches the number 0 as x becomes positively infinite.

It is important to note that a limit, as just presented, is a two-way, or bilateral, concept: A dependent variable approaches a limit as an independent variable approaches a number or becomes infinite. The limit concept can be extended to a variable that is dependent on several independent variables. The statement "u is an infinitesimal" meaning "u is a variable approaching 0 as a limit," found in a few present-day and in many older texts on calculus, is confusing and should be avoided. Further, it is essential to distinguish between the limit of $f(x)$ as x approaches x_0 and the value of $f(x)$ when x is x_0, that is, the correspondent of x_0. For example, if $f(x) = \sin x/x$, then $\lim_{x \to 0} f(x) = 1$; however, no value of $f(x)$ corresponding to $x = 0$ exists, because division by 0 is undefined in mathematics.

The two branches into which elementary calculus is usually divided are differential calculus, based on the consideration of the limit of a certain ratio, and integral calculus, based on the consideration of the limit of a certain sum.

Differential Calculus. Let the dependent variable y be a function of the independent variable x, expressed by $y = f(x)$. If x_0 is a value of x in its domain of definition, then $y_0 = f(x_0)$ is the corresponding value of y. Let h be a real number (Δx, read "delta x," is used quite frequently in place of h), and let $y_0 + k = f(x_0 + h)$. When Δx is used in place of h, Δy is used in place of k. Then clearly

$$k = f(x_0 + h) - f(x_0)$$

and

$$\frac{k}{h} = \frac{f(x_0 + h) - f(x_0)}{h}$$

This ratio is called a difference quotient. Its intuitive meaning can be grasped from the geometrical interpretation of the graph of $y = f(x)$. Let A and B be the points (x_0, y_0), $(x_0 + h, y_0 + k)$, respectively, as in Fig. 1. Draw the secant AB and the lines AC and CB, parallel to the x and y axes, respectively, so that $h = AC$, $k = CB$. Then the differential quotient k/h equals the tangent of angle BAC and is therefore, by definition, the slope of the secant AB. It is evident that if an insect were crawling along the curve from A to B, the abscissa x would always increase along its path but the ordinate y would first increase, slow down, then decrease. Thus, y varies with respect to x at different rates between A and B. If a second insect crawled from A to B along the secant, the ordinate y would vary at a constant rate, equal to the difference quotient k/h, with respect to the abscissa x. As the two insects start and end at the same points, the differential quotient may be regarded as the average rate of change of $y = f(x)$ with respect to x in the interval AC.

If the limit of the ratio k/h exists as h approaches 0, this limit is called the derivative of y with respect to x, evaluated at $x = x_0$. For example, let $y = x^2$ and $x = 3$, so that $y = 0$. Then $9 + k = (3 + h)^2$; $k = (3 + h)^2 - 9 = 6h + h^2$; $k/h = 6 + h$; and $\lim_{h \to 0} k/h = 6$. Referring back to Fig. 1, the secant AB pivots around A and approaches a limiting position, the tangent AT, as h approaches 0. The derivative of y with respect to x, at $x = x_0$, may be interpreted as the slope of the tangent AT, and this slope is defined as the slope of the curve $y = f(x)$ at $x = x_0$. Further, the derivative of y with respect to x, at $x = x_0$, may be

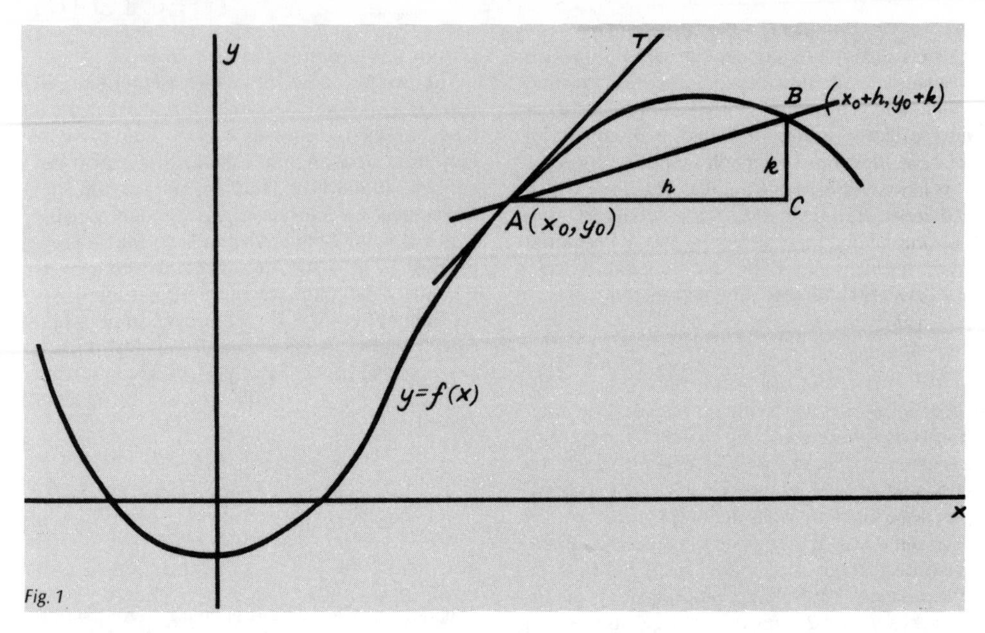

Fig. 1

interpreted as the instantaneous rate of change of y with respect to x at x_0.

If the derivative of y with respect to x is found for all values of x (in its domain) for which the derivative is defined, a new function is obtained, the derivative of y with respect to x. If $y = f(x)$, the new function is written as y' or $f'(x)$, D_xy or $D_xf(x)$, $\frac{dy}{dx}$ or $\frac{df(x)}{dx}$. Thus, if $y = x^2$, $y + k = (x + h)^2$; $k = (x + h)^2 - x^2 = 2xh + h^2$; $k/h = 2x + h$, whence $D_xx^2 = \lim_{h \to 0} k/h = 2x$. Thus, as before, $y' = f'(x) = 6$ at $x = 3$, or $f'(3) = 6$; also, $f'(2) = 4$, $f'(0) = 0$, and $f'(-2) = -4$.

As the derivative $f'(x)$ of a function $f(x)$ of x is itself a function of x, its derivative with respect to x can be found; it is called the second (order) derivative of y with respect to x, and is designated by any one of the symbols y'' or $f''(x)$, D_x^2y or $D_x^2f(x)$, $\frac{d^2y}{dx^2}$ or $\frac{d^2f(x)}{dx^2}$. Third- and higher-order derivatives are similarly designated.

Every application of differential calculus stems directly or indirectly from one or both of the two interpretations of the derivative as the slope of the tangent or curve and as the rate of change of the dependent variable with respect to the independent variable. In a detailed study of the subject, rules and methods developed by the limit process are provided for rapid calculation of the derivatives of various functions directly by means of various known formulas. Differentiation is the name given to the process of finding a derivative.

Differential calculus provides a method of finding the slope of the tangent to a curve at a certain point; related rates of change, such as the rate at which the area of a circle increases (in square feet per minute) in terms of the radius (in feet) and the rate at which the radius increases (in feet per minute); velocities (rates of change of distance with respect to time) and accelerations (rates of change of velocities with respect to time, therefore represented as second derivatives of distance with respect to time) of points moving on straight lines or other curves; and absolute and relative maxima and minima.

Integral Calculus. Let $y = f(x)$ be a function defined for all x's in the interval $[a, b]$, that is, the set of x's from $x = a$ to $x = b$, including a and b, where $a < b$ (suitable modifications can be made in the definitions to follow for more restricted ranges or domains). Let $x_0, x_1, \ldots, x_n$ be a sequence of values of x such that $a = x_0 < x_1 < x_2 < \ldots < x_{n-1} < x_n = b$, and let $h_1 = x_1 - x_0$, $h_2 = x_2 - x_1, \ldots, h_n = x_n - x_{n-1}$, in brief, $h_i = x_i - x_{i-1}$, where $i = 1, 2, \ldots, n$. The x's form a partition of the interval $[a, b]$; an h with a value not exceeded by any other h is called the norm of the partition. Let n values of x, for example, $X_1, X_2, \ldots, X_n$, be chosen so that $x_{i-1} < X_i < x_i$, where $i = 1, 2, \ldots, n$. The sum of the area of the rectangles, indicated in Fig. 2, is given by

$$f(X_1)h_1 + f(X_2)h_2 + \ldots + f(X_n)h_n,$$

usually abbreviated to $\sum_{i=1}^{n} f(X_i)h_i$. (Σ is the Greek capital letter *sigma.*) Aside from the given function $f(x)$ and the given a and b, the value of the sum clearly depends on n and on the choices of the x_i's and X_i's. In particular, if, after the x_i's are chosen, the X_i's are chosen so that $f(X_i)$, for each i, is a maximum in the interval $[x_{i-1}, x_i]$ (that is, no ordinate from x_{i-1} to x_i exceeds the ordinate at X_i), the sum is called an upper sum; similarly, if, after the x_i's are chosen, the X_i's are chosen so that $f(X_i)$, for each i, is a minimum in the interval $[x_{i-1}, x_i]$, the sum is called a lower sum. It can be proved that the upper and lower sums will have limits, $\bar{S}$ and $\underline{S}$, respectively, as the norm approaches 0. If $\bar{S}$ and $\underline{S}$ are equal and have the common value S, S is called the definite integral of $f(x)$ from a to b and is written

$$S = \int_a^b f(x)\,dx$$

The symbol $\int$ is an elongated S (for sum); the $f(x)\,dx$ is suggested by a term $f(X_i)h_i = f(X_i)\,\Delta x_i$ of the sum which is used in defining the definite integral.

If $y = g(x)$, then by differentiation $y' = g'(x)$. Let $g'(x) = f(x)$, and C be any constant. Then $f(x)$ is also the derivative of $g(x) + C$. The expression $g(x) + C$ is called the antiderivative of $f(x)$, or the indefinite integral of $f(x)$, and it is represented by

$$\int f(x)dx = g(x) + C$$

The dual use of the term *integral* is justified by one of the fundamental theorems of calculus, namely, if $g(x)$ is an antiderivative of $f(x)$, then, under suitable restrictions on $f(x)$ and $g(x)$,

$$\int_a^b f(x)dx = g(b) - g(a)$$

The process of finding either an indefinite or a definite integral of a function $f(x)$ is called integration; the fundamental theorem relates differentiation and integration.

If the antiderivative, $g(x)$, of $f(x)$ is not readily obtainable or is not known, the definite integral $\int_a^b f(x)dx$ can be approximated by the trapezoidal rule, $\frac{b-a}{2}\,[f(a) + f(b)]$ or by the more accurate Simpson's rule:

$$\frac{b-a}{6}\left[f(a) + 4f\left(\frac{a+b}{2}\right) + f(b)\right]$$

If $|b - a|$ is small, Simpson's rule gives a fairly close result. If $|b - a|$ is large, a good approximation can be obtained by dividing the interval from a to b into a number of small intervals and applying Simpson's rule to the subintervals.

Integral calculus involves the inverse process of finding the derivative of a function, that is, it is the process of finding the function itself when its derivative is known. For example, integral calculus makes it possible to find the equation of a curve if the slope of the tangent is known at an arbitrary point; to find distance in terms of time if the velocity (or acceleration) is known; and to find the equation of a curve if its curvature is known. Integral calculus can also be used to find the lengths of curves, the areas of plane and curved surfaces, volumes of solids of revolution,

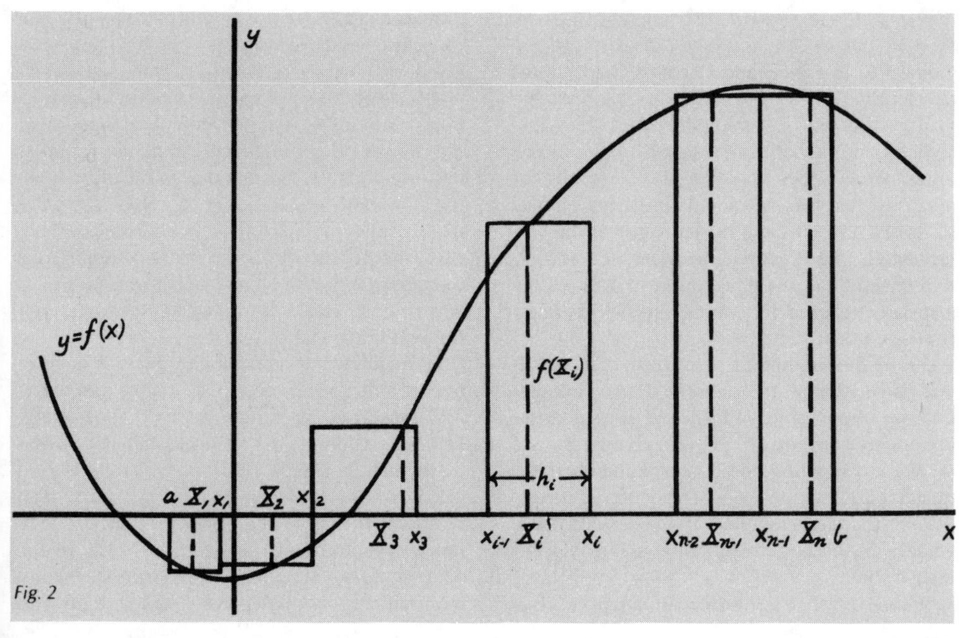

Fig. 2

centroids, moments of inertia, and total mass and total force.

Differential Equations. Calculus leads directly to the branch of mathematics called differential equations, which is extremely useful in engineering and in the physical sciences. An ordinary differential equation is an equation involving an independent variable, a dependent variable (one or both of these two may be missing), and one or more derivatives (at least one derivative must be present). Many physical laws or statements are initially expressed as differential equations. For example, the law that the acceleration of gravity is a constant g can be expressed mathematically by the differential equation $d^2x/dt^2 = g$; the principle that the rate of disintegration of radium is proportional to the amount present is expressed as $dR/dt = -kR$. A differential equation is solved if an equivalent equation is found involving only the independent and dependent variables.

This article has considered functions of a single independent variable only. Partial derivatives, multiple integrals, and partial differential equations are defined and studied in investigating functions of two or more independent variables.

Development of Calculus. The English and German mathematicians, respectively, Isaac Newton and Gottfried Wilhelm Leibniz invented calculus in the 17th century, but isolated results about its fundamental problems had been known for thousands of years. For example, the Egyptians discovered the rule for the volume of a pyramid as well as an approximation of the area of a circle. In ancient Greece, Archimedes proved that if c is the circumference and d the diameter of a circle, then $3\frac{1}{7}\ d < c < 3\frac{10}{71}\ d$. His proof extended the method of inscribed and circumscribed figures developed by the Greek astronomer and mathematician Eudoxus. Archimedes used the same technique for his other results on areas and volumes. Archimedes discovered his results by means of heuristic arguments involving parallel slices of the figures and the law of the lever. Unfortunately, his treatise *The Method* was only rediscovered in the 19th century, so later mathematicians believed that the Greeks deliberately concealed their secret methods.

During the late middle ages in Europe, mathematicians studied translations of Archimedes' treatises from Arabic. At the same time, philosophers were studying problems of change and the infinite, such as the addition of infinitely many quantities. Greek thinkers had seen only contradictions there, but medieval thinkers aided mathematics by making the infinite philosophically respectable.

By the early 17th century, mathematicians had developed methods for finding areas and volumes of a great variety of figures. In his *Geometry by Indivisibles,* the Italian mathematician F. B. Cavalieri (1598–1647), a student of the Italian physicist and astronomer Galileo, expanded on the work of the German astronomer Johannes Kepler on measuring volumes. He used what he called "indivisible magnitudes" to investigate areas under the curves $y - x^n$, $n = 1 \ldots 9$. Also, his theorem on the volumes of figures contained between parallel planes (now called Cavalieri's theorem) was known all over Europe. At about the same time, the French mathematician René Descartes' *La Géométrie* appeared. In this important work, Descartes showed how to use algebra to describe curves and obtain an algebraic analysis of geometric problems. A codiscoverer of this analytic geometry was the French mathematician Pierre de Fermat, who also discovered a method of finding the greatest or least value of some algebraic expressions—a method close to those now used in differential calculus.

About 20 years later, the English mathematician John Wallis (1616–1703) published *The Arithmetic of Infinites,* in which he extrapolated from patterns that held for finite processes to get formulas for infinite processes. His colleague at Cambridge University was Newton's teacher, the English mathematician Isaac Barrow (1630–77), who published a book that stated geometrically the inverse relationship between problems of finding tangents and areas, a relationship known today as the fundamental theorem of calculus.

Although many other mathematicians of the time came close to discovering calculus, the real founders were Newton and Leibniz. Newton's discovery (1665–66) combined infinite sums (infinite series), the binomial (q.v.) theorem for fractional exponents, and the algebraic expression of the inverse relation between tangents and areas into methods we know today as calculus. Newton, however, was reluctant to publish, so Leibniz became recognized as a codiscoverer because he published his discovery of differential calculus in 1684 and of integral calculus in 1686. It was Leibniz, also, who replaced Newton's symbols with those familiar today.

In the following years, one problem that led to new results and concepts was that of describing mathematically the motion of a vibrating string. Leibniz's students, the Bernoulli family of Swiss mathematicians (*see* BERNOULLI, DANIEL), used calculus to solve this and other problems, such as finding the curve of quickest descent connecting two given points in a vertical plane. In the 18th century, the great Swiss-Russian mathematician Leonhard Euler, who had studied with

Johann Bernoulli (1667–1748), wrote his *Introduction to the Analysis of Infinites,* which summarized known results and also contained much new material, such as a strictly analytic treatment of trigonometric and exponential functions.

Despite these advances in technique, calculus remained without logical foundations. Only in 1821 did the French mathematician A. L. Cauchy succeed in giving a secure foundation to the subject by his theory of limits, a purely arithmetic theory that did not depend on geometric intuition or infinitesimals. Cauchy then showed how this could be used to give a logical account of the ideas of continuity, derivatives, integrals, and infinite series. In the next decade, the Russian mathematician N. I. Lobachevsky and German mathematician P. G. L. Dirichlet (1805–59) both gave the definition of a function as a correspondence between two sets of real numbers, and the logical foundations of calculus were completed by the German mathematician J. W. R. Dedekind (1831–1916) in his theory of real numbers, in 1872. J.Si.; J.Le.B.

For further information on this topic, see the Bibliography in volume 28, sections 367–68, 371.

CALCUTTA, city, E India, capital of West Bengal State, on the Hooghly R., near the Bay of Bengal. The hub of a populous metropolitan area, it is a major port and the chief commercial, financial, and manufacturing center of E India. The principal manufactures of the city include jute products, processed food, silk and cotton textiles, iron and steel, chemicals, electric and transportation equipment, and rubber goods.

One of the world's most crowded and colorful cities, Calcutta is located close to sea level in a formerly swampy area. It has a subtropical climate known for its high heat and humidity during the summer rainy season. The city's main business district centers on Dalhousie Square, situated just E of the busy waterfront. To the S is an area of parkland and elegant Victorian office buildings and residences, built during the long period of British control. Housing in Calcutta is in critically short supply, and thousands of people live on the streets or in crowded slums of mud huts lacking adequate sanitary facilities. The city's principal suburbs, some linked to Calcutta by a subway system built chiefly in the 1970s and still being expanded in the mid-80s, are Howrah (site of the region's main railroad station), Garden Reach, South Suburban, Behala, South Dum Dum, Bally, Baranagar, and Barrackpore.

Points of Interest. Calcutta's major landmark is the Maidan, a large park along the Hooghly containing many fine drives, a racecourse, a cricket ground, and historic Fort William (1696, rebuilt 1757). To the SE is the domed, marble Victoria Memorial (1921), commemorating Queen Victoria's rule of India. Other places of interest are fashionable Jawaharlal Nehru (formerly Chowringhee) Road, the city's main thoroughfare; the Writers' Building (on Dalhousie Square), once the headquarters of the British East India Co.; the old Government House (now called Raj Bhavan); the Indian Museum, with noted displays on archaeology and natural history; the Birla Industrial and Technological Museum; and botanical gardens. Religious structures in Calcutta include Saint Paul's Cathedral, the Hindu Kali Temple, the Muslim Nakhoda Mosque, and the Parasnath Jain Temple. The University of Calcutta (1857), Jadavpur University (1955), Rabindra Bharati University (1962), and the Institute of Radiophysics and Electronics (1949) are here.

History. Modern Calcutta was founded in 1690 by the British trader Job Charnock (fl. 1655–93) as a trading post of the British East India Co. Fort William was built to protect the post in 1696, and three older villages—Kalikata (later altered by the British to Calcutta), Sutanati, and Govindpur—were purchased from the Mughal emperor in 1698. The city became famous in 1756, when Siraj-ud-Dawlah (1732–57), nawab of Bengal, captured it and stifled a number of British residents to death in a small guardroom—called the Black Hole of Calcutta (q.v.)—of Fort William. The city was recaptured by Robert Clive in 1757 and subsequently was the capital of British India from 1772 to 1912, when it was replaced by Delhi.

As the British expanded their control over the Indian subcontinent in the late 18th and 19th centuries, Calcutta developed as a busy port and industrial center. Millions came from other parts of India in search of greater economic opportunities. Unemployment and poverty, already major social problems in the early 20th century, became increasingly acute after the partition of British India in 1947, when large numbers of Hindus from East Pakistan sought refuge in Calcutta. Pop. (1981, greater city) 9,194,018.

For further information on this topic, see the Bibliography in volume 28, section 1082.

CALDER, Alexander (1898–1976), American sculptor of great vitality and versatility, best known for his creation of mobile sculpture, and generally regarded as one of the 20th century's most innovative and witty artists.

Calder, the son and grandson of distinguished American sculptors, was born July 22, 1898, in Philadelphia. He graduated from Stevens Institute of Technology in 1919 with a degree in mechanical engineering. In 1923 Calder enrolled at the Art Students League in New York City; in the

Black Widow *(1959), by Alexander Calder, a stabile of painted sheet steel.*
Collection, The Museum of Modern Art, New York, Mrs. Simon Guggenheim Fund

fall of 1926 he moved to Paris. His sculptures in wire—satirical portraits as well as delightful miniature circus figures (1927-32, Whitney Museum of American Art, New York City)—brought him worldwide recognition. He returned to the U.S. in 1933; in later years he divided his time between the U.S. and France, with numerous highly successful exhibitions in Paris and New York City.

In the early 1930s Calder experimented with abstraction, first as a painter and later as a sculptor. He was influenced by his meetings with such European abstract artists as Joan Miró, Jean Arp, and Piet Mondrian. He also began to experiment with motion, a process that led to his development of the two modes of sculpture for which he is famous, the mobile and the stabile.

Calder's mobiles (so named by the French Dada artist Marcel Duchamp) are suspended, elegantly balanced arrangements of abstract, organic forms. The stabiles (so named by Arp) are stationary abstract forms that frequently convey a humorous suggestion of animal shapes. Although Calder's stone, wood, and bronze sculptures; his drawings; and his later paintings (almost exclusively gouaches) are important, his reputation rests primarily upon his mobiles and stabiles. These works, increasingly monumental, achieved an enthusiastic popular acceptance seldom enjoyed by abstract art; this led to numerous important commissions following World War II. Giant stabiles and mobiles by Calder grace dozens of public buildings and plazas in Brussels, Chicago, Mexico City, Montréal, New York City, and many other cities. They culminate in his last work, the huge red-and-black mobile (1976) suspended in the multistory central court of the National Gallery of Art's East Wing (completed 1978) in Washington, D.C. Calder died Nov. 11, 1976, in New York City, just after supervising the installation of his largest retrospective exhibition, at the Whitney Museum of American Art.

CALDERÓN DE LA BARCA Y HENAO, Pedro (1600-81), Spanish dramatist and poet, the last prominent figure of the golden age of Spanish literature.

Calderón was born in Madrid, on Jan. 7, 1600, and educated at the Jesuit college in Madrid and at the University of Salamanca. At the age of 23 he became a playwright and competed successfully in a poetry contest held in honor of St. Isidore, the patron saint of Madrid. His reputation as a playwright grew rapidly, and upon the death of the Spanish dramatist Lope de Vega in 1635, Calderón was recognized as the foremost dramatist of the period. In 1636 his brother José edited a volume of his plays that contained *Life Is a Dream* (1635; trans. 1925), generally regarded as his masterpiece and as one of the greatest of European dramas. The drama is outstanding for its high moral concepts and philosophic symbolism. The thesis expressed by the title is convincingly unfolded in religious terms.

In 1636 King Philip IV, who had commissioned

Calderón to write a series of plays for the royal theater, made him a knight of the Order of Santiago. He joined (1640) in a military campaign to suppress the Catalan revolt against the Crown. During the following decade of his life, it is known only that he was ordained in 1651.

Calderón took up residence as a prebendary of Toledo Cathedral in 1653 and was appointed honorary chaplain to the king in 1666. Subsequently, he devoted himself chiefly to writing *autos sacramentales,* allegorical plays that emphasized the moral aspects of life and dramatized in an original way the mystery of the Holy Eucharist. He died in Madrid on May 25, 1681.

Calderón is considered one of the greatest of Spanish dramatists, equally distinguished for his religious and his secular plays. He gave artistic form to the traditional *autos sacramentales* and became the acknowledged master of this type of religious drama. In these plays Calderón vividly dramatized abstract concepts of Roman Catholic theology through personification, thus making them real to his audience. Two of his plays in this genre, *El gran teatro del mundo* (The Great Theater of the World, 1649) and *La cena de Baltasar* (Belshazzar's Feast, c. 1634), are still performed in Spain. The chief themes of Calderón's secular plays are devotion to the church and exaltation of

Pedro Calderón de la Barca, depicted in an 18th-century engraving by Mariano Brandi. Bettmann Archive

the Castilian code of honor requiring husband, father, or brother to punish the transgressions of an unfaithful woman. The ways in which he treats that code are the basis for the designation "Calderonian," which in Europe is used to describe dramatic conflicts of honor arising from a wife's infidelity or the vaguest suspicion of it. Among the 140 plays and sketches Calderón wrote for the secular stage are dramas based on historical and legendary material, such as *The Mayor of Zalamea* (1642; trans. 1906) and *La hija del aire* (The Daughter of the Air, 1653); dramas of intrigue, such as *La dama duende* (The Phantom Lady, 1629) and *Casa con dos puertas* (House with Two Doors, 1629); dramas of jealousy and male honor, such as *El médico de su honra* (The Doctor of His Own Honor, c. 1629); the philosophical plays *El magico prodigioso* (The Prodigious Magician, 1637) and *Life Is a Dream;* and mythological dramas, including *La estatua de Prometeo* (The Statue of Prometheus, 1669).

CALDWELL, Erskine Preston (1903–87), American novelist, born in White Oak, Ga., and educated at the universities of Virginia and Pennsylvania. He is best known for his novels and short stories that concern the poverty-stricken lives of black and white sharecroppers in rural Georgia. With vivid humor, an earthy indignation, and considerable profanity, he describes the unforgettable family of Jeeter Lester in *Tobacco Road* (1932), his most famous novel. Dramatized in 1933, the play had a seven-year run on Broadway; it was also made into a successful film (1940).

CALEB (Heb. *keleb,* "dog"), in the Old Testament (see Num. 13, 14, 34; Josh. 14–15), member of the Israelite tribe of Judah. After Moses and Aaron had led the Israelites out of Egypt to the borders of Canaan, the promised land, Moses appointed Caleb and others, including Joshua, to reconnoiter the land. All but Caleb and Joshua brought back a false and discouraging report on the walled cities and warlike inhabitants of Canaan. On the basis of the false report, the Israelites refused to enter Canaan, defying their leaders and God. God, however, put down the revolt and ordained that no Israelite over the age of 20 who had spoken out against him should live to enter Canaan. He also caused the immediate death of all who had gone ahead to spy out the land of Canaan, excepting Caleb and Joshua. Before he died, Moses distributed the lands of Canaan among the tribes, and Joshua and Caleb led in their conquest.

CALEDONIA, ancient Roman name for the country north of the firths of Forth and Clyde in Britain. Constituting most of present-day Scotland, the region was inhabited by the Picts, a warlike people who successfully resisted conquest by the Romans. In poetic and rhetorical usage, the name is a synonym for Scotland.

CALENDAR, system of measuring time for the needs of civil life, by dividing time into days, weeks, months, and years. Calendar divisions are based on the movements of the earth and the regular appearances of the sun and the moon. A day (q.v.) is the average time required for one rotation of the earth on its axis. The measurement of a year (q.v.) is based on one revolution of the earth around the sun and is called a seasonal, tropical, or solar year. A solar year contains 365 days, 5 hr, 48 min, and 45.5 sec. A month (q.v.) was originally calculated by ancient peoples as the time between two full moons, or the number of days required for the moon to circle the earth (29.5 days). This measurement, called a synodic, or lunar month, resulted in a lunar year of 354 days, 11¼ days shorter than a solar year. In modern calendars, however, the number of days in a month is not based on the phases of the moon. The length of the months is approximately one-twelfth of a year (28 to 31 days) and is adjusted to fit the 12 months into a solar year. For information concerning the names or arrangement of the months, see the articles on each of the 12 months. The week (q.v.) was derived from the Judeo-Christian tradition requiring rest from labor every seventh day. It is not based on a natural phenomenon. The Romans named the days of the week in honor of the sun, moon, and various planets.

The variations among the many calendars in use from ancient to modern times have been caused by the inaccuracy of the earliest determinations of the duration of the year, together with the fact that a year cannot be divided evenly by any of the other time units: days, weeks, or months. The earliest calendars based on lunar months eventually failed to agree with the seasons. A month occasionally had to be intercalated, or added, to reconcile lunar months with the solar year. A calendar that makes periodic adjustments of this kind is a lunisolar calendar.

Ancient Calendars. The ancient Babylonians had a lunisolar calendar of 12 lunar months of 30 days each, and they added extra months when necessary to keep the calendar in line with the seasons of the year. The ancient Egyptians were the first to replace the lunar calendar with a calendar based on the solar year. They measured the solar year as 365 days, divided into 12 months of 30 days each, with 5 extra days at the end. About 238 BC King Ptolemy III ordered that an extra day be added to every fourth year, similar to the modern leap year. In ancient Greece a lunisolar calendar was in use, with a year of 354 days. The Greeks were the first to intercalate extra months into the calendar on a scientific basis, adding months at specific intervals in a cycle of solar years.

The Roman Calendar. The original Roman calendar, introduced about the 7th century BC, had 10 months with 304 days in a year that began with March. Two more months, January and February,

Aztec calendar stone, now in the National Museum of Anthropology, Mexico City. Dating from 1479, it represents the solar calendar derived from the Mayan system of 400 BC. In the center is the head of the sun god; around it, in concentric circles, is the history of the world according to Aztec mythology. The stone is 3.9 m (13 ft) in diameter and weighs 21 metric tons. George Holton–Photo Researchers, Inc.

were added later in the 7th century BC, but because the months were only 29 or 30 days long, an extra month had to be intercalated approximately every second year. The days of the month were designated by the awkward method of counting backward from three dates: the calends, or first of the month; the ides, or middle of the month, falling on the 13th of some months and the 15th of others; and the nones, or 9th day before the ides. The Roman calendar became hopelessly confused when officials to whom the addition of days and months was entrusted abused their authority to prolong their terms of office or to hasten or delay elections.

In 45 BC Julius Caesar, upon the advice of the Greek astronomer Sosigenes (fl. 1st cent. BC), decided to use a purely solar calendar. This calendar, known as the Julian calendar, fixed the normal year at 365 days, and the leap year, every fourth year, at 366 days. Leap year is so named because the extra day causes any date after February in a leap year to "leap" over one day in the week and to occur two days later in the week than it did in the previous year, rather than just one day later as in a normal year. The Julian calendar also established the order of the months and the days of the week as they exist in present-day calendars. In 44 BC Julius Caesar changed the name of the month Quintilis to Julius (July), after himself. The month Sextilis was renamed Augustus (August) in honor of the Roman emperor Caesar Augustus, who succeeded Julius Caesar. Some authorities maintain that Augustus established the length of the months we use today.

The Gregorian Calendar. The Julian year was 11 min and 14 sec longer than the solar year. This discrepancy accumulated until by 1582 the vernal equinox (*see* ECLIPTIC) occurred 10 days early and church holidays did not occur in the appropriate seasons. To make the vernal equinox occur on March 21, as it had in AD 325, the year of the First Council of Nicaea, Pope Gregory XIII issued a decree dropping 10 days from the calendar. To prevent further displacement he instituted a calendar, known as the Gregorian calendar, that provided that century years divisible evenly by 400 should be leap years and that all other century years should be common years. Thus, 1600 was a leap year, but 1700 and 1800 were common years.

The Gregorian calendar, or New Style calendar, was slowly adopted throughout Europe. It is used today throughout most of the Western world and in parts of Asia. When the Gregorian calendar was adopted in Great Britain in 1752, another correction of an 11-day discrepancy was made; the day after Sept. 2, 1752, became September 14. The British also adopted January 1 as the day when a new year begins. The Soviet Union adopted the Gregorian calendar in 1918, and Greece adopted it in 1923 for civil purposes, but many countries affiliated with the Greek church retain the Julian, or Old Style, calendar for the celebration of church feasts.

The Gregorian calendar is also called the Christian calendar because it uses the birth of Jesus Christ as a starting date. Dates of the Christian era (*see* CHRONOLOGY) are often designated AD (Lat. *anno domini,* "in the year of our Lord") and BC (before Christ). Although the birth of Christ was originally given as Dec. 25, 1 BC, modern scholars now place it about 4 BC.

Because the Gregorian calendar still entails months of unequal length, so that dates and days of the week vary through time, numerous proposals have been made for a more practical, reformed calendar. Such proposals include a fixed calendar of 13 equal months and a universal calendar of 4 identical quarterly periods. Thus far, none has been adopted (*see* CALENDAR REFORM).

Religious Calendars. As indicated, the Gregorian calendar is basically a Christian calendar. The official Christian church calendar is a table containing the holy days, saints' days, and festivals of the church, with the dates of the civil calendar on which they occur. These include the fixed feasts, such as Christmas, and the movable feasts, which depend on the date of Easter. The most important early church calendar was compiled by Furius Dionisius Philocalus about 354. After the Reformation, the German Lutheran church retained the Roman calendar, as did the Church of England and some other Anglican churches. The calendar of the Protestant Episcopal church retains only those festivals that have a scriptural origin. The principal seasons of the church calendar observed by most Christians are, in order, Advent, Christmas, Epiphany, Lent, Easter, Ascension, Pentecost, and Trinity (qq.v.).

Several other calendars based on religious doctrine can also be described. For example, the Jewish calendar, derived from the ancient Hebrew calendar, has remained unchanged since about AD 900. It is the official calendar of the modern state of Israel and is used by Jewish people throughout the world as a religious calendar. The starting point of Hebrew chronology is the year 3761 BC, the date for the creation of the world as described in the Old Testament. The Jewish calendar is lunisolar, based on lunar months of 29 days alternating with 30 days. An extra month is intercalated every 3 years, based on a cycle of 19 years. Dates of the Jewish calendar are designated AM (Lat. *anno mundi,* "the year of the world") and BCE (before the common era).

Another major religious calendar is the Islamic calendar, a lunar one used in most Muslim countries. It is reckoned from AD 622, the day after the Hegira (q.v.), or flight of Mohammed from Mecca to Medina. The Islamic year consists of 12 lunar months. Thirty years constitute a cycle in which the 2d, 5th, 7th, 10th, 13th, 16th, 18th, 21st, 24th, 26th, and 29th years are leap years of 355 days; the others are common years of 354 days. The Islamic date corresponding to a date in the Gregorian calendar can be computed by the following rule, with a maximum error of one day: multiply 970,224 by the Islamic year, divide by 6 decimal places, and add 621.5774. The figure to the left of the decimal point is the year AD, and the decimal fraction multiplied by 365 is the day of the year.

For information concerning the Aztec calendar and Mayan calendar, *see* AZTEC; MAYA.

For further information on this topic, see the Bibliography in volume 28, section 388.

CALENDAR REFORM. Calendar improvements have often been proposed to correct defects in the Gregorian calendar. Suggestions for official reform of the calendar have all failed, however, probably because people resist changing their traditional economic, religious, and social activities. Critics of the Gregorian calendar point out that it has 12 months of unequal length; no month is exactly one-twelfth of a year; the number of weeks in the quarter-year and half-year is uneven; and dates and days of the week vary from one year to the next.

One of the best-known proposals for calendar reform is the so-called World Calendar that was considered, but not adopted, in the UN in 1954. This calendar is based on a 52-week, 364-day year starting on Sunday, January 1, with the 365th day, called Year-End Day, intercalated, or added, without date or day of the week. In leap years an extra Leap-Year Day, also without date or day of the week, is inserted at the end of the 26th week, between the last day of June and the first day of July. The first month of each quarter has 31 days, and all the others have 30 days. The chief disadvantage of this calendar is that the Year-End Day interferes with regular religious observances.

The International Fixed Calendar (Thirteen-Month Calendar) is a proposal based on a year divided into 13 months of 28 days each, with the 365th day a Year Day, belonging to no week or month. In leap years an extra Leap Day is added after June 28. Half-years contain exactly 26 seven-day weeks and quarter-years exactly 13 weeks. All Sundays occur on the 1st, 8th, 15th, and 22d of each month. The additional month, called Sol, is inserted as the seventh month between June and July. Although this calendar is uniform, it is criticized because national holidays would have to be changed.

A third fixed calendar, the Perpetual Calendar, has been proposed to the U.S. Congress without success. This calendar, like the World Calendar, has four 3-month quarters and adds an extra Year-End Day and Leap-Year Day. Monday is the first day of every week, and the quarters all begin on Monday, which is useful for business concerns.

CALENDULA, genus of ornamental, both annual and perennial plants belonging to the family Compositae (*see* COMPOSITE FLOWERS). Calendulas are native to temperate regions, particularly the Mediterranean, and the genus contains about 20 species. The plants have large yellow- or orange-rayed flower heads and alternate, generally oblong leaves. The best-known species is the pot marigold, *Calendula officinalis,* a popular garden plant in North America growing up to 61 cm (24 in) in height and having leaves 5 to 15 cm (2 to 6 in) long. The bright flower heads, up to 10 cm (4 in) in diameter, close at night. The petals of the pot marigold are used in cooking.

CALGARY, city, S Alberta, Canada, at the confluence of the Bow and the Elbow rivers; inc. as a city 1893. The largest city in the province, Calgary is a commercial, manufacturing, and transportation center for a region producing much petroleum and natural gas, grain, and cattle. The principal industries of the city are food processing, oil refining, tourism, and the manufacture of chemicals, building materials, and fertilizer. As the headquarters for more than 300 oil and natural gas companies, the city has become known as the Oil and Gas Capital of Canada.

The University of Calgary (1945), Mount Royal College (1910), and the Provincial Institute of Technology and Art (1916) are in Calgary. Among the city's points of interest are the Glenbow-Alberta Institute Museum and Art Gallery; the Calgary Centennial Planetarium; Husky Tower; Heritage Park, a reproduction of a late 19th-century village; the Calgary Zoo and Dinosaur Park; and the Southern Alberta Jubilee Auditorium. Calgary is the site of the Calgary Exhibition and Stampede, a rodeo and livestock show, first held in 1912 and an annual event since 1923.

The first settlement here, established in 1875, was an outpost for the North West Mounted Police called Fort Brisebois. In 1876 the post was renamed Fort Calgary, a name probably derived from a Gaelic term for "clear running water." The community grew after the arrival of the Canadian

Pacific Railway in 1883. In the 20th century the development of irrigated agriculture nearby, the discovery of the Turner Valley (1914) and Leduc (1947) oil and gas fields, and the construction of the Trans-Canada Highway further stimulated economic growth. The city's population increased tremendously after 1960. In 1988 Calgary was the site of the Winter Olympic Games. Pop. (1981) 592,743; (1986) 636,104.

John C. Calhoun National Archives

CALHOUN, John Caldwell (1782-1850), seventh vice-president of the U.S. (1825-32).

Calhoun was born on March 18, 1782, near Abbeville, S.C., and educated at Yale College (now Yale University). After serving in the South Carolina legislature, he was elected to the U.S. House of Representatives in 1811 and served three terms. In Congress he and the Speaker of the House, Henry Clay, in 1812 persuaded the House to declare war on Great Britain. From 1817 to 1825 Calhoun was secretary of war in the cabinet of President James Monroe. He was elected vice-president of the U.S. in 1824 under President John Quincy Adams. Calhoun was reelected in 1828, when Andrew Jackson won the presidency. In the course of his opposition to the high tariff of 1828, which benefited the industrial North but adversely affected the slaveholding South, Calhoun wrote an essay, *The South Carolina Exposition and Protest,* in which he asserted the right of the states to nullify federal laws. In 1832 Calhoun persuaded the South Carolina legislature to nullify the federal tariff acts of 1828 and 1832. Later in 1832 he became the first U.S. vice-president to resign; he was then named U.S. senator from South Carolina. A compromise tariff, proposed by Clay, resolved the nullification conflict.

The following year Calhoun and Senator Daniel Webster engaged in a historic debate in the Senate over slavery and states' rights. The opposing views expressed in this debate crystallized the theories of government of the opponents and supporters of slavery. Calhoun was secretary of state in the cabinet of President John Tyler in 1844-45. In the latter year he was reelected to the Senate, where he employed his great oratorical abilities to support the annexation of Texas and to defeat the Wilmot Proviso. He died in Washington, D.C., on March 31, 1850.

For further information on this person, see the section Biographies in the Bibliography in volume 28.

CALI, city, W Colombia, capital of Valle del Cauca Department, on the Cali R. Cali is a major transportation, commercial, and industrial center for the Cauca R. valley, where sugarcane, coffee, tobacco, cotton, cacao, bananas, rice, and corn are grown and cattle and hogs are raised. Coal mines are also in the region. In the city, textiles, clothing, shoes, pharmaceuticals, tobacco products, soap, cement, processed food, and furniture are manufactured.

Cali is the site of the University of Valle (1945) and Santiago University of Cali (1958). Also in the city are San Pedro Cathedral and the Church and Monastery of San Francisco. Cali was founded in 1536 by the Spanish conquistador Sebastian de Belalcázar (c. 1495-1551). Pop. (1985 prelim., greater city) 1,654,000.

CALICO, a plain-weave cotton fabric commonly printed with simple, two-colored designs or patterns and used to make colorful dresses and shirts. The fabric, one of the oldest textiles known, originated as a fine weave in Calicut (now Kozhikode), India, for which it was named. Calicoes were first imported into Europe from India during the Renaissance and since then have been manufactured in both Europe and the U.S. Calico was especially popular in America during the 19th century.

CALICUT. *See* KOZHIKODE.

CALIFORNIA, one of the Pacific Coast states of the U.S., bounded on the N by Oregon, on the E by Nevada and Arizona, on the S by the Mexican state of Baja California Norte, and on the W by the Pacific Ocean. The Colorado R. forms the S portion of its E border.

California entered the Union on Sept. 9, 1850, as the 31st state. Agriculture and mining have always been important to the economy of California. Industrial activity has expanded rapidly in the 20th century along with a booming population. By the 1980s California had a larger population than any other state and was the leading producer by value of both agricultural and manufactured goods. The name California was first given to the Baja California Peninsula by the Spanish explorer Hernán Cortés in the early 16th century and was applied by other explorers to more N areas. The word is derived from the name of an imaginary island in a popular Spanish romance of the time. California is called the Golden State.

LAND AND RESOURCES

California, with an area of 411,047 sq km (158,706 sq mi), is the third largest state in the U.S.; 46.6% of the land area is owned by the federal government. The state most resembles an arc; its extreme dimensions are about 1240 km (about 770 mi) from N to S and about 595 km (about 370 mi) from E to W. California has a great complexity of relief, with elevations from 86 m (282 ft) below sea level in Death Valley (the lowest point on the continent), to 4418 m (14,494 ft), atop Mt. Whitney, the highest peak in the conterminous states.

Physical Regions. In the NE corner of California is a segment of the Great Basin. Part of the Basin and Range Region, it includes the Warner Mts., Honey Lake Plain, and the volcanic Modoc Plateau. Farther S, separated by a spur of the Sierra Nevada, is another Basin and Range wedge. The N half of this wedge is also part of the Great Basin and is sometimes called the Trans-Sierra. The entire region contains worn mountain ranges separated by numerous low-lying arid basins, the most famous of which is Death Valley. The Mojave Desert alone occupies approximately one-fifth of the state. In the Colorado Desert to the S, the fertile soils of the Imperial Valley are irrigated and productive.

In the N central part of the state is the Cascade Range, which extends N into British Columbia. It is a volcanic tableland capped by cones, the most prominent of which is the extinct Mt. Shasta (4317 m/14,162 ft). The active volcano Lassen Peak (3187 m/10,457 ft) protrudes from the core of ancient Mt. Tehama.

South of the Cascades is the Sierra Nevada, a rugged granitic mountain range. Its dramatic E escarpment rises sharply above the deserts of the Great Basin. This region is of much importance to California, as a source of numerous rivers and for its scenic beauty. Six peaks, including Mt. Whitney, exceed about 4270 m (about 14,010 ft).

The Central Valley, wedged between the Sierra

Sand dunes in Death Valley, a desert region, in southwestern California, in which is the lowest point in the U.S., 86 m (282 ft) below sea level. Carl R. Mappes

Coastline at Santa Barbara, a residential city and popular resort in southern California. Cecil W. Stoughton

Nevada on the E and the Coast Ranges on the W, is a downfolded basin with deep fertile alluvial soils. This sizable lowland supports most of the agriculture for which California is renowned.

Occupying much of NW California are the Klamath Mts. This rugged mass has been cut by the Klamath R. and its tributaries.

South of the Klamath Mts. and W of the Central Valley are the California Coast Ranges. This region consists basically of low parallel (N-S) ranges, interspersed with structural depressions, the best known of which are the Salinas Valley and the lowlands around San Francisco Bay.

The Lower California Ranges of S California make up a region that includes two major landform areas. Along its N portion are the Transverse Ranges, which unlike other ranges in the state trend along an E-W axis. The two major masses here are the San Gabriel and San Bernardino mountains. A structural depression, the Los Angeles Basin, separates the Transverse Ranges from the Peninsular Ranges to the S. These are granitic ranges that differ from the Sierra Nevada in their lower elevations and absence of glacial features. Two island groups are found offshore, the rocky Farallon Islands off the N coast and the larger Channel, or Santa Barbara, Islands off the S coast. California's coastline is geologically unstable, with many faults, or fractures, the most prominent of which is the San Andreas Fault.

Rivers and Lakes. The longest river in California, the Sacramento, rises near Mt. Shasta and flows S into San Francisco Bay. The second longest is the San Joaquin R., which rises in the Sierra Nevada and flows into the Sacramento R. near its mouth. Both rivers lie mostly in the Central Valley and with their numerous tributaries drain the Sierra Nevada, the Cascades, and much of the NE. The Colorado R., situated along the SE border, receives no additional volume within California. NW rivers, principally the Klamath, Smith, and Eel, have small drainage basins but heavy seasonal volume. California has numerous small lakes; among the few larger lakes are Lake Tahoe (shared with Nevada), Clear Lake, Honey Lake, and Mono Lake. Sizable artificial bodies of water include Shasta Lake and Oroville Reservoir. The Salton Sea, which lies below sea level, was formed (1905–07) by floodwaters of the Colorado R. Extensive water transfer projects have been built in California for both irrigation and supply. Most water is taken from the well-watered N to the dry S, but also from the Sierra in the E to San Francisco and Los Angeles.

Climate. Climate in California varies widely, but is essentially subtropical; in almost all areas pre-

Woodland scene Yosemite National Park, which contains stands of some of the oldest and tallest timber in North America. Cecil W. Stoughton–National Park Service

cipitation is concentrated in the winter months. Favored by maritime influences and summer fog, the Pacific coast enjoys mild winters and relatively cool summers. NW California receives some of the nation's heaviest winter-season precipitation. By contrast, the coast S of Los Angeles has less than 200 mm (less than 8 in) of rain a year. Inland the climate becomes more continental; the Central Valley gets desert hot on summer afternoons, but winters are mild. The E California mountain ranges are dry and range from mild summers and cold winters in the N to extremely hot summers in the S. Death Valley's highest recorded temperature of 56.7° C (134° F) in 1913 is near the world record. Increasingly cooler climates are found at higher elevations in the mountains. The state's lowest recorded temperature was −42.8° C (−45° F), recorded in 1937 N of Lake Tahoe.

Plants and Animals. Forest covers about 40% of California's total land area, somewhat less than half of which is commercially valuable. Approximately 50% of the commercial-forest area is part of the national forest system. No state approaches the plant variety of California; approximately 40% of species found naturally in the U.S. are indigenous to California.

California's richest forests are found in the N and NW highlands. Forests of coast redwoods, the world's tallest trees, are found near the ocean. Inland in the Klamath Mts. Douglas fir predominates. Farther E are pine forests, with the western yellow pine especially widespread. Stands of sierra redwood, or giant sequoia, are found in the Sierra Nevada; alpine meadows are found here above the timberline. California is well known for its spring-blooming wild flowers; California poppy and lupine are among the most common.

In the coastal areas S of San Francisco Bay, coast sage and grasslands are typical, replaced inland by chaparral, consisting of drought-tolerant evergreen shrubs. Over much of the Coast Ranges at high elevations the typical vegetation consists of groves of live oak amid grasslands. At elevations higher than 1970 m (6000 ft), forests include both conifers and oaks. Before the advent of agricultural development much of the Central Valley was covered with grasses, with a lusher prairie vegetation in the more humid Sacramento Valley.

The SE deserts contain indigo bushes, various species of cacti and shrubs, creosote bushes, and the Joshua tree, a giant lily with white flowers.

California's diversity of vegetation furnishes habitats for many different animals. In the SE

Cities and Towns

City	Map
Adelanto	H 9
Alameda	J 2
Alamo	K 2
Albany	J 2
Alhambra	C 10
Altadena	C 10
Alturas ⊙	E 2
Alum Rock	L 3
Anaheim	D 11
Anderson	C 3
Antioch	L 1
Apple Valley	H 9
Arcadia	D 10
Arcata	A 3
Arden	B 8
Arroyo Grande	E 8
Artesia	C 11
Arvin	G 8
Ashland	K 2
Atascadero	E 8
Atherton	K 3
Atwater	E 6
Auburn ⊙	C 8
Azusa	D 10
Bakersfield ⊙	F 8
Baldwin Park	D 10
Banning	J 10
Barstow	H 9
Beaumont	J 10
Bell	C 11
Bellflower	C 11
Bell Gardens	C 11
Belmont	J 3
Benicia	K 1
Berkeley	J 2
Beverly Hills	B 10
Bishop	G 6
Bloomington	E 10
Blythe	L 10
Brawley	K 11
Brea	D 11
Brentwood	L 2
Bridgeport ⊙	F 5
Brisbane	J 2
Broderick	B 8
Bryte	B 8
Buena Park	D 11
Burbank	C 10
Burlingame	J 3
Calexico	K 11
Camarillo	F 9
Campbell	K 3
Canoga Park	B 10
Cardiff-by-the-Sea	H 10
Carlsbad	H 10
Carmel	C 7
Carmichael	C 8
Carpinteria	F 9
Carson	C 11
Castro Valley	K 2
Cerritos	C 11
Chatsworth	B 10
Chico	D 4
China Lake	H 8
Chino	D 10
Chula Vista	J 11
Citrus Heights	C 8
Claremont	D 10
Clovis	F 7
Coachella	J 10
Colton	E 10
Colusa ⊙	C 4
Commerce	C 10
Compton	C 11
Concord	K 1
Corcoran	F 7
Corning	C 4
Corona	E 11
Coronado	H 11
Corte Madera	J 2
Costa Mesa	D 11
Cotati	C 5
Covina	D 10
Crescent City ⊙	A 2
Cucamonga (Ranch Cucamonga)	E 10
Cudahy	C 11
Culver City	B 10
Cupertino	K 3
Cypress	D 11
Daly City	H 2
Danville	K 2
Davis	B 8
Delano	F 8
Del Mar	H 11
Desert Hot Springs	J 9
Dinuba	F 7
Dixon	B 9
Downey	C 11
Downieville ⊙	E 4
Duarte	D 10
East Los Angeles	C 10
El Cajon	J 11
El Centro ⊙	K 11
El Cerrito	J 2
El Monte	D 10
El Paso de Robles (Paso Robles)	E 8
El Segundo	B 11
Encino	B 10
Enterprise	C 3
Escondido	H 10
Eureka ⊙	A 3
Exeter	F 7
Fairfax	H 1
Fairfield ⊙	K 1
Fair Oaks	C 8
Fallbrook	H 10
Fillmore	G 9
Folsom	C 8
Fontana	E 10
Fort Bragg	B 4
Fortuna	A 3
Foster City	J 2
Fountain Valley	D 11
Fremont	K 3
Fresno ⊙	F 7
Fullerton	D 11
Gardena	C 11
Garden Grove	D 11
Gilroy	D 6
Glendale	C 10
Glendora	D 10
Granada Hills	B 10
Grand Terrace	E 10
Grass Valley	D 4
Gridley	D 4
Grover City	E 8
Guadalupe	E 9
Gustine	D 6
Half Moon Bay	H 3
Hanford ⊙	F 7
Harbor City	C 11
Hawthorne	C 11
Hayward	K 2
Healdsburg	B 5
Hemet	H 10
Hercules	J 1
Hermosa Beach	B 11
Highland	H 9
Hillsborough	J 2
Hollister ⊙	D 7
Hollywood	C 10
Huntington Beach	C 11
Huntington Park	C 10
Imperial	K 11
Imperial Beach	H 11
Independence ⊙	H 7
Indio	J 10
Inglewood	B 11
Irvine	D 11
Isla Vista	F 9
Jackson ⊙	C 9
Kerman	E 7
King City	D 7
Kingsburg	F 7
La Canada	C 10
La Crescenta	C 10
Lafayette	K 2
Laguna Beach	G 10
Laguna Hills	D 11
Laguna Niguel	H 10
La Habra	D 11
La Jolla	H 11
Lake Arrowhead	H 9
Lakeport ⊙	C 4
Lakewood	C 11
La Mesa	H 11
La Mirada	D 11
Lamont	G 8
Lancaster	G 9
La Puente	D 10
Larkspur	H 1
La Verne	D 10
Lawndale	B 11
Lemon Grove	J 11
Lemoore	F 7
Lennox	C 11
Leucadia	H 10
Lincoln	B 8
Linda	D 4
Lindsay	G 7
Live Oak	D 4
Livermore	L 2
Livingston	E 6
Lodi	C 9
Loma Linda	E 10
Lomita	C 11
Lompoc	E 9
Long Beach	C 11
Los Alamitos	D 11
Los Altos	K 3
Los Altos Hills	J 3
Los Angeles ⊙	C 10
Los Banos	E 6
Los Gatos	K 4
Lynwood	C 11
Madera ⊙	E 7
Malibu	B 10
Manhattan Beach	B 11
Manteca	D 6
Marina	D 7
Mariposa ⊙	F 6
Markleeville ⊙	F 5
Martinez ⊙	K 1
Marysville ⊙	D 4
Maywood	C 10
Menlo Park	J 3
Merced ⊙	E 6
Millbrae	J 2
Mill Valley	H 2
Milpitas	L 3
Mira Loma	E 10
Mission Viejo	D 11
Modesto ⊙	D 6
Monrovia	D 10
Montclair	D 10
Montebello	C 10
Monterey	D 7
Monterey Park	C 10
Montrose	C 10
Moraga	K 2
Morgan Hill	L 4
Morro Bay	D 8
Mountain View	K 3
Mount Shasta	C 2
Napa ⊙	C 5
National City	J 11
Needles	L 9
Nevada City ⊙	D 4
Newark	K 3
Newhall	G 9
Newport Beach	D 11
Norco	E 11
North Highlands	B 8
North Hollywood	B 10
Norwalk	C 11
Novato	H 1
Oakdale	E 6
Oakland ⊙	J 2
Oceanside	H 10
Oildale	F 8
Ontario	D 10
Orange	D 11
Orinda	J 2
Orland	C 4
Oroville ⊙	D 4
Oxnard	F 9
Pacifica	H 2
Pacific Beach	H 11
Pacific Grove	C 7
Palmdale	G 9
Palm Desert	J 10
Palm Springs	J 10
Palo Alto	K 3
Palos Verdes Estates	B 11
Paradise	D 4
Paramount	C 11
Pasadena	C 10
Paso Robles	E 8
Patterson	D 6
Pebble Beach	C 7
Perris	F 11
Petaluma	H 1
Pico Rivera	C 10
Piedmont	J 2
Pinole	J 1
Pismo Beach	E 8
Pittsburg	L 1
Placentia	D 11
Placerville ⊙	C 8
Pleasant Hill	K 2
Pleasanton	L 2
Pomona	D 10
Porterville	F 7
Port Hueneme	F 9
Portola Valley	J 3
Quincy ⊙	E 4
Rancho Cordova	C 8
Rancho Cucamonga	E 10
Rancho Mirage	J 10
Rancho Palos Verdes	B 11
Red Bluff ⊙	C 3
Redding ⊙	C 3
Redlands	H 9
Redondo Beach	B 11
Redwood City ⊙	J 3
Reedley	F 7
Reseda	B 10
Rialto	E 10
Richmond	J 1
Ridgecrest	H 8
Rio Linda	B 8
Riverbank	E 6
Riverside ⊙	E 10
Rocklin	B 8
Rodeo	J 1
Rohnert Park	C 5
Rolling Hills Estates	B 11
Rosemead	D 10
Roseville	B 8
Rubidoux	E 10
Sacramento (cap.) ⊙	B 8
Saint Helena	C 5
Salinas ⊙	D 7
San Andreas ⊙	E 5
San Anselmo	H 1
San Bernardino ⊙	E 10
San Bruno	J 2
San Buenaventura (Ventura) ⊙	F 9
San Carlos	J 3
San Clemente	H 10
San Diego ⊙	H 11
San Dimas	D 10
San Fernando	C 10
San Francisco ⊙	H 2
San Gabriel	C 10
Sanger	F 7
San Jacinto	H 10
San Jose ⊙	L 3
San Juan Capistrano	H 10
San Leandro	J 2
San Lorenzo	K 2
San Luis Obispo ⊙	E 8
San Marcos	H 10
San Marino	D 10
San Mateo	J 3
San Pablo	J 1
San Pedro	C 11
San Rafael ⊙	J 1
Santa Ana ⊙	D 11
Santa Barbara ⊙	F 9
Santa Clara	K 3

⊙ County seat

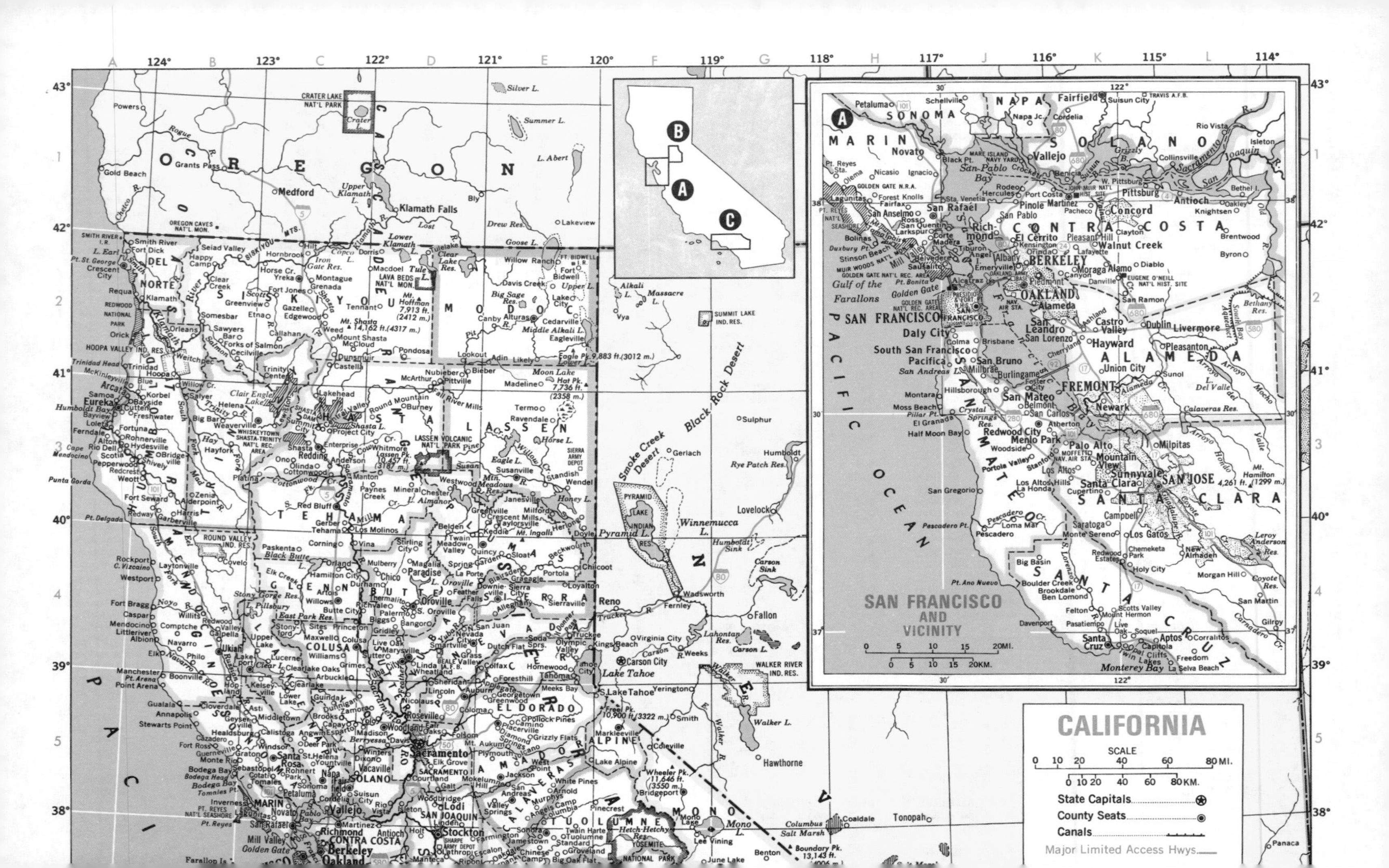
CALIFORNIA
SCALE
0 10 20 40 60 80 MI.
0 10 20 40 60 80 KM.
State Capitals
County Seats
Canals
Major Limited Access Hwys.
SAN FRANCISCO AND VICINITY
PACIFIC OCEAN
OREGON
NEVADA

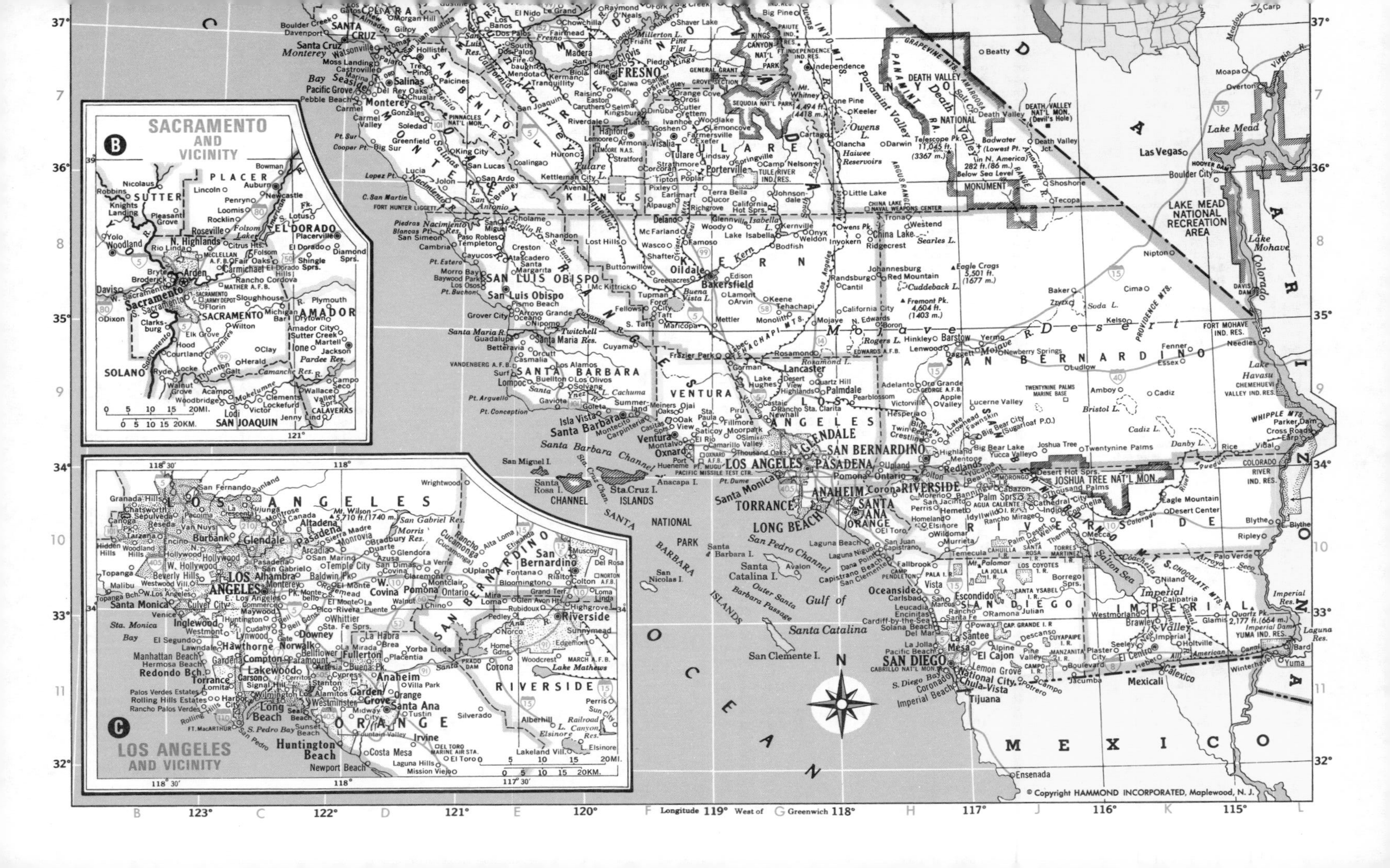

SACRAMENTO AND VICINITY
LOS ANGELES AND VICINITY
SAN DIEGO
LOS ANGELES
SAN BERNARDINO
PASADENA
GLENDALE
ANAHEIM
RIVERSIDE
LONG BEACH
TORRANCE
SANTA ANA
FRESNO
Bakersfield
Santa Barbara
San Luis Obispo
Las Vegas
Mojave Desert
Death Valley
LAKE MEAD NATIONAL RECREATION AREA
JOSHUA TREE NAT'L MON.
Salton Sea
Santa Barbara Channel
Gulf of Santa Catalina
CHANNEL ISLANDS
SANTA BARBARA ISLANDS
OCEAN
MEXICO
Tijuana
Mexicali
Ensenada
Longitude 119° West of Greenwich 118°
© Copyright HAMMOND INCORPORATED, Maplewood, N. J.

Index to Map of California

Santa Cruz ⊙ . . . . K 4
Santa Fe Springs . . . . C 11
Santa Maria . . . . E 9
Santa Monica . . . . B 10
Santa Paula . . . . F 9
Santa Rosa ⊙ . . . . . . C 5
Santee . . . . J 11
Saratoga . . . . K 4
Sausalito . . . . H 2
Scotts Valley . . . . K 4
Seal Beach . . . . C 11
Seaside . . . . D 7
Sebastopol . . . . C 5
Selma . . . . F 7
Sepulveda . . . . B 10
Shafter . . . . F 8
Sierra Madre . . . . D 10
Signal Hill . . . . C 11
Simi Valley . . . . G 9
Soledad . . . . D 7
Sonoma . . . . C 5
Sonora ⊙ . . . . E 6
South El Monte . . . . . . C 10
South Gate . . . . C 11
South Lake Tahoe . . . . F 5
South Pasadena . . . . . C 10
South Sacramento . . . . B 8
South San Francisco . . J 2
Stanford . . . . J 3
Stanton . . . . D 11
Stockton ⊙ . . . . D 6
Suisun City . . . . K 1
Sunland . . . . C 10
Sunnymead . . . . F 11
Sunnyvale . . . . K 3
Susanville ⊙ . . . . E 3
Taft . . . . F 8
Tarzana . . . . B 10
Tehachapi . . . . G 8
Temple City . . . . D 10
Thousand Oaks . . . . . . G 9
Tiburon . . . . J 2
Torrance . . . . C 11
Tracy . . . . D 6
Tujunga . . . . C 10
Tulare . . . . F 7
Turlock . . . . D 6
Tustin . . . . D 11
Twentynine Palms . . . . K 9
Ukiah ⊙ . . . . B 4
Union City . . . . K 2
Upland . . . . E 10
Vacaville . . . . D 5
Vallejo . . . . J 1
Van Nuys . . . . B 10
Venice . . . . B 11

⊙ County seat

Ventura ⊙ . . . . F 9
Victorville . . . . H 9
Villa Park . . . . D 11
Visalia ⊙ . . . . F 7
Vista . . . . H 10
Walnut . . . . D 10
Walnut Creek . . . . K 2
Wasco . . . . F 8
Watsonville . . . . D 7
Weaverville ⊙ . . . . B 3
Weed . . . . C 2
West Covina . . . . D 10
West Hollywood . . . . . . B 10
West Los Angeles . . . . B 10
Westminster . . . . D 11
West Sacramento . . . . . B 8
Westwood Village . . . . . B 10
Whittier . . . . D 11
Willits . . . . B 4
Willows ⊙ . . . . C 4
Wilmington . . . . C 11
Woodlake . . . . G 7
Woodland ⊙ . . . . B 8
Woodland Hills . . . . . . B 10
Woodside . . . . J 3
Yorba Linda . . . . D 11
Yreka ⊙ . . . . C 2
Yuba City ⊙ . . . . D 4
Yucaipa . . . . J 9

Other Features

Aqua Caliente Ind.
Res. . . . . J 10
Alamo (river) . . . . K 10
Alcatraz (island) . . . . . . J 2
All American (canal) . . . K 11
Almanor (lake) . . . . D 3
Amargosa (river) . . . . . . J 7
American (river) . . . . . . C 8
Anacapa (island) . . . . . . F 10
Angel (island) . . . . J 2
Ano Nuevo (point) . . . . . J 4
Arena (point) . . . . B 5
Arguello (point) . . . . E 9
Argus (range) . . . . H 7
Beale AFB . . . . D 4
Berryessa (lake) . . . . . . D 5
Black Butte (lake) . . . . . C 4
Bodega (bay) . . . . B 5
Bristol (lake) . . . . K 9
Buena Vista (lake) . . . . . F 8
Cabrillo Nat'l Mon. . . . . H 11
Cadiz (lake) . . . . K 9
Cahuilla Ind. Res. . . . . . J 10
Calaveras (res.) . . . . L 3
California Aqueduct . . . . E 7

Campo Ind. Res. . . . . . . J 11
Capitan Grande Ind.
Res. . . . . J 11
Cascade (range) . . . . . . D 1
Castle AFB . . . . E 6
Channel Is. Nat'l Park . F 10
Chemehuevi Valley
Ind. Res. . . . . L 9
Chocolate (mts.) . . . . . . K 10
Clair Engle (lake) . . . . . C 3
Clear (lake) . . . . C 4
Clear Lake (res.) . . . . . . D 2
Coachella (canal) . . . . . K 10
Coast (ranges) . . . . B 2
Colorado (river) . . . . L 8
Colorado River
Aqueduct . . . . K 10
Colorado River Ind.
Res. . . . . L 10
Conception (point) . . . . . E 9
Cooper (point) . . . . D 7
Copco (lake) . . . . C 2
Cosumnes (river) . . . . . . C 9
Coyote (res.) . . . . L 4
Crowley (lake) . . . . G 6
Crystal Springs (res.) . . . J 3
Cuyama (river) . . . . E 8
Cuyapaipe Ind. Res. . . . J 11
Danby (lake) . . . . K 9
Death Valley Nat'l Mon. . H 7
Delgada (point) . . . . A 3
Devils Postpile Nat'l
Mon. . . . . F 6
Donner (pass) . . . . E 4
Dume (point) . . . . G 10
Eagle (peak) . . . . E 2
Eagle Crags (mt.) . . . . . J 8
Earl (lake) . . . . A 2
East Park (res.) . . . . C 4
Edison (lake) . . . . F 6
Edwards AFB . . . . H 9
Eel (river) . . . . B 4
Elsinore (lake) . . . . E 11
El Toro Marine Air
Sta. . . . . D 11
Estero (point) . . . . D 8
Estrella (river) . . . . E 8
Eugene O'Neill Nat'l
Hist. Site . . . . K 2
Farallon (islands) . . . . . B 6
Farallons (gulf) . . . . H 2
Feather (river) . . . . D 4
Florence (lake) . . . . G 6
Folsom (lake) . . . . C 8
Fort Bidwell Ind. Res. . . . E 2
Fort Hunter Liggett . . . . . D 8
Fort Independence
Ind. Res. . . . . G 7

Fort MacArthur . . . . C 11
Fort Mohave Ind. Res. . . L 9
Fort Ord . . . . D 7
Fort Point Nat'l Hist.
Site . . . . J 2
Freel (peak) . . . . F 5
Fremont (peak) . . . . H 8
Fresno (river) . . . . E 7
General Grant Grove
Park . . . . G 7
George AFB . . . . H 9
Golden Gate (chan.) . . . H 2
Golden Gate Nat'l
Rec. Area . . . . H 2
Goose (lake) . . . . E 1
Grapevine (mts.) . . . . . . H 7
Grizzly (bay) . . . . K 1
Guadalupe (river) . . . . . K 3
Haiwee (res.) . . . . H 7
Hamilton (mt.) . . . . L 3
Havasu (lake) . . . . L 9
Hetch Hetchy (res.) . . . . F 6
Hoffmann (mt.) . . . . D 2
Honey (lake) . . . . E 3
Hoopa Valley Ind. Res. . . A 2
Humboldt (bay) . . . . A 3
Imperial (valley) . . . . . . K 10
Ingalls (mt.) . . . . E 3
Inyo (mts.) . . . . G 6
Inyokern Naval Ord.
Test Sta. . . . . H 8
Isabella (lake) . . . . G 8
John Muir Nat'l Hist.
Site . . . . K 1
Joshua Tree Nat'l
Mon. . . . . J 10
Kern (river) . . . . G 8
Kings (river) . . . . F 7
Kings Canyon Nat'l
Park . . . . G 7
Klamath (river) . . . . B 2
Laguna (res.) . . . . L 11
La Jolla Ind. Res. . . . . . J 10
Lassen (peak) . . . . D 3
Lassen Vol. Nat'l Park . . D 3
Lava Beds Nat'l Mon . . . D 2
Leroy Anderson (res.) . . L 4
Los Angeles Aqueduct . G 8
Los Coyotes Ind. Res. . J 10
Lost (river) . . . . D 1
Mad (river) . . . . B 3
Manzanita Ind. Res. . . . J 11
March AFB . . . . E 11
Mare Island Navy Yard . . J 1
Mather AFB . . . . B 8
Mathews (lake) . . . . E 11
McClellan AFB . . . . B 8
Mendocino (cape) . . . . . A 3

Merced (river) . . . . E 6
Millerton (lake) . . . . F 6
Moffett Naval Air Sta. . . . K 3
Mojave (desert) . . . . H 9
Mokelumne (river) . . . . . C 9
Mono (lake) . . . . G 5
Monterey (bay) . . . . K 4
Morongo Ind. Res. . . . . J 10
Mountain Meadows
(res.) . . . . E 3
Muir Woods Nat'l
Mon. . . . . H 2
Nacimiento (river) . . . . . D 8
Navarro (river) . . . . B 4
New (river) . . . . K 11
Norton AFB . . . . F 10
Noyo (river) . . . . B 4
Old (river) . . . . L 1
Owens (lake) . . . . H 7
Owens (river) . . . . G 6
Paiute Ind. Res. . . . . . . G 6
Pala Ind. Res. . . . . H 10
Palomar (mt.) . . . . J 10
Panamint (range) . . . . . . H 7
Pendleton, Camp . . . . . H 10
Pescadero (point) . . . . . J 3
Picacho (mt.) . . . . L 11
Piedras Blancas (pt.) . . . D 8
Pine (creek) . . . . D 3
Pine Flat (lake) . . . . F 7
Pinnacles Nat'l Mon. . . . D 7
Pit (river) . . . . D 2
Point Mugu Pacific
Missile Test Center . . . F 9
Point Reyes Nat'l
Seashore . . . . H 1
Providence (mts.) . . . . . K 8
Punta Gorda (point) . . . . A 3
Railroad Canyon (res.) . E 11
Redwood Nat'l Park . . . . A 2
Reyes (point) . . . . B 6
Rogers (lake) . . . . H 9
Rosamond (lake) . . . . . . G 9
Round Valley Ind.
Res. . . . . B 4
Russian (river) . . . . B 4
Sacramento (river) . . . . . D 5
Saint George (point) . . . . A 2
Salinas (river) . . . . D 7
Salmon (river) . . . . B 2
Salton Sea (lake) . . . . . K 10
San Andreas (lake) . . . . H 2
San Benito (river) . . . . . . D 7
San Bernardino (mts.) . J 10
San Clemente (island) . G 11
San Diego (bay) . . . . . . H 11
San Francisco (bay) . . . . J 2
San Gabriel (res.) . . . . . D 10

San Joaquin (river) . . . . E 6
San Lorenzo (river) . . . . K 4
San Martin (cape) . . . . . D 8
San Miguel (island) . . . . E 9
San Nicolas (island) . . . F 10
San Pablo (bay) . . . . J 1
San Pedro (bay) . . . . . . C 11
Santa Ana (river) . . . . . E 11
Santa Barbara (island) . G 10
Santa Barbara
(islands) . . . . F 10
Santa Catalina (island) G 10
Santa Cruz (island) . . . . F 10
Santa Maria (river) . . . . . E 9
Santa Monica Mts.
Nat'l Rec. Area . . . . . B 10
Santa Rosa (island) . . . E 10
Santa Rosa Ind. Res. . . J 10
Santa Ynez (river) . . . . . E 9
Santa Ysabel Ind. Res. . J 10
Scott (river) . . . . B 2
Searles (lake) . . . . H 8
Sequoia Nat'l Park . . . . . G 7
Shasta (lake) . . . . C 3
Shasta (mt.) . . . . C 2
Shasta (river) . . . . C 2
Sierra Nevada (mts.) . . . . E 4
Sierra Army Depot . . . . . E 3
Siskiyou (mts.) . . . . C 2
Smith River Ind. Res. . . . A 2
Suisun (bay) . . . . K 1
Sur (point) . . . . D 7
Susan (river) . . . . D 3
Tahoe (lake) . . . . F 4
Tamalpais (mt.) . . . . H 1
Tehachapi (mts.) . . . . . . G 9
Telescope (peak) . . . . . . H 7
Tomales (point) . . . . B 5
Torres Martinez Ind.
Res. . . . . J 10
Travis AFB . . . . L 1
Trinidad (head) . . . . A 2
Trinity (river) . . . . B 3
Truckee (river) . . . . F 4
Tulare (lake) . . . . F 7
Tule River Ind. Res. . . . . G 7
Twitchell (res.) . . . . E 9
Vandenberg AFB . . . . . . E 9
Wheeler (peak) . . . . F 5
Whipple (mts.) . . . . L 9
Whiskeytown-Shasta-
Trinity Nat'l Rec.
Area . . . . C 3
Whitney (mt.) . . . . G 7
Wilson (mt.) . . . . D 10
Yosemite Nat'l Park . . . . F 6
Yuba (river) . . . . D 4
Yuma Ind. Res. . . . . L 11

View of Yosemite National Park, with the rocky cliffs of the Sierra Nevada Mts. in the background. M. Woodbridge Williams–National Park Service

deserts many animals are nocturnal; found here are rabbits, foxes, rats, various reptiles, and insects. In the chaparral regions are rabbits, ring-tailed cats and many species of birds. The state's forestlands host a variety of wildlife, including deer, skunk, fox, and rattlesnake, of which the state has six species. Larger mammals, found principally in the N and in mountain areas, are bear, elk, and pronghorn antelope.

Mineral Resources. In spite of depletion of reserves of gold, petroleum, natural gas, and mercury, California remains an important storehouse of minerals. In the E Sierra Nevada is found a major world source of tungsten. Borates are important in the Mojave Desert; salt is recovered in San Francisco and San Diego bays. Petroleum and natural-gas deposits are located in the Los Angeles Basin and the San Joaquin Valley. Other minerals present in significant quantities include asbestos, sand and gravel, iron ore, magnesium, silver, and gemstones. D.W.L.

POPULATION

According to the 1980 census, California had 23,668,562 inhabitants, an increase of 18.5% over 1970. It was the most populous state in the U.S. in 1980, when its average population density was 58 people per sq km (149 per sq mi). The state had a great diversity of ethnic and racial groups. Whites made up 76.2% of the population and blacks 7.7%; additional population groups included some 357,514 people of Filipino background, 322,340 people of Chinese descent, 261,817 people of Japanese ancestry, 198,095 American Indians, 103,891 people of Korean descent, and 89,587 people of Vietnamese background. A major component of California's population, especially in the S, were the 4,543,800 persons of Hispanic (mainly Mexican) background, constituting nearly one out of every five persons in the state. Roman Catholics formed the largest single religious group in the state, and they were followed in size by several Protestant groups; Jews formed a significant religious minority. California was the most urbanized state in the U.S. About 91% of all Californians lived in areas defined as urban, and the rest lived in rural areas. The largest cities were Los Angeles; San Diego; San Francisco; San Jose; Long Beach; Oakland; and Sacramento, the capital.

EDUCATION AND CULTURAL ACTIVITY

California is well known for its progressive attitude toward education and its high academic standards. Its support of the arts has made it one of the major cultural centers of the country.

Education. Although the state constitution of 1849 provided for a public school system, it was not until 1866, when the legislature adopted the

Revised School Law, that free state schools were actually established in California. In 1903 state support was extended to secondary schools and then in 1917 to junior colleges.

In the early 1980s, California had about 7170 public elementary and secondary schools. The public primary schools each year enrolled about 2,737,000 pupils, and the public secondary schools about 1,324,000 students. In addition, about 520,400 students attended private schools.

In the same period California had some 268 institutions of higher education, including one of the largest systems of state colleges and universities in the U.S. Combined enrollment in all institutions of higher education was about 1,791,000 students. The ten campuses of the University of California alone provided higher education for approximately 133,350 students each year; the California State University system has 19 campuses. Other notable institutions of higher education include Stanford University, in Stanford; Claremont University Center (1925), in Claremont; Mills College (1852), in Oakland; the University of Southern California, in Los Angeles; California Institute of Technology, in Pasadena; Whittier College (1901), in Whittier; and two of the state's oldest institutions of higher education, the University of Santa Clara (1851), in Santa Clara, and the University of the Pacific (1851), in Stockton.

Cultural Institutions. California contains numerous cultural institutions of the highest quality. Among the most notable of these are the Los Angeles County Museum of Art, in Los Angeles; the J. Paul Getty Museum, in Malibu, a replica of an ornate Roman villa housing an extensive collection of antiquities and European painting; the Hearst-San Simeon State Historical Monument, in San Simeon; the Norton Simon Museum, in Pasadena; and the M. H. de Young Memorial Museum, in San Francisco, the oldest and largest municipal museum in the West. Also of note are the Natural History Museum of Los Angeles County and the Griffith Observatory and Planetarium, both in Los Angeles; the San Francisco Museum of Modern Art, the California Palace of the Legion of Honor, and the California Academy of Sciences, in San Francisco; and Balboa Park, a cultural center in San Diego. The state has many public libraries, and the University of California at Berkeley library is a major research facility.

Each of California's largest cities—Los Angeles, San Diego, and San Francisco—has a professional ballet company, an opera company, and a sym-

The San Francisco-Oakland Bay Bridge, completed in 1936, has two decks and an overall length of more than 12 km (more than 8 mi). Transamerica Corporation

The Chinese district of downtown Los Angeles.
American Airlines

phony orchestra. The Music Center of Los Angeles County is a notable building devoted to music and theater.

Historical Sites. Many of California's historical sites commemorate early Spanish settlements and the pioneering, gold-rush days. Located in the state are Spanish missions, belonging to a system established in the 18th century by Father Junípero Serra; one of the most notable of these, Mission San Carlos Borromeo (1770), is located in Carmel. Other sites of particular interest are Pioneer Village, in Bakersfield; El Pueblo de Los Angeles State Historic Park, in Los Angeles; the Old Customs House, in Monterey; and Sutter's Fort, in Sacramento.

Sports and Recreation. California's diverse landscape and large urban centers furnish opportunities for almost every type of indoor and outdoor sport, and more than one-fourth of the state's total land area is included in the national and state park systems. Ideal conditions are furnished by coast and mountains for swimming, boating, and fishing, as well as hiking, skiing, and hunting. The state also has a number of hot-spring health spas. California is also the home of many major league sports teams. In addition, the state contains some of the country's most outstanding entertainment park facilities including Disneyland, in Anaheim; Sea World, in San Diego; Knott's Berry Farm, in Buena Park; and Busch Gardens, in Van Nuys.

Communications. California has one of the most comprehensive communications systems in the country; it includes some 232 AM and 204 FM commercial radiobroadcasting stations and 54 commercial television stations. The first radio station in California, KQW in San Jose, initiated regular broadcasts in 1912. The first commercial television station in California, KTLA in Los Angeles, went into operation in 1947. The state's first newspaper, the *Californian,* began publication in Monterey in 1846. By the early 1980s California had 122 daily newspapers with a total daily circulation of some 6 million. Influential dailies included the *Los Angeles Times,* with a daily circulation of about 1 million; the *Los Angeles Herald Examiner;* the *Chronicle,* published in San Francisco; and the *San Diego Union.* California is also a major center of book publishing.

GOVERNMENT AND POLITICS

California is governed under a constitution adopted in 1879, with subsequent revisions and amendments. An earlier constitution had been adopted by the territorial government in 1849. An amendment to the constitution may be proposed by the legislature, voter initiative, or a constitutional convention. To become effective it must be approved by a majority of the persons voting on the issue in an election.

Executive. The chief executive of California is a governor, who is popularly elected to a 4-year term and may serve any number of terms. The same requirements apply to the lieutenant governor, who succeeds the governor should the latter resign, die, or be removed from office. Other state elected officials include the secretary of state, attorney general, treasurer, controller, and superintendent of public instruction.

Legislature. The bicameral California legislature comprises a Senate and an Assembly. The 40 members of the Senate are popularly elected to 4-year terms; the 80 members of the Assembly are popularly elected to 2-year terms. California's citizens can pass laws directly, through their power of initiative, or can prevent a law from going into effect by calling for a referendum. The governor may call for a special session of the legislature.

Judiciary. California's highest court, the supreme court, is made up of a chief justice and 6 associate judges. The intermediate appellate courts are the five district courts of appeal with a total of 59 judges. Judges of both these courts are appointed by the governor, with the approval of

CALIFORNIA

DATE OF STATEHOOD: September 9, 1850; 31st state

CAPITAL:	**Sacramento**
MOTTO:	***Eureka*** **(I have found it)**
NICKNAME:	**Golden State**
STATE SONG:	**"I Love You, California" (words by F. B. Silverwood; music by A. F. Frankenstein)**
STATE TREE:	**California redwood**
STATE FLOWER:	**Golden poppy**
STATE BIRD:	**California valley quail**
POPULATION (1980):	**23,668,562; 1st among the states**
AREA:	**411,047 sq km (158,706 sq mi); 3d largest state; includes 6234 sq km (2407 sq mi) of inland water**
COASTLINE:	**1352 km (840 mi)**
HIGHEST POINT:	**Mt. Whitney, 4418 m (14,494 ft)**
LOWEST POINT:	**86 m (282 ft) below sea level, in Death Valley**
ELECTORAL VOTES:	**47**
U.S. CONGRESS:	**2 senators; 45 representatives**

POPULATION OF CALIFORNIA SINCE 1850

Year of Census	Population	Classified As Urban
1850	93,000	8%
1860	380,000	21%
1880	865,000	43%
1900	1,485,000	52%
1910	2,378,000	62%
1930	5,677,000	73%
1950	10,586,000	81%
1960	15,717,000	86%
1970	19,953,000	91%
1980	23,669,000	91%

POPULATION OF TEN LARGEST CITIES

	1980 Census	1970 Census
Los Angeles	2,966,763	2,811,801
San Diego	875,504	697,471
San Francisco	678,974	715,674
San Jose	636,550	459,913
Long Beach	361,334	358,879
Oakland	339,288	361,561
Sacramento	275,741	257,105
Anaheim	221,847	166,408
Fresno	218,202	165,655
Santa Ana	203,713	155,710

CLIMATE	LOS ANGELES	SAN FRANCISCO
Average January temperature range	8.3° to 19.4° C (47° to 67° F)	7.8° to 13.3° C (46° to 56° F)
Average July temperature range	17.8° to 28.3° C (64° to 83° F)	11.7° to 17.8° C (53° to 64° F)
Average annual temperature	18.3° C (65° F)	13.9° C (57° F)
Average annual precipitation	356 mm (14 in)	533 mm (21 in)
Average annual snowfall	negligible	negligible
Mean number of days per year with appreciable precipitation	34	66
Average daily relative humidity	53%	67%
Mean number of clear days per year	185	162

NATURAL REGIONS OF CALIFORNIA

CASCADE RANGE
KLAMATH MTS.
BASIN & RANGE REGION
COAST RANGES
Sacramento R.
SIERRA NEVADA
CENTRAL VALLEY
San Joaquin R.
COAST RANGES
BASIN & RANGE REGION
LOWER CALIFORNIA RANGES
Colorado R.

ECONOMY

State budget	revenue $42.2 billion
	expenditure $40.4 billion
State and local taxes, per capita	$1372
Personal income, per capita	$13,239
Assets, commercial banks (499)	$227.9 billion
Labor force (civilian)	12,333,000
Employed in services	19%
Employed in wholesale and retail trade	19%
Employed in manufacturing	16%
Employed in government	14%

	Quantity Produced	Value
FARM PRODUCTS		**$11.3 billion**
Crops		**$7.1 billion**
Vegetables	10 million metric tons	$1.8 billion
Grapes	4.5 million metric tons	$886 million
Hay	6.7 million metric tons	$732 million
Cotton	429,000 metric tons	$699 million
Citrus fruits	3.6 million metric tons	$510 million
Livestock and Livestock Products		**$4.2 billion**
Milk	6.7 million metric tons	$2.0 billion
Cattle	753,000 metric tons	$889 million
Eggs	8.2 billion	$372 million
Chickens (broilers)	358,000 metric tons	$253 million
Turkeys	189,000 metric tons	$146 million
MINERALS		**$12.6 billion**
Petroleum	404.7 million barrels	$8.7 billion
Natural gas	13.7 billion cu m	$1.2 million
Cement	5.9 million metric tons	$402 million
Boron	1.1 million metric tons	$385 million
Sand, gravel	75.6 million metric tons	$299 million
FISHING	**240,000 metric tons**	**$202 million**
		Annual Payroll
FORESTRY		**$7 million**
MANUFACTURING		**$43.7 billion**
Electric and electronic equipment		$7.7 billion
Transportation equipment		$7.6 billion
Nonelectric machinery		$5.6 billion
Food and kindred products		$3.3 billion
Fabricated metal products		$2.8 billion
Printing and publishing		$2.4 billion
Instruments and related products		$2.0 billion
Apparel and textile mill products		$1.3 billion
Chemicals and allied products		$1.2 billion
Stone, clay, and glass products		$1.1 billion
Rubber and plastics products		$1.1 billion
OTHER		**$144.5 billion**
Services		$35.2 billion
Government		$41.3 billion
Contract construction		$10.1 billion
Transportation and public utilities		$12.6 billion
Finance, insurance, and real estate		$12.4 billion
Wholesale trade		$12.2 billion
Retail trade		$18.1 billion

ANNUAL PRODUCTION OF GOODS BY SECTOR

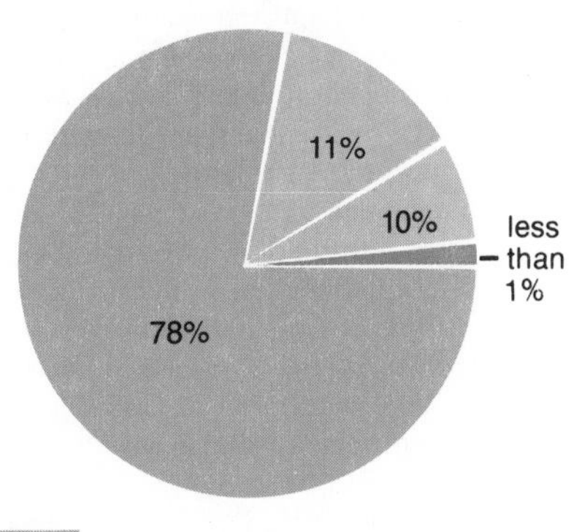

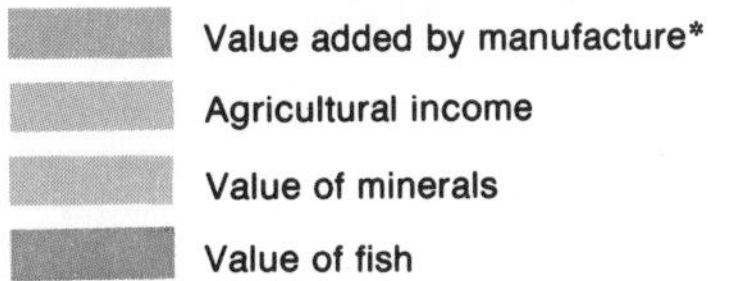

*The value added by an industry is a measure of the value created in its products, not counting such production costs as raw materials and power.

Sources: U.S. government publications

The 254-ha (103 acre) main lot of the Burbank Studios, in Burbank, Calif., includes facilities for the production of feature films, television shows, records, and videotapes.
Burbank Studios

the commission on judicial appointments, to 12-year terms. Subsequent terms are subject to approval by popular election. The major trial court justices, superior court judges, as well as municipal and justice court judges, are elected on nonpartisan ballots to 6-year terms.

Local Government. California has 58 counties, most of them governed by a five-member board of supervisors. Other county officials include the district attorney, treasurer, assessor, auditor, clerk, coroner, sheriff, and superintendent of schools. A large proportion of California's cities operate under the council-manager form of government.

National Representation. California elects 2 senators and 45 representatives to the U.S. Congress. The state has 47 electoral votes in presidential elections.

Politics. Despite a Democratic edge in voter registration, California has generally supported the Republican ticket in presidential voting. Republicans have also fared well in contests for the governorship and the U.S. Senate.

ECONOMY

Since the earliest settlement of the region by the Spanish in the 18th century, agriculture has been vital to the California economy. The gold rush of the mid-19th century was followed by the intensive exploitation of petroleum and other minerals. As the population grew, fishing and forestry emerged, and by the late 19th century light manufacturing industries had developed. Industrial diversification proceeded apace in the early 20th century. The motion picture industry, radiobroadcasting, and, later, television added other dimensions to the economy. World War II accelerated industrial development and inaugurated the growth of the state's large aerospace industry. Government and educational services expanded rapidly after the war, as did tourism and other service industries. In the early 1980s the state's several major military bases also were important contributors to the economy, as were its large financial institutions.

Agriculture. California produces a larger volume of agricultural products than any other state in the U.S. Farming accounts for about 11% of the total annual value of goods produced in the state. Farms number about 78,000 and average 171 ha (423 acres) in size; many holdings are, however, considerably larger. With about 3% of the farms in the U.S., California accounts for ap-

Wine-grape vineyards near Salinas, in the western part of the state of California. The state produces almost 90 percent of the wines of the U.S.
Joe Munroe–Photo Researchers, Inc.

proximately 10% of national farm income. Livestock and livestock products account for some 37% of the state's farm income; most important are dairy products, beef cattle, eggs, and broiler chickens. Crops account for about 63% of farm income. California produces more than 200 commercial crops, and in nearly 50 of these it leads the nation. Leading crops include grapes, hay, cotton, sugar beets, potatoes, and rice. An extraordinary array of vegetables, fruits, and nuts are also grown. Most important of these are tomatoes, lettuce, spinach, citrus fruit, peaches, apricots, and almonds.

The state's agricultural strength is based to a significant degree on irrigation and the long growing season; California has more land under irrigation than any other state. The chief agricultural areas are the Central Valley, the Imperial Valley, and to a lesser extent smaller valleys and coastal lowlands.

Forestry. California ranks behind only Oregon and Washington in value of annual production of sawtimber and accounts for about one-tenth of the nation's total. Nearly all trees harvested are softwoods, with the Douglas fir and other firs responsible for nearly half the yearly take; red-

California farms, occupying almost 40 percent of the land area of the state, are noted for their high productivity. This is due largely to the fertile soils and long growing season of much of the region. Oranges are a major crop.
Photo Researchers, Inc.

wood is also important. Production is heaviest in the coastal ranges and Sierra Nevada of N California.

Fishing. Although the fishing industry accounts for less than 1% of the yearly value of goods produced in California, the state is a major national producer of fish, ranking only behind Alaska and supplying about one-twelfth of the value of the national total. Principal species caught are tuna, anchovy, and jack mackerel; others include crab and other shellfish, sole, rockfish, squid, bonito, and sablefish. Essentially all the commercial catch is taken from salt water.

Mining. The mining industry accounts for some 10% of the value of goods produced each year in California. Petroleum output accounts for over two-thirds of the total value of all minerals extracted and for about one-eighth of the nation's annual production of petroleum. Leading fields are in the San Joaquin R. valley and in SW California, which has some offshore oil deposits. Natural gas, occurring mainly with petroleum, is second in annual value among California's minerals. Other mineral commodities of note include cement, boron, and sand and gravel, as well as smaller amounts of tungsten, asbestos, stone, magnesium, iron, gold, and gemstones.

Manufacturing. The more than 40,000 manufacturing firms in California account for about 78% of the annual value of goods produced in the state and are responsible for the employment of over 1.9 million workers. The state's principal manufactures are electric and electronic equipment, aircraft and other transportation equipment, nonelectric machinery, food and kindred products, and fabricated metal goods. Regionally, manufacturing is clustered mainly within the Los Angeles metropolitan area (which contains about half the state's manufacturing employment), the San Francisco-Oakland-San Jose metropolitan area, and the San Diego area.

Tourism. Tourism is a major industry in California. Each year more than 25 million visitors produce an estimated $16 billion for the state economy. The major attractions include the S California beaches, Disneyland, Hollywood, Palm Springs, Lake Tahoe and vicinity, the San Francisco Bay area, and the wine country of the Napa and Sonoma valleys. Yosemite and Sequoia national parks are leading attractions among a group of national parks and numerous other areas that are managed by the National Park Service. The state maintains a system of 237 parks, reserves, historic parks, and recreation areas.

Visitors walk along a flower-lined thoroughfare of Disneyland, one of southern California's best-known tourist attractions, located at Anaheim. Disneyland

Transportation. San Francisco, Los Angeles, and San Diego are the principal hubs of California's highly developed road network. About 280,080 km (about 174,030 mi) of federal, state, and local roads serve all sections of the state. Some 3830 km (about 2380 mi) of Interstate Highways link the three major metropolitan areas with one another and with the cities of the Central Valley as well as with points N and E of the state boundaries.

California is served by about 10,400 km (about 6465 mi) of operated railroad track. The major railway pattern is oriented N-S along the main axis of the state, with lines extending E from the major metropolitan areas. The Bay Area Rapid Transit system (BART) carries thousands of daily commuters in the San Francisco-Oakland metropolitan area.

Of the approximately 60 water ports in the state the foremost is the San Francisco Bay area, with its deepwater ports that include Oakland and lesser outlets. Facilities at Long Beach and Los Angeles rank second and third, with San Diego a minor fourth. Sacramento, Stockton, and other cities have inland ports on the Sacramento and San Joaquin rivers and are linked by deepwater channel to San Francisco Bay.

A major crude oil pipeline system connects the San Francisco and Los Angeles metropolitan areas, through fields in the S San Joaquin Valley and extending to the marine terminal at San Luis Obispo. It also connects to the national crude pipeline system via a line to producing fields in Texas. Natural-gas lines reach not only between the two major cities but also to fields in Alberta, Canada, and the Rocky Mt. states.

The airports at Los Angeles, Oakland, San Diego, San Francisco, and Santa Ana are among the busiest in the nation. California has 568 airports, 277 heliports, and 13 seaplane bases.

Energy. The electrical generating plants of California have a total capacity of nearly 40 million kw and produce each year some 118 billion kwh of electricity. Some 48% of all electrical energy is produced in hydroelectric facilities, 47% in conventional steam generators, 4.8% in nuclear plants, and the rest from geothermal, solar, and wind-powered sources. In addition, some power is transferred to the state from electrical systems outside California's borders. Major hydroelectric projects include the Hoover, Glen Canyon, and Davis dams on the Colorado R. The Geysers Power Plant, N of San Francisco, harnesses geothermal steam. R.S.Th.

HISTORY

The California Indians comprised 105 tribes and spoke the dialects of six linguistic families. Half of them resided in central California grasslands, where acorns, game, and fish were abundant. The Yuma and the Mojave of the Colorado River area were the only tribes to practice farming. Basketry was the most developed art of the peaceful California Indians, who occupied the land for several thousand years before the arrival of the Spaniards.

The Spanish and Mexican Periods. Hernán Cortés, the Spanish conqueror of Mexico, initiated Spanish efforts to colonize California, sending expeditions northward along the coast; one of these, led by Fortún Jiménez, discovered Baja California in 1533 before being wiped out by local Indians. Viceroy Antonio de Mendoza (c. 1490–1552) of New Spain in 1542 ordered Juan Rodríguez Cabrillo to explore farther north, and he became the first European to explore what is now the state of California. Spain's opulent Pacific trade attracted English and Dutch pirates to the area; the English navigator Francis Drake landed north of present-day San Francisco in 1579, claiming the region as Nova Albion.

Sebastián Vizcaíno surveyed (1602–03) the entire California coast, but it was not until 1769 that an expedition led by Gaspar de Portolá (c. 1723–c. 1784) and Father Junípero Serra settled San Diego. Portolá then settled Monterey. In 1776 Juan Bautista de Anza (1735–88) brought colonists overland from Sonora to found San Francisco. To convert the Indians, Franciscan padres built a chain of 21 missions. The Spaniards also established 4 presidios (forts) and 3 pueblos (towns), maintaining a precarious control over California until 1822, when it became a part of independent Mexico.

The Mexican era (1822–46) was a transition from Spanish to U.S. rule. During this time more foreign commerce and immigration were allowed, and incoming foreigners engaged in the sea otter, hide and tallow, and fur trades. The Mexican government's neglect of California, however, caused much political unrest among the settlers. Governmental institutions were then democratized, and between 1835 and 1840 the Franciscans were expelled, and mission land was distributed for private use.

The U.S. conquest of northern California began (1846) without any serious resistance, when the U.S. Navy occupied Monterey, San Francisco, and Sonoma. John C. Frémont's California Battalion, Stephen Kearny's Army of the West, and Jonathan D. Stevenson's Regiment of New York Volunteers then defeated Mexican forces in southern California. In 1848 Mexico ceded California to the U.S. by the Treaty of Guadalupe Hidalgo.

A point of historic interest in Santa Barbara, Calif., is the mission, founded in 1786. It is the western headquarters of the Franciscan order. Walter S. Clark

The Gold Rush and Statehood. The discovery of gold by James W. Marshall (1810–85) at Coloma, in January 1848, resulted in a local rush to the mines. The gold rush of 1849, international in scope, prepared California for immediate statehood. Delegates to a convention meeting at Monterey in 1849 adopted a free-state constitution. The people approved the document and elected Peter H. Burnett (1807–95) as governor; the first legislature met at San José to organize the machinery of government. The sectional conflict between the northern and southern states, however, delayed the official admission of California to the Union as the 31st state until Sept. 9, 1850. The state capital was located in several places before it was moved to Sacramento in 1854. During the American Civil War, the state sided with the Union, most Californians being of northern origin. The completion of the transcontinental railroad in 1869 ended the state's isolation and expanded the market for its growing agricultural wealth.

From 1850 to 1870 California profited from its mining and agriculture, and some advances were made in industry. For several decades, however, the lack of capital, raw materials, and adequate markets slowed industrial growth. During the 1870s the state suffered from unemployment and business failures; the Chinese, who had helped build the California railroads, were blamed for the depression. Agrarian interests and a Workingmen's party, led by the labor leader Denis Kearney, then drafted the new constitution of 1879, with provisions for regulating the railroads and monopolies and for discouraging Chinese employment and immigration.

The distress of the 1870s was followed by a real estate boom, particularly in southern California, that was stimulated by improved railroad facilities. Moreover, an increase in wheat and citrus production furthered the return of prosperity. By 1890 San Francisco was the largest city on the Pacific Coast and a commercial center on a world scale that traded in the agricultural and mineral products of the area.

The Progressive Era and World War I. In Los Angeles the boom peaked in 1887, and by 1889 the city's economy began to decline; in 1892 that of San Francisco followed suit. The so-called Panic of 1893 led to a serious depression in California, characterized by bank and business failures and labor violence. Many farmers and a few laborers joined the Populist party in a futile attempt to implement economic reforms. Railroad interests dominated the state's politics, and corruption existed at all levels of government. The Lincoln-Roosevelt League, organized in 1907 by liberal Republicans, became the spearhead of the Progressives, who elected Hiram W. Johnson (1866–1945) as governor in 1910, ushering in an era of significant economic and political reforms.

World War I stimulated an expansion of agriculture and industry in California. Farmers doubled their acreage, and Oakland's shipyards produced 10 percent of the nation's emergency shipping. Thousands of soldiers were trained at Camp Frémont and Camp Kearny, and the state's naval installations were fully mobilized.

The Interwar Period. Although demobilization initially caused a decline in jobs, California quickly boomed again. In the 1920s, 2 million newcomers poured into the state. By 1924 the population of Los Angeles reached 1 million. With the advent of the automobile, petroleum became a major industry, and in 1925 more than one-fifth of the world's oil was produced in California. The motion picture industry, centering in Hollywood, prospered, and the citrus groves of southern California increased in number.

Following the 1929 stock market crash, the Great Depression hit California hard as farm income dropped and unemployment spread. In 1932 those on relief totaled about 25 percent of the population. Many Californians embraced unorthodox schemes to restore the economy. Almost 1 million voters supported the socialistic EPIC (End Poverty in California) program of the novelist Upton Sinclair, the unsuccessful Democratic gubernatorial candidate of 1934. Culbert L. Olson (1876–1962), another Democrat, defeated the incumbent Republican governor in 1938 and proposed his own New Deal reforms, but a hostile legislature rejected them.

World War II and After. During World War II prosperity returned to the state as the aircraft plants of southern California and the shipyards of the San Francisco Bay area suddenly multiplied to meet the production demands of a global war. The steel, oil, machinery, rubber, and electric equipment industries also advanced, and farm income more than doubled. An influx of war workers caused the state's population to increase by almost 2 million between 1940 and 1945. For fear of their disloyalty, however, some 100,000 residents of Japanese descent were placed in so-called relocation centers—actually detention, or concentration, camps—during the war.

When peace came, many war workers and returning veterans remained in the state. The population explosion continued, resulting in temporary shortages in housing and schools. The aerospace and electronics industries now helped to provide jobs. Earl Warren, governor from 1943 to 1953, created a "rainy day" fund from surplus state revenue during the war for a later expansion of freeways and public higher education. By 1950 California had become the second most populous state in the U.S., and in 1962 it took the lead.

In the mid-1950s Governor Goodwin J. Knight (1896–1970) initiated labor and welfare reforms. The next governor, Edmund G. Brown, Sr. (1905–), dealt with sectional problems involving legislative reapportionment and water distribution. California, like the rest of the nation, had to deal with racial violence in its slums and student unrest on its campuses in the mid-1960s. In 1966 Ronald Reagan was elected governor, and in his two terms he reduced state funding of such items as higher education and mental health. In 1974 Edmund G. Brown, Jr. (1938–), secretary of state since 1971, and son of the earlier governor, was himself elected to that position. He was reelected in 1978, the same year that California voters approved Proposition 13, a state constitutional amendment limiting local property taxes. George Deukmejian (1928–) was elected to the governorship in 1982.

The growing importance of California in national politics was demonstrated in 1980, when former governor Reagan was elected to the U.S. presidency. B.F.G.

For further information on this topic, see the Bibliography in volume 28, sections 1212, 1221–24.

CALIFORNIA, GULF OF, arm of the Pacific Ocean, separating the peninsula of Baja California from the mainland of Mexico. The gulf was known originally as the Sea of Cortés, because the Spanish conqueror Hernán Cortés in 1539 sent an expedition to explore the area. The gulf is more than 1126 km (700 mi) long and varies in width from 48 to nearly 241 km (30 to 150 mi). It receives at its upper end the Colorado R., and from the E several streams, chief of which are the Sonora, Yaqui, and Fuerte. Its shores are bordered by highlands, broken by the river valleys on the E but presenting an almost unbroken mountain wall on the W. The coastline is irregular and forms numerous small bays. The gulf contains many islands, particularly in the upper part, the largest of which are Ángel de la Guarda and Tiburón. On its W shore are the ports of San Felipe, San José del Cabo, and La Paz; on its E shore, the ports of Mazatlán and Guaymas. Pearl fisheries are on the W coast.

CALIFORNIA, LOWER. *See* BAJA CALIFORNIA.

CALIFORNIA, UNIVERSITY OF, state institution of higher learning, with campuses throughout California: in Berkeley, Davis, Irvine, Los Angeles, Riverside, San Diego, San Francisco, Santa Barbara, and Santa Cruz. One of the largest institutions of its kind in the world, the university was established in 1868, when the state assumed control of the College of California. The latter had been chartered as a private institution in 1855. Instruction was begun at Oakland in 1869, and the university was transferred to the Berkeley campus in 1873. The largest number of courses are offered at Berkeley and Los Angeles. Other facilities include the veterinary school at Davis; the dental schools at Los Angeles and San Francisco; the medical schools at Davis, Irvine, Los Angeles, San Diego, and San Francisco; the law schools at Berkeley, Davis, and Los Angeles; and the Scripps Institution of Oceanography at La Jolla. The university also operates more than 100 research facilities in the state, including Lick Observatory. All basic undergraduate and graduate degrees are conferred.

CALIFORNIA, UNIVERSITY OF SOUTHERN. *See* SOUTHERN CALIFORNIA, UNIVERSITY OF.

CALIFORNIA INSTITUTE OF TECHNOLOGY, school of higher learning, in Pasadena, Calif. The institute was founded in 1891 by Amos Gager Throop (1811-94) and known successively as Throop Polytechnic Institute and Throop College of Technology. The present name was adopted in 1920. The institute confers B.S. degrees in science and engineering, English literature, history, economics, and social science, and M.S. and Ph.D. degrees. Off-campus facilities that are a part of the institute include the Hale Observatories (formerly the Mount Wilson and Palomar observatories), the Jet Propulsion Laboratory, and the Guggenheim Aeronautical Laboratory.

CALIFORNIUM, radioactive element, symbol Cf, a member of the transuranium elements (q.v.) in group III b of the periodic table (*see* PERIODIC LAW); at.no. 98, at.wt. 251 (most stable isotope). The isotope of californium with atomic mass 245 was first produced in 1950 at the University of California by a group of scientists working under the direction of the American chemist Glenn Seaborg. It was produced by bombarding curium-242 with alpha particles (helium nuclei) in a 152-cm (60-in) cyclotron. Californium-245 rapidly decays, with the emission of alpha particles, having a half-life of 44 min. Other isotopes, with atomic mass numbers from 240 to 255, were subsequently prepared. Californium-249 is the result of beta decay of berkelium-249. The heavier californium isotopes are produced by neutron bombardment of berkelium-249, which increases the number of protons in the nucleus. Californium-252, with a half-life of 2.6 years, has an unusually high rate of spontaneous fission, with an abundant emission of neutrons. It has practical application as a high-intensity neutron source in electronic systems and in medical research.

See also ACTINIDE SERIES.

CALIGULA, real name GAIUS CAESAR (12–41), Roman emperor (37–41), born probably in Antium (now Anzio, Italy), the youngest son of the Roman general Germanicus Caesar and the grandnephew of the Roman emperor Tiberius. His early life in military camps earned him the nickname Caligua (Lat., "Little Boot") because of the small military shoes he wore. Tiberius named his

A bust of Caligula (from the Capitoline Museum, Rome). Bettmann Archive

grandson, Tiberius Gemellus (19-38), and Caligula joint heirs to the throne, but the Roman Senate and people chose Caligula as sole emperor. Caligula adopted Gemellus as his son but subsequently had him murdered. A clement ruler during the first six months of his reign, he became a vicious tyrant after a severe illness. Historians believe that he probably went insane. He squandered his fortune on public entertainment and building projects; banished or murdered most of his relatives; enjoyed having people tortured and killed while he dined; made his favorite horse a consul; declared himself a god; and had temples erected and sacrifices offered to himself. In 41 he was assassinated by his guard.

CALIPER, mechanical device used to determine small lengths with reasonable accuracy. Simple calipers have two movable legs of some desired shape to meet the surfaces whose separation is to be measured. The adjusted width between the leg tips is then placed against some length scale. The more complex vernier caliper is wrenchlike and has a scale that allows direct reading of the adjusted width between the jaws of the wrench.

CALIPHATE, office and realm of the caliph as supreme leader of the Muslim community and successor of the Prophet Muhammad. Under Muhammad the Muslim state was a theocracy, with the Sharia, the religious and moral principles of Islam, as the law of the land. Although both secular and religious leaders, the caliphs were not empowered to promulgate dogma, because it was considered that the revelation of the faith had been completed by Muhammad.

The Sunnites (followers of the Sunna, the body of Islamic custom or the Way of the Prophet), who constitute a majority of Muslims, generally consider the period of the first four caliphs the golden age of Islam. Other sects, however, as they were formed, came to regard this period and subsequent caliphates differently, and as a result great hostility has frequently arisen between the Sunnites and other Muslims, such as the Shiites (q.v.), concerning the caliphate. During the course of Islamic history the issue of the caliphate probably has created more dissension than any other article of faith. Based on the examples of the first four "rightly guided" caliphs and companions of the Prophet, the Sunnites formulated the following requirements of the caliphate: the caliph should be an Arab of the Prophet Muhammad's tribe, the Quraysh; he should be elected and approved by a council of elders representing the Muslim community; and he should be responsible for enforcing divine law and spreading Islam by whatever means necessary, including war. In the history of the caliphate, however, all these requirements were rarely met.

The Shiites, in contrast, believing that the Prophet himself had designated his son-in-law, Ali, as both his temporal and spiritual successor, accepted only Ali's descendants (by Fatima, Muhammad's daughter) as legitimate caliphs.

The Immediate Successors. Muhammad died in 632, leaving no instructions for the future government of the Muslim community. Islamic leaders met in Medina (now in Saudi Arabia), the capital of the Muslim world at that time, and elected Abu Bakr, the Prophet's father-in-law and closest associate, as caliph. Abu Bakr took the title *khalifat Rasul Allah* (Arab., "successor to the Messenger of God"), from which the term *caliph* (Arab., khalifah, "successor") is derived.

Umar I (581?–644) became the second caliph in 634, designated by Abu Bakr as his successor and accepted by all the important members of the Muslim community. Under his leadership, the first great expansion of Islam outside of Arabia took place. Egypt, Syria, Iraq, and the northern part of Mesopotamia became Islamic territories, and the armies of the Persian Empire were routed several times. Umar added the title *amir-al-muminin* (Arab., "commander of the believers") to that of caliph.

After Umar's death in 644, Uthman ibn Affan (575?–656), Muhammad's son-in-law and one of his first converts, was appointed the third caliph by a panel of six Meccan electors. Although an elderly man, he carried on Umar's policy of territorial expansion. Eventually, however, Uthman earned the enmity of many of his subjects, who felt he favored the Meccan aristocracy in political and commercial affairs. Uthman also antagonized the Islamic preachers by issuing an official text of the Koran, with an accompanying order to destroy all other versions. Rebellious Muslim troops from al-Kufah (Iraq) and Egypt besieged Uthman in Medina and assassinated him in 656.

Ali, a cousin and son-in-law of Muhammad, was acknowledged as the fourth caliph by the Medinians and the rebellious Muslim troops. Muawiyah I (602?–80), then governor of Syria, refused to recognize Ali as caliph and called for vengeance for the death of Uthman (who was Muawiyah's kinsman). In 657 the rival parties met at Siffin, near the site of the modern city of ar-Raqqah, Syria. There, after an inconclusive battle, they agreed to arbitrate the dispute. Ali found himself being considered as a mere candidate for the caliphate on equal grounds with Muawiyah. Angered by this indignity, and with Ali for submitting to it, a group of his followers, later known as the Kharijites, deserted and vowed to assassinate both Ali and Muawiyah. They succeeded in killing only Ali. Ali's son, Hasan (c. 624–79), then claimed (661) the still disputed caliphate but abdicated within a few months under pressure from Muawiyah's supporters, who greatly outnumbered Ali's followers, the Shiites.

The Umayyad Caliphs (661–750). The Umayyad caliphs were descendants of aristocratic caravan merchants, the Umayya, to which Muawiyah, the first Umayyad caliph, belonged. Muawiyah(r. 661–80) restored stability to the Muslim community after Ali's assassination. He moved the capital of Islam from Medina to Damascus, bringing the Muslim rulers into contact with the more advanced cultural and administrative traditions of the Byzantine Empire. Muawiyah also dispensed with the practice of electing the caliph by designating his son Yazid (d. 683) as heir apparent. The principle of election was acknowledged formally, however, by having the council of elders pledge to support the designated heir. The practice of hereditary succession continued throughout the Umayyads and in subsequent dynasties. Many Muslims, however, later disapproved of it as a deviation from the essential nature of Islam.

Yazid I (r. 680–83) succeeded his father but was faced immediately with two rebellions, each supporting a rival claimant to the caliphate. The Kufan Shiites recognized Ali's second son (and the Prophet's grandson), Husayn (626?–80), as caliph. Greatly encouraged, Husayn left Medina for al-Kufah, despite warnings that Yazid's troops had quelled the Kufic uprising. On the plain of Karbala, in Iraq, he and his small escort were intercepted and slaughtered. This event, more than any other, marks the true beginning of the Shiite schism. A second rebellion by Meccans was not finally quelled until the caliphate of Abdal-Malik (r. 685-705), Yazid's third successor.

Shiite, Kharijite, and other groups of Muslims and non-Arabic converts (Arab. *mawali*) frequently revolted against the Umayyads. The mawali accused the Umayyads of religious laxity and of indifference to their demands for full brotherhood in the Muslim community. Umayyad caliphs, nevertheless, vastly enlarged the Muslim empire and created a bureaucracy capable of administering it. Under the Umayyads, Muslim armies swept eastward to the borders of India and China, westward across North Africa to the Atlantic Ocean, then northward through Spain and over the Pyrenees Mountains into France, where the Frankish infantry under the Carolingian ruler Charles Martel checked them near Poitiers in 732.

The caliphs, as political and religious leaders, helped spread Islam by building fine mosques, such as the Mosque of Ahmad Ibn Tulun in Cairo, commissioned by a 9th-century Abbasid caliph. G. R. Richardson–Taurus Photos

The Abbasid Caliphs (750–1258). The Umayyads were overthrown by a combination of Shiite, Iranian, and other Muslim and non-Muslim groups dissatisfied with the Umayyad regime. The rebels were led by the Abbasid family, descendants of the Prophet's uncle Abbas. From about 718 the Abbasids had plotted to take the caliphate, sending agents into various parts of the Muslim empire to spread propaganda against the Umayyads. By 747 they had secured enough support to organize a rebellion in northern Iran that led to the defeat of the Umayyad caliphate three years later. The Abbasids executed most of the Umayyad family, moved the capital of the empire to Baghdad, and assimilated much of the pomp and ceremony of the former Persian monarchy into their own courts.

Beginning in 750 with Abu al-Abbas (721?–54), the Abbasid caliphate lasted five centuries; it is the most durable and most famous Islamic dynasty. The Abbasids became patrons of learning and encouraged religious observance. They were the first Muslim rulers to become leaders of an Islamic civilization and protectors of the religion rather than merely an Arab aristocracy imposing an Arab civilization on conquered lands. Under their caliphate Baghdad replaced Medina as the center of theological activity, industry and commerce developed greatly, and the Islamic empire reached a peak of material and intellectual achievement.

The 8th- and 9th-century caliphs Harun ar-Rashid and his son Abdullah al-Mamun (r. 813–33) are especially renowned for their encouragement of intellectual pursuits and for the splendor of their courts. During their reigns scholars were invited to the court to debate various topics, and translations were made from Greek, Persian, and Syriac works. Embassies also were exchanged with Charlemagne, emperor of the West.

Later in the 9th century, the Abbasid caliphs increasingly began to delegate administrative responsibility to ministers of state and other government officials and to lose control over their Baghdad guards. As they gradually gave up personal political power, the caliphs placed more and more emphasis on their role as protectors of the faith. One result of this change in emphasis was the increased persecution of heretics and non-Muslims. About the same time, several successful revolts in the eastern provinces led to the establishment of independent principalities, and independent caliphates were subsequently established in North Africa and in Spain. Eventually, the power of the Abbasids barely extended outside Baghdad, and by the middle of the 10th century, the Abbasid caliphs had virtually no power, serving merely as figureheads at the mercy of the military commanders. The final defeat of the Abbasid dynasty came from outside the Muslim world, when al-Mustasim (r. 1242–58) was put to death by the invading Mongols at the order of Hulagu Khan (1217–65), the grandson of Genghis Khan.

The Abbasids in Cairo (1261–1517). When the Mongols sacked Baghdad in 1258, two members of the Abbasid family escaped to Egypt, where they took refuge with Baybars I, the Mameluke sultan. Each was named caliph, successively, by the sultan; but they were allowed to assume only religious duties, and the descendants of the second caliph remained politically powerless under the Mameluke sultans.

The Fatimid Dynasty and the Umayyads of Spain. During the decline of Abbasid power, two rival caliphates were established, one in North Africa and another in Spain. The first, ruled by the Fatimid dynasty, was founded by Ubayd Allah (d. 933), who proclaimed himself caliph in Tunisia in 909. The Fatimids were Shiites, claiming descent from Fatima (thus the name Fatimid), Muhammad's daughter, and her husband Ali, the fourth caliph. At the height of its power, in the latter half of the 10th century, the Fatimid caliphate constituted a serious threat to the Abbasids in Baghdad. The Fatimids ruled most of northern Africa from Egypt to present-day Algeria, as well as Sicily and Syria. In addition the Fatimids claimed the allegiance of other Shiites, both within and outside their domain. They sent missionaries from their capital in Cairo to the rest of the Muslim world, proclaiming the Fatimid caliphs to be infallible and sinless and the bearers of divine illumination handed down directly from Ali. Their dynasty was overthrown in 1171 by Saladin, sultan of Egypt.

The second rival caliphate was established by Abd-ar-Rahman III, who proclaimed himself caliph in Spain in 929. He was the descendant of an Umayyad prince who fled the Abbasid massacre of his family and settled (755) in Spain. The Umayyad dynasty of Spain, responsible for a brilliant period in Spanish history, ruled from its capital in Córdoba until 1031, when the caliphate broke up into numerous petty states.

The Ottomans and the Modern Period. From about the 13th century various monarchs throughout the Muslim world, particularly the Ottoman sultans, assumed the title caliph indiscriminately without regard to the prescribed requirements of the caliphate. The title held little significance for the Ottoman sultans until their empire began to decline. In the 19th century, with the advent of Christian powers in the Near East, the sultan began to emphasize his role as caliph in an effort to gain the support of Muslims living outside his realm. The Ottoman Empire collapsed during World War I (1914-18). After the war, Turkish nationalists deposed the sultan, and the caliphate was finally abolished (March 1924) by the Turkish Grand National Assembly.

The abolition of the caliphate brought consternation to many sections of the Muslim world, and protests were directed against the action of the Turkish government. Subsequently, King Husein ibn Ali (1856-1931) of al-Hijaz (Hejaz, now part of Saudi Arabia) laid claim to the title by virtue of his direct descent from the Prophet and his control of the two holy cities, Mecca and Medina. His claim, however, received little attention outside of Palestine, Syria, and parts of Arabia. The conquest (1925) of al-Hijaz by Abdul Aziz ibn Saud, ruler of Najd, Arabia, made Husein's claim even less significant.

An international Muslim congress held in Cairo in 1926 to choose an acceptable successor to the caliphate proved abortive, resulting only in an appeal to the Muslims of the world to work together to reestablish a caliphate. Ever since World War II, however, the preoccupation of Muslim nations has been with national independence and economic problems, and the restoration of the caliphate may now be regarded as irrelevant.

For additional information on historical figures, see biographies of those whose names are not followed by dates.

For further information on this topic, see the Bibliography in volume 28, section 875.

CALIXTUS. *See* CALLISTUS.

CALLA, genus of plants of the family Araceae (*see* ARUM). The only species of this genus, *Calla palustris,* the water arum, is a perennial herb found in the cold bogs of Canada, Eurasia, and the U.S. The calla is about 25 cm (about 10 in) tall, has heart-shaped leaves, and bears an oval white leaf surrounding a cluster of yellow blossoms that develop into red berries. The name is applied also to other plants of the same family, especially the golden calla, *Zantedeschia elliottiana,* and the calla lily, *Z. aethiopica,* both native to southern Africa. The calla lily, also called lily of the Nile, grows about 76 cm (about 2.5 ft) high and has large spear-tip leaves around a cluster of tiny flowers. The black calla, *Arum palaestinum,* found in Palestine and Syria, has beautiful black-purple flowers.

CALLAGHAN, James (1912-), British prime minister (1976-79), born in Portsmouth. He served in the Royal Navy during World War II and was elected to Parliament for the Labour party in 1945. Callaghan was chancellor of the Exchequer (1964-67), home secretary (1967-70), and foreign secretary (1974-76) in the two governments headed by Harold Wilson, and he succeeded Wilson as party leader and prime minister in 1976. Inheriting a severely troubled economy and a slender majority in Parliament, he depended on support from the Liberals and (after 1978) the Scottish Nationalist party (SNP). His government, destabilized by labor unrest and deserted by the SNP, fell to the Conservative onslaught led by Margaret Thatcher in 1979. He resigned as party leader in 1980.

CALLAGHAN, Morley Edward (1903-), Canadian writer, who sought to present truly Canadian characters in realistic situations. His first novel, *Strange Fugitive* (1929), and several of his later works examine problems faced by individuals who fail to conform to the accepted social patterns. Particularly popular were *They Shall Inherit the Earth* (1935) and *The Loved and the Lost* (1951). *A Fine and Private Place* (1975) is the story of a writer who desires recognition in his own country. His short stories—a collection of which was published in 1967—as well as his novels show a lean style, the legacy of his friendship with the American novelist Ernest Hemingway. At the age of 80, Callaghan wrote another novel, *A Time for Judas* (1984), a retelling of the story of Christ's betrayal.

CALLAO, city and chief seaport of Peru, W Peru, capital of Callao Province, on Callao Bay on the Pacific coast, near Lima. The harbor, sheltered by the island of San Lorenzo, is one of the safest and most spacious in South America. The port is equipped with wharves fit for the simultaneous berthage of more than ten ships, steam cranes, modern warehouses and cold-storage plants, and extensive dry-dock facilities. Chief exports are minerals, cotton, foodstuffs, wool, and hides. The imports include textiles, grain, machinery, paper, coal, and foodstuffs. Callao has manufacturing industries, including lumber making, sugar refining, brewing, and iron making. The National Technical University (1966) is here.

Callao was founded by the Spanish in 1537, and thereafter it developed as one of the most active ports on the W coast of South America. Frequently raided by British buccaneers, the town was destroyed by an earthquake and tidal wave in 1746, with the loss of 6000 lives. It was later rebuilt, and remained a possession of Spain until the 1820s, when Peruvian independence from Spain was proclaimed. Pop. (1981) 441,374.

CALLAS, Maria, professional name of MARIA ANNA SOFIA CECILIA KALOGEROPOULOS (1923-77),

American operatic soprano, the preeminent prima donna of her day, and the first modern soprano to revive forgotten operas of the *bel canto* repertoire. Born in New York City, she moved to Athens at age 13, making her first major appearance there in 1941 as Tosca. Callas began her career in dramatic roles such as Isolde, Brünnhilde, and Aida. After 1949, encouraged at the La Scala opera by her mentor, the Italian conductor Tullio Serafin (1878–1968), she turned toward coloratura *bel canto* roles; they included Norma, Lucia di Lammermoor, and many roles in long-unperformed operas. Praised for the distinctive color of her voice, her dramatic presence, and her careful musicianship, she sang principally at La Scala, the Rome and Paris operas, Covent Garden in London, and the Metropolitan Opera in New York City.

CALLES, Plutarco Elías (1877–1945), Mexican soldier and statesman, born in Guaymas, in the state of Sonora. Calles gave up a teaching career to help the revolt of Gen. Venustiano Carranza against President Victoriano Huerta in 1914. During the Carranza administration, Calles was governor of Sonora and secretary of industry, commerce, and labor from 1919 to 1920. In 1920 Calles assisted Gen. Álvaro Obregón in overthrowing Carranza and was made secretary of the interior from 1920 to 1923 while Obregón was president. In 1924 Calles succeeded Obregón as president of Mexico. Notable among the achievements of his administration were the construction of many new highways and a number of irrigation projects; the founding of the Bank of Mexico; amortization of the public debt; encouragement of public education and the organization of labor; and the effective application of land reform laws, including division of large estates among small farmers. In 1928 Calles retired to private life, but returned to serve in various offices and was an adviser to the three presidents who succeeded him. He was exiled in 1936 because of his criticism of the social reform policies of President Lázaro Cárdenas; he returned to Mexico in 1941.

CALLICRATES (fl. 5th cent. BC), Greek architect. Callicrates collaborated with the architect Ictinus in designing the Parthenon (dedicated 438 BC) on the Acropolis in Athens in the severe Doric style. He also built temples in the lighter Ionic style, including the Temple of Athena Nike (427 BC), or Wingless Victory, in Athens.

CALLIGRAPHY, the art of fine writing or script. The term *calligraphy* is derived from the Greek *kalligraphia,* meaning "beautiful writing," and is applied to individual letters as well as to entire documents; it also refers to an aesthetic branch of paleography (q.v.). In Islamic countries and in India, China, and Japan, calligraphy is done with a brush and has been a highly respected art form for many centuries (*see* CHINESE ART AND ARCHITECTURE; JAPANESE ART AND ARCHITECTURE). In the West, calligraphy eventually evolved from the earliest cave paintings, such as those (20,000–35,000 BC) at Lascaux, France, into the abstractions that became the familiar letterforms of the alphabet (q.v.).

Calligraphy in the Ancient World. About 3500 BC the ancient Egyptians created a form of picture writing called hieroglyphs (q.v.)—sacred inscriptions—usually incised on monuments or inside tombs. Hieroglyphs were also written on papyrus, an early form of paper made from a rushlike plant growing along the Nile; the earliest examples date from the 5th Dynasty (c. 2544–2407 BC). The scribes used either a brush or a flat-edged pen cut from a river reed to write on papyrus scrolls.

In Sumeria, about the same period, people used a stylus of hard wood or bone to press wedged shapes—cuneiform (q.v.)—into clay tablets, which were then baked in the sun. The writing, a complex system of syllables and words, was adopted by their Babylonian conquerors and by neighboring Semitic peoples.

The Phoenicians, traders and seafarers of the eastern Mediterranean, were the first to invent, sometime before 1000 BC, a system with 24 letters, written from right to left. The word *alphabet* is derived from the first two letters of the Phoenician alphabet, aleph and bet.

About 850 BC the Greeks took over alphabetic writing from the Phoenicians. The first line was written from right to left, followed by a line written from left to right, as a farmer would plough a field. This method is called boustrophedon. Finally they settled on left to right, as Westerners still write today. Greek letters were carved into stone, cast in metal, painted on pottery, and written on papyrus.

The Romans, before the end of the 2d century BC, had adapted the Greek alphabet to the Latin language, changing the shapes to the capital letters used today. The proportions of Roman letters on monumental inscriptions, such as those on Trajan's Column (106–13) in Rome, have never been surpassed. They were painted on stone with a brush and then carved with chisel and mallet.

In day-to-day use, writing was pressed with a stylus on wax tablets, which could be erased and reused. For correspondence, a speedier script called cursive was developed. For books or scrolls, a more lasting material was used—either vellum, the skin of a calf, or parchment, the skin of a sheep. The script called uncial, a rounded capital letter, was the book hand used between the 4th and 9th centuries.

Medieval European Calligraphy. During the decline of the Roman Empire and the ensuing ages of turmoil, the Christian church was the principal guardian of Western culture. Monasteries became centers of learning, establishing libraries and scriptoriums (copying chambers). Monks copied mostly religious books, as well as some ancient texts; many produced decorated books called illuminated manuscripts (q.v.).

Scribes gradually developed the first minuscules—small letters of the alphabet—most notably in England and Ireland. Irish half-uncials were especially beautiful, as evident in the famous Book of Kells (c. 800, Trinity College, Dublin).

Many obscure styles of writing had developed by the 8th century. After Charlemagne was crowned Holy Roman emperor in 800, he asked the English scholar and ecclesiastic Alcuin of York to reform handwriting and to have it taught to all government officials and to everyone in the monastery schools. The new writing was slightly sloped, extremely rhythmic, and clear; by joining letters (eliding) now and then, it could be written at greater speed. The script, which became known as Carolingian, is the source of today's printed minuscule.

By the 12th century the merchant class had become powerful. Professional scribes set up their own workshops, artisans worked in groups or guilds, universities were founded, and trade increased with Islamic countries. Through the Arabs, the knowledge of papermaking came from China to Europe, where paper replaced expensive vellum and parchment.

Between the 12th and 13th centuries Carolingian letters were turned into compressed and broken forms. Today they are called black letter. Eventually this writing became a model for early printing.

By 1450 Johann Gutenberg had printed the Bible on his press in Mainz, Germany, with movable letters cast from lead; soon printing spread all over the world. The characters used by printers copied the scribal styles of the period; for a century, nevertheless, initial letters of major sections were still hand drawn (*see* BOOK).

A more spiky, cursive script was developed (called bâtarde, for bastard letter), which combined book hand, secretary hand, and Gothic script. In Italy and Spain a rounder form called rotunda was preferred to the compressed Gothics; the fraktur type of black letter, half round, half broken, was popular in Germany during the 16th and 17th centuries and continued in use there until it was officially abolished during World War II. Today it has only decorative and ornamental uses.

Renaissance Calligraphy. About 1400 classical scholarship was revived, and the Renaissance age began, first manifesting itself in Italy. With Carolingian and later book hands as a model, Italian scribes developed an elegant, slightly sloped cursive style now called italic.

In 1522 Ludovici degli Arrighi, secretary at the papal offices in Rome, published the first writing manual, a teaching guide entitled *La operina*. Other 16th-century writing masters followed with their copybooks, among them Giovanni Antonio Tagliente, Giovanni Battista Palatino, and Gianfrancesco Cresci, in Italy; Juan de Yciar, in Spain; and Geofroy Tory (c. 1480–1533), in France. The italic style soon spread throughout Europe.

Calligraphy in the 17th and 18th Centuries. In Renaissance books calligraphy was printed from woodblocks, but in the 17th century wood was replaced by copperplates. These engravings resulted in much finer lines and increasingly elaborate writing books. One of the finest calligraphic artists was Jan van de Velde (1561–1623) of Holland. Maria Strick of Rotterdam and Ester Inglis of Scotland were 17th-century professional calligraphers. In England, Edward Cocker (1631–76), Charles Snell (1667–1733), and John Clark (1683–1736) and other calligraphers in France and Spain spread the new copperplate styles.

In the 18th century, *The Universal Penman* (1733–41), by the English calligrapher George Bickham (d. 1769), appealed to businessmen, administrators, and schoolmasters. Calligraphic scripts continued to serve as models for type designs. For the businessman and student it was not easy to attain the perfection of the engraved scripts with the use of quill pens, To speed up writing, the pen was held at a far steeper angle, hairlines were thin, and curves and downstrokes swelled with pressure from the hand. As commerce took over, penmanship declined.

19th-Century Inventions and Calligraphy. Two inventions of the 19th century—the steel pen (imitating the shape of the quill) and the fountain pen—became part of daily life, but handwriting, overembellished, often vulgar, could hardly be considered calligraphy any longer.

In mid-19th-century England, the poet and artist William Morris, engaged in a revival of arts and crafts (*see* ARTS AND CRAFTS MOVEMENT), rediscovered the use of the flat-edged pen. In London, the educator Edward Johnston (1872–1944) carried this revival of interest in calligraphy fur-

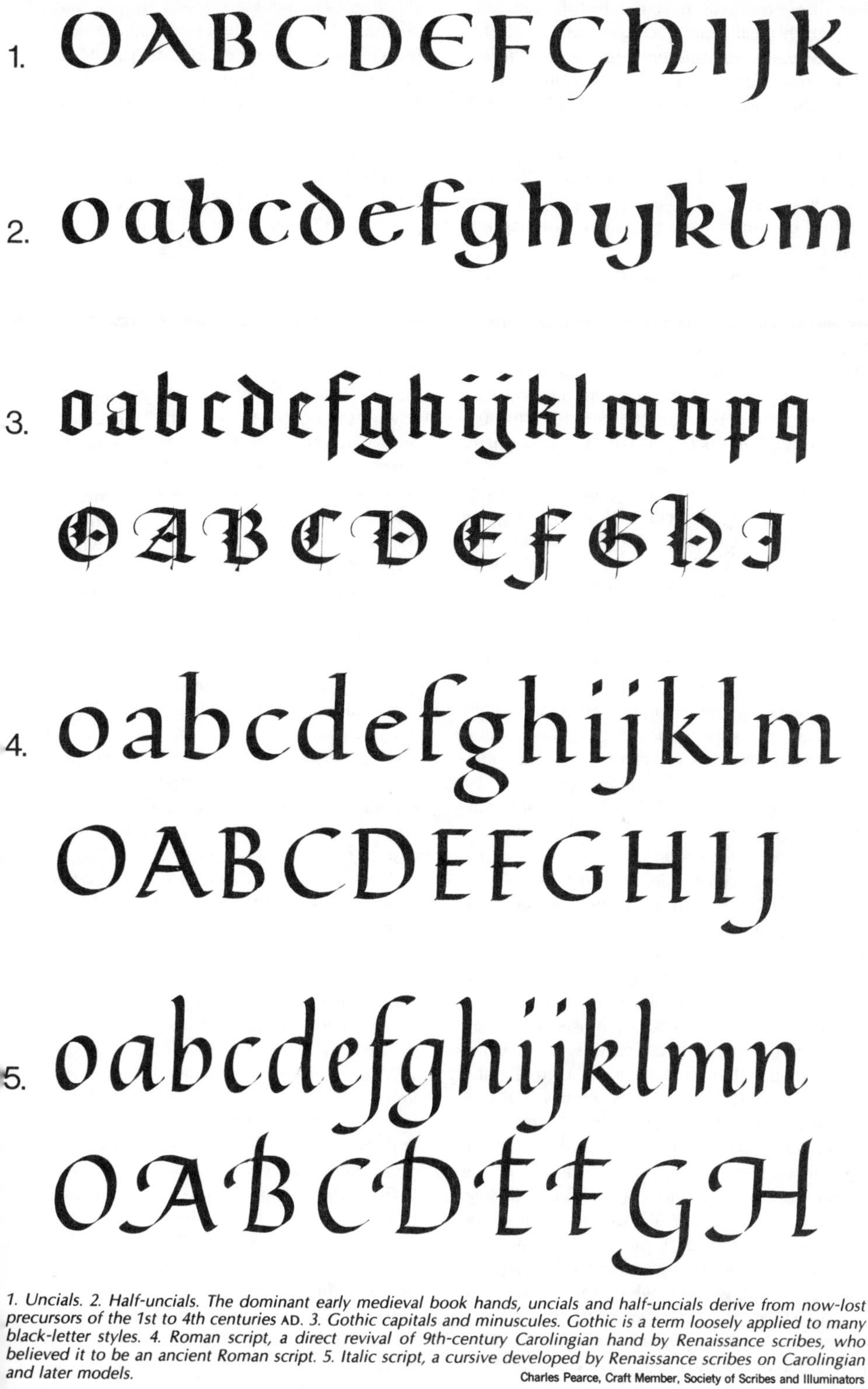

1. OABCDEFGHIJK

2. oabcdefghijklm

3. oabcdefghijklmnpq

OABCDEFGHI

4. oabcdefghijklm

OABCDEFGHIJ

5. oabcdefghijklmn

OABCDEFGH

1. Uncials. 2. Half-uncials. The dominant early medieval book hands, uncials and half-uncials derive from now-lost precursors of the 1st to 4th centuries AD. *3. Gothic capitals and minuscules. Gothic is a term loosely applied to many black-letter styles. 4. Roman script, a direct revival of 9th-century Carolingian hand by Renaissance scribes, who believed it to be an ancient Roman script. 5. Italic script, a cursive developed by Renaissance scribes on Carolingian and later models.*

Charles Pearce, Craft Member, Society of Scribes and Illuminators ther through research at the British Museum, through his calligraphy classes, and with his book *Writing and Illuminating, and Lettering* (1906), reprinted to this day. In 1922 his students in London founded the Society of Scribes and Illuminators.

In the U.S., the writing systems of various specialists such as Platt Rogers Spencer (1800–64) and proponents of the "push-pull" Palmer Method of penmanship carried on the copperplate tradition.

20th-Century Revival of Calligraphy. In the 20th century the typewriter did not replace handwriting altogether. In England Alfred Fairbank (1895–1982) revived italic with his teaching sets of the 1920s. Tom Gourdie (1913–) brought italic to schools in Great Britain, Scandinavia, and East Germany. Rudolf von Larisch (1856–1935) in Austria and Rudolf Koch (1874–1934) in Germany taught calligraphy and design.

Those who promoted calligraphy and handwriting in the U.S. include William Dwiggins (1880–1956), Oscar Ogg (1908–71), Ray DaBolla (1892–), Paul Standard (1896–), Arnold Bank (1908–), and George Salter (1897–1976).

When Donald Jackson (1938–), a prominent English calligrapher, first visited the U.S. in 1974, he inspired a fresh interest in calligraphy and illumination, through television interviews, lectures, and workshops, suggesting that Americans might form their own societies for teaching and exhibitions. More than 30 calligraphic societies currently flourish in the U.S. and Europe.

See also entries for individual letters of the alphabet; WRITING. L.C.W.

For further information on this topic, see the Bibliography in volume 28, sections 354, 698.

CALLIMACHUS (fl. 3d cent. BC), Alexandrian poet and grammarian, born in Cyrene (now Shahat, Libya), Africa, and educated in Athens. After teaching at Eleusis, near Alexandria, Egypt, Callimachus was appointed by Ptolemy II as chief librarian of the famous library in Alexandria, an office he held for about 20 years. By his teaching and writing Callimachus exerted a great influence on scholars and poets of the day. Callimachus reputedly wrote more than 800 books. Of his learned works in prose one of the most important was the *Pinakes,* a huge catalog of the works contained in the Alexandrian library. Through this catalog Callimachus became the founder of the critical study of Greek literature. As a poet he won distinction chiefly through his short poems, of which 6 hymns and about 60 epigrams are extant. Also surviving are fragments of his most outstanding poetic work, *Aetia,* a collection of Greek legends in elegaic verse, and the short epic *Hecale.* He extolled the short, highly elaborated poem in preference to the lengthier forms in which his rival and former pupil Apollonius of Rhodes excelled. In this field Callimachus greatly influenced the Roman poets, especially Catullus, Ovid, and Propertius.

CALLIOPE. *See* MUSES.

CALLISTO. *See* JUPITER.

CALLISTUS *or* **CALIXTUS I, Saint** (c. 160–c. 222), pope (c. 217–c. 222), whose pontificate was the first to be opposed by an antipope.

A Roman by birth, Callistus was originally a slave. His first appearance in history was in connection with fraudulent banking operations, after which he was sentenced to work (c. 186–89) in the Sardinian mines. Upon his return to Rome, he was ordained a deacon and appointed chief adviser to Pope Zephyrinus (d. 217). One of the principal accomplishments of Callistus as archdeacon was the establishment on the Appian Way of the Cemetery of Callistus, a shrine of martyrs where all 3d-century popes but him are buried.

As pope, Callistus was opposed by Hippolytus (*see* HIPPOLYTUS OF ROME, SAINT), an antipope who accused him of Monarchianism, a doctrine that denied personal distinctions in the Godhead (*see* TRINITY). He was also accused of laxity for admitting repentant adulterers to Holy Communion. Callistus probably died a martyr. His feast day is October 14.

CALLISTUS II *or* **CALIXTUS II** (d. 1124), pope (1119–24), who was instrumental in ending the investiture controversy (q.v.) with Holy Roman Emperor Henry V and in implementing the church reform program of Pope Gregory VII.

Born Guido or Guy di Borgogne, he was the fifth son of Count William of Burgundy. In 1088 he was appointed archbishop of Vienne, France. Soon he became an outspoken advocate of church reform and opposed Henry V on the issue of investiture, which involved the church appointments being made by the emperor or lay princes. Upon the death of Pope Gelasius II(r. 1118–19), Callistus was elected his successor. He immediately called a council at Reims (1119); lay investiture was condemned and Henry and the antipope Gregory VIII (r. 1118–21) were excommunicated. Public opinion sided strongly with Callistus, and Gregory VIII was imprisoned. A truce was reached with Henry V; on Sept. 23, 1122, he signed the famous Concordat of Worms, thus ending the investiture controversy and guaranteeing the church full freedom in its elections. In 1123 Callistus called the first great ecumenical council of the West, the First Lateran Council, which ratified the Concordat. He died in Rome.

CALLISTUS III *or* **CALIXTUS III** (1378–1458), pope (1455–58), who led the Crusade to recover Constantinople from the Ottoman Turks, who had taken the city in 1453. He was born Alonso de Borja (Ital. Alfonso Borgia) near Játiva, Spain. A successful jurist, he was appointed cardinal in 1444 by Pope Eugene IV. At the time of his election to the papacy, Callistus was 77 years old, but he demonstrated great vitality, particularly in his Crusade againt the Turks. Although his overall plan failed, Callistus did have the satisfaction of seeing Hungary's János Hunyadi defeat the Turks at Belgrade on Aug. 6, 1456. During the pontificate of Callistus, Joan of Arc's trial was revised, and she was declared innocent.

In his personal life, Callistus was good, honest, and austere, but he did practice nepotism. He raised his nephew Rodrigo Borgia (the future Alexander VI) to the cardinalate in 1456. Callistus died in Rome.

CALLOT, Jacques (1592–1635), French engraver and etcher, who was an important innovator in both the technique and subject matter of printmaking. As a court printmaker for the Medici in Florence from 1612 to 1621, he developed a new engraving medium (a varnish of linseed oil and mastic), the hardness of which made possible greater fineness and detail. This innovation facilitated the work of the great printmakers of the 1600s, such as Rembrandt. Callot, in works such as the monumental *Fair at Impruneta* (1620), was one of the first artists to depict a complete cross section of society. Returning to his native Lorraine in 1621, he adapted a more realistic, less courtly style. His masterpieces are the two series, each entitled *Miseries of War* (both 1633), in which he stripped war of its glory and romance, showing with a merciless eye the distress of the common people.

CALLUS, thickened, horny area on the outer layer of the skin. The hands and feet are particularly susceptible to calluses, which commonly form as a result of heavy footwork or exertion in manual work or sports. *See also* BUNION.

CALMAR. *See* KALMAR.

CALOOCAN, city, National Capital Region, N Philippines, on the island of Luzon. It is a residential and industrial suburb to the N of Manila on the E shore of Dagatdagatan Lagoon. Shoes and other consumer items are made here. The city has grown rapidly since World War II. In 1975 it was merged with Manila and other nearby urban areas to form a single administrative division under the Metropolitan Manila Commission. Pop. (1980 prelim.) 471,289.

CALORIE, metric unit of heat measurement. The small, or gram, calorie (cal) is usually specified in science and engineering as the amount of heat required to raise the temperature of 1 g of water from 14.5° to 15.5° C. The temperature interval is sometimes specified in other ways. The definition now generally accepted in the U.S., and standard in thermochemistry, is that 1 cal equals 4.1840 joules (J).

A slightly different calorie is used in engineering, the international calorie, which equals 1/860 international watt-hour (W h). A large calorie, or kilocalorie (Cal), usually referred to as a calorie and sometimes as a kilogram calorie, equals 1000 cal and is the unit generally used to express the energy-producing value of food in the calculation of diets.

CALORIMETRY, science of measuring a quantity of heat (expressed in calories), as distinct from thermometry, the science of measuring the intensity of heat (expressed as temperature). A calorimeter is the instrument used to measure the amount of heat; one widely used type consists of an insulated container of water, a stirring device, and a thermometer (q.v.). A heat source is placed in the calorimeter, the water is stirred until equilibrium is reached, and the rise of temperature is noted by reading the thermometer. Because the heat capacity of the calorimeter is known (or can be measured by using a standard heat source), the amount of heat liberated can be readily calculated. When the heat source is a hot object of known temperature, the specific and latent heat may be measured as the object cools. Latent heat, which is not associated with a change in temperature, is the heat evolved or absorbed by a substance as it changes from one state to another, as from liquid to solid or vice versa (*see* MATTER, STATES OF). When the heat source is a chemical reaction, such as the burning of a fuel, the reacting substances are placed in a heavy steel vessel called a bomb. The bomb is placed within the calorimeter, and the reaction is started by ignition with an electric spark. *See* HEAT.

See also TEMPERATURE.

CALPE. *See* PILLARS OF HERCULES.

CALUMET CITY, industrial city, Cook Co., NE Illinois, between the Little Calumet and Grand Calumet rivers, near Lake Calumet; inc. as a city 1925. Manufactures include processed food, chemicals, and fertilizer. The community, settled in 1868, developed as a suburb of Hammond, Ind., and was called West Hammond until 1924, when it was renamed for the Calumet peace pipe of the American Indians. Pop. (1970) 33,107; (1980); 39,673.

CALVARY (Lat. *calvaria,* "skull"), hill just outside Jerusalem on which the crucifixion of Jesus Christ took place. It has been identified as a place of execution where malefactors were flung from cliffs or stoned to death.

In Roman Catholic countries a calvary is a representation, either in a chapel or outside a church, of the scenes of the passion and crucifixion of Jesus Christ. The representation is usually of three crosses with the life-size figures of Christ and the thieves, surrounded by figures of the various personages who took part in the crucifixion. Representations of Christ's sufferings on his way to be executed, known as Stations of the Cross, line the way to Calvary. The Via Dolorosa is the name given to the approach to Calvary.

CALVERT, Cecilius. *See* BALTIMORE, CECILIUS CALVERT, 2D BARON.

CALVERT, Charles. *See* BALTIMORE, CHARLES CALVERT, 3D BARON.

CALVERT, George. *See* BALTIMORE, GEORGE CALVERT, 1ST BARON.

CALVIN, John (1509-64), French theologian, church reformer, humanist, and pastor, whom Protestant denominations in the Reformed tradition regard as a major formulator of their beliefs.

Life. Calvin was born in Noyon, France, on July 10, 1509. He received formal instruction for the priesthood at the Collège de la Marche and the Collège de Montaigue, branches of the University of Paris. Encouraged by his father to study law instead of theology, Calvin also attended universities at Orléans and Bourges. Along with several friends he grew to appreciate the humanistic and reforming movements, and he undertook studies in the Greek Bible. In 1532 he published a commentary on Seneca's *De Clementia,* proving his skills as a humanist scholar. His association with Nicholas Cop, newly elected rector of the University of Paris, forced both to flee when Cop announced his support in 1535 of Martin Luther. Although he seldom spoke of it, Calvin underwent a personal religious experience about this time.

Calvin moved frequently during the next two years, avoiding church authorities while he studied, wrote, and formulated from the Bible and Christian tradition the primary tenets of his theology. In 1536 he published the first edition of his *Institutes of the Christian Religion,* a succinct and provocative work that thrust him into the forefront of Protestantism as a thinker and spokesman. During the same year, Calvin visited Geneva on his way to Strasbourg and was asked by Guillaume Farel to assist in the city's reformation movement. Calvin remained in Geneva with Farel until 1538, when the town voted against Farel and asked both men to leave. Calvin went to Strasbourg and participated in that community's religious life until September 1541. While there, he married Idelette de Bure, a widow. They had one child, who died in infancy. At Strasbourg, Calvin also published his *Commentary on Romans* (1539), the first of his many commentaries on books of the Bible.

John Calvin Swiss National Tourist Office

In 1541 Genevans asked Calvin to return and lead them again in reforming the church. He remained in that city for the rest of his life, except for brief journeys in the interest of church reform. His wife died in 1549, and he did not remarry. Although he received a house and stipend from the government, he did not hold office in the government, and he did not even become a citizen of Geneva until 1559. Until the defeat of the Perrin family in 1555, there was significant opposition to Calvin's leadership in the city.

Calvin drafted the new ordinances that the government modified and adopted as a constitution for Geneva governing both secular and sacred matters. Calvin also supported development of a municipal school system for all children, with the Geneva Academy as the center of instruction for the very best students. In 1559 the academy was begun, with Theodore Beza as rector of what soon became a full university.

While Calvin served Geneva, the city was almost constantly threatened by Catholic armies under Emanuel Philibert, duke of Savoy (1528–80), and other leaders. Indeed, the city was a walled fortress, receiving little benefit from surrounding farmlands and nearby allies. Thus, the threat of conquest contributed to Geneva's harsh quality of life and to its need for commerce. Dissenting Christians were frequently expelled, and one man was put to death as a heretic. A man of his time, Calvin approved the burning of Michael Servetus (although he recommended decapitation), when the Unitarian was captured in the city.

Calvin sought to improve the life of the city's citizens in many ways. He supported good hospitals, a proper sewage system, protective rails on upper stories to keep children from falling from tall buildings, special care for the poor and infirm, and the introduction of new industries. He encouraged the use of French in churches, and he personally contributed to its formation as a modern language by his vernacular writings.

Calvin's writings are his most lasting contribution to the church. He wrote hymns and encouraged others to do so. The famous Genevan Psalter, composed mostly by his colleague Louis Bourgeois (c. 1510–c. 1561), became the basis for much Protestant hymnody. He wrote an influential catechism, hundreds of letters to fellow reformers, and commentaries on almost all books of the Bible. Most of his collected sermons and manuscripts are available in English.

Calvin's health was never robust; his illnesses included chronic asthma, indigestion, and catarrh. He became very frail with the onslaught of quartan fever in 1558. He died on May 27, 1564, and was buried in an unmarked grave in Geneva.

Calvin's Theology. According to Calvin, the Bible specified the nature of theology and of any human institutions. Thus, his statements on doctrine began and ended in Scripture, although he frequently cited the church fathers and medieval Catholic thinkers. He sought to minimize speculation on divine matters and instead to draw on the Word of God. He also urged the church to recover its original vitality and purity.

In Calvin's masterwork, *Institutes of the Christian Religion,* which he revised at least five times between 1536 and 1559, Calvin sought to articulate biblical theology in a sensible way, following the articles of the Apostles' Creed (q.v.). The four books in the definitive edition (1559) focus on the articles "Father," "Son," "Holy Spirit," and "Church."

On the Father. Knowledge of God is bound up with self-knowledge. In the world and in the human conscience, spiritual demands are manifest. God created the world and made it good. Since the fall, however, humanity, by its own powers, has been able to apprehend God only rarely and imperfectly. On their own, human beings can never achieve a true religious life based on the knowledge of God. In God's grace (q.v.), however, conveyed through Jesus Christ as described in the Bible, the Creator resolved this destructive dilemma and enabled humanity to gain a clear view of revelation. Those people who learn the truth about human depravity—that even the best deeds are tainted and none is pure—can repent and depend on God the Father for salvation.

On the Son. Human sin, inherited from Adam and Eve, produces in each person an "idol factory" (*see* ORIGINAL SIN). All individuals deserve destruction, but Jesus Christ served as prophet, priest, and king to call the elect into eternal life with God. Christ summons the chosen into new life, interceding for them in his atonement, and he reigns at God's right hand. Calvin took pains to emphasize the continuity of his doctrines with Christian orthodoxy as expressed in the Nicene and Chalcedonian creeds. *See* NICENE CREED.

On the Spirit. God's Holy Spirit, the third person of the Trinity, gives power to the writing and the reading of Scripture, to the devotional life of believers, and to Christian growth in Christ (sanctification). It also permits faith that God's resurrection of the dead will bring the saved into perfection in God's presence. Any assurance of election to grace is given by the Spirit, and even the condemnation of the damned according to God's justice works by the power of the Spirit. *See* PREDESTINATION.

On the church. God's church and the sacraments are also given in God's grace for the edification of the elect and the good of the world. The church, one through all time, can be known by the preaching and hearing of God's Word and the proper administration of the sacraments. Although the true church is known only to God, the visible church is thoroughly related to it on earth. Officers and leaders in the church should be those individuals who try responsibly to follow in Christian discipleship, but their authority cannot depend on their righteousness. The offices should be only those designated in the New Testament. Sacraments (baptism and the Eucharist, qq.v.) should be celebrated as mysteries in which Christ is spiritually present. Calvin stressed the sovereignty of God, the nature of election and predestination, the sins of pride and disobedience, the authority of Scripture, and the nature of the Christian life. Each of these teachings has been seized upon at some time by those following him as the central doctrine of Calvinism (q.v.). Calvin expounded biblical teaching on various issues of his day, in light of particular controversies within the church. His theology has been recognized as lying in the Pauline-Augustinian tradition; he tried to steer what he perceived to be a middle course between an exclusive emphasis on either divine providence or human responsibility.

See also REFORMATION. L.B.W.

For further information on this person, see the section Biographies in the Bibliography in volume 28.

CALVIN, Melvin (1911–), American chemist and Nobel laureate, noted for his study of photosynthesis and for his work with certain plant species that produce fuel oil. Calvin was born in Saint Paul, Minn., and educated at the Michigan College of Mining and Technology (now Michigan Technological University) and at the universities of Minnesota and Manchester, England. At the University of California at Berkeley, which he joined in 1937, Calvin started his experiments in photosynthesis. Using radioactive carbon-14, he detected the sequence of chemical reactions produced by plants in converting gaseous carbon dioxide and water into oxygen and carbohydrates. For this work he received the 1961 Nobel Prize in chemistry.

CALVINISM, Christian theology of the French church reformer John Calvin. Calvin's *Institutes of the Christian Religion* (1536–59; trans. 1561) was most influential in the development of the Protestant churches of the Reformed tradition.

Calvinist doctrine lies within the Pauline and Augustinian theological tradition. Its central tenets include belief in the absolute sovereignty of God and the doctrine of justification by faith alone (*see* FAITH). As did the German religious reformer Martin Luther, Calvin denied that human beings were capable of free will after the Fall of Adam, but he went farther than Luther in elaborating a doctrine of predestination (q.v.)—that certain persons are elected by God to salvation, while others are rejected by him and consigned to eternal damnation. Calvin also shared Luther's belief in the Bible as the unique rule for the life of faith, but differed from his fellow reformer in defending the subjugation of the state to the church and in his interpretation of the Eucharist (q.v.). Many of the tenets of Calvinism have had profound social implications—in particular, that thrift, industry, and hard work are forms of moral virtue and that business success is an evidence of God's grace. Because these views helped to create a climate favorable to commerce, Calvinism played a role in the establishment of capitalism.

By the early 17th century, Calvinism had been adopted by Protestant groups in many lands. The Synod of Dort (1618–19) in Holland fixed this form of belief as Dutch orthodoxy (*see* ARMINIANISM). French Calvinists founded the Huguenot movement (*see* HUGUENOTS), which was suppressed by the Roman Catholic church. In England, Puritanism (q.v.) developed and briefly achieved ascendancy during the period when the monarchy was suspended under Oliver Cromwell. The Westminster Confession (1646) represents the systematic expression of Puritan theology. It was adopted by the Church of Scotland in 1648 and has become the basic creed of Presbyterian groups in Great Britain and throughout the world. Many English Puritans, dissatisfied with the Church of England, immigrated to America during the colonial period. Settling in New England, they contributed greatly to shaping the religious character of the U.S., mainly through the preaching of Jonathan Edwards and other leaders during the Great Awakening (q.v.).

Calvinism remains an important strain within Protestant thought. In the 20th century, the influential Swiss theologian Karl Barth revived the Calvinist doctrine of God's supremacy, beside which all human activity is seen as worthless.

For a summary of Calvin's theology, *see* CALVIN, JOHN. For a more detailed discussion of Calvinist history and doctrine, *see* PRESBYTERIANISM.

For further information on this topic, see the Bibliography in volume 28, sections 85, 93, 95.

CALVINO, Italo (1923–85), Italian writer. Born in Cuba, of Italian parents, Calvino moved to Italy in his youth. After World War II activity as a partisan in the Italian Resistance, he settled in Turin, where he earned his degree in literature.

He was a realistic writer in his first novel, *The Path to the Nest of Spiders* (1947; trans. 1956). He then turned to techniques of a genre that became known as magic realism, characteristic of his allegorical novels *The Nonexistent Knight & The Cloven Viscount* (1952–59; trans. 1962). These and the later works *Cosmicomics* (1965; trans 1968); *If on a Winter's Night a Traveler* (1979; trans. 1981); and *Mr. Palomar* (1983; trans. 1985) demonstrate Calvino's unique blend of fantasy, scientific curiosity, and methaphysical speculation.

CALVO, Carlos (1824–1906), Argentine diplomat, historian, and specialist in international law, born in Buenos Aires. As a diplomat Calvo represented at various times both Paraguay and Argentina as minister to Berlin, Belgium, Paris, London, Saint Petersburg (now Leningrad), and Vienna. Today he is remembered for his writings on international law and as one of the founders of the Institute of International Law at Ghent, Belgium, in 1873. His principal work, *The Theoretical and Practical International Law of Europe and America,* was first published in 1863. Calvo also compiled a 15-volume collection of Latin American treaties, published from 1862 to 1867. In the latter part of his career Calvo enunciated the so-called Calvo Doctrine that has since become a part of several Latin American constitutions. This doctrine states that people living in a foreign nation should settle claims and complaints by submitting to the jurisdiction of local courts and not by using either diplomatic pressure or armed intervention from their own government. The Calvo Doctrine is sometimes confused with the

Drago Doctrine, which is a narrower application of the same principle. Calvo justified his doctrine as necessary to prevent the abuse of the jurisidiction of weak nations by more powerful nations. Calvo's writings had a decided influence on the development of international law in the 20th century.

CALVO DOCTRINE. *See* CALVO, CARLOS.

CALYPSO, in Greek mythology, a sea nymph and daughter of the Titan Atlas. Calypso lived alone on the mythical island of Ogygia in the Ionian Sea. When the Greek hero Odysseus was shipwrecked on Ogygia, she fell in love with him and kept him a virtual prisoner for seven years. Although she promised him immortality and eternal youth if he would stay with her, she could not make him overcome his desire to return home. At the bidding of the god Zeus, she finally released Odysseus and gave him materials to build a raft to leave the island. She died of grief after he left.

CALYPSO, form of folk music developed in Trinidad, West Indies, and originally sung at carnivals. Frequently improvised, the words of calypso songs usually concern topical or satirical themes, and they are characterized technically by arbitrary shifts in the accentuation of everyday English words. In Trinidad, calypso music is generally sung to a guitar and maraca accompaniment that establishes a complex counterrhythm with the voice of the singer in a style probably based on the percussive rhythms of native African music. Since about 1945, steel drums (oil drums, modified and tuned) are also used, often played in bands.

CAM, part of a machine used to provide a repetitive straight-line or back-and-forth motion to a second part, known as the follower. Cams are used to open and close the inlet and exhaust valves of an automotive engine, to index parts of automatic machinery for mass production, to operate a sequence of control switches in electrical equipment, and in many other machines. Complex cam shapes may be required to produce a desired motion.

Three types of cams are in common use, the most common being the disk cam illustrated in Fig. a. The cam profile here is cut from a disk mounted on a rotating shaft. The follower can be a flat plate moving vertically in a straight line, or it can be a roller or knife-edge that moves in a straight line or is pivoted. The follower is usually spring loaded to retain contact with the cam. The second type of cam commonly used is the cylinder cam shown in Fig. b, the follower in which is a pivoted roller moving along a groove cut into a cylindrical cam rotor. The third type is the translation cam shown in Fig. c, in which the required profile that defines the motion is cut into a flat plate that moves back and forth. The follower shown in the figure is a spring-loaded knife edge that moves up and down. It can be observed from the figures that the motion of the follower can be changed easily, in order to obtain a desired sequence, by altering the shape of the cam profile.

CAM, *or* **CÃO, Diogo** (fl. 15th cent.), Portuguese navigator and explorer. During voyages made between 1482 and 1484 and again in 1485 and 1486, he discovered the mouth of the Congo River and was the first European to explore the W coast of Africa as far S as Cape Cross, near what is now Walvis Bay, in SW Africa. He marked the territories he discovered by erecting four pillars inscribed with the Portuguese royal arms, three of which have since been transferred to museums. In recognition of his services, John II of Portugal made Cam a noble in 1484, promoted him to the rank of cavalier, and granted him an annuity.

CAMACHO, Manuel Ávila. *See* ÁVILA CAMACHO, MANUEL.

CAMAGÜEY, formerly PUERTO PRÍNCIPE, city, E Cuba, capital of Camagüey Province, near the port of Nuevitas. It is the largest inland city of

Three types of cam. (a) Disk cam; (b) Cylinder cam; (c) Translation cam.

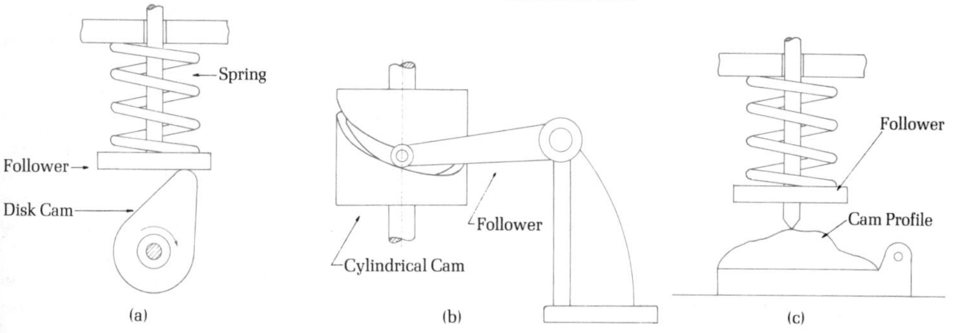

Cuba. Lying at the junction of railroads and highways, it is an important commercial center with a large trade in cattle, hides, and sugar, which are produced in the province. Industries in Camagüey include sawmilling, distilling, tanning, and processing of meat and dairy products. The city has a cathedral and many beautiful churches and mansions. Founded in 1514 by the Spanish governor of Cuba, Diego Velázquez, the original settlement occupied a site on the N coast of Cuba; it was moved to its present site about 1530. In 1668 the city was seized and sacked by pirates under the Welsh buccaneer Sir Henry Morgan. Pop. (1981 prelim.) 245,235.

CAMARGO, Marie Anne de Cupis de (1710–70), French ballerina, the first female dancer to adopt the brilliant leaping steps of male dancers. Born in Brussels, she studied with the celebrated French ballerina Françoise Prévost (1680–1741) and in 1726 made her debut at the Paris Opéra. To gain technical freedom, Camargo broke with custom by dancing in slippers without heels and a skirt shortened to calf length. She may have introduced ballet's fundamental 90-degree turnout of the legs, and was probably the first woman to dance the virtuosic entrechat-quatre, a movement in the air, with the criss-crossing of legs four times.

CAMARILLO, city, Ventura Co., SW California; inc. 1964. It is the processing and shipping center of a diversified farming area. Electronic and aerospace equipment is manufactured. Saint John's College (1939) and a state mental hospital are here. Settled in the 1800s, the community is named for Juan Camarillo (1812–80), a local landowner. Pop. (1970) 19,219; (1980) 37,732.

CAMBACÉRÈS, Jean Jacques Régis de (1753–1824), French statesman and jurist, born in Montpellier. Educated as a lawyer, Cambacérès became president of the criminal court in Montpellier in 1791. During the French Revolution, he was elected to the National Convention and voted somewhat reluctantly for the execution of King Louis XVI. Avoiding party politics, Cambacérès concentrated on legal matters and formulated the civil code from which the Code Napoléon was eventually derived. In 1796 he became a member of the Council of Five Hundred, the lower house of the new legislature set up by the constitution of 1795. In June 1799, he became minister of justice, and in November of that year he assisted in the coup d'état that brought Napoleon Bonaparte to power as First Consul; in 1804 Bonaparte became emperor of France as Napoleon I. In 1799 Cambacérès was appointed to the second highest position in the nation as Second Consul, in 1804 he was made archchancellor of the empire, and in 1808, Napoleon created him duke of Parma. In 1813–14, Cambacérès directed civil affairs as president of the Council of Regency, finally voting for Napoleon's abdication. During the Hundred Days, however, he again served Napoleon as minister of justice and president of the House of Peers. After Waterloo and the permanent restoration of the Bourbons under Louis XVIII, Cambacérès was exiled because of his involvement in the death of Louis XVI and went to live in Belgium. His legal and political rights were restored to him in 1818, and he returned to France.

CAMBAY, GULF OF, inlet of the Arabian Sea, W India, between the Kathiawar Peninsula and the mainland of India. The gulf, which is cone-shaped, is 209 km (130 mi) long and about 200 km (about 125 mi) wide at the mouth and is noted for high tides of from 9 to 12 m (30 to 40 ft). Four rivers empty into the gulf, the Sabarmati, Mahi, Narmada, and Tapti. The city of Cambay at the head of the gulf was a prosperous port in the 15th century but later lost its importance when silting almost sealed it off from the gulf. Surat, a port on the mouth of the Tapti R., has also been affected by silting. The most important trading center today is the deep-sea port of Bhavnager on the Kathiawar Peninsula.

CAMBODIA, also known as Kampuchea, nation of SE Asia, bounded on the NE by Laos, on the E and SE by Vietnam, on the SW by the Gulf of Thailand, and on the W and NW by Thailand. Cambodia covers a total area of 181,035 sq km (69,898 sq mi).

LAND AND RESOURCES

Cambodia's terrain is dominated by a large, low-lying alluvial plain that occupies most of the central part of the country. The main features of the plain are the Mekong R., which flows from N to S through Cambodia, and the Tonle Sap (Great Lake), which covers an area of about 2600 sq km (about 1000 sq mi) in the dry season to about 10,400 sq km (about 4015 sq mi) in the rainy season. The outlet of Tonle Sap is a river of the same name, which during the dry season flows S into the Mekong R.; during the rainy season the floodwaters of the Mekong R. back into the Tonle Sap, inundating the central part of the country. To the E of the alluvial plain lies an undulating plateau region. Mountain ranges fringe the plain on the SW, where the Cardamom Mts. form a physical barrier along the country's coast, and on the N by the Phnum Dangrek.

Known mineral resources are limited; phosphate and gemstones are most important. Cambodia has an enormous waterpower potential, but its development has been hindered by the warfare and civil strife of the 1970s and '80s.

Climate. Cambodia has a tropical monsoon climate. The average annual temperature is about 26.7° C (about 80° F). A rainy season extends from mid-April through mid-October. Average annual rainfall is about 1400 mm (about 55 in) on the central plains and more than 3800 mm (150 in) in mountainous areas and along the coast.

Plants and Animals. More than half of Cambodia is forested. The densest forests are found in the mountains and along the SW coast. Savannas, covered with high, sharp grass, are present in the higher plains and plateaus. Such trees as rubber, kapok, palm, coconut, and banana are common.

Wildlife is varied and includes elephant, deer, wild oxen, buffalo, panther, bear, and tiger. Cormorant, crane, pheasant, and wild duck are also found, as are poisonous snakes, including cobra.

POPULATION

About 90% of the people are Cambodians, ethnically known as Khmer. Chinese and Vietnamese make up most of the remaining 10%. Others include Laotians, Thai, and the Cham-Malays, who inhabit the moutainous regions. The population is over 85% rural.

Population Characteristics. The population of Cambodia (1986 est.) was 7.47 million. The overall population density was 41 per sq km (107 per sq mi). During the late 1970s the larger cities were systematically depopulated, with residents being sent to rural areas.

The capital and largest city is Phnom Penh (pop., 1983 est., 600,000), situated at the junction of the Mekong and Tonle Sap rivers. Other major cities are Batdambang (est. pop., 40,000), Kampong Cham (30,000), and Kampot (13,000). The major port is Kampong Saom, formerly Sihanoukville, on the Gulf of Thailand.

Language and Religion. The official language is Khmer, or Cambodian. French was formerly an important secondary language, but its use has been discouraged.

Theravada (Hinayana) Buddhism is the dominant religion and is adhered to by about 90% of the population. Other religions include Roman Catholicism, Islam, and Mahayana Buddhism; the mountain tribes are animists.

Education. About 48% of the Cambodian population is literate. Government plans to reestablish and expand the educational system, which was disrupted by warfare in the late 1970s, are being realized. All public education is free. In the early 1980s about 1,505,000 pupils attended some 3600 primary schools. Secondary and higher education remains limited, however. Institutions of higher education were closed in the late 1970s, and many instructors were murdered or died of starvation or disease. By the early 1980s a teacher-training institution and a medical school had reopened, but student enrollment in higher education was only about 600.

A Cambodian princess, wearing a ceremonial costume that includes a mokot, *or tiara, takes part in a traditional Cambodian dance.* UPI

Culture. The cultural heritage of the Khmer dynasties is reflected in many facets of contemporary Cambodia. Many buildings, such as the Royal Palace in Phnom Penh, are decorated in the Khmer architectural style and use such motifs as the garuda, a mythical symbolic bird in the Hindu religion. Handicraft items, often in woven gold or silver lamé, also reflect ancient motifs. The classical Cambodian dance mimes in the most traditional style the legendary lives of ancient religious deities.

The ruins of the ancient Khmer empire, found in NW Cambodia, constitute one of the richest and most remarkable archaeological sites in the world. Particularly noteworthy are the ruins of the Khmer capital of Angkor Thom, built about 850, and to the S, the temple of Angkor Wat (or Angor Vat), built between 1112 and 1152.

A family of Cambodian farmers work in their rice paddies near Phnom Penh. UPI

ECONOMY

Agriculture is the mainstay of the Cambodian economy. Before the onset of warfare and civil disorder during the 1970s and '80s, Cambodia was largely self-sufficient in food products, and in spite of low yields per unit area and the planting of only one crop a year, the country exported sizable amounts of rice. By 1974 rice had to be imported. Production of rubber, the other major crop, also fell. In 1975 the new Khmer Rouge government nationalized all means of production, and agriculture was collectivized. Crop production rose slightly until warfare in 1978 and 1979 disrupted the harvesting and planting of rice. Widespread famine followed. Disruption was also severe in the country's small manufacturing sector, and many transportation and communication links were destroyed. By the mid-1980s both agriculture and manufacturing had begun to recover from the effects of years of warfare. Nevertheless, Cambodia remained one of the world's poorest countries, with an average monthly wage of less than $7 a month.

Agriculture. Rice is the most important crop of Cambodian agriculture. In peacetime some 80% of the cultivated land is planted in rice; annual production during the mid-1980s was estimated at 1.3 million metric tons. Rubber, the other leading crop, is primarily grown in the E plateaus. Other important agricultural products include corn, cassava, soybeans, sesame, palm sugar, and pepper. Mangoes, bananas, and pineapples are grown for local consumption.

Forestry, Fishing, and Mining. Of the extensive, potentially valuable forests, only a small proportion has been exploited, mainly because of Cambodia's poor transportation facilities. The annual timber harvest was about 5.2 million cu m (183.6 million cu ft) during the mid-1980s.

Fishing is an important economic activity; most of the catch is consumed locally. The Tonle Sap provides one of the largest freshwater fishery resources in Southeast Asia. Carp, perch, and smelt are the principal varieties of fish caught.

Zircons, sapphires, and rubies are mined in

Cambodian peasant cleans and prepares for cooking fish caught in the Mekong River. UPI

INDEX TO MAP OF CAMBODIA (KAMPUCHEA)

limited amounts in the W, and salt is found in the central provinces. Other mineral resources include bauxite and phosphates.

Manufacturing. Cambodia's limited industry was severely damaged during the 1970s and has been only partially rebuilt since that time. Industrial products in the early 1980s included 42,000 metric tons of meat and 4.1 billion cigarettes.

Currency and Banking. The unit of currency is the new riel, consisting of 100 sen. The National Bank of Kampuchea (1980) is the sole bank of issue. Money, which had been officially abolished in 1978, was reintroduced in 1980, but the new riel was not traded on world currency markets.

Commerce and Trade. In peacetime the principal Cambodian exports were rice and rice products, rubber, corn, and wood products. The total annual value of exports dropped from about $60 million in the early 1970s to less than $10 million in the early 1980s. The chief imports were metals, machinery, textiles, mineral products, and foodstuffs; their total value was less than $30 million annually in the early 1980s. By the mid-1970s the country had become a net importer of rice; the export of rubber was also adversely affected by wartime activities.

Transportation. In the early 1980s Cambodia had about 13,350 km (about 8295 mi) of roads of all types; some one-fifth of these were paved. A modern highway links Phnom Penh with the port of Kampong Saom. A railway links the capital with Batdambang and extends NE to the Thai frontier. A link completed in 1969 connects Phnom Penh with Kampong Saom. The aggregate rail mileage was about 650 km (about 400 mi) in the early 1980s. Inland waterways, including navigable sections of the main rivers, total about 1400 km (about 870 mi) in the rainy season, but diminish to less than 650 km (less than 400 mi) at other times. An international airport is located near Phnom Penh.

Communications. All major Cambodian communications systems are controlled by the government. Radio services link the large cities; telephone, telegraph, and postal services were resumed in 1979. In the early 1980s the country had some 7300 telephones, 200,000 radios, and 52,000 television receivers.

Labor. About 75% of the Cambodian labor force is engaged in agriculture. The Cambodian Federation of Trade Unions is the leading labor organization.

GOVERNMENT

In April 1975, Cambodia came under the rule of the Khmer Rouge, as Democratic Kampuchea, thus ending its 600-year-old monarchy. In 1979 a rebel organization, the KNUFNS (Kampuchean National United Front for National Salvation), with the backing of Vietnamese troops deposed the Khmer Rouge government and established the People's Republic of Kampuchea. The KNUFNS established a 14-member People's Revolutionary Council to govern the country. A draft constitution was promulgated in March 1981, and in May elections were held for the 117 seats of the National Assembly. Executive power was vested in the chairperson of the Council of State and the chairperson of the Council of Ministers (the premier). Remnants of the Khmer Rouge, organized as the Coalition Government of Democratic Kampuchea in resistance to the Vietnamese-backed regime, retained Cambodia's seat at the UN and diplomatic recognition from the U.S. and China.

Health and Welfare. Dispensaries and first-aid stations are being established throughout the country to help combat such widespread illnesses as yaws, trachoma, tuberculosis, malaria, and dysentery. Welfare programs are still limited. Internationally organized aid programs helped the victims of the 1979–80 famine.

Defense. In the mid-1980s Cambodia had an estimated 35,000 persons in the armed forces. A force of about 140,000 Vietnamese troops was also in the country.

HISTORY

The Mon and the Khmer peoples moved into Southeast Asia before the Christian era. They probably came from southern China, although some scholars believe they migrated from Indonesia. The Khmer and Mon peoples are thought to have arrived before their present neighbors—the Vietnamese, Lao, and Thai. Indian missionaries, traders, and soldiers of fortune greatly influenced the early kingdoms of Cambodia, providing a writing system, architectural styles, religions (Hinduism and Buddhism), the concept of the god-king (*deva-raja*), and a highly stratified class system.

The Khmer Kingdoms. Funan, the first kingdom to occupy the present area of Cambodia, was formed in the 1st century AD, probably by Mon-Khmer peoples. Funan's culture, however, came mainly from India. Its port, Oc Eo, on the Gulf of Thailand, was a major trade link between China and India. Chenla, located northeast of the Tonle Sap, was originally a vassal of Funan, but in the 6th and 7th centuries AD it conquered that kingdom. In AD 706, however, Chenla was split in two. The northern half, Land Chenla, was in Laos, and the southern half, called Water Chenla, in the area of modern Cambodia, fell under the control of Java. *See* CHENLA, KINGDOM OF.

Angkor era. The reign of Jayavarman II (r. about 802–50) began the Angkor era in Khmer history (*see* ANGKOR). In the early 9th century he returned from exile in Java, rejected Javanese suzerainty, and instituted the cult of the god-king. The great temples of the Angkor era were built by his successors to house their royal lingas, the phallic emblems of the Hindu god Shiva. The kings of Angkor ruled over much of the Southeast Asian mainland until the early 15th century. Their capital was the center of a network of reservoirs and canals that controlled the supply of water for rice farming and enabled the people to produce a surplus of wealth to finance wars and temple building. One king, Jayavarman VII (c. 1130–1219), built hospitals and rest houses along the roads that crisscrossed his kingdom.

Early signs of imperial weakening could be seen in the rebellions of the 1100s. These were caused by the rulers' excessive demands on their people and by neglect of the irrigation system. Epidemics of malaria, plague, and other diseases undermined the population. The introduction of Theravada Buddhism—which taught that all could hope for spiritual advancement through meditation—may also have upset Angkor's imperial drive and its rigid social order. Loss of control over the Chao Phraya River Basin in Thailand further weakened the Angkor Empire.

A view of the causeway leading to Angkor Wat; the balustrades in foreground represent the naga, or cobra, of Hindu mythology. UPI

Decline. After Thailand—or Siam, as it was then called—defeated Angkor in 1431, the Cambodian court was moved southeastward to Phnom Penh. Despite almost constant fighting with Siam in the west, everyday life in Cambodia's interior was little changed until Siam took Phnom Penh in 1594 and established a degree of political control. Vietnam's slow advance southward reached the Mekong delta a few years later. In 1620 the Khmer king Chetta II (r. 1618–25) married a Vietnamese princess and allowed Vietnam to set up a customs collection house on the site of present Ho Chi Minh City (Saigon). Thereafter, Siam and Vietnam each tried to control the Khmer kingdom by military occupation and enthronement of puppet monarchs.

French Rule. In 1863 France, by then rapidly expanding its control in Indochina, intervened to slow the process of Cambodia's dismemberment by Vietnam and Siam, proclaiming a protectorate over the country. French rule in Cambodia was indirect, through resident advisers whose word was final on major subjects. The Cambodian monarchy was retained and strengthened, and a Khmer civil service was gradually trained. Roads, port facilities, and other public works were built, with an eye to internal security and the export of rubber and rice. The restoration of the vast temple complex at Angkor Wat in the 1930s helped rekindle the Khmer people's pride in their past. During World War II, when Japanese forces overran Indochina (1940), they left the French administration in place. On the verge of defeat in 1945, however, the Japanese overthrew the French and installed a nominally independent Khmer government under King Norodom Sihanouk. France quickly reestablished control after the war, but Sihanouk gained full independence for his country in 1953.

The Modern State. Two years later King Sihanouk abdicated in favor of his father. As Prince Sihanouk he retained an aura of majesty but was much freer to manipulate the urban elite, who constantly jockeyed for high-status jobs. Sihanouk controlled them by organizing a popular movement that centered on village notables. Foreign powers, such as the U.S., the Soviet Union, and China, seeking influence in the region, courted Sihanouk, who drew them into competition for the privilege of aiding Cambodia's development. His success in diplomacy abroad enhanced Sihanouk's political control at home. For more than 15 years he walked the neutralist tightrope and kept Cambodia relatively isolated from the turmoil raging in neighboring Vietnam. In so doing, however, he had to close his eyes to more and more blatant abuse of Cambodia's neutrality by North Vietnamese and Vietcong forces. *See* VIETNAM WAR.

Coup of 1970. In March 1970, while Sihanouk was abroad, his prime minister, Gen. Lon Nol, seized power and sent his army to fight the Vietcong in the border areas. This drew the North Vietnamese into Cambodia, and shortly afterward both U.S. and South Vietnamese troops invaded the kingdom in order to destroy enemy bases there. For the next two years Cambodia was a major battleground of the Vietnam (or Indochina) War. The U.S. and South Vietnam supplied Lon Nol's army and supported it with air power, hoping to gain a breathing space for the Saigon regime. Meanwhile, Khmer Communist party guerrillas, called the Khmer Rouge, had become active in battling Lon Nol's regime, and they were aided by the North Vietnamese and by Prince Sihanouk, who had found asylum in China. Hundreds of thousands of peasants sought the relative safety of towns that were under Lon Nol's control.

Vietnamese domination. In April 1975, just before Saigon fell to the North Vietnamese, the Khmer Rouge seized Phnom Penh. Their subsequent regime, headed by Pol Pot, forced the entire population into rural communes, where death was the penalty for disobeying orders or even for revealing middle-class status. The Khmer Rouge tried to isolate Cambodia from all foreign influence. The brutality of their regime, however, during which 2 to 3 million people may have perished, gave Hanoi in December 1978 the pretext for launching an invasion, which quickly brought the main towns and highways under the control of a new, Vietnamese-backed puppet regime led by Heng Samrin (1934–) as head of the Council of State. The Vietnamese-backed government restored much of the pre-1970 way of life, including Buddhism, but not the monarchy. Khmer Rouge remnants, meanwhile, with forces loyal to Sihanouk, continued resistance in border areas, and their insurgent government retained Cambodia's UN seat. P.A.P.

A refugee camp in Thailand harbors some of the hundreds of thousands of Cambodians who fled their country in 1979 following the Vietnamese invasion.
T. Schmitt-Sygma

For further information on this topic, see the Bibliography in volume 28, sections 120, 668, 670, 678, 1092, 1098.

CAMBON, Jules Martin (1845-1935), French diplomat. In 1891 he was appointed governor-general of Algeria, and was largely responsible for establishing administrative autonomy there. As ambassador (1897-1902) to the U.S., he helped negotiate the peace ending the Spanish-American War. He served as chairman (1919-31) of the Council of Ambassadors responsible for enforcing the Treaty of Versailles (See VERSAILLES, TREATY OF).

CAMBON, (Pierre) Paul (1843-1924), French diplomat, brother of Jules Martin Cambon. He was ambassador (1898-1920) to Britain and worked on the Entente Cordiale (q.v.), an Anglo-French alliance, and the Anglo-Russian agreement of 1907.

CAMBRAI (Flemish *Kambryk*), city, N France, in Nord Department, on the Scheldt (Escaut) R., in Flanders. It is a farm-trade and manufacturing center; products include textiles, metal items, and processed food. The city formerly was a major center for producing cambric, a fine linen fabric named for the city and first made here. Notable structures in Cambrai include the Cathedral of Notre Dame, the Church of Saint Géry, and the city hall.

In Roman times the city was known as Camaracum. It became the capital of a Frankish kingdom in AD 445 and later (about 800) was fortified by Charlemagne. Much of the medieval history of Cambrai is a record of strife between the ruling bishops (archbishops from the 16th cent.) and the citizenry. In the late 15th century the city came under the Holy Roman Empire. At Cambrai, in 1508, the kings of France and Spain, the pope, and the Holy Roman emperor formed the League of Cambrai, an alliance against the Venetian Republic. The Peace of Cambrai, signed here in 1529, concluded a war (1527–29) between Francis I of France and Holy Roman Emperor Charles V. The treaty is sometimes referred to as the Paix des Dames (Ladies' Peace), the preliminary negotiations having been conducted by Louise of Savoy (1476–1531), mother of the French king, and Margaret of Austria (1480–1530), aunt of the Holy Roman emperor. Cambrai was annexed by the French crown in 1677. The city was occupied by the Germans and badly damaged in World Wars I and II. Pop. (1982) 36,618.

CAMBRIAN MOUNTAINS, rugged upland region, occupying much of Wales. The region, which receives abundant rainfall, is the source of the Severn, Towy, and Wye rivers and contains many reservoirs for supplying water to the industrial communities of S Wales and the Midlands of England. The highest point in the Cambrian Mts. is Aran Fawddwy (905 m/2970 ft).

CAMBRIAN PERIOD, first division of the Paleozoic era (q.v.) of the geologic time scale (*see* GEOLOGY), spanning an interval of about 70 million years, from 570 to 500 million years ago. It was named in 1835 by the English geologist Adam Sedgwick for sedimentary rocks found in Wales, which was known to the ancient Romans as "Cambria."

By the dawn of the Paleozoic era, the steadily increasing oxygen content of the atmosphere and oceans had made it possible for the marine environment to support new forms of life (*see* ATMOSPHERE). Thus, for the first time in the history of the earth, creatures evolved that could derive energy from respiration.

The earliest of these new organisms were relatively large, complex marine invertebrates. With hard shells and skeletons of chitin or lime, these creatures had far better chances of preservation in the fossil record than the soft-bodied life of the Precambrian era. Of the latter, only sparse carbonized remains are found.

With their relatively rich fossil content, sedimentary rocks of Cambrian age are the oldest strata that lend themselves to extensive stratigraphic correlation (*see* DATING METHODS). For this reason, in attempting to draw a picture of the earth as it existed during the remote geologic past, scientists have been far more successful with the Cambrian and succeeding periods than with the far older, longer Precambrian era.

The Cambrian is the earliest geologic period for which science has sufficient evidence to hypothesize the existence of crustal plates and to attempt to delineate them (*see* PLATE TECTONICS). Multiple collisions between these plates gave rise, during this period, to a vast landmass or supercontinent. Known to geologists as Gondwanaland, it incorporated the beginnings of today's four southern continents—South America, Africa, Antartica, Western Australia—and included, in addition, India and parts of present-day Mexico and Florida, southern Europe, and possibly China.

As can well be imagined, the distribution of Cambrian continents was vastly different from that of today. Most landmasses were situated in either the tropics or the southern hemisphere. Evidence for the tropical location of ancestral North America and Northern Europe is provided by salt deposits and coral reefs found in the Cambrian rocks of those land areas. Gondwanaland, covering a much more extensive area than the northern landmasses, stretched from the tropics and the south temperate zone almost to the South Pole.

Although life had not yet invaded dry land or the air, the seas of Cambrian time teemed with a great variety of marine invertebrates, including sponges, worms, bryozoans ("moss animals" q.v.), hydrozoans, brachiopods, mollusks (among them the gastropods and species ancestral to the nautilus), primitive arthropods such as the trilobite (q.v.), and a few species of stalked echinoderms. The only plant life of the time consisted of marine algae.

For further information on this topic, see the Bibliography in volume 28, sections 417, 436.

CAMBRIDGE, city, administrative center of Cambridgeshire, central England, on the Cam R. Cambridge is important as a center of learning and is the seat of the University of Cambridge, one of the great educational institutions of Europe. It is also a market center for the surrounding agricultural region and has research industries; the chief manufactures include electronic equipment and precision instruments. Cambridge has retained much of its medieval appearance and has many outstanding edifices, including the Church of Saint Bene't, a 10th-century Saxon structure; and the restored Church of the Holy Sepulchre, one of the four round Norman churches in England. King's College Chapel (begun in 1446) is one of the finest examples of Gothic architecture in Europe. The city has numerous parks and gardens and many museums and galleries, including the noteworthy Fitzwilliam Museum. Cambridge and County Folk museums are here. Cambridge is host to an annual arts festival and of a midsummer fair in existence since the early 16th century.

A Roman military outpost probably existed in the vicinity of present-day Cambridge. In Anglo-Saxon times trade between central England and continental Europe passed over the bridge on the Cam R. here. During the 12th century various religious orders established monasteries and affiliated schools in Cambridge; the university originated from these institutions in the 13th century. Cambridge received its first charter in 1207. Pop. (1981) 90,440.

CAMBRIDGE, city, a seat (with Lowell) of Middlesex Co., NE Massachusetts, on the Charles R., opposite Boston; inc. as a city 1846. It is a noted educational and research center, seat of Harvard University, Massachusetts Institute of Technology, Radcliffe College, and Lesley College (1909). Its printing and publishing industry dates from 1638, when the first printing press in America was established here. Rubber goods, electronic equipment, scientific instruments, candy, and meat products also are manufactured. The city's historic structures include the house George Washington used as headquarters after assuming command of the Continental army here in 1775; it later became the home of the poet Henry Wadsworth Longfellow. Among the many other notable people who lived in Cambridge were the author-physician Oliver Wendell Holmes and the poet-diplomat James Russell Lowell. Founded as New Towne in 1630, the city was the capital of Massachusetts Bay Colony until 1634. It was renamed in 1638 for Cambridge, England. Pop. (1970) 100,361; (1980) 95,322.

CAMBRIDGE, city, Waterloo Regional Municipality, S Ontario Province, Canada, between the Grand and Eramosa rivers. Cambridge was formed in 1973 by the amalgamation of the municipalities of Galt, Preston, and Hespeler with parts of the townships of Waterloo and North Dumfries. It is an agricultural trade center and has some manufacturing industries. Pop. (1981) 77,183; (1986) 79,920.

CAMBRIDGE, UNIVERSITY OF, institution of higher education, the second oldest university (after the University of Oxford) in Great Britain, in the municipal borough of Cambridge.

Academic Organization. The University of Cambridge is a system of 29 independent colleges. Although the colleges and the university per se are separate corporations, all are parts of an integrated educational entity. The university, governed by a senate headed by the chancellor, conducts entrance examinations, examines candidates for degrees during their residency and at the conclusion of their studies, and confers degrees. In addition, it regulates the system of education, deals with disciplinary problems, and administers facilities, such as libraries, lecture rooms, and laboratories, that are beyond the scope of the colleges. The colleges provide their students with lodgings and meals, assign tutors, and offer social, cultural, and athletic activities.

The academic year is divided into three terms of approximately eight weeks each: Michaelmas (autumn), Lent (late winter), and Easter (spring). Students are required to be in residence for the duration of each term. Much of the year's work is done, however, out of term time, during the vacations. Students study under the direct supervision of tutors, members of college faculties who maintain close relationships with the small groups of students in their charge and assist them in preparing for university exams.

Bachelor of arts degrees may be conferred, upon the satisfactory completion of exams, after nine terms, or three years of residency. The majority of students, candidates for honors degrees, take a special examination called a tripos (after the three-legged stools on which examiners formerly sat). Successful candidates for triposes are classified according to their standing; first, second, or third class. The university also confers the master of arts and doctor of philosophy degrees in law, theology, medicine, science, and music.

History. Several religious orders, including the Franciscans and Dominicans, established monasteries and affiliated schools in Cambridge early in the 12th century. Students of the University of Oxford and the University of Paris left to study in Cambridge in the 13th century. The origin of the colleges is traced to the associations of students, distinct from religiously affiliated groups, who began to reside in independent hostels, or halls. Over the centuries these halls were endowed by

College	Founded
Christ's	1505
Churchill	1960
Clare	1326
Clare Hall	1966
Corpus Christi	1352
Darwin	1964
Downing	1800
Emmanuel	1584
Fitzwilliam	1966
Girton (women)	1869
Gonville and Caius	1348
Hughes Hall (graduate women)	1885
Jesus	1496
King's	1441
Lucy Cavendish Collegiate Society (graduate women)	1965
Magdalene	1542
New Hall (women)	1954
Newnham (women)	1871
Pembroke	1347
Peterhouse	1284
Queens'	1448
Saint Catherine's	1473
Saint Edmund's House (graduate men)	1896
Saint John's	1511
Selwyn	1882
Sidney Sussex	1596
Trinity	1546
Trinity Hall	1350
Wolfson (coeducational graduate)	1965

The name of Cambridge University in Cambridge, England, is derived from the Cam River, here shown flowing under the bridge at St. John's College. Cecile Brunswick

private benefactors, beginning with Hugh de Balsham, bishop of Ely (fl. 1256–86), who in 1284 founded Peterhouse, the first of Cambridge's colleges. In 1318 Pope John XXII issued a bull recognizing Cambridge as a *studium generale,* or place of study, that is, a university. Five new colleges were established during the 14th century, four in the 15th, and six in the 16th; not until the 19th century were other colleges founded. For a list of all the Cambridge colleges and their founding dates, see the accompanying table.

The University of Cambridge figured prominently in the Protestant Reformation. The Dutch scholar Desiderius Erasmus was a professor of Greek and divinity at Cambridge from 1511 to 1514 and translated the New Testament from Greek into Latin there; the religious reformers William Tyndale, Hugh Latimer, and Thomas Cranmer were educated at Cambridge. As a result of the decrees of King Henry VIII establishing the Church of England, the humanistic method of study replaced the Scholastic. Canon law studies were ended, public lectures in Latin and Greek were held, and the Bible was studied in the light of contemporary learning.

A reaction took place, however, during the reign of Queen Elizabeth I, when Cambridge became a stronghold of Puritanism. Restrictive legislation enacted in 1570 transferred teaching authority to the heads of the colleges. In 1604, early in the reign of King James I, the university was granted the right to elect two members to Parliament; the right was ended in 1949. During the 17th century the group of scholars known as the Cambridge Platonists (q.v.) emerged, and, through the influence of such faculty members as the scientists Isaac Barrow (1630–77) and Isaac Newton, an emphasis on the study of mathematics and natural sciences developed for which Cambridge has been subsequently noted.

Important 19th-century developments included the repeal of the restrictive Elizabethan statutes and, accordingly, greater academic freedom; the abolition in 1871 of religious tests for admission; and the adoption of a broader curriculum. Girton College, the first such establishment for undergraduate women, was founded in 1869. Among major changes in the second half of the 20th century were a marked increase in the size of the older colleges and the establishment of seven new ones and a growing emphasis on research and advanced studies. State aid has been granted to all British universities since 1926.

John Harvard, founder of Harvard College (later Harvard University), was a graduate of Cambridge, as were the statesman Oliver Cromwell, the poet John Milton, the naturalist Charles Darwin, and the economist John Maynard Keynes. Charles, prince of Wales, studied at Trinity College (as did his forebears Edward VII and George VI) and received a degree in June 1970.

Special Facilities. The Fitzwilliam Museum, founded in 1816 by the English statesman William Wentworth Fitzwilliam (1748-1833), is part of the university and houses a renowned collection of art and archaeological objects. Science buildings at Cambridge include the Cavendish Laboratory of Experimental Physics, the Sedgwick Museum of Geology, and the Scott Polar Research Institute. The University Library ranks, with the British Library and Bodleian Library at Oxford, as one of the greatest collections in Great Britain; its holdings are supplemented by the manuscripts and printed books housed in the libraries of the colleges and associated university facilities. King's College Chapel, a late 15th-century building, is famed for the beauty of its architecture as well as for its choral music. The Cambridge University Press, established in 1521, publishes books of scholarly and general interest. S.D.P.

For further information on this topic, see the Bibliography in volume 28, section 309.

CAMBRIDGE PLATONISTS, school of English Christian philosphers, centered at the University of Cambridge, in the late 17th century. Derived from a group known as the Latitudinarians that reacted against Calvinism, and basing their doctrines largely on the teachings of Plato, the Cambridge Platonists were the theological liberals of their age. Stressing morality rather than dogma, they sought to reconcile fundamental Christian ethics with the new rationality of Renaissance philosophy, science, and humanism. Although their theological background was Puritan, they rejected the Puritan separation of theology and morals. The school was fundamentally antagonistic to the doctrines of the English philosopher Thomas Hobbes, who founded his dogma on the senses and ignored the moral and religious postulates of human nature. The extent of their liberalism often caused the Cambridge Platonists to be condemned as atheists, and they generally were viewed with suspicion. The two best-known Cambridge Platonists are the English philosophers Ralph Cudworth and Henry More (1614-87).

CAMBRIDGESHIRE, county, E England; Cambridge is the administrative center. Cambridgeshire is dominated in the N by The Fens, a largely drained marshland region; in the S and W are low, undulating hills. The county is predominantly agricultural, producing wheat and other grains, sugar beets, fruit, and vegetables. Light industry is concentrated chiefly in Cambridge and Peterborough. Cambridgeshire was formed in 1974 with the merging of the former counties of Cambridgeshire and Isle of Ely, and Huntingdon and Peterborough (qq.v.). Area, 3409 sq km (1316 sq mi); Pop. (1981) 575,177.

CAMBRIDGESHIRE AND ISLE OF ELY, former county, E England; Cambridge was the administrative center. The county was formed in 1965 with the amalgamation of the previously separate administrative divisions of Cambridgeshire and the Isle of Ely. The latter is not truly an island; it is so-named because the town of Ely rises on a hill above surrounding marshes. In 1974 Cambridgeshire and Isle of Ely became a part of the new county of Cambridgeshire (q.v.).

CAMBYSES I (fl. 6th cent. BC), Persian king of the Achaemenid dynasty who ruled (c. 600-559 BC) over Anshan (now Baghdad Province, Iraq) as a vassal of the Medes, then preeminent in Persia. Cambyses I was the son of Cyrus I (fl. 7th cent. BC), whom he succeeded, and the father of Cyrus the Great, who founded the Persian Empire. According to the Greek historian Herodotus, Cambyses I married the daughter of Astyages, king of Medes (r. about 584-550 BC).

CAMBYSES II (r. 529-522 BC), king of Persia, son of Cyrus the Great, whom he succeeded. In order to maintain control over the Persian Empire, Cambyses II had his younger brother, Smerdis (fl. 6th cent. BC), murdered. He then led an expedition to conquer Egypt, the sole independent kingdom in the Middle East after the conquest of Asia by his father. Cambyses defeated Psamtik III, king of Egypt (r. 526-525 BC), and succeeded in conquering Egypt as far south as Nubia, but he failed in later attacks on the Egyptian oasis of Ammonium (now Siwa) and in campaigns in Ethiopia. During his absence in Egypt, a usurper, Gaumata (r. 522), claimed to be Smerdis and seized the throne of Persia. The death of Smerdis had been kept secret; so Gaumata's claim was believed, and he was acknowledged king throughout Persia for about seven months. Cambyses was on his way to Persia to punish Gaumata when he either died by accident or committed suicide. According to Herodotus,

Cambyses II was a dissolute and inhuman despot, prone to drunken or insane rages in which he committed sacrilegious and cruel acts.

CAMDEN, town, Knox Co., S Maine, on Penobscot Bay; settled 1769, inc. 1791. It is a tourist resort located in a scenic area. Manufactures include textiles and leather. A large state park is nearby. The town is named for Charles Pratt, 1st Earl Camden (1714–94), a British jurist sympathetic to the American colonies. Pop. (1970) 4115; (1980) 4584.

CAMDEN, industrial city, seat of Camden Co., SW New Jersey, a port of entry on the Delaware R., opposite Philadelphia; settled 1681, platted 1773, inc. 1828. Camden is a trade, manufacturing, and transportation center. It has two deep-water docking areas and major railroad freight yards. Two bridges connect the city with Philadelphia. Chief products are electronic equipment, office supplies, and processed foods; the Campbell's Soup plant has been here since 1862. The Camden campus (1927) of Rutgers University and a community college are in the city. Camden's historic structures include the house in which the poet Walt Whitman lived from 1873 until his death in 1892. The city's Fairview Historic District was built in 1917 to house shipyard workers. Also of note is the Campbell Museum. A ferry was operated between Camden and Philadelphia from 1688. Following the arrival of the railroad in 1834, the city began a rapid industrial growth. Camden is named for the British jurist Charles Pratt, 1st Earl Camden (1714–94), a champion of colonial rights. Pop. (1970) 102,551; (1980) 84,910.

CAMDEN, city, seat of Kershaw Co., central South Carolina; settled 1730s, inc. 1791. Camden is an important horse-training center and a winter resort; manufactures include textiles and cotton products. During the American Revolution, the British held Camden (1780–81); they repelled the Americans at the Battle of Camden (August 1780), fought on a site adjacent to the present city, but evacuated the community after suffering heavy losses at nearby Hobkirk Hill in April 1781. The city was an important Confederate supply base during the American Civil War. Camden is named for Charles Pratt, 1st Earl Camden (1714–94), a British jurist who championed colonial rights. Pop. (1970) 8532; (1980) 7462.

CAMDEN, BATTLE OF, engagement of the American Revolution fought on Aug. 16, 1780, about 5 km (about 3 mi) north of Camden, S.C., then occupied by the British. The American force, about 1500 regulars and 2000 poorly trained militiamen, was commanded by Gen. Horatio Gates. Gen. Charles Cornwallis commanded the British force, numbering about 2000 men. Shortly after the action began, the American militiamen, many of whom were ill with dysentery, broke ranks, left their arms, and fled in disorder. The regulars, under Gen. Johann Kalb (called Baron de Kalb), stood firm and were almost annihilated. De Kalb was wounded and captured; he died three days later. Through their victory, the British gained temporary control of the entire South. American casualties were about 1000 killed and wounded and about 1000 taken prisoner. British losses were about 325 killed and wounded. After the battle, Gates was replaced as commander of the Army of the South by Gen. Nathanael Greene.

CAMEL, common name for two species of large ruminant, constituting the typical genus, *Camelus,* of the family Camelidae, and native to the desert regions of Asia and northern Africa. Both species have been domesticated since ancient times. The dromedary, or Arabian camel, *C. dromedarius,* has one hump, and the Bactrian camel, *C. bactrianus,* has two humps. The humps are stores of flesh and fat, absorbed as nutrition when food is unavailable. A camel can subsist without water for several days. Its stomach has many diverticula, or pouches, each closed by a sphincter muscle; water is stored in these pouches and is released as required. The Arabian camel usually stands 1.8 m (6 ft) tall at the shoulders. The hump rises about 30 cm (about 12 in) above the back. The Bactrian camel has shorter legs, is about 1.5 m (about 5 ft) in height at the shoulders, but usually has a heavier torso than the dromedary.

The Arabian camel, unknown in the wild state, is found from northwestern India and the lowlands of Afghanistan to the extremity of the Arabian Peninsula and the Somali Republic to the south and westward across the African deserts. Attempts have been made to introduce the species into Australia, Spain, Zanzibar, and the southwestern U.S., but without lasting success. The Arabian camel is singularly adapted to subsistence in the desert by its structural qualities and by its ability to bite off and consume the thorny plants that grow there. Thick, broad sole pads and thick callosities on the joints of the legs and on the chest, upon which it rests in a kneeling position, enable it to withstand the heat of the desert sand. Moreover, its nostrils may be closed against flying dust, and its eyes are shielded by very long eyelashes. Its acute sense of smell is valuable in locating supplies of water.

The Bactrian camel is better adapted, by virtue of its smaller size and heavier build, harder and more cloven feet, longer and finer wool, and other qualities, to a rocky and cooler region; its home is Central Asia, from northern Chinese Turkistan (now part of Xinjiang Uygur Autonomous Region) to Mongolia. Its endurance is as remarkable, under different circumstances, as that of the Arabian camel, for it withstands the rigorous climate of the Tibetan Plateau, where the temperature rises to 60° C (140° F) in summer and sinks to arctic cold in winter. A wild race of the Bactrian species is found in Central Asia.

The endurance and strength of the camel have made it a valuable beast of burden. Loads as great as 454 kg (1000 lb) can be carried by the Bactrian camel, and although its pace is slow (about 2.4 km/hr [about 1.5 mph]), they will travel as many as 48 km (30 mi) in a day. The Arabian camel, generally used as a saddle animal, can cover more than 161 km (100 mi) in a day. The flesh and milk of the camel are used as food and the hide for leather. The long hair, shed every summer, is made into cordage, fine paintbrushes, and a light, warm, long-napped cloth.

CAMELLIA, genus of about ten species of evergreen shrubs or trees of the family Theaceae (*see* TEA), native in tropical and subtropical Asia. The best-known and most valued species is *Camellia japonica,* varieties of which are cultivated in China, Korea, and Japan for their beautiful, fragrant, waxlike flowers. In the wild state this species grows up to 12 m (40 ft) high and has red flowers; white, red, pink, and double varieties also have been developed. Camellias are grown in warm, damp regions in southern and western areas of the U.S. Popular as an ornamental plant, the camellia is also the state flower of Alabama.

CAMELOT. *See* ARTHURIAN LEGEND.

CAMEO, precious or semiprecious gemstone with carved decoration. A cameo may also be of shell, colored glass, or porcelain. Cameos may have intaglio decoration (design engraved below the surface) or, for cameos proper, relief decoration (design carved above the surface). Motifs may be heads in profile, figures, coats of arms, or other devices. Most relief cameos consist of two or more layers of different colors. The top layer is carved and the darker, lower layer forms a background. Cameos are used as jewelry, such as brooches, pendants, and rings. Although the art

Arabian camel and its Bedouin owner near Beersheba, Israel. Trans World Airlines

Crucifixion with the Virgin and St. John on a 17th-century cameo pendant mounted in a gold and enamel frame. Metropolitan Museum of Art–Gift of Mrs. Ethel Weil Worgelt

of gem carving was known in very early times, cameo carving did not become an art until the 4th or 3d century BC in Greece. Cameos were popular in Rome and from the Renaissance to the present day.

CAMERA. *See* PHOTOGRAPHY.

CAMERON, Julia Margaret (1815–79), English 19th-century photographer, whose portrait techniques represented an important advance in the aesthetics of photography. She produced her first photograph—entitled *Annie, My First Success*—in 1864, and thereafter turned to a series of portraits of great men of her day, including Alfred, Lord Tennyson, Charles Darwin, Henry Wadsworth Longfellow, Robert Browning, and Sir John Herschel. Unlike most Victorian portrait photographers, she conceived of the photograph not as a detailed, visually precise record of the sitter but as a reflection of the sitter's personality and inner spirit. She pioneered several techniques designed to heighten the expressive possibilities of the portrait, among them soft focus and carefully blurred images; narrow closeup; and harsh lighting. She also produced many studio tableaux and book illustrations; unaccountably, their overripe sentimentality and elaborate poses were the stylistic opposite of her splendid portraits.

CAMERON, Richard (1648–80), Scottish Covenanter, born in Falkland, Fife Co. During his early career Cameron was a schoolteacher and private tutor. Subsequently he espoused the cause of the Covenanters, who worked to maintain Presbyterianism as the only religion in Scotland. Because Covenanters were being persecuted during the reign of Charles II, king of England, who was Roman Catholic, Cameron went into exile in 1678 and joined other exiled friends in Holland. Returning in 1680, he and others antagonized the government by strenuously resisting the measures that reinstated the Episcopal church in Scotland and proscribed public worship by unauthorized religious bodies. In June 1680, with 20 well-armed companions, he entered the town of Sanquhar and publicly renounced allegiance to Charles II for abuse of power, declaring war against him and his followers. Cameron and his men were surprised by royal troops in Ayr Co. in July 1680, and Cameron was killed. His hands and head were cut off and publicly displayed in Edinburgh. In 1689 the survivors of the skirmish organized a military unit that became the nucleus of the Cameronians, a famous regiment of the British army. In 1681 Cameron's followers organized the religious group later known as the Reformed Presbyterians.

CAMERON, Simon (1799–1889), Pennsylvania politician prominent during and after the American Civil War. Cameron was elected as a Republican to the U.S. Senate in 1857, and for the next two decades he controlled the party's political machine in Pennsylvania. In 1860 he was an unsuccessful candidate for the Republican presidential nomination; the following year he became secretary of war under President Lincoln. Complaints against Cameron, alleging corruption and favoritism, became so embarrassing, however, that he was asked to resign in January 1862; for a while after that he was U.S. minister to Russia. He was reelected U.S. senator in 1867 and served until 1877, when he arranged to have his son, James Donald Cameron (1833–1918), elected in his place. Cameron is considered the first powerful state "boss" in American politics.

CAMERON, Verney Lovett (1844–94), British explorer, born near Weymouth and Melcombe Regis, England. Cameron entered the British navy in 1857, and in 1873 he was sent to Africa by the Royal Geographical Society on a second expedition to relieve the British missionary and explorer David Livingstone. Soon after the expedition landed at Zanzibar and began its journey inland, Cameron and his party met servants bearing Livingstone's body. Cameron continued on, becoming the first European to cross tropical Africa from east to west when he reached the Atlantic Ocean in November 1875. On this expedition he found some of Livingstone's papers, which he sent back to England, and also explored the southern half of Lake Tanganyika. When he returned home Cameron was made a commander in the British navy and a companion of the Order of the Bath. In 1878-79 he traveled in Turkey, and in 1882, with the British explorer Sir Richard Burton, he visited the African Gold Coast in search of gold. Cameron retired from the navy in 1883 and spent the rest of his life directing commercial projects in Africa. His writings include *Across Africa* (2 vol., 1877).

CAMERONIANS, followers of Richard Cameron, one of the Covenanters of Scotland. The Cameronians were known officially as Reformed Presbyterians and date from 1681; except for a few seceding congregations, they united with the Free Church of Scotland in 1876 and thus became part of the Church of Scotland in the 1929 reunion. The Cameronians refused to recognize the civil government of 17th-century Scotland. Moderate Calvinists, they asserted that human will is determined only by the practical judgment of the mind; that the cause of doing good or evil proceeds from the knowledge that God infuses into one; and that God does not move the will physically, but only morally, by virtue of its dependence on the mind.

CAMEROON, MOUNT, active volcanic peak, SW Cameroon, near the Gulf of Guinea. It is the highest mountain in W Africa, with an elevation of 4069 m (13,350 ft). On the rich soils of its lower slopes rubber, cacao, and tea are grown.

CAMEROON, UNITED REPUBLIC OF, country, W Africa, bounded on the N by Lake Chad; on the E by Chad and the Central African Republic; on the S by the Congo, Gabon, and Equatorial Guinea; and on the W by the Bight of Bonny (an arm of the Atlantic Ocean) and Nigeria. The country is shaped like an elongated triangle, and forms a bridge between W Africa and central Africa. Until 1972 the republic was divided into two states, East Cameroon, the former French Cameroons, and West Cameroon, part of the former British Cameroons. The country has a total area of 475,442 sq km (183,569 sq mi).

LAND AND RESOURCES

Cameroon has four distinct topographical regions. In the S is a coastal plain, a region of dense equatorial rain forests. In the center is the Adamawa Massif, a plateau region with elevations reaching about 1370 m (about 4500 ft) above sea level. This is a transitional area where forest gives way in the N to savanna country. In the far N the savanna gradually slopes into the marshland surrounding Lake Chad. In the W is an area of high, forested mountains of volcanic origin. Located here is Mt. Cameroon (4069 m/ 13,350 ft), the highest peak in W Africa and an active volcano. The country's most fertile soils are found in this region. Among the principal streams, the Sanaga and Nyong rivers flow generally W to the Atlantic Ocean, and the Mbéré and Logone rivers flow N from the central plateau

Waterfall on a river deep in the rain forests of Cameroon. Such rapids make river travel hazardous, especially during the rainy season. P. Ware–Bruce Coleman, Inc.

Dancers of the Bamileke tribe of western Cameroon with their elaborate beaded masks and headdresses. As these intricate, many-hued costumes suggest, the Bamileke are known for their skill in embroidery and beadwork.
George Holton–Photo Researchers, Inc.

into Lake Chad. A network of rivers in the Chad Basin, including the Benue R., links the country with the vast Niger R. system to the E and N.

Climate. Cameroon has a tropical climate, humid in the S but increasingly dry to the N. On the coast the average annual rainfall is about 3890 mm (about 153 in). On the exposed slopes of the Cameroon Mts. in the W, rainfall is almost constant and sometimes reaches 10,160 mm (400 in) a year. In the semiarid NW annual rainfall averages about 380 mm (about 15 in). A dry season in the N lasts from October to April. The average temperature in the S is 25° C (77° F), on the plateau it is 21.1° C (70° F), and in the N it is 32.2° C (90° F).

Plants and Animals. Cameroon's valuable rain forests contain a number of species of trees, including oil palms, bamboo palms, mahogany, teak, ebony, and rubber. Wildlife is diverse and abundant and includes monkeys, chimpanzees, gorillas, antelopes, lions, and elephants, as well as numerous species of birds and snakes.

Natural Resources. Cameroon is dependent primarily on its agricultural and timber resources. High-yield deposits of bauxite exist in N Cameroon. Natural gas is found near Douala, and offshore deposits of petroleum are exploited. A small amount of gold is mined. Hydroelectric potential is significant; the largest power station is at Edéa, on the Sanaga R.

POPULATION

The majority of the people are farmers who live in small towns or villages in S and central Cameroon. Seminomadic herders inhabit the N.

Population Characteristics. The population of Cameroon (1985 official est.) was 10,106,000. The overall population density was 21 persons per sq km (55 per sq mi).

The capital is Yaoundé (pop., 1981 est., 435,900). Douala, on the Bight of Bonny, with an estimated population of 637,000, is the chief port. Other principal towns include Nkongsamba, Foumban, Maroua, and Bafoussam. Less than one quarter of the population adheres to traditional religions; about 20 percent of the population is Muslim; the remainder is Christian. Muslims predominate in the N and Christians in the S. Cameroon contains about 140 ethnic groups who speak 24 major languages. In general, Bantu-speaking peoples inhabit the S, and Sudanic-speaking peoples dominate in the N. Among the more important ethnic groups are the Bamileke, a Bantu-speaking people, and the Fulani, a Muslim people. French and English are

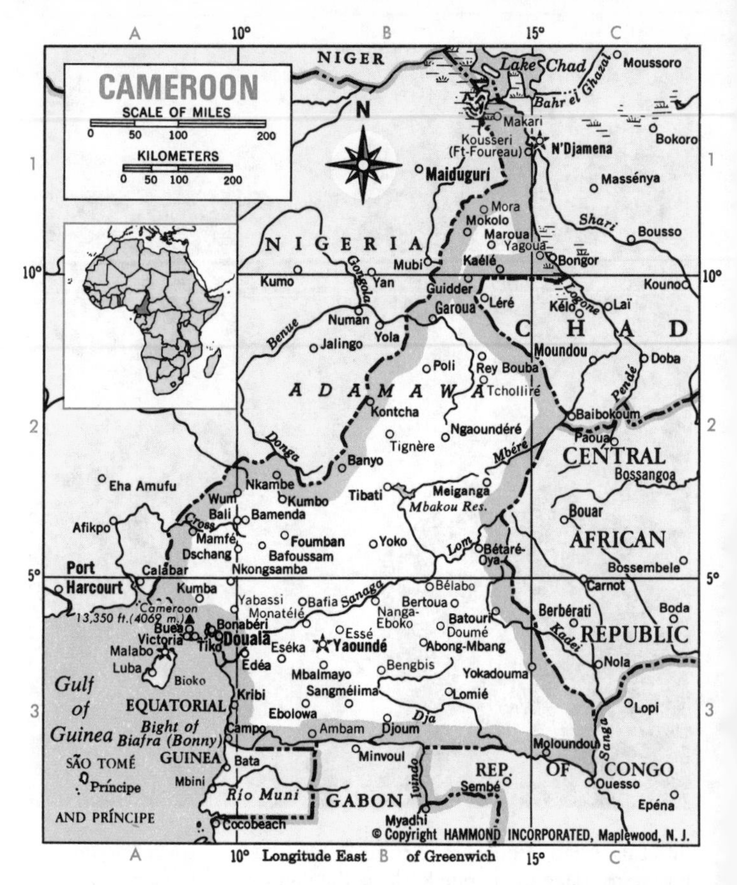

both official languages. French dominates, however; English is confined mainly to the W.

Education. French principles of education predominate in Cameroon's secondary and technical schools. Mission schools play an important role in education and are partly subsidized by the government. In the mid-1980s total annual enrollment in primary schools was about 1,638,600, and in secondary schools, about 238,100. The University of Yaoundé, which was established in 1962, has faculties of law, arts, and science. A total of more than 13,700 students are enrolled in institutions of higher education.

ECONOMY

Agricultural activities are the main occupation of the vast majority of the population of Cameroon. Agricultural and forestry products constitute more than half of all exports. In the mid-1980s the estimated national budget showed revenues of about $1.8 billion and expenditures of about $1.6 billion annually.

Agriculture. The principal commercial crops in Cameroon are coffee, cacao, tobacco, cotton, and bananas. In the mid-1980s yearly production of coffee and cacao, the leading export commodities, amounted to about 127,000 metric tons for the former and 115,000 metric tons for the latter. Other commercial products include rubber, palm products, and sugarcane. Subsistence crops include plantains, sweet potatoes, cassava, corn, and millet.

Livestock raising is important in the Adamawa Massif region. In the mid-1980s the livestock population included 3.7 million head of cattle, 2 million goats, 1 million pigs, and 2.2 million sheep.

Forestry and Fishing. Timber is traditionally one of Cameroon's most valuable exports, consisting mainly of mahogany, ebony, and teak. The annual timber cut in the mid-1980s amounted to some 10.4 million cu m (367.3 million cu ft). Fishing is dominated by freshwater subsistence activity. Deep-sea fishing activity, however, is increasing, especially from the port of Douala. About 84,000 metric tons of fish are caught annually.

Mining and Manufacturing. One of the largest single industrial enterprises in Cameroon is the aluminum smelting plant at Edéa, which produces more than 50,000 metric tons annually from imported bauxite. The processing of agri-

INDEX TO MAP OF CAMEROON

Cities and Towns

Place	Grid
Abong-Mbang	B 3
Ambam	B 3
Bafia	B 3
Bafoussam	B 2
Bali	A 2
Bamenda	B 2
Banyo	B 2
Batouri	B 3
Bélabo	B 3
Bengbis	B 3
Bertoua	B 3
Bétaré-Oya	B 2
Bonabéri	A 3
Buea	A 3
Campo	B 3
Djoum	B 3
Douala	A 3
Doumé	B 3
Dschang	A 2
Ebolowa	B 3
Edéa	B 3
Eséka	B 3
Essé	B 3
Fort-Foureau (Kousseri)	B 1
Foumban	B 2
Garoua	B 2
Guidder	B 2
Kaélé	B 1
Kontcha	B 2
Kousseri	B 1
Kribi	B 3
Kumba	A 3
Kumbo	B 2
Lomié	B 3
Makari	B 1
Mamfé	A 2
Maroua	B 1
Mbalmayo	B 3
Meiganga	B 2
Mokolo	B 1
Moloundou	C 3
Monatélé	B 3
Mora	B 1
Nanga-Eboko	B 3
Ngaoundéré	B 2
Nkambe	B 2
Nkongsambe	B 2
Poli	B 2
Rey Bouba	B 2
Sangmélima	B 3
Tchollіré	B 2
Tibati	B 2
Tignére	B 2
Tiko	A 3
Victoria	A 3
Wum	A 2
Yabassi	B 3
Yagoua	B 1
Yaoundé (cap.)	B 3
Yokadouma	B 3
Yoko	B 2

Other Features

Feature	Grid
Adamawa (reg.)	B 2
Benue (river)	B 2
Biafra (Bonny) (bight)	A 3
Cameroon (mt.)	A 3
Chad (lake)	C 1
Cross (river)	A 2
Dja (river)	B 3
Donga (river)	B 2
Guinea (gulf)	A 3
Ivindo (river)	B 3
Kadei (river)	C 3
Logone (river)	C 2
Lom (river)	B 2
Mbakou (res.)	B 2
Mbéré (river)	B 2
Sanaga (river)	B 3
Sanga (river)	C 3
Shari (river)	C 1

cultural products, however, dominates industrial activity; other manufactures include textiles, fertilizers, and cement. Offshore petroleum exploitation began in the late 1970s, and an oil refinery has been built. Cameroon's output of crude petroleum reached 47.5 million barrels a year during the mid-1980s. Small amounts of gold and tin concentrates are also produced.

Currency and Banking. The unit of currency of Cameroon is the CFA franc, consisting of 100 centimes (302.80 CFA francs equal U.S.$1; 1987). The currency is issued by the Bank of the States of Central Africa (headquartered in Yaoundé), the central bank of a monetary union formed by five Central African states.

Transportation and Communications. Cameroon is engaged in an effort to improve its transportation network. Of the approximately 64,900 km (about 40,325 mi) of roads, about 5 percent are paved. Unpaved roads are frequently impassable during the rainy season. The country has nearly 1200 km (almost 750 mi) of railroad. The overwhelming majority of port traffic is handled at Douala; Kribi is the country's second port. The port of Garoua on the Benue R. in the N is open two to three months a year and handles most of the trade with Nigeria. Cameroon Airlines provides domestic and international service. The principal international airport is at Douala, and a number of smaller airfields exist. The national radiobroadcasting system has its main station at Yaoundé and local stations in Douala, Garoua, and Buea. In the early 1980s about 790,000 radio receivers and 26,000 telephones were in use. A national television network was established in 1985.

GOVERNMENT

Cameroon is governed under a constitution promulgated in 1972. The president of the republic is chief of state and commander of the armed forces and is elected to a 5-year term by universal suffrage. The federal ministers, incuding the prime minister, are appointed by the president and by statute are not permitted to be members of the legislature. The president also appoints the governors of the 10 provinces.

Legislature. Legislative power in Cameroon is vested in the unicameral National Assembly, which consists of 120 members elected to 5-year terms. The sole political party is the Democratic Rally of the Cameroonian People (1966).

Judiciary. The judicial system of Cameroon is largely based on the French system with an admixture of elements from the British system. The highest judicial body is the supreme court. Other courts are the appeals courts, regional courts, and magistrates' courts.

HISTORY

The coast of present-day Cameroon was explored late in the 15th century by the Portuguese, who named the estuary to the south of Mount Cameroon Rio das Camerões ("river of prawns"). Merchants established trading stations along the coast in the 17th century, buying slaves, ivory, and rubber. British traders and missionaries were especially active in the area after 1845. The Germans and British began to explore inland after 1860, and in 1884 the former established a protectorate over the Douala area; the British, taken by surprise, offered no resistance to their claim.

European Rule. Transportation difficulties and local resistance slowed German development of the area, but they managed to cultivate large cacao, palm, and rubber plantations. They also built roads and began the construction of a railroad and the port of Douala on the Atlantic coast.

Anglo-French forces invaded the German colony in 1916. In 1919 one-fifth of the territory, which was contiguous with eastern Nigeria, was assigned to Great Britain, and the remaining four-fifths were assigned to France as mandates under the League of Nations.

The British Cameroons consisted of the Northern and Southern Cameroons, which were separated by a 72-km (45-mi) strip along the Benue River. The northern territory, peopled by tribes of Sudanese origin, was always administered as a part of Northern Nigeria. The Southern Cameroons, peopled by a variety of tribes, was administered as part of the Nigerian federation but had a locally elected legislature. The French Cameroons was administered as a separate territory. Neither area, however, experienced much social or economic progress.

Independence. After World War II the mandates were made trust territories of the UN. In the following years political ferment grew enormously in the French territory, where more than 100 parties were formed between 1948 and 1960. The campaign for independence, intermittently violent, gained steady momentum during the 1950s, until the French granted self-government in December 1958; full independence was achieved on Jan. 1, 1960. Ahmadou Ahidjo, prime minister since 1958, became the first president. The new republic was admitted to the UN in September 1960.

The following year the UN sponsored a plebiscite in the British Cameroons. As a result, the Southern Cameroons was federated with the Republic of Cameroon in October 1961, while the Northern Cameroons joined Nigeria.

Rebellion and Unity. When Cameroon became independent, President Ahidjo's government was faced with a rebellion incited by the Cameroon People's Union, a pro-Communist party. By 1963, however, the revolt had been suppressed, and as Ahidjo succeeded in establishing the authority of his regime, the opposition lost strength. In 1966 the six major parties merged into the National Cameroonian Union, which was then declared the only legal party in the country. In 1972 Ahidjo sponsored a national referendum that changed Cameroon from a federal to a unitary state, called the United Republic of Cameroon.

Reaffirmed in office in 1975 and again in 1980, President Ahidjo resigned unexpectedly in November 1982. He was succeeded in office by Paul Biya (1933–), the former prime minister. Relations between Biya and Ahidjo deteriorated, and in July 1983 Ahidjo (who had retained the leadership of the National Cameroonian Union) went into exile in France and gave up his party post, which Biya assumed. Biya won election to his first full term as president in January 1984 and suppressed a coup attempt that April.

In late August 1986, an explosive discharge of gas from a volcanic lake near the Nigerian border killed more than 1700 people. International medical and economic aid was sent to the area, and by August 28 the emergency was declared under control. In the country at the time was Shimon Peres, prime minister of Israel. He and President Biya announced the resumption of diplomatic ties between their countries on August 26.

For further information on this topic, see the Bibliography in volume 28, sections 1009, 1028.

CAMEROONS (Fr. *Cameroun*), former region of W Africa that included what is now the United

Market day in Maroua, in northern Cameroon. From their villages, women bring the pottery they have crafted in a variety of sizes. Diane Rawson-Photo Researchers, Inc.

Republic of Cameroon and part of E Nigeria. *See* CAMEROON, UNITED REPUBLIC OF.

CAMILLUS, Marcus Furius (d. 365 BC), Roman soldier and statesman. During the period of the Roman Republic, Camillus was made military tribune of Rome several times, made censor, and finally made dictator about 403 BC. He led the Roman army against rival cities in Etruria (now in Italy), conquering Veii (396), Capena (395), and Falerii (394). It is believed that he went into exile near Rome soon afterward because he had mishandled distribution of booty after his Etruscan campaigns. About 387, while he was in exile, the Gauls plundered and burned Rome. During the recovery of Rome, Camillus became a folk hero, and it is believed that he again served as military tribune and dictator several times, although legends have obscured the facts about his life. According to legend, he raised an army and forced the Gallic leader Brennus out of Rome. In fact, however, the Gauls retired unharmed after Rome ransomed itself with gold. Afterward, Camillus resisted efforts of the plebs (commoners) to move the capitol building to Veii and worked instead to rebuild and fortify Rome. He reorganized the Roman army and made administrative reforms. His military exploits ensured Roman supremacy in central Italy. Camillus is also credited with persuading the Roman patricians to make concessions to the plebs, thus keeping peace between the two groups.

CAMISARDS (Fr. dialect *camisa,* "shirt"), name applied to the French Huguenot (Protestant) peasants of the Cévennes mountain region who rose in rebellion in 1702 against King Louis XIV. The Camisards, so called because of the black smocks they wore during night raids, had sought refuge in the Cévennes after Louis XIV in 1685 had revoked the religious freedom granted to them by the Edict of Nantes. The revolt was sparked by a religious "awakening" among the Huguenots. Led principally by the French soldier Jean Cavalier, the Camisards conducted guerrilla warfare from mountain strongholds against the royal troops. Roman Catholic churches were burned, and their priests were killed or forced to flee. Urged on by Pope Clement XI, who issued a papal bull excoriating the Camisards, the Roman Catholics razed more than 450 villages and exterminated most of the inhabitants. In 1704 the Royalist commander Duc Claude Louis Hector de Villars (1653-1734) met with Cavalier and persuaded the rebel leader to surrender in return for a commission in the royal army and a pardon for his followers. These terms of surrender were rejected by the majority of the Camisards, who demanded full restoration of the rights granted by the Edict of Nantes. The struggle continued sporadically until the death of Cavalier's successor, Abraham Mazel, in 1710.

CAMÕES *or* **CAMOËNS, Luís (Vaz) de** (1524?-80), one of the greatest Portuguese poets, whose principal work, *The Lusiads* (1572; trans. 1655), is considered Portugal's national epic. Camões, whose life was one of high adventure, was probably born in Lisbon. He was apparently educated at the University of Coimbra. Subsequently, he became a tutor at the court of John III, from which he was banished in 1546 because of a love affair with one of the queen's ladies-in-waiting, Caterina de Ataíde; she was presumably the inspiration of his love poetry.

Virtually an exile, Camões pursued a military career and in 1547 lost an eye in battle in Morocco. In 1550 he returned to Lisbon, was imprisoned after a street brawl, and, upon being pardoned in 1553, sailed for India. It is thought that he may already have begun work on *The Lusiads;* at any rate, the central theme of the poem is the discovery of the sea route to India by the Portuguese explorer Vasco da Gama.

After fighting in India, Camões was posted to Macao, but in 1558 was accused of extortion and ordered back to India. Surviving shipwreck, he made his way home to Lisbon via Mozambique in 1570, with the manuscript of his epic intact. Two years later it was published. Despite a small royal pension and the beginnings of world fame, Camões's last years were spent in obscurity, and he died in poverty in Lisbon on June 10, 1580.

The Lusiads, written in ten cantos in ottava rima, was patterned after both the *Aeneid,* the Latin epic of Vergil, and *Orlando furioso* by the Italian poet Ludovico Ariosto. Woven into the story of Vasco da Gama's voyage are lively narrative and prophetic references to other events in Portuguese history, as well as certain Christian and humanist concepts. Although the work extols the achievements of the sons of Lusus—that is, the Lusiads, or Portuguese—it also reflects the poet's bitterness about the punitive aspects of Portuguese colonialism. The same vein of pessimism pervades many of his lyrics and his few surviving letters.

Camões's fame rests also on his substantial number of posthumously published shorter poems: odes and sonnets, elegies, and canzoni. In addition, he also wrote three plays, two of which were based on classical models. The main theme of his verse is the conflict between passionate, sensual love and the Neoplatonic ideal of spiritual love. It is noted for its formal perfection and simplicity, expressive of deep sentiment.

CAMOMILE. *See* CHAMOMILE.

CAMORRA, secret criminal and terrorist society in the former Italian kingdom of the Two Sicilies. Members of the Camorra, called Camorristi, plundered and terrorized the country for many years. The society, originating from a fraternal organization among prisoners, became prominent about 1830. During the turmoil in Italy in the fight for Italian unity, the Camorra prospered. The society allied itself with the forces of the Italian patriot Giuseppe Garibaldi and helped expel the ruling house of Bourbon from Italy. In the period after unification in 1870, a brief, unsuccessful attempt was made to employ the Camorristi in police service. The society continued to terrorize the country, and during the early 1900s it practically dominated the city of Naples. The power of the Camorra was ended in 1911 when the Camorristi were brought to trial for murder.

CAMOUFLAGE (Fr. *camoufler,* "to disguise"), word introduced by the French at the beginning of World War I to designate scientific disguise of objects through imitation of natural surroundings. Early in the war front-line camouflage, or concealment from ground observation, played the principal role. Later the development of the bomber plane made camouflage of industrial centers far in the rear of the fighting front a necessity. To camouflage an object, the surrounding landscape is imitated by the use of fabric screens, grass, or shrubs, genuine or artificial. Fortifications or factories may be given the appearance of farm buildings, and well-known landmarks may be altered or duplicated. During World War II the use of aerial survey and the development of infrared photography, which distinguishes between natural and artificial vegetation, led to the development of sophisticated devices for camouflage.

CAMP, Walter Chauncey (1859–1925), American football authority, born in New Britain, Conn., and educated at Yale University. He became the head football coach at Yale in 1888 and later athletic director. In football, he invented the system of downs, created the position of quarterback, and set the number of players at 11. In 1889, Camp, with Caspar W. Whitney (1864?–1929), began the practice of honoring the best college football players of each season by naming them to an "All-American Team."

CAMPAGNA DI ROMA, undulating plain of central Italy, surrounding Rome, in Latium region. The name is applied to the district of about 2100 sq km (about 810 sq mi) extending along the coast of the Tyrrhenian Sea from the city of Civitavecchia to the city of Terracina. From the coast the district extends inland to the Alban and the Sabine hills. The ground, which never rises higher than 61 m (200 ft) above sea level, is almost entirely volcanic. The many lakes were formed in the craters of extinct volcanoes. Until the 5th and 6th centuries AD the Campagna di Roma was well populated and was filled with luxurious villas, ruins of which have been found. During the Middle Ages the political insecurity of the region following the fall of Rome, as well as the poor soil resulting from misuse of the land and the failure of the water supply, led to a gradual depopulation and to an increase of unhealthful conditions, including malaria. Reclamation of the district was begun in the 19th century and largely completed in the 1930s. Today the district has grazing land for sheep and cattle and land suitable for growing grain, vegetables, and fruit.

CAMPANELLA, Roy (1921–), American professional baseball player, who starred as a catcher for the Brooklyn Dodgers (National League) from 1948 to 1957. As a result of an automobile accident in 1958 he was paralyzed, and his career came to an end. His account of this, *It's Good to Be Alive,* was published in 1959. Campy, as he is known, was voted most valuable player in the league three times (1951, 1953, and 1955). In 1969 he was elected to the Baseball Hall of Fame.

CAMPANELLA, Tommaso, real name GIOVANNI DOMENICO CAMPANELLA (1568–1639), Italian philosopher, born in Stilo, and educated in the Order of the Dominicans. He dissented from the teaching of his time, and in 1599 he was arrested on charges of heresy and of conspiring against the Spanish government in Naples. He spent the next 27 years in prison in Naples, where he wrote *Civitas Solis* (City of the Sun, 1623), a description of an ideal society patterned after the *Republic* of Plato. He was released from prison in 1626, but renewed persecutions compelled him to seek refuge in France. Many of the tenets of his philosophy were similar to the views of the French philosopher René Descartes and the later German philosopher Immanuel Kant. Campanella's works, 82 in all, treat many different philosophical subjects. Among his treatises are *Theologia* (1613–14) and *Metafisica* (1638).

CAMPANIA, administrative region, S Italy, on the Tyrrhenian Sea, between Latium and Basilicata, comprising the provinces of Avellino, Benevento, Caserta, Naples, and Salerno. The islands of Capri and Ischia in the Bay of Naples form part of the region. The capital is Naples. The E section of Campania is crossed by the Apennines. The coastal plain, which is exceptionally fertile and thickly populated, is noted for the production of citrus fruits and garden vegetables. Corn, oats, tobacco, olives, and wine grapes also are grown here. Other leading regional industries are live-

The waterfront of Naples, the capital of Campania. In the distance is Mt. Vesuvius.
A. L. Goldman–Photo Researchers, Inc.

stock raising; fishing; lumbering; tanning; canning; oil refining; shipbuilding; and the manufacture of glass, ceramics, chemicals, machinery, textiles, and iron and steel. The tourist industry is also important. Among the notable landmarks are Mt. Vesuvius and Lake Avernus.

Greeks settled on the Campanian coast about 1030 BC and founded, among other colonies, the cities of Cumae and Neapolis (Naples). In the 4th century BC the district fell under Roman rule and became a favorite resort of wealthy Romans. After the fall of the Western Roman Empire in the 5th century AD, Campania was occupied successively by Goths, Byzantines, and Lombards. The Normans, who conquered it in the 11th century, ruled it as part of the kingdom of the Two Sicilies. The region was incorporated subsequently in the kingdom of Naples and united in 1861 with the kingdom of Italy. During the invasion of Italy by the Allies in World War II, Campania suffered extensive destruction. Area, 13,595 sq km (5249 sq mi); pop. (1983 est.) 5,513,500.

CAMPANILE, a bell tower, either freestanding or attached to a church building, derived from *campana* (Ital., "bell"). Probably the world's most famous campanile is the Leaning Tower of Pisa (1174–1350), the freestanding Tuscan Romanesque bell tower of Pisa Cathedral. The cylindrical eight-story, 56-m (185-ft) building began to tilt during its construction because of weak foundations, for which the builders tried to compensate by stacking the upper stories in a curve against the tilt. The Campanile of Florence Cathedral, a slim, freestanding Gothic tower 82 m (269 ft) tall, is renowned for its beauty. It was begun by the Florentine artist Giotto in 1334 and completed by his compatriot Francesco Talenti (c. 1300–69) in the mid-14th century. Its seven stories are faced with richly colored marbles and with bas-reliefs by Giotto, Andrea Pisano, and Luca della Robbia. A notable 20th-century campanile, designed by the Hungarian-American architect Marcel Breuer in 1967 for Saint John's Abbey Church in Collegeville, Minn., is a high freestanding slab on splayed piers; the bells are hung in variously sized spaces that pierce the slab. *See also* ARCHITECTURE.

CAMPANULA. *See* BELLFLOWER.

CAMPBELL, noble Scottish family of the former county of Argyllshire (q.v.) bearing the hereditary titles of earls, marquesses, and dukes of Argyll. The lineage of the family has been traced to Sir Colin Campbell of Loch Awe, who was knighted in 1286, and who bequeathed to the chiefs of his line the title Mac Callum More ("great Colin's son"). Sir Duncan Campbell was made a peer as

Lord Campbell in 1445; his son Colin (fl. 1453-93) was created 1st earl of Argyll in 1457. The Campbells were among the first Scottish noble families to adopt Protestantism. Archibald Campbell, 1st marquess of Argyll, led the Scottish Covenanters during the wars of the English Revolution, and his descendants, the 1st, 2d, and 3d dukes of Argyll, were prominent Whigs who supported the Revolution of 1688, the Union of England and Scotland, and the Hannoverian kings, in opposition to the Scottish Jacobites. *See also* individual listings under ARGYLL.

CAMPBELL, city, Santa Clara Co., W California; settled by Benjamin Campbell (1826-1907) in 1851, inc. 1952. The city was a major fruit-processing center until the 1960s. It now is chiefly residential, with some small-scale manufacturing (electronic equipment, commercial flowers, processed fruit). Pop. (1970) 23,797; (1980) 27,067.

CAMPBELL, Alexander (1788-1866), American minister and a founder of the Christian Church (Disciples of Christ), or Campbellites. He was born in Ireland and studied for one year at the University of Glasgow. After immigrating to the U.S. in 1809, he later settled in Bethany, W.Va. At first a member of the Baptist church, he organized the nucleus of the Disciples of Christ about 1827, merging his group with that led by the American revivalist Barton Stone in 1832.

Campbell founded Bethany College in 1840 and served as its president until his death. In 1823 he established the magazine *Christian Baptist,* which became the *Millennial Harbinger* in 1830; Campbell continued the publication until 1863. He also engaged in many public debates and published approximately 60 volumes, including hymnbooks and a translation of the New Testament. His most important doctrinal work is *The Christian System* (1839). Campbell also wrote (1861) a biography of his father, Thomas Campbell (1763-1854), who had been associated with him in organizing the Disciples of Christ.

CAMPBELL, Colin, Baron Clyde (1792-1863), British field marshal, born in Glasgow, Scotland. As a field commander during the Crimean War (1854-56), he was largely responsible for the British victory at the Alma River and for driving back the Russian attack on Balaklava. Called to India at the outbreak of the Sepoy Mutiny in 1857, he effected the relief of Lucknow and quelled the revolt. He was created Baron Clyde in 1858.

CAMPBELL, Sir Malcolm (1885-1948), British corporation director and automobile racer, born in Chislehurst, Kent, England, and educated in Uppingham and abroad. He was prominent in the business world of England as a director and officer in a number of corporations, but he is known in the U.S. chiefly for the world speed records he set, beginning in the 1920s, in his specially constructed racing cars on the flat sands in Daytona Beach, Fla., and on the Bonneville Salt Flats, Utah. He was knighted in 1931. Campbell is the author of *Speed* (1931), *The Romance of Motor-Racing* (1936), *The Roads and the Problem of Their Safety* (1937), and *Drifting to War* (1937).

Mrs. Patrick Campbell on her first American tour.

CAMPBELL, Mrs. Patrick, *née* BEATRICE STELLA TANNER (1865-1940), English actor, born in London. Her first important stage success was in 1893 in the title role of *The Second Mrs. Tanqueray* by Sir Arthur Wing Pinero. Mrs. Campbell was noted for her performances of the Shakespearean roles of Juliet, Ophelia, and Lady Macbeth. She also appeared in a number of dramas by Henrik Ibsen, the most notable being the title role in *Hedda Gabler* in 1907. After she met George Bernard Shaw, he wrote the role of Eliza Doolittle in *Pygmalion* (1912) for her. Mrs. Campbell made several tours of the U.S.; she retired from the stage in 1938. She wrote an autobiography, *My Life and Some Letters* (1922); her lively correspondence with Shaw was published in 1952.

CAMPBELL, Robert. *See* ROB ROY.

CAMPBELL, (Ignatius) Roy Dunnachie (1901-57), South African poet of British descent. In *The Flaming Terrapin* (1924) and *Flowering Rifle* (1939) he presented virile, witty verses somewhat like those of the English romantic poets. Although he fought for the Fascist side in the Spanish civil war (1936–39), he joined the British forces in Africa in World War II. Campbell's prose work *Light on a Dark Horse* (1951) is his autobiography.

CAMPBELL, Thomas (1777–1844), Scottish poet, born in Glasgow. His first work, "The Pleasures of Hope" (1799), a poem in couplets, met with immediate success. Much of his fame rests on the poems "Hohenlinden," "Ye Mariners of England," and "The Battle of the Baltic." His volumes of poetry include *Gertrude of Wyoming* (1809), *Theodoric* (1824), and *The Pilgrim of Glencoe* (1842). In addition, he compiled *Specimens of the British Poets* (7 vol., 1819).

CAMPBELL, William Wallace, (1862–1938), American astronomer, who pioneered in the use of spectroscopy to study the motions of stars. Born in Hancock Co., Ohio, Campbell was educated at the University of Michigan. His *Stellar Motions* (1913) and catalog of nearly 1000 stellar velocities became the classic works in the field. Through his studies of planetary atmospheres, Campbell was also one of the first to declare (1894) Mars unsuitable to life as known on earth. Campbell was director of Lick Observatory (1901–30) and president of the University of California (1923–30). He later served as president of the National Academy of Sciences (1931–35).

CAMPBELL-BANNERMAN, Sir Henry (1836–1908), British statesman, born in Glasgow, Scotland, and educated at Trinity College, University of Cambridge. He entered Parliament as member for Stirling, Scotland, in 1868 and allied himself with the Liberal party of Prime Minister William Gladstone. In 1886 he was secretary for war under Gladstone, and from 1892 to 1895 he held the same position in the ministries of Gladstone and Archibald Philip Primrose, 5th earl of Rosebery (1847–1929). Campbell-Bannerman was chosen leader of the Liberal party in 1899 and became prime minister in 1905. During his ministry, he granted responsible government to the Transvaal and Orange Free State in South Africa, but he failed in his ambition to gain home rule for Ireland. He resigned his post because of illness two weeks before his death.

CAMPBELL ISLAND, mountainous island in the South Pacific Ocean, part of New Zealand. Although only about 48 km (about 30 mi) in circumference, the semicircular island has good harbors that are used as provision depots but are not permanently inhabited. Campbell Island is rich in fur seals. Area, 166 sq km (64 sq mi).

CAMPBELLITES. *See* CAMPBELL, ALEXANDER; CHRISTIAN CHURCH (DISCIPLES OF CHRIST).

CAMPBELLTON, city, Restigouche Co., N New Brunswick, Canada, a port on the Restigouche R., near the head of Chaleur Bay; inc. 1889. It is a shipping, fishing, and resort center and contains some manufacturing firms. The community, established in the late 18th century as Martin's Point, was laid out in 1833 and renamed, probably in honor of Sir Archibald Campbell (1769–1843), lieutenant governor of New Brunswick at the time. In 1910 the settlement was almost destroyed by fire, but it was subsequently rebuilt. Pop. (1976) 10,177; (1981) 9818.

CAMPECHE. *See* LOGWOOD.

CAMPECHE, Bay of, shallow bay, S Mexico, an inlet of the Gulf of Mexico, bordered by the Yucatán Peninsula on the E, the Isthmus of Tehuantepec on the S, and the state of Veracruz on the W. Significant petroleum deposits are located beneath the floor of the bay; large-scale oil production began in the late 1970s. Shrimping is an important industry in coastal areas. The cities of Veracruz, Campeche, and Coatzacoalcos are on the bay.

CAMP FIRE, INC., national organization for girls and boys up to the age of 21. It was founded in 1910 as Camp Fire Girls by the American physical education specialist Luther Halsey Gulick (1865–1919). Boys were admitted in 1975, and the present name was adopted in 1979.

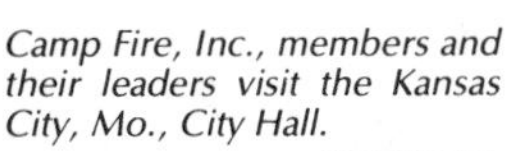

Camp Fire, Inc., members and their leaders visit the Kansas City, Mo., City Hall.

Camp Fire, Inc.

The purpose of Camp Fire is to provide, through a program of informal education, opportunities for young people to realize their potential and to function responsibly as caring, self-directed individuals, and as an organization to seek to improve those conditions in society that affect youth. The watchword of the organization is Wohelo, composed of the first two letters of the words *work, health,* and *love.* "Give Service" is the Camp Fire slogan.

Camp Fire members are organized into four age groups: Blue Birds, first through third grades; Adventurers, fourth through sixth grades; Discovery members, junior high school age; and Horizon members, high school age. The Blue Bird program encourages members to learn about themselves and their community. Adventure members take part in home and community activities and explore the outdoors. In the Discovery program members learn more about their physical, emotional, and intellectual development. Horizon members are helped in defining their goals and abilities. Groups are led by trained adult volunteers.

Present membership is over 400,000, and 300 local councils are located throughout the U.S. National headquarters is in Kansas City, Mo.

CAMPHOR, volatile, white, crystalline compound, $C_{10}H_{16}O$, with a characteristic aromatic odor. Ordinary camphor is obtained from the camphor tree, *Cinnamomum camphora,* which grows in Asia and Brazil. The camphor is distilled by steaming chips of the root, stem, or bark. The leaves of certain plants, such as tansy and feverfew, contain a second form of camphor, which is not used commercially. A racemic form is present in the oil of an Asian chrysanthemum and is also produced synthetically for most commercial uses. Camphor is used in the manufacture of celluloid and explosives and medicinally in liniments and other preparations for its mild antiseptic and anesthetic qualities. It is poisonous if ingested in large amounts.

Camphor is insoluble in water, soluble in organic solvents, and melts at 176° C (349° F) and boils at 209° C (405° F).

CAMPI, family of 16th-century Italian painters of Cremona. The most important members of the family were the four sons of Galeazzo Campi (1470-1536), who painted religious pictures.

Giulio Campi (1500-72). Trained by his father and the Italian architect-painter Giulio Romano, he is best known for building and decorating Santa Margherita in Cremona. He also painted frescoes in the cathedral in Cremona and in other churches in Cremona and Milan. Among his students were his three brothers.

Bernardino Campi (1522-91). He is best known for the frescoes in the cupola of San Sigismondo in Cremona.

Antonio Campi (1525?-87). He was one of the artists commissioned by Philip II of Spain to decorate the Escorial. He painted the *Birth of Christ* fresco in San Paolo, Milan. He was also a sculptor, architect, and writer.

Vincenzo Campi (1525?-91). He specialized in still lifes and portraits, some of which are in the Bergamo Gallery, Bergamo, and the Brera Gallery, Milan.

CAMPIN, Robert (c. 1378-1444), called the Master of Flémalle, one of the founders and great masters of the Flemish school of painting, born in Tournai, Flanders. He became a master painter in Tournai in 1406 and remained active there until his death, painting mainly altarpieces and religious panel paintings. He broke with the idealized, artificial International Gothic style to pursue a revolutionary interest in realism.

Three principal innovations distinguish Campin's art and set it apart from the Gothic: his conception of the human figure in solid, three-dimensional terms; his awareness of perspective; and his preoccupation with the details of everyday life. These qualities are tentatively evident in early works such as the famous triptych the *Mérode Altarpiece* (c. 1425, The Cloisters, New York City). They reach their full development in his late masterwork, the *Werl Altarpiece* (1438, Prado, Madrid). The St. Barbara panel, for instance, is set in a highly realistic contemporary Flemish interior, rich with detail, and the skillful perspective of the room is continued through an open window into an outdoor landscape; the figure of St. Barbara is rounded and realistic, draped in rich, almost sculptural folds of material. Campin's work exerted an important influence on the two later masters of Flemish art, his pupil Rogier van der Weyden and Jan van Eyck.

CAMPINA GRANDE, city, NE Brazil, in Paraíba State, at the edge of the arid Borborema Plateau. It is an industrial processing and export center for a large cotton-growing region that also produces sugar, fruit, tobacco, textiles, and leather goods. Deposits of tantalite and columbite are nearby. Campina Grande is the site of a thermoelectric station. Pop. (est.) 236,400.

CAMPINAS, city, SE Brazil, in the highlands of São Paulo State, on the main São Paulo-Brasília highway. It is an important manufacturing and commercial center for a rich agricultural area in which coffee, sugarcane, and cotton are produced. Textiles, machinery, and agricultural equipment are manufactured in the city, which is the seat of the noted Institute of Agronomy

(1887), the Pontifical Catholic University of Campinas (1941), and the State University of Campinas (1962). Campinas dates from the 18th century and grew rapidly during the Brazilian coffee boom of the late 19th and early 20th centuries. Pop. (1979 est., greater city) 562,400.

CAMPING, popular recreation, involving living temporarily in the outdoors, usually in a shelter such as a tent, lean-to, or special recreational vehicle (familiarly referred to as an RV). Most camping is done in forest areas, on mountains, or near oceans, lakes, or streams.

Although people, such as nomads and gypsies, have lived outdoors since antiquity, camping in the modern sense, as a leisure-time recreation, did not begin until after World War II. Increased availability of automobiles and advances in the design of camping gear enabled more people to journey longer distances into the backcountry and to live there in relative comfort for extended periods of time.

Purposes. The purposes of camping are varied, although most people go camping to get away from everyday routines and to place themselves in a healthy outdoor environment. From a campsite, campers can hike, fish, and hunt, find secluded places to swim, or study and photograph flora and fauna. At the campsite itself, campers enjoy such activities as pitching a tent, gathering wood and starting a campfire, cooking, and sleeping in fresh air.

Camping Areas. Selection of a camping area depends on the camper's purposes. Some campers, desiring to be on their own in isolated areas, stow gear and food in a backpack and either hike or canoe into forest or mountain areas. Others, preferring to live in a campsite with people nearby, drive to a public or privately owned site and set up a tent there. Since about 1965 camping with an RV has also become popular. Such mobile homes range from large vans equipped with beds, showers, and kitchens to two-wheeled trailers towed by an automobile. These trailers, constructed of heavy-duty plastic or fiberglass tops and canvas sides, can be converted into tents by lifting the top, which is then held in place by poles. The bottom of the trailer forms the tent floor. Elderly campers or families with young children frequently choose mobile-home camping; younger people or families with older children often prefer paddling or hiking to secluded areas.

Finding a place to suit the camper's needs is not difficult today. Travel-guide books and magazines, state and national tourism departments, and even road maps pinpoint many places of in-

Recreational camping has been spurred by the development of self-contained vans and campers. Keith Gunner–Bruce Coleman, Inc.

A couple sets up camp on the Continental Divide near Ferry Lake in Wyoming. Modern lightweight tents and equipment have increased the popularity of backwoods camping. Pat O'Hara–West Stock, Inc.

terest where camping is allowed and encouraged. Persons desiring to get farther away from civilization may consult a topographical map of a specific area, which will show hiking trails, primitive shelters, elevations, watercourses, and wooded areas.

Camping Gear. Equipment for camping has progressed greatly since post-World War II campers hiked into the woods with canvas tents, wool-filled sleeping bags, and woven pack baskets. Today, experienced backpackers may tote such items as lightweight aluminum-frame packs, 1-kg (2-lb) nylon tents, down-filled sleeping bags, and tiny camp stoves.

Proper clothing, lightweight but warm and worn in layers, is essential, regardless of where the person camps. In cold weather, a camper may wear a pair of lug-soled hiking boots, wool socks, underwear consisting of a thermal undershirt and long johns, wool trousers (wool, even when wet, keeps the body warm), a cotton shirt, and a down-filled vest or jacket, as well as an anorak or parka, to protect against inclement weather. The camper may always discard layers of such clothing if too warm.

A wide range of equipment for shelter and sleep is available for modern camping. Tents made of nylon are generally preferred, as they will protect the camper from the most adverse conditions. Tent size and design depend on the number of people in the camping group and on the type of climate and terrain in the camping area. Sleeping bags must also be selected carefully. Bags filled with goose down or duck down will keep a person warm in cold temperatures, but bags made of synthetic materials are more resistant to wetness.

Gear for cooking varies according to the site the camper chooses. A long hike to a backcountry area generally calls for a small, lightweight gas stove, but a stay in a developed campground, where portability is not as important, enables the camper to use a larger two-burner stove. Many campers also cook over fires, although gas- or propane-fueled stoves are more reliable in poor weather. Most campers require aluminum pots and pans, a spatula, and plastic utensils, plates, and cups for preparing and eating meals. Other related equipment includes a water bottle or canteen, a sharp knife, a grill, and a cooler. People staying in a developed campground or in an RV, where it is convenient to have a cooler for the storage of perishable foods, may have a variety of foodstuffs on hand; but backpackers also can maintain a nutritious and varied diet by supplementing conventional nonperishable foods with dehydrated and freeze-dried items.

Other essential camping equipment includes an ax, camp lantern, flashlight, map and compass, first-aid kit, rope, and matches.

Safety and Conservation. Wherever a camper stays, safety and conservation should be foremost concerns. The rule at any campsite, whether primitive (without any modern conveniences or facilities) or modern (with accommodations such as bathrooms, electrical hookups for RVs, and perhaps a small grocery store), is to leave the area clean and undefiled. Thoughtful campers respect the privacy of others and keep noise to a minimum. All fires should be extinguished before the camper leaves for the day; all sharp implements should be stored in a safe place, and food should be kept either in a vehicle or tied up in a tree to prevent attracting animals such as bears.

Organized Camping. Today more than 800,000 private and 310,000 public campsites have been established in the U.S. alone; these figures do not include primitive campsites that campers set up in the backcountry. In addition, fully maintained day and sleep-away camps are attended primarily by youngsters during the summer. Day camps, which generally run all day, five days a week, are usually oriented toward outdoor sports such as swimming, hiking, baseball, and tennis. Sleep-away camps, which have programs lasting from a week to two months, offer the same sports and crafts activities as day camps and may also provide campers with the chance to take overnight hikes and canoe trips. The American Camping Association annually publishes a parents' guide to accredited camps.

Sources of Information. The following organizations can provide information about campgrounds and camping in the U.S.: the National Park Service (q.v.), the National Campground Owners Association, the Sierra Club, the Adirondack and the Appalachian Mountain clubs, the Boy Scouts and Girl Scouts of America, and the tourism departments in every state. Information about camping in Canada is provided by the Environmental Management Service of Canada, the National and Provincial Parks Association of Canada, and the provincial tourism departments. The tourist offices of other nations are also sources of camping information. J.H.C.

For further information on this topic, see the Bibliography in volume 28, sections 794, 796, 1144.

CAMPION, Saint Edmund (1540–81), best known of the English Jesuits martyred during the reign of Queen Elizabeth I.

Born in London on Jan. 25, 1540, Campion was educated at the University of Oxford, where he showed early promise as a scholar and orator. Although ordained a deacon in 1567, he could not accept the Protestant formulary as required by the Church of England. Accordingly, he left England for Ireland in 1569; later he went to Douay, France, joined the newly founded English College there, and was received into the Roman Catholic church. In 1573, after being ordained subdeacon, he went to Rome and entered the Society of Jesus (Jesuits). He was ordained priest in 1578 and returned to England in 1580 on a mission to reestablish Roman Catholicism there. To avoid capture by the government, he rarely spent more than a day in any one place. Despite persecution he wrote a bold attack on the Church of England, *Decem Rationes* (Ten Reasons), which was distributed at the Oxford commencement in 1581. A few weeks later he was captured and brought before Queen Elizabeth, who offered him honors and fortune if he would recant. When he refused the offer, he was imprisoned, tortured, and hanged as a traitor on Dec. 1, 1581. He was beatified in 1886 and was one of the "Forty English Martyrs" canonized by Pope Paul VI in 1970. Campion's feast day is December 1.

CAMPION, Thomas (1567–1620), English poet and musician, born in London. A successful London physician, Campion was also a writer and a lutenist and a composer of delicate, expressive vocal music. His reputation rests chiefly on his lyric poems, which are distinguished for their musical quality and charm; they were set to music by Campion and his contemporaries. Among them are "Cherry Ripe" and "Whether Men Do Laugh or Weep." His other works include *Poemata* (1595), Latin epigrams; the words and music for such court masques as *The Lord's Masque* (1613); *Observations on the Arte of English Poesie* (1602), an argument against the use of rhyme in poetry (Campion himself nevertheless employed rhyme); and four books of *Ayres* for lute and voice (1601–c. 1617).

CAMPOAMOR Y CAMPOOSORIO, Ramón de (1817–1901), Spanish poet and philosopher, born in Navia. Campoamor was one of the most popular poets of his day. His short, philosophical verse epigrams, called *doloras,* were usually sentimental and humorous and were based on an unsophisticated philosophy of life. Campoamor's poetry is typified by *Doloras* (1846), *Pequeños poemas* (Little Epics, 1872–94), and *Humoradas* (Humorous Sayings, 1886–88).

CAMPOBASSO, city, central Italy, capital of Campobasso Province and Molise Region. Located in the Apennines, Campobasso is an agricultural center and has factories producing textiles, building materials, and soap. A 15th-century castle is here. Pop. (1979 est.) 46,552.

CAMPO FORMIO, TREATY OF. *See* NAPOLEON I.

CAMPOS, city SE Brazil, in Rio de Janeiro State, on the lower Paraíba R. Coffee, tobacco, sugarcane, and tropical fruits are grown in the surrounding region. Among industries in the city are sugar refining, alcohol distilling, and fruit preserving. Pop. (1979 est., greater city) 352,500.

CAMPTOSAURUS, genus of plant-eating, beaked dinosaurs of the late Jurassic period, about 140 million years ago (*see* DINOSAUR). The largest adult camptosauruses were more than 7 m (23 ft) long. They had heavy bodies but could rear up and walk on two legs as well as four. The genus is probably linked to the later iguanodon and hadrosaur dinosaurs.

CAMUS, Albert (1913–60), French novelist, essayist, and dramatist, regarded as one of the finest philosophical writers of modern France. His work, characterized by a vigorous, concise style, is based on the post–World War II philosophy of the futility and meaninglessness of human life, but also reveals a more hopeful outlook.

Camus was born in Mondovi (now Drean), Algeria, on Nov. 7, 1913, and educated at the University of Algiers. His studies were cut short because of a recurrence of tuberculosis. Active in social reform, he established an amateur theater to bring worthwhile drama to working-class audiences; he also worked as a journalist and traveled extensively in Europe. In 1939 he published *Noces* (Weddings), a collection of essays inspired by his reading and travels. In 1940 he moved to Paris and joined the staff of the newspaper *Paris-Soir.* During World War II he was active in the French Resistance and from 1945 to 1947 was editor of *Combat,* an underground paper.

An Algerian background provides the setting for Camus's first published novel, *The Stranger* (1942; trans. 1946), and for most of his subsequent fiction. This work and the essay on which it is based, *The Myth of Sisyphus* (1942; trans. 1955), reveal the influence of existentialism (q.v.) on his thought. Of the plays that develop existentialist themes, *Caligula* (1944), produced in New York City in 1960, is one of the best known. Although in the novel *The Plague* (1947; trans. 1948) Camus still was concerned with the fundamental absurdity of existence, he recognized human courage in the face of disasters. His later works include the novel *The Fall* (1957; trans. 1957), also based on an earlier essay, *The Rebel* (1951; trans. 1951); a play, *State of Siege* (1948; trans. 1958); and a collection of stories, *Exile and the Kingdom* (1957; trans. 1958), in various styles but reworking earlier ideas. Collections of his articles came out under the titles *Actuelles* (3 vol., 1950, 1953, and 1958) and *L'été* (Summer, 1954). *A Happy Death* (1971; trans. 1972), although posthumously published, is actually his first novel. His *Notebooks,* covering the years 1935 to 1951, were also posthumously issued in two volumes (1962 and 1964; trans. 1963 and 1966). Camus, who was awarded the 1957 Nobel Prize in literature, was killed in an automobile accident at Villeblerin, France, on Jan. 4, 1960.

Albert Camus French Embassy Press & Information Div.

CANAAN, in the Old Testament, designation of the land to the west of the Jordan River, later known as Palestine, and the name of the reputed ancestor of the Canaanites, the original inhabitants of that land. The Israelites gradually conquered and occupied this territory during the 2d millennium BC or earlier. It was probably the Canaanites who gave the Israelites the language now known as Hebrew.

CANAANITES, in the Old Testament, original inhabitants of the land of Canaan. According to the Book of Judges, the Israelites, during the 2d millennium BC or earlier, gradually subjugated the Canaanite cities. By the end of the reign of Solomon, king of Israel, the Canaanites had virtually been assimilated into the Hebrew people, among whom they appear to have exerted a reactionary religious influence. The Canaanite religion itself was based on the worship of the divinities Baal and Ashtoreth. Biblical scholars now believe that the Hebrew language was derived from Canaanite sources, and that the Phoenician language was an early form of Hebrew. Recent discoveries indicate that, before the Hebrew conquest of the south of Canaan, the Canaanites and the Phoenicians were a single nation, and the people now known as the Phoenicians subsequently developed as a separate nation.

CANADA, federated state of North America, formerly known as the Dominion of Canada. It is bounded on the N by the Arctic Ocean; on the NE by Baffin Bay and Davis Strait, which separate it from Greenland; on the E by the Atlantic Ocean; on the S by the U.S.; and on the W by the Pacific Ocean and Alaska. Occupying all of

Snowcapped peaks of the Canadian Rocky Mts. in Mt. Robson Provincial Park, British Columbia.
John M. Burnley–Bruce Coleman, Inc.

North America N of the conterminous U.S., except Alaska, Greenland, Saint-Pierre Island, and the Miquelon Islands, Canada includes many islands, notably the Canadian Arctic Islands (Arctic Archipelago) in the Arctic Ocean. Among the larger members of this group, which in aggregate area is about 1,424,500 sq km (about 550,000 sq mi), are Baffin, Victoria, Ellesmere, Banks, Devon, Axel Heiberg, and Melville islands. Cape Columbia, a promontory of Ellesmere Island at lat 83°07′ N, is the northernmost point of Canada; its southernmost point is Middle Island in Lake Erie, at lat 41°41′ N. The easternmost and westernmost limits are delineated, respectively, by long 52°37′ W, which lies along Cape Spear, Newf., and long 141° W, which coincides with part of the Alaskan-Canadian frontier. Canada has a total land area of 9,922,330 sq km (3,831,033 sq mi); areas occupied by rivers, lakes, including those portions of the Great Lakes under Canadian jurisdiction, and other bodies of fresh water total 755,165 sq km (291,571 sq mi).

Canada, which is the world's second largest country (surpassed in size only by the USSR), contains great reserves of natural resources, notably timber, petroleum, natural gas, iron ore, and fish. It is also an important manufacturing country, and its major cities, such as Toronto, Montréal, Winnipeg, Calgary, Edmonton, Vancouver, and Ottawa (the country's capital) are bustling centers of commerce and industry. Most of Canada's inhabitants live in the S part of the country, and vast areas of the N are very sparsely inhabited. The country is divided into ten provinces (Alberta, British Columbia, Manitoba, New Brunswick, Newfoundland, Nova Scotia, Ontario, Prince Edward Island, Québec, Saskatchewan) and two territories (Northwest Territories, Yukon Territory). The name Canada is derived from an Iroquoian Indian term meaning "village" or "community."

THE LAND

The coast of the Canadian mainland, about 58,500 km (about 36,350 mi) in length, is extremely broken and irregular. Large bays and peninsulas alternate, and Canada has numerous coastal islands, in addition to the Arctic Archipelago, with a total insular coastline of some 185,290 km (some 115,135 mi). Off the E coast the largest islands are Newfoundland, Cape Breton, Prince Edward, and Anticosti. Off the W coast, which is fringed with fjords, are Vancouver Island and the Queen Charlotte Islands. Southampton Island, covering 41,214 sq km (15,913 sq mi), and many smaller islands are in Hudson Bay, a vast inland sea in E central Canada.

Canada contains more lakes and inland waters than any other country. In addition to the Great

Lakes on the U.S. border (all partly within Canada except Lake Michigan), the country has 33 lakes more than 1300 sq km (502 sq mi) in area. Largest among these lakes are Great Bear, Great Slave, Dubawnt, and Baker in the mainland Northwest Territories; Nettilling and Amadjuak on Baffin Island; Athabasca in Alberta and Saskatchewan; Wollaston in Saskatchewan; Reindeer in Saskatchewan and Manitoba; Winnipeg, Manitoba, Winnipegosis, and Southern Indian in Manitoba; Nipigon and Lake of the Woods in Ontario; Mistassini in Québec; and Smallwood Reservoir and Melville in Newfoundland.

Among the many great rivers of Canada are the Saint Lawrence, draining the Great Lakes, and emptying into the Gulf of St. Lawrence; the Ottawa and the Saguenay, the principal affluents of the St. Lawrence; the Saint John, emptying into the Bay of Fundy, between Nova Scotia and New Brunswick; the Saskatchewan, flowing into Lake Winnipeg, and the Nelson, flowing from this lake into Hudson Bay; the system, formed by the Athabasca, Peace, Slave, and Mackenzie rivers, which empties into the Arctic Ocean; the upper course of the Yukon, which flows across Alaska into the Bering Sea; and the Fraser and the upper course of the Columbia, emptying into the Pacific Ocean.

Excluding the Arctic Archipelago, five physiographic regions are distinguishable in Canada. The largest region, designated either as the Canadian Shield (q.v.) or the Laurentian Plateau, extends from Labrador to the Mackenzie R. and from the Arctic Ocean to the Thousand Islands in the St. Lawrence R. and into the U.S. west of Lake Superior and into N New York. This region of ancient granite rock, sparsely covered with soil and deeply eroded by glacial action, comprises all of Labrador, most of Québec, N Ontario, Manitoba, and most of the Northwest Territories, with Hudson Bay in the center.

Eastern Canada consists of the Appalachian-Acadian region and the St. Lawrence and Lower Lakes region. The former embraces Newfoundland, Nova Scotia, New Brunswick, and Prince Edward Island, and the Gaspé Peninsula of Québec. This region is an extension of the Appalachian mountain system (continuations of the Green Mts. of Vermont and the White Mts. of New Hampshire) and of the Atlantic Coastal Plain. The St. Lawrence and Lower Lakes region, covering an area of about 98,420 sq km (about 38,000 sq mi) in S Québec and Ontario, is a generally level plain. In this region is the largest expanse of cultivable land in E Canada and most of the manufacturing industries of the nation.

Bordering the Canadian Shield on the W is the Interior Plain, an extension of the Great Plains of the U.S. About 1290 km (about 800 mi) wide at the U.S. border, it narrows to about 320 km (about 200 mi) W of Great Bear Lake and widens again at the mouth of the Mackenzie R. on the

A farm in Saskatchewan, in west-central Canada. Saskatchewan, Manitoba, and Alberta are known as the Prairie provinces. Annan Photo Features

coast of the Arctic Ocean to about 480 km (about 300 mi). Within the Interior Plain are the NE corner of British Columbia, most of Alberta, the S half of Saskatchewan, and the S third of Manitoba, the most fertile sections of Canada.

The fifth and westernmost region of Canada embraces the uplifts W of the Interior Plain. The region belongs to the Cordillera (q.v.), the vast mountain system extending from the southernmost extremity of South America to westernmost Alaska. In Canada the Cordillera has an average width of some 805 km (some 500 mi). Part of W Alberta, much of British Columbia, Inuvik Region and part of Fort Smith Region of the Northwest Territories, and practically all of Yukon Territory lie within this region. The E portion of the Cordillera in Canada consists of the Rocky Mountains (q.v.) and related ranges, including the Mackenzie, Franklin, and Richardson mountains. Mt. Robson (3954 m/12,972 ft) is the highest summit of the Canadian Rockies, and eight other peaks reach elevations of more than 3350 m (10,991 ft). To the W of the Canadian Rockies is a region occupied by numerous isolated ranges, notably the Cariboo, Stikine, and Selkirk mountains, and a vast plateau region. Deep river valleys and extensive tracts of arable land are the chief features of the plateau region, particularly in British Columbia. Flanking this central belt on the W and generally parallel to the Pacific Ocean is another great mountain system. This system includes the Coast Mts., an extension into British Columbia of the Cascade Range (q.v.) of the U.S., and various coastal ranges. The loftiest coastal uplift is the Saint Elias Mts., on the boundary between Yukon Territory and Alaska. Among noteworthy peaks of the W Cordillera in Canada are Mt. Logan (5951 m/19,524 ft), the second highest mountain in North America, Mt. St. Elias (5489 m/18,008 ft), Mt. Lucania (5226 m/17,147 ft), and King Peak (5173 m/16,971 ft); all are in the St. Elias Mts.

Geology. The Canadian Shield, which occupies the eastern half of Canada's landmass, is an ancient craton, or stable platform, made up of rocks that formed billions of years ago, during the Precambrian era (q.v.) of earth history. The shield, with its assemblage of 2–4 billion-year-old granites, gneisses, and schists, became the nucleus of the North American plate at the time that the earth's crust first began experiencing the tectonic forces that drive continental drift. *See also* NORTH AMERICA: *Geological History;* PLATE TECTONICS.

During the Paleozoic era (q.v.), large parts of Canada were covered by shallow seas. Sediments deposited in these seas formed the sandstone, shale, and limestone that now surround the Canadian Shield. The Cambrian and Silurian systems are represented by great thicknesses of strata that appear in outcroppings in Nova Scotia, New Brunswick, and Newfoundland, along the St. Lawrence Valley, and on the shores of Lake Ontario. Flat-lying beds of Paleozoic and younger rocks extend westward across the Interior Plains throughout the prairie provinces of Alberta, Saskatchewan, and Manitoba. In these areas, the rocks contain valuable deposits of oil and gas. In the Cordilleran region of western Canada, the rocks were subjected to tectonic forces generated by the collision of the North American plate with the Pacific plate. In the ensuing upheavals, which began during the Cretaceous period (q.v.), mountain ranges rose throughout the Cordilleran region. The easternmost of these ranges, the Rocky Mountains, are similar in structure to the mountains of Colorado, Wyoming, and Montana, having been built by uplift and folding of sedimentary rocks and, in lesser degree, by volcanic activity. The strata of which they are composed range in age from Paleozoic to Tertiary and contain valuable deposits of base and precious metals as well as fossil fuels.

During the Quaternary period (q.v.), nearly all of Canada was covered by a vast ice sheet, the Laurentian glacier, that terminated in the northern U.S. Landscapes were profoundly modified by the erosive action of this vast mass of moving ice, particularly in the creation of Canada's many thousands of lakes and its extensive deposits of sand, clay and gravel. *See also* ICE AGES.

Climate. Part of the Canadian mainland and most of the Arctic Archipelago fall within the Frigid Zone; the remainder of the country lies in the N half of the North Temperate Zone. As a consequence, general climatic conditions range from the extreme cold characteristic of the Arctic regions to the moderate temperatures of more southerly latitudes. The Canadian climate is marked by wide regional variations. In the Maritime provinces extremes of winter cold and summer heat are modified by oceanic influences, which also cause considerable fog and precipitation. Along the W coast, which is under the influence of warm ocean currents and moisture-laden winds, mild, equable summers and winters, high humidity, and abundant precipitation are characteristic. In the Cordilleran region the higher W slopes of certain uplifts, particularly the Selkirks and the Rockies, receive sizable amounts of rain and snow, but the E slopes and the central plateau region are extremely arid. A feature of the Cordilleran region is the chinook, a warm, dry westerly wind that substantially ameliorates

A polar bear family of mother and two cubs along the shore of Hudson Bay near Churchill, Man. Cubs are born in spring and weaned during the summer.
Bob & Clara Calhoun–Bruce Coleman, Inc.

winter conditions in the Rocky Mt. foothills and adjoining plains, often causing great diurnal changes. For further information see articles on the individual provinces.

Natural Resources. Canada is richly endowed with valuable natural resources that are commercially indispensable to the economy. The country has enormous areas of fertile, low-lying land in the Prairie provinces (Alberta, Manitoba, Saskatchewan) and bordering the Great Lakes and St. Lawrence R. in S Québec and S Ontario. Canadian forests cover about 37% of the country's land area and abound in commercially valuable stands of timber. Commercial fishing in Canada dates back nearly 500 years. The waters of the Atlantic and Pacific oceans, inland lakes, and rivers continue to yield abundant catches. The mining industry of Canada has a long history of exploration and development that predates confederation in 1867. The Canadian Shield contains a wealth of minerals; the nation is also rich in reserves of crude petroleum and natural gas. The river and lake systems of the country combine with the mountainous topography to make energy produced by waterpower one of the permanent natural assets of Canada. The wildlife of the country is extensive and varied.

Plants. The flora of the entire N part of Canada is arctic and subarctic (*see* TUNDRA). A good part of the Maritime provinces is covered by forests of mixed hardwoods and softwoods. The Prairie provinces are comparatively treeless as far N as the Saskatchewan R. system; prairie grasses, herbage, and bunchgrasses are the chief forms of vegetation. N of the Saskatchewan a broad belt of rather small and sparse trees extends from Hudson Bay to Great Slave Lake and the Rocky Mts. Spruce, tamarack, and poplar are the principal species. The dry slopes and valleys of the Rocky Mts. support thin forests, mainly pine, but the forests increase in density and the trees in size westward toward the region of greater rainfall. On the coast ranges, especially on their W slopes, are dense forests of mighty evergreen trees. The principal trees are the spruce, hemlock, Douglas and balsam firs, jack and lodgepole pines, and cedar.

Animals. The animals of Canada bear a close resemblance or are identical to those of N Europe and Asia. Among the carnivores are several species of the weasel subfamily, such as the ermine, sable, fisher, wolverine, and mink. Other representative carnivores include the black bear, grizzly bear, lynx, wolf, coyote, fox, and skunk. The polar bear is distributed throughout the arctic regions; the puma, or American lion, is found in British Columbia. Of the rodents, the most characteristic is the beaver. The Canadian porcupine, muskrat, and many smaller rodents are numerous, as are hare, and in the W plains a variety of burrowing gopher is found.

Several varieties of Virginia deer are indigenous to S Canada; the black-tailed deer occurs in British Columbia and parts of the plains region. This region is also the habitat of the pronghorn antelope. The woodland caribou and the

INDEX TO MAP OF CANADA

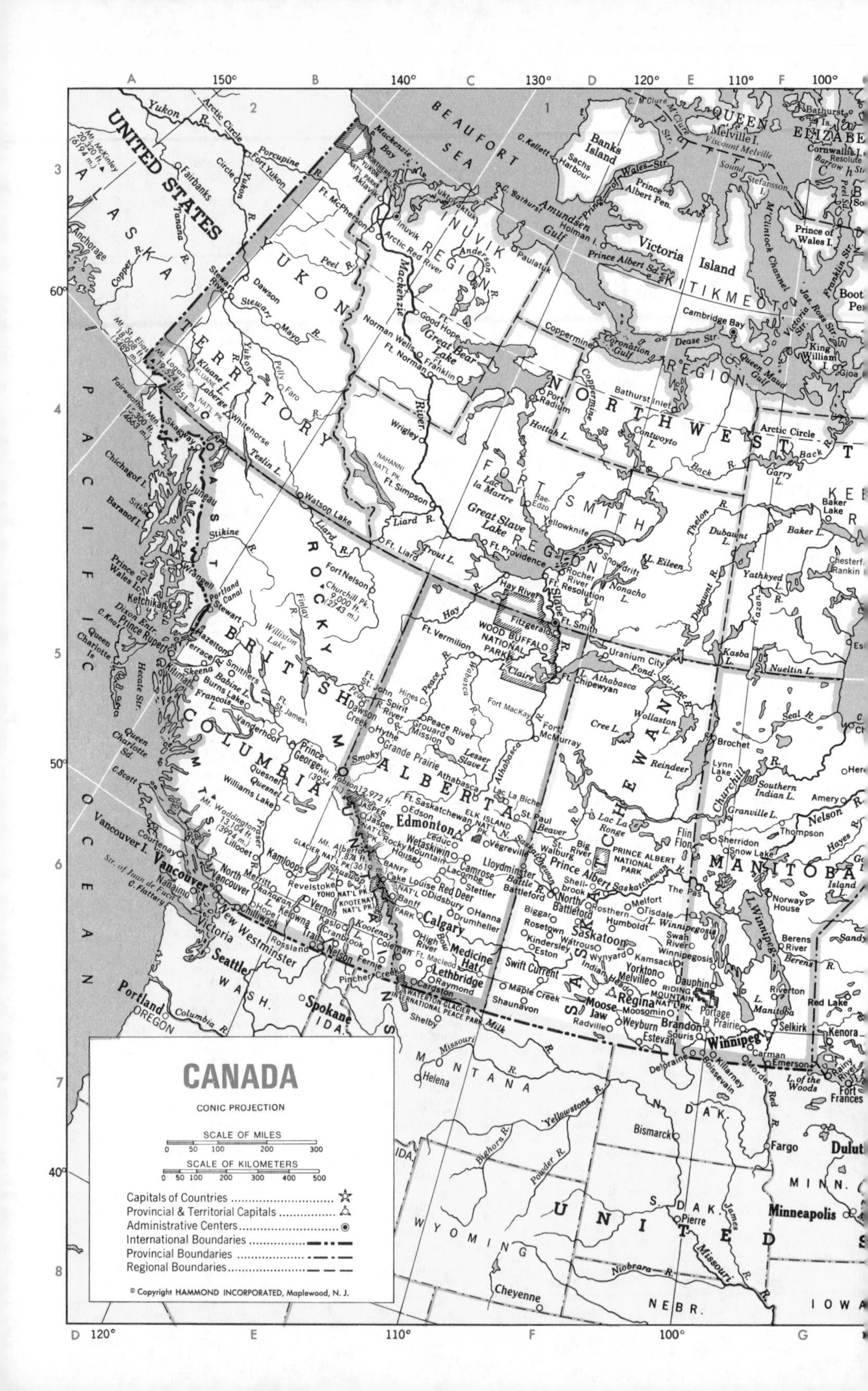

CANADA
CONIC PROJECTION
SCALE OF MILES
0 50 100 200 300
SCALE OF KILOMETERS
0 50 100 200 300 400 500
Capitals of Countries
Provincial & Territorial Capitals
Administrative Centers
International Boundaries
Provincial Boundaries
Regional Boundaries
© Copyright HAMMOND INCORPORATED, Maplewood, N. J.
BEAUFORT SEA
UNITED STATES
ALASKA
PACIFIC OCEAN
YUKON TERRITORY
BRITISH COLUMBIA
ALBERTA
SASKATCHEWAN
MANITOBA
NORTHWEST TERRITORIES
INUVIK REGION
KITIKMEOT REGION
FORT SMITH REGION
ROCKY MOUNTAINS
QUEEN ELIZABETH
Banks Island
Victoria Island
Great Bear Lake
Great Slave Lake
L. Athabasca
L. Winnipeg
Vancouver I.
Queen Charlotte Is.
Whitehorse
Dawson
Yellowknife
Inuvik
Edmonton
Calgary
Regina
Saskatoon
Winnipeg
Vancouver
Victoria
Prince George
Prince Rupert
Kamloops
Lethbridge
Medicine Hat
Moose Jaw
Prince Albert
Brandon
Seattle
Spokane
Portland
Helena
Bismarck
Pierre
Cheyenne
Fargo
Minneapolis
Anchorage
Fairbanks
Juneau
MONTANA
WYOMING
N. DAK.
S. DAK.
MINN.
NEBR.
IOWA
WASH.
IDA.
OREGON
WOOD BUFFALO NATIONAL PARK
PRINCE ALBERT NATIONAL PARK
JASPER NAT'L PK.
BANFF NAT'L PARK
Mt. Robson 12,972 ft. (3954 m.)
Mt. Logan 19,524 ft. (5951 m.)
Mt. McKinley 20,320 ft. (6194 m.)
Arctic Circle

H
80°
J
70°
K
60°
L
50°
M
40°
N
30°
O
Grise Fiord
GREENLAND
(KALATDLIT-NUNAT)
BAFFIN
BAY
Upernavik
Svartenhuk Pen.
Ūmának Fjord
Nûgssuaq
Disko
Godhavn
Disko Bay
DAVIS
STRAIT
Holsteinsborg
Lancaster Sound
Bylot I.
Arctic Bay
Pond Inlet
Clyde
Clyde Inlet
C. Raper
Home Bay
AUYUITTUQ NAT'L PARK
Padloping I.
C. Dyer
C. Walsingham
Cumberland Pen.
Pangnirtung
Cumberland Sound
BAFFIN ISLAND
Nettilling L.
Amadjuak L.
Hall Pen.
Frobisher Bay
Frobisher Bay
Lake Harbour
Resolution I.
Amadjuak
Cape Dorset
Salisbury I.
Igloolik
Jens Munk
FOXE BASIN
Prince Charles I.
Melville Pen.
Committee Bay
Bowman Bay
Foxe Pen.
Isthmus
Frozen Str.
Foxe Chan.
Roes Welcome Sound
Southampton I.
Coral Harbour
Evans Str.
Nottingham I.
Fisher Str.
Coats I.
C. Low
Mansel I.
Hudson Str.
Ivujivik
Saglouc
Maricourt
C. Chidley
Akpatok I.
Ungava Bay
Ungava
Bellin
Port-Nouveau-Québec
Povungnituk
C. Smith
L. Payne
Peninsula
R. aux Feuilles
R. Koksoak
Ft. Chimo
R. George
R. à la Baleine
R. Caniapiscau
L. Minto
Ottawa Is.
Inoucdjouac
HUDSON BAY
Nain
Hopedale
C. Harrison
Hamilton Inlet
Cartwright
Rigolet
L. Melville
LABRADOR
LABRADOR SEA
Smallwood Res.
Goose Bay
Goose Airport P.O.
Churchill R.
Schefferville
Lac à l'Eau Claire
Belcher Is.
Poste-de-la-Baleine
Grande R. de la Baleine
Lac Bienville
C. Henrietta Maria
Pte. Louis-XIV
James Bay
Ft-George
La Grande Rivière
R. Opinaca
R. Eastmain
Eastmain
Rupert House
Charlton I.
Akimiski I.
Fort Albany
Albany R.
Moosonee
Wabush
Gagnon
L. Plétipi
R. Moisie
R. Natashquan
R. Romaine
Mingan
Sept-Îles (Seven Is.)
Port-Cartier
Havre-St-Pierre
Île d'Anticosti
Port Menier
QUEBEC
L. Mistassini
Chibougamau
R. Nottaway
R. Mistassibi
R. Péribonca
R. Manicouagan
R. Betsiamites
NEWFOUNDLAND
Battle Harbour
Belle Isle
C. Bauld
Str. of Belle Isle
Bell I.
White Bay
Fogo I.
Grand Falls
Gander
Bonavista
Harbour Grace
St. John's
C. Race
Corner Brook
Stephenville
Channel-Port aux Basques
C. Ray
Cabot Strait
Gulf of St. Lawrence
ST. PIERRE & MIQUELON (Fr.)
Gaspé
FORILLON NAT'L PK.
Cap-Chat
Chandler
Magdalen Is.
C. North
Glace Bay
Sydney
Cape Breton I.
Inverness
Souris
PRINCE EDWARD I.
Charlottetown
St. Lawrence R.
Mont-Joli
Rimouski
Campbellton
Bathurst
Rivière-du-Loup
Edmundston
NEW BRUNSWICK
Newcastle
Chatham
Moncton
Amherst
Truro
Saint John
Fredericton
Woodstock
St. Stephen
Bay of Fundy
Windsor
NOVA SCOTIA
Dartmouth
Halifax
Lunenburg
Bridgewater
Yarmouth
C. Sable
Sable I.
Chicoutimi
Jonquière
Roberval
L. St-Jean
Tadoussac
Baie-St-Paul
Rés. Gouin
La Tuque
Québec
Rés. Baskatong
Shawinigan
Trois-Rivières
Mont-Laurier
MONTRÉAL
Hull
Sherbrooke
Ottawa
Cornwall
Kingston
Amos
Val-d'Or
Noranda
Rouyn
L. Abitibi
La Sarre
R. Bell
L. Timiskaming
North Bay
Ottawa R.
Pembroke
Renfrew
Mattawa
Callander
Sturgeon Falls
Sudbury
Parry Sound
Peterborough
Kirkland Lake
Englehart
New Liskeard
Cobalt
Cochrane
Iroquois Falls
Timmins
Kapuskasing
Abitibi R.
Missinaibi R.
Hearst
Oba
Geraldton
Nakina
Armstrong
L. Nipigon
Nipigon
Marathon
White River
PUKASKWA NAT'L PK.
Thunder Bay
I. Royale
Lake Superior
Chapleau
Sault Ste. Marie
Sault Ste. Marie
Thessalon
Blind River
Manitoulin I.
Georgian Bay
Owen Sound
Lake Huron
TORONTO
Guelph
Hamilton
London
Sarnia
L. Ontario
Niagara Falls
Niagara Falls
Buffalo
L. Erie
Windsor
DETROIT
Cleveland
Albany
NEW YORK
N.Y.
N.J.
PA.
MICH.
L. Michigan
ILLINOIS
Milwaukee
VT.
Montpelier
N.H.
MAINE
Augusta
MASS.
BOSTON
C. Cod
CONN.
R.I.
Gulf of Maine
ATLANTIC OCEAN
Winisk R.
Ekwan R.
Attawapiskat R.
Ogoki R.
Kenogami R.
ONTARIO
West of Greenwich
3
4
5
6
7
8
60°
50°
40°
A
QUEEN ELIZABETH ISLANDS
0 50 100 200 MI.
0 100 200 KM.
140° 130° 120° 110° 100° 90° 80° 70° 60°
C. Columbia
Alert
UNITED STATES RA.
ELLESMERE
Kennedy Chan.
Kane Basin
Nares Str.
ARCTIC OCEAN
Meighen I.
Peary Chan.
Axel Heiberg Island
Eureka
SVERDRUP ISLANDS
Borden I.
Brock I.
Ellef Ringnes I.
Amund Ringnes I.
Mackenzie King I.
Prince Patrick I.
Cornwall I.
Graham I.
Smith B.
Grise Fiord
NORTH MAGNETIC POLE
PARRY ISLANDS
Eglinton I.
Melville Island
Bathurst I.
Jones Sd.
Devon I.
M'Clure Str.
Banks I.
Viscount Melville Sd.
Cornwallis I.
Resolute Bay
Lancaster Sd.
120° 110° 100° 90° 80°

Index to Map of Canada

Kazan (river) F 3
Kellett (cape) D 1
Kennedy (chan.) N 3
King William (island) G 2
Lancaster (sound) H 1
Liard (river) D 4
Low (cape) H 3
M'Clintock (chan.) F 1
M'Clure (cape) E 1
M'Clure (strait) E 1
Mackenzie (bay) C 2
Mackenzie (river) C 2
Mackenzie King (island) M 3
Mansel (island) H 3
Martre (lake) E 3
Meighen (island) M 3
Melville (island) M 3
Melville (pen.) H 2
Nahanni Nat'l Park D 3
Nares (strait) N 3
Nettilling (lake) J 2
North Magnetic Pole F 1
Nottingham (island) J 3
Nueltin (lake) G 3
Ottawa (islands) H 4
Padloping (island) K 2
Parry (chan.) E 1
Parry (islands) M 3
Peel (sound) G 1
Prince Albert (sound) E 1
Prince Charles (island) J 2
Prince of Wales (island) G 1
Prince of Wales (strait) E 1
Prince Patrick (island) M 2
Prince Regent (inlet) G 1
Queen Elizabeth (islands) M 2
Queen Maud (gulf) F 2
Rae (isthmus) H 2
Resolution (island) K 3
Roes Welcome (sound) H 3
Salisbury (island) J 3
Slave (river) E 3
Somerset (island) G 1
Southampton (island) H 3
Sverdrup (islands) M 3
Thelon (river) F 3
Trout (lake) D 3
Victoria (island) E 2
Victoria (strait) G 2
Viscount Melville (sound) F 1
Wager (bay) G 3
Walsingham (cape) L 2
Wellington (chan.) G 1
Wood Buffalo Nat'l Park E 4
Yathkyed (lake) G 3

NOVA SCOTIA

Cities and Towns

Amherst K 6
Bridgewater K 7
Dartmouth K 7
Glace Bay L 6
Halifax (cap.) K 7
Inverness K 6
Lunenburg K 7
Sydney L 6
Truro K 6
Windsor K 7
Yarmouth K 7

Other Features

Cabot (strait) K 6
Cape Breton (island) K 6
Fundy (bay) K 7
Maine (gulf) K 7
North (cape) L 6
Sable (cape) K 7
Sable (island) L 7

ONTARIO

Cities and Towns

Armstrong H 5
Atikokan G 6
Blind River H 6
Callander H 6
Chapleau H 6
Cobalt H 6
Cochrane H 6
Cornwall J 7
Fort Albany H 5
Fort Frances G 6
Geraldton H 6
Guelph H 7
Hamilton H 7
Hearst H 6
Ignace G 6
Iroquois Falls H 6
Kapuskasing H 6
Kenora G 5
Kingston J 7
Kirkland Lake H 6
London H 7
Marathon H 6
Mattawa J 6
Moosonee H 5
New Liskeard H 6
Niagara Falls J 7
Nipigon H 6
North Bay J 6
Ottawa (cap.), Canada J 6
Owen Sound H 7
Parry Sound J 6
Pembroke J 6
Peterborough J 7
Rainy River G 6
Red Lake G 5
Renfrew J 6
Sarnia H 7
Sault-Ste.-Marie H 6
Sioux Lookout G 6
Steep Rock Lake G 6
Sturgeon Falls H 6
Sudbury H 6
Thessalon H 6
Thunder Bay H 6
Timmins H 6
Toronto (cap.) H 7
White River H 6
Windsor H 7

Other Features

Abitibi (lake) H 6
Abitibi (river) H 5
Albany (river) H 5
Attawapiskat (river) H 5
Erie (lake) H 7
Georgian (bay) H 6
Henrietta Maria (cape) H 4
Huron (lake) H 7
Kenogami (river) H 5
Lake of the Woods (lake) G 6
Manitoulin (island) H 6
Missinaibi (river) H 6
Nipigon (lake) H 6
Ogoki (river) H 5
Ontario (lake) J 7
Pulaskwa Nat'l Park H 6
Rainy (lake) G 6
Saint Joseph (lake) G 5
Severn (river) G 5
Superior (lake) H 6
Winisk (river) H 5
Woods (lake) G 6

PRINCE EDWARD ISLAND

Cities and Towns

Charlottetown (cap.) K 6
Souris East K 6

QUÉBEC

Cities and Towns

Amos J 6
Baie-Saint-Paul J 6
Bellin J 3
Cap-Chat K 6
Chandler K 6
Chibougamau J 6
Chicoutimi J 6
Eastmain J 5
Fort-Chimo K 4
Fort-George J 5
Gaspé K 6
Havre-Saint-Pierre K 5
Hull J 6
Inoucdjouac J 4
Ivujivik J 3
Jonquière J 6
La Tuque J 6
Maricourt J 3
Monti-Joli K 6
Mont Laurier J 6
Montréal J 6
Noranda J 6
Port-Cartier K 6
Port-Menier K 6
Port-Nouveau-Québec J 4
Poste-de-la-Baleine J 4
Povungnituk J 3
Québec (cap.) J 6
Rimouski K 6
Rivière-du-Loup K 6
Roberval J 6
Rouyn J 6
Rupert House J 5
Saglouc J 3
Schefferville K 4
Sept-Îles K 5
Seven Islands (Sept-Îles) K 5
Shawinigan J 6
Sherbrooke J 6
Tadoussac J 6
Trois-Rivières J 6
Val-d'Or J 6

Other Features

Anticosti (island) K 6
Baleine (river) K 4
Baskatong (res.) J 6
Bell (river) J 6
Betsiamites (river) K 5
Bienville (lake) J 5
Caniapiscau (river) K 4
Eastmain (river) J 5
Eau Claire (lake) J 4
Feuilles (river) J 4
Forillon Nat'l Park K 6
Gouin (res.) J 6
Grande (river) J 5
Grande de la Baleine (river) J 4
Koksoak (river) K 4
Louis-XIV (point) H 5
Magdalen (islands) K 6
Manicouagan (river) K 5
Minto (lake) J 4
Mistassibi (river) J 6
Mistassini (lake) J 5
Moisie (river) K 5
Natashquan (river) K 5
Nottaway (river) J 5
Opinaca (river) J 5
Ottawa (river) J 6
Péribonca (river) J 5
Plétipi (lake) J 5
Romaine (river) K 5
Saint-Jean (lake) J 6
Saint Lawrence (gulf) K 6
Saint Lawrence (river) K 6
Timiskaming (lake) J 6
Ungava (pen.) J 3

SASKATCHEWAN

Cities and Towns

Battleford F 5
Big River F 5
Estevan F 6
Eston F 5
Humboldt F 5
Indian Head F 5
Kindersley F 5
Maple Creek F 6
Melfort F 5
Melville F 5
Moose Jaw F 6
Moosomin F 5
North Battleford F 5
Prince Albert F 5
Radville F 6
Regina (cap.) F 5
Rosetown F 5
Rosthern F 5
Saint Walburg F 5
Saskatoon F 5
Shaunavon F 6
Shellbrook F 5
Swift Current F 5
Tisdale F 5
Uranium City F 4
Watrous F 5
Weyburn F 6
Wynyard F 5
Yorkton F 5

Other Features

Athabasca (lake) F 4
Beaver (river) F 5
Cree (lake) F 4
Fond-du-lac (river) F 4
Prince Albert Nat'l. Park F 5
Reindeer (lake) F 4
Ronge, La (lake) F 5
Saskatchewan (river) F 5
Wollaston (lake) F 4

YUKON TERRITORY

Cities and Towns

Dawson C 3
Faro C 3
Mayo C 3
Stewart River B 3
Watson Lake D 3
Whitehorse (cap.) C 3

Other Features

Kluane (lake) C 3
Kluane Nat'l Park C 3
Laberge (lake) C 3
Logan (mt.) C 3
Northern Yukon Nat'l Park C 2
Peel (river) C 2
Pelly (river) C 3
Porcupine (river) B 2
Saint Elias (mt.) B 3
Stewart (river) C 3
Yukon (river) C 3

Vancouver is Canada's third largest city and its principal west coast port. It is a railroad, shipping, and forestry products manufacturing center. Bill Staley–West Stock, Inc.

moose are numerous and widely distributed, but the Barren Ground caribou is found only in the more N areas, which are the habitat also of the musk-ox. Elk and bison are found in various W areas. In the mountains of British Columbia bighorn sheep and Rocky Mountain goats are numerous. An immense variety of birds abounds, and fish are numerous in all the inland waters and along all the coasts. Reptiles and insects are scarce, except in the far S.

Soils. Large areas of Canada are covered by boggy peat characteristic of the tundra and adjoining forest areas. It is generally infertile and frequently mossy. A formation of rich dark brown and black prairie soils runs from S Manitoba W across Saskatchewan and into Alberta, forming Canada's best farmland. The gray-brown soil of the St. Lawrence Basin and the Great Lakes is also good farmland. However, only about 8% of Canada's land is suitable for farming, the remainder being too mountainous, rocky, wet, or infertile.

POPULATION

The racial and national makeup of the Canadian people is diversified. About 40% of the population, which consists predominantly of native-born citizens, is composed of persons of British origin. Persons of French origin total about 29% of the population. The vast majority of French-speaking Canadians reside in Québec, where they make up about 80% of the population; large numbers also live in Ontario and New Brunswick, and smaller groups inhabit the remaining provinces. French-speaking Canadians maintain their language, culture, and traditions, and the federal government follows the policy of a bilingual and bicultural nation. The remainder of the population is composed of people of various ethnic origins, mainly German, Italian, Ukrainian, Netherlands Dutch, Scandinavian, Polish, Native Indian, Jewish, Hungarian, and Greek.

Blacks have never constituted a major segment of the Canadian population, but their history has been an interesting one. Although Louis XIV in 1689 authorized the importation of slaves from the West Indies, black immigration into Canada has been almost entirely from the U.S. Some Loyalists brought slaves north with them during and after the American Revolution. The British troops that burned Washington in the War of 1812 brought many slaves back with them to Halifax. As early as 1787, however, Nova Scotia, and six years later, Upper Canada, abolished slavery, thus setting precedents for the whole British Empire. The fact of free soil in Canada was a major influence in the operation of the Underground Railroad (q.v.), which, during the abolition campaign in the U.S., transported many slaves into Canada, particularly to Chatham and Sarnia. Blacks made up less than 1% of the Canadian population in the 1970s.

American Indians and Inuit (Eskimo) made up, respectively, about 1.4% and 0.1% of Canada's inhabitants. Close ethnic relatives of the aborigines of the U.S. (*see* AMERICAN INDIANS), the Indians

The Toronto City Hall, dedicated in 1965, in which two curvilinear office buildings are innovatively "wrapped" around a domed council chamber. Metal arches span a skating rink in the foreground. Bill Brooks–Bruce Coleman, Inc.

of Canada belong predominantly to the Algonquian linguistic group; other representative linguistic stocks are the Iroquoian, Salishan, Athabascan, and Inuit (Eskimoan). The Indians are divided into some 570 groups.

Population Characteristics. The population of Canada (1986) was 25,354,064, compared with 24,343,181 in 1981. The overall population density in 1986 was 2.6 persons per sq km (6.6 persons per sq mi).

Approximately three-quarters of the people of Canada inhabit a relatively narrow belt along the U.S. frontier, with about 62% concentrated in Québec and Ontario. Nearly 18% of the population lives in the Prairie provinces of Alberta, Manitoba, and Saskatchewan; about 9% in the Atlantic provinces, which include Newfoundland and the Maritime provinces of Prince Edward Island, Nova Scotia, and New Brunswick; and about 11% in British Columbia. Yukon Territory and the Northwest Territories are sparsely inhabited, having only about 0.3% of the total population. About 76% of the population is urban.

Political Divisions. Canada comprises ten provinces, each with a separate legislature and administration, and Yukon Territory and Northwest Territories, which are governed by commissioners, assisted by councils. In descending order of population (1986 census) the provinces are the following: Ontario, Québec, British Columbia, Alberta, Manitoba, Saskatchewan, Nova Scotia, New Brunswick, Newfoundland, and Prince Edward Island.

Principal Cities. Among the leading cities of Canada are Toronto, Ont., a port and manufacturing city (pop., 1986, 612,289); Montréal, Qué., a port and major commercial center (1,015,420); Vancouver, B.C., a railroad, shipping, and forest-products manufacturing center (431,147); Ottawa, Ont., the capital of Canada and a commercial and industrial city (300,763); Winnipeg, Man., a major wheat market and railroad hub (594,551); Edmonton, Alta., a farming and petroleum center (573,982); Québec City, Qué., a shipping, manufacturing, and tourist center (164,580); Hamilton, Ont., an important shipping and manufacturing center (306,728); Calgary, Alta., a railroad, mining, and farm-trade center (636,104); St. Catharines, Ont., an industrial and commercial city (123,455); Kitchener, Ont., a city of diverse manufacturing industries (150,604); London, Ont., a railroad and industrial center (269,140); and Halifax, N.S., a seaport and manufacturing city (113,577). See the separate article on each city mentioned above.

Religion. The largest religious community in Canada is Roman Catholic. Considerably more than half of the communicants of the Roman Catholic faith live in Québec. Of the Protestant denominations in Canada the largest is the United Church of Canada (q.v.), followed by the Anglican Church of Canada. Other important religious groups are the Presbyterian, Lutheran, Baptist, Greek Orthodox, Jewish, Ukrainian Greek Orthodox, and Pentecostal.

Education. The educational system in Canada is derived from the British and American traditions and the French tradition, particularly in the province of Québec. English or French is the language of instruction, and some schools provide instruction in both official languages. Each of the ten provinces has responsibility for establishing and maintaining its own school system. In Québec the French-Canadian tradition is followed with Roman Catholic schools. The province also maintains Protestant schools, however, which are widely attended. Although Canada does not have a central ministry of education, the federal government provides schools for Indian and Inuit children, inmates of federal penitentiaries, and the children of military personnel in Europe.

The earliest Canadian schools, which were conducted by French Catholic religious orders, date from the early 17th century. Higher education was inaugurated in 1635 with the founding of the Collège des Jésuites in the city of Québec. It was not until the transfer of Canada from French to British jurisdiction in 1763 that an educational system began to emerge that encompassed church, governmental, and private secular schools. The early 19th century saw the establishment of the large universities, beginning with McGill in 1821 and followed by Ottawa in 1848 and Toronto in 1850. Since World War II a notable expansion in higher education has occurred. Many new institutions have been founded, and the older universities have increased in size, scope, and influence. Universities still are the predominant institutions offering higher education, but the number of nonuniversity postsecondary institutions, particularly community colleges, has increased sharply in recent decades.

Elementary and secondary schools. Education is generally compulsory for children from ages 6 to 14 or 16, depending on the province in which they live, and it is free until the completion of secondary school studies. In the mid-1980s Canada had about 15,600 elementary and secondary schools, with a total enrollment of approximately 4.9 million students.

Specialized schools. In the mid-1980s Canada had some 21 specialized schools for the blind and the deaf. These institutions together enrolled about 2900 pupils, who were instructed by some 835

Montréal, Québec, Canada's largest city, is a major commercial and industrial center with an active cultural life. Dick Huffman–Monkmeyer Press

teachers. Canada had several schools for mentally handicapped children.

Nursing education, formerly concentrated at special schools attached to hospitals, has been transferred to community colleges. Similarly, teacher training has been shifted from specialized institutions to colleges and universities.

Universities. In the mid-1980s Canada had 67 degree-granting universities and colleges, which together enrolled some 461,000 full-time students. Among the country's larger universities are the following: the University of Alberta and the University of Calgary, in Alberta; the University of British Columbia and Simon Fraser University, in British Columbia; the University of Manitoba; the University of Moncton and the University of New Brunswick, in New Brunswick; Memorial University of Newfoundland; Acadia University and Dalhousie University, in Nova Scotia; Carleton University, McMaster University, the University of Ottawa, the University of Toronto, the University of Waterloo, and York University, in Ontario; the University of Prince Edward Island; Concordia University, Laval University, McGill University, the University of Montréal, and the University of Québec, in Québec; and the University of Saskatchewan.

CULTURAL LIFE

As Canada developed from a rural pioneer land, primarily absorbed in economic and political concerns, into a more urbanized, sophisticated nation, it has given more attention to cultural pursuits. The federal government especially encourages the arts through the Canada Council, established in 1957, which awards fellowships and grants. It favors decentralizing policies that bring cultural resources within reach of the most isolated communities. Since 1972 it has supported a multicultural policy to reflect the varied influences that make up the mosaic of Canadian life—British and American, which predominate; French, affecting about 30% of the population; and German, Polish, Scandinavian, Italian, Hungarian, and Ukrainian, as a result of late 19th- and 20th-century immigration.

Museums and Libraries. The National Museums of Canada in Ottawa are the most important in the country. An outgrowth of the 1842 Canadian geological survey, they include the National Museum of Natural Sciences and the National Museum of Science and Technology. Another constituent is the National Museum of Man, which deals with Canadian archaeology and history and the culture of peasants, Indians, Inuit, and Métis. The fourth constituent, the National Gallery of Canada, contains European art and a large collection of Canadian art. These museums oversee the National Museum Policy (1972), which encourages regional museums, sends out museumobiles, and maintains a national inventory of collections as well as conservation and assistance programs.

The Royal Ontario Museum in Toronto has collections of art, life and earth sciences, and Canadiana. Among more specialized museums are Upper Canada Village, a restoration of 18th- and 19th-century buildings in Morrisburg, Ont.; the Museum of Ukrainian Culture in Saskatoon, Sask.; and the British Columbia Provincial Museum, in Victoria, which contains important displays of Indian artifacts.

The National Library of Canada, in Ottawa, issues the national bibliography and maintains a union catalog of the collections of more than 300 other libraries. Its holdings in humanities, the social sciences, and Canadiana, including the largest collection of Canadian newspapers, amount to more than 1 million volumes. The Canada Institute for Scientific and Technical Information, also in Ottawa, is the center of a network of scientific and technical information. Provinces and cities have their own libraries. Particularly outstanding university libraries are those of McGill, Toronto, and Montréal.

Theater and Music. The performing arts in Canada are supported by government and private grants. The National Arts Centre, in Ottawa, opened in 1969, has a resident symphony orchestra and theater companies in French and English. Visiting opera and dance companies perform there, and in summer its terraces along the Rideau Canal are the scene of band concerts and arts and crafts fairs.

A number of major theater, opera, dance, and musical groups are found in the large cities; these groups also tour the provinces and travel abroad. The chief theatrical centers are Québec, Montréal, and Toronto. The theaters of these cities make an effort to present new Canadian plays as well as imports and classics. Opera companies include the Canadian Opera, in Toronto, and four in the west—in Vancouver, Calgary, Edmonton, and Winnipeg—that pool their costumes and sets. The principal dance companies are the National Ballet of Canada, the Royal Winnipeg Ballet, and Les Grands Ballets Canadiens (Montréal). The Toronto Dance Theatre presents modern dance. The prominent orchestras are the Montréal Symphony, the Toronto Symphony, and the Vancouver Symphony. Among chamber music and choral groups are Les Jeunes Chanteurs d'Acadie.

Canadians and visitors also enjoy summer festivals, such as the Stratford Festival of classical drama in Ontario; the Shaw Festival at Niagara-on-the-Lake, Ont.; and Festival Canada, a series of cultural events in Ottawa. Local traditions are preserved in the Highland Games on Cape Breton; the Sherbrooke Festival de Cantons (Québec), celebrating French-Canadian culture and cuisine; and the Ukrainian Festival in Dauphin, Man. Discovery Day in Dawson City, Yukon Territory, marks the 1896 discovery of gold.

ECONOMY

Until the early 20th century, Canada was primarily an agricultural nation. Since then it has become one of the most highly industrialized countries in the world. Manufacturing is by far the leading economic activity. To a large extent the manufacturing industries are supplied with raw materials produced by the agricultural, mining, forestry, and fishing sectors of the Canadian economy.

Between 1950 and 1984 Canada's total output, or gross national product, increased from $18.5 billion to $421 billion. In the 1984–85 fiscal year the estimated national budget showed revenues of about $63.3 billion, compared to $2.7 billion in 1949–50. Expenditures in 1984–85 were estimated at about $99.9 billion, leaving a deficit of $36.6 billion. (All monetary values in this section are given in Canadian dollars.)

Agriculture. The Canadian economy depends heavily on agriculture, which employs about 4% of the labor force. Farm cash receipts amounted to $18.7 billion in 1983. Because of its abundant production and relatively small population, Canada is a leading exporter of food products. Field crops account for more than 40% of cash receipts from farming operations. Wheat is the most important single crop, and the Prairie provinces of Alberta, Manitoba, and Saskatchewan form one of the greatest wheat-growing areas of the world, each year producing more than three-quarters of Canadian wheat. These provinces also grow a large percentage of the coarse grains and oilseeds produced in Canada. After wheat, the major cash receipts from field crops are obtained from sales of barley, rapeseed, tobacco, vegetables, potatoes, corn, flaxseed, soybeans, and oats.

Livestock and livestock products account for about 48% of yearly farm cash receipts. Ranching prevails in the W, and the raising of livestock is a general enterprise, except in parts of Alberta and Saskatchewan, where beef cattle form a specialized industry. Ontario and Québec rank highest in production of dairy products, with about 70% of the national output; in poultry farming, with 64%; and in egg production, with 57%. Québec produces 82% of the maple products, and Ontario produces 87% of the nation's tobacco crop.

In 1984 the livestock population of Canada included about 12.3 million cattle and calves, of which some 2.4 million were milk cows; 10.8 million hogs; 791,000 sheep and lambs; and 23.5 million laying hens. Fruit farming is done in Ontario, British Columbia, and Québec, with apples contributing about one-third the total value. Berries, peaches, grapes, and cherries are other important crops. Tomatoes, onions, carrots, turnips, peas, and beans are major vegetable crops; Ontario produces about one-half of the total crop, followed by Québec and British Columbia.

Forestry and Fishing. Forestry is a major source of Canada's wealth, and forest products annually account for about 13% of Canadian exports. Forests cover some 4.4 million sq km (some 1.7 million sq mi), with about 59% suitable for regular harvest. Canada has more than 150 varieties of native trees; about 80% of them are softwoods, such as spruce, Douglas fir, hemlock, cedar, and balsam. The annual timber harvest in the early 1980s was about 156 million cu m (about 5.5 billion cu ft). Forestry sustains a complex and diversified export and domestic industry, employing more than 330,000 persons and supporting about 1290 sawmills and planing mills and 3450 manufacturing plants that use wood. Canada leads the world in newsprint production, with about 32%, and accounts for about two-thirds of world exports; most of the Canadian export is sent to the U.S. The sawmill and planing-mill industry is centered in British Columbia. Québec and Ontario lead the nation in pulp and paper production.

The fishing resources of the country are harvested from the NW Atlantic and NE Pacific oceans and from the most extensive bodies of fresh water in the world. In the early 1980s the number of people employed in primary fishing operations was approximately 87,000. In addition, 37,000 persons worked in plants that processed fish. Most of the yearly output of the fishing industry, which has a market value exceeding $1.7 billion per year, is exported, making Canada one of the world's preeminent fish-processing nations. The catch includes cod, haddock, herring, salmon, flounder, lobster, scallops, squid, halibut, and whitefish.

Furs. A minor Canadian industry is fur farming and trapping. The farming operations consist mainly of raising mink, which contributes more than 95% of the annual value of pelts from fur farms, and small quantities of chinchilla, fox, and nutria. The fur farms are mainly concentrated in Ontario, Nova Scotia, Québec, and British Columbia. In the early 1980s, 1.5 million mink pelts with a total value of nearly $50 million were produced each year on farms. Trapping is carried on

The Corner Brook Paper Mill in Newfoundland. The forestry industry in Canada's eastern provinces is devoted mainly to pulp and paper production.

C. L. Brown–Shostal Associates

Manufacturing provides about 60 percent of the value added by the goods-producing industries in Canada. Among key products is iron, shown here being poured in a foundry.
National Film Board of Canada

primarily in N Canada; Ontario, Québec, Alberta, Saskatchewan, and Manitoba are the main producers of wildlife pelts. In the early 1980s the aggregate yearly output was about 2.9 million wildlife pelts, worth some $41.8 million.

Mining. The mining industry in Canada has a long history of exploration. The most significant period of growth, however, has been since World War II, with mineral discoveries in almost every region of the country. Mining is an important source of national wealth; in 1984 mineral production was valued at about $43.1 billion. The Canadian mining industry is strongly oriented toward exports, and Canada is one of the world's leading mineral exporters. The U.S. is by far the leading purchaser of Canadian minerals.

The growth of the mining industry is due in part to petroleum and natural gas discoveries in W Canada; development of huge iron-ore deposits in Labrador and Québec; the discovery and development of large deposits of nickel in Manitoba, uranium in Ontario and Saskatchewan, and potash in Saskatchewan; extraction of sulfur from natural gas in the W provinces; development of copper, lead, and zinc deposits; and the production of asbestos in Québec, British Columbia, and Newfoundland. The leading minerals of Canada are crude petroleum, natural gas and natural gas by-products, copper, nickel, iron ore, zinc, asbestos, cement, sand and gravel, and coal, which together typically account for more than 80% of the annual value of mineral production. Alberta leads the country by a wide margin in the yearly value of mineral output; it is usually followed by Ontario, British Columbia, Québec, Saskatchewan, and Newfoundland. Canada usually leads the world in the annual production of nickel and zinc and ranks among the top countries in the annual production of asbestos, copper, gold, iron ore, lead, molybdenum, natural gas, platinum-group metals, potash, silver, sulfur, and uranium.

Manufacturing. The Canadian economy is largely dependent on manufacturing, which employs about 20% of the labor force and accounts for about 19% of the yearly national product. Manufacturing has grown remarkably since World War II, with the total value of Canadian shipments increasing by more than 1600%. The leading manufactures, ranked by value of shipments, are refined petroleum, motor vehicles and vehicle parts, processed foods, paper and paper products, refined metals, machinery, sawn and planed timber, industrial chemicals, printed materials, communications equipment, plastics, and animal feeds. The most important manufacturing provinces are Ontario, which now accounts for about one-half the manufacturing production of Canada, and Québec, which accounts for about 26%. The chief manufacturing cities include To-

In the town of St. Philips, a chapel of the Church of England overlooks Conception Bay. The bay, an inlet of the Atlantic Ocean, is on the southeastern coast of Newfoundland Island.

ronto, Montréal, Hamilton, Vancouver, Windsor, Winnipeg, and Kitchener.

Energy. Endowed with many fast-flowing rivers, Canada is the world's second leading producer of hydroelectricity, exceeded only by the U.S. About three-fourths of the country's hydroelectric output is generated in the provinces of Québec, Ontario, Newfoundland, and British Columbia. In the late 1970s the largest facility was at Churchill Falls (q.v.), in the Labrador region of Newfoundland. In 1979 the first of three planned hydroelectric stations on La Grande-Rivière, near James Bay, in Québec, began operations; when completed in 1985, the three installations, called Hydro-Québec, had a capacity of 10.3 million kw, more than any other hydroelectric complex in Canada or in the U.S.

Since the early 1950s, Canada has sought to use its abundant resources of natural uranium to generate electricity. The first nuclear power plant, a demonstration station at Rolphton, Ont., was completed in 1962. A small full-scale nuclear station was opened in 1966 at Douglas Point, on Lake Huron, and it was followed, in the early 1970s, by a huge nuclear plant at Pickering, Ont. In addition, a great complex of nuclear facilities on the Bruce Peninsula, in Ontario, called Hydro-Ontario, was scheduled for completion in 1987.

In the early 1980s Canada had an installed electrical generating capacity of some 89.5 million kw, 57% of which was provided by hydroelectric plants. During that period, the annual output of electricity was about 395.9 billion kwh.

Tourism. The natural variety of seasons and scenic wonders of Canada draw large numbers of tourists. In the spring, blossom festivals flourish across Canada, especially in the Annapolis Valley of Nova Scotia and the Okanagan Valley in British Columbia. Noteworthy is the Ottawa Festival of Spring (Tulip Festival) in May. Alberta's Calgary Exhibition and Stampede in July is world famous. The Niagara Grape and Wine Festival and autumn-color tours in central Ontario and the Laurentian Mts. of Québec are among the other attractions. In the winter the abundant snowfall has been exploited; skiing centers are expanding. About 375,000 sq km (about 144,790 sq mi) of scenic areas have been preserved in the natural state for use as national and provincial parks.

Tourism has become one of the leading industries of Canada. In the early 1980s the country was visited each year by some 34.3 million tourists, of whom about 94% came from the U.S. Expenditures were about $3.8 billion a year, with U.S. residents spending some 70% of the total.

Currency and Banking. The unit of currency is the Canadian dollar, which consists of 100 cents (1 Canadian dollar equals U.S. $0.75; 1987). The Bank of Canada has the sole right to issue paper money for circulation. The commercial banking system of Canada consists of 13 Canadian-owned banks, which have been chartered by Parliament and which operate under the provisions of the Bank Act. Of the six leading Canadian-owned banks, five are nationwide, with branches in all ten provinces and the two territories; the other maintains branches in nine provinces only. Commercial banks operated more than 7000 domestic branches in the early 1980s. A total of 58 foreign-owned banks have branches in Canada. Among these are 15 U.S. banks, six British banks, and five Japanese banks. Foreign-owned banks usually have their head offices in Toronto. The country also has many credit unions and several large savings banks.

Foreign Trade. From the 16th to the 18th century the leading Canadian items of export were fish and furs. During the 19th century exploitation of the white-pine forests of the Laurentian region was initiated, and timber became the staple item of export. With the improvement of railroad communications early in the 20th century, the W prairie regions were opened, and wheat became the chief item of export. The mining industry began to grow at about the same time; valuable mineral deposits were discovered in the Laurentian region (previously mining had been confined largely to iron and coal in Nova Scotia, and gold, silver, and copper in British Columbia), and exploitation of the spruce timber of N Ontario and Québec began. Manufacturing industries developed to supply and process the goods of the three primary industries, agriculture, forestry, and mining. Aiding economic expansion in the Canadian North was the advance of hydroelectric and thermoelectric technology.

The per capita foreign trade of Canada ranks among the highest of any nation in the world. The growth since World War II of Canada's external trade has been remarkable. The value of exports in 1946 was $2.34 billion; this figure increased to $3.16 billion in 1950, to $5.39 billion in 1960, to $16.82 billion in 1970, and to $64.3 billion in 1980. By 1984 the export total was $112.5 billion. Imports showed a comparable increase, from $1.93 billion in 1946 to $3.17 billion in 1950, to $5.50 billion in 1960, to $13.95 billion in 1970, and to $58.5 billion in 1980. The import total rose to $95.8 billion in 1984.

Most of Canada's foreign trade is with the U.S., which typically takes about 76% of Canada's exports and supplies about 72% of its imports. A

Seal Cove, on Grand Manan Island, a popular resort area in southwest New Brunswick, one of the Maritime provinces. Burdick, Leo DeWys Inc.

large proportion of this trade is made up of motor vehicles and motor-vehicle parts. Japan and Great Britain usually are Canada's next leading trade partners. Other countries with which Canada has significant trade include the USSR, China (a major purchaser of wheat), West Germany, Venezuela, the Netherlands, Belgium and Luxembourg, Italy, France, Venezuela, Australia, India, South Korea, Taiwan, Mexico, and Brazil.

The leading commodities Canada sells abroad include motor vehicles and motor-vehicle parts, minerals and mineral products (especially crude and refined petroleum, natural gas, copper ore and copper, nickel, aluminum, and iron ore), grain (principally wheat and barley), and forest products (notably wood pulp, newsprint, and lumber). Among Canada's main imports are motor vehicles and motor-vehicle parts, heavy machinery, crude petroleum, consumer goods, and chemicals.

Transportation. The natural water and mountain barriers of Canada, combined with a dispersed population, necessitate efficient and economical transportation facilities. Since the earliest explorations of the country, water transportation has been indispensable. The St. Lawrence-Great Lakes navigation system extends some 3670 km (some 2280 mi) from the Gulf of St. Lawrence into the center of the continent. The opening of the St. Lawrence Seaway in 1959 contributed greatly to industrial expansion. In the early 1980s some 5200 transits were made per year; cargo carried totaled more than 49 million metric tons. Some 24,790 vessels engaged in foreign trade entered and cleared Canadian ports annually; cargo unloaded totaled some 48.7 million metric tons, and about 125.3 million metric tons were loaded. Vancouver, Sept-Îles, Port-Cartier, Montréal, Halifax, Québec, Saint John (New Brunswick), Baie-Comeau, Sorel, Thunder Bay, and Hamilton together handled most of the total. Vessels of Canadian registry numbered about 35,600, with a gross tonnage of about 5.4 million.

The government-owned Canadian National Railways is the largest public utility in Canada and operates about 36,420 km (about 22,630 mi) of the approximately 66,385 km (approximately 41,250 mi) of first main track in the country. The system serves all ten provinces and the Northwest Territories. The privately owned Canadian Pacific Limited railroad (CP Rail) serves all of Canada except Newfoundland, Prince Edward Island, and the two territories; it operates about 24,650 km (about 15,315 mi) of track. Regional railroads include the following: the British Columbia Railway, Northern Alberta Railways, the Ontario Northland Railway, the Algoma Central Railway (in Ontario), and the Québec North Shore and Labrador Railway (a carrier of iron ore and concentrate).

The Château Frontenac, a landmark hotel of Québec City, was opened in 1893.
Canadian Pacific photo from Québec National Tourist Office

The total length of the federal, provincial, and territorial road system in Canada in the early 1980s was about 283,800 km (about 176,345 mi); there is also an extensive local road system. The Trans-Canada Highway, completed in 1962, stretches from St. John's, Newf., to Vancouver, B.C. In the early 1980s about 9.7 million passenger cars, 2.7 million commercial vehicles, and 398,000 motorcycles and mopeds were in use.

Two major airlines, Air Canada and Canadian Pacific Air Lines Limited (CP Air), maintain a broad network of domestic and international routes. Other smaller carriers are licensed.

Communications. The publicly owned Canadian Broadcasting Corporation (CBC) operated 60 originating radio stations, including AM, FM, and shortwave, and 29 originating television stations in the early 1980s. More than 460 private radio stations and over 80 private television stations were operating.

In the mid-1980s Canada had more than 100 telephone systems, the largest being Bell Canada (serving Ontario, Québec, and the Northwest Territories) and the British Columbia Telephone Co. The country had a total of more than 16 million telephones. Teleglobe Canada provided international telephone service.

Telesat Canada was established in 1969 by the federal government and private firms to provide commercial communications via satellite. In 1972 it launched the world's first stationary communications satellite designed for domestic commercial use. Called Anik I, after an Inuit word for "brother," the satellite helps provide television broadcasting and telephone service to remote N Canada. Backup satellites were put into orbit in the mid-1970s.

In the early 1980s Canada had 120 daily newspapers, with an aggregate daily circulation of over 5.5 million copies. Widely read dailies included the *Calgary Herald;* the *Journal,* published in Edmonton; the *Province,* published in Vancouver; the *Vancouver Sun;* the *Winnipeg Free Press;* the *Globe and Mail,* published in Toronto; the *Toronto Star;* the *Toronto Sun;* and the *Gazette, La Presse,* and *Le Journal de Montréal,* all published in Montréal. The country also was served by many other publications, including *Maclean's,* a weekly news magazine; *Chatelaine,* a women's journal published in English and French; *Canadian Geographic;* and *Financial Post.*

The government-run Canadian Postal Service provides mail delivery throughout the country. It operated some 8400 post offices in the late 1970s.

Labor. The civilian labor force in Canada during the mid-1980s was made up of approximately 12.6 million persons. Employment was concentrated in commercial, business, and personal services (3 million), in manufacturing (1.8 million), and in trade (1.6 million). Approximately 512,000 persons worked in agriculture.

Union membership in the early 1980s totaled some 3.1 million persons, or about 35% of all nonagricultural workers. About 61% of the union members belonged to organizations affiliated with the Canadian Labour Congress (CLC); most of these unions were also linked with the American Federation of Labor and Congress of Industrial Organizations. Smaller union groupings included the Québec-based Confederation of National Trade Unions (CNTU), the Centrale des Syndicats Démocratiques, and the Confederation of National Trade Unions.

GOVERNMENT

Canada is mainly governed according to principles embodied in the Constitution Act, 1982, which came into effect in 1982 when the country gained full control of its constitution. Previously, the British North America Act (q.v.) of 1867 and subsequent laws enacted in Great Britain formed the basis for Canadian government. Canada is a federal union, with a division of powers between the central and provincial governments. Under the original 1867 act, the central government had considerable power over the provinces, but, through amendments to the act and changes brought by practical experience, the provincial governments increased the scope of their authority. In the 1970s and early '80s considerable tension existed between the federal government and the provincial governments over the proper allocation of power in the country.

The head of state of Canada is the sovereign of Great Britain. In theory the head of the national government is the governor-general, who represents the British monarch; the actual head of government, however, is the prime minister, who is responsible to Parliament.

Central Government. The central government of Canada exercises all powers not specifically assigned to the provinces; it has exclusive jurisdiction over administration of the public debt, currency and coinage, taxation for general purposes, organization of national defense, fiscal matters, banking, fisheries, commerce, navigation and shipping, postal service, census, statistics, patents, copyright, naturalization, aliens, Indian affairs, marriage, and divorce. Among the powers assigned to the provincial governments are education, hospitals, provincial property and civil rights, taxation for local purposes, the regulation of local commerce, and the borrowing of money. With respect to certain matters, such as immigration, the federal and provincial governments possess concurrent jurisdiction.

The nominal head of the government is the governor-general, the representative of the British crown, who is appointed by the reigning monarch on the recommendation of the prime minister of Canada. The governor-general adheres to the advice of the majority in the House of Commons (the lower chamber of the legislature) in appointing the prime minister, who is the effective head of government, and follows the prime minister's wishes in appointing the cabinet. The cabinet consists of some 30 members, most of whom are ministers presiding over departments of the federal government. The cabinet has no formal legal power, but submits its decisions to the governor-general, who is constitutionally bound to approve them in almost all circumstances.

Health and Welfare. All levels of government share the responsibility for social welfare in Canada. The federal government administers comprehensive income-maintenance measures, such as the Canada Pension Plan, Canada Assistance Plan, old-age security pensions, family allowances, youth allowances, and unemployment insurance, in which nationwide coordination is necessary. The federal government also gives aid to the provinces in meeting the costs of public assistance; it also provides services for special groups, such as Indians, Inuit, veterans, and immigrants. Administration of welfare services is mainly the responsibility of the provinces, but local authorities, generally with financial aid from the province, often assume the provision of services. Provincial governments have the major responsibility for health services in Canada, with the municipality also assuming authority over matters delegated to it by provincial legislation. The department of health and welfare is the chief federal agency in health matters.

The Medical Care Act, passed in 1966, has permitted the federal government to contribute about half the cost of the Medical Care Insurance Program (Medicare), with the respective province contributing the remainder. The program establishes the following minimum criteria: (1) comprehensive coverage, to cover all medically required services rendered by physicians and surgeons; (2) universal availability to all residents; (3) portability, to cover temporary or permanent change in residence to another province; and (4) nonprofit basis.

Legislature. The Canadian Parliament consists of two houses, a Senate composed of 104 members appointed by the governor-general on the advice of the prime minister, and a House of Commons composed of 295 members apportioned according to provincial population. Senators serve until the age of 75, and members of the House are elected for five years (or until the House is dissolved) by popular vote. Women have the franchise and are eligible for election to the House of Commons or appointment to the Senate. Elections are held at the discretion of the prime minister. Laws must be passed by both houses and signed by the governor-general.

Political Parties. The strongest national political parties in Canada in the late 1980s were the Liberal Party of Canada and the Progressive Conservative party (PC). They agreed on most issues, and at times intraparty divisions were more acute than differences between the parties. The Liberals, however, tended to place greater emphasis on government intervention to promote the general welfare. The PC favored individualism, free enterprise, and free trade. A relatively small party represented in the House of Commons during the 1980s was the New Democratic party, a social democratic grouping associated with the labor movement.

Several regional parties also were in existence. Notable among them was the Parti Québecois, limited to Québec, which strongly advocated a form of separatism for the province. It controlled the provincial legislature from 1976 to 1985.

Local Government. The government of each of Canada's ten provinces is in theory headed by a lieutenant governor, who represents the sovereign of Great Britain and is appointed by the governor-general on the advice of the federal prime minister. Like the governor-general, however, the lieutenant governor has little actual power, and in practice the chief executive of each province is the premier (known in Québec as the prime minister), who is responsible to a unicameral provincial legislature. Yukon Territory and the Northwest Territories are both governed by federally appointed commissioners, who are assisted by elected territorial councils.

Judiciary. The legal system in Canada is derived from English common law, except in Québec, where the provincial system of civil law is based on the French Code Napoléon (q.v.). The federal judiciary is headed by the Supreme Court of Canada, made up of a chief justice and eight puisne (associate) judges. It sits in Ottawa and is the final Canadian appellate court for all civil, criminal, and constitutional cases. The next leading tribunal, the Federal Court of Canada, is divided into a Trial Division and an Appeal Division. It hears a variety of cases, notably involving claims against the federal government. Provincial courts are established by the provincial legislatures, and, although the names of the courts are not uniform, each province has a similar three-tiered court system. Judges of the Supreme Court and the Federal Court and almost all judges of the higher provincial courts are appointed by the federal government.

Defense. The Canadian armed forces are integrated and are headed by the chief of the defense staff, who reports to the civilian minister of national defense. Under the defense staff are five separate commands, organized according to function: the mobile command, the air command, the maritime command, the communications command, and the training command. Canada is a member of the North Atlantic Treaty Organization (NATO), and Canadian Forces Europe comprises the air and land forces allocated to support NATO in Europe. Canada also participates jointly with the U.S. in the North American Defense Command (NORAD; *see* DEFENSE SYSTEMS). It also contributes troops to UN peacekeeping operations. In the early 1980s the Canadian armed forces included about 78,650 persons.

HISTORY

The history of Canada was shaped by the encounter of its people with the rigors and riches of a vast new land. It was also marked by the achievements and conflicts of its diverse inhabitants—indigenous tribes and French, English, and other European immigrants. A pervasive influence was Canada's southern neighbor, the U.S.

A MEETING OF PEOPLES

The New World received waves of immigrants from West and East over many millennia.

Indians and Inuit. In a series of migrations at the end of the last ice age, Mongoloid peoples from Asia entered North America, probably crossing the Bering Strait. Gradually they spread over the continent and into South America. By AD 1600 perhaps 250,000 of their Indian and Inuit (Eskimo) descendants inhabited what is now Canada. Developing a stone age economy, they hunted, fished, and gathered food and in warmer areas also farmed. The basic social unit was the band, which varied from a few families to several hundred people. In more sophisticated Indian cultures, bands were organized into tribes.

The largest linguistic group was the Algonquian, which included migratory hunting tribes such as the Cree and Naskapi in the eastern subarctic region and the Abnaki and Micmac in the eastern woodlands on the coast. By the 18th century, Algonquians had spread west, where the Ottawa, Ojibwa, Blackfoot, Plains Cree, and others roamed the prairies and plains in search of buffalo. More advanced were the Iroquoian-speaking tribes—the Huron and especially the Iroquois—who lived in permanent farm settlements and had a highly developed tribal organization in the St. Lawrence Valley and around Lakes Ontario and Erie.

Weakly organized tribes of Salishan, Athabascan, and other linguistic groups occupied semipermanent fishing villages along the rivers of interior British Columbia. On the Pacific coast, Salishan tribes, such as the Bellacoola, and related Wakashan-speaking tribes—the Kwakiutl and Nootka—developed a rich culture based on salmon fishing and expressed in elaborate potlatch ceremonies and carved wood totem poles. In the western subarctic, the Athabascan group—Carrier, Dogrib, and others—led a primitive hunting existence similar to that of the Algonquians. Small, isolated Inuit bands developed a unique culture based on hunting seals and caribou, which enabled them to survive the harsh environment of the Arctic.

European Intruders. The first Europeans to reach North America were probably the Icelandic colonizers of Greenland. According to Icelandic sagas, Leif Ericson reached Vinland—somewhere along the North Atlantic coast—about AD 1000. Archaeological evidence suggests that Nordic people later established short-lived settlements in Labrador and Newfoundland. Claims that they penetrated deep into the mainland have not been substantiated.

A second wave of European exploration, between 1480 and 1540, firmly established the existence of the new land in European minds. Many of the explorers, under government auspices, were in search of a northwest passage by sea from Europe to the riches of Asia and thus regarded the Canadian landmass as an obstacle as well as a potentially useful discovery. The voyage to Newfoundland in 1497 of John Cabot, a Venetian in English service, inspired a series of further explorations and laid the basis for English claims to Canada.

In the 1530s and '40s the French explorer Jacques Cartier sailed up the St. Lawrence River, claiming the land for France. His failure to find a northwest passage—or gold, as the Spanish had found in Peru—discouraged further exploration. France was also too preoccupied with domestic religious wars to make any substantial commitment. The discovery of Canada was important, however, to English, French, Spanish, and Portuguese fishing fleets, all of which regularly fished the Grand Banks off the coast of Newfoundland.

English and French interest in Canada revived in the late 16th century, largely for commercial reasons. The English explorers Martin Frobisher in the 1570s and Henry Hudson (in Dutch service) in 1610–11 continued the fruitless search for a passage to Asia. English fishing interests in the 1630s secured a virtual prohibition on efforts to colonize Newfoundland.

Earliest French Settlements. The French were more successful. Fishermen had noticed the abundance of beaver, whose pelts merchants were eager to market in Europe. The French government, motivated by visions of building an empire in the New World, decided to work through commercial monopolies, which in return for control of the fur trade would foster colonization. A monopoly granted to the sieur de Monts in 1603 established trade settlements in Acadia (later Nova Scotia) and at Québec City on the St. Lawrence. The settlement of Québec (1609) owed much to Samuel de Champlain, an explorer hired by de Monts, who became the foremost champion of French colonization. Eventually Champlain convinced Cardinal Richelieu, chief adviser to Louis XIII, of the importance of North America to his mercantilist system of state-aided economic development. In 1627 Richelieu organized a joint-stock company, the Company of One Hundred Associates, to found a powerful center of French civilization in the New World.

This European intrusion over the next 300 years completely disrupted the native Indian cultures, which, although stable, lacked the numbers, technology, and organization to withstand it. The introduction of liquor and of smallpox and other European diseases decimated many tribes. Missionaries undermined old systems of belief, as, for example, Roman Catholics among the Huron and Protestants among Pacific coast Indians. Perhaps most destructive, the Europeans' demand for land deprived the natives of their freedom of movement, eventually eliminating some tribes. As their indigenous way of life was slowly but steadily destroyed, the Indians, ill adapted to European ways, became a subjugated minority, remaining so until the 20th century.

NEW FRANCE (1627-1763)

As a French possession, New France reflected the interests of the parent country.

A Proprietary Colony. Under the proprietorship of Richelieu's company, and later its colonial agent, the Community of Habitants (1645-63), the new French colony took shape along the St. Lawrence. In the French feudal tradition, large fiefs of land were granted to seigneurs, men who promised to parcel it out among habitants, or tenant farmers. Frenchmen were induced to emigrate, resulting in a population of about 2000 by 1663. Hardy, adaptable, and tenacious, many entered the lucrative fur trade, which was brought under central control. New trade settlements were founded, notably at Trois-Rivières (1634) and Montréal (1642). Further explorations of the interior were carried out by *coureurs de bois,* adventurous, unlicensed fur traders who wanted to escape company restrictions. One of them, Pierre Esprit Radisson, explored west of Lake Superior in the 1650s.

Of more lasting significance was the role of the Roman Catholic church. French Protestants, defeated in France, were prohibited from settling in the new colony. Roman Catholic religious orders were charged with maintaining and spreading the faith. Franciscan Récollet friars arrived in 1614 to convert the Indians, but were replaced in 1625 by the heroic priests of the richer, better-organized Society of Jesus. Later came Ursuline nuns (1639), who educated girls, and Sulpicians (1657), who ran missions. In 1659 a vicar apostolic, the Jesuit-trained Bishop F. X. de Laval-Montmorency (1623-1708), arrived to take command of the missions and to found parishes. The church increasingly became a powerful, rigidly moralistic force in colonial life.

The survival of New France was uncertain, however, because of almost continuous warfare with the Iroquoian Confederacy. In 1608 Champlain had allied himself with the Algonquians and with the Hurons, who were amenable to missionary activities and acted as the principal suppliers of furs. This alliance, however, antagonized the Iroquoian Confederacy, traditional rivals of the Huron and suppliers of furs to the Dutch in New Amsterdam. After the Iroquois had brutally ravaged Huron country north of the St. Lawrence in 1648 and 1649, they turned against New France itself. The fur trade was no longer profitable, and the threat to the colony was now so great that the French considered abandoning it.

A Crown Colony. In 1663, Louis XIV's brilliant minister J. B. Colbert reorganized New France directly under royal authority. Administration was divided between a military governor and a more powerful intendant, both ruling from Québec City but under orders from Paris. The fur trade was granted to a new monopoly, the Company of the West Indies. Defense was improved by the arrival in 1665 of the French Carignan-Salières regiment, many of whose members stayed on as settlers. The Iroquois menace was ended, although Indian attacks continued sporadically throughout the 17th century. Restructuring the seigneurial system, the Crown deprived uncooperative landowners of their fiefs, granted new blocs of land to promising candidates, and laid down rules to govern seigneurs and habitants. The church received land and special payments. The comte de Frontenac, as governor, encouraged further explorations. Those of Louis Jolliet and Father Jacques Marquette led to the discovery of the Mississippi River (1673) and those of Robert Cavelier, sieur de La Salle, to the acquisition of Louisiana (1682).

Jean Talon (c. 1625-94), intendant from 1665 to 1672, set out to establish New France as a prosperous, expanding colony rivaling the thriving English colonies to the south. He invited many new settlers, including young women, until by 1675 the population was almost 8000. He also tried to diversify the economy beyond furs and build trade with Acadia and the West Indies. Talon was recalled before he could carry out his policies, however. After Colbert's death in 1683, French interest in the colony waned, and by 1700 it was clear that New France was not going to be self-sufficient.

Under the governor, the intendant, and the bishop, officials, military officers, and seigneurs constituted a little colonial nobility, overconscious of their rank. Leading merchants, also pursuing status, were influential in the towns. The clergy, almost a separate class altogether, controlled the morals, education, and social welfare of the colonists.

The theoretical authoritarianism of this regime

The Acadians, French inhabitants, were deported from Nova Scotia by the British in 1755 during the French and Indian War. Some were later returned, but many found refuge in Louisiana. New York Public Library

was in fact limited by the vigorous spirit of independence among the people. The artisans were organized into strong guilds, each the focus of its own rituals and ways. They and the rural habitants successfully resisted the colonial government when it infringed on what they considered their traditional rights. Besides, if a man felt restricted, he could always escape into the wilderness to engage in the fur trade.

Anglo-French Rivalry. As the colony developed, it was caught up in the imperial rivalries of England and France, which, in the late 17th and early 18th centuries, were locked in a struggle for worldwide hegemony. Europe was one battlefield, North America another. The burgeoning English colonies along the Atlantic Ocean were hemmed in by Acadia and New France in the north and by French expansion in the Mississippi Valley. At the same time, the French felt themselves caught between the Hudson's Bay Company (q.v.; chartered in England in 1670), which dominated northern Canada, and the English colonies to the south. The inevitable conflict broke out in 1689 as King William's War (the American counterpart of the War of the Grand Alliance in Europe). After almost a decade of guerrilla warfare, the Peace of Ryswick (1697) merely confirmed the status quo, even returning Acadia, captured by the English, to the French.

This short-lived truce collapsed in 1702 with the outbreak of Queen Anne's War (paralleling the European War of the Spanish Succession). In the course of the war, the English recaptured Acadia (1710), this time permanently. By the Treaty of Utrecht (1713), the French ceded Newfoundland and the Hudson Bay region as well. They retained Cape Breton and the Île Saint-Jean (Prince Edward Island).

To compensate for their loss, the French in 1720 built a fortress at Louisbourg on the southeast tip of Cape Breton. This expensive endeavor was in vain, however. When hostilities recommenced in King George's War (the American counterpart of the War of the Austrian Succession), the fortress fell to a joint British-New England force. Louisbourg was returned to France by the Peace of Aix-la-Chapelle (1748).

The succeeding French and Indian War (counterpart of the Seven Years' War) was disastrous for France. France had attempted to strengthen its position in North America by refurbishing Louisbourg, building forts in the Ohio Valley, and arranging new Indian alliances. New France, however, with a population of roughly 60,000 and an indifferent, war-weary parent country, was weak. It could not uphold French imperial-

The victorious British general James Wolfe died shortly after the Battle of the Plains of Abraham (1759), in which British forces gained control of Québec from the French.
National Gallery of Canada, Ottawa–Gift of the Duke of Westminster, 1918

ism against a British population of more than 1 million in the 13 American colonies, backed by the military and naval capacity of an expanding Britain. Anglo-French competition in the Ohio Valley sparked conflict in 1754. The next year the British, presuming that their Acadian subjects were disloyal and urged by New Englanders fearing northern invasion, deported the Acadians. In 1758 a British expedition reconquered Louisbourg. A British army under the impulsive young James Wolfe won the crucial battle of the Plains of Abraham against the French, led by the experienced Marquis L. J. de Montcalm, and so gained Québec. British land forces won control of the west, and the arrival of a British fleet led to the surrender of Montréal in 1760. The result, confirmed by the Treaty of Paris (1763), was that New France came under British rule.

BRITISH NORTH AMERICA (1763–1867)

Under British rule, the population rapidly increased, and ethnic tensions developed.

The Shaping of a British Colony. British North America was formed more by historical chance than by design. In 1763 it consisted of four distinct regions. Three, long disputed with France, had been won in 1713. Newfoundland was considered merely a series of fishing stations even after settlement, until it became self-governing in the 19th century. The Hudson Bay region (Rupert's Land and the adjoining North-Western Territory) was a wilderness where the Hudson's Bay Co. and small, aggressive Scottish companies competed for the fur trade. Acadia, conquered to protect New England and renamed Nova Scotia, was populated largely with New Englanders to replace the exiled French. Its capital, Halifax, was founded in 1749. Annexed to Nova Scotia was Prince Edward Island, which became a separate colony in 1769.

The conquest of the fourth region, New France, or Québec, placed the British, as rulers of French colonists, in something of a quandary. Eventually, two successive governors, James Murray (1721–94) and Sir Guy Carleton, finding that they could not govern effectively without the cooperation of the seigneurs, persuaded the Crown to guarantee the traditional language, civil law, and faith of its new subjects. This decision, embodied in the Québec Act of 1774, ensured the loyalty of the seigneurs and the clergy to the new regime. Indeed, they stood by the government during the American Revolution, although the habitants generally remained neutral. American troops captured Montréal in 1775 but, failing to take Québec City or elicit local support, soon withdrew.

The success of the rebellious 13 American colonies left the British with the poorest remnants of their New World empire and the determination to prevent a second revolution. They had, however, to accommodate the roughly 50,000 refugees from the American Revolution who settled in Nova Scotia and the upper St. Lawrence. There these United Empire Loyalists soon began to agitate for the political and property rights they had previously enjoyed. In response to Loyalist demands, the Crown created New Brunswick out of Nova Scotia in 1784 and by the Constitutional Act of 1791 divided Québec into Lower Canada (mostly French) and Upper Canada (mostly English from America).

In so doing, the Crown hoped to create a stable society that was distinctly non-American. Although French-Canadians retained the privileges granted by the Québec Act, the Anglican church received preferred status. An Anglo-French colonial aristocracy of rich merchants, leading officials, and landholders was expected to work with the royal governors to ensure proper order. Legislative assemblies, although elected by propertied voters, had little power. The threat of revolution, it appeared, had been banished.

This system worked surprisingly well, at least for a generation. Despite the arrival of large numbers of land-hungry Americans, the aristocracy managed to dominate the society. Minor trouble arose after 1806 when a governor attempted to anglicize Lower Canada, but he was able to quell dissent if not to achieve his goal. In the War of 1812, most Canadians, convinced that Americans were the aggressors, rallied to the British flag. Indeed, the militia aided the British army in the defense of Upper and Lower Canada. After the war, large-scale emigration of English, Scots, and Irish from Europe swelled the ranks of the English-speaking population.

Agitation for Reform. The older order came under attack during the 1820s and collapsed before the forces of reform in the succeeding two decades. The underlying cause was the emergence in all the colonies of a self-conscious bourgeoisie composed of businesspeople (especially in the newly thriving timber and shipbuilding industries), lawyers and other professionals, and rich farmers. All resented the power and arrogance of the English-speaking, largely Anglican ruling class. Some, notably egalitarian American immigrants, objected on political and economic grounds. Others, such as Methodists and Baptists in Upper Canada, French-Canadians in Lower Canada, and Irish Roman Catholics in Newfoundland, were opposed on the basis of religious and ethnic differences. The parallel development of political parties—proestablishment Tories and antiestablishment reform groups—and an energetic press enabled the champions of reform to reach more and more people.

Some reformers were moderate, especially in the Maritime colonies—New Brunswick, Nova Scotia, and Prince Edward Island—which had Loyalist populations. Others were radical. In Lower Canada, although the Roman Catholic church supported moderates, the seigneur Louis Joseph Papineau led radicals in a nationalist agitation for ethnic autonomy. In Upper Canada, William Lyon Mackenzie, a Scot, led a demand for a more Americanized, that is, republican, form of government. The radicals, frustrated by the opposition of Canadian Tories and the indifference of Britain, led rebellions in Upper and Lower Canada in 1837–38. The uprisings were swiftly quelled by the army and local militia. Suppression was particularly severe in Lower, or French, Canada.

Stirred by these events, the Crown appointed a liberal English aristocrat, John George Lambton, 1st earl of Durham, the first governor-general of all British North America, and ordered him to find a solution to colonial ills. Believing that the colonies must make economic progress in the pattern of the U.S., he recommended in the important Durham Report (1839) the reunification of Upper and Lower Canada, the anglicization of the French-Canadians, and the creation of an executive responsible to the elected legislature. The next year the British Parliament passed the Act of Union, which joined the two Canadas into the Province of Canada and gave each equal representation in the joint legislature. Responsible government was secured in 1849 after much agitation by moderate reformers. The French-Canadians held enough political power to retain their language and institutions, however.

Progress and Tension. During the 1840s and early 1850s colonial life underwent a general liberalization. Municipal corporations were organized, government-aided common schools were founded, prisons were reformed, and Anglican church privileges and seigneurial tenure were abolished. Politics, once the domain of the elite, became the game of party politicians. Most important, the business community became dominant among conflicting interest groups. Its strength was reflected in the politics of the 1850s and '60s, which often centered on economic is-

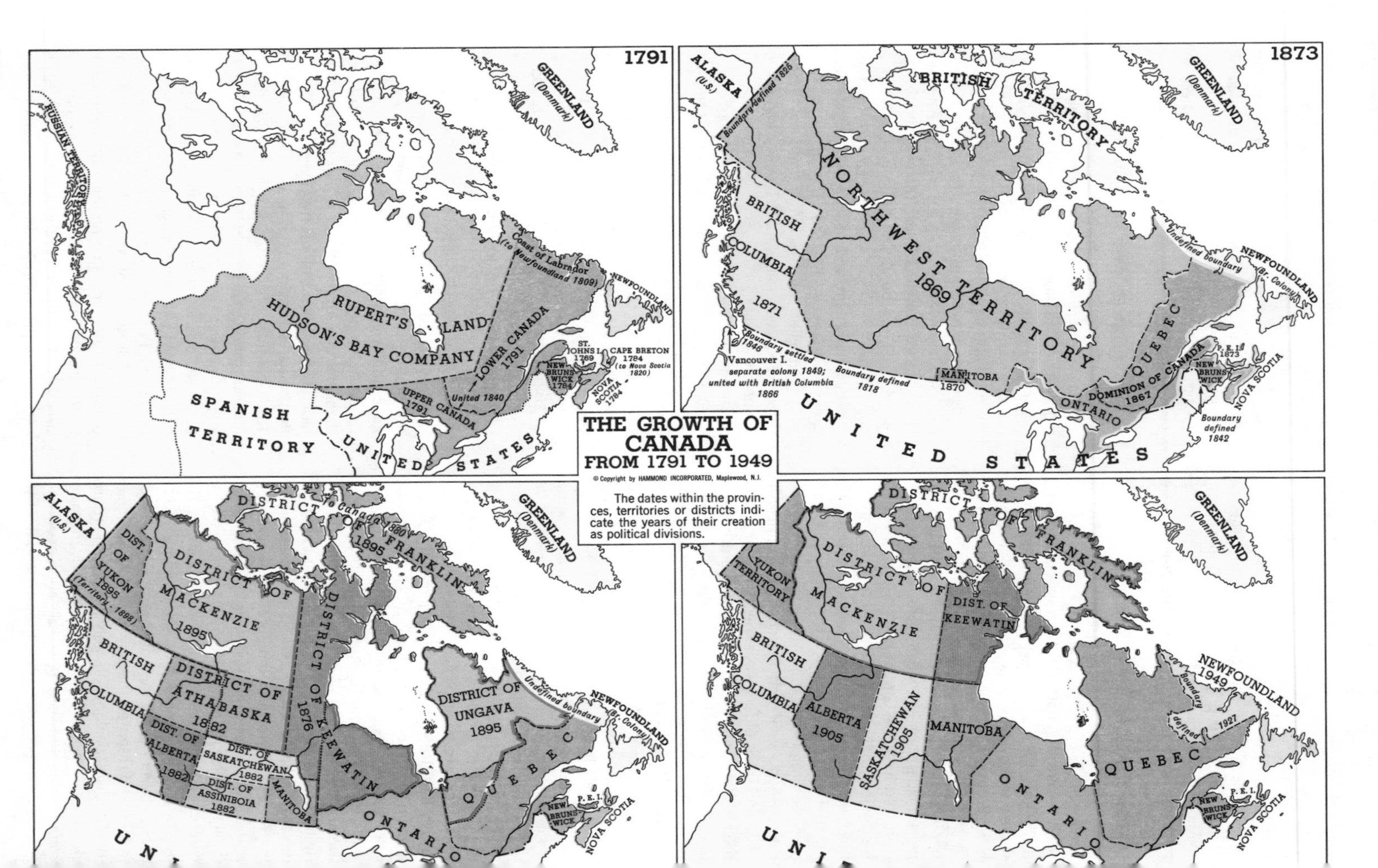
THE GROWTH OF CANADA FROM 1791 TO 1949
© Copyright by HAMMOND INCORPORATED, Maplewood, N.J.
The dates within the provinces, territories or districts indicate the years of their creation as political divisions.
1791
GREENLAND (Denmark)
RUSSIAN TERRITORY
RUPERT'S LAND
HUDSON'S BAY COMPANY
Coast of Labrador (to Newfoundland 1809)
NEWFOUNDLAND
LOWER CANADA 1791
United 1840
UPPER CANADA 1791
ST. JOHNS I. 1769
CAPE BRETON 1784 (to Nova Scotia 1820)
NEW BRUNSWICK 1784
NOVA SCOTIA 1784
SPANISH TERRITORY
UNITED STATES
1873
ALASKA (U.S.)
Boundary defined 1825
BRITISH TERRITORY
GREENLAND (Denmark)
NORTHWEST TERRITORY 1869
BRITISH COLUMBIA 1871
Undefined boundary
NEWFOUNDLAND (Br. Colony)
QUEBEC
DOMINION OF CANADA 1867
ONTARIO
P. E. I. 1873
NEW BRUNSWICK
NOVA SCOTIA
Boundary defined 1842
Boundary settled 1846
Vancouver I. separate colony 1849; united with British Columbia 1866
Boundary defined 1818
MANITOBA 1870
UNITED STATES
ALASKA (U.S.)
DIST. OF YUKON 1895 (Territory - 1898)
DISTRICT OF MACKENZIE 1895
DISTRICT OF FRANKLIN 1895
to Canada 1880
GREENLAND (Denmark)
BRITISH COLUMBIA
DISTRICT OF ATHABASKA 1882
DISTRICT OF KEEWATIN 1876
DISTRICT OF UNGAVA 1895
Undefined boundary
NEWFOUNDLAND (Br. Colony)
DIST. OF ALBERTA 1882
DIST. OF SASKATCHEWAN 1882
DIST. OF ASSINIBOIA 1882
MANITOBA
ONTARIO
QUEBEC
NEW BRUNSWICK
P. E. I.
NOVA SCOTIA
DISTRICT OF FRANKLIN
GREENLAND (Denmark)
YUKON TERRITORY
DISTRICT OF MACKENZIE
DIST. OF KEEWATIN
BRITISH COLUMBIA
ALBERTA 1905
SASKATCHEWAN 1905
MANITOBA
ONTARIO
QUEBEC
NEWFOUNDLAND 1949
Boundary defined 1927
NEW BRUNSWICK
P. E. I.
NOVA SCOTIA

sues such as the immigration of cheap labor, the building of railways, and commercial and industrial development. The last was much enlarged by the Reciprocity Treaty (1854-66) with the U.S.

Despite this progress, ethnic tensions reemerged, especially in the two Canadas. Deep misunderstanding continued to separate urban, profit-minded British businesspeople from largely rural French farmers and professionals concerned with maintaining tradition. The Protestant British in Upper Canada particularly disliked what they considered undue Roman Catholic French influence in local affairs. The French in Lower Canada resented English efforts to dominate and anglicize the colony. In addition, a host of Irish Roman Catholics, fleeing famine in Ireland in the late 1840s, inspired much bigotry among Protestants. No coalition of parties was able to overcome these differences to win a stable majority, and by the mid-1860s the two Canadas were almost ungovernable. Furthermore, the American Civil War seemed to threaten the survival of British North America. Colonists feared that a victorious North, angered by Britain's sympathy for the South, would retaliate by invading the British colonies.

Confederation. Out of these concerns came a movement for the unification of the colonies of British North America. The initiators were three political leaders—George Étienne Cartier and John A. Macdonald of the Conservative party, successor to the Tories, and George Brown of the Liberal party, successor to the reformers—who formed a coalition government in 1864. A preliminary conference on unification was held at Charlottetown, Prince Edward Island, in September of that year; a second conference, which met in Québec City in October, actually designed the Confederation. Many Maritimers objected, but Great Britain, hoping to strengthen its territory against U.S. influences, gave its support. The Québec resolutions, slightly modified, were passed by the British Parliament as the British North America Act in March 1867 and proclaimed in Canada on July 1, 1867. It was the first time a colony had achieved responsible government without leaving the empire.

The new nation, called the Dominion of Canada, was a federation of Nova Scotia, New Brunswick, Québec (Lower Canada), and Ontario (Upper Canada). Prince Edward Island and Newfoundland refused to join. The Dominion continued to be subject to the full authority of the Crown. Indeed, political rights remained limited, because the cautious unionists wished to avoid what they saw as the perils of American democracy. The federal government, established in Ottawa, Ont., consisted of an appointed Senate and an elected House of Commons with the power to tax and grant subsidies. The provincial governments, under federal supervision, were granted powers sufficient to develop their own resources and fashion their own social institutions. That division of labor, unionists hoped, would prevent the kind of sectional squabbles that had disrupted the American republic.

BUILDING A NATION (1867-1929)

Confederation had created a nation of comparatively few people in a vast territory, most of it uninhabitable. According to the census of 1871, the Dominion's population was 3.7 million (compared to about 40 million Americans in a smaller but more usable area). Of the total, about 1 million were French Roman Catholic, 850,000 Irish Roman Catholic and Protestant, and more than 1 million English and Scottish Protestants—all better known for mutual suspicion than for brotherly love. Three-fourths of the population was rural. Only Montréal, Québec, and Toronto could be considered big cities. A mere 4185 km (2600 mi) of railroad linked the disparate provinces. The gross national product was $459 million, with agriculture the leading occupation.

Expansion Under Macdonald. Sir John A. Macdonald, elected prime minister in 1867, immediately took up the task of nation building. Astutely, he began with a coalition government that drew support from all provinces and interests, although it soon became Conservative in cast. He extended Canada's domain north and west by purchasing Rupert's Land and the North-Western Territory from the Hudson's Bay Co. in 1870, largely to block possible American expansion. This move aroused the existing inhabitants, mostly of mixed European and Indian extraction, and especially the French-speaking métis, who considered themselves a distinct nation. Both English- and French-speaking inhabitants were worried by the threatened incursion of Ontario settlers. The métis, led by Montréal-educated Louis Riel, revolted. The government subdued this first Riel rebellion and then created the province of Manitoba (1870), wherein political power and school policy were supposed to reflect the French and English duality.

Expanding Canada still further, Macdonald added Prince Edward Island (1873) and British Columbia (1871). The latter had been explored by Spanish and British naval expeditions in the 18th century. It was opened to the fur trade through the efforts of Sir Alexander Mackenzie and others and then, in the 1860s, flooded by European and American prospectors in search of gold. The colony joined the Canadian Confeder-

The conference of unification held in Québec City in October 1864 led to the formation of the Dominion of Canada, a Confederation of four provinces that retained allegiance to the British crown. House of Commons, Government of Canada

ation on Macdonald's promise of a federally financed railway to connect it to centers of population. Indeed, railways were necessary to bind the nation together. The government funded the Intercolonial Railway to the Maritimes and contracted with an entrepreneur with U.S. financial backing for the difficult and costly task of building the Canadian Pacific Railway across the prairies and the Rockies to the coast. The disclosure of corruption in the contract led to a scandal that produced a liberal victory in the election of 1874.

A National Policy. The Liberal triumph, however, was short-lived. The onset of an economic depression, which the Liberals were unable to check, soon rehabilitated Macdonald. He was reelected in 1878 on the promise of a "National Policy" to make Canada economically self-sufficient. Presuming an alliance of business and government, he set out to construct an east-west market with an industrial heartland in Québec and Ontario and an agricultural frontier in the prairies. Over the next 13 years he imposed a tariff on imports to foster industry, revived and aided the transcontinental railway (completed in 1887), and encouraged prairie settlement. The last policy provoked métis and some Indians to join in the second Riel rebellion, on the Saskatchewan River. This uprising was crushed by the army, which was rushed to the scene on the new railway, and Riel was hanged in 1885. His execution enraged sympathetic French-Canadians, inflaming the ethnic tensions that, together with provincial demands for more power, had already weakened the Macdonald government.

During these years, the Dominion underwent considerable social change. In the vast new western lands the Indians were dying off or settling on reservations as a result of government treaties offering them money, supplies, and farming aid in exchange for their hunting grounds. In the east, despite a long depression, cities and indus-

try grew rapidly, producing an urban proletariat. In response, churches, schools, newspapers, and department stores emerged as mass institutions to serve the new public. Ethnic differences notwithstanding, the middle-class citizenry embarked on a moral crusade to "Victorianize" the masses, that is, to defeat the liquor traffic, protect the Sabbath, elminate prostitution and gambling, ban impure literature, and improve the moral education of schoolchildren. The U.S., struggling with similar difficulties, did not seem to be so successful in surmounting them. Gradually, the image of a pure Canada and an immoral U.S. became fixed in the national mind.

The Laurier Years. The death of Macdonald in 1891 left the Conservatives without an effective leader. Thus, the election of 1896 was won by the Liberals, led by the French-Canadian lawyer Wilfrid Laurier. A period of prosperity ensued as he carried forward Macdonald's national policy. Protective tariffs supported rapid industrial expansion. A host of emigrants was attracted from Britain and central and eastern Europe and from the U.S., where free land was running out. The prairies were finally settled, with Alberta and Saskatchewan becoming provinces in 1905. Two new transcontinental railways were built with public funds to serve the prairie granary. Private entrepreneurs with provincial aid extended railways to northern Ontario and Québec, where gold, silver, and base metals were discovered.

Laurier also won notice as a stalwart champion of Canadian rights against the U.S. in a dispute (1903) over the Alaskan boundary, which cut northwestern Canada off from the Pacific. He preserved Canadian autonomy by skillfully managing to limit its involvement in British imperialist expansion during the Boer War (1899–1902).

The business community benefited most from the Laurier years. Indeed, by 1911 railway development, industrial growth, and corporate mergers had produced a powerful big-business sector.

Some Canadians, however, worried about the social costs of rapid growth, began to attack the supposed evils of plutocratic rule. The spread of slums and disease in overcrowded cities led to demands for government action to improve public health, welfare, and morality. Reformers agitated for the modernization of government and its services, along the lines of a similar reform movement in the U.S. Other Canadians feared that their way of life was being threatened by alien influences. One such influence was the nearly 600,000 "New Canadian" emigrants from central and southern Europe, many of them Slavs. The other was the steady Americanization of Canada through heavy industrial investment, the domination of the labor movement by the American Federation of Labor, and the enormous popularity of American culture in the cities of English Canada.

In addition to these new discontents, the old ethnic frictions were exacerbated by recent developments. Objecting to the establishment of a single English school system in Manitoba (1890) and the new provinces (1905), and to even limited Canadian military support of Britain, French-Canadians began again to agitate for autonomy. Consequently, when Laurier negotiated a new reciprocal trade agreement with the U.S. that seemed to increase American influence, both French-Canadian and business interests defeated him in the election of 1911.

World War I and Its Effects. Robert L. Borden, the new Conservative prime minister, was responsive to reform demands but soon found his government's energies absorbed by World War I. The Canadian war effort was impressive. The population of 8 million spent $1.67 billion. It raised an armed force of 600,000, at first under British command but by 1917 under Canadian, and lost about 48,000 troops in such actions as Vimy Ridge and Passchendaele. As a result, in foreign affairs Canada's autonomy was expressed by its independent participation in the Paris Peace Conference. On the domestic scene, however, the war effort had undermined national unity. Borden's policy of military conscription had split the Liberal party, driving French-Canadians, who objected to fighting Britain's war, into the arms of a rump Liberal opposition in the bitter "khaki election" of December 1917.

The English-dominated coalition known as the Union government granted woman suffrage in 1918 and briefly legalized prohibition. It could not, however, handle postwar problems. The government, struggling under war debt, was further burdened by the acquisition of bankrupt railways, including the two subsidized by Laurier. All these were amalgamated as the Canadian Railways in 1923. Wartime inflation followed by peacetime depression heightened class tensions. Winnipeg was crippled by a general strike in 1919, raising fears of a Communist takeover. Farmers in Ontario and the west, caught between the high cost of manufactured goods and declining wheat prices, revolted against the established parties. They formed the new National Progressive party, which swept the Prairie provinces in the election of 1921. The Progressives gave limited support to the Liberals, enabling them to form a minority government.

The Prosperous 1920s. The 1920s were a time of healing. Prosperity returned, principally in the cities, attracting ambitious rural youth escaping farm drudgery or seeking new economic opportunity. The latter was based on a third wave of industrial development, especially of mineral and forest products from the north. Reflecting this economic upturn, the labor movement declined; farmers turned from political action to economic cooperatives; and businesspeople, as apparent creators of the good life, regained their prestige. People spent more on personal items such as cars and radios, setting off a retail boom. The moral rigor of the previous generation relaxed, as manifested by the popularity of hockey, horse racing, and other organized sports; the rising sales of liquor and tobacco; and the enthusiasm for American motion pictures and radio programs.

The new Liberal prime minister, the Ontario labor expert William Lyon Mackenzie King, benefited from the new mood of confidence and ease as he strove to unify the nation. He insisted that Canada determine its own domestic and foreign policies as an equal of Britain, a right recognized at the Imperial Conference of 1926 and confirmed by the British Statute of Westminster (1931). His defense of Canadian autonomy was popular with both French-Canadians and western Canadians. He partly satisfied farmers by mildly reducing the tariff, won business support by cautious budgeting, and even earned praise from reformers for passage of an Old Age Pension Act (1927). Conservatives were a minority, and Progressives were in decline.

THE PURSUIT OF WELL-BEING (1929–57)

After the prosperity of the 1920s, Canada underwent depression and war and emerged into another era of material progress.

The Depression. In four short years the worldwide Great Depression shook the foundations of the nation. The gross national product fell from a high of $6.1 billion in 1929 to a low of $3.5 billion in 1933. The value of industrial production was halved. In 1933 about 20 percent of the labor force was unemployed. The Maritimes, an economic backwater, were poor anyway, but the drought-stricken western provinces were particularly hard hit as grain prices toppled from $1.60 a bushel in 1928 to $0.28 in 1932. Total exports dropped by about $600 million, a disaster for a country so dependent on foreign markets. The consequence was a shift in the government's priority from nation building to the pursuit of social well-being—the security, health, and comfort of the mass of people.

Canadians quickly turned to politics for a solution. Rejecting Mackenzie King, they chose the dynamic Conservative lawyer Richard Bennett, who promised swift action. He immediately granted relief for unemployment, which by 1935 was reaching one-tenth of the population. He dramatically raised tariffs to protect industry and force concessions from foreign countries, and at the Imperial Economic Conference at Ottawa in 1932 he arranged preferential trade agreements with Britain and other Commonwealth countries. He enlarged the sphere of government by creating the Canadian Radio Broadcasting Commission (1932), the centralized Bank of Canada (1934), and a Wheat Board (1935). The economy did not recover, however, and the government lost prestige. In 1935, Bennett announced a more radical reform package similar to the American New Deal: unemployment insurance, a reduced workweek, a minimum wage, industrial codes, and permanent economic planning.

The new policy did not save the Conservatives, however. Many voters turned to three small new parties, which promised solutions to the depression—the Reconstruction party, a Conservative offshoot; the Co-operative Commonwealth Federation, a socialist group; and the Social Credit party, a right-wing radical movement based in Alberta. Almost by default, Mackenzie King and the Liberals won the election of 1935.

Mackenzie King dropped Bennett's New Deal package, which was eventually declared unconstitutional in 1937 by the British Privy Council, then the final court of appeal. He did, however, make a new Reciprocity Treaty (1936) with the U.S., convert the radio commission into the Canadian Broadcasting Corp., and fully nationalize the Bank of Canada. Fending off provincial demands for money to support relief programs, he instituted the Rowell-Sirois Royal Commission (1937), which recommended federal responsibility for many provincial social services and a more even distribution of revenue.

The War Years. World War II intervened to save Mackenzie King and the Canadian economy. Although Canada had followed an isolationist policy in the 1930s, when Britain went to war in 1939, Canada too joined the anti-Axis coalition. At first the government concentrated mainly on economic contributions of food, raw materials, and goods, thereby avoiding the conscription so odious to French-Canadians. The German invasion of France in 1940, however, forced Canadians to accept the realities of total war.

Quickly taking command of the economy, the Liberal government set up boards to regulate resources and industry, wages and prices, and a rationing system. In 1944 it approved labor's right to collective bargaining. Most important, it agreed to a large army, which required conscription. Again, the war effort was impressive: Expenditure amounted to $21 billion by 1950. Out of a population of 12 million, about 1.5 million men and women served, 41,700 of whom died in action in Europe.

During the war the government planned a peacetime society that would ensure the well-being of the populace according to the recommendations of the Rowell-Sirois Commission. One key element in the plan was a minimum social-welfare package that would establish a basic living standard. It consisted of unemployment insurance (1940), family allowance payments (1944), generous veterans' benefits, improved old-age pensions, subsidized housing, and various health plans. The other key element was an economic program to foster full employment with a minimum of inflation. After the war the government swiftly dismantled industrial controls, encouraged foreign trade, and stemmed the tide of postwar inflation.

After 22 years as prime minister, Mackenzie King retired in 1948, to be succeeded by Louis St. Laurent, a Québec lawyer. St. Laurent led the Liberals to an overwhelming victory in 1949, indicating national approval of the Liberal design for Canada. Another sign of approval was the decision of Newfoundland, including Labrador, to become a Canadian province. This union, in 1949, completed the Confederation.

Postwar Prosperity. The success of the Liberal design and the continued rule of the Liberal party were ensured by an enormous postwar economic boom. New oil supplies in Alberta and new iron-ore reserves in Ungava (in northern Québec) and Labrador were discovered during the late 1940s. In the next decade uranium resources were developed in northern Ontario, and hydroelectric power stations were built across the country. Manufacturing expanded and diversified, increasing in gross value from $8 billion in 1946 to $22 billion in 1953. The government encouraged modernization of the transportation system. The Trans-Canada Highway, a federal-provincial project, was begun in 1949. Trans-Canada Airways, a crown corporation founded in 1938, expanded. In 1956 the privately owned Trans-Canada Pipeline was approved to carry oil and gas from Alberta to Canadian and American markets. The boom was further fueled by the arrival of some 1.5 million immigrants, chiefly British and other Europeans, who provided a pool of cheap labor and a body of new consumers.

The gross national product rose from $12 billion in 1946 to more than $30 billion in 1957. The trade unions made significant economic gains for their members. In 1956 the two largest, the Canadian Congress of Labour and the Trades and Labour Congress, merged into the Canadian Labour Congress, which became a potent force in political as well as economic life. Much of this economic expansion, however, depended on heavy American investment in Canadian natural resources and American control of much Canadian manufacturing.

New Foreign Ties. Canada's postwar affluence enhanced its status in a world of devastated European countries and underdeveloped African and Asian lands. The government was especially active in foreign aid. In 1950 it joined the Colombo Plan for assisting underdeveloped members of the Commonwealth.

As the old ties with Britain slowly dissolved, Canada came gradually into the political orbit of the U.S. Even before the war, in 1940, Mackenzie King and U.S. President Franklin D. Roosevelt had signed the Ogdensburg Agreement providing for permanent joint planning of North American defense. After the war, Canada's foreign policy was closely linked to U.S. strategy of containing Communist expansion. In 1949 Canada approved the North Atlantic Treaty Organization (NATO), guaranteeing the defense of Europe under U.S. leadership. It sent troops to the largely American-staffed UN army during the Korean War (1950–53). In 1956, at the time of the Anglo-French occupation of the Suez Canal, it proposed, with American approval, a UN Emergency Force to preserve a new truce in the Middle East. Canada also negotiated the North American Air Defense Command (NORAD, 1958), confirming that Canadian defense was a U.S. responsibility. Thus, relations between the U.S. and Canada became, to the Canadian mind, as significant and problematic as had been the ties with Britain.

A TIME OF TROUBLES (1957–)

The success of the Liberal design had undermined the traditional supports of the nation: the connection with Britain, a decentralized federalism, and social conservatism. Beginning in the late 1950s, a series of challenging problems emerged to threaten the very survival of Canada.

Mounting Opposition. One of the most serious dangers to the Confederation was the old issue of French-Canadian separatism, newly inflamed by French resentment of English and American control of most of the new industry in Québec. After 1960 a new Liberal government in Québec sponsored a "Quiet Revolution" to achieve modernization of provincial institutions and greater French-Canadian self-determination within the Confederation. Soon more extreme separatist organizations appeared, including the terrorist Front de Libération du Québec (FLQ) and René Lévesque's democratic Parti Québecois (PQ). Other provinces shook off their subservience to Ottawa and joined Québec in demanding more autonomy.

As in the U.S., during the 1960s a surge of social criticism challenged the authority of existing conventions and institutions. On the national level, the prolabor New Democratic party (NDP) was formed to champion social democracy. A new wave of anti-Americanism, sparked by increasing fears of American economic and political dominance, led to widespread demands for an assertion of Canadian independence.

GOVERNORS-GENERAL OF CANADA SINCE 1867

Charles Stanley Monck, 4th Viscount Monck, 1867–68
Sir John Young, Baron Lisgar, 1869–72
Frederick Temple Blackwood, 1st marquess of Dufferin and Ava, 1872–78
John Douglas Sutherland Campbell, 9th duke of Argyll, 1878–83
Henry Charles Keith Petty-Fitzmaurice, 5th marquess of Lansdowne, 1883–88
Frederick Arthur Stanley, Baron Stanley of Preston, 1888–93
John Campbell Gordon, 1st marquess of Aberdeen and Temair, 1893–98
Gilbert John Elliot-Murray-Kynynmound, 4th earl of Minto, 1898–1904
Albert Henry George Grey, 4th Earl Grey, 1904–11
Prince Arthur William Patrick Albert, duke of Connaught, 1911–16
Victor Christian William Cavendish, 9th duke of Devonshire, 1916–21
Julian Hedworth George Byng, Viscount Byng of Vimy, 1921–26
Freeman Freeman-Thomas, 1st marquess of Willingdon, 1926–31
Vere Brabazon Ponsonby, 9th earl of Bessborough, 1931–35
Sir John Buchan, Baron Tweedsmuir of Elsfield, 1935–40
Alexander Augustus Frederick William Alfred George Cambridge, 1st earl of Athlone, 1940–46
Harold Rupert Leofric George Alexander, 1st Earl Alexander of Tunis, 1946–52
Vincent Massey, 1952–59
Georges P. Vanier, 1959–67
Roland Michener, 1967–74
Jules Léger, 1974–79
Edward R. Schreyer, 1979–84
Jeanne Sauvé, 1984–

The Conservative government of the Saskatchewan lawyer John Diefenbaker had won the elections of 1957 and 1958, the latter by a sweeping majority; but it fell victim to this fragmentation of the national consensus. The Liberals, under the diplomat Lester Pearson, who formed a minority government after 1963, proved more responsive to the public mood. The Pearson government implemented "cooperative federalism," which allowed Québec and other provinces a greater say in national affairs. It created a royal commission to study bilingualism and biculturalism and launched an investigation of U.S. domination of the economy. The government also unified the armed forces under a single command, revamped the broadcasting system, and negotiated a federal-provincial agreement on medical care for the aged.

In the election of 1968, the charismatic personality and reasoned policies of Pierre Elliott Trudeau, a French-Canadian, brought the Liberals a majority. Trudeau, unlike his two predecessors, had a vision of Canada as bilingual, multicultural, collectivist, and non-American. In domestic affairs, his government passed the Official Languages Act (1969), which established the equality of French and English in all government activities. The government encouraged the strengthening of French culture outside Québec and the idea of multiculturalism championed by new immigrants. It even funded efforts to revitalize and improve Indian life and culture. In addition, it greatly expanded payments to the underprivileged, the young, and the aged in an effort to realize a social democracy in the European style.

In foreign affairs the Trudeau government reduced Canada's contribution to NATO in 1969 and in 1971 recognized the People's Republic of China as part of an effort to forge links with countries outside the American orbit. More hesitantly, through the Foreign Investment Review Agency (1974), the administration moved to control American presence in the economy.

Economic and Political Crises. Trudeau's efforts to remake Canada ran into increasing difficulties. The western provinces, especially oil-rich Alberta, resented the central Canadian bias implicit in Trudeau's vision of the nation. The business community bitterly criticized the government's expensive program of social equity and apparent indifference to galloping inflation. The formation of an Anti-Inflation Board (AIB) in 1975 displeased business and infuriated organized labor.

The economic crisis was overshadowed by the specter of the nation's dissolution. In 1976 the PQ won political control of Québec and began a campaign to win support for its goal of independence. This in turn led other Canadians to reconsider the ethnic and political character of their Confederation. The country showed its dissatisfaction with the Liberals by voting Trudeau out of office in May 1979. His successor, Progressive Conservative Joseph Clark, was unable to form a stable majority in Parliament, and Trudeau returned to power in February 1980. The central government won a victory the following May, when Québec voters defeated a referendum proposing separation from Canada; at the same time, however, it became involved in a dispute with Alberta over control of that province's petroleum resources. In Alberta and other western provinces, more and more voices were raised

Prime Minister Pierre Elliott Trudeau signs the proclamation of Canada's new constitution in the presence of Queen Elizabeth II, after she formally transferred constitutional power from Britain to Canada on April 17, 1982. UPI

protesting the power exercised by the central government. Trudeau hoped to resolve the problems of the Confederation by adopting a new federal constitution to replace the British North America Act, and in late 1981 he reached agreement with the English-speaking provinces on the form of the proposed new constitution. It was proclaimed by Queen Elizabeth II in Ottawa on April 17, 1982, and later approved by Québec in 1987. In February 1984, Trudeau announced his intention to resign as soon as the Liberals could pick a successor, and John Napier Turner became prime minister in June. In parliamentary elections that September, the Conservatives, led by Brian Mulroney, swept into power. Mulroney and President Ronald Reagan signed an agreement in January 1988 providing for the gradual elimination of all trade barriers between Canada and the U.S. In November, in an election that hinged on the free-trade issue, Mulroney's government was returned to power, but with a reduced majority in parliament. P.R.

For further information on this topic, see the Bibliography in volume 28, sections 261, 664-65, 695, 727, 834, 1109-17, 1148, 1150, 1152.

CANADA, UNITED CHURCH OF. *See* UNITED CHURCH OF CANADA.

CANADA BALSAM, an oleoresin obtained from the balsam secreted by the bark of the evergreen fir tree *Abies balsamea,* or balsam fir. The balsam fir, a member of the family Pinaceae (*see* PINE), grows in the forests of Canada and the northern U.S. The balsam exudes from the tree as a greenish-yellow liquid with the consistency of honey, which becomes hard and transparent as it dries. Although balsam is sometimes an ingredient of varnishes, it is valued as an adhesive for mounting microscopic specimens and in the manufacture of lenses and optical systems. Balsam is used to cement the elements of compound lenses and other glass surfaces because it is transparent, and its index of refraction is so close to that of optical glass that it introduces little distortion.

CANADA COMPANY, private venture in the colonization of Upper Canada (now Ontario Province), organized in 1825 by the British novelist John Galt. The company, which received a royal charter in 1826, played an important part in settling southern Ontario between Lakes Ontario and Huron, where large tracts of land were cleared and many English and Scottish settlers established farms. In 1827 the town of Guelph was founded by the company. Goderich and Saint Marys were established shortly thereafter. The region became one of the richest in Ontario.

CANADIAN, also South Canadian, unnavigable river, southwestern U.S., 1451 km (906 mi) long. The Canadian R. is formed in NE New Mexico by the union of several branches from the southern Rocky Mts. The river flows S through New Mexico and then turns E, crossing the Texas Panhandle into Oklahoma. Following a meandering course in Oklahoma, it finally joins the Arkansas R. The only major tributary of the Canadian R. is the North Canadian R., 1260 km (784 mi) long, which runs almost parallel to the Canadian R. in Oklahoma. The tributary joins the Canadian R. at Eufaula in E Oklahoma to form the Eufaula Reservoir. In NE New Mexico, a semiarid region, the Canadian R. provides an important water source at the Conchas Dam, a flood-control and irrigation project.

CANADIAN ART AND ARCHITECTURE, the paintings, sculpture, and buildings created by the European settlers, and their descendants, in Canada. For the art of native Canadian cultures, *see* AMERICAN INDIANS: *Art;* INUIT: *Arts and Crafts.*

EARLY ART IN NEW FRANCE

Artistic activity began in Canada in the 1660s when New France was first colonized. Unlike the Protestant inhabitants of New England, the settlers of New France were Roman Catholics; the construction of new church buildings in the towns and villages along the Saint Lawrence River created a demand for ecclesiastical decorations. Local artisans were trained to produce the required works using native woods for altars, tabernacles, retables, and statues painted to imitate stone and metal. These artisans transformed complex European baroque and rococo models into simplified folk-art forms. Wood carving thus became the most common and sophisticated art form in New France. Early Québec had few painters. Most easel pictures painted in New France before 1760 were executed by self-taught amateurs. The church remained the primary patron, and the few surviving paintings of the period are restricted to biblical or other religious subjects, portraits of priests and nuns, or votive paintings. Although many of these works are ambitious attempts to imitate baroque figure compositions, most are folk-art productions.

PAINTING AFTER THE ENGLISH CONQUEST

With the English conquest of New France in 1759, an entirely new class of artists was introduced into Canada. These were army officers trained in topographical watercolor painting, who produced picturesque views of urban and wilderness subjects that reflected contemporaneous English landscape ideals. Among the most outstanding soldier-artists were Thomas Davies (c. 1737-1812), George Heriot (1766-1844), and James Cockburn (1778-1847).

The secularization of art under the English extended to portraiture as well. In the early 1800s, the leading portraitists were Robert Field (c. 1769–1819) and William Berczy (1744–1813), who were professionally trained in Europe and painted in the then fashionable neoclassical manner. In the first half of the 19th century, the demand for portraits in English-speaking Canada was satisfied by itinerant folk portraitists who traveled through pioneer settlements.

Art Before 1860. In Montréal and Québec City, local schools of portraiture developed in the 1820s and '30s that depended for patronage on wealthy merchants rather than the church. Many of these "primitive" portraits are by anonymous artists; others, however, are sophisticated, neoclassical productions executed by such native-born, European-trained painters as Antoine Plamondon (1817–95) and Théophile Hamel (1817–70). Joseph Legaré (1795–1855) was an extremely versatile self-taught Québec artist; his wilderness scenes of the 1840s are the earliest known Canadian landscapes in oil. One of the most prolific artists to work in Québec in the mid-19th century was European-born Cornelius Krieghoff (1815–72), whose portraits, detailed genre scenes of rural French-Canadian life, and snow scenes proved enormously popular with English colonial patrons.

The most ambitious painter in Ontario in the 1840s and '50s was Paul Kane (1810–71). Directly influenced by the example of the American artist George Catlin, Kane set out to record the life of the Indians of western Canada before it was altered by contact with whites. By 1855 he had completed a cycle of 100 scenes and portraits.

In the mid-19th century, a number of professionally trained English amateur artists—working mostly in watercolor—appeared in pioneer settlements in Ontario. Their work, like that of the vast majority of painters active in Canada at the time, was provincial; emulating conservative British art, they produced Canadian landscapes with a curiously English look to them, such as those by Robert Whale (1805–87).

Establishment of Art Academies and Exhibitions After 1860. By the 1860s (in Montréal) and the 1870s (in Toronto), artists had secured a more professional footing with the establishment of art associations, artists' societies, and annual exhibitions. With the increased emigration of professional painters from England, Germany, and the U.S., artistic endeavors were strongly augmented. During the period 1860–90, the wilderness landscape emerged as a primary symbol for Canadian artists. After the confederation of Canada as a single nation in 1867 and its expansion to the Pacific Ocean in 1871, English-speaking artists in particular were imbued with a spirit of national pride and sought to express the physical grandeur of their immense new country. Landscapists such as Otto Jacobi (1812–1901), Alan Edson (1846–88), John Fraser (1838–98), and Lucius O'Brien (1832–99) painted picturesque wilderness scenes in a romantic-realist style similar in many respects to the art of the Hudson River school in the U.S. The culmination of the nationalist mood in Victorian Canada was the establishment, in Ottawa, of the Royal Canadian Academy in 1880, which created a bond among artists often widely separated by geography and language differences. The diploma pieces required of academicians became the basis of the collection of the National Gallery of Canada, founded in Ottawa in the same year.

After 1875 a younger generation of Canadian-born painters committed to figural rather than landscape painting traveled to Paris, then at the height of its fame as a cosmopolitan art center. Many of them enrolled in private academies or in the official Académie des Beaux-Arts. Among the leading Anglo-Canadian exponents of academic figure painting were William Brymner (1855–1925), Robert Harris (1849–1919), Paul Peel (1860–92), and George Reid (1860–1947). The sober propriety and sentimentality of their works and those of their French-Canadian compatriots, who also studied in Paris, reflected tightly conservative ideals in figural art.

Two Canadian-born artists were strongly influenced by French realist landscape painting, especially that of the famed Barbizon school. Homer Watson (1855–1936) of rural Ontario and Horatio Walker (1850–1938) of Ile d'Orléans near Québec City painted monumental landscapes and scenes of their respective locales. Walker's art was immensely popular in New York City.

Canadian Impressionism. Not all Canadians who worked in Paris in the 1890s emulated academic French painting. Several important Québec painters were attracted instead to impressionist and postimpressionist art. Maurice Cullen (1866–1934) and Marc Aurèle de Foy Suzor-Coté (1869–1937) introduced a decorative impressionism into Canadian landscape painting. The bright colors and clear light of the French impressionists were transformed on their return to Canada into a low-keyed, atmospheric tonalism.

The single truly avant-garde artist among the Canadians in Paris about 1900 was Montréal-born James Wilson Morrice (1865–1924), the first native-born painter to achieve an international reputation. At first, his oil paintings reflected the simplified shapes and delicate tones of the American expatriate artist J. A. M. Whistler. Later,

The Ferry, Québec, *oil painting by James Wilson Morrice.* The National Gallery of Canada–Ottawa

Morrice absorbed the formal values of the Parisian Fauves ("Wild Beasts"), especially those of Henri Matisse. Although his intellectual and artistic home remained France, Morrice regularly returned to Canada in the winter, to paint and to exhibit his work.

The Group of Seven. In the years just before World War I, a number of younger artists based in Toronto reacted strongly against the ubiquitous espousal of outmoded European art ideals. Instead, they promoted painting that was distinctively Canadian in spirit. As their primary subject, they chose the raw, sparsely inhabited wilderness of northern Ontario. To these artists and their supporters, the north was the true spiritual symbol of Canada. Never before had landscapists painted the vast stretches of forests, lakes, and rock that make up the spectacular geography of the Canadian Shield. One of the Toronto painters, Tom Thomson, was an inspiration to the others. His brightly colored outdoor sketches (directly executed on wilderness canoe trips) became the basis for large-scale, decorative studio canvases, the bold and stirring compositions of which were strongly influenced by the flat patterns of Art Nouveau graphic design. In 1920, after Thomson's untimely death (1917) and the end of World War I, the remaining artists reassembled in Toronto and formed the famous Group of Seven. Nationalistic in their stance, they set out to create a "living Canadian art." Original members included Lawren Harris, A. Y. Jackson, J. E. H. Macdonald, Arthur Lismer, F. H. Varley, Frank Carmichael (1890–1945), and Frank Johnston (1888–1949). Together with like-minded artists, the group exhibited annually from 1920 to 1931. The visual energy of their works and the nationalistic basis of their philosophy proved extraordinarily popular with English-speaking Canadians, who identified with their aggressive, expansive spirit. Many of their dramatic canvases have become national icons and remain among the best-loved works of Canadian art.

Independent Artists of the 1920s and '30s. The vision of the Group of Seven dominated painting in the 1920s and '30s. During a period in which American artists focused on social issues, Canadians represented the uninhabited landscape. Among the exceptions to this rule are Carl Schaefer (1903–) and Charles Comfort (1900–), whose regionalist works of the 1930s approximate American Midwest regionalist painting of the same period. They and others formed the Canadian Group of Painters in Toronto in 1933. Three independent and individualistic artists stand out from the mainstream of English-speaking artists at this time. David Milne (1882–1953) painted landscapes and still lifes, the arbitrarily flattened compositions and refined color harmonies of which reflect his study of avant-garde art in New York City between 1904 and 1914. Emily Carr created expressionistic and highly original sculpturesque paintings of forest interiors and Indian totem pcles in British Columbia. The Winnipeg artist L. L. Fitzgerald (1890–1956) painted precisely modeled, smoothly finished backyard scenes; their logic is akin to that of the American precisionist painter Charles Sheeler.

The Contemporary Art Society of Montréal. Artists in Québec failed to respond to the nationalism of the Group of Seven. For them, the artistic culture of modern France exerted a stronger attraction than the Canadian wilderness. John Lyman (1886–1967) lived and worked in Paris for some 24 years before his return in the 1930s to Montréal. Like Morrice before him, Lyman was deeply influenced by the art of Matisse. In 1940 Lyman founded the Contemporary Art Society, whose members, in contrast to those of the Canadian Group of Painters, produced experimental works firmly based on Parisian modes such as Fauvism and cubism, little known in isolationist Toronto art circles. Another influential artist to return to Montréal from Paris was Alfred Pellan (1906–). He was among the earliest to introduce surrealism into French Canada, where it flourished brilliantly in the 1940s and '50s.

The Automatistes of Montréal. The most outstanding modern Québec artist was Paul Émile Borduas (1905–60). At first a symbolist, Borduas joined the Contemporary Art Society. Studying surrealist theory, he developed an "automatic," or spontaneous, painting style. After 1945, a group of young French-Canadian painters gathered around Borduas; they were called Automatistes because of their adherence to spontaneous creation. In rebellion against the figural tradition of Lyman's group, they created a wholly abstract movement that was unprecedented in Canada. Among their members was Jean Paul Riopelle, considered Canada's leading abstract expressionist painter, whose highly colored, mosaiclike canvases have achieved international renown.

Painters Eleven—Canadian Abstract Expressionists. In the early 1950s a group of younger Toronto painters began to move beyond representationalism. Their route to abstraction was through New York's abstract expressionist movement. In 1953 these Toronto artists formed Painters Eleven, a group that challenged the inherent conservatism of the city's art circles. Members included Jock Macdonald (1897–1960), William Ronald (1926–), and Harold Town (1924–). Unlike the Automatistes of Montréal, Painters Eleven were not concerned with pure abstraction but rather, like many American abstract expressionists, with a figural abstraction derived from cubism.

In the 1960s other forms of abstraction were practiced by English-speaking artists. Under the direct influence of the American formalist critic Clement Greenberg (1909–), several important

The Jack Pine *(1916–17), an oil painting by Tom Thomson, reveals Art Nouveau influence in the sharply silhouetted, curving tree branches, but also shows his pioneering depiction of the vast Canadian wilderness. Thomson was the prime influence on the artists of the Canadian nationalist Group of Seven.*

National Gallery of Canada, Ottawa

painters, chief among them Jack Bush (1909-77), engaged in color-field painting. In Montréal, a group of artists known as Plasticiens developed a hard-edge, geometric abstraction utilizing stripes of dazzling color, a mode ultimately derived from the art of the Dutch painter Piet Mondrian and the Russian constructivists. A diametrically opposing point of view, that of the precise representational style known as "super" or "magic" realism, was practiced contemporaneously in parts of eastern Canada and Ontario and remained popular through the 1970s.

Internationalists and Nationalists—Debates of the 1960s and '70s. From the late 1960s through the '70s, an often acrimonious debate raged in Canadian art circles between internationalists, adhering to the formal modernism of recent American art, and the nationalists, attempting to create an aggressive, national self-consciousness through the use of specifically Canadian imagery. An anti-Americanism, generated by opposition to the war in Vietnam and to the continued domination of Canadian culture by American values, permeated the debate. In response to this, a group of populist artists based in London, Ont., concentrated on regional themes and popular imagery as means by which to effect a self-conscious Canadianism in the visual arts. Important among these new nationalists were Greg Curnoe (1936-), who paints in an idiosyncratic, neo-Dadaist manner, and Joyce Wieland (1931-), a filmmaker as well as a painter and celebrated for reviving the art of quiltmaking.

The Present. During the 1970s, art in Canada emerged not only from reliance on American or European art but also from a crisis of identity. Newly confident in their ability to pursue goals irrespective of their connection with internationalist or nationalist aims, a generation of younger painters, sculptors, and printmakers, along with video and performance artists, have created an unprecedented artistic diversity. Conceptual issues preoccupy most of this generation. Since the late 1950s, the single figure of Michael Snow (1929-) has exemplified the recent advance among Canadian artists toward self-reliance. Emerging from the figural abstraction of Toronto painting, Snow soon became known outside Canada for his avant-garde filmmaking activities and has earned a worldwide reputation as a pioneer in the conceptual use of this medium. While sculpture never aroused as much interest in Canada as painting, and only in the 1930s began to reflect contemporary European styles, a few artists, such as the minimalist sculptor David Rabinovitch (1943-) have become known internationally. More recently, increased interest has centered on contemporary Inuit and Indian carving.

ARCHITECTURE

Canadian architecture, like painting in Canada, before the 1960s remained essentially provincial, adopting first European and then American styles. Vernacular transformations often occurred, creating distinctively Canadian characteristics. The parish churches and homes constructed after the colonization of New France in the 1660s were made of stone rather than wood. Medieval and baroque architectural forms in France directly influenced those erected in Canada in the late 17th and early 18th centuries. Parish churches, plain on the exterior, with characteristic high-pitched roofs with flaring eaves and tall, single steeples, were richly decorated on the interior with carved and painted decoration. By contrast, public and church architecture in Québec City and Montréal was on a much grander scale, reflecting the aristocratic preferences of colonial administrators and ecclesiastical leaders.

Neoclassicism. During the early decades of English rule, neoclassicism predominated. Italian Renaissance forms, particularly those of Andrea Palladio, strongly influenced the design of large buildings constructed by the English in the early 1800s. The Province House (1808-11) in Halifax, N.S., and the Anglican Cathedral (1804) in Québec City typify the massive neoclassicism favored by the English authorities. French-Canadians, on the other hand, retained a French cultural allegiance and adopted the more delicate neoclassicism of Louis XVI architecture for their religious edifices. In the late 1700s, a third form of classical design was introduced into Canada by New Englanders who settled eastern Canada before the American Revolution and imported their indigenous Georgian style. After 1789 and the arrival of large numbers of Loyalist settlers from the U.S., the templelike structures of Greek Revival architecture made their appearance in Ontario border settlements.

Gothic Revival. Renaissance and antique forms were supplanted by Gothic-inspired designs. The eclecticism of the early Gothic Revival is clearly exhibited in Montréal's Church of Notre Dame (1823); the more archaeologically correct High Victorian Gothic is best seen in the Anglican Cathedral of Christ Church (1845) in Fredericton, N.B. Gothicism remained the predominant architectural mode in English-speaking Canada in the last half of the 19th century. Its widespread popularity was based on its expression of British monarchical cultural values. In its most sophisti-

An aerial view of the civic center (1979) in Vancouver, B.C., designed by Arthur Charles Ericson. This three-block-long complex houses law courts and provincial offices in a unified design. Extensive roof gardens, pools, and fountains are an important feature of the exterior. Ezra Stoller–ESTO

cated and monumental form, High Victorian Gothic is manifested in two important Ontario monuments: University College (1856) in Toronto and the Parliament Buildings (1859) in Ottawa. In its more simple and vernacular form, it is seen in the high-steepled, white-painted wooden Protestant churches of the period and the ubiquitous gable-fronted Ontario farmhouse with its characteristic pointed window above the front door.

Continuation of Eclectic Revivals. In the late Victorian era in Canada, historical eclecticism was rampant. Alongside the more florid Gothic style of the late 1800s existed the simpler forms of the Italianate style and the grander massing of the Parisian Second Empire style, the latter particularly popular in French Canada. In the last decade of the century, the massive Romanesque style developed by the American architect H. H. Richardson was also introduced into Canada. Toronto's Old City Hall (1890) is perhaps the best-known Canadian example of this American architectural mode. A singular form that appeared on the Canadian scene in the 1890s was the distinctive "château" style enthusiastically adopted by the Canadian Pacific Railway for its cross-Canada chain of hotels.

20th-Century Conformity. Victorian historicism continued to shape the architectural landscape in the early decades of the 1900s. Neoclassical or Gothic detailing was regularly applied to the exterior of such functional structures as skyscrapers. The bleak new buildings of the 1930s depression era were influenced by the severity of the International Style. Decoration was minimal and limited to geometric, Art Deco motifs. In the 1940s and early '50s Canadian architecture remained cautious and conservative. Large-scale buildings of this period were bland adaptations of the International Style.

Emergence of Indigenous Canadian Architecture. A creative quickening occurred after 1956 and the establishment of annual national awards—the Massey Medals—for excellence in Canadian architectural design. The publication of winning entries familiarized architects across the country with one another's work. A spirit of competition resulted, which by 1960 caused architecture in Canada to emerge from its provincial status. Some of the most enlightened projects undertaken in the early '60s remain among the most widely respected produced to date: intimate Massey College (1963) at the University of Toronto, designed by Ron Thom (1923–); monumental Scarborough College (1965) outside Toronto, designed by John Andrews (1933–); and airy Simon Fraser University (1965), designed by Arthur Erickson, which stretches across a mountaintop near Vancouver, B.C. The celebrations of Canada's centennial in 1967 included the construction of large numbers of new public buildings across the country. A wave of national self-confidence and excitement over the event resulted in the production of numerous lighthearted and structurally romantic works. Chief among them are the spectacular theme buildings erected for Expo '67 in Montréal. Another large-scale Montréal project was the monumental, multipurpose Place Bonaventure (1967–68), designed by Ray Affleck (1922–), which contains a railroad station, trade center, hotel, shops, and convention facilities. One of the most outstanding architectural designs in the post-Expo period was the elegant Canadian Pavilion by Erickson and Geoffrey Massey (1924-) at the world exhibition held in 1970 at Osaka, Japan. A configuration of four adjoining, triangular structures covered with mirror glass, it reflected the continuously changing light of the sky.

In reaction to the grandiose scale of architecture in the '60s, many Canadian architects, instead of designing monumental new edifices that dominated their environments, increasingly turned to the renovation of existing buildings in the old downtown cores of larger Canadian towns and cities. The picturesque variety and human scale of the urban landscape was preserved, and multiuse structures attracted people to the inner city. A new romanticism flourished, and new projects often exhibited a lively, eccentric quality. One of the most significant new complexes realized in the 1970s was the Eaton Center in downtown Toronto. The product of an architectural and planning collaborative headed by Zeidler Associates, it is a multilevel, two-block-long retail complex that wittily merges high-tech machine aesthetic with the elegance of a glass-enclosed European *galleria.* Admired by critics and the public is Erickson's Robson Square (1979), the three-block civic center of Vancouver that combines law courts, provincial offices, and a cultural center, each in a distinctive structure linked to the others by galleries, terraces, waterfalls, and landscaping.

For additional information on individual artists and architects, see biographies of those whose names are not followed by dates. J.A.

For further information on this topic, see the Bibliography in volume 28, section 664.

CANADIAN LITERATURE, literature written in English and French by the peoples of Canada. As a young, pioneering country, Canada put more of its energies into economic development than into the arts. As material circumstances improved, however, two literatures developed, reflecting Canada's dual cultural heritage. At first they evinced a common interest in the wilderness and in regional locales and tended to imitate European styles. In the 20th century a growing sense of national identity was reflected in literatures of maturity and distinction.

CANADIAN LITERATURE IN ENGLISH

Because English-speaking Canadians were more numerous and diversified than French-speaking Canadians, Canadian literature written in English has been until recently more abundant and varied than that written in French.

Colonial Period. Among early Canadian works in English were the accounts of 18th- and early 19th-century explorers such as Samuel Hearne (1745-92), Alexander Mackenzie, Simon Fraser (1776-1862), and David Thompson. The first novel produced in Canada, indeed in North America, was *The History of Emily Montague* (1769), an account of contemporary Québec, realistically written by Frances Moore Brooke (1724-89), wife of an English army chaplain.

In the early 19th century, Oliver Goldsmith (1794-1861) wrote *The Rising Village* (1825), a book-length poem extolling a pioneer community, in reply to *The Deserted Village* (1770) by the British writer Oliver Goldsmith, his great-uncle. Charles Sangster (1822-93), in *St. Lawrence and the Saguenay* (1856), was one of the first poets to describe the natural beauties of the land.

Wacousta (1832) by John Richardson (1796-1852), about Pontiac's Rebellion (1763) was the first novel based on Canadian history. In the humorous essays of *The Clockmaster* (1836), Thomas Chandler Haliburton (1796-1865) presented the vulgar but enterprising Yankee peddler Sam Slick as a satire on the comparatively lazy Nova Scotians. The rigors of pioneer life were described in two autobiographical books, *Backwoods of Canada* (1836) by Catherine Parr Traill (1802-99) and *Roughing It in the Bush* (1852) by her sister Susanna Moodie (1803-85).

Confederation to World War I. The Confederation of 1867 encouraged a sense of national identity, which stimulated literary activity. Inspired by the English romantics' and early Victorians' love of nature. Canadians looked for themes in their own natural landscape.

Poetry. The first significant Canadian poets were those of the Confederation school, led by Sir Charles G. D. Roberts (1860-1943). His romantic *Orion and Other Poems* (1880) stimulated other writers, and in his *Songs of the Common Day* (1893) he vividly described his native New Brunswick countryside. Bliss Carman, Roberts's cousin, gained fame through love songs and nature poems, tinged with romantic melancholy and nostalgia. Among his best-known collections are *Low Tide on Grand Pré* (1893) and *The Pipes of Pan* (5 vol., 1902-05).

Other important Confederation poets were Archibald Lampman (1861-99) and Duncan Campbell Scott. Lampman described rural Ontario in *Among the Millet* (1888) and *Lyrics of the Earth* (1893). Scott took the most dramatic view of the Ontario landscape in *New World Lyrics and Ballads* (1905) and *Beauty and Life* (1921). As head of the Department of Indian Affairs, he wrote poems sympathetic to Indian culture. His volumes of short stories, *In the Village of Viger* (1896) and *The Witching of Elspie* (1923), reveal a deep interest in psychology as well. Wilfred Campbell (1858?-1918) described contrasts in Canadian climate and landscape.

The most popular Canadian poet of the early 20th century was English-born Robert W. Service. His *Songs of a Sourdough* (1907), including "The Shooting of Dan McGrew," was the product of his years in the Yukon. Although his work has been highly praised, Service himself never pretended to be anything but a rhymester.

Prose. The two principal novelists of the late 19th century, William Kirby (1817-1906) and Sir Gilbert Parker, wrote historical romances concerning the trials and pleasures of life in a vast new land. Kirby's *Golden Dog* (1877) and Parker's *The Seats of the Mighty* (1897), both set in Québec, began a trend toward colorful novels of a glorified past.

Around the turn of the century, a literary taste developed for regional novels that gave a rather idyllic description of rural life of the time. Ralph Connor (pseudonym of C. W. Gordon, 1860-1937), once a missionary in the Rockies, wrote *Black Rock* (1898) and *The Man from Glengarry* (1901) about the west. Lucy Maud Montgomery (1874-1942) set her classic children's story, *Anne of Green Gables* (1908), on her native Prince Edward Island; perennially popular, it has been staged and filmed several times.

The English-born humorist Stephen Leacock, a professor of economics at McGill University, wrote sharp, witty social criticism in such works as *Sunshine Sketches of a Little Town* (1912), set in Ontario, and *Arcadian Adventures with the Idle Rich* (1914).

1920s to World War II. During the 1920s realist writers were critical of Canadian values and institutions, a tendency strengthened by Canadians' experience of the Great Depression and World War I.

Poetry. One of the finest poets of this period was the Newfoundland-born English professor Edwin John Pratt (1882-1964). His poetry reflects his fascination with the sea, his sense of the impersonal violence of nature, and his fundamentally tragic world view. In *The Titanic* (1935) and *Brébeuf and His Brethren* (1940), he amply proved that the ancient epic form is vital in the 20th century.

Poets living in Montréal made the 1930s and 1940s one of the most exciting periods in the history of Canadian poetry in English. They published in little literary magazines, cheaper than books in a depressed economy, which encouraged rivalry and urged them to be aware of their roots and guard against excessive British or American influence. The leaders were Francis Reginald Scott (1899-1985) and A. J. M. Smith (1902-80), who were also concerned with social issues and with literary criticism. Later they compiled *The Blasted Pine: An Anthology of Satire, Invective, and Disrespectful Verse: Chiefly by Canadians* (1957), which perhaps belies the cliché that Canadians are incapable of self-criticism. Another of these early Montréal poets was Abraham Moses Klein (1909-72). Steeped in Jewish tradition, he wrote lyrically and with deep understanding of Jews and other minorities.

Prose. One of the first writers of sociological novels was the European-born Frederick Philip Grove (1871-1948). Years as a farmhand and schoolmaster on the Manitoba prairies inspired his book of sketches. *Over Prairie Trails* (1922), and the two powerful novels *Settlers of the Marsh* (1925) and *Fruits of the Earth* (1933), in which he described pioneer life with strength, vigor, and an astute eye. He is often weak and tedious in style and characterization, however.

Combining the traditions of the late 19th-century historical romances and early 20th-century regional idylls was Mazo de la Roche, the most widely read Canadian novelist of her day. Beginning with *Jalna* (1927), she created a 16-volume chronicle of the Whiteoak family and of Jalna, their Ontario estate.

Morley Callaghan sympathetically explored individuals in conflict with society in *They Shall Inherit the Earth* (1935) and *The Loved and the Lost* (1961). Hugh MacLennan studied various strains of the Canadian heritage in *Barometer Rising* (1941), *Two Solitudes* (1945), and *The Watch That Ends the Night* (1959). Early in their careers both Callaghan and MacLennan were commended for their realism, psychological honesty, and contributions to defining Canadian character. Since then, however, their reputations have declined. Other social realist novels are *As for Me and My House* (1941), an affecting picture of the depression years on the prairies, by Sinclair Ross (1908-), and *Who Has Seen the Wind?* (1947), a boy's experience of a Saskatchewan village, by W. O. Mitchell (1914-).

Late 20th Century. Since World War II, Canadian literature has gained in volume and creativity, reflecting and encouraging a heightened national consciousness. Produced in a time of rebellion and of breaks with tradition, it has become more experimental in approach and universal in theme. Many critics considered Canadian poetry of the 1970s the best being written in the English-speaking world.

Poetry. Perhaps the most significant voices in poetry were those of Earle Birney (1904-) and Dorothy Livesay (1909-), both of whom had written of social problems in the 1930s. Birney's

David (1942), set in the Canadian Rockies of his youth, continues to captivate readers by its powerful language and intriguing story of a man's search for truth through encountering nature. Birney's lyrical style and controlled humanism have never faltered in such later works as *Ice, Cod, Bell, or Stone* (1962) and *Near False Creek Mouth* (1964). His *Collected Poems* appeared in 1975. Livesay has been humanistically concerned with the individual's efforts to overcome the forces of destruction within and without. Her work, such as *The Unquiet Bed* (1967), *Collected Poems* (1972), and *The Phases of Love* (1982), seemed to become more youthful and accomplished as she grew older, revealing a sensitive, understanding mind.

Raymond Souster (1921–) Louis Dudek (1918–), and Irving Layton (1912–) criticized materialist Canadian society. Using colorful, earthy language, the Romanian-born Layton attacked smugly complacent middle-class morality in *The Laughing Rooster* (1964) and *Periods of the Moon* (1967). A selection of his verse was published in 1977. Also important were Patricia K. Page (1916–), interested in psychology, the neoromantic Anne Wilkinson (1910–61), and Miriam Waddington (1917–), who emphasized the beneficence of nature.

Margaret Avison (1918–), in *Winter Sun* (1960) and *The Dumbfounding* (1966), lyrically expressed her Christian faith. Leonard Cohen (1934–) wrote emotionally of his own love and art and of 20th-century evil. Margaret Atwood (1939–) explored the anxieties accompanying poetic self-realization. Other noteworthy figures were Al Purdy (1918– ; *The Stone Bird,* 1981), Phyllis Webb (1927–), Alden Nowlan (1933–83), and experimental aural and oral poets Bill Bissett (1939–) and B. P. Nichol (1944–).

Robertson Davies Viking Press–Jill Krementz

Margaret Atwood John Reeves

Prose. Major novelists of the 1950s included Ernest Buckler (1908–84), whose *Mountain and the Valley* (1952) concerns frustrated artists in Nova Scotia, and Ethel Wilson (1890–1980), who wrote of women's self-fulfillment in *The Equations of Love* (1952) and *Swamp Angel* (1954), both set in British Columbia. Aspects of the Jewish experience are treated by Abraham Moses Klein in his novel *The Second Scroll* (1951), a modern search for Israel, and by Mordecai Richler in his satiric, antimaterialist *Apprenticeship of Duddy Kravitz* (1959).

According to many critics, the best novelists of the 1960s and 1970s were Robertson Davies (1913–) and Margaret Laurence. Davies moved from satirical novels and plays to Jungian psychological examination of oddly assorted characters in his *Deptford Trilogy: Fifth Business* (1970), *The Manticore* (1972), and *World of Wonders* (1975). His popularity continued with *The Rebel Angels* (1982) and *What's Bred in the Bone* (1985). Laurence's writing is distinguished by penetrating characterizations and fine technique. In *The Stone Angel* (1964), *A Jest of God* (1966), and *The Diviners* (1974), she traces a heroine's progress toward self-realization.

Other contemporary novelists produced more experimental works, such as *The Double Hook*

(1959) by Sheila Watson (1919-), *The Studhorse Man* (1969) by Robert Kroetsch (1927-), and *Bear* (1976) by Marian Engel (1933-85). Several poets turned to fiction, including Leonard Cohen, who wrote *The Favorite Game* (1963) and *Beautiful Losers* (1966), and Margaret Atwood. Her feminist outlook shapes her several novels, including *Surfacing* (1972), *Life before Man* (1979), *Bodily Harm* (1981), and *The Handmaid's Tale* (1986). Among writers of short stories are Alice Munro (1931-), Norman Levine (1924-), and Jane Rule (1931-). Mavis Gallant (1922-), although a longtime resident of France, appraises her native country clearly in *Home Truths: Selected Canadian Stories* (1981).

Farley Mowat (1921-) has written several very popular nonfiction books on Native Americans (*People of the Deer,* 1952), on the survival of endangered species (*Never Cry Wolf,* 1963, and *A Whale for the Killing,* 1972), and on problems of the Canadian North (*The Great Betrayal: Arctic Canada Now,* 1976). Mordecai Richler's nonfictional *Home Sweet Home: My Canadian Album* (1984) mingles autobiography and journalistic essays.

Drama has been slower to develop in a country of widely spaced small communities. In the mid-20th century, increased interest in drama was reflected in the establishment of theaters such as the repertory theater in Stratford, Ont.; the Shaw Festival in Niagara, Ont.; and the Vancouver Playhouse in British Columbia.

Two of the most noteworthy literary critics are George Woodcock (1912-) and Northrop Frye (1912-). Woodcock, a believer in social revolution, has written poetry, history, drama, and travel books in addition to criticism. Frye's *Anatomy of Criticism* (1957) is a highly influential study of English literary themes; he also wrote *The Bush Garden: Essays on the Canadian Imagination* (1971) and *The Great Code: The Bible and Literature* (1981). University of Toronto professor Marshall McLuhan received wide attention for his theory proclaiming that printed literature is being superseded by electronic means of mass communication. Somewhat ironically, his own book *The Medium Is the Massage* (1967) enjoyed a great vogue.

CANADIAN LITERATURE IN FRENCH

Until the mid-20th century Canadian literature in French focused primarily on religion, Canadian history, and patriotism. Since then it has become more involved in the concerns of contemporary Western society.

Colonial Period. The earliest Canadian works in French were written by 16th- and 17th-century explorers and missionaries. Particularly informative are the accounts of the 1534-35 voyage of Jacques Cartier and Samuel de Champlain's *Voyages de la Nouvelle France occidentale, dicte Canada* (Voyages in Western New France, called Canada, 2 vol., 1632) and *Les relations des Jésuites* (Jesuit Reports, 1632-73), annual reports of Jesuit missionaries about their lives among the Indians. Letters by the Ursuline nun Marie de l'Incarnation (1599-1672) are filled with details of life in New France.

19th Century. Resentment of the English conquest, intensified by the Union Act of 1840 and Confederation in 1867, strengthened a deep sense of French-Canadian patriotism. It affected the first novelists, P. I. F. Aubert de Gaspé (1814-41), who filled his *Influence d'un livre* (Influence of a Book, 1837) with Québec folklore, and P. J. O. Chauveau (1820-90), who described the decline of French Canada after the conquest in *Charles Guérin* (1852). It found its classic expression in the *Histoire du Canada* (1845-48), written by François Xavier Garneau (1809-66) to disprove Governor-General Lord Durham's statement that French Canada had neither a history nor a literature.

Taking Garneau as their prophet, poets, novelists, historians, and journalists met at the Québec city bookshop of Octave Crémazie. At its height in the 1860s, this Québec group set the style for oratorical patriotic works, modeled on French romantic poetry, that dominated French-Canadian literature for the rest of the century. Crémazie, considered the father of French-Canadian poetry,

Philippe Joseph Aubert de Gaspé, author of the 19th-century classic Les anciens Canadiens.

Public Archives Canada—PA-74099

influenced the younger poet Louis Honoré Fréchette, who based his *Légenae d'un peuple* (1887) on French-Canadian history. Pamphile Lemay (1837-1918), author of *Les gouttelettes* (1904), and William Chapman (1850-1917) in *Les rayons du nord* (The Northern Lights, 1910) vividly recreated rural Québec life in poetic form.

Also prominent in the Québec group was Abbé Henri Raymond Casgrain, who wrote *Légendes canadiennes* (1861), literary criticism, and histories such as *Montcalm et Lévis* (1891; *Wolfe and Montcalm,* 1964). Joseph Charles Tache (1820-94) told tales of lumbermen and trappers in *Forestiers et voyageurs* (1884), and Antoine Gérin-Lajoie (1824-82) tried to discourage French-Canadian emigration in the propaganda novel *Jean Rivard: le defricheur* (Jean Rivard: the Settler, 1862). Other novelists wrote historical romances set in New France; they include Napoléon Bourassa (1827-1916) and Philippe Joseph Aubert de Gaspé (1786-1871), whose *Anciens canadiens* (1863) became a classic.

Early 20th Century. French-Canadian life continued to be a major theme in early 20th-century literature through the *terroir* ("country"), or regionalist, school, which stressed the bonds between the habitant, or farmer, and the ancestral land. One of the best *terroir* poets was Nérée Beauchemin (1850-1931), whose *Floraisons matutinales* (Morning Efflorescence, 1897) and *Patrie intime* (Intimate Birthplace, 1928) express his devotion to Québec. Among *terroir* novelists were Ernest Choquette (1862-1941), Harry Bernard (1898-), and especially French-born Louis Hemon, who lived with a habitant family in order to write *Maria Chapdelaine* (1914; trans. 1934). Abbé Lionel Adolphe Groulx (1878-1967) vehemently expressed his patriotism in *Vers L'émancipation* (Towards Emancipation, 1921) and *Histoire du Canada Français . . .* (2 vol., 1962).

The Montréal school of poets, which flourished in Montreal between 1895 and 1930, was influenced by French Parnassians and symbolists; its members emphasized aesthetics and technique. Particularly original and sensuous was the work of Émile Nelligan (1879-1941) before he lost his reason at the age of 20. Paul Morin (1889-1963) drew on his Mediterranean travels for the vivid, technically complex *Paon d'émail* (Enamel Peacock, 1911) and *Poèmes de cendre el d'or* (Poems of Ashes and Gold, 1922). Also noteworthy are the nostalgic lyrics of the lapsed Jesuit Louis Dantin (pseudonym of Eugène Seers, 1865-1945) and the reflective works of Albert Lozeau (1878-1924) and Jean Charbonneau (1875-1960).

As a result of urbanization, the Great Depression, and World War II, the proud cultural isolation of French Canada began to break down, and writers became more introspective, realistic, and innovative. The poets Hector de Saint-Denys-Garneau (1912-43), François Hertel (pseudonym of Rodolphe Dubé, 1905-), and Alain Grandbois (1900-75) experimented with free verse and symbolism to express philosophical abstractions and awareness of death. The novelist Albert Laberge (1871-1960) had already subjected Québec tradition to harsh realism in *La scouine* (1918; *Bitter Bread,* 1977). That culture was further criticized and exposed by Claude Henri Grignon (1894-) in *Un homme et son peché* (A Man and His Sin, 1933), Jean Charles Harvey (1891-1967) in *Les demi-civilisés* (1934; *Sackcloth for Barner,* 1938), and Ringuet (pseudonym of Philippe Panneton, 1895-1960) in *Trente arpents* (1938; *Thirty Acres,* 1940).

Late 20th Century. After World War II and especially in the nationalist 1960s, new writers appeared, writing in many different modes with great technical skill.

A poet of major stature was Anne Hébert, whose surrealist, symbolist works such as *Les songes en équilibre* (Dreams in Equilibrium, 1942) and *Le tombeau des rois* (The Tomb of Kings, 1953) concerned mental anguish, solitude, and death. Pierre Trottier (1925-) in *Le combat contre Tristan* (The Battle Against Tristan; 1951) presented a tragic drama of love and death that evoked the troubled disunity of Canada. Also criticizing or lamenting the modern world were Paul Marie Lapointe (1929-), Gatien Lapointe (1931-), and Fernand Ouellette (1930-). Among other notable poets was Jacques Poulin (1937-), author of the experimental "novel-poem" *Coeur de la baleine bleue* (Heart of the Blue Whale, 1970).

Many novelists turned to social satire. In *Bonheur d'occasion* (1945; *The Tin Flute,* 1947) and *Alexandre Chenevert* (1954; *The Cashier,* 1955), Gabrielle Roy (1909-83) described the disturbing effect of industrialization and the city on human dignity, suggesting that such pressures may be withstood by cultivating compassion and love. *La détresse et l'enchantement* (Distress and Enchantment), the first volume of her autobiography, was published posthumously in 1984. Roger Lemelin (1919-) wrote of urban workingclass life in *Les Plouffe* (1948; *The Plouffe Family,* 1948). This seemingly benign satire, popular in both French- and English-speaking Canada, was made into a film in 1982. Germaine Guèvremont (1900-68), on the other hand, realistically depicted rural life. The prolific writer Yves Thériault

Marie Claire Blais Culver Pictures

(1916–83), as well as Gerard Bessette (1920–), and Jean Simard (1916–), criticized the puritanical attitudes and other negative aspects of French-Canadian culture.

Other novelists were concerned with human inner nature. André Giroux (1916–) and Robert Élie (1915–) expressed some confidence in the human spirit. Particularly sensitive is *Poussière sur la ville* (1953; *Dust over the City,* 1955), a study of despair, by André Langevin (1927–). The French Jewish immigrant Monique Bosco (1927–) wrote of postwar rootlessness in *Un amour maladroit* (An Awkward Love, 1961), and the symbolist Hubert Aquin (1929–77) concluded the impossibility of freedom in *Prochain episode* (The Next Installment, 1965). One of the most devastating psychological novels is *Une saison dans la vie d'Emmanuel* (1965; *A Season in the Life of Emmanuel,* 1966) by Marie Claire Blais. Also notable is *L'avalée des avalés* (1966; *The Swallower Swallowed,* 1968) by Rejean Ducharme (1942–). Reflecting French-Canadian nationalism, Michel Tremblay (1942–) used the Montréal vernacular in dramas, which, in translation, were also enjoyed by English audiences. His first play was *Les belles-soeurs* (The Sisters-in-law, 1973). D.G.S.

For further information on this topic, see the Bibliography in volume 28, section 834.

CANADIAN SHIELD *or* **LAURENTIAN PLATEAU,** vast horseshoe-shaped geologic or physiographic region, composed mainly of granitic and metamorphic Precambrian rocks, the deeply eroded roots of ancient mountains, located primarily in central and eastern Canada and also including small parts of the northern U.S. The oldest part of the North American crustal plate, its rocks contain some of the earliest forms of life on earth—fossils of algae and bacteria over 2 billion years old. The shield extends in a great semicircle around Hudson Bay, ranging from the Arctic coast north of Great Bear Lake in the Northwest Territories to northern Québec Province and Labrador. It covers about 4.4 million sq km (about 1.7 million sq mi) and occupies almost one-half of Canada's total area. In the U.S. it includes the Superior Upland of northern Minnesota, northern Wisconsin, and northern Michigan and the Adirondack Mountains of northeastern New York.

During the most recent of the Ice Ages (q.v.), beginning about 2 million years ago, continental ice sheets covered the region, stripping away soil, depositing glacial drift, and creating many lake basins and riverbeds. Present-day elevations in the shield are mostly between 300 and 600 m (984 and 1969 ft), except in limited areas, such as the Québec-Labrador Peninsula, where they rise about 1070 m (about 3510 ft). The shield has a poorly integrated drainage system.

The climate is arctic in the northern shield, where the mean January temperature is about −32° C (−25° F), the growing season is less than 40 days a year, and lakes are free of ice for only about three months annually. Permanently frozen subsoil is continuous northwest of Hudson Bay and is sporadic east of it. The more temperate southern shield has forests of pine and northern hardwoods. Such vegetation gives way northward to open tundra carpeted with sedges, grasses, lichens, and dwarf shrubs. Muskegs, swamps, and lakes are found throughout the shield area.

The northern Canadian Shield is sparsely populated, mainly by Inuit (Eskimo) and Indians, but the southern shield has numerous urban areas, which have developed principally as centers for exploiting natural resources. The southern shield is Canada's main source of metallic minerals, hydroelectricity, and pulpwood. Minerals recovered include iron, nickel, copper, zinc, uranium, gold, silver, platinum, and molybdenum. Many of the mines are located south of James Bay.

CANAL, artificial waterway constructed for purposes of irrigation, drainage (qq.v.), or navigation, or in connection with a hydroelectric dam. This article deals only with navigational waterways, which are generally of two kinds: ship canals, which are deep enough to accommodate oceangoing vessels, and shallower canals used mainly by barges.

Construction. Canal construction consists chiefly of opencut excavation with ordinary power tools and construction machinery. The sides of the cut are often faced with masonry to prevent erosion of the banks by the wash of passing vessels and the subsequent blocking of the channel by a buildup of silt.

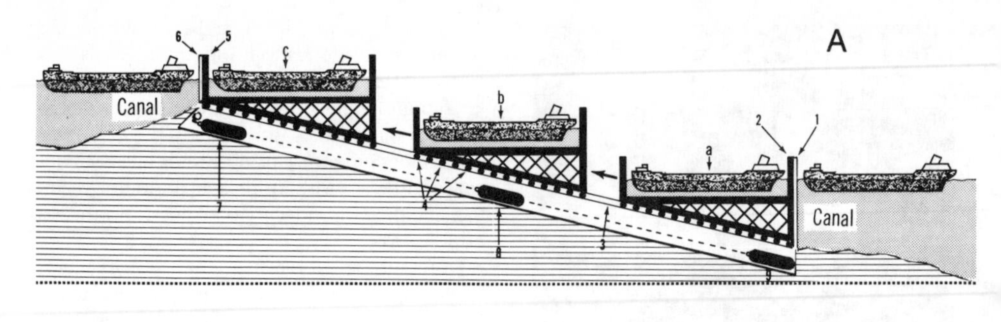

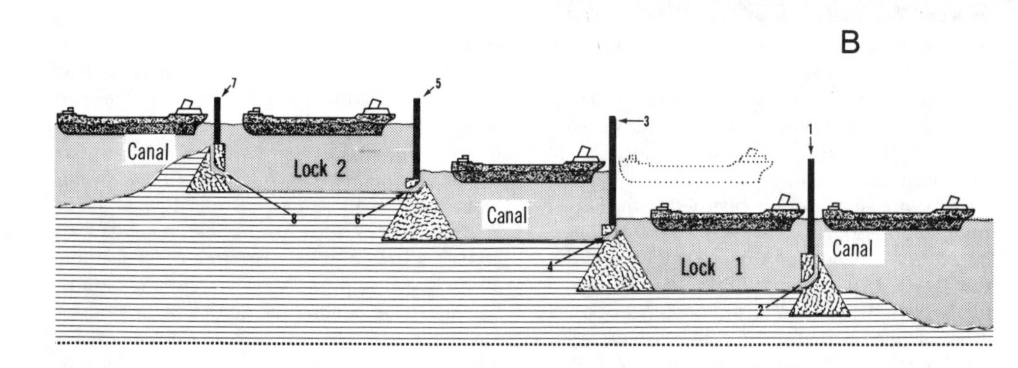

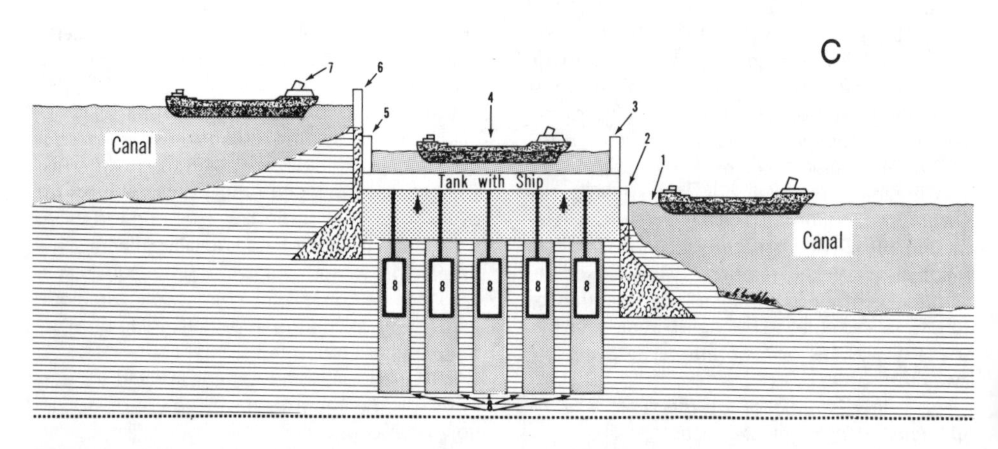

Types of canal. Part A, Incline: A ship traveling along a canal reaches the downstream side of the incline. The lower gate (1) and the incline tank gate (2) open to admit the ship. With the ship in the tank (a) and the gates closed, the tank begins traveling up the railroad rails (3) of the incline to the middle level (b), riding on steel wheels (4). At the upper level (c), the tank gate (5) and the incline gate (6) open and the ship enters the upper canal. The tank containing the ship is pulled up the incline by counterweights weighing up to 4000 tons. The counterweight is at the top of the incline (7) when the tank is in the lower position, at the middle of the incline (8) when the tank is halfway up or down, and at the lower end (9) when the tank is at the upper level. Part B, Locks: A ship moving through a canal reaches a lock. The lock gate (1) opens to admit the ship. A valve (4) opens and water flows into the lock, raising the ship to the level of the upper canal. The upper lock gate (3) opens and the ship moves out into the next canal section. The lower valve (2) opens to let water run out of the lock. The ship reaches Lock 2. The lower gate (5) opens to admit the ship, and the outlet valve (6) closes. The upper gate (7) opens to admit the ship into the next section of the canal after the valve (8) has opened and water has run into the lock to raise the ship to the next level. Part C, Hydraulic Lift: A ship sailing up a canal (1) reaches the hydraulic lift. The gate (2) and the lift tank gate (3) open to admit the ship, after which both gates close. The lift tank (4), shown midway between lower and higher canal sections, rises straight up until it reaches the level of the upper canal section, whereupon the tank gate (5) and the lift gate (6) open and the ship sails into the canal (7). Hydraulic lifts (8) raise and lower the tank.

Unlike roads and railways, canals cannot be made to conform to irregularities in terrain, but must consist of one or more level stretches, or reaches. Where reaches of different levels meet, vessels are transferred from one reach to the next usually by means of locks. A lock is a walled section of the channel, closed by water gates at both ends, in which the water level can be raised or lowered by means of valves or sluiceways to match the level in the upper or lower reach, as desired; when the levels are the same, the corresponding water gate is opened to permit a vessel to enter or leave the lock.

Other devices sometimes used to raise and lower small vessels are inclines and lifts. Inclines are paved or railed ramps over which vessels are hauled from one reach to the other by means of cables. In a lift the vessel is floated into a movable tank from one reach, water gates are closed, and the tank with the floating vessel is raised or lowered to the level of the next reach.

Locks, which are used in most multilevel canals, have certain disadvantages; frequently they are uneconomic because of the expense of construction and operation. Also, when traffic is heavy, the supply of water for the highest reach is difficult to maintain; in addition to the natural current flow, a lockful of water is lost from the upper reach in each locking operation. Consequently, to avoid construction of locks, canals are sometimes carried across depressions on embankments, over rivers on aqueducts, and through mountains in tunnels.

History. Canals date from a period long before the Christian era and served as means of navigation and communication for the Assyrians, Egyptians, Hindus, and Chinese. The remains of a canal near Mandali, Iraq, date from about 4000 BC; the 1782-km-long (1107-mi-long) Grand Canal of China, connecting Tianjin City (Tientsin) and Hangzhou (Hangchow), was begun in the 6th century BC (completed AD 1327) and is still in use. The lock was invented in Europe in the late 15th century. Several important French canals were built in the 17th century, including the Brière, Orléans, and Languedoc canals. During the 18th century in Russia a great system of canals connecting Saint Petersburg (now Leningrad) with the Caspian Sea was built. The Göta (q.v.) Canal, a 386-km-long (240-mi-long) system of lakes, rivers, and canals, about 87 km (about 54 mi) of which can accommodate oceangoing vessels, connects Stockholm and Göteborg and was completed in 1832; the Ludwig Canal, joining the Danube with the Main and Rhine rivers and totaling about 177 km (about 110 mi), was built in 1832. The Suez Canal (q.v.), opened in 1869, links the Mediterranean and Red seas. The Panama Canal (q.v.), first used in 1914, joins the Atlantic and Pacific oceans. In Germany the opening (1938) of the Mittelland Canal system (467 km/290 mi long) completed the east-west link in a system of about 11,265 km (about 7000 mi) of inland waterways, extending from the Dortmund-Ems Canal east of the Rhine to the Elbe north of Magdeburg.

The first canal in England was completed in 1134, during the reign of King Henry I; it joined the Trent and Witham rivers. Canal building in Great Britain and Ireland flourished in the late 18th and early 19th centuries. Two of the most notable canals of that period are the Grand Canal in Ireland (begun 1756), which extends 134 km (83 mi) east-west between Dublin and the Irish town of Shannon Harbor on the Shannon River, and the Caledonian Canal (completed 1847), a 97.3-km-long (60.5-mi-long) waterway including 37 km (23 mi) of canals, across Scotland. The Manchester Ship Canal (opened 1894) opened Manchester Port to oceangoing vessels.

The Canadian canal system includes the Saint Lawrence River canals, the Ottawa River canals, the Chambly Canal, the Rideau Canal, and the Trent Canal. Of these the St. Lawrence system has long been the most important, because it provides a waterway 4.3 m (14 ft) deep from the head of Lake Superior to the Gulf of St. Lawrence. As part of the St. Lawrence Seaway project, completed in 1959, the waterway was deepened to 8.2 m (27 ft) to permit oceangoing vessels with drafts up to 7.8 m (25.5 ft) to sail from the Atlantic Ocean to such Great Lakes ports as Chicago and Duluth. *See* SAINT LAWRENCE SEAWAY.

The first navigation canal in the U.S was built around the rapids of the Connecticut River at South Hadley, Mass., in 1793. It had two levels connected by an incline, over which boats were transported in tanks filled with water and dragged by cables operated by waterpower. The construction of the Erie Canal (q.v.), started in 1817, marked the beginning of an era of canal building, which produced an aggregate of more than 7242 km (4500 mi) of canals (mostly in the Middle Atlantic and Central states) and was largely responsible for opening the American Midwest to settlement. Many of the early canals are no longer in active service, having been superseded by railroads and by modern, enlarged waterways. These include the Mississippi River system, which is navigable for 2956 km (1837 mi) and has 30 locks and dams; the Illinois Waterway, which links Lake Michigan with the Mississippi River; the 1579-km (981-mi) Ohio River waterway system, extending from Pittsburgh, Pa., to the Mississippi River; and the New York State Barge Canal System (q.v.), a principal section of which connects Lake Erie with the Hudson River. The intracoastal waterways along the Atlantic and Gulf coasts are an important part of the inland-waterway system of the U.S., which in the late 1960s totaled 40,845 km (25,380 mi).

Barge Canals. On most large canals barges are pushed or pulled by tugboats and towboats; one towboat may pull as many as 40 barges lashed together. Modern barges are designed to carry specific types of cargo. Open-hopper barges carry coal, gravel, and large equipment; covered dry-cargo barges are used for grain, dry chemicals, and other commodities that must be kept dry; tank barges carry petroleum and liquid chemicals. On some European canals barges are towed in trains of two or more by gasoline- or diesel-powered tractors running on a towpath beside the canal. In certain areas men and draft animals are still used for haulage.

River Canalization. Formerly, when important rivers were found to be unnavigable at certain points, shallow side canals running parallel to the river were built with pick and shovel so that vessels could bypass that part of the river and reenter it at a more suitable point. With the advent of power machinery, this practice has been largely discarded in favor of canalization of the river itself; that is, a river may be dredged at unnavigable points and provided with dams and bypass locks that control the level of the river from end to end. Construction of 40 locks and dams on the Ohio River was completed in 1929; redevelopment, begun in 1955 to replace the present system with 18 high-lift locks, was completed in 1981. Canalization of the upper Mississippi River from Minneapolis, Minn., to Alton, Ill. (just above Saint Louis, Mo.), was completed in 1939–40. In May 1954, the U.S. Congress authorized the federal government to join with Canada in the construction of the St. Lawrence Seaway; as its share of the project, the U.S. built two canals, three locks, and various other improvements along the St. Lawrence River from Montréal, Qué., to Ogdensburg, N.Y. Canalization of the Arkansas River, which includes 13 locks and dams and a 14-km (9-mi) canal linking the Arkansas to the White and Mississippi rivers, opened the river to navigation to Catoosa, Okla., in 1970. The Tennessee-Tombigbee Waterway, a 407-km-long (253-mi-long) project that was completed in 1984, includes five dams, ten locks, and a 72-km-long (45-mi-long) canal linking the two rivers in Alabama, Mississippi, and Tennessee.

See also DAM; INTRACOASTAL WATERWAY; SHIPPING INDUSTRY.

Ship Canals. Ship canals are generally of two kinds: those that connect two lakes or oceans, such as the Suez Canal and the Panama Canal, and those that link an inland port to the ocean, such as the Manchester Ship Canal and the Houston Ship Channel. The accompanying table includes the major ship canals of the world.

For further information on this topic, see the Bibliography in volume 28, sections 334, 563.

MAJOR SHIP CANALS OF THE WORLD

Name and Location	Length (km/mi)	Year Opened
Baltic-White Sea, USSR	226.91/141.00	1933
Suez, Egypt	162.13/100.76	1869
Albert, Belgium	130.36/81.00	1939
Moscow-Volga, USSR	128.75/80.00	1937
Nord-Ostsee, Germany	96.56/60.00	1895
Göta, Sweden	86.91/54.00	1832
Panama, Panama	81.63/50.72	1914
Houston Ship, U.S.	80.47/50.00	1914
Amsterdam-Rhine, Netherlands	62.76/39.00	1947
Manchester Ship, England	57.13/35.50	1894
Chicago Sanitary & Ship, U.S.	48.28/30.00	1900
Welland Ship, Canada*	44.42/27.60	1932
Juliana, Netherlands	33.80/21.00	1934
Chesapeake-Delaware, U.S.	30.58/19.00	1829
North Sea-Amsterdam, Netherlands	28.97/18.00	1876
Cape Cod, U.S.	28.16/17.50	1914
Kronshtadt-Leningrad, USSR	27.36/17.00	1885
Lake Washington Ship, U.S.	12.88/8.00	1916
New Orleans Industrial, U.S.	9.66/6.00	1923
Sault Ste. Marie (N.), U.S.	2.57/1.60	1919
Sault Ste. Marie, Canada	2.09/1.30	1895

*Reconstructed from the old Welland Canal, which was originally completed in 1833.

CANALETTO, real name GIOVANNI ANTONIO CANAL (1697–1768), Italian painter, known for his sparkling views of Venice. He was born in Venice on Oct. 28, 1697, and died there on April 19, 1768. Canaletto received instruction in painting and perspective from his father, a scene designer in the high baroque tradition. He took as his specialty the relatively new and rare form of painting, the city view (*veduta*). His principal patrons were English aristocrats on the Grand Tour, for whom his scenes were souvenirs of the sights of Venice—the Grand Canal, the basin of Saint Mark's, plus innumerable scenes of regattas and water festivals, such as the annual celebration of the Marriage of Venice to the Sea.

Canaletto's technique had the traditional Venetian hallmarks of luminous light and glowing color, to which he added a Dutch-influenced attention to clear and accurate detail. His early works often feature dark, saturated colors that

The Piazzetta, *an oil painting by Antonio Canaletto.*
Metropolitan Museum of Art–Kennedy Fund

depict a moist, palpable atmosphere under a stormy or dark sky. Later works—after 1740, when Canaletto began to develop a somewhat looser, less precise style of brushwork—often portray bright sunlit scenes with rich colors highlighted by red and gold. He went to England in 1746 after the War of the Austrian Succession had drastically curtailed the stream of English visitors to Venice. He painted many scenes of English landscapes and country houses before returning to Venice in 1755. Canaletto was elected to the Venice Academy in 1763, but the paintings of his later years were increasingly criticized for their facile manner and mechanical repetition of overly familiar themes. The atmospheric quality of his best works was an important influence on 19th-century landscape painting.

CANAL ZONE. *See* PANAMA CANAL ZONE.

CANARY, common name for a small finch, *Serinus canarius,* native to the Azores, Madeira, and the Canary and Cape Verde islands. It is bred as a cage bird throughout the world. In its wild state, the canary builds its nest of moss, feathers, or hair in thick, bushy, high shrubs or trees and produces from two to four broods in a season; its plumage is olive green or greenish yellow, tinged with brown. The birds produced by selective breeding are predominantly yellow. In confinement the canary often breeds three or four times a year, laying from four to six pale blue eggs in each clutch. The canary can be taught various notes or series of notes, which it in turn will teach to its young. Many varieties of canaries have been produced by selective scientific breeding. Particularly noted as a songbird is the Harz Mountain canary, bred in Germany.

Some canaries are bred for beauty and trained to perch in a manner that will best display their attractiveness. These ornamental species include the crested Norwich; the Scotch fancy, a slender bird with high-arched shoulders; and the Manchester, a show variety noted for its size.

Canary songs consist of bass and flute notes, as well as "bell" and "bubbling water" sounds. The songs are classified as either "roller" or "chopper." The roller song is soft and is sung with a nearly closed beak. The chopper song is loud, natural, and produced with an open beak; distinct "chop-chop" sounds are heard. Some breeds of canary sing a warblerlike song combining both types.

CANARY GRASS, common name for an annual grass, *Phalaris canariensis,* of the grass family (Gramineae), native to the Temperate Zones of Europe and the U.S. (*see* GRASSES). The grass is frequently cultivated commercially for the seeds,

Canary, Serinus canarius, *a popular cage bird.*
Jeanne White–National Audubon Society

Aerial view of Las Palmas, Canary Islands.
Spanish National Tourist Office

which are sold as birdseed. Canary grass grows to a height of 61 cm (24 in) and has slender leaves about 15 cm (about 6 in) long. The seeds are egg-shaped. Reed canary grass, *P. arudinacea,* particularly the variety *picta,* is cultivated in gardens and is called ribbon grass.

CANARY ISLANDS *or* **CANARIES** (Span. *Islas Canarias*), group of islands in the Atlantic Ocean, off the NW coast of Africa, comprising two Spanish provinces, Las Palmas and Santa Cruz de Tenerife. Their capitals are, respectively, Las Palmas on Grand Canary and Santa Cruz de Tenerife on Tenerife Island. The chief islands of the group, in descending order of size, are Tenerife; Fuerteventura, the nearest to the African mainland; Grand Canary (Gran Canaria); Lanzarote; La Palma; Gomera; and Hierro. In addition, several barren islets are included in the group.

The islands are of volcanic origin. Of the volcanic peaks the highest is the dormant Pico de Teide, or Pico de Tenerife (3710 m/12,172 ft). The Canaries are noted for their scenery and mild, dry climate. Precipitation occurs mainly during the winter season. In areas below about 400 m (about 1310 ft) elevation, the vegetation is typically N African; characteristic varieties are the date palm, dragon tree, and cactus. Growing at higher levels are laurels, holly, myrtle, eucalyptus, pine, and a variety of other types of flowering plants.

Farming and fishing are the principal industries. The volcanic soil of the Canaries is extremely fertile. The islands have no rivers, however, and severe droughts are common; artificial irrigation is therefore a necessity in most cultivable areas. Among important crops are bananas, citrus fruits, sugarcane, peaches, figs, wine grapes, grain, tomatoes, onions, and potatoes. Manufactured products include textiles and fine embroideries. Tourism is also important, and the islands are a popular winter-resort area.

In the view of some authorities the Canaries are the Fortunatae Insulae of antiquity. The islands were probably known to the Phoenicians and Carthaginians. As described by the Roman scholar Pliny, large numbers of wild dogs (Lat. *canes*), roamed the islands, which he therefore named Canaria. Arab mariners reached the group in the 12th century, and it was visited in 1334 by French navigators. Pope Clement VI awarded the islands to Castile in 1344. The French mariner Jean de Bethéncourt (c. 1360–c.1422) began the conquest of the islands in 1402 and was made king of the Canaries in 1404 by the Castilian ruler Henry III. Claimed by Portugal, the islands were recognized as Spanish possessions by a treaty negotiated in 1479. Spanish conquest of the islands was completed by the late 1490s. The indigenous population, the Guanche, a Berber people, eventually became extinct.

In 1927 the Canaries, previously a single province of Spain, were divided into two provinces. Area, 7273 sq km (2808 sq mi); pop. (1981) 1,444,626.

For further information on this topic, see the Bibliography in volume 28, section 968.

CANASTA, variant of rummy, played with a pack made up of two regular 52-card decks and 4 jokers. In the U.S. it was for a time one of the most popular card games. Of Uruguayan or possibly Argentine origin, canasta apparently was devised to provide a common meeting ground between poker and rummy devotees. As in all rummy games, the grouping of cards into melds is the main feature of canasta; but, unlike other games of this family, its object is not to match up cards as quickly as possible, but to build up melds of 7 like cards, called canastas, because such cards have a high scoring value. In the two-handed games each player receives 15 cards, dealt one at a time alternately; in the partnership game hands of 11 cards are distributed in clockwise rotation. The remainder of the pack is placed face down in the center of the table to form a drawing stock, with the top card turned faceup alongside to begin a discard pile. If this top card is an ace, deuce, joker, or three, other cards must be turned until a card of any denomination from king to four appears.

Melds in canasta are restricted to sets of cards of the same denominations, and sequences are not played. Melds may start with three or four of a kind and may be added to as play progresses, players building always on their own and never on the melds of an opponent. However, melds must contain at least two natural cards and not more than three wild cards, which consist of the deuces and jokers. The bonus for "going out" by matching the hand completely is small compared to the premiums for establishing canastas.

The playing rules of canasta are more complicated than those of other rummy games. Like all rummy games, however, canasta lends itself to numerous variations.

CANBERRA, city, capital of Australia, in SE Australia, in the Australian Capital Territory. It is a rapidly expanding city of modern design located on the Molonglo R. (a tributary of the Murrumbidgee R.) in a predominantly agricultural region. It is built around the artificial Lake Burley Griffin and is the economic center for the nearby communities of Woden-Weston Creek, Belconnen, and Queanbeyan. The government is the chief employer in Canberra, but tourism and light-manufacturing industries are growing. Major landmarks include Parliament House, the Church of Saint John the Baptist (1840s), Captain Cook Memorial Water Jet (in Lake Burley Griffin), the Australian War Memorial (a museum and art gallery devoted to the wars in which Australia has participated), the National Library, and the civic center. Major educational institutions and academic organizations in Canberra are the Australian National University (1946), Canberra College of Advanced Education (1967), Canberra School of Music (1965), the Australian Academy of Science (1954), and the Australian Academy of the Humanities (1969). Mt. Stromlo and Siding Spring observatories also are here.

The site of Canberra was settled by whites in 1824, and in 1908 the sparsely populated area was chosen the capital of Australia. Construction of a new city, designed by the American architect Walter Burley Griffin (1876–1937), was begun in 1913, when Canberra officially became the capital. Building was interrupted by World War I, and only in 1927 was the national parliament moved here from Melbourne (the temporary capital until 1913). Canberra's population grew rapidly following World War II. Pop. (1986, greater city) 248,441.

CANCAN, French dance in $\frac{4}{4}$ time, derived from the quadrille and noted for high kicking and suggestive bodily movements. The cancan, danced by women, became popular in the music halls of Paris about 1840. It was considered vulgar. The name of the dance is derived from the French word *cancan* ("scandal"). The French composer Jacques Offenbach wrote a well-known cancan melody for his light opera, *Orpheus in the Underworld* (1858), and the French painter Henri de

Moulin Rouge (1891), the first poster designed by Henri Toulouse-Lautrec, advertises the cancan at the famous nightclub in Montmartre, the Bohemian section of Paris. Museum of Modern Art

Toulouse-Lautrec produced several notable paintings of cancan dancers.

CANCER (Lat., "crab"), in astronomy and astrology, the fourth constellation of stars or sign of the zodiac in the ecliptic, the apparent annual path of the sun through the stars. The name is derived from a Greek myth about a crab who fought the Greek hero Heracles (better known by his Roman name, Hercules) as he attacked the Hydra, a many-headed monster. The ancient Greeks discovered that the sun entered Cancer at the summer solstice, at which time the sun is 23°27′ N. For this reason that parallel of latitude was called the tropic of Cancer. A loose cluster of more than 300 faint stars, known as Praesepe or the Beehive, is a feature of the constellation.

CANCER, new growth of tissue resulting from a continuing proliferation of abnormal cells that have the ability to invade and destroy other tissues. Cancer, which may arise from any type of cell and in any body tissue, is not a single disease but a large number of diseases classified according to the tissue and type of cell of origin. Several hundred such classes exist, constituting three major subtypes:

· *Sarcomas* arise from connective and supportive tissue, such as bone, cartilage, nerve, blood vessel, muscle, and fat.

· *Carcinomas,* which include the most frequently occurring forms of human cancer, arise from epithelial tissue, such as the skin and the lining of the body cavities and organs, and the glandular tissue of the breast and prostate. Carcinomas with a structure resembling skin are termed squamous cell carcinomas. Those that resemble glandular tissue are called adenocarcinomas.

· *Leukemias* and *lymphomas* include the cancers that involve blood-forming tissue and are typified by the enlargement of the lymph nodes, the invasion of the spleen and bone marrow, and the overproduction of immature white cells.

NATURE OF THE DISEASE

A cancerous growth, or neoplasm, is clonal; that is, all its cells are descendants of a single cell. These cells have escaped the control of the normal forces regulating cellular growth. Resembling embryonic cells, they are unable to differentiate or mature into an adult, functioning state. As these cells multiply, they may form a mass, called a tumor (q.v.), which enlarges and continues to grow without regard to the function of the tissue of origin.

Tumors. Almost all cancers form tumors, but not all tumors are cancerous, or malignant; the greatest number are benign. Benign tumors are characterized by entirely localized growth and are usually separated from neighboring tissue by a surrounding capsule. Benign tumors generally grow slowly, and in structure closely resemble the tissue of origin. In some instances they may endanger the patient by obstructing, compressing, or displacing neighboring structures, as in the brain. A few benign tumors, such as polyps of the colon, may be precancerous.

Invasion and Spreading. The most significant attribute of malignant tumors is their ability to spread beyond the site of origin. Cancer may invade neighboring tissues by direct extension or infiltration or may disseminate to distant sites, forming secondary growths known as metastases. The routes and sites of metastases vary with different primary cancers: (1) When a cancer extends through the surface of the organ of origin into a cavity, cells may break away from the surface and implant on the surface of adjacent organs. (2) Tumor cells may migrate into the lymphatic channels and be carried to the draining lymph nodes, or they may penetrate the blood vessels. Once in the bloodstream the tumor cells are carried to the point at which the vessels become too small for the large tumor cells to pass. Cells from tumors of the gastrointestinal tract will be stopped in the liver. Later they may go on to the lungs. Cells from all other tumors will go to the lungs before being carried to other organs. The lungs and liver are therefore common sites of metastases. (3) Many cancers tend to shed cells into the bloodstream early in their course. Most such cells die in the bloodstream, but some lodge against the surface and penetrate the wall into the tissue. A few may find themselves in a favorable tissue in which they are able to survive and grow into a tumor, a metastasis. Others may divide only a few times, forming a small nest of cells that then remain dormant as a micrometastasis. They may remain dormant for many years, only to begin to grow again as recurrent cancer for reasons unknown.

Cancer cells, even when widely disseminated, may retain the physical and biological characteristics of their tissue of origin. Thus the pathologist can often determine the site of origin of metastatic tumors by microscopic examination of the cancerous tissue. Identification of tumors of endocrine glands is simplified because they may produce excessive amounts of the hormone elaborated by the parent tissue. Such tumors may also respond to administration of the hormones that normally control that tissue.

In general, the less closely a cancer resembles its tissue of origin, the more malignant and rapidly invasive it tends to be, but the rate of growth of a cancer depends not only on cellular type and

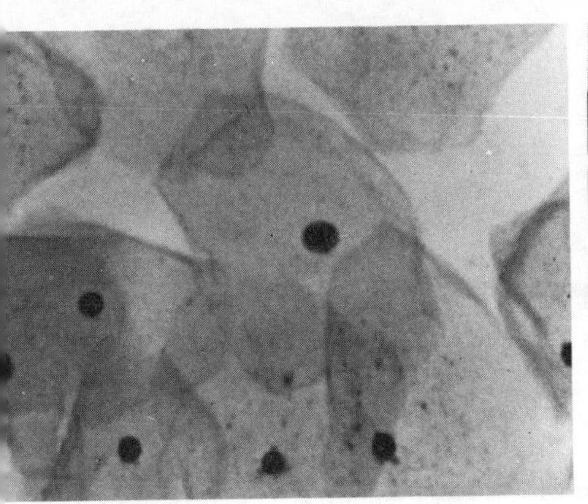

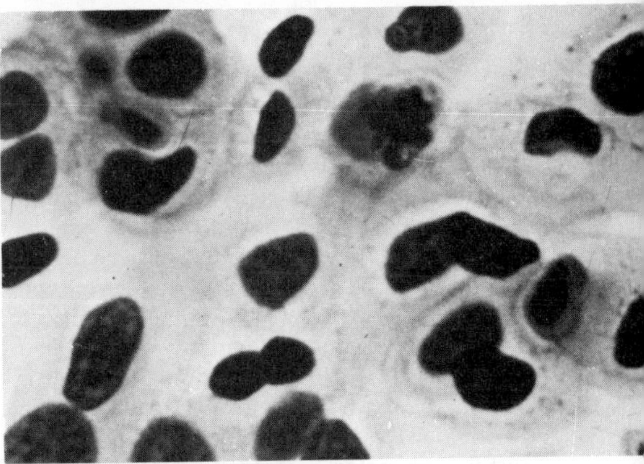

Left: A microscope reveals the structure of normal cells from the uterine cervix. Right: Cancerous cells from the cervix have a different appearance.

American Cancer Society

degree of undifferentiation, but also on various host factors. A characteristic of malignancy is tumor cell heterogeneity. Because of the abnormalities of proliferation in tumor cells, they are more susceptible to mutation. With time a tumor tends to become less differentiated and to grow more rapidly. It may also develop increased resistance to chemotherapy or irradiation.

CAUSES OF CANCER

A number of factors produce cancer in a proportion of exposed individuals (see Table 1). Among these factors are heredity, viruses, ionizing radiation, chemicals, and alterations in the immune system. For a long time these various factors seemed to work in different ways, but now researchers are studying how they might interact in a multifactorial, sequential process resulting in malignancy. Basically, cancer is a genetic process. Gene abnormalities may be inherited or they may be induced in a body cell by a virus or by damage from an outside source. Probably a series of sequential mutations eventually leads to a single cell that is malignant and proliferates as a clone. Originally it was thought that a malignant clone was completely abnormal and that the only way to cure cancer was to rid the body of all of the abnormal cells. Considerable evidence now indicates that the problem may be a loss of the ability of the cell to differentiate into its final, functioning state, perhaps because of the inability to produce a necessary factor.

Heredity Factors. It is estimated that no more than 20 percent of cancers are based on inheritance. Several types of cancer, however, do run in families. Breast cancer is one example. Cancer of the colon is more common in families with familial polyposis of the colon. A type of retinoblastoma has been demonstrated to occur only when a specific gene is deleted. In some hereditary disorders the chromosomes exhibit a high frequency of breakage; such diseases carry a high risk of cancer.

Viral Factors. Viruses are the cause of many cancers in animals. In humans the Epstein-Barr virus is associated with Burkitt's lymphoma and lymphoepitheliomas, the hepatitis virus with hepatocarcinoma, and a papilloma virus with carcinoma of the cervix. These viruses associated with human tumors are DNA viruses. The HTLV (q.v.) virus that produces a T-cell leukemia is an RNA virus, or retrovirus, as are most of the viruses associated with animal tumors. In the presence of an enzyme called reverse transcriptase, they induce the infected cell to make DNA copies of the virus's genes, which can be incorporated into the cell genome (the full complement of DNA). Such viruses may contain a gene, called a viral oncogene, capable of transforming normal cells into malignant cells. Research indicates that each viral oncogene has a counterpart in the normal human cell called a proto-oncogene, or cellular oncogene. Oncogene gene products (proteins for which they code) have been identified as growth factors or proteins necessary for the action of growth factors. They are therefore importantly related to cell proliferation.

Radiation Factors. Ionizing radiation is a potent cause of cancer. Radiation induces changes in DNA, including chromosome breaks and transpositions, in which the broken-off ends of two chromosomes are exchanged. It acts as an initiator of carcinogenesis, inducing a change that progresses to cancer after a latent period of years. This delay provides opportunity for exposure to other factors.

Chemical Factors. The process by which chemical agents cause cancer has been extensively studied. Some chemicals act as initiators. Only a single exposure is required, but cancer does not follow until after a long latent period and after exposure to another agent that acts as a promotor. Initiators produce irreversible changes in DNA. Promotors do not change DNA, but they do increase synthesis of DNA and stimulate expression of genes. They have no effect if given before the initiator, only if given after the initiator and given repeatedly over a period of time. Tobacco smoke contains many chemical initiators and promotors. The promotor action of cigarettes is very important, and if smoking is stopped, the risk of lung cancer falls rapidly. Alcohol is an important promotor; chronic abuse greatly increases the risk of cancers known to be induced by other agents, such as lung cancer in smokers. Carcinogenetic chemicals also produce chromosome breaks and translocations. *See also* CARCINOGEN.

Immune System Factors. The immune system appears to be able to recognize malignant cells and stimulate the production of cells able to destroy them. An important factor in the development of cancer may be a disease or other damaging event leading to a state of immune deficiency. Such states are a consequence of AIDS (*see* ACQUIRED IMMUNE DEFICIENCY SYNDROME), inherited immune deficiency diseases, and the administration of immunosuppressive drugs.

Environmental Factors. It is estimated that about 80 percent of cancers may be caused by environmental factors. The best established cause is tobacco smoke, actively or passively inhaled, which is responsible for about 30 percent of all deaths from cancer in the U.S. Dietary factors may account for about 40 percent, but the causative relationship is not as clear, and the responsible constituents of the diet are not clearly defined. Obesity is a risk factor for a number of cancers, especially cancers of the breast, colon, uterus, and prostate. Dietary fat and low dietary fiber are associated with high incidence of colon cancer. Dietary fat and obesity, like alcohol, appear to act as promoters.

TABLE 1 CAUSES OF CANCER

Causes	Range of Plausible Estimates (percent of all cancer deaths in the U.S., 1981)
Tobacco	25–40
Alcohol	2–4
Diet	10–70
Food additives	<2
Reproduction and sexual behavior	1–13
Occupation	2–8
Pollution	<1–5
Industrial products	<1–2
Medicine and medical procedures	0.5–3
Geophysical factors	2–4
Infection	1–?

Source: Doll, R., and Peto, R., "The Causes of Cancer: Quantitative Estimates of Avoidable Risks of Cancer in the United States Today." *Journal of the National Cancer Institute* 66:1191–1308 (1981).

Killer T cells surround a large cancer cell. T cells, or T lymphocytes, both kill harmful cells directly and amplify or suppress the body's overall immune response. Defects in the immune system prevent the proper working of this normal surveillance mechanism and allow the malignant cells to escape and grow.

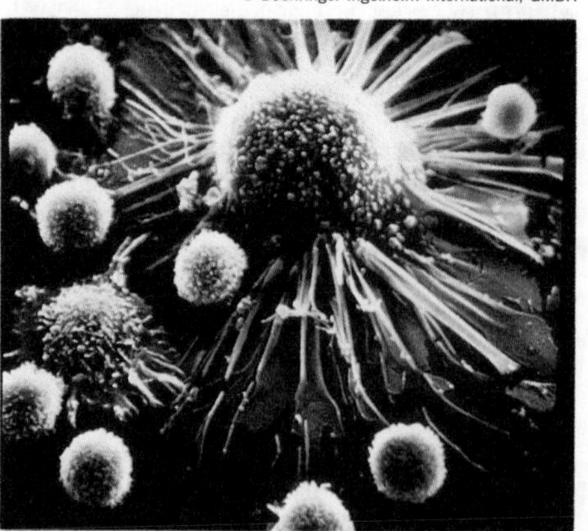

The Oncogene Factor. The common component that unites these seemingly disparate mechanisms may be the oncogene. Oncogenic viruses may insert their genes at many loci in the animal genome. A viral oncogene that is inserted in connection with a cellular oncogene influences the expression of the oncogene and induces cancer. Radiation and carcinogenetic chemicals produce DNA damage, mutations, and chromosome changes, and oncogenes are often located on the chromosome near the fragile site or breakpoint.

A malignancy appears to be the result of a series of mishaps beginning with an abnormal gene or a somatic mutation, probably more than one, followed by a promoting activity that stimulates the expression of one or more oncogenes, leading to the release of growth factors. Perhaps the earlier event leads to the loss of production of metabolites necessary for the normal differentiation of the cell. The stimulation of growth factors then causes the clone of undifferentiated cells to proliferate, and a defect in the immune system permits the abnormal cells to escape destruction by the normal surveillance mechanism.

OCCURRENCE

More than 1 million new cases of cancer occur in the U.S. each year. It is the second leading cause of death in the nation, accounting for about 500,000 deaths annually, and is the leading cause of death from disease in children between the ages of 1 and 14. The incidence of cancer varies enormously among different geographic areas. The age-adjusted death rate from all cancers in males is 310.9 per 100,000 in Luxembourg (the highest) as compared to 37.5 in El Salvador (the lowest). For women it is 175.2 in Denmark and 48.7 in El Salvador. The figures for the U.S. are 216.6 per 100,000 men and 136.5 per 100,000 women. For particular cancers the difference between countries may be as high as 40-fold. Evidence from studies of populations that have migrated from one geographic area to another suggests that these variations are due to differences in life-style rather than ethnic origin. This is consistent with other evidence that most cancers are predominantly related to environmental causes rather than heredity, although the two interact.

The cancers that cause the most deaths in the U.S. are lung cancer (first in each sex), colorectal cancer (second in both sexes combined), breast and uterine cancers in women, and prostate cancer in men. Together they account for more than 55 percent of all deaths from cancer. The most frequently occurring cancers are cancers of the skin, with over 500,000 cases per year, which, except for malignant melanoma, are not counted in the statistics.

Since 1949 cancer mortality in the U.S. has been higher among men than among women. The sex ratios of different cancers vary considerably. Cancer mortality is higher among blacks than whites for reasons that are not fully understood but are under intensive study.

DETECTION AND DIAGNOSIS

The earlier a cancer is diagnosed and treated, the greater the chance of cure. The regular screening of apparently healthy people has a high premium because it permits diagnosis before development of symptoms, when the cancer is most curable. The cancers for which excellent or reasonably good screening is available are among the major killers: breast, colon and rectum, uterus, and prostate.

Early diagnosis of cancers not susceptible to screening depends upon recognition of early signs of disease by the patient. The following is a list of the classic seven danger signals of cancer:

· Change in bowel or bladder habits
· A sore that does not heal
· Unusual bleeding or discharge
· Thickening or lump in breast or elsewhere
· Indigestion or difficulty in swallowing
· Obvious change in a wart or mole
· Nagging cough or hoarseness

TABLE 2 TRENDS IN SURVIVAL BY SITE OF CANCER, BY RACE
Cases Diagnosed in 1960-63, 1974-76, 1979-84

Site	White			Black		
	Relative 5-Year Survival			Relative 5-Year Survival		
	1960–63[1]	1974–76[2]	1979–84[2]	1960–63[1]	1974–76[2]	1979–84[2]
All Sites	39%	50%	50%	27%	38%	37%
Oral Cavity & Pharynx	45	54	54	—	35	31
Esophagus	4	5	7	1	4	5
Stomach	11	14	16*	8	15	17
Colon	43	50	54*	34	45	49
Rectum	38	48	52*	27	40	34
Liver	2	4	3	—	1	5
Pancreas	1	3	3	1	2	5
Larynx	53	66	66	—	58	55
Lung & Bronchus	8	12	13*	5	11	11
Melanoma of Skin	60	78	80*	—	62††	61†
Breast (females)	63	74	75*	46	62	62
Cervix Uteri	58	69	67	47	61	59
Corpus Uteri	73	89	83*	31	61	52*
Ovary	32	36	37*	32	41	36
Prostate Gland	50	67	73*	35	56	60*
Testis	63	78	91*	—	77†	82†
Urinary Bladder	53	73	77*	24	47	57*
Kidney & Renal Pelvis	37	51	51	38	49	53
Brain & Nervous System	18	22	23	19	27	31
Thyroid Gland	83	92	93	—	88	95
Hodgkin's Disease	40	71	74*	—	67†	69
Non-Hodgkin's Lymphoma	31	47	49*	—	47	49
Multiple Myeloma	12	24	24	—	28	29
Leukemia	14	34	32	—	30	27

Source: Surveillance and Operations Research Branch, National Cancer Institute/American Cancer Society (1989).
[1] Rates are based on End Results Group data from a series of hospital registries and one population-based registry.
[2] Rates are from the SEER Program. They are based on data from population-based registries in Connecticut, New Mexico, Utah, Iowa, Hawaii, Atlanta, Detroit, Seattle-Puget Sound and San Francisco-Oakland. Rates are based on follow-up of patients through 1985.
* The difference in rates between 1974–76 and 1979–84 is statistically significant ($p < .05$).
† The standard error of the survival rate is between 5 and 10 percentage points.
†† The standard error of the survival rate is greater than 10 percentage points.
– Valid survival rate could not be calculated.

Diagnostic study for cancer begins with a thorough history and physical examination, including inspection and palpation of all accessible sites, especially the skin, neck, breasts, abdomen, testicles, and lymph-node-bearing areas. It specifically includes examination of bodily orifices, particularly rectal examination for cancers of the rectum or prostate and pelvic examination for cancers of the cervix or body of the uterus.

Biopsy. The biopsy remains the only definitive method for the diagnosis of a cancer. It involves examination of a section of tissue removed from the tumor itself or from a metastasis. Modern technology has greatly reduced the need for open surgical biopsy. Guided by palpation or computerized axial tomography (CAT or CT) scan, a tumor in almost any part of the body can be biopsied through a thin, flexible needle. This permits diagnosis before surgery and therefore better choice of therapeutic approach and better planning of surgery, should it be necessary.

Staging. Once a tissue diagnosis of cancer has been made, the extent, or stage, of the disease must be evaluated because prognosis and appropriate treatment vary with the stage of the disease. For each type of tumor, the stage (I, II, III, or IV) is defined in terms of findings with progressively more severe prognostic implications: small local tumor, more extensive local tumor, regional lymph node involvement, and distant metastases. The clinical stage, defined by information obtained prior to surgical exploration, is used to decide appropriate initial treatment. The surgical stage, which may be different from the clinical, incorporates the findings of the surgical exploration, and is used as a basis for subsequent treatment and for prognosis. It is also used for any analyses of effects of different treatments.

TREATMENT

The traditional means of treating cancer have been surgery, radiation, and chemotherapy. Currently, studies are under way of the usefulness of immunotherapy and biologic response modifiers.

Surgery. The principal approach to curing cancer is to remove all of the malignant cells by a surgical operation. In the past this meant the removal of all of the involved tissue and as much potentially involved tissue as possible, including adjacent tissues and lymph nodes. For some tumors, notably cancer of the breast, this radical degree of surgery (*see* MASTECTOMY) is not always necessary. Refinements in surgical techniques, improved knowledge of physiology, advances in anesthesiology, ready availability of blood products, and potent antibiotics have permitted more extensive surgery with more rapid recovery and less resulting disability. Many cancers, though, are at too advanced a stage at the time of diagnosis to permit cure by surgery. If local extension involves neighboring tissues that cannot be sacrificed or if distant metastases are already present, surgery will not be curative. Even when it is clear that surgical cure is not possible, however, palliative surgery may be helpful to relieve symptoms, as of obstruction, or to reduce the size of the tumor in an effort to improve response to subsequent radiation or chemotherapy.

Radiation Therapy. Ionizing radiation, which may be either electromagnetic or particulate, is destructive to tissue. Electromagnetic radiation includes gamma rays, emitted by radioactive decay, and X rays, produced when a beam of electrons strikes a heavy-metal target. Particulate radiation includes beams of electrons, protons, neutrons, alpha particles (helium nuclei), and negative pi mesons (pions).

Tumors vary greatly in their sensitivity to radiation. A "sensitive" tumor is one that is more sensitive than surrounding normal tissues. When such a tumor is readily accessible—a superficial tumor, for example, or one in an organ like the uterus, into which a radiation source can be introduced—it may be curable by radiation therapy. Because of its relatively sparing effect on normal tissues, radiation is useful when a tumor is located where it cannot be removed because surgery would damage vital adjacent tissue or because a tumor has begun to infiltrate adjacent structures that cannot be sacrificed. Radiation therapy is also extremely useful for palliation, especially of metastatic tumors.

Radiation can also be useful as an adjunct to surgery. Preoperative radiation may rapidly sterilize the tumor cells and prevent seeding at surgery. It may also shrink the tumor and make surgery easier or shrink an inoperable tumor so that it becomes operable. In other tumors postoperative radiation is used.

Chemotherapy. Chemotherapy is the use of drugs in the treatment of cancer. Since a drug is distributed throughout the body by the bloodstream, chemotherapy is useful for tumors that have spread beyond the area accessible by surgery or radiotherapy. A number of different types of anticancer drugs are used, but nearly all work by interfering with DNA synthesis or function. Rapidly dividing cells are therefore more sensitive to chemotherapy. Cancers have a larger proportion of dividing cells than do normal tissues, in which stem, or replenishing, cells are dormant and therefore resistant to drug effect. The most

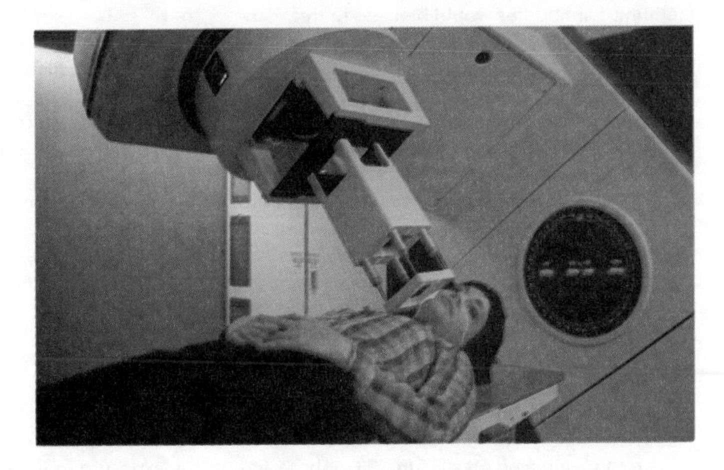

A cancer patient is placed so that a beam of radiation from a linear accelerator is aimed precisely at the tumor. This high-energy device can generate both X-ray and electron beams. Such radiotherapy is usually employed together with other kinds of treatment, and its effectiveness depends on the form of cancer involved. Geisinger Medical Center

rapidly proliferating normal tissues are the bone marrow and the lining cells of the gastrointestinal tract. These are the most sensitive normal areas of chemotherapeutic effect and constitute the sites of toxicity that will limit the tolerable dose of most drugs. To be effectively treated, a tumor must have a sensitivity greater than that of the most sensitive normal tissue. Some tumors may be many times more sensitive, but many are only slightly more sensitive. Fortunately the normal bone marrow cells can divide faster than malignant cells and thus recover more rapidly. This permits a repeat cycle of the drug before the tumor has regrown very much. Repeated cycles can steadily deplete a tumor before resistance occurs. Some tumors are so sensitive to chemotherapy that a chemotherapeutic cure is possible in a high percentage: choriocarcinoma in the female; acute leukemia (q.v.), especially in children; Hodgkin's disease (q.v.) and diffuse large-cell lymphoma; testicular carcinoma; ovarian carcinoma; small-cell carcinoma of the lung; and several of the cancers of children are examples. These cancers are often already disseminated at the time of diagnosis and cannot be treated by other means. Still other advanced cancers respond well to chemotherapy and can be controlled for a long time, so chemotherapy is commonly used for palliation.

Two major problems limiting the usefulness of chemotherapy are toxicity and resistance. Techniques that avoid or control toxicity and reduce the risk of resistance have steadily improved. It is important to begin treatment as early as possible, to use the optimal dose of the drug, and to repeat cycles as quickly as possible consistent with reasonable recovery from toxicity.

The use of multiple drugs is effective. Combination chemotherapy employs several drugs (often three to six at a time), each of which is effective as a single agent. The drugs used have different mechanisms of action, making cross-resistance less likely, and different types of toxicity, so that each may be given at optimal dose without causing fatal additive toxicity.

Chemotherapy may be used together with surgery or radiation as combined modality therapy. It is often used as an adjuvant, or helper, when surgery is the primary therapy. As such it is usually given after surgery. This type of therapy has greatly increased the cure rate of breast cancer. The major purpose of chemotherapy as an adjuvant is to kill off micrometastases that may have been established before surgery. Recently, chemotherapy has been used before surgery as a neoadjuvant. This therapy has the same effect as adjuvant chemotherapy but may also shrink a tumor, making it more easily resectable.

Hormone Therapy. Many cancers arising from tissues that are hormone-dependent, such as the breast, the prostate, the endometrium, and the thyroid, are responsive to hormone manipulation. This may consist of the removal of the source of the stimulating hormone or the administration of various hormones and antihormones.

Other Approaches. Several promising new approaches to the treatment of cancer are being taken. In one, biological agents known as biological response modifiers are used to modify the response of the body to cancer. Another approach involves biological agents that stimulate certain cells, which can then attack the malignant cells. The best example is the use of interleukin-2 to stimulate the patient's lymphokine-activated killer lymphocytes (LAK cells). Research has been very active concerning tumor-specific antigens against which antibodies could be raised. These antitumor antibodies would be used to treat cancer either directly or by coupling to a chemotherapeutic agent. The antibody could identify the malignant cell and adhere to it, thus delivering the drug directly to the target.

Even if cured, a cancer patient may be left with serious handicaps. Every effort must be made to achieve the maximum possible quality of life through rehabilitative techniques, including reconstructive surgery. For the patient who is not cured, palliative therapy may achieve comfort and good function for months or years. Pain is a severe problem and can be relieved much more than in the past.

CURABILITY OF CANCER

For decades the number of deaths from cancer has risen rapidly and steadily, from 298,000 in 1965 to an estimated 500,000 in 1989. These figures give an inaccurate picture of progress in that they reflect the increasing population and the increasing percentage of older people, who have a higher incidence of cancer. They also reflect a failure until recently to reduce significantly the number of people who smoke tobacco (*see* SMOKING). As a result, the incidence of lung cancer, the most common cause of death from cancer, has continued to rise. This rate has risen 10-fold in 50 years. The recent dramatic fall in the use of tobacco should bring about a falling mortality from lung cancer in the future. If lung cancer is excluded, the age-adjusted death rate from cancer has leveled off. Other cancers have a rising incidence, but for many of these, improvement in the cure rate has exceeded the increase in incidence.

The treatment of cancer has improved remarkably since 1920, when less than 20 percent of U.S. white patients with cancer survived more than five years. In 1960, 39 percent did so, and the figures improved to 43 percent in 1970 and 50 percent in 1980. An estimated more than 5 million living Americans have had cancer. Three million of these have survived more than five years, and nearly all of the survivors can be regarded as cured. The changes in survival over time are shown in tables 2 and 3.

The death rate from cancer has fallen progressively for all age groups below the age of 55, probably because more-healthful habits and environment have reduced prolonged exposure to carcinogens and because of earlier diagnosis. This drop is expected to extend to older age groups as these younger people age.

The risk of lung cancer falls dramatically within a few years if smoking is stopped. Efforts at early diagnosis of lung cancer, however, have had little influence on the cure rate. Skin cancers, most of which are easily curable, cause only about 2200 deaths a year, and because they are caused by exposure to the sun, they are preventable.

CANCER CONTROL

The most important preventive measure in controlling cancer is the cessation of tobacco use, which is the cause of 30 percent of all deaths from cancer. A large reduction might follow better diet: optimal calorie intake to avoid obesity, reduction of calories from fat to 20 percent of the diet (about half of the current U.S. intake), reduction of red meat intake, and increased intake of dietary fiber (whole grain, fruits, and vegetables) and protective foods (foods that contain vitamins C and A, as well as such cruciferous vegetables as cabbage, cauliflower, broccoli, and Brussels sprouts). Moderation in eating salt-cured, smoked, and nitrite-cured foods and in the consumption of alcohol is also advised. The avoidance of exposure to sunlight and the routine use of sunscreens is most important to prevent cancer of the skin.

The environment can be improved by the elimination of carcinogenic chemicals from the workplace and the home, by the elimination of exposure to asbestos fiber dust, and by the reduction of excess radon accumulation in homes.

TABLE 3 SURVIVAL RATES BY TYPE OF CANCER, SPREAD, AND SEX

	Total Population % 5-Year Survival		Males		Females	
Type of Cancer	Localized	Spread	% of Total Cancers	% 5-Year Survival	% of Total Cancers	% 5-Year Survival
Lung	33	7	20	12	11	13
Colo-rectal	85	37	14	52	15	52
Breast	90+	60	—	—	28	69
Uterus	—	—	—	—	9	78
(in situ)	100	NA	—	—	—	—
(invasive)	89	48	—	—	—	—
Prostate	84	47	21	71	—	—
Lymphomas & Leukemias	—	—	8	43	7	42

Source: American Cancer Society (1989).

Effective screening is available for cancer of the uterus, breast, colon and rectum, and prostate. People without symptoms should have a cancer-related checkup every three years from age 20 to 40 and every year after 40. Women past 20 should do breast self-examination every month and have a breast examination and pelvic examination yearly. A mammogram should be done between age 35 and 39, every one or two years from 40 to 49, and yearly thereafter. Women who are sexually active or have reached the age of 18 should have the so-called Pap test (*see* GYNECOLOGY) yearly for three negative tests and less frequently thereafter. A digital rectal exam should be done every year after age 40 and a stool blood test every year after 50. A flexible proctoscopy should be done annually for two negative examinations and then every 3 to 5 years. Young men should do monthly self-examinations of the testes.

Widespread adoption of these measures could virtually eliminate lung cancer, reduce the incidence of breast and colon cancer, and assure a high rate of cure of cancers of the breast, colon and rectum, uterus, and prostate. Such measures, together with full use of present technology for diagnosis and treatment, may permit the achievement of the goal, announced in 1985, of a 50 percent reduction in cancer deaths in the U.S. by the year 2000.

For further information on this topic, see the Bibliography in volume 28, sections 443, 448–49, 508–9.

CANDELA. *See* INTERNATIONAL SYSTEM OF UNITS.

CANDELA OUTERIÑO, Felix (1910–), Mexican architect and engineer, known for his innovative design and construction of concrete shell structures. His sculpturally beautiful churches and public buildings, such as the Church of the Virgen Milagrossa, Mexico City (1955), are characterized by seamless concrete vaults, double vaults, hyperbolic paraboloids (saddle-shaped surfaces), and free-form organic shapes. One of his most important works is the Manantiales Restaurant (1958) in Xochimilco, the flower shape of which is derived from eight curved concrete membranes.

CANDIA. *See* IRÁKLION.

CANDLE, illuminating device made of a fiber wick enclosed in a cylinder of wax or fatty material. Beeswax candles were used by the Romans, and tallow (animal fat) candles have been made in Europe since the Middle Ages. In the 18th century, spermaceti, a wax obtained from the heads of whales, was introduced for candles. Since the mid-19th century, ordinary candles have been made from mixtures of paraffin wax (a mixture of saturated hydrocarbons), stearic acid (a solid fatty acid), and beeswax. Hydrogenated vegetable oils and other waxes are also used.

The earliest method of candlemaking was by dipping the wick, usually made of flax or cotton fibers, into melted wax or fat and removing it to let it cool and solidify in the air. The candle was built up to the required thickness by successive dippings. Taper candles are still made by dipping, but most candles used today are molded, usually by machine.

CANDLEBERRY. *See* BAYBERRY.

CANDLEFISH, common name for a small saltwater fish, *Thaleichthys pacificus,* of the family Osmeridae (*see* SMELT). The candlefish is found in the northern Pacific Ocean. Used primarily as a food, candlefish are about 30 to 38 cm (about 12 to 15 in) long and are silvery in appearance. From February to April they swim up western freshwater streams to spawn. The name is derived from a practice of the Alaskan Indians, who use the dried fish, which is very oily, as a lamp by pushing a piece of bark through the fish as a wick.

CANDLEMAS, Christian festival observed on February 2 in honor of the presentation of the infant Christ in the Temple and the purification of the Virgin Mary. The festival was probably meant to replace the great feast of expiation and purification (*Februa*) that was held in ancient Rome in mid-February. The date of the pagan feast was then transferred to February 2, the 40th day after Christmas; the 40-day period was in accordance with the Jewish law that required the ritual purification at the Temple of every mother of a male child 40 days after the child's birth. The Candlemas festival is believed to have been instituted in 541 or 542 by the Byzantine emperor Justinian I.

CANDY. *See* CONFECTIONERY.

CANDYTUFT, common name for more than 30 species of herbs, forming the genus *Iberis,* of the family Cruciferae (*see* MUSTARD). Both annual and perennial plants, they are natives of Mediterranean countries and are cultivated in gardens. The perennial *I. sempervirens* is popular as edging for rock gardens because of its evergreen leaves and fragrant white flower clusters; *I. amara* and *I. umbrellata* are the most popular annuals. The latter has flowers of many colors.

CANISIUS, Saint Peter (1521–97), German Jesuit theologian. His original name was Pieter de Hondt. Born in Nijmegen (now in the Netherlands), he was the first German to join (1543) the Jesuit order. He established Jesuit centers in many parts of Germany and taught at German universities, including those at Cologne and Vienna. Canisius was a leader of the Counter Reformation, the reform movement that arose in the Roman Catholic church in answer to the Protestant Reformation. He participated actively in the Council of Trent and the Diet of Augsburg (1556). His triple catechism, written for different age levels, is his most important work. He was canonized in 1925 and in the same year was named Doctor of the Church. Canisius's feast day is December 21. Canisius College in Buffalo, N.Y., a Jesuit institution founded in 1870, is named for him.

CANIS MAJOR and CANIS MINOR (Lat., "greater dog" and "lesser dog"), two constellations of stars, the former lying southeast and the latter east of Orion, and separated by the Milky Way. According to ancient mythology, these constellations represent dogs trotting at the heels of the Greek hunter Orion. Canis Major contains Sirius (also called the Dog Star), the brightest star in the heavens, and Canis Minor contains Procyon, far less bright than Sirius but still a star of the first magnitude. Midsummer, when Sirius rises at dawn, was associated by the ancients with the Dog Star, and this period is still known as the dog days or canicular days.

ÇANKAYA, district of Ankara, central Turkey, formerly an independent city. Çankaya, which includes the residential section of Kavaklıdere, is the site of foreign embassies and of the presidential palace. Textiles, mohair, and leguminous plants are produced. Çankaya was formerly called Yenişehir, or New City.

CANKER, common name for a wide range of plant diseases, most often of woody plants, that are characterized by the development of local lesions on the trunk, branches, or stems. The lesions swell or sink and become discolored as the affected areas die, and they often crack open to reveal underlying tissues. As such lesions spread, they may encircle a branch and kill foliage growth beyond that point.

Cankers are produced by many different kinds of bacteria and fungi. Citrus cankers, for example, are caused by variants of the bacterium *Xanthomonas campestris.* The diseases tend to develop in plants that are already weakened by inadequate growth conditions or by insect attacks. No cure thus far exists for a number of cankers, but others can be treated by pruning and by taking various common preventive measures. The use of special soils may be required to deal with certain particular cankers. Foliage loss through infestation by the caterpillars called cankerworms is an unrelated phenomenon. *See* DISEASES OF PLANTS.

CANKERWORM, common name for several destructive caterpillars known as inchworms, especially *Paleacrita vernata,* the spring cankerworm, and *Alsophila pometaria,* the fall cankerworm, of the family Geometridae. They are found in the U.S. from Maine to Texas. The male moth of both species has silky wings; the female is wingless. The females crawl up the trunks of fruit or shade trees to lay their eggs, and the caterpillars, which hatch about the time the tree comes into leaf, often skeletonize the leaves of an entire orchard in a few days. The common name of these two species is derived from the season in which the female lays eggs.

CANNA, family of flowering plants, the Cannaceae, herbaceous in habit, with large, showy flowers. The one genus, *Canna,* includes about 50 species that occur in the West Indies and Central America. In temperate areas several forms are used for summer plantings both for their flowers and their luxuriant foliage.

The canna family is a member of the Zingiberales (*see* GINGER) and, like many members of that order, exhibits a reduction in the number of fertile stamens and a corresponding development of showy staminodes, sterile floral structures derived from stamens.

Other than horticultural forms, several species yield useful extracts from their rhizomes, including an easily digestible starch, purple arrowroot, from *C. edulis.* M.R.C.

CANNABIS, a genus of coarse, tall, hairy annual herbs in the family Cannabaceae (*see* HEMP) that provides fiber from its stems, oil from its seeds, and drugs from its leaves and flowers. The only species, *C. sativa,* is a native of Central Asia but is widely cultivated and found as a weed throughout North America. The plant grows up to 1.8 m (6 ft) tall, with coarsely toothed, palmately divided leaves and inconspicuous clusters of flowers. Depending on the product desired, the methods and areas of production vary. Hemp is grown mainly in temperate regions, and the Soviet Union is the world's largest producer. Seeds yield a drying oil used in the manufacture of varnish, paints, and soap. The seeds are also used as bird feed. The drugs derived from *Cannabis* contain as their principal component narcotic resins found mostly in the glandular hairs of the plants. These resins are most abundant under hot, tropical conditions. In the U.S., cannabis can be grown only under government permit. *See also* MARIJUANA.

CANNAE, ancient town of Italy, in the Apulia region, near the mouth of the Aufidus (now Ofanto) River. In 216 BC, during the Second Punic War, the Carthaginian general Hannibal defeated the Romans at Cannae.

CANNES, city, SE France, in Alpes-Maritimes Department, on the Mediterranean Sea, near Nice. A fashionable resort of the French Riviera, the city is built on an elevation that slopes to the sea and is sheltered by a range of hills. Tourism is the chief industry, but Cannes also has a busy port and is a trade center for flowers and fruit produced in the region. An important international film festival is held here each year.

Points of interest in the city include the Church of Notre Dame d'Espérance (15th cent.); the Lycklama Museum, which has a fine collection of antiquities; and the Promenade de la Croisette, a street with splendid hotels and shops. On a nearby island in the Mediterranean is the Abbey of Lérins, a noted intellectual center in the 5th century.

For centuries Cannes was a small fishing village. Since the 1830s, however, when the British statesman Henry Peter Brougham, 1st baron Brougham and Vaux, built a villa here, Cannes has been a popular winter and summer resort. Pop. (1982) 72,787.

CANNIBALISM, eating of human flesh by human beings. The term *cannibalism* is derived from Canibales, the Spanish name for the man-eating Carib Indians who lived in the West Indies when Christopher Columbus arrived. The practice of cannibalism is ancient and has been reported in many parts of the world. Evidence indicates that it may have been practiced as early as Neolithic times. The Greek historian Herodotus and other ancient writers described various cannibalistic peoples. In medieval times the Italian traveler Marco Polo reported that tribes from Tibet to Sumatra practiced cannibalism. It was practiced among many North American Indians, especially the tribes of the western coast of the Gulf of Mexico. Until recent times cannibalism prevailed throughout much of central and western Africa, Australia, New Zealand, Melanesia, Sumatra, New Guinea, Polynesia, and remote parts of South America.

Motives for practicing cannibalism were numerous. In some cultures, the belief that the person who ate the dead body of another would acquire the desired qualities of the person eaten, particularly of a brave enemy, promoted this practice. In a few instances cannibalism seems to have been dictated by no other motive than revenge. It was even believed that an enemy's spirit would be utterly destroyed if the body were eaten, thus leaving nothing in which the ghost could live. Cannibalism was sometimes part of a religious practice. The Binderwurs of central India ate their sick and aged in the belief that the act was pleasing to their goddess Kali. In Mexico thousands of human victims were sacrificed annually by the Aztecs to their deities. After the ceremony of sacrifice, the priests and the populace ate the bodies of the victims, believing that this would bring them closer to their gods.

Among Western peoples cannibalism is rare, although starvation has sometimes driven humans to eat the flesh of other humans. One instance in America involved members of the ill-fated Donner party in the Sierra Nevada in California during the winter of 1846–47. Another occurred in Chile in 1972, when 16 members of a Uruguayan soccer team survived for 70 days after their airliner crashed in the Andes Mountains.

CANNING, process of preserving food by heating and sealing it in airtight containers. The process was invented (1809) by François Appert (c. 1750–1841), a French chef. In the Appert process, the food was cooked in open kettles and placed in glass jars, which were sealed by corks wired in place. The jars were then heated by submersion in boiling water. Canning was introduced into the U.S. soon after its invention.

Early Canning Methods. In 1810 an English inventor, Peter Durand, patented the idea of using tin-plated cans; despite their comparatively lower cost, they did not replace glass containers until the mid-19th century. The early form of tin can was sealed with a disk of metal soldered over a hole in the end of the can. Later, calcium chloride was added to the water used to sterilize the food sealed in the cans, to raise the temperature of the water above 100° C (212° F). Although the food was heated faster, the increased internal pressure often burst the cans. In 1874 the closed-vessel process, in which the cans were heated by

Field-ripened tomatoes go through a series of high-powered spray washes, inspections, and sortings before being placed in individual cups by automatic feeders; they are then checked and hand oriented for proper position before they enter the peeler. Hunt-Wesson Foods

Tomatoes move along conveyors to rotary fillers, where they are packed in cans, ready for sealing and cooking.
Hunt-Wesson Foods

steam under pressure, was invented; the pressure of the steam compensated for pressure that developed in the can, largely eliminating the bursting of cans.

Later Developments. Gradual improvements in machinery and techniques for producing cans resulted in better lining materials, such as lacquers and enamels, and in the development of the sanitary open-top can, in which the top is crimped to the can after filling, producing an airtight seal by means of a rubber gasket. During World War II, the critical shortage of tin resulted in a revival of the use of glass containers, which have the advantage of not reacting chemically with the food contents. Other recent developments include the use of aluminum cans, very thin steel cans, and tin-free cans. The last-named may be coated with plastic on the inner surface to eliminate a metallic taste. Cans made entirely of plastic have also been market-tested. The use of can openers has been eliminated in many containers that are opened by pulling a metal tab or ring attached to the top of the can, which is designed to pull free of the can.

Pull-tape containers are used for a variety of vacuum-packed products. American Can Company

Home canning became an important method of preserving food after the American John Landis Mason (1832-1902) invented (1858) a practical glass jar and lid, now called the mason jar. Home canning is still popular as an economical means of preserving homegrown fruits and vegetables. The preferred method for canning foods at home is the hot-pack method, in which precooked, hot food and part of the liquid in which it was cooked are placed in a clean, hot mason jar. The mouth of the jar is covered with a metal disk that has a rubber ring seal. A screw-type lid is then partially screwed onto the glass jar. After the jar has been processed in boiling water for the length of time required for the type of food, the screw top is tightened completely. Heat and pressure during processing force most of the air from the jar and minimize the danger of multiplication of disease-causing organisms. Jams and jellies are usually prepared by the open-kettle method. The jam is cooked to the proper consistency, then poured into hot, sterilized jars, which are then sealed. Further heating is not required; the sugar used in preparing jams and jellies acts as a preservative.

See BOTULISM; FOOD PROCESSING AND PRESERVATION.

CANNING, George (1770-1827), British statesman, born in London, and educated in law at the University of Oxford. A Tory, he entered the House of Commons in 1794 as the protégé and supporter of Prime Minister William Pitt the Younger. In 1796 Canning was made undersecretary of state for foreign affairs. In 1801, when Pitt resigned, Canning left his post on the Privy Council. When Pitt again became prime minister in 1804, Canning was appointed treasurer of the navy, an office he held until the death of Pitt in 1806. In 1807 Canning became foreign minister. His resignation three years later was prompted by his continuing feud with the secretary of war, Viscount Castlereagh. (The two men fought a duel in 1809.) Canning held a series of minor offices until 1822, when he succeeded Castlereagh as foreign secretary and leader of the House of Commons. From then until his death, Canning guided the foreign affairs of Great Britain. He supported nationalist movements throughout

Latin America, discouraging foreign intervention in American affairs, a policy that accorded with the Monroe Doctrine of the U.S.; he aided Portugal against Spanish aggression and aided the Greeks in their struggle against the Turks. At home, Canning worked for emancipation of Roman Catholics. When the British prime minister Robert Banks Jenkinson, 2d earl of Liverpool (1770–1828), left office in 1827, Canning succeeded him as prime minister, but his ministry lasted only until his death four months later.

CANNIZZARO, Stanislao (1826–1910), Italian chemist, born in Palermo, Sicily. After participating in the 1848 Sicilian revolution, Cannizzaro worked (1849–51) in a laboratory in Paris. He was appointed professor of chemistry at the institute in Alessandria (1851) and at the universities of Genoa (1855), Pisa (1861), and Rome (1871). At Alessandria he discovered the reaction that bears his name, Cannizzaro's reaction, which proves that aldehydes in the presence of concentrated alkali are reduced to a mixture of their corresponding alcohol and acid; for example, benzaldehyde yields benzyl alcohol and benzoic acid.

Cannizzaro made a great contribution to atomic theory by clarifying (1858) the distinction between atomic weight and molecular weight. He showed how unknown atomic weights of elements in volatile compounds can be arrived at from known molecular weights of the compounds. Cannizzaro also determined that atomic weights of elements in compounds can be determined if specific heats are known even though vapor densities are unknown. His work on atomic theory was based on Avogadro's law, which states that equal volumes of any two gases contain an equal number of molecules when held under identical conditions of temperature and pressure.

CANNON, general term for large military weapons supported on carriages or fixed mounts, as opposed to small arms (q.v.). In modern military usage the term is synonymous with artillery. The invention of cannon is generally credited to a German monk, Berthold Schwarz (fl. early 14th cent.). The first cannon used gunpowder charges to fire stones or metal balls. Early cannon were smoothbore metal tubes loaded from the muzzle and aimed and elevated manually; recoil was absorbed by allowing the carriage to run backward. The modern cannon, loaded through the breech (at the rear of the bore), consists of a forged steel tube, rifled (that is, having a grooved bore) to give the projectile a spin in flight, and enclosed for strength in a steel jacket. The carriage is equipped with mechanisms to absorb the force of recoil on firing and return the cannon to firing position. Elevating and traversing mechanisms provide for accurate aiming by hand, by electric power, or by a completely automatic system that locates and tracks targets by radar. In 1975 the U.S. Army demonstrated a laser-guided artillery shell, or "cannon-launched guided projectile," that can be fired with great accuracy.

Ammunition includes high-explosive shells, antitank shells, smoke and signal shells, shells containing chemical agents, and shells with nuclear warheads. Shells filled with propaganda leaflets or that deliver vital medical supplies to isolated troops are also fired by cannon.

See also ARTILLERY; PROJECTILE.

CANNON, Annie Jump (1863–1941), American astronomer, born in Dover, Del., and educated at Wellesley and Radcliffe colleges. She was an assistant at the Harvard College Observatory from 1897 until 1911, when she was appointed curator of astronomical photographs. She was responsible for the photographic discovery of 5 novas and about 300 variable stars. She is best known for compiling a bibliography of about 200,000 references to variable stars and for completing a catalog of about 250,000 stellar spectra; the catalog is still accepted as an international standard. Regarded as the first great woman astronomer, she was also the first woman to receive an honorary doctor's degree from the University of Oxford.

CANNON, Joseph Gurney (1836–1926), American lawyer and politician, born in New Garden, N.C., and educated at the Cincinnati Law School. In 1858 Cannon moved to Illinois and was admitted to the Illinois bar. He was elected as a Republican to the U.S. House of Representatives in 1873 and served 23 terms in Congress, failing to

Joseph G. Cannon UPI

be reelected for the two terms beginning in 1891 and 1913. From 1903 until 1911 he was Speaker of the House. Cannon was noted for his strong partisan leadership as speaker and his conservative political views. He was opposed to the so-called progressive reforms advocated by such political leaders as President Woodrow Wilson, and he was an outspoken opponent of the League of Nations. Cannon's opponents in Congress felt that he had arbitrary power over legislative procedure in the House, and in 1910 they passed a resolution reducing the powers of the office of Speaker.

CANO, Alonso (1601-67), Spanish painter, sculptor, and architect, who was one of the foremost masters of Spanish baroque art. All of his work is notable for its religious connotations, and the human figures in his paintings and sculptures radiate devout feeling. His most notable works were the seven paintings illustrating *Mysteries of the Virgin* (1654, Granada Cathedral) and the carved polychrome altarpiece of Santa Maria, Lebrija (1631). As architect for Granada Cathedral, he executed designs for a new facade (designed 1667) that was one of the most lushly imaginative creations of baroque architecture. He also produced a great quantity of drawings and is considered the foremost Spanish baroque draftsman.

CANO, Juan Sebastián del, called El Cano (d. 1526), Spanish navigator, born in Guetaria. In 1519 he was made captain of the *Concepción,* one of the five vessels commanded by the Portuguese navigator Ferdinand Magellan during his expedition in the service of Spain. After the death of Magellan on April 27, 1521, Cano assumed command of the expedition. On Sept. 6, 1522, he arrived in Spain on board the *Victoria,* becoming the first man to circumnavigate the earth, although Magellan is usually given credit for the voyage. Cano died off the western coast of South America while in command of a subsequent expedition.

CANOE, light, narrow boat, generally with identically shaped bow and stern and curved sides, and usually propelled by at least one oar or paddle. The canoe was developed by many early cultures throughout the world. It varies in shape, size, and construction, according to its place of origin. The oldest form of canoe was probably a tree trunk hollowed out by tools or fire.

The North American Indians created the birchbark canoe, a vessel with a frame of light wood that is covered with pieces of bark sewn together and made watertight with melted pitch. Similar in design to the birchbark is the canvas canoe created by the Penobscot Indians of Maine in the 19th century. Indians living in treeless regions made canoes of tule or other bulrushes lashed together; Indians living on the shores of Lake Titicaca in South America still make them this way.

The Inuit (Eskimo) created two kinds of canoe, both of which had whalebone or wooden frames and were covered with animal skins, generally those from whales or seals. The kayak, a boat used only by the male Eskimo, is completely enclosed except for an opening for the occupant. The umiak, used only by the female, is open. The

Recreational canoes constructed of lightweight metals such as aluminum are sturdier and more easily handled than their wooden predecessors. Alumacraft

canoe of Greenland and Hudson Strait is flat bottomed and flat sided.

The dugout is still used by the peoples of Africa, South America, and Polynesia. Another type of canoe used by the natives of the southwest Pacific islands is made of planks fastened together. This type is often equipped with an outrigger, a device that ensures stability in heavy seas. Many of the ancient war canoes used by natives of the Pacific islands were elaborately carved.

In recent years the canoe has been used increasingly by vacationists and sports enthusiasts, and since 1886 canoeists have engaged in official competitions. Today canoes, usually about 5.2 m (about 17 ft), are constructed of molded plastic or fiberglass, aluminum and magnesium alloys, rubber, canvas, and other materials. A modern development is the foldboat, a small collapsible canoe of rubberized sailcloth stretched over a knockdown frame.

For further information on this topic, see the Bibliography in volume 28, sections 557, 806.

CANON (Gr. *kanon,* "standard"), musical composition in which one voice or part introduces a melody (the "subject") and, after a given number of beats, a second voice repeats or answers the melody note for note, either on the same pitch or at a higher or lower pitch. A third voice may enter, or begin the melody, at the given number of beats after the start of the second voice, and so on. If the imitation is at a different pitch, the subject may be altered slightly to fit the tonality of the composition. If the subject melody leads back into its own beginning so that the piece can be repeated endlessly, the canon is termed *circular.* The most common kind of circular canon is called a round (q.v.).

More complicated ways of writing the answer in a canon include augmentation and diminution (lengthening or shortening the notes of the answering voice); inversion (turning the subject upside down by making each rising interval a falling one and vice versa); retrogression (giving the subject notes in reverse order); writing the answer in both inversion and retrogression; and repeating the melody pitches of the subject but changing its meter and note durations (mensuration canons). Canonic imitation is often employed for several measures in contrapuntal compositions (*see* COUNTERPOINT). The earliest known piece that is a canon from start to finish is the 13th-century English composition "Sumer is Icumen In."

CANON, in Christian usage, a rule or standard. By the middle of the 3d century the word had come to refer to those doctrines recognized as orthodox by the Christian church. It was later used to designate collectively the list of books accepted as Scripture (*see* BIBLE).

The term *canon* is also used to denote the catalog or register of saints. The use of the plural form to denote church precepts originated about the year 300; this form began to be applied specifically to the decrees of the church councils about the middle of the 4th century (*see* CANON LAW). The term is also applied to the part of the Roman Catholic Mass (q.v.) that opens with the Preface, or prayer of thanksgiving, and closes just before the recitation of the Lord's Prayer. In some Christian churches, *canon* is also an ecclesiastical title given to the clergy attached to a cathedral church or to certain types of priests living under a semimonastic rule, such as the Augustinians (q.v.).

CANONICAL HOURS. *See* DIVINE OFFICE.

CANONIZATION, in the Roman Catholic church, an act by which the pope publicly proclaims the sanctity of a deceased person, whom he thereupon proposes for the veneration of the universal church. Canonization is usually the final act of a lengthy process that begins with beatification (q.v.). The decree of beatification is an official declaration that a person lived a holy life and can be venerated as one of the "blessed"; canonization awards the full title of "saint." In the Orthodox church, the process of canonization is less formal and is carried out by local synods of bishops.

The modern custom of canonization originated in the early Christian practice of paying public honor to the martyrs. For many centuries thereafter the title of saint was bestowed by popular acclamation. Not until a comparatively late period was a procedure equivalent to canonization adopted.

The earliest acknowledged instance of a solemn decree of canonization is that of Udalric or Ulric, bishop of Augsburg, declared a saint by Pope John XV (d. 996) in 993. Pope Alexander III in 1171 reserved the right of canonizing exclusively for the papacy. Pope Urban VIII, in two constitutions promulgated in 1625 and 1634, made more stringent regulations and laid down the canonization procedure that, with slight modifications, is still followed.

Canonization, without a special dispensation, cannot be decreed until 50 years have elapsed since the claimant's death. The process that precedes the decree of canonization seeks to establish two characteristics of the claimant according to the testimony of competent witnesses: eminent virtues, technically referred to as virtues in a "heroic degree," and the performance of at least two authentic miracles.

Pope Paul VI during the ceremony of canonization in June 1977 that conferred sainthood upon Bishop John Neumann of Philadelphia. Wide World Photos

If the initial investigation is satisfactory, the pope takes the cause into his own hands and issues letters assigning the cause to a committee of the Congregation for the Causes of Saints, which then examines the virtues and miracles specifically. The claimant's cause is now said to be introduced. The introduction of the cause, that is, of the pontifical process, entitles the *beatificandus,* or candidate for beatification, to be called "venerable." Many candidates have reached this point in the proceedings and have failed to go beyond it. If the candidate passes successfully through the proceedings, a decree of beatification is pronounced. Before the further process of canonization can be instituted, witnesses must testify that the candidate has worked a certain number of miracles since beatification. The case then once more passes through the hands of several congregations, the last of which is held in the presence of the pope, when the final decree is agreed upon.

The ceremony of canonization occurs in Saint Peter's Basilica in the Vatican and is one of the most solemn and imposing of all papal functions.

Equipollent or equivalent canonization is founded upon proof of immemorial veneration, or of some papal sanction given to veneration, prior to the date of Urban VIII's constitution. In such cases the pope may at once pronounce the decree of canonization. Equipollent beatification is a summary process of a similar kind. The pope accepts the results of the preliminary process and at once decrees beatification.

CANON LAW (Gr. *kanon,* "rule" or "measure"), usually, the body of legislation of various Christian churches dealing with matters of constitution or discipline. Although all religions have regulations, the term applies mainly to the formal systems of the Roman Catholic, Orthodox, and Anglican communions. It is distinguished from civil or secular law, but conflict can arise in areas of mutual concern (for example, marriage and divorce).

Components. In its origins canon law consisted of the enactments of councils or synods of bishops, and the Anglican and Orthodox churches so restrict it today. The Roman Catholic church also recognizes the authority of the pope to make universal law and that certain customary practices may acquire the force of law. The Roman Catholic church has by far the most elaborate body of law and, to provide training in it, has chartered graduate faculties in a number of universities throughout the world. The doctorate in canon law requires at least four years of study beyond the bachelor of arts degree. Each diocese has a church court or tribunal staffed by canon lawyers. In modern times church courts have dealt almost exclusively with marriage nullity cases.

The full range of canon law in contemporary times may be seen in the Roman Catholic church, which promulgated a revised code for its Latin, or Western, members in 1983 and has projected a first-ever code for its Eastern communicants. The planned *Lex Fundamentalis* setting forth the constitutive or organizational principles common to both proved to be inopportune. The 1983 (Latin) Code of Canon Law promulgated by the authority of Pope John Paul II consists of seven books for a total of 1752 canons. Each book is divided into titles, but in the larger books the titles are grouped in parts and even in sections.

Book One, "General Norms," includes 203 canons under 11 titles: ecclesiastical laws (definition and application); custom; general decrees and instructions; individual administrative acts (precepts, rescripts, privileges, and dispensations); statutes and rules of order; physical and juridic persons; juridic acts; the power of governance; ecclesiastical offices; prescription; and the computation of time.

Book Two, "The People of God," is, from a theological perspective, the most significant book. Its 543 canons are organized in three parts: "The Christian Faithful," "The Hierarchical Constitution of the Church," and "Institutes [communities] of Consecrated Life and Societies of Apostolic Life." Among the Christian faithful a distinction is made between clergy and laity, and their respective rights and duties are spelled out. The hierarchical constitution of the church establishes the supreme authority (the Roman pontiff and the college of bishops, the synod of bishops, the cardinals, the Roman Curia, and papal legates) and the particular churches (dioceses, archdioceses [ecclesiastical provinces], episcopal conferences, as well as parishes and deaneries). Part Three regulates the various types of religious communities: institutes of consecrated Life (e.g., Jesuits, Franciscans, Visitation nuns), secular institutes (e.g., Opus Dei), and societies of apostolic life (e.g., Paulists, Sulpicians, Vincentians).

Book Three, "The Church's Teaching Mission," consists of 87 canons concerned with preaching, catechizing, missionary activity, Christian education, publications, and the profession of faith.

Book Four, "The Church's Sanctifying Role," regulates in 420 canons the seven sacraments: baptism, confirmation, the Holy Eucharist, penance, the anointing of the sick, holy orders, and matrimony. The canons prescribe the proper minister for each, the necessary dispositions on the part of the recipient, and the ceremonial to be observed. The second part of the book discusses other religious acts: sacramentals (e.g., blessings and exorcisms); the Liturgy of the Hours, or Divine Office (q.v.); funerals; devotion to the saints (sacred images and relics); vows and oaths. The third part is concerned with sacred places (churches and cemeteries) and sacred times (holy days and days of fast and abstinence).

Book Five, "The Temporal Goods of the Church," regulates property in 57 canons: its acquisition, administration, and alienation. It also deals with pious wills and pious foundations.

Book Six, "Sanctions in the Church," consists of 89 canons concerned with ecclesiastical penalties such as excommunication, interdict, and suspension. Various crimes and offenses are listed with specific sanctions attached. Types of delicts (or offenses against the law) are as follows: apostasy, heresy, and schism (against religion and the unity of the church); physical violence, incitement to disobedience, and unauthorized alienation of property (against ecclesiastical authorities and the liberty of the church); simulation of the sacraments, unauthorized ordinations, and violation of the seal of confession (usurpation of ecclesiastical functions); falsification of church documents and injury of a person's good name; clerics engaging in business or trade or attempting marriage (against special obligations); homicide and abortion (against human life and liberty).

Book Seven, "On Processes," treats procedural law in 353 canons. Every diocesan bishop is required to appoint a judicial vicar, or officialis, who is to have ordinary jurisdiction over all cases except those that the bishop may reserve to himself. Other officials include the promoter of justice and the defender of the bond (relating to holy orders and matrimony). The tribunal of second instance, or court of appeal, is the archdiocesan, or metropolitan, court. The pope, as the supreme judge for the whole Roman Catholic world, may hear cases himself. The ordinary tribunal for receiving appeals to the Holy See is the Roman Rota. The Supreme Tribunal of the Apostolic Signatura is competent to hear complaints against a sentence of the Rota or any act of an ecclesiastical administrative power alleging error of law or procedure. The code concludes with a section on administrative procedure. In each diocese an office or council may be permanently established to resolve disputes arising from the exercise of an administrative authority in the church. A special procedure is provided for the removal and transfer of pastors.

Laws of the church as well as those of the state bind their subjects in conscience. The obligation in conscience does not arise immediately from the laws themselves but from the divine plan, in which people are envisioned as living in both a civil and an ecclesiastical society. Church and state are the judges of what is necessary to realize the common good. Their laws carry a legal obligation of greater or lesser weight, depending on the importance of specific statutes in achieving that end.

The Code of Canon Law itself lays down certain principles of interpretation. Laws that impose a penalty, for example, or restrict the free exercise of rights, or contain an exception from the law are to be strictly interpreted. In canon law, unlike common law, an interpretation given by a court in a judicial sentence does not set a precedent; it has no force of law and binds only those persons affected. For an authentic interpretation of the code, a special Roman commission was established in 1917.

History. The beginning of canon law may be seen in the New Testament (see Acts 15; 1 Cor. 11). During the 2d and 3d centuries a number of church orders (for example, the *Didache* and the *Apostolic Tradition*) described as normative certain customary practices of the community. Canon law in the sense of enacted legislation originated in the 4th-century regional councils held in Asia Minor. The enactments of these councils (Ancyra, Neocaesarea, Antioch, Gangra, and Laodicea), together with those of the ecumenical councils of Nicaea (325), Constantinople (381), and Chalcedon (451), formed the nucleus of subsequent collections. They dealt with the structure of the church (the provincial and patriarchal organization), the dignity of the clergy, the process of reconciling sinners, and Christian life in general.

The oldest Greek canonical collection preserved in the original text is the *Synagoge Canonum* (c. 550) in 50 titles by Johannes Scholasticus (d. 577). Instead of a chronological arrangement, the canons are grouped systematically according to subject matter. Another innovation was the accordance of canonical authority to rulings of church fathers, especially St. Basil. The Council of Trullo (692), in giving formal approval to the preceding conciliar legislation and patristic writings, established the basic code for the Eastern churches that is still normative for the Orthodox.

In the West, the most important canonical collection of the early centuries was made in the 6th century by Dionysius Exiguus. He translated into Latin the canons of the Eastern councils and added 39 papal decretals. The rulings of the popes were thus put on a level with conciliar law. After the disintegration of the Roman Empire, canon law developed independently in the different kingdoms. National collections were made in which local legislation, intermingled with elements of Germanic law, were added to the ancient code. Because conciliar activity was particularly intense in Spain, the collection known as the *Hispana* (later called the *Isidoriana* after St. Isidore of Seville) proved to be outstanding. Of great significance for the future was the institution of the practice of private penance by the Irish monks.

Collections made at the time of Charlemagne (c. 800) and the Gregorian reform (c. 1050) reflect the attempt to restore traditional discipline. Great confusion persisted, however, insofar as certain practices accepted in the Germanic law and the penitentials (for example, remarriage after adultery) were in conflict with the program of the reformers. Ivo of Chartres (c. 1040–1116) prepared (c. 1095) a set of rules and principles for interpreting and harmonizing texts. The actual work of harmonization was done (c. 1140) by Gratian, who is called the father of the science of canon law. Shortly after the revival of Roman law studies at the University of Bologna, Gratian collected all the canon law from the earliest popes and councils up to the Second Lateran Council (1139) in his *Decretum,* or *Concordance of Discordant Canons.* With its appearance the period of the *ius antiquum* came to a close.

The scientific study of law stimulated by the *Decretum* encouraged the papacy to resolve disputed points and supply needed legislation, thus inaugurating the *ius novum.* Over the next century thousands of papal decretals were issued and gradually collected in five *compilationes. Compilatio Tertia,* consisting of decretals from the first 12 years of his reign, was ordered by Innocent III in 1210 to be used in courts and law schools, thus becoming the first collection in the West to be officially promulgated. Gregory IX commissioned Raymond of Peñafort (c. 1185–1275) to organize the five *compilationes* in one collection, which was promulgated in 1234 and became known as the *Extravagantes.* Two other official collections were made later: the *Liber Sextus* (1298) of Boniface VIII and the *Constitutiones Clementinae* (1317). The *Extravagantes of John XXII* and the *Extravagantes Communes* were privately compiled. In 1503 the legist Jean Chappuis printed and published in Paris, under the title *Corpus Iuris Canonici,* the *Decretum* of Gratian and the three official and two private collections of decretals. The *Corpus,* together with the decrees of the Council of Trent (1545-63), remained the fundamental law of the Roman Catholic church until the appearance of the *Codex Iuris Canonici* in 1917 (*see* TRENT, COUNCIL OF). The *Corpus* continues to have some validity for the Church of England, which issued a Code of Canons in 1603. The medieval law is presupposed except where it has been affected by contrary statute or custom in England. The Convocations of Canterbury and York in 1964 and 1969 promulgated a revised code with the same understanding.

After the theological updating of the Second Vatican Council (1962-65; *see* VATICAN COUNCIL, SECOND), it became necessary for the Roman Catholic church to undertake a thorough revision of the 1917 code. A special commission was established in 1963, which in 1980 presented the draft of a completely new code. Pope John Paul II, after making a number of revisions, promulgated it on Jan. 25, 1983; it took effect on Nov. 27, 1983.

Plans have been underway since a presynodal meeting at Chambesy, Switzerland, in November 1976 for the first Great Synod of Eastern Orthodoxy to be held since the 8th century. Among the topics for further study is the codification of the Holy Canons. J.E.L.

For further information on this topic, see the Bibliography in volume 28, section 81.

CANONSBURG, borough, Washington Co., SW Pennsylvania; inc. 1802. It is an industrial center located in an agricultural and coal-mining area; major manufactures include metal products and pottery. Settled about 1773, the community was platted in 1787 by Col. John Canon (hence its name). The Whiskey Rebellion of 1794, a protest against a federal excise tax, was organized here at the Black Horse Tavern. Pop. (1970) 11,439; (1980) 10,459.

CANOPUS, star of the first magnitude, the second brightest star in the heavens, located in the southern constellation Argo. Although Canopus is about 98 light-years away from the earth, it is only half a magnitude fainter than the brightest star, Sirius, which is 8.8 light-years distant. Because of its brightness, Canopus is used as a reference point for navigation of spacecraft launched on interplanetary missions. The star is in the extreme southern part of the sky and cannot be seen at latitudes north of Norfolk, Va.

CANOSSA, village in Reggio nell'Emilia Province, northern Italy, southwest of the city of Reggio nell'Emilia. In January 1077, Henry IV, Holy Roman emperor, who had been excommunicated by Pope Gregory VII, traveled from Germany to Canossa, where Gregory was staying at the castle of Countess Matilda of Tuscany (1046-1115), to seek an audience with the pope. The emperor stood for three days in the courtyard of the castle, bareheaded and barefooted. Following this display of humility, the pontiff granted Henry absolution. The phrase *going to Canossa* was probably coined by the Prussian statesman Prince Otto von Bismarck during the *Kulturkampf,* his struggle with the Roman Catholic church. The phrase has since alluded to a place or occasion of submission, penance, or humiliation.

CANOVA, Antonio (1757-1822), Italian sculptor, who, with the Danish sculptor Bertel Thorvaldsen, was the leading exponent of neoclassicism. Born in Possagno, he studied sculpture in nearby Venice. He won distinction with such marble statues as *Daedalus and Icarus* (1779, Museo Correr, Venice). On visits to Rome and Naples he was exposed to classical art, and after settling in Rome in 1781, he took an active part in the current revival of interest in antique Greek and Roman styles. For such works as the tombs of Clement XIV (begun 1784, Santi Apostoli, Rome) and Clement XIII (begun 1787, St. Peter's, Rome) and the *Perseus with Medusa's Head* (1801, Metropolitan Museum of Art, New York City), he became recognized as the foremost neoclassical sculptor of his day. Canova also received commissions from Napoleon, including the famous Maria Paulina Borghese as *Venus Victrix* (1805-07, Galleria Borghese, Rome), a serenely sensuous portrait of Napoleon's sister Pauline reclining. After the fall of Napoleon, Canova was sent to Paris to retrieve the art treasures the emperor had taken from Italy. He also worked on commissions in England. Canova died in Venice.

CANSO, STRAIT OF, also Gut of Canso, strait, SE Canada, separating Cape Breton Island from the mainland of Nova Scotia. It is about 27 km (about 17 mi) long and up to 3.2 km (2 mi) wide and links the Gulf of Saint Lawrence and the North Atlantic Ocean. The Canso Causeway (opened 1955) carries vehicular and rail traffic across the strait; at the E end of the causeway are a canal and lock that enable large vessels to navigate the waterway.

CANTABRIAN MOUNTAINS, mountain range, N Spain, extending about 480 km (about 300 mi) W from the Pyrenees to the Atlantic Ocean along the S shore of the Bay of Biscay. Torre de Cerredo, 2648 m (8687 ft) above sea level, is the highest peak; others exceed 2134 m (7000 ft).

CANTACUZENE, John. *See* JOHN VI CANTACUZENE.

CANTACUZENE, Serban (1640–88), Romanian statesman. He was hospodar (governor) of the Romanian region of Walachia from 1679 to 1688, when the region was part of the Ottoman Empire. In 1683 he was forced to help the Turks in their unsuccessful siege of the city of Vienna. In return for his aid, the Turkish sultan recognized the descent of his family from the Byzantine emperor John VI Cantacuzene. He is noted for introducing the cultivation of Indian corn into his country, for establishing the first Romanian school in the city of Bucharest, and for replacing Old Church Slavonic with Romanian in the liturgy of the church.

CANTALOUPE. *See* MELON.

CANTATA, in music, a vocal composition with instrumental accompaniment. The cantata originated in the early 17th century simultaneously with opera and oratorio. The earliest type of cantata, known as the *cantata de camera,* was written for solo voice on a secular text. It contained several sections in contrasting vocal styles, such as recitative and aria. Italian composers who wrote in this form include Giulio Caccini, Claudio Monteverdi, and Jacopo Peri (1561–1633). During the late 17th century, the *cantata de camera* developed into a composition for two or three voices; written mainly for churches, this form was known as the *cantata da chiesa.* Its chief Italian exponents were Giacomo Carissimi and Alessandro Scarlatti. In Germany during this period, the *cantata da chiesa,* under the leadership of Heinrich Schütz, Georg Philipp Telemann, Dietrich Buxtehude, Johann Sebastian Bach, and other composers, developed into a far more elaborate form than its Italian model.

Since the time of Bach the cantata has usually been a choral composition with instrumental accompaniment, containing choruses, solos, arias, recitatives, and instrumental interludes. The text may be sacred, in which case the cantata resembles the oratorio, or secular, in which case it resembles opera. In its sacred form it differs from an oratorio by being considerably shorter and less elaborate in both its vocal writing and its accompaniment. In its secular form it differs from opera by being sung without scenery, costumes, or staged action. Among composers of the cantata since the period of Bach are Felix Mendelssohn, Franz Liszt, Robert Schumann, Johannes Brahms, Hector Berlioz, Aaron Copland, Béla Bartók, and Sergey Prokofiev.

CANTERBURY (anc. *Durovernum*), city, Kent, SE England, on the Stour R. The present city, formed in 1974, incorporates the former city and county borough of Canterbury and an area that includes the seaside towns of Whitstable and Herne Bay. Canterbury is the ecclesiastical center of England. Trade in grain and hops, the chief crops of the region, is conducted here. Among the industrial establishments are textile mills, brickworks, and breweries; tourism is also important to the economy. At Whitstable are oyster fisheries.

The town of Canterbury is dominated by its huge cathedral, seat of the Primate of the Church of England since the late 6th century. The present cathedral was constructed between 1070 and 1180, with important additions dating from the 15th and 19th centuries. Trinity Chapel, to the rear of the altar, contains the site of the shrine of St. Thomas à Becket, who was murdered here in 1170. At the E terminus of the cathedral is the circular tower known as Corona Chapel or Becket's Crown. On the N side of the cathedral are the cloisters, chapter house, baptistery, deanery, library, and the King's School (a grammar school, originally est. in the 7th cent.). Among the Roman relics in Canterbury are the remains of the town walls and the mosaic floors of a villa. Canterbury is the seat of Saint Augustine's College (1848) for training Anglican clergy, the University of Kent at Canterbury (1965), and the City of Canterbury College of Art (1874).

Canterbury is a town of ancient British origins. It was occupied by the Romans in the 1st century AD. In the late 6th century it became the capital of Ethelbert, king of Kent. The first Christian missionary to England, St. Augustine, arrived here from Rome in 597, founded the abbey, and converted Ethelbert to Christianity. The town subsequently became a Saxon religious and cultural center. From the 8th to the 11th century it was raided periodically by the Danes, who burned the cathedral in 1011. The cathedral's shrine of St. Thomas à Becket was the object of pilgrimage from the 12th century to 1538, when it was dismantled and its accumulated treasures confiscated, by command of Henry VIII. During the 16th century French and Flemish Protestant refugees introduced the textile industry to Canterbury. The cathedral and surrounding buildings were damaged by German aerial bombing in World War II but have since been repaired. Pop. (1981) 116,829.

CANTERBURY, ARCHBISHOP OF, Primate of all England, chief bishop of the Church of England, with jurisdiction over 29 dioceses in the ecclesiastical province of Canterbury, and bishop of the diocese of Canterbury, which consists of the eastern part of the county of Kent and the rural deanery of Croyden. The archbishop has palaces at Canterbury and at Lambeth in London. He presides over the upper house of the Convocation of Canterbury; the Church Assembly, the representative body for the entire Church of England; and the Lambeth Conference, a decennial assembly of bishops of the Anglican Communion (q.v.). By tradition he is a member of the House of Lords in the British Parliament and crowns the British monarch.

The archbishopric began in AD 597 with the arrival of St. Augustine of Canterbury at Kent and the baptism of King Ethelbert in Saint Martin's Church, Canterbury. During the Middle Ages a long struggle for precedence between Canterbury and York was settled in the 14th century in favor of Canterbury. In the 16th century Thomas Cranmer was archbishop when the Act of Supremacy (1534) separated the Church of England from the Roman Catholic church. In 1960 Archbishop Geoffrey Francis Fisher visited Pope John XXIII in Rome, inaugurating a new era of fellowship between the divided churches. A total of 102 archbishops have occupied the see of Canterbury since 597; the current archbishop, Robert A. K. Runcie (1921-), was elevated in 1980.
J.E.B.

CANTERBURY TALES. *See* CHAUCER, GEOFFREY.

CAN THO, city, S Vietnam, on the Bassac R. (Song Hau Giang), in the Mekong delta. Hub of an important rice- and fruit-growing area, Can Tho has an agricultural experimental station. Industries include rice milling, sawmilling, coconut-oil extracting, and soap and cigarette manufacturing.

Situated in an area of Cochin China formerly dominated by the Khmer people, Can Tho was captured by the Annamese in the 18th century and eventually became a part of French Indochina. Pop. (est.) 182,400.

A winter view of Canterbury Cathedral, seat of the archbishops of Canterbury for almost 1400 years.
British Tourist Authority

The cantilever principle is used here in a jutting wing of the Milwaukee County War Memorial (1953–57), Milwaukee, Wis., designed by Eero Saarinen. Ezra Stoller–ESTO

CANTILEVER, in engineering or construction, beam or truss rigidly supported at one end, or in the middle, but not at both ends, which has forces applied along the free arm or at the free end. A typical example of a cantilever is a diving springboard. Cantilever construction is used for canopies, balconies, large construction cranes, airplane hangars, and in cantilever bridges where the span is supported not at the ends but toward the center of the bridge truss. Many drawbridges are basically cantilevers. A cantilever beam of given cross section is much weaker than a similar beam twice as long but supported at both ends.

CANTON, also Guangzhou, Kuang-chou, or Kwangchow, city, S China, capital of Guangdong (Kwangtung) Province. It is a busy port and a commercial and industrial center on the Pearl R. (Zhu Jiang or Chu Chiang). Manufactures include processed food (especially sugar), textiles, steel, paper, cement, fertilizer, chemicals, motor vehicles, and machinery. The city, which is served by an outer deepwater port at Whampoa (Huangpu), is linked by rail with Hong Kong and Peking. About 15 percent of China's foreign trade is conducted here, and the city is the site of a twice-yearly major international trade fair (est. 1957). A leading educational center of China, Canton is the site of Zhongshan (Chungshan or Sun Yat-sen) University (1924), a school of medicine, a technical university, and an agricultural institute.

Landmarks in the city include Sha Mian (Shameen) Island, where foreign traders formerly lived; a Ming dynasty (1368–1644) temple, now the Peasant Movement Institute; a pagoda in the Temple of the Six Banyan Trees; a 14th-century watchtower (now Guangzhou Museum) in Yue Xiu (Yue Hsiu) park; the blue-roofed Sun Yat-sen Memorial Hall; and a mosque said to be the oldest in China.

An ancient settlement of obscure origins, Canton was brought into the Chinese Empire in the 3d century BC. Arab, Persian, Hindu, and other merchants traded here for centuries before the Portuguese arrived in quest of silk and porcelain in the 16th century. They were followed by British merchants in the 17th century and French and Dutch traders in the 18th century. Canton became a treaty port in 1842, but restrictions on trade continued until a sandbank in the Pearl R. (later developed into Sha Mian Island) was ceded (1861) for unrestricted foreign trading and settlement; it was returned to Chinese control in 1946. Canton was a center of activity during the Republican Revolution (1911), led by Sun Yat-sen, which resulted in the establishment of the Republic of China, and it was the early headquarters of the Kuomintang, the leading political party. The Japanese occupied and heavily damaged the city during 1938–45. Extensive urban redevelopment, begun in the 1920s, was resumed after 1949, when it was combined with a major program of beautification, industrial expansion, and port improvement. Pop. (1980 est.) 3,000,000.

CANTON, industrial city, seat of Stark Co., NE Ohio, on Nimishillen Creek; settled 1805, inc. as a city 1854. Among its many manufactures are iron and steel, refined petroleum, electrical equipment, engines, processed food, metal items, and ceramics. The city is the site of Malone College (1892) and the National Professional Football Hall of Fame. President William McKinley lived in Canton and is buried here. Pop. (1970) 110,053; (1980) 94,730.

CANTON AND ENDERBURY ISLANDS. *See* Phoenix Islands.

CANTOR. *See* Jewish Music.

CANTOR, Georg (1845–1918), German mathematician, born in Saint Petersburg (now Leningrad). He taught at the University of Halle and was professor there after 1872. His early work with the Fourier Series led to his development of a theory of irrational numbers. Cantor also formulated the theory of sets, upon which modern mathematical analysis is based. This theory extended the concept of number by introducing infinite or, as he called them, transfinite numbers. Cantor's work was largely responsible for the subsequent critical investigation of the foundations of mathematics and mathematical logic.

CANUTE II, called The Great (994?–1035), king of England (1016–35), Denmark (1018–35), and Norway (1028–35).

Canute, the son of Sweyn I Forkbeard, king of the Danes, conquered England in 1013. When his father died the following year, he was proclaimed king of England by his Danish warriors. However, the witenagemot, an advisory body to the Anglo-Saxon kings, reinstated King Ethelred, and Canute fled. He returned in 1015 and soon subjugated all of England, except London. After Ethelred's death in 1016, the Londoners named his son, Edmund II, king. During an ensuing struggle, the Londoners' brave fight ended in defeat at Ashingdon, Essex, in October 1016. The following month Edmund died and Canute emerged the undisputed king. A wise and effective ruler, he reconciled with the English and maintained peace with the Continental powers. To that end he married King Ethelred's widow, Emma of Normandy (fl. 1002–52), supported the church, and in 1027 went to Rome to attend the coronation of Holy Roman Emperor Conrad II. For administrative purposes he divided England into the four earldoms of Mercia, Northumberland, Wessex, and East Anglia.

Canute continued to reside in England even after he inherited the crown of Denmark in 1018. He soon began his conflict with Olaf II of Norway, whose realm he claimed. Forcing Olaf into exile in 1028, Canute installed his young son, Sweyn (r. 1029–35; d. 1036), to govern Norway; after Olaf's fall at Stiklestad in 1030 his rule was unchallenged. Canute's North Sea empire fell apart after his death. Two sons separately ascended the thrones of England and Denmark, while the son of Olaf II succeeded in Norway.

CANVAS, closely woven fabric made of natural or synthetic fibers. The firm cloth is used in making sails, awnings, tarpaulins, artist's canvas, and—in lightweight form—clothing.

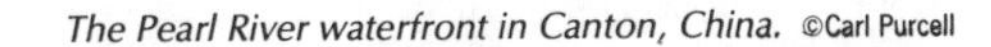

The Pearl River waterfront in Canton, China. ©Carl Purcell

CANVASBACK, North American bay or sea duck, *Aythya valisineria,* much esteemed as a table delicacy. It is named from the wavy, dusky markings on the white feathers of its upperparts. It has a reddish-brown head and neck. It is larger than the redhead (*A. americana*), with a bill deeper at the base and larger. It is found from Minnesota and the Dakotas north to the Arctic Circle and winters on the tidewaters of the middle and southern states. The canvasback has a length of about 53 cm (about 21 in) and weighs about 1 kg (about 2 lb). *See* DUCK.

CANYON, deep gorge created by the erosive action of a river. The best-known examples in North America are the Grand Canyons of the Colorado R. and the Yellowstone R.

CANYON DE CHELLY NATIONAL MONUMENT, NE Arizona, established in 1931. The monument, located within a Navajo Indian reservation, contains ruins of numerous prehistoric cliff dwellings, the earliest of which date from the 4th century and the most recent from the 14th century. The sheer red sandstone walls of Canyon de Chelly and Canyon del Muerto rise to a height of about 300 m (about 1000 ft) above the canyon floors. Ruins are found on the floors and in caves in the canyon walls. Notable are the White House Pueblo, occupied from about 1060 to 1275, and the Mummy Cave, dating from 1253. The Navajo settled in the region about 1700. Area, 339.3 sq km (131.0 sq mi).

CANYONLANDS NATIONAL PARK, SE Utah, established in 1964. The park is located in a scenic desert region surrounding the confluence of the Green and Colorado rivers. Each river passes through deep, winding gorges, the most dramatic of which is Cataract Canyon below the rivers' junction. Here, erosion has produced monumental formations in the red and white sandstone, with spires and pillars reaching about 90 m (about 300 ft) in height. The park contains Indian petroglyphs (rock carvings) and traces of villages approximately 1000 years old. Area, 1366.1 sq km (527.5 sq mi).

CANZONE, in poetry, a short lyric poem that developed in Provence, France, and became popular in Italy during the Middle Ages. The subject of canzoni (Ital., "songs") was usually love, nature, or feminine beauty. In form a canzone was composed of stanzas of equal length and closed with an envoy, a shorter stanza. The number of lines in the stanzas varied from 7 to 20. The most famous writers of canzoni were the 14th-century Italians Dante and Petrarch.

In music, a canzone (or, usually, canzona) was a 16th-century multipart vocal setting of a literary canzone and a 16th- and 17th-century instrumental composition. At first based on Franco-Flemish polyphonic songs (chansons) later independently composed, the instrumental canzona influenced the fugue and was the direct ancestor of the sonata.

Canvasback, Aythya valisineria
Arthur W. Ambler–National Audubon Society

CÃO, Diogo. *See* CAM, DIOGO.

CAPA, Robert (1913–1954), Hungarian-American, who was an outstanding war photographer. His original name was André Friedmann. He covered the Spanish civil war, World War II, and the war in Indochina, where he was killed in 1954. To Capa, technical considerations were secondary to catching a dramatic moment. His slightly blurred action photographs, such as those taken during the 1944 Normandy invasion, portray the violence of war with unique impact.

CAPABLANCA, José Raúl (1888–1942), Cuban chess grand master, born in Havana, and educated at Columbia University. He learned to play chess at the age of 4 and won the championship of Cuba at the age of 12. Later, in international tournaments in Europe, he defeated a number of the best players of the time and established himself as a grand master. In 1921 he won the world championship from the German player Emanuel Lasker, but in 1927 Capablanca lost his title to the Russian grand master Alexander Alekhine in a match that lasted three months. Relying less on theory than on intuitive perceptions, intense concentration, and precise positional analysis, Capablanca was what is called a "natural player."

CAPACITANCE, ability of a circuit system to store electricity. The capacitance of a capacitor (q.v.) is measured in farads and is determined by the formula $C = q/V$, where q is the charge (in coulombs) on one of the conductors and V is the potential difference (in volts) between the conductors. The capacitance depends only on the thickness, area, and composition of the capacitor's dielectric.

CAPACITOR, or electrical condenser, device for storing an electrical charge. In its simplest form a capacitor consists of two metal plates separated by a nonconducting layer called the dielectric. When one plate is charged with electricity from a direct-current or electrostatic source, the other plate will have induced in it a charge of the opposite sign; that is, positive if the original charge is negative and negative if the charge is positive. The Leyden jar is a simple form of capacitor in which the two conducting plates are metal-foil coatings on the inside and outside of a glass bottle or jar that serves as the dielectric. The electrical size of a capacitor is its capacitance (q.v.), the amount of electric charge it can hold.

Capacitors are limited in the amount of electric charge they can absorb; they can conduct direct current for only an instant but function well as conductors in alternating-current circuits. This property makes them useful when direct current must be prevented from entering some part of an electric circuit. Fixed-capacity and variable-capacity capacitors are used in conjunction with coils as resonant circuits in radios and other electronic equipment. Large capacitors are also employed in power lines to resonate the load on the line and make it possible for the line to transmit more power.

Capacitors are produced in a wide variety of forms. Air, mica, ceramics, paper, oil, and vacuums are used as dielectrics, depending on the purpose for which the device is intended.

CAP-DE-LA-MADELEINE, city, Champlain Co., S Québec Province, Canada, at the confluence of the Saint-Maurice and Saint Lawrence rivers, near Trois-Rivierès; inc. as a city 1922. Major manufactures include printed materials, paper, aluminum and asbestos products, clothing, and abrasives. Of note is the Church of Notre-Dame du Cap (early 18th cent.). The main growth of the community, settled in 1651, began in the early 20th century. Pop. (1981) 32,626; (1986) 32,800.

CAPE AGULHAS (Port., "needles"), the southernmost point of Africa, Cape of Good Hope Province, SW South Africa. Fog, uncertain currents, and rocks make passage around the point dangerous for ships. The meridian of Cape Agulhas is used as the boundary between the Atlantic and Indian oceans.

CAPE ANN, peninsula, NE Massachusetts, at the N limit of Massachusetts Bay. The rocky peninsula, rich in stone quarries, projects 14 km (9 mi) into the Atlantic Ocean. It is the location of several old fishing centers and resorts, notably Gloucester, Essex, and Rockport.

CAPE BRETON HIGHLANDS NATIONAL PARK, N Cape Breton Island, N.S., Canada, established in 1936. It includes a scenic tableland region with a rugged Atlantic coastline characterized by high cliffs. The thickly forested hills of the park harbor diverse wildlife. The Cabot Trail is in the N part of the park. Area, 951 sq km (367 sq mi).

CAPE BRETON ISLAND, irregularly shaped, hilly island of NE Nova Scotia, Canada, located between the Atlantic Ocean and the Gulf of Saint Lawrence. The island is 177 km (110 mi) long and up to 137 km (85 mi) wide. It is separated from the mainland of Nova Scotia by the Strait of Canso and is divided into two parts by the large Bras d'Or Lake.

Friars Head, Inverness Co., Cape Breton Island.
Nova Scotia Communications & Information Centre

The rugged landforms and cool summer climate of Cape Breton Island lure many tourists. Attractions include the Cabot Trail, a scenic road that offers spectacular views along the NE coast. The road also passes through Cape Breton Highlands National Park (q.v.), which has uplands ranging up to 532 m (1747 ft) in height. Besides tourism, important industries on the island include coal mining, steel making, fishing, and lumbering. The principal coal mines are located near Sydney, the island's main urban center, which has large steel mills. Other towns include Glace Bay, New Waterford, North Sydney, and Sydney Mines. Most of the inhabitants of Cape Breton Island are descended from the Highland Scots who settled here in the early 19th century. Some French-Canadians and a small number of Micmac Indians also live on the island.

The first European to see the island was probably John Cabot in 1497. In 1534 Jacques Cartier named the island Breton, after the French region of Brittany. In 1629 a group of Scots founded the island's first European settlement, which soon after was captured by the French. The island was formally assigned to France in 1713 by the Peace of Utrecht, and it was renamed Île Royale. At Louisbourg, in the SE, the French built (1720–45) a large fortress (now part of Louisbourg National Historic Park) to help defend the sea approaches to the Saint Lawrence R. The fortress was seized by British colonial forces in 1745, during King George's War, but was returned to French control three years later. In 1758, during the French and Indian War, the British destroyed the fortress and gained possession of the island. Cape Breton Island has been administered as part of Nova Scotia since 1763, except from 1784 to 1820, when it was made a separate British colony.

Area, 10,311 sq km (3981 sq mi); pop. (1976) 170,866; (1981) 170,088.

CAPE CANAVERAL, cape, E Florida, on a barrier island. Occupying the cape area and a part of nearby Merritt Island is the John F. Kennedy Space Center, operated by the National Aeronautics and Space Administration (q.v.). The space center is the principal U.S. launching site for earth satellites and space flights. Patrick Air Force Base is nearby. Neighboring communities have experienced great industrial expansion and population growth caused largely by the space center. The area also attracts many tourists. From 1963 to 1973 the cape was known as Cape Kennedy in honor of President John F. Kennedy.

CAPE CHARLES, promontory, E Virginia, at the entrance to Chesapeake Bay. On Smith's Island, near the cape, is a lighthouse with a revolving light 55 m (180 ft) above high water.

CAPE CHELYUSKIN, promontory, N Siberian USSR, on the Boris Vil'kitskiy Strait, the northernmost point of the Asian mainland. It is a portion of the tundra extending N from the Taymyr Peninsula to lat 77°41′ N.

CAPE COAST, city and port, S Ghana, capital of the Central Region. Products of the district that are exported from the city include frozen fish, cacao, coconuts, citrus fruits, corn, and cassava. It is the site of a university college. The area was settled by the Portuguese in 1610, and the city, formerly called Cape Coast Castle, is the site of an old castle and several forts. The Swedes in 1652 built the fort of Carolusberg, which passed to the Dutch in 1659 and to the British in 1667. Cape Coast was the capital of the British Gold Coast possessions until the 1870s, when the capital was transferred to Accra. The city was chartered in 1905. Pop. (1984) 57,700.

CAPE COD peninsula, SE Massachusetts, crossed at its base by the Cape Cod Canal. The cape is surrounded by Cape Cod Bay to the N; the Atlantic Ocean to the E; Nantucket Sound to the S; and Buzzards Bay to the SW. The cape is deeply indented; in shape it resembles a flexed arm. It extends eastward about 56 km (about 35 mi) and then northward about 48 km (about 30 mi). The width varies from about 32 km (about 20 mi) between the towns of Sandwich and Woods Hole at the neck to a few hundred meters at the tip near the town of Provincetown. The cape is sandy, hilly, and thickly forested in spots and contains many lakes and ponds. Cape Cod is well known as a popular summer resort and has excellent facilities for swimming, fishing, and boating. Fishing is an important industry, especially in Provincetown, which has one of the largest and safest harbors on the Atlantic seaboard. Cranberries are the chief crop. Other communities on Cape Cod are Barnstable, Yarmouth, Orleans, Falmouth, Bourne, and Hyannis. The cape has a number of lighthouses, including Chatham Light at Chatham, and Cape Cod Light at Truro. Cape Cod was discovered and named in 1602 by the English explorer Bartholomew Gosnold, who was impressed by the abundance of codfish in the surrounding waters. In 1620 the Pilgrims dropped anchor in Provincetown Harbor. Cape Cod National Seashore covers much of the NE part of the peninsula.

CAPE COD CANAL, sea-level ship canal, SE Massachusetts, crossing the base of the Cape Cod Peninsula. It connects Cape Cod Bay on the N to Buzzards Bay on the S, a distance of 12.4 km (7.7 mi). The maximum width is 165 m (540 ft), and the depth is 10 m (32 ft). The approach channels at the extremities are each almost 8 km (5 mi) long. A breakwater protects the Cape Cod Bay entrance. Except for one turn, the canal is straight. It shortens the water route from New York City and other major ports to Boston and eliminates the hazardous alternative route around Cape Cod. The Cape Cod Canal was built (1909–14) by private interests. The federal government purchased the canal in 1928 and since that time has operated it as a toll-free waterway.

CAPE COLONY. *See* CAPE PROVINCE.

CAPE CORAL, city, Lee Co., SW Florida, on the Caloosahatchee R., near Fort Myers; inc. 1971. It is primarily a residential center, with many retired persons. The city has some 645 km (some 400 mi) of canals. Cape Coral grew rapidly in the 1970s. Pop. (1980) 32,103.

CAPE DEZHNEV, also East Cape, cape, NE Russian SFSR, Far Eastern USSR. It forms the easternmost part of the Chukchi Peninsula and of the entire mainland of Asia. The cape is separated from Cape Prince of Wales, Alaska, by the Bering Strait. It is named for the Russian explorer S. I. Dezhnyov (1605–1672?), who sailed around it in 1648.

CAPE FEAR, promontory, S North Carolina, on the S tip of Smith Island, jutting into the Atlantic Ocean, near the mouth of the Cape Fear R. It was so named because of the treacherous waters surrounding it. A prominent landmark on Cape Fear is its lighthouse.

CAPE FEAR, river rising in central North Carolina. It flows SE for about 322 km (about 200 mi) before emptying into the Atlantic Ocean. The river is formed by the junction of the Haw and Deep rivers. The largest tributaries are the South R. from the E and the North East Cape Fear R. from the NE. It is the longest river wholly within the state and is navigable inland to Fayetteville. Rice growing is an important industry along the lower river.

CAPE FINISTERRE (Lat., "land's end"), promontory, NW Spain, extending into the Atlantic Ocean. It is noted as the scene of two British naval victories over France, on May 3, 1747, in the War of the Austrian Succession, and on July 22, 1805, in the Napoleonic Wars.

CAPE FLATTERY, high promontory, NW Washington State, extending into the Pacific Ocean, at the entrance to Juan de Fuca Strait. It was discovered by the British explorer and navigator Capt. James Cook in 1778, on his last voyage. When the American explorers Meriwether Lewis and William Clark arrived at the cape in 1806, it was inhabited by the Makah Indians. In 1855 the Makah ceded all their lands to the federal government, except for the cape and a small adjacent area; a Makah reservation still occupies this land.

CAPE GIRARDEAU, city, Cape Girardeau Co., SE Missouri, on the Mississippi R.; inc. as a city 1843. The city is a manufacturing, commercial, and transportation center situated in an agricultural region; products include paper and plastic goods, footwear, and electrical appliances. Southeast Missouri State University (1873) is here. The name of the community, settled about 1793, is derived from that of Jean B. Girardot, a French-Canadian who built a trading post nearby in the early 18th century. Pop. (1970) 31,282; (1980) 34,361.

CAPE OF GOOD HOPE, headland, SW Cape Province, South Africa, near Cape Town. Rising 256 m (840 ft) above sea level, the headland marks the turning point for vessels plying between the South Atlantic and Indian oceans. It is erroneously regarded as the extremity of the continent; Cape Agulhas, to the SE, is the southernmost point of Africa. The Cape of Good Hope was discovered by the Portuguese navigator Bartholomeu Dias in 1488 and named by him Cabo Tormentoso (Port., Cape of Storms). It was renamed Cabo da Bōa Esperança (Port., Cape of Good Hope) by John II of Portugal, because of the commercial importance of the new route to the E. The cape was not rounded again by a European until 1497, when the Portuguese navigator Vasco da Gama made the first voyage from Europe to India.

CAPE OF GOOD HOPE, PROVINCE OF THE. *See* CAPE PROVINCE.

CAPE GUARDAFUI. *See* RAS ASIR.

CAPE HATTERAS, promontory, E North Carolina. It projects into the Atlantic Ocean from Hatteras Island, a long and narrow beach separated from the mainland of North Carolina by Pamlico Sound. Shoals and frequent gales and storms make the surrounding waters dangerous for navigation. Southbound coasting vessels are apt to be crowded toward the cape by the E and W vibrations of the Gulf Stream, which is about 32 km (about 20 mi) to the E. Cape Hatteras National Seashore is noted for points of historical interest, including Cape Hatteras Lighthouse.

CAPE HORN (Span. *Cabo de Hornos*), promontory, S Chile, in the Tierra del Fuego archipelago, on Horn Island. It marks the southernmost point of South America and extends into Drake Passage, the antarctic strait connecting the South Atlantic and South Pacific oceans. The rocky terrain of the cape rises to a height of 424 m (1391 ft). Storms, strong currents, and icebergs make passage around the cape extremely hazardous. During the time of sailing ships, hundreds of vessels were wrecked while "rounding the horn." The Dutch navigator Willem Cornelis Schouten, the

A view of the arid central plateau, or Karroo, that occupies the interior of Cape Province, South Africa. In the distance are the Nieuwveld Mts.
Douglas Waugh–Peter Arnold, Inc.

first to sail around the cape (1616), named it for his birthplace, Hoorn, Netherlands.

ČAPEK, Karel (1890–1938), Czech novelist, playwright, and theatrical producer, born in Malé Svatoňovice, and educated at the University of Prague. Čapek was a close friend of the first Czech president, Tomáš Masaryk, with whom he worked to preserve the Czech nation after World War I. Simultaneously Čapek was an editor for a Prague newspaper, founder and director of the Vinohradsky Art Theater in Prague, and political essayist, playwright, and novelist.

Čapek is best known for his plays, the most famous of which is *R.U.R.* (1921; trans. 1923), a dramatic fantasy in which people are dehumanized by the machine age. *R.U.R.* stands for "Rossum's Universal Robots" and is the source of the English word *robot*. Čapek is also well known for two other dramas: *The Insect Play* (1921; trans. 1923), known in the U.S. as *The World We Live In,* a satire that foretells the evils of totalitarianism; and *Power and Glory* (1937; trans. 1938), an attack on dictatorship. His novels include fanciful romances, science fiction, and a philosophical trilogy. Čapek also wrote travel sketches and impassioned political essays.

CAPE KENNEDY. *See* CAPE CANAVERAL.

CAPE KRUSENSTERN NATIONAL MONUMENT. *See* NATIONAL PARK SERVICE (table).

CAPELLA, (Lat., "she-goat"), first-magnitude star in the northern constellation Auriga. It is also known as Aurigae. A giant yellow star with a spectrum much like that of the sun, it is one of the brightest stars visible in the sky. Capella is a spectroscopic binary (double star) with a rotation period of 104 days. Capella is approximately 40 light-years from earth and is much larger and brighter than the sun. The star's name is derived from a Roman myth about a goat that suckled the infant god Jupiter.

CAPE MAY, southernmost point of New Jersey, at the N entrance to Delaware Bay. It has a revolving light 49 m (160 ft) above sea level.

CAPE MAY, city, Cape May Co., southernmost tip of New Jersey, on the Atlantic Ocean; settled 1630s, inc. as a city 1851. It is one of the nation's oldest coast resorts; commercial fishing is also important. It was a whaling community in the 18th century and developed as a fashionable resort in the early 19th century. The city is named for the Dutchman Cornelius Mey, who explored this coast in 1621. Pop. (1970) 4392; (1980) 4853.

CAPE PRINCE OF WALES, westernmost point of the mainland of Alaska and of the North American continent, separated by the Bering Strait from Cape Dezhnev, Far Eastern USSR. Cape Prince of Wales is on the Seward Peninsula.

CAPE PROVINCE, also Province of the Cape of Good Hope, formerly CAPE COLONY, largest province of South Africa, occupying the S extremity of Africa, and bordered on the N by Botswana, on the NE and E by the provinces of Transvaal, Natal, and Orange Free State, as well as by the independent state of Lesotho and the black-African homeland of Transkei, and on the NW by Namibia. Two other black-African homelands, Bophuthatswana, in the N, and Ciskei, in the SE, form enclaves in the province. Cape Town is the provincial capital and the largest city. Other cities include Port Elizabeth, East London, Kimberley, Uitenhage, and Paarl. Area of Cape Province, 648,302 sq km (250,311 sq mi).

Land. Most of the province is a rolling plateau region, averaging about 915 m (about 3000 ft) in height. This region is demarcated on the S by a series of steep ranges, including the Drakensberg and Stormberg mountains. To the S of these ranges is a vast, barren tableland, known as the Karroo (q.v.), which varies between about 305 and 915 m (about 1000 to 3000 ft) in elevation. The Karroo is fringed to the S by coastal mountain ranges. Cape Agulhas, SW of the Cape of Good Hope, is the southernmost extremity of Africa. The principal river is the Orange, which flows westerly into the Atlantic Ocean.

Around Cape Town the annual average temperature is a mild 16.7° C (62° F); generally lower temperatures prevail in the upland areas, particularly during the winter season. Rainfall is heaviest along the S coast; the interior is semiarid.

Population. Bantu-speaking peoples, principally Xhosa, constitute a majority of the black population, which numbers some 1.6 million. Persons of unmixed European origin number about 1.3 million. This section of the population consists of a slight majority of Afrikaans speakers as opposed to English speakers. Coloureds—people of mixed ancestry (black, white, Asian)—and Asians make up the remainder. Pop. (1980) 5,091,360.

Economy. A principal industry in Cape Province is the raising of livestock, extensive areas being highly suitable for pasturage and grazing. Cattle, sheep, goats, ostriches, horses, and donkeys are raised. Crop cultivation is limited largely to areas in the E, S, and SE. Among the chief crops of the province are wine grapes, olives, citrus and other fruits, oats, barley, wheat, and tobacco.

Diamond mining is a major source of wealth; the diamond mines in the vicinity of Kimberley are among the most productive in the world. Blue asbestos, tin, copper, and manganese are mined also. Among other leading industries are wine and brandy making, fruit canning, food processing, brewing, fishing, lumbering, and the manufacture of textiles, building materials, furniture, shoes, and metal products.

History. European colonization of the region began in 1652, when the Dutch East India Co. (*see* EAST INDIA COMPANY) established a settlement on Table Bay, near modern Cape Town. Dutch immigration to the colony increased during the 18th century. In 1795, during the French Revolution, British military forces seized the colony. It was returned to Dutch control in 1803 but was ceded to the British in 1806 and formally became a colony of Great Britain in 1814.

Various reforms, including the abolition (1833) of slavery, were instituted by the British, but the first few decades of their rule were marked by a series of wars with the Xhosa and other Bantu-speaking peoples and by growing antagonisms between the Dutch, or Boers (q.v.), and the British sections of the population. A mass migration (the Great Trek) from the Cape Province by angered Dutch farmers led to the establishment of Transvaal and Orange Free State (qq.v.).

The discovery (1867) of diamonds in Griqualand West, a part of Transvaal, tremendously stimulated the industrial and population growth of the colony. Cape Colony annexed Griqualand West in 1871 and Transvaal in 1877, provoking profound hostility among the Boers.

Relations between the British and Boers deteriorated, finally culminating in 1899 in war (*see* BOER WAR). British annexation in 1900 of Transvaal and Orange Free State and the subsequent collapse of the Boers created conditions favorable to the establishment of a federal dominion in South Africa. In 1910 the British colonies in South Africa were confederated as the Union of South Africa (now the Republic of South Africa), and Cape Colony became the Province of the Cape of Good Hope (or Cape Province).

CAPER, common name for the order Capparales, a diverse group of flowering plants important for their vegetable and oil crops and garden flowers, and for its representative genus *Capparis*. The order is cosmopolitan in distribution, but species are concentrated in the tropical and Mediterranean regions. Capparales includes 8 families and about 4000 species; all but about 100 of these belong to two large families: Capparaceae, the capers, and Brassicaceae, the mustards. The mustards include cabbage, cauliflower, turnip, horseradish, and wallflower (*see* MUSTARD).

Ruins of an ancient synagogue (2d–4th cent. AD) excavated in Capernaum. Björn Bölstad–Peter Arnold, Inc.

Although the caper and mustard families share many floral, chemical, and vegetative features, indicating a close relationship between the two, questions concerning the relationships of the smaller families remain because of insufficient knowledge of their diverse structures.

The caper family contains about 45 genera and 1000 species, which occur in tropical and subtropical areas, especially Africa and the Mediterranean region. It contains herbs, shrubs, trees, and some vines. Flowers are usually irregular, and some are showy. Although the number and arrangement of the flower parts are variable, the ovary (female flower part) is characteristically borne on a gynophore, an elongation of the floral tissue between the stamens and ovary, resulting in a distinctive stalked appearance of the mature ovary and fruit. The spider flower, *Cleome hassleriana,* a well-known garden annual, is a member of this family. The capers that are used as a seasoning or condiment are the pickled, unopened buds of *Capparis spinosa,* a spiny shrub native to dry, rocky areas in the Mediterranean.

Plants of the order Capparales are dicots (q.v.) in the class Angiospermae (*see* ANGIOSPERM).

See also SPICES.

CAPERNAUM, town of ancient Palestine, on the northwestern shore of the Sea of Galilee (now Lake Tiberias), northeast of the modern town of Tiberias, Israel. Excavations begun at the village of Tell Hum in 1905 identified it with Capernaum, the home of Jesus Christ during much of his ministry. It is also the home of his first disciples St. Andrew, St. Matthew, and St. Peter. A hill nearby is thought to have been the site of the Sermon on the Mount. Today only a few ruins of the ancient town remain, among them a synagogue built between the 2d and 4th centuries AD. In the late 19th century Franciscan monks restored part of the synagogue and built a monastery, which they still maintain.

CAPE SABLE, southernmost point of the mainland U.S. and of mainland Florida. It is a peninsula extending W from the S tip of Florida, between Ponce de Leon and Florida bays. It is part of Everglades National Park.

CAPET, family name of the dynasty of kings that ruled France from 987 to 1328. In 987, on the death of Louis V, the last of the Carolingian kings of France, Hugh Capet, duke of France and count of Paris, was elected king by the nobility and the clergy. The feudal domain of the Capet family was Île de France, the area around Paris. The Capetian kings greatly strengthened the royal power in France by insisting on the principles of heredity, primogeniture, and indivisibility of crown lands. Shortly after Hugh became king, he had his son Robert crowned as Robert II (known as the Pious). Hugh appointed Robert his associate, and this practice of the father having his eldest son rule with him was followed until the late 12th century. The greatest of the Capetian kings were Philip II Augustus, Louis IX (St. Louis), and Philip IV. The dynasty secured direct overlordship of almost all France by the process of incorporating additional fiefs, large and small, with their own territories. In 1328, when Charles IV died without male heirs, the Capetians were succeeded by the Valois, a younger branch of the family, which ruled France until 1589.

CAPE TOWN (Afrik. *Kaapstad*), city, legislative capital of South Africa and capital of Cape of Good Hope Province. It is located at the N end of the Cape Peninsula and is one of South Africa's major ports and industrial centers; associated suburbs and satellite towns of the fast-growing metropolitan area extend S across the neck of the Cape Peninsula to False Bay (Vaalsbaai). The old part of the city, now marked by tall, high-rise buildings and sprawling suburbs, is located between Table Bay to the N and the steep slopes of Table Mt. (1082 m/3549 ft) to the S. Several lesser peaks, including Lion's Head to the SW, and Signal Hill to the W, rise above the city and overlook the Atlantic Ocean. Cape Town is also a popular vacation resort, noted for natural scenic beauty and fine beaches.

Economy. Port activities are concentrated in a large artificial harbor in Table Bay. Equipped with dry docks and modern cargo-handling facilities, it is a regular port of call for freight and passenger vessels rounding the Cape of Good Hope to the S. Gold, diamonds, and citrus are leading exports. Major industries include oil refining, shipbuilding and repairing, diamond cutting, printing, food processing, and the manufacture of clothing, plastics, and leather goods.

Points of Interest. Table Mt., with cable car service to the top, dominates the city landscape and provides an excellent point from which to view the surrounding area. Historic points of interest include the Castle, the oldest building in Cape Town (begun 1665); the Dutch Reformed Church (begun 1699); Old Town House (1755); and the old Dutch-style buildings and mosques found in the Malay Quarter on Signal Hill. Other important landmarks are the houses of Parliament; the South African Museum (1825); the South African National Gallery (1871); the famous Michaelis Collection of 17th-century Dutch and Flemish paintings; the South African Library; and Groote Schuur, official residence of the prime minister on the city outskirts. The University of Cape Town (1829) is in the city, and the University of the Western Cape (1960) is on the outskirts.

History. Cape Town was founded (1652) by Jan van Riebeeck (1618–77) as a supply base for the Dutch East India Co. and is the oldest city of European origin in South Africa. It remained under Dutch control, aided by the presence (1781–95) of a French garrison, until captured by British forces in 1795 during the Napoleonic Wars. The settlement briefly reverted to Dutch control in 1803 and was again reoccupied by British troops in 1806. In the 18th and early 19th centuries, before the building of the Suez Canal, Cape Town was a major station for ship provisioning. It be-

A view of Cape Town from a cable station on Table Mt.
South African Tourist Corp.

came the capital of the British Cape Colony in 1814 and subsequently was made the legislative capital of the Union of South Africa (1910–61) and the present republic of South Africa. Pop. (1985, greater city) 1,911,521.

For further information on this topic, see the Bibliography in volume 28, section 1035.

CAPE VERDE, republic, comprising the Cape Verde Islands, in the Atlantic Ocean, due W of the westernmost point of Africa, Cape Verde. The archipelago consists of ten islands and five islets, which are divided into windward and leeward groups. The windward group on the N includes Santo Antão, São Vicente, São Nicolau, Sal, and Boa Vista; the leeward group on the S includes São Tiago, Brava, Fogo, and Maio. Cape Verde has a total area of approximately 4033 sq km (approximately 1557 sq mi).

Land and Resources. The Cape Verde Islands are volcanic in origin, and all but three—Sal, Boa Vista, and Maio—are mountainous. The highest point, Pico do Cano (2829 m/9281 ft) on Fogo, is also the group's only active volcano. The climate is tropical and dry and subject to extended droughts. The average annual temperature is about 24° C (about 75° F). The annual rainfall averages about 250 mm (about 10 in) and is concentrated in the months from August to October. Vegetation is sparse and consists of various shrubs, aloes, and other drought-resistant species. Wildlife is also limited and includes lizards, monkeys, wild goats, and a variety of birdlife. Mineral resources are meager and include pozzolana (a volcanic rock used in making cement), salt, and kaolin.

Population. The majority of the people of Cape Verde are of mixed African and European descent and are known as Creoles, or *mestiços.* Nearly all of the remainder are of pure African stock. The total population (1986 est.) of Cape Verde was 342,000. The overall population density was about 85 persons per sq km (about 220 per sq mi). The official language is Portuguese; the national language, however, is Crioulo, a Creole dialect of Portuguese incorporating many African elements. Roman Catholicism is the dominant religion. The principal urban centers are Praia (pop., 1980, 37,500), the capital, on São Tiago, and Mindelo (est. 28,000) on São Vicente.

Government. Under the 1980 Cape Verde constitution, executive authority rests with a president, who is assisted by a cabinet headed by a prime minister. The president is chosen by the National Assembly, the country's legislative body. The 83 members of the National People's Assembly are elected by universal adult suffrage. The leading political grouping is the African Party for the Independence of Cape Verde.

Economy. Farming and fishing are by far the chief economic activities of Cape Verde. The principal subsistence crops are corn, beans, cassava, sugarcane, and bananas. Some coffee, bananas, and palm products are exported. Tuna and lobsters are taken from surrounding waters, and goats, pigs, and cattle are raised. Industries include sugar refining, fish processing, tobacco processing, and the distilling of liquors. The ports of Mindelo and Porto Novo serve as transatlantic fueling stops, and an international airport is located on Sal. The basic unit of currency is the Cape Verde escudo (89.2698 escudos equal U.S.$1; 1987).

History. The islands were used by Senegalese fishers before the first Europeans arrived, about 1456. They were claimed by Portugal in 1460; Portuguese settlers began to land shortly afterward. In 1495 the archipelago was declared a Crown possession, and slaves were subsequently imported from the African continent to cultivate the land. After gaining prosperity, the islands became attractive to pirates and foreign raiders—English, Dutch, and French—who repeatedly attacked during the following centuries. When the slave trade (for which the islands had served as a port of call) was abolished in 1876, their importance dwindled, although a coaling station and a submarine cable station at Mindelo still attracted many ships until World War I. Trade increased again toward the middle of the 20th century.

Like other Portuguese possessions in Africa, the islands were designated an overseas province rather than a colony, in 1951. Unlike the other territories, however, Cape Verde had relatively little agitation for independence until the 1970s. After the coup in Portugal in April 1974, self-determination was promised to the archipelago, and it became independent on July 5, 1975. Aristides Pereira (1923-), the country's first president, kept his nation nonaligned, maintaining good relations with all, while relying mainly on the Western powers for economic aid.

CAPE VERDE, also Cap Vert, peninsula, W Senegal, forming the westernmost part of Africa. It is about 32 km (about 20 mi) long and, at its maximum, 11 km (7 mi) wide. Cape Almadies forms its W tip. The city of Dakar is located here.

CAPE WRATH, promontory, extreme NW Scotland, 112 m (368 ft) high, extending into the Atlantic Ocean. It is noted for its wildness and grandeur. A lighthouse on the cape is visible for up to 43 km (27 mi).

CAP-HAÏTIEN, also Le Cap, city and seaport, N Haiti, capital of Nord Department, on the Bahía de Manzanillo, an inlet of the Atlantic Ocean. Cap-Haïtien has a spacious harbor and is an export center for coffee, cocoa, hides, honey, and logwood. In the 17th century the Spaniards built on the site of Cap-Haïtien a settlement that became a French possession in 1697. Under the French, who made it the capital of their colony of Saint-Domingue, it was a flourishing town, referred to as Little Paris. From 1811 to 1820 Cap-Haïtien was the capital of Henri Christophe, king of Haiti, when he ruled N Haiti. The town was almost destroyed by an earthquake in 1842. Pop. (1982 prelim.) 64,406.

CAPILLARITY, elevation or depression of the surface of a liquid where it is in contact with a solid, such as the sides of a tube. This phenomenon is an exception to the hydrostatic law that a liquid seeks its own level. It is most marked in capillary tubes (Lat. *capillus,* "hair"), that is, tubes of very small diameter. Capillarity, or capillary action, depends on the forces created by surface tension and by wetting of the sides of the tube. If the forces of adhesion of the liquid to the solid (wetting) exceed the forces of cohesion within the liquid (surface tension), the surface of the liquid will be concave, and the liquid will rise up the tube, that is, it will rise above the hydrostatic level. This action is typified by water in clean glass tubes. If the forces of cohesion exceed the forces of adhesion, the surface of the liquid will be convex, and the liquid will be repelled from the sides of the tube, that is, it will fall below the hydrostatic level. This action is typified by water in greasy glass tubes (in which the adhesion is small) and by mercury in clean glass tubes (in which the cohesion is great). The absorption of water in a sponge and the rise of molten wax in a wick are familiar examples of capillary rise. Water rises in soil partly by capillarity.

CAPILLARY, one of the minute blood vessels that form the connection between the arteries and the veins. These tiny vessels vary in diameter from 0.0127 to about 0.2032 mm (0.0005 to about 0.008 in) and are present in great numbers throughout the entire body. The walls of capillaries are exceedingly thin and readily permeable. They are surrounded by lymph (q.v.), and there is a constant interchange between the substances in the blood within the capillaries and the waste products in the body tissues and lymph outside. This interchange facilitates the processes of nutrition and elimination and enables the exchange of oxygen and carbon dioxide to take place. Lymph capillaries assist the blood capillaries in this process.

CAPITAL, collective term for a body of goods and monies from which future income can be derived. Generally, consumer goods and monies spent for present needs and personal enjoyment are not included in the definition or economic theory of capital. Thus, a business regards its land, buildings, equipment, inventory, and raw materials, as well as stocks, bonds, and bank balances available, as capital. Homes, furnishings, cars, and other goods that are consumed for personal enjoyment (or the money set aside for purchasing such goods) are not considered capital in the traditional sense.

In the more precise usage of accounting, capital is defined as the stock of property owned by an individual or corporation at a given time, as distinguished from the income derived from that property during a given period. A business firm accordingly has a capital account (frequently called a balance sheet), which reports the assets of the firm at a specified time, and an income account, which reckons the flow of goods and of claims against goods during a specified period.

Among the 19th-century economists, the term *capital* designated only that segment of business wealth that was the product of past industry. Wealth that is not produced, such as land or ore deposits, was excluded from the definition. Income from capital (so defined) was called profit, or interest, whereas the income from natural resources was called rent. Contemporary economists, for whom capital means simply the aggregate of goods and monies used to produce more goods and monies, no longer make this distinction.

The forms of capital can be distinguished in various ways. One common distinction is between fixed and circulating capital. Fixed capital includes all the more or less durable means of production, such as land, buildings, and machinery. Circulating capital refers to nonrenewable goods, such as raw materials and fuel, and the funds required to pay wages and other claims against the enterprise.

Frequently, a business will categorize all of its assets that can be converted readily into cash, such as finished goods or stocks and bonds, as liquid capital. By contrast, all assets that cannot be easily converted to cash, such as buildings and equipment, are considered frozen capital.

Another important distinction is between productive capital and financial capital. Machines, raw materials, and other physical goods constitute productive capital. Claims against these goods, such as corporate securities and accounts receivable, are financial capital. Liquidation of productive capital reduces productive capacity, but liquidation of financial capital merely changes the distribution of income.

Theories of Capital. The 18th-century French economists known as physiocrats were the first to develop a system of economics. Their work was developed by the British economist Adam Smith and emerged as the classic theory of capital after further refinements by the British economist David Ricardo in the early 19th century. According to the classic theory, capital is a store of values created by labor. Part of capital consists of consumers' goods used to sustain the workers engaged in producing items for future consumption. Part consists of producers' goods channeled into further production for the sake of expected future returns. The use of capital goods raises labor productivity, making it possible to create a surplus above the requirements for sustaining the labor force. This surplus constitutes the interest or profit paid to capital. Interest and profits become additions to capital when they are plowed back into production.

Karl Marx and other socialist writers accepted the classic view of capital with one major qualification. They regarded as capital only the productive goods that yield income independently of the exertions of the owner. An artisan's tools and a small farmer's land holding are not capital in this sense. The socialists held that capital comes into being as a determining force in society when a small body of people, the capitalists, owns most of the means of production and a much larger body, the workers, receives no more than bare subsistence as reward for operating the means of production for the benefit of the owners.

In the mid-19th century the British economists Nassau William Senior (1790–1864) and John Stuart Mill, among others, became dissatisfied with the classic theory, especially because it lent itself so readily to socialist purposes. To replace it, they advanced a psychological theory of capital based on a systematic inquiry into the motives for frugality or abstinence. Starting with the assumption that satisfactions from present consumption are psychologically preferable to delayed satisfactions, they argued that capital originates in abstinence from consumption by persons hopeful of a future return to reward their abstinence. Because such people are willing to forgo present consumption, productive power can be diverted from making consumers' goods to making the means of further production; consequently, the productive capacity of the nation is enlarged. Therefore, just as physical labor justifies wages, abstinence justifies interest and profit.

Inasmuch as the abstinence theory rested on subjective considerations, it did not provide an adequate basis for objective economic analysis. It could not explain, in particular, why a rate of interest or profit should be what it actually was at any given time.

To remedy the deficiencies of the abstinence theory, the Austrian economist Eugen Böhm-Bawerk (1851–1914), the British economist Alfred Marshall, and others attempted to fuse that theory with the classic theory of capital. They agreed with the abstinence theorists that the prospect of future returns motivates individuals to abstain from consumption and to use part of their income to promote production, but they added, in line with classic theory, that the amount of returns depends on the gains in productivity resulting from accretions of capital to the productive process. Accretions of capital make production more roundabout, thus causing greater delays before returns are realized. The amount of income saved, and therefore the amount of capital formed, would accordingly depend, it was held, on the balance struck between the desire for present satisfaction from consumption and the desire for the future gains expected from a more roundabout production process. The American economist Irving Fisher (1867–1947) was among those who contributed to refining this eclectic theory of capital.

The British economist John Maynard Keynes rejected the theory because it failed to explain the discrepancy between money saved and capital formed. Although, according to the eclectic theory and, indeed, all previous theories of capital, savings should always equal investments, Keynes showed that the decision to invest in capital goods is quite separate from the decision to save. If investment appears unpromising of profit, saving still may continue at about the same rate, but a strong "liquidity preference" will appear that will cause individuals, business firms, and banks to hoard their savings instead of investing them. The prevalence of a liquidity preference causes unemployment of capital, which, in turn, results in unemployment of labor.

History of Capital. Although theories of capital are of relatively recent origin, capital itself has existed in civilized communities since antiquity. In the ancient empires of the Middle East and to a larger degree in the Greco-Roman world, a considerable amount of capital, in the form of simple tools and equipment, was employed to produce textiles, pottery, glassware, metal objects, and many other products that were sold in international markets. The decline of trade after the fall of the Roman Empire led to less specialization in the division of labor and a reduced use of capital in production. Medieval economies engaged almost wholly in subsistence agriculture and were therefore essentially noncapitalist. Trade began to revive during the time of the Crusades. The revival was accelerated throughout the period of exploration and colonization that began late in the 15th century. Expanding trade fostered greater division of labor and mechanization of production and therefore a growth of capital. The flow of gold and silver from the New World facilitated the transfer and accumulation of capital, laying the groundwork for the Industrial Revolution. With the Industrial Revolution, production became increasingly roundabout and dependent on the use of large amounts of capital. The role of capital in the economies of western Europe and North America was so crucial that the socioeconomic organization prevailing in these areas from the 18th century through the first half of the 20th century became known as the capitalist system, or capitalism.

In the early stages of the evolution of capitalism, investments in plant and equipment were relatively small, and merchant, or circulating, capital—that is, goods in transit—was the preponderant form of capital. As industry developed, however, industrial, or fixed, capital—for example, capital frozen in mills, factories, railroads, and other industrial and transportation facilities—became dominant. Late in the 19th and early in the 20th centuries, financial capital in the form of claims to the ownership of capital goods of all sorts became increasingly important. By creating, acquiring, and controlling such claims, financiers and bankers exercised great influence on production and distribution. After the Great Depression of the 1930s, financial control of most capitalist economies was superseded in part by state control. A large segment of the national income of the U.S., Great Britain, and various other countries flows through government, which exerts a great influence in regulating that flow, thereby determining the amounts and kinds of capital formed. D.L.K.

For further information on this topic, see the Bibliography in volume 28, sections 211-13, 230.

CAPITALISM, economic system in which private individuals and business firms carry on the production and exchange of goods and services through a complex network of prices and markets. Although rooted in antiquity, capitalism is primarily European in its origins; it evolved through a number of stages, reaching its zenith in the 19th century. From Europe, and especially from England, capitalism spread throughout the world, largely unchallenged as the dominant economic and social system until World War I ushered in modern communism (or Marxism) as a vigorous and hostile competing system.

The term *capitalism* was first introduced in the mid-19th century by Karl Marx, the founder of communism (q.v.). *Free enterprise* and *market system* are terms also frequently employed to describe modern non-Communist economies. Sometimes the term *mixed economy* is used to designate the kind of economic system most often found in Western nations.

The individual who comes closest to being the originator of contemporary capitalism is the Scottish philosopher Adam Smith, who first set forth the essential economic principles that undergird this system. In his classic *An Inquiry into the Nature and Causes of the Wealth of Nations* (1776), Smith sought to show how it was possible to pursue private gain in ways that would further not just the interests of the individual but those of society as a whole. Society's interests are met by maximum production of the things that people want. In a now famous phrase, Smith said that the combination of self-interest, private property, and competition among sellers in markets will lead producers "as by an invisible hand" to an end that they did not intend, namely, the well-being of society.

Characteristics of Capitalism. Throughout its history, but especially during its ascendency in the 19th century, capitalism has had certain key characteristics. First, basic production facilities—land and capital—are privately owned. Capital in this sense means the buildings, machines, and other equipment used to produce goods and services that are ultimately consumed. Second, economic activity is organized and coordinated through the interaction of buyers and sellers (or producers) in markets. Third, owners of land and capital as well as the workers they employ are free to pursue their own self-interests in seeking maximum gain from the use of their resources and labor in production. Consumers are free to spend their incomes in ways that they believe will yield the greatest satisfaction. This principle, called consumer sovereignty, reflects the idea that under capitalism producers will be forced by competition to use their resources in ways that will best satisfy the wants of consumers. Self-interest and the pursuit of gain lead them to do this. Fourth, under this system a minimum of government supervision is required; if competition is present, economic activity will be self-regulating. Government will be necessary only to protect society from foreign attack, uphold the rights of private property, and guarantee contracts. This 19th-century view of government's role in the capitalist system has been significantly modified by ideas and events of the 20th century.

Origins. Merchants and trade are as old as civilization itself, but capitalism as a coherent economic system had its origins in Europe in the 13th century, toward the close of the feudal era. Human beings, Adam Smith said, have always had a propensity to "truck, barter, and exchange one thing for another." This inclination toward trade and exchange was rekindled and stimulated by the series of Crusades that absorbed the energies of much of Europe from the 11th through the 13th centuries. The voyages of discovery in the 15th and 16th centuries gave further impetus to business and trade, especially following the vast flood of precious metals that poured into Europe after the discovery and conquest of the New World. The economic order that emerged from these events was essentially commercial or mercantile; that is, its central focus remained on the exchange of goods rather than on their production. Emphasis on production did not come until the rise of industrialism in the 19th century.

Before that time, however, an important figure in the capitalistic system began to emerge: the entrepreneur (q.v.), or risk taker. A key element in capitalism is the undertaking of activity in the expectation that it will yield gain in the future. Because the future is unknown, both the risk of loss and the possibility of gain always exist. The assumption of risk involves the specialized role of the entrepreneur.

The thrust toward capitalism from the 13th century onward was furthered by the forces of the Renaissance and the Reformation (qq.v.). These momentous developments changed society enormously and paved the way for the emergence of the modern nation-state, which eventually provided the essential peace, law, and order crucial for the growth of capitalism. This growth is achieved through the accumulation of an economic surplus by the private entrepreneur and the plowing of this surplus back into the system for further expansion. Without some minimum of peace, stability, and continuity this process cannot continue.

Mercantilism. From the 15th to the 18th century, when the modern nation-state was being born, capitalism not only took on a commercial flavor but also developed in another special direction known as mercantilism. This peculiar form of capitalism attained its highest level in England.

The mercantilist system rested on private property and the use of markets for the basic organization of economic activity. Unlike the capitalism of Adam Smith, the fundamental focus of mercantilism was on the self-interest of the sovereign (that is, the state), and not the self-interest of the individual owners of economic resources. In the mercantilist era, the basic purpose of economic policy was to strengthen the national state and to further its aims. To this end the government exercised much control over production, exchange, and consumption.

The most distinctive feature of mercantilism was the state's preoccupation with accumulating national wealth in the form of gold and silver. Because most nations did not have a natural abundance of such precious metals, the best way to acquire them was through trade. This meant striving for a favorable trade balance—that is, a surplus of exports over imports. Foreign states would then have to pay for imports in gold or silver. Mercantilist states also favored maintaining low wages, believing that this would discourage imports, contribute to the export surplus, and thus swell the influx of gold.

More sophisticated proponents of the mercantilist doctrine understood that the real wealth of a nation was not its hoard of precious metals, but its ability to produce. They correctly saw that the influx of gold and silver from a favorable trade balance would serve as a stimulus to economic activity generally, thus enabling the state to levy more taxes and gain more revenue. Only a few states that practiced mercantilism, however, understood this principle.

Beginnings of Modern Capitalism. Two developments paved the way for the emergence of modern capitalism; both took place in the latter half of the 18th century. The first was the appearance of the physiocrats in France after 1750; and the second was the devastating impact that the ideas of Adam Smith had on the principles and practice of mercantilism.

The physiocrats. *Physiocracy* is the term applied to a school of economic thought that suggested the existence of a natural order in economics, one that does not require direction from the state for people to be prosperous. The leader of the physiocrats, the economist François Quesnay, set forth the basic principles in his *Tableau économique* (1758), in which he traced the flow of money and goods through the economy. Simply put, this flow was seen to be both circular and self-sustaining. More important, however, was that it rested on the division of society into three main classes: (1) The productive class was made up of those engaged in agriculture, fishing, and mining, representing one-half of the population. (2) The proprietary class consisted of landed proprietors and those supported by them, which amounted to one-quarter of the population. (3) The artisan, or sterile, class, made up the rest of the population.

Quesnay's *Tableau* is significant because it expressed the belief that only the agricultural classes are capable of producing a surplus or net product, out of which the state either could find the capital to support an expansion of the flow of goods and money or could levy taxes to meet its needs. Other activities, such as manufacturing, were regarded as essentially sterile, because they did not produce new wealth but simply transformed or circulated the output of the productive class. It was this aspect of physiocratic thought that was turned against mercantilism. If industry did not create wealth, then it was futile for the state to try to enhance society's wealth by a detailed regulation and direction of economic activity.

The doctrine of Adam Smith. The ideas of Adam Smith represented more than just the first systematic treatise on economics; they were a frontal attack on the doctrines of mercantilism. Like the physiocrats, Smith tried to show the existence of a "natural" economic order, one that would function most efficiently if the state played a highly limited role. Unlike the physiocrats, however, Smith did not believe that industry was unproductive or that only the agricultural sector was capable of producing a surplus above the subsistence needs of society. Rather, Smith saw in the division of labor and the extension of markets almost limitless possibilities for society to expand its wealth through manufacture and trade.

Thus, both the physiocrats and Smith contributed to the belief that the economic powers of governments should be limited and that there existed a natural order of liberty applicable to the economy. It was Smith, however, far more than the physiocrats, who opened the way for industrialization and the emergence of modern capitalism in the 19th century.

The Rise of Industrialization. The ideas of Smith and the physiocrats provided the ideological and intellectual background for the Industrial Revolution—the material side of the sweeping transformations in society and the world that characterized the 19th century. No precise date can be given for this "revolution"; it is generally conceded to have begun in the late 18th century.

The fundamental characteristic of the industrialization process was the introduction of mechanical power (originally steam) to replace human and animal power in the production of goods and services. As the mechanization of production gained momentum in England and gradually spread to other parts of the world, several fundamental changes occurred. Production became more specialized and concentrated in larger units, called factories. The artisans and small shops of the 18th century did not disappear, but they were relegated to the periphery of economic activity in the leading nations, especially in England, the U.S., and Germany. The modern working class began to emerge; workers no longer owned their tools, they had little property, and generally they had to exchange their labor for a money wage. The application of mechanical power to production brought with it a great increase in worker efficiency, which made goods abundant and cheap. Consequently, the real standard of living rose throughout much of the world during the 19th century.

The development of industrial capitalism had serious human costs. The early days of the Industrial Revolution were marred by appalling conditions for large numbers of workers, especially in England. Abusive child labor, long working hours, and dangerous and unhealthy workplaces were common. These conditions led Karl Marx, who spent most of his adult life in England, to produce his massive indictment of the capitalistic system, *Das Kapital* (3 vol., 1867–94). Marx's work, which is the intellectual foundation for the kind of Communist economic systems now in use in the USSR and China, struck at the fundamental principle of capitalism—private ownership of the means of production. Marx believed that land and capital should be owned collectively (that is, by society) and that the products of the system should be distributed according to need.

Capitalism was also beset by cycles of "boom and bust," periods of expansion and prosperity followed by economic collapse and waves of unemployment. The classical economists who refined the ideas of Adam Smith had no ready explanation for the ups and downs of economic life, being content to view such cycles as the inevitable price that society had to pay for the material progress experienced under capitalism. Marxian criticisms, along with frequent depressions in the major capitalist nations, helped to establish vigorous trade-union movements that fought to raise wages, shorten working hours, and improve working conditions.

In the late 19th century, especially in the U.S., the modern corporation (q.v.), with its limited liability and immense financial power, began to emerge as the dominant form of business organization. The tendency toward corporate control of manufacturing led to many attempts to create combines, monopolies, or trusts (q.v.) that could control an entire industry. Eventually, the public outcry against such practices was great enough in the U.S. to lead Congress to pass antitrust legislation. This legislation attempted to make the pursuit of monopoly by business illegal, using the power of the state to force at least a bare minimum of competition in industry and commerce. The antitrust laws never succeeded in restoring to industry the competition of many small businesses that Adam Smith had envisaged, but it did impede the worst tendencies toward creating monopolies and restraining trade.

Despite such difficulties, capitalism continued to expand and prosper almost without limit throughout the 19th century. It was successful because it demonstrated an enormous ability to create new wealth and to raise the real standard of living for nearly everyone touched by it. As the century closed, capitalism was the dominant economic and social system.

20th-Century Capitalism. In the 20th century, capitalism has been continually buffeted by wars, revolution, and depression. More than anything else, war proved to be the undoing of capitalism in major areas. World War I brought revolution and a Marxist-based communism to Russia. The war also spawned the Nazi system in Germany, a malevolent mixture of capitalism and state socialism, brought together in a regime whose violence and expansionism eventually pushed the world into another major conflict. In the aftermath of World War II, Communist economic systems took hold in China and Eastern Europe. At present, many of the developing nations are strongly influenced by Marxist ideas as they struggle to turn former colonial areas into independent states. More than one-third of the world's population now lives under Marxist-inspired regimes, most of which are authoritarian to some degree.

In the industrial democracies of Western Europe and North America, the sharpest challenge to capitalism came from the catastrophic depression of the 1930s. This was by far the most severe economic upheaval endured by modern capitalism since its beginnings in the 18th century. Contrary to the logic of Marx's prophesy, however, Western nations failed to collapse into revolution. Rather, in meeting the challenge of the Great Depression, these capitalist systems demonstrated remarkable abilities for survival and adaptability to change. Democratic governments began to intervene in the economy to correct the worst abuses inherent in capitalism.

In the U.S., for example, the New Deal administration of President Franklin D. Roosevelt restructured the financial system so as to prevent a repeat of the speculative excesses that had led to financial collapse in 1929. Action was taken to encourage collective bargaining and build a strong labor movement in order to offset the concentration of economic power in large industrial corporations. The foundation for the modern welfare state was laid through the introduction of social security and unemployment insurance, measures designed to protect people from the economic hazards endemic to a capitalist system.

The most important intellectual event in the development of contemporary capitalism was the publication of the British economist John Maynard Keynes's *General Theory of Employment, Interest and Money* (1936). Like Adam Smith's ideas from an earlier era, Keynes's thought profoundly affected the way in which capitalism worked in Western democracies.

Keynes demonstrated that it is possible for a modern government to use its powers to spend money, vary taxes, and control the money supply in ways that can dampen down, if not eliminate, the age-old curse of capitalism—cycles of "boom and bust." According to Keynes, in a depression, government should increase its spending, even at the cost of unbalanced budgets, to offset the decline in private spending. The process should be reversed if a boom threatens to get out of hand, leading to excessive speculation and inflation. The Keynesian viewpoint became incorporated into U.S. law when Congress passed the Employment Act of 1946. This act, which committed the American government to maintaining high levels of employment and production, is a legal landmark representing the formal abandonment of laissez-faire (q.v.) as national policy.

Outlook for the Future. For 25 years after World War II the mixture of Keynesian ideas with traditional forms of capitalism proved extraordinarily successful. Western capitalist countries, including the defeated nations of World War II, enjoyed nearly uninterrupted growth, low rates of inflation, and rising living standards. Beginning in the late 1960s, however, inflation erupted nearly everywhere, and unemployment rose. In most capitalist countries the Keynesian formulas apparently no longer worked. Critical shortages and rising costs of energy, especially petroleum, played a major role in this change. New demands imposed on the economic system included ending environmental pollution, extending equal opportunities and rewards to women and minorities, and coping with the social costs of unsafe products and working conditions. At the same time, social-welfare spending by governments continued to grow; in the U.S., these expenditures (along with those for defense) account for the overwhelming proportion of all federal spending.

A major means of raising capital for the modern corporation is the sale of interest-bearing bonds, like the ones shown here. Edward C. Topple

The current situation needs to be seen in the perspective of the long history of capitalism, particularly its extraordinary versatility and flexibility. The events of this century, especially since the Great Depression, show that modified "mixed" or "welfare" capitalism has succeeded in building a floor under the economy. It has so far been able to prevent economic downturns from gaining enough momentum to bring about a collapse of the magnitude of the 1930s. This is no small accomplishment, and it has been achieved without the surrender of personal liberty or political democracy.

The accelerating inflation of the 1970s came to an end in the early 1980s, mainly because of two developments. First, restrictive monetary and fiscal policies led in 1981–82 to the sharpest recession since the 1930s, both in the U.S. and in Western Europe. As unemployment rose, inflation moderated. Second, energy prices dropped drastically, primarily as a result of conservation measures enacted in the 1970s; worldwide petroleum surpluses developed, thereby putting pressure on prices. By the mid-1980s the Western economies had recovered from the recession, although unemployment remained unusually high by post-World War II standards. This was part of the price paid for containing inflation.

The elusive goal for capitalist nations is to secure, simultaneously, high employment and stable prices. This is a formidable task, but given the historical flexibility of capitalism, the goal is both reasonable and attainable.

See also BUSINESS CYCLE; SOCIALISM; TRADE UNION; TRADE UNIONS IN THE UNITED STATES. For additional information on individual economists, see biographies of those mentioned. W.C.P.

For further information on this topic, see the Bibliography in volume 28, sections 211–13.

CAPITAL PUNISHMENT, legal infliction of the death penalty; in modern law, corporal punishment in its most severe form. Lynching, in contrast to capital punishment, is the unauthorized, illegal use of death as a punishment. The usual alternative to the death penalty is long-term or life imprisonment.

History. The earliest historical records contain evidence of capital punishment. It was mentioned in the Code of Hammurabi (1750 BC). The Bible prescribed death as the penalty for more than 30 different crimes, ranging from murder (see Exod. 21:12) to fornication (see Deut. 22:13). The Draconian Code of ancient Greece imposed capital punishment for every offense.

In England, during the reigns of King Canute and William the Conqueror, the death penalty was not used, although the results of interrogation and torture were often fatal. By the end of the 15th century, English law recognized seven major crimes: treason (grand and petty), murder, larceny, burglary, rape, and arson. By 1800, more than 200 capital crimes were recognized, and as a result, 1000 or more persons were sentenced to death each year (although most sentences were commuted by royal pardon). In the American colonies before the Revolution, the death penalty was commonly authorized for a wide variety of crimes. Blacks, whether slave or free, were threatened with death for many crimes that were punished less severely when committed by whites.

The Reform Movement. Efforts to abolish the death penalty did not gather momentum until the end of the 18th century; in England and America this reform was led by the Quakers (Society of Friends). In Europe, a short treatise, *On Crimes and Punishments* (1764), by the Italian jurist Cesare Beccaria, inspired influential thinkers such as the French philosopher Voltaire to oppose torture, flogging, and the death penalty. Encouraged by the writings of the philosopher Jeremy Bentham, England repealed all but a few of its capital statutes during the 19th century. Several states in the U.S. (led by Michigan in 1847) and a few countries (beginning with Venezuela in 1853 and Portugal in 1867) abolished the death penalty entirely.

Where complete abolition could not be achieved, reformers concentrated on limiting the scope and mitigating the harshness of the death penalty. Pennsylvania adopted a law in 1794 to distinguish first- and second-degree murder and limited the death penalty to murders committed with premeditation or in the course of carrying out another felony (first-degree murder). In 1846, Louisiana abolished the mandatory death penalty and authorized the option of sentencing a capital offender to life imprisonment rather than to death, a reform universally adopted in the U.S. during the following century. After the 1830s, public executions ceased to be commonplace, but did not cease entirely until after 1936.

Methods of Execution. The death penalty has been inflicted in many ways now regarded as barbaric and forbidden by law almost everywhere: Crucifixion, boiling in oil, drawing and quartering, impalement, beheading, burning alive, crushing, tearing asunder, stoning, and drowning are examples.

In the U.S., the death penalty is currently authorized in one of five ways: hanging (the traditional method of execution throughout the English-speaking world), electrocution (introduced by New York State in 1890), the gas chamber (adopted in Nevada in 1923), firing squad (used only in Utah), or lethal injection (introduced in 1977 by Oklahoma). In most nations that still retain the death penalty for some crimes, hanging or the firing squad are the preferred methods of execution. In some countries that adhere strictly to the traditional practices of Islam, beheading or stoning are still occasionally employed as punishment.

Effectiveness of Capital Punishment. The fundamental questions raised by the death penalty are whether it is an effective deterrent to violent crime, and whether it is more effective than the alternative of long-term imprisonment.

Defenders of the death penalty insist that because taking an offender's life is a more severe punishment than any prison term, it must be the better deterrent. Public opinion, which in the U.S. currently supports the death penalty for murder by a more than two-to-one margin, rests largely on this conviction. Supporters also argue that no adequate deterrent in life imprisonment is effective for those already serving a life term who commit murder while incarcerated; those who have not yet been caught but who would be liable to a life term if arrested; and revolutionaries, terrorists, traitors, and spies.

Those who argue against the death penalty as a deterrent to crime cite the following: (1) Adjacent states, in which one has a death penalty and the other does not, show no significant long-term differences in the murder rate; (2) states that use the death penalty seem to have a higher number of homicides than states that do not use it; (3) states that abolish and then reintroduce the death penalty do not seem to show any significant change in the murder rate; (4) no change in the rate of homicides in a given city or state seems to occur following a local execution.

In the early 1970s, some published reports purported to show that each execution in the U.S. deterred eight or more homicides, but subsequent research has discredited this finding. The current prevailing view among criminologists is that no conclusive evidence exists to show that the death penalty is a more effective deterrent to violent crime than long-term imprisonment.

Moral Concerns. The classic moral arguments in favor of the death penalty have been biblical and retributive. "Whosoever sheds man's blood, by man shall his blood be shed" (Gen. 9:6) has usually been interpreted as a divine warrant for putting the murderer to death. "Let the punishment fit the crime" is its secular counterpart; both maxims imply that the murderer deserves to die. Proponents of capital punishment have also claimed that society has the right to kill in defense of its members, just as the individual may kill in self-defense. The analogy to self-defense, however, is somewhat doubtful, as long as the effectiveness of the death penalty as a deterrent to violent crimes has not been proved.

Critics of the death penalty have always pointed to the risk of executing the innocent, although definitely established cases of this sort in recent years are rare. They have also argued that one can accept a retributive theory of punishment without necessarily resorting to the death penalty; proportioning the severity of punishment to the gravity of the crime does not require the primitive rule of "a life for a life."

In the U.S., the chief objection to capital punishment has been that it was always used unfairly, in at least three major ways. First, women are rarely sentenced to death and executed, even though 20 percent of all homicides in recent years have been committed by women. Second, a disproportionate number of nonwhites are sentenced to death and executed. Before the 1970s, when the death penalty for rape was still used in many states, no white men were executed for raping nonwhite women, whereas most black offenders found guilty of raping a white woman were executed. Third, poor and friendless defendants, those with inexperienced or court-appointed counsel, are most likely to be sentenced to death and executed. Defenders of the death penalty, however, have insisted that, because nothing inherent in the laws of capital punishment causes sexist, racist, or class bias in its use, these kinds of discrimination are not a sufficient reason for abolishing the death penalty either on grounds of fairness or on grounds that it is a "cruel and unusual punishment," violating the 8th Amendment to the U.S. Constitution. Opponents have replied that the death penalty is inherently subject to caprice and mistake in practice and that it is impossible to administer fairly.

Current Status. A series of U.S. Supreme Court decisions in the 1970s made the death penalty in the U.S. unconstitutional if it is mandatory, if it is imposed without providing courts with sufficient guidance to determine the appropriateness of the sentence, or if it is imposed for a crime that does not take or threaten life. Apart from crimes such as treason and espionage, about which the Supreme Court has rendered no decisions, the death penalty was confined to crimes of murder, including felony murder (that is, any homicide committed in the course of committing another felony, such as rape or robbery). Thirty-seven states revised and reenacted their death penalty laws after the 1972 Court ruling that all but a few capital statutes were unconstitutional. The Court upheld some revised death penalty laws in 1976; since then more than 100 executions have been carried out. In 1986 the Court ruled that opponents of capital punishment may be barred from juries in murder cases even if this increases the likelihood of conviction, thus sweeping away one of the last appeals available to death row inmates. The Supreme Court widened the possible use of the death penalty in two 1987 decisions, first ruling that it may be applied to some accomplices in crimes that led to murder and then rejecting a challenge to capital punishment based on statistics indicating that killers of whites are sentenced to die more often than killers of blacks.

In many other countries the death penalty is still lawfully inflicted for a wide range of crimes against people, property, public order, and the state. Few African and no Middle Eastern (Arab) or Asian nations have abolished it. About a dozen European countries (many from the Soviet bloc) have carried out executions since the 1970s. In the 1980s, however, certain Western nations have no capital punishment, while others have abolished it except for military or national security offenses. H.A.B.

For further information on this topic, see the Bibliography in volume 28, sections 37, 302.

CAPITOLINE HILL, one of the Seven Hills of Rome. Originally it had two peaks, and in ancient times the Arx, or Citadel, occupied the N summit and the great temple of Jupiter (originally built 508 BC) the S summit. In the central depression is the Piazza del Campidoglio, a plaza that, with its surrounding buildings designed by Michelangelo, is the civic center of modern Rome.

CAPITOL REEF NATIONAL PARK, S Utah, established as a national monument in 1937, as a national park in 1971. The park contains a massive sandstone ridge, 97 km (60 mi) long. The ridge is cut by numerous deep canyons and possesses unusual and colorful rock formations, such as those found in Cathedral Valley, where monoliths reach heights of 215 m (705 ft). Also found here are prehistoric Indian petroglyphs (rock carvings) and remnants of ancient cliff dwellings. The park's name is taken from the white dome-shaped rock formations on the Fremont R. Area, 979.0 sq km (378.0 sq mi).

CAPITOL OF THE UNITED STATES, seat of the U.S. Congress in Washington, D.C. Built on a hill popularly called Capitol Hill, the Capitol contains floor space equivalent to 1.6 ha (4 acres); its grounds cover 62.7 ha (155 acres). A neoclassical-style building, the Capitol is constructed of white marble, except for the center part of the west

The central dome of the Capitol building was completed in 1863. Crowning the cupola is a great bronze statue of a woman, representing freedom. Wearing classical robes and a crested helmet, she holds a sword in one hand and a wreath in the other. The dome, designed by Thomas Crawford, is modeled after the one designed by Michelangelo for St. Peter's Basilica in Rome. UPI front, which is Virginia sandstone painted white. The iron dome, also white, is surmounted by a statue of a woman representing Freedom (5.943 m/19.5 ft), by the American sculptor Thomas Crawford (1813–57). The height of the Capitol from the baseline on the east front to the top of the statue is 87.6 m (287.5 ft). Important parts of the Capitol include the Rotunda, directly under the dome, the Senate Chamber in the north wing, the House Chamber in the south wing, the National Statuary Hall (housing statues of famous Americans from every state), and the President's Room. Until 1935, the U.S. Supreme Court met in the Old Senate Chamber, which was located in the original north wing.

The original design of the Capitol, by William Thornton (1759–1828), a physician, was made in 1792, and the cornerstone was laid by George Washington on Sept. 18, 1793; Congress occupied the original north wing in 1800. Seven years later the main building was completed. During the War of 1812, invading British troops set fire to the structure, gutting the interior, but it was reconstructed after the war. Charles Bulfinch became Capitol architect in 1818; he built the Rotunda and the west central portico. The Capitol was completed and given its present appearance by Thomas U. Walter (1804–87), who finished the new north and south wings in the 1850s and the cast-iron dome in 1863. J. George Stewart (1890–1970) renovated the east front in 1962.

CAPO D'ISTRIA, Giovanni Antonio, Count. *See* KAPODÍSTRIAS, IOÁNNIS ANTÓNIOS, COUNT.

CAPONE, Al, full name ALFONSO CAPONE (1899–1947), Italian-American gangster of the Prohibition era. Born in Naples and raised in Brooklyn, N.Y., Capone was known as "Scarface" because of a knife cut on his cheek. In 1925 he took over a Chicago organization dealing in illegal liquor, gambling, and prostitution from the gangster Johnny Torrio (1882–1970). In the following years he eliminated his competitors in a series of gang wars, culminating in the St. Valentine's Day massacre of 1929, that won him control of Chicago's underworld. Convicted of income tax evasion in 1931 and sentenced to 11 years in prison, he was released in 1939 and spent the rest of his life an invalid, crippled by syphilis.

CAPORETTO, BATTLE OF, engagement of World War I, fought between October and December 1917, that resulted in a disastrous defeat of the armed forces of Italy by the armies of the Central Powers. On October 24, German and Austrian troops launched a sudden attack on Italian positions near the Austrian town of Caporetto (now Kobarid, Yugoslavia). Within 24 hours, units of the Italian army, under the command of the general Conte Luigi Cadorna (1850–1928), collapsed along the entire Isonzo River front, precipitating a retreat that continued until November 12. During this period, the forces of the Central Powers occupied Italy as far south as the Piave River, captured vast quantities of matériel, and inflicted casualties totaling about 320,000 killed, wounded, and missing. British and French troops that had arrived early in November saved Italy from total defeat. Gen. Armando Diaz replaced Cadorna as Italian commander in chief.

CAPOTE, Truman (1924–84), American writer, born in New Orleans, La. He was educated chiefly at Trinity School and Saint John's Academy, both in New York City. His first novel, *Other Voices, Other Rooms,* about a southern boy's search for identity, was published when he was 23 years old. His other works include *A Tree of Night and Other Stories* (1949), *The Grass Harp* (1951), *The Muses Are Heard* (1956), and *Breakfast at Tiffany's* (1958). His widely acclaimed *In Cold Blood* (1966), a "nonfiction novel," is an account of the murder of four family members in Garden City, Kans.; it was made into a film in 1967. *Music for Chameleons* (1980) is a collection of essays. Capote wrote the script for the musical stage play *House of Flowers* (1954) and collaborated on the scenario of the motion picture *Beat the Devil* (1954). His work has received critical praise for its technical virtuosity and keen observation. Capote died in Los Angeles on Aug. 25, 1984.

Truman Capote Rudy Valenzuela

CAPPADOCIA, ancient country in eastern Asia Minor, extending from the Pontus Euxinus (now the Black Sea) to the Taurus Mountains in present-day Turkey. As early as 1900 BC, merchants from Assyria established a colony in Cappadocia. From about 1750 BC to the formation of the Persian Empire of the Achaemenid dynasty in the 7th century BC, this region was the center of power of the Hittites. Later, the Persians controlled the area and divided it into two satrapies, or provinces. The northern province became known as Cappadocia near the Pontus, or merely Pontus; the southern area retained the name Cappadocia, by which it was known in classical times. After the conquest of Persia by Alexander the Great early in the 4th century BC, Cappadocia became independent. The first king of the Cappadocian dynasty, Ariarathes I (d. 322 BC), paid tribute to Alexander, but Alexander's successors were unable to conquer the country. Later, the kings of Cappadocia sided with Rome, then a rising power, against the Seleucids and against Pontus. Cappadocia changed sides often in its support of the various factions during the Roman civil wars of the 1st century BC. The independence of the country ended when the Romans supplanted the Cappadocian dynasty with a puppet king about 40 BC. In AD 17 the Roman emperor Tiberius made Cappadocia a province of the Roman Empire. Thereafter, the importance of Cappadocia as a separate political unit declined. Among the important towns of Cappadocia were the capital of the kingdom, Mazaca (now Kayseri), known in Roman times as Caesarea Mazaca; Tyana; and Melitene (now Malatya). The modern town of Boğazköy is on the site of the Cappadocian town of Pteria, which was built on the site of the city of Hattushash, capital of the Hittite Empire.

CAPRA, Frank (1897-), American film director and producer, born in Palermo, Italy. Capra was six years old when his family immigrated to the U.S., settling in Los Angeles. His first important job in Hollywood was as a writer for the Mack Sennett studios. Capra later joined Columbia Pictures, where he gained his greatest success as a director of sophisticated comedies that had appealing characters, social overtones, and happy endings. Such films include three that won Capra Academy Awards for best director: *It Happened One Night* (1934), *Mr. Deeds Goes to Town* (1936), and *You Can't Take It with You* (1938). During World War II Capra produced military documentaries. Other films he directed or produced include *Lost Horizon* (1937), *Mr. Smith Goes to Washington* (1939), *Arsenic and Old Lace* (1941), *State of the Union* (1948), *A Hole in the Head* (1959), and *A Pocketful of Miracles* (1961). His autobiography, *The Name Above the Title,* was published in 1971 (reprinted, 1985).

CAPRERA, small rocky island of Italy, in the Tyrrhenian Sea, off the NE coast of Sardinia, connected with the island of Maddalena by a causeway and drawbridge. It is famous as the residence of the Italian patriot Giuseppe Garibaldi, who died and was buried here in 1882. Area, 16 sq km (6 sq mi).

CAPRI (anc. *Capreae*), island, S central Italy, at the entrance of the Bay of Naples, near the city of Naples. It is about 6 km (about 4 mi) long and about 2 km (about 1.5 mi) at its widest point. Limestone cliffs, 274 m (900 ft) high, rise from the sea in the E; Monte Solaro, in the W, the highest point on the island, is 585 m (1920 ft) above sea level. The town of Capri, 136 m (450 ft) high, is an episcopal see. From the town 784 steps, carved in the rock, lead upward to Anacapri. To the W of the town of Capri is the Grotta Azzurra (Blue Grotto), a cavern, entered from the sea by a narrow opening not more than 91 cm (3 ft) high, but which inside is of magnificent proportions. Elliptical in form, it is 53 m (175 ft) long, 30 m (100 ft) at the widest part, and 12 m (41 ft) high; the water in the cavern is 15 m (48 ft) deep. Stalactites hang from the roof and sides. The blue color within the grotto is caused by the light passing through the water. Capri contains relics of prehistoric ages and numerous remains of Roman times, including the ruins of the 12 villas built by the emperor Tiberius, who resided in Capri for ten years. No springs or streams are on Capri, but it has abundant rainfall and is fertile, producing olive oil, wine, and fruit. The tourist trade provides the principal source of income for the islanders. Area, 10.4 sq km (4 sq mi); pop. (est.) 12,000.

CAPRICORNUS (Lat., "goat horn"), constellation of stars, the 10th of the 12 constellations of the zodiac. Capricornus is situated in the heavens far south of the equator, between the constellations Sagittarius and Aquarius. The name of the constellation is derived from Greek myths about the god Pan, who was often represented as a goatlike figure. Capricornus has no stars brighter than those of the third magnitude; its brightest star, Alpha Capricornus, is a wide multiple of which two separate stars can be distinguished by the naked eye. In the North Temperate Zone the constellations can be seen near the southern horizon in June. The ancient Greeks named the tropic of Capricorn after this constellation, because about 2000 years ago the sun entered Capricornus at the winter solstice about December 22; now it enters Sagittarius.

Capuchin, Cebus capucinus American Museum of Natural History

CAPRIVI, Georg Leo, Graf von (1831–99), German statesman, born in Berlin. Chosen by Emperor William II to replace Otto von Bismarck as imperial chancellor in 1890, Caprivi initiated a "new course" following 20 years of Bismarckian rule. By abandoning Bismarck's Reinsurance Treaty with Russia, however, he permitted the formation of a Franco-Russian alliance against Germany (1894). At home, he alienated German agricultural interests by lowering duties on imported grain. A target of increasing criticism, he was dismissed in 1894, and thereafter he lived in retirement. The Caprivi Strip, a narrow piece of land jutting east out of northeast Namibia that Caprivi acquired for Germany from Great Britain in 1890, is named for him.

CAPSICUM, red pepper plant, about 2 m (about 6 to 8 ft) in height, a genus of the family Solanaceae (*see* NIGHTSHADE). The fruit is a many-seeded berry, known variously as pod pepper, red pepper, chili, or capsicum, and is pungently flavored. Some species of the plant are bushy and are cultivated in tropical and subtropical countries. Under its Mexican name, chili, the fruit is used in sauces and mixed pickles. Cayenne pepper is made from the dried, ground seeds and pods.

CAPSTAN. *See* WHEEL AND AXLE.

CAPUA, town, S Italy, in Campania Region, on the Volturno R. Notable buildings include the Cathedral of San Stefano (856) and a Roman amphitheater.

Ancient Capua, founded before the 6th century BC near the site of the modern town, was the largest city in Italy except for Rome. During the Second Punic War Capua renounced its allegiance to the Romans for the Carthaginian general Hannibal, after which the city lost its autonomy. Capua continued to be an important city, despite its temporary destruction by the Vandals in 456, until about 840, when the Saracens destroyed it. In 856 the Lombards refounded Capua nearby on the site of ancient Casilinum. Pop. (est.) 14,000.

CAPUCHIN MONKEY, also sapajou, any of four species of New World monkey (q.v.) constituting the genus *Cebus* of the family Cebidae, suborder Anthropoidea, order Primates, and familiar as "organ-grinder" monkeys. Capuchins are found in the tropical forests of Central and South America. The name is derived from the cap of dark hair on the monkey's crown, which resembles the cowl worn by a Capuchin monk. One species, *C. apella,* also has tufts of hair on its head. The sturdy, roundheaded capuchins are about 30 to 55 cm (about 12 to 22 in) long, with a hairy, slightly prehensile tail of the same length. The tail is usually carried coiled at the tip—hence the alternative name, ringtail monkey. The monkeys are active by day and go about in troops, mainly in the tops of tall trees, feeding on fruits and small animals. The dominant male in a troop's social hierarchy breaks up fights between other troop members, keeps watch for enemies, and puts himself between the troop and intruders.

CAPUCHINS, branch of the Roman Catholic order of Franciscans, so designated from the *cappuccio* ("cowl") worn by them as their headdress. The Italian monk Matteo da Bascio (c. 1495–1552) founded the branch in 1528 at Montefalco in Umbria to restore the literal observance of the Rule of St. Francis. An order of Capuchin nuns, properly a branch of the Poor Clare order, was founded in Naples in 1538.

CAPULIN MOUNTAIN NATIONAL MONUMENT, NE New Mexico, established in 1916. The monument contains Capulin Mt. (2504 m/8215 ft), an extinct volcanic cone estimated to have been active about 2000 years ago. The crater of the mountain is about 460 m (about 1500 ft) wide and about 120 m (about 400 ft) deep. Area, 3.1 sq km (1.2 sq mi).

Capybara, Hydrochoerus hydrochoeris
Guyana Information Service

CAPYBARA, common name for *Hydrochoerus hydrochoeris,* the largest living rodent, of the Caviidae family. The capybara, also known as the carpincho, grows to a length of about 1 m (about 4 ft), weighs about 45 kg (about 100 lb), is semiaquatic in its habits, and is a vegetarian. The rodent runs clumsily because of slightly webbed feet, but swims well and can remain underwater for several minutes. A plump animal, with coarse, thin, brownish hair, it is easily tamed. It lives in pairs or families along the banks of rivers and lakes in South America.

CARABOBO, BATTLE OF, decisive engagement in the Venezuelan war of independence against Spain, fought on June 24, 1821. The revolutionary army, under the command of Simón Bolívar and José Antonio Páez, was intercepted during an advance on the city of Caracas by Spanish troops. The action, which lasted little more than an hour, took place on the plains of Carabobo southwest of Valencia and resulted in defeat of the Spanish. Four days later Bolívar entered Caracas in triumph, and freedom for Venezuela was ensured.

CARACAL, also Persian lynx, lynxlike member of the cat family (q.v.), Felidae, species *Caracal caracal,* native to the savannas and dry, rocky hills of Africa and Asia. Somewhat larger than a fox, the caracal has a reddish-brown coat, white belly, and tufts of black hair on the tips of its ears (the name caracal means "black ears" in Turkish). Caracals live on small deer, hare, and birds. In India and Iran they are sometimes tamed and used for hunting because of their speed and agility. They also go after nesting or roosting birds at the tops of trees and have been known to attack eagles. The caracal has been overhunted but is now a protected species.

CARACALLA, nickname of the Roman emperor who ruled as Marcus Aurelius Antoninus (188–217). Originally named Bassianus, he was born in Lugdunum, Gaul (now Lyon, France), and was nicknamed Caracalla because he introduced into Roman fashion a long cloak or tunic from Gaul

Marble bust of Caracalla Metropolitan Museum of Art

called the caracalla. When his father, Emperor Lucius Septimius Severus, died in 211, Caracalla became joint emperor with his younger brother, Publius Septimius Geta (189–212). In 212 Caracalla became sole emperor after causing the murder of Geta and the massacre of several thousand of Geta's followers. Caracalla's reign was marked by cruelty, extravagance, and treachery, particularly in military campaigns against the Alamanni and the peoples of Gaul and Parthia. During his reign the Baths of Caracalla and the Arch of Septimius were constructed in Rome. Caracalla was assassinated in Mesopotamia by Marcus Opelius Macrinus (164–218), who then succeeded him as emperor.

CARACARA, common name for members of the New World bird genus *Caracara* in the falcon (q.v.) family. One species, *C. plancus,* ranges from the Amazon basin through southern South America; the other, *C. cheriway,* extends northward from the Amazon into the southwestern U.S. Although a good flyer, the caracara has relatively long legs and is adapted to walking and running. It feeds on carrion and small animal life. The face and underbill are red, the body and crest black, and the neck white. The bird is about 60 cm (24 in) long. The caracara is the national emblem of Mexico.

CARACAS, capital and chief city of Venezuela, in N Venezuela, capital of the Federal District, in the fertile Caracas Valley, near the Caribbean port of La Guaira. Caracas is the commercial and industrial center of Venezuela and a great variety of industries are located here: auto assembly, sugar refining, meat packing, brewing, leather tanning, and the manufacture of paper, tobacco products, glassware, textiles, rubber goods, and pharmaceuticals. Oil refining is a leading industry. The city of Caracas is linked by air routes, by railroads, and by highways with La Guaira, with W Venezuela, and with Ciudad Bolívar.

The Plaza Bolívar, one of many squares and public gardens in Caracas, contains a bronze equestrian statue of Simón Bolívar, South American statesman and revolutionary, who was born in Caracas. Near the plaza are many Caracas landmarks, including the gilt-domed capitol building, the Central University of Venezuela (1725), and the National Pantheon, where Bolívar is buried. Another notable building is the Roman Catholic cathedral built in 1636; Caracas is the seat of the Roman Catholic archbishop of Venezuela.

The city was founded in 1567 as Santiago de León de Caracas and became one of the most prosperous Spanish colonial communities in South America. It was sacked by English buccaneers under the English navigator Sir Francis Drake in 1595. In 1810, under the leadership of Bolívar, it became the center of the first revolt in the war for independence from Spain (1810–21). Caracas became the capital of the Venezuelan Republic in 1829. During its history the city has suffered several earthquakes: 12,000 people were

University City, Caracas. Creole Petroleum Corp.

killed and most of the city was destroyed in 1812, and 277 people were killed and many buildings collapsed or were damaged in 1967. Pop. (1981) 2,299,700.

CARAT, term expressing the ratio of precious metal to base metal in an alloy, also a unit of weight for precious stones. In the first sense, a carat (usually spelled karat) indicates $\frac{1}{24}$ part by weight of a precious metal, such as gold, in an alloy. Thus, 18-karat gold is $\frac{18}{24}$, or $\frac{3}{4}$, gold, and 24-karat gold is pure gold. As a unit of weight for precious stones, the international metric carat, now used by most countries, was standardized by the U.S. government in 1913 at 200 mg, or 0.2 g. This standard carat is divided decimally; 0.01 carat is usually called a point.

CARAVAGGIO (1573–1610), Italian baroque painter, who played a pivotal role in the development of a naturalistic style in 17th-century painting. His use of models from the lower echelons of society in his early secular works and later religious compositions appealed to the Counter Reformation taste for realism, simplicity, and piety in art. Equally important is his introduction of dramatic light-and-dark effects—termed *chiaroscuro* (q.v.)—into his works.

Originally named Michelangelo Merisi, Caravaggio was born Sept. 28, 1573, in the Lombardy hill town of Caravaggio, from which his popular name is derived. He may have spent four years as apprentice to Simone Peterzano (fl. 1573–96) in Milan before going to Rome in 1593, where he entered the employ of the Mannerist painter Cesare d'Arpino (1568–1640), for whom he executed fruit and flower pieces (now lost). Among his best-known early works are genre (everyday) scenes with young men—for example, *The Musicians* (c. 1591–92, Metropolitan Museum, New York City)—which were done for his first important patron, Cardinal Francesco del Monte. Scenes such as the *Fortune Teller* (1594, versions in the Louvre, Paris, and the Museo Capitolino, Rome) were especially appealing to the artist's followers. Caravaggio's mature manner commenced about 1600 with the commission to decorate the Contarelli Chapel in San Luigi dei Francesi in Rome with three scenes of the life of St. Matthew. The *Calling of Saint Matthew* (c. 1599–1600) is noted for its dramatic use of "cellar light," streaming in from a source above the action, to illuminate the classically composed Christ (based on Michelangelo's Adam on the Sistine ceiling) and the other figures, most of whom are in contemporary dress. About 1601, Caravaggio received his second major commission, from Santa Maria del Popolo in Rome for a *Conversion of Saint Paul* and *Martyrdom of Saint Paul.* In the former, a bright shaft of light carries symbolic meaning, indicating the bestowal of faith upon the former pagan Saul.

Caravaggio's personal life was turbulent. He was often arrested and imprisoned. He fled Rome for Naples in 1607 when charged with murder. There he spent several months executing such works as the *Flagellation of Christ* (San Domenico Maggiore, Naples), which were crucial to the development of naturalism among the artists of that city. Later in 1607 he traveled to Malta, was made a knight, or *cavaliere,* of the Maltese order, and executed one of his few portraits, that of his fellow *cavaliere* Alof de Wignacourt (1608, Louvre). In October of 1608, Caravaggio was again arrested and, escaping from a Maltese jail, went to Syracuse in Sicily. While in Sicily he painted several monumental canvases, including the *Burial of Saint Lucy* (1608, Santa Lucia, Syracuse) and the *Raising of Lazarus* (1609, Museo Nazionale, Messina), paintings of densely packed yet simple compositions with large figures clothed in swirling masses of drapery. These works were among Caravaggio's last, for the artist died on the beach at Port'Ercole in Tuscany on July 18, 1610, of a fever contracted after a mistaken arrest.

Although the use of both realistic types and strong chiaroscuro originated in northern Italian art of the previous century, Caravaggio brought new life and immediacy to these aspects of painting, with which he effected a transformation of anticlassical Mannerism in early baroque Rome. Despite his personal protestations that nature was his only teacher, Caravaggio obviously studied and assimilated the styles of the High Renaissance masters, especially that of Michelangelo. Caravaggio's impact on the art of his century was considerable. He discouraged potential students, but throughout the century a true naturalist school flourished in Italy and abroad based on an enthusiastic emulation of his style.

See also BAROQUE ART AND ARCHITECTURE. E.J.S.

CARAVAN, name applied to groups of pilgrims or merchants organized for mutual help and protection against the hazards of travel, particularly on the deserts of Asia and Africa. On these journeys, many of which cover long distances, the beasts of burden most frequently used are the camel, donkey, and, in South America, the llama. The animals are traditionally arranged in a single file, which in larger caravans may extend for a distance of almost 10 km. Pilgrims on their way to the holy city of Islam, Mecca, particularly the groups that assemble annually in Cairo and in Damascus, Syria, form the most celebrated caravans. Groups en route from these cities some-

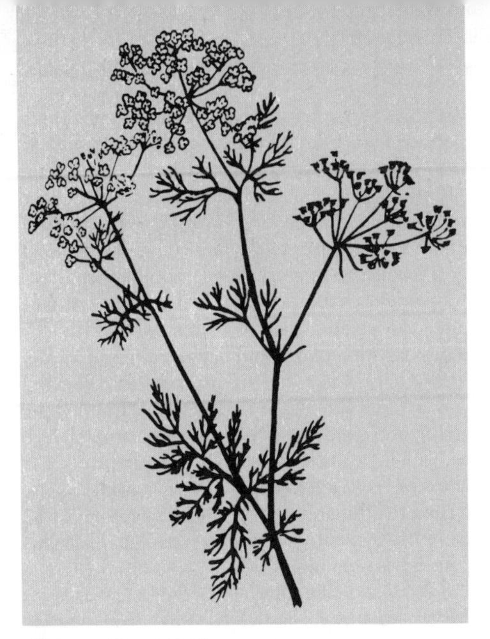

Caraway, Carum carvi

times consist of several thousand people, and the number of camels used for the journey may be more than 10,000.

Trade caravans figured prominently in the ancient history of Asia and Africa. Wars were fought for control of caravan routes, many of which, for centuries, were the only arteries of communication and trade between parts of the various empires. Although trade caravans are still used in parts of Africa and Asia, in recent times camels and donkeys have been replaced by specially equipped motor vehicles and, to a certain extent, by the airplane.

CARAVEL. *See* SHIPS AND SHIPBUILDING.

CARAWAY, common name for a plant, *Carum carvi,* of the family Umbelliferae (*see* PARSLEY), that has long been cultivated in temperate zones for its aromatic fruit, called caraway seeds. These seeds are used in cookery, confectionery, and medicine. The caraway plant is a biennial herb; it grows up to 61 cm (up to 2 ft) high and has finely divided leaves and clusters of white flowers. The large oil glands of the seed contain caraway oil, which is used to flavor the liqueur aquavit. This oil is also used in perfumery and in pharmacy, as an aromatic stimulant and as a flavoring agent.

CARBIDES, compounds of carbon with metals or metalloids. These compounds have high melting points and are not readily volatilized. They are produced by heating appropriate mixtures to high temperatures in electric furnaces. The largest of the carbides is the acetyledic group, including carbides of beryllium, calcium, strontium, sodium, potassium, copper, silver, gold, and nickel. The acetylides, the most important of which is calcium carbide, form acetylene by reaction with water or acids. Another group, consisting of aluminum, beryllium, and manganese carbides, is termed the methanides. These yield methane on reaction with water or acids.

Important metallic carbides include iron carbide, or cementite, the hardening constituent in steel; tungsten carbide, from which are made hard tools for the machining of tough metals; and boron carbide, a material almost as hard as diamond. An important nonmetallic carbide is silicon carbide, or Carborundum, which is used as an abrasive.

CARBINE, light, short-barreled rifle. The carbine is essentially the same as the rifle, but has a

A camel caravan plods its way to a remote area of Niger, in western Africa. Camels can travel over tracks impassable even for four-wheel-drive trucks. UPI

shorter barrel, a generally smaller caliber, and a more limited range. The carbine was formerly carried only by mounted cavalry troops, but during World War II the M2 carbine was substituted for the .45-caliber pistol as the personal weapon of artillery personnel and service troops. Carbines were also modified for semiautomatic firing, but they were replaced officially by the M14 rifle in the early 1960s. *See also* SMALL ARMS.

CARBOHYDRATE, any of a large group of compounds in which hydrogen and oxygen, in the proportions in which they exist in water, are combined with carbon; the formula of most of these compounds may be expressed as $C_m(H_2O)_n$. Structurally, however, these compounds are not hydrates of carbon, as the formula would seem to indicate.

Carbohydrates, as a class, are the most abundant organic compounds found in nature. They are produced by green plants and by bacteria using the process known as photosynthesis (q.v.), in which carbon dioxide is taken from the air by means of solar energy to yield the carbohydrates as well as all the other chemicals needed by the organisms to survive and grow.

The carbohydrate group consists principally of sugar, starch, dextrin, cellulose (qq.v.), and glycogen, substances that constitute an important part of the human diet and that of many animals. The simplest of them are the simple sugars, or monosaccharides, which contain either an aldehyde or a ketone (qq.v.) group. The most important is glucose (q.v.). Two monosaccharide molecules joined together by an oxygen atom, with the elimination of a molecule of water, yield a disaccharide, of which the most important are sucrose (ordinary cane sugar), lactose, and maltose (qq.v.). Polysaccharides have enormous molecules made up of one type or several types of monosaccharide units—about 10 in glycogen, for example; 25 in starch; and 100 to 200 in cellulose.

Within living organisms, carbohydrates serve both essential structural and energy-storage functions. In plants, cellulose and hemicellulose are the main structural elements. In invertebrate animals, the polysaccharide chitin (q.v.) is the main component of the exoskeletons of arthropods. In vertebrate animals, the cell coatings of connective tissues contain carbohydrates. Cell membranes are rich in glycoproteins, and so forth. Plants use starch and animals use glycogen to store energy; when the energy is needed, the carbohydrates are broken down by enzymes.

Carbohydrates are used in the manufacture of fabrics, photographic film, plastics, and other products. Cellulose, a carbohydrate, can be converted into viscose rayon, acetate rayon, and paper products. Nitrocellulose (cellulose nitrate) is used in the production of motion picture film, cement, guncotton, celluloid, and similar kinds of plastics. Starch is used in the preparation of foods for livestock and humans; pectin, a jelling agent; gum arabic; and agar, used in the production of adhesive materials, sizing materials, and emulsions. Gum arabic is also used in demulcent medicines. Agar, a constituent of some laxatives, is also used as a thickening agent in food and as a medium for bacterial culture. Hemicellulose is used to modify paper during its manufacture. The carbohydrate dextran is a polysaccharide used in medicine as a blood-plasma-volume expander to counteract acute shock; another carbohydrate, heparin sulfate, is a blood anticoagulant.

CARBOLIC ACID. *See* PHENOL.

CARBON, element, symbol C, in group IVa of the periodic table (*see* PERIODIC LAW); at.no. 6, at.wt. 12.01115.

Carbon has the unique ability to link with other carbon atoms to form complex chains and rings. This property leads to an almost infinite number of carbon compounds, the most common being those containing carbon and hydrogen. The first carbon compounds were identified in living matter in the beginning of the 19th century, and therefore the study of carbon compounds was called "organic" chemistry.

The most common isotope of carbon is carbon-12; in 1961 this isotope was chosen to replace the isotope oxygen-16 as the standard for atomic weights, and was assigned the atomic weight of 12.

Occurrence. Carbon is a widely distributed element in nature, although it makes up only about 0.025 percent of the earth's crust. It occurs there mostly in the form of carbonates (q.v.). Carbon dioxide (q.v.), CO_2, is an important constituent of the atmosphere and is the main source of carbon incorporated in living matter. Plants, using photosynthesis (q.v.), convert carbon dioxide into organic carbon compounds, which are subsequently consumed by other organisms (*see* CARBON CYCLE). Elemental carbon occurs in nature in three forms: diamond (q.v.), graphite (q.v.), and amorphous carbon. Amorphous carbon is found in varying degrees of purity in charcoal, coal, coke, carbon black, and lampblack. In 1985, scientists vaporized graphite to produce a stable form of carbon molecule consisting of 60 carbon atoms in a roughly spherical shape, looking like a soccer ball. The molecule was named buckminsterfullerene—"buckyball" in short—in honor of R. Buckminster Fuller, the inventor of the geodesic dome. The molecule may be common in interstellar dust.

Properties. At normal temperatures carbon is characterized by a low reactivity. At high temperatures it reacts directly with most metals to form carbides (q.v.), and with oxygen to form carbon monoxide (q.v.), CO, and CO_2. Carbon in the form of coke is used to remove oxygen from metal oxide ores in order to obtain the pure metal. Carbon also forms compounds with most of the nonmetallic elements, although some of these, such as carbon tetrachloride, CCl_4, must be formed indirectly.

The three forms of elemental carbon—diamond, graphite, and amorphous carbon—are solids with extremely high melting points and are insoluble in all solvents at ordinary temperatures. The physical properties of the three forms differ widely because of the differences in crystalline structure. In diamond, the hardest material known, each atom is linked to four other atoms in a three-dimensional framework, whereas graphite consists of weakly bonded plane layers of atoms that are arranged in hexagons.

Amorphous Carbon. Amorphous carbon is characterized by a very low degree of crystallinity. Pure amorphous carbon can be obtained by heating purified sugar at 900° C (1652° F) in the absence of air. Lampblack, sometimes incorrectly called carbon black, is made by burning liquid hydrocarbons, such as kerosene, with an insufficient quantity of air, producing a smoky flame. The smoke or soot is collected in a separate chamber. For a long time lampblack was used as a black pigment in inks and paints, but it is now displaced by carbon black, which is composed of finer particles. Carbon black, also called gas black, is produced by incomplete combustion of natural gas and is mainly used as a filler and reinforcing agent for rubber.

Scientific Applications. The isotopes carbon-13 and carbon-14 are used extensively as tracers (*see* ISOTOPIC TRACER) in biochemical research. Carbon-14 is also used in the technique called radiocarbon dating (*see* DATING METHODS), which permits the estimation of the age of fossils and other organic materials. Carbon-14 is continuously produced in the atmosphere by cosmic rays and is incorporated into all living matter. As carbon-14 decays, with a half-life of 5760 years, the proportion of carbon-14 to carbon-12 in a specimen is a measure of its approximate age.

CARBONARI (Ital., "charcoal burners"), early 19th-century secret revolutionary society active in Italy and France. It originated in Naples during the Napoleonic period and later spread to France. The Carbonari borrowed ritual terminology from the Italian charcoal burners of the mountains where they held their first meetings. The members, mostly from the middle and upper classes, were organized in a hierarchy of lodges in two parallel structures, one in the civil population and the other in the armed forces.

The Carbonari led an unsuccessful uprising in Naples in 1820. They participated in the French revolution of 1830, after which most French Carbonari supported the government of King Louis Philippe. About 1831 Giuseppe Mazzini, an active member of the Carbonari, founded a new secret society called Young Italy. This group absorbed most of the membership of the Carbonari, which then ceased to be effective.

CARBONATES, compounds containing the carbonate radical CO_3^{-2}. Carbonates may be considered derivatives of carbonic acid, H_2CO_3, formed when carbon dioxide, CO_2, dissolves in water. If the hydrogen atoms in carbonic acid are replaced by metal atoms, an inorganic carbonate is formed, exemplified by sodium carbonate, Na_2CO_3. If the hydrogen atoms are replaced by organic radicals, organic carbonates, or carbonic acid, esters are formed. An example is ethyl carbonate, $(C_2H_5)_2CO_3$.

Several inorganic carbonates occur in nature and are important minerals or ores; these include calcite, $CaCO_3$; magnesite, $MgCO_3$; siderite, $FeCO_3$; and smithsonite, $ZnCO_3$. As a class, they can be recognized by their effervescence when treated with hydrochloric acid. All these carbonates decompose when heated, yielding CO_2 gas and usually a solid metal oxide.

Only the alkali metal carbonates dissolve readily in water, and the resulting solutions are alkaline. Because of their alkalinity, solutions of sodium carbonate, known as washing soda, are used as cleaning agents and water softeners. Although sodium carbonate occurs to some extent in nature, most of this substance is made commercially by the Solvay process.

Replacement of only half the hydrogen of carbonic acid produces bicarbonates, or hydrogen carbonates, which contain the bicarbonate radical, HCO_3^-. Only the alkali metal bicarbonates are stable enough to be isolated. Among the bicarbonates, the best known and most useful is sodium bicarbonate, $NaHCO_3$, or baking soda.

CARBON BLACK. *See* CARBON.

CARBON CYCLE, or carbon-nitrogen-oxygen cycle, in astronomy, one of the two series of nuclear reactions that provide the energy of a main-sequence star (q.v.). The carbon cycle starts and ends with carbon-12, which acts as a catalyst in the sequential production of helium from hydrogen; neutrinos and gamma rays are also produced. When the hydrogen is used up, the cycle stops. The carbon cycle is common in massive stars, whereas in low-mass stars, such as the sun, the proton-proton chain of reactions converts hydrogen into helium.

CARBON CYCLE, in ecology (q.v.), the cycle of carbon usage by which energy flows through the earth's ecosystem. The basic cycle begins when photosynthesizing plants (*see* PHOTOSYNTHESIS) use carbon dioxide (CO_2) found in the atmosphere or dissolved in water. Some of this carbon is incorporated in plant tissue as carbohydrates, fats, and protein; the rest is returned to the atmosphere or water by respiration. Carbon is thus passed on to herbivores that eat the plants and thereby use, rearrange, and degrade the carbon compounds. Much of it is given off as CO_2 in respiration, as a by-product of metabolism (q.v.), but some is stored in animal tissue and is passed on to carnivores feeding on the herbivores. Ultimately, all the carbon compounds are broken down by decomposition, and the carbon is released as CO_2 to be used again by plants.

Air-Water Exchanges. On a global scale the carbon cycle involves an exchange of CO_2 between two great reservoirs: the atmosphere and the earth's waters. Atmospheric CO_2 enters water by diffusion across the air-water surface. If the CO_2 concentration in the water is less than that in the atmosphere, it diffuses into water, but if the CO_2 concentration is greater in the water than in the atmosphere, CO_2 enters the atmosphere. Additional exchanges take place within aquatic ecosystems. Excess carbon may combine with water

This diagram of the carbon cycle shows the routes—from the atmosphere to deep-lying fossil fuel deposits—by which carbon passes through the earth's ecosystem.
From E. O. Wilson et al. *Life on Earth*, 2nd Edition, 1978, Sinauer Associates, Inc.

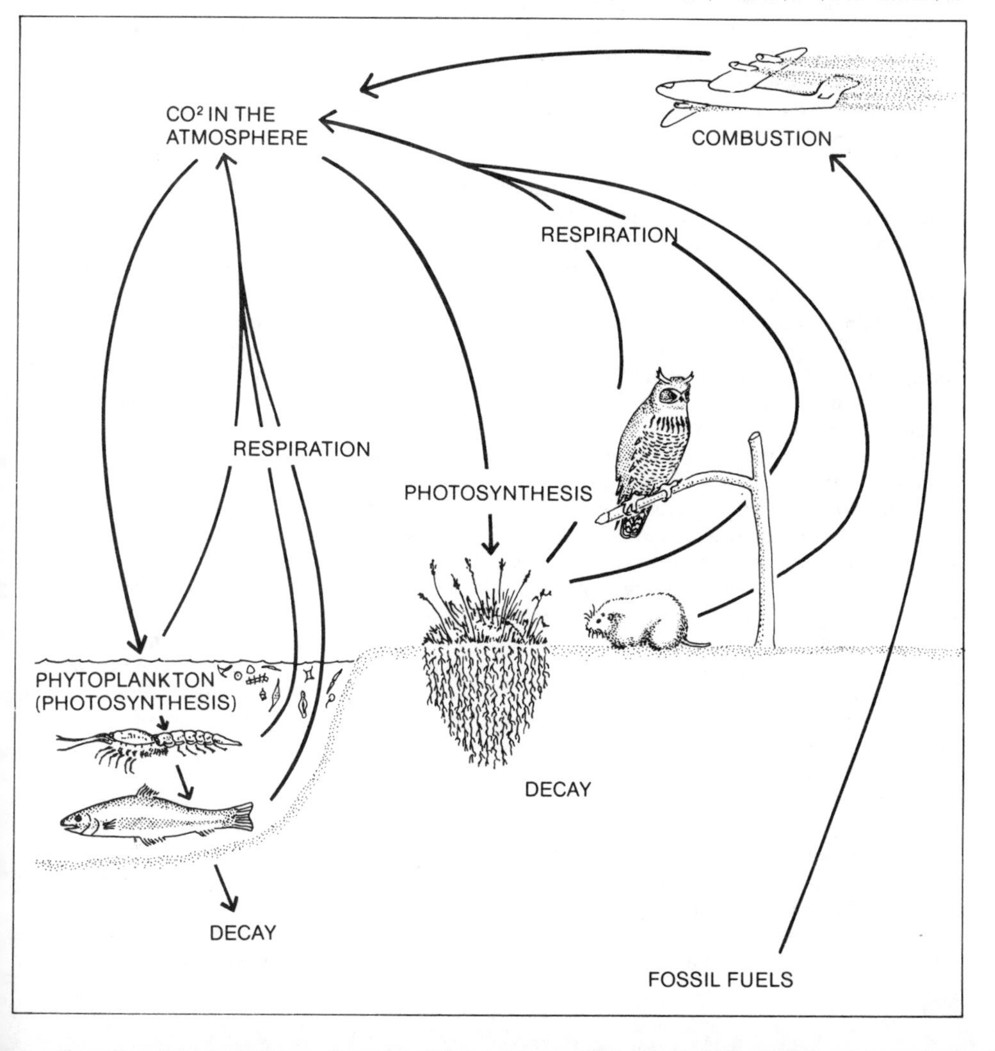

to form carbonates and bicarbonates. Carbonates may precipitate out and become deposited in bottom sediments. Some carbon is incorporated in the forest-vegetation biomass (living matter) and may remain out of circulation for hundreds of years. Incomplete decomposition of organic matter in wet areas results in the accumulation of peat (q.v.). Such accumulation during the Carboniferous period created great stores of fossil fuels: coal, oil, and gas.

Total Carbon Pool. The total carbon pool, estimated at about 49,000 metric gigatons (1 metric gigaton equals 10^9 metric tons), is distributed among organic and inorganic forms. Fossil carbon accounts for 22 percent of the total pool. The oceans contain 71 percent of the world's carbon, mostly in the form of bicarbonate and carbonate ions. An additional 3 percent is in dead organic matter and phytoplankton. Terrestrial ecosystems, in which forests are the main reservoir, hold about 3 percent of the total carbon. The remaining 1 percent is held in the atmosphere, circulated, and used in photosynthesis.

Additions to Atmosphere. Because of the burning of fossil fuels, the clearing of forests, and other such practices, the amount of CO_2 in the atmosphere has been increasing since the Industrial Revolution. Atmospheric concentrations have risen from an estimated 260 to 300 parts per million (ppm) to 330 ppm today. This increase accounts for only half of the estimated amount of carbon dioxide poured into the atmosphere. The other 50 percent has probably been taken up by and stored in the oceans. Although terrestrial vegetation may take up considerable quantities of carbon, it is also an additional source of CO_2.

Atmospheric CO_2 acts as a shield over the earth; it is penetrated by shortwave radiation from outer space but blocks the escape of longwave radiation. As increased quantities of CO_2 are added to the atmosphere, therefore, the shield thickens and more heat is retained. This acts to increase global temperatures. Although such increases have not yet been large enough to cancel out natural climatic variability, projected increases in CO_2 from the burning of fossil fuels suggest that global temperatures could rise by some 2° to 3° C (about 3.6° to 5.4° F) early in the 21st century. This increase would suffice to alter global climates and thereby affect human welfare. *See also* AIR POLLUTION; GREENHOUSE EFFECT. R.L.S.

For further information on this topic, see the Bibliography in volume 28, section 452.

CARBONDALE, city, Jackson Co., SW Illinois; inc. 1856. The city is a commercial and rail center for an agricultural and coal-mining area. Southern Illinois University at Carbondale (1869) is here, and Crab Orchard National Wildlife Refuge, Shawnee National Forest, and Giant City State Park are nearby. Settled in the mid-19th century, the community is named for the local coalfields. The annual U.S. Memorial Day holiday on May 30 was started here in 1868. Pop. (1970) 22,816; (1980) 27,194.

CARBON DIOXIDE, colorless, odorless, and slightly acid-tasting gas, sometimes called carbonic acid gas, the molecule of which consists of one atom of carbon joined to two atoms of oxygen (CO_2). It was called "fixed air" by the Scottish chemist Joseph Black, who obtained it by the decomposition of chalk and limestone and recognized that it entered into the chemical composition of these substances. The French chemist Antoine Lavoisier proved that it is an oxide of carbon by showing that the gas obtained by the combustion of charcoal is identical in its properties with the "fixed air" obtained by Black. Carbon dioxide is about 1.5 times as dense as air. It is soluble in water, 0.9 volume of the gas dissolving in 1 volume of water at 20° C (68° F).

Carbon dioxide is produced in a variety of ways: by combustion, or oxidation, of materials containing carbon, such as coal, wood, oil, or foods; by fermentation of sugars; and by decomposition of carbonates under the influence of heat or acids. Commercially, carbon dioxide is recovered from furnace or kiln gases; from fermentation processes; from reaction of carbonates with acids; and from reaction of steam with natural gas, a step in the commercial production of ammonia. The carbon dioxide is purified by dissolving it in a concentrated solution of alkali carbonate or ethanolamine and then heating the solution with steam. The gas is evolved and is compressed into steel cylinders.

The atmosphere contains carbon dioxide in variable amounts, usually 3 to 4 parts per 10,000. It is used by green plants in the process known as photosynthesis, by which carbohydrates are manufactured.

Carbon dioxide is used in the manufacture of sodium carbonate, $Na_2CO_3 \cdot 10H_2O$ (washing soda); sodium bicarbonate, $NaHCO_3$ (baking soda); and basic carbonate of lead, $Pb_3(OH)_2(CO_3)_2$ (white lead). Dissolved under a pressure of 2 to 5 atmospheres, carbon dioxide causes the effervescence in carbonated beverages. Carbon dioxide does not burn and does not support ordinary combustion, and because of these properties it is used for extinguishing fires. The CO_2 extinguisher is a steel cylinder filled with liquid carbon dioxide, which, when released, expands suddenly and causes so great a lowering of temperature that it solidifies into powdery "snow." This snow volatilizes (vaporizes) on contact with the burning substance, producing a blanket of gas that cools and smothers the flame. Solid carbon dioxide, known as dry ice, is widely used as a refrigerant. Its cooling effect is almost twice that of water ice; its special advantages are that it does not melt as a liquid but turns into gas, and that it produces an inert atmosphere that reduces bacterial growth.

The presence of carbon dioxide in the blood stimulates breathing. For this reason, carbon dioxide is added to oxygen or ordinary air in artificial respiration and to the gases used in anesthesia.

CARBON DISULFIDE, colorless, extremely volatile and flammable compound, CS_2, with a disagreeable, fetid odor. It is used as a solvent for oils, fats, and waxes; as a reagent in the manufacture of regenerated cellulose; as the starting material in the manufacture of carbon tetrachloride; in rayon and cellophane production; and in the vulcanization of rubber. Carbon disulfide is made by heating carbon and sulfur together or by the reaction between methane and sulfur vapor. It freezes at −111.53° C (−168.75° F) and boils at 46.25° C (115.25° F).

CARBONIFEROUS PERIOD, fifth division of the Paleozoic era (q.v.) of the geologic time scale (*see* GEOLOGY), spanning a time interval of from 345 to 280 million years ago. The name originated in Great Britain, where it was first applied, in 1822, to the coal-bearing strata (Lat. *carbo,* "coal"; *ferre,* "to bear") of England and Wales.

In North America, this 65-million-year interval of geologic time is considered to comprise two periods rather than one. The earlier of the two, called the Mississippian, ranges in age from 345 to 310 million years, while the later, called the Pennsylvanian, ranges from 310 to 280 million years.

At the beginning of the Pennsylvanian portion of Carboniferous time, when most of the world's coal was forming, lush forests and tropical peat swamps covered large areas of what would eventually become eastern North America and Northern Europe. These areas, situated as they then were in the Tropics, immediately north of the Equator, had climates that were uniformly warm and humid. Such conditions promoted growth of the vegetation and marine organisms from which would form not only coal but also oil and gas.

Of the ancient landmasses, only the protocontinent of Siberia lay north of the Tropics, extending almost to the North Pole. The supercontinent of Gondwanaland, comprising what would someday be South America, Africa, India, Australia, and Antarctica, lay entirely within the Southern Hemisphere, covering a vast area the center of which was near the South Pole.

A fossilized crinoid, or sea lily, from the Carboniferous period, embedded in limestone. Its stalk held the sea lily to the ocean floor. American Museum of Natural History

Gondwanaland and the various protocontinents had been drifting toward each other since early in the Paleozoic era. By the time the Carboniferous period was drawing to a close, crustal movements had begun to culminate in a four-way collision, so that when the Permian period began, collisions between plates of the earth's crust had welded all the world's landmasses into the single, giant supercontinent known as Pangaea (*see* PLATE TECTONICS).

Global climatic changes were a major consequence of this redistribution of land and sea. The climate, which had been warm and wet earlier in the Carboniferous, became cooler and drier as the period drew to a close, with the result that a long interval of glaciation, known as the Permo-carboniferous, ensued (*see* ICE AGES).

Flora and Fauna. Animal and vegetable remains are abundant in the Carboniferous period and are, in many cases, well preserved. Great uniformity is observed in the character of plant life, the same genera and often the same species being found in widely separated regions. About 2000 species are known, most of which belong to the flowerless, spore-producing plants. Early club mosses, horsetails, and forest trees (*Cordaites*) were common, in addition to numerous ferns. The contemporary land fauna left few traces, but the fauna of seas and lagoons are much better represented. The first true reptiles began to appear, developing from the earlier amphibians. Corals, crinoids, and minute foraminifers were abundant. A few trilobites and eurypterids were to be found. Snails and mollusks, including cephalopods and nautiloids, were widespread. Insects were frequent, particularly a giant form of dragonfly. Polyzoa and brachiopods were common, and sharks and primitive, hard-scaled fish were well represented. *See* PALEONTOLOGY.

For further information on this topic, see the Bibliography in volume 28, sections 417, 436.

CARBON MONOXIDE, chemical compound of carbon and oxygen with the formula CO. It is a colorless, odorless gas, about 3 percent lighter than air, and is poisonous to all warm-blooded animals and to many other forms of life. When inhaled it combines with hemoglobin in the blood, preventing absorption of oxygen and resulting in asphyxiation.

Carbon monoxide is formed whenever carbon or substances containing carbon are burned with an insufficient air supply. Even when the amount of air is theoretically sufficient, the reaction is not always complete, so that the combustion gases contain some free oxygen and some carbon monoxide.

An incomplete reaction is especially probable when it takes place quickly, as in an automobile engine; for this reason, automobile-exhaust gases contain harmful quantities of carbon monoxide, sometimes several percent, although antipollution devices are intended to keep the level below 1 percent. As little as 1/1000 of 1 percent of carbon monoxide in air may produce symptoms of poisoning, and as little as $\frac{1}{5}$ of 1 percent may prove fatal in less than 30 min. Carbon monoxide is a major ingredient of the air pollution in urban areas.

Because it is odorless, carbon monoxide is an insidious poison. It produces only mild symptoms of headache, nausea, or fatigue, followed by unconsciousness. An automobile engine running in a closed garage can make the air noxious within a few minutes; a leaking furnace flue may fill a house with unsuspected poison. Fuel gas, which may contain as much as 50 percent carbon monoxide, often has small quantities of unpleasant-smelling sulfur compounds purposely added to make leaks noticeable.

Carbon monoxide is an important industrial fuel because it contains more than two-thirds of the heating value of the carbon from which it was formed. It is a constituent of water gas, producer gas, blast furnace gas, and coal gas. In smelting iron ore carbon monoxide formed from coke used in the process acts as a reducing agent, that is, it removes oxygen from the ore. Carbon monoxide combines actively with chlorine to form carbonyl chloride, or phosgene, and it combines with hydrogen, when heated in the presence of a catalyst, to form methyl alcohol. The direct combination of carbon monoxide with certain metals, forming gaseous compounds, is used in refining those metals, particularly nickel.

Carbon monoxide melts at −205° C (−337° F) and boils at −191.5° C (−312.7° F).

CARBON TETRACHLORIDE, heavy, colorless liquid, CCl_4, with a characteristic nonirritating odor. It has a freezing point of −22.92° C (−9.26° F), a boiling point of 76.72° C (170.10° F), and a density of 1.5947 g/ml at 20° C. It is made by treating carbon disulfide, CS_2, with sulfur monochloride, S_2Cl_2, or by the chlorination of hydrocarbons. Carbon tetrachloride is used to make compounds such as chlorofluoromethanes, used as refrigerants and as aerosol-spray propellants. It is also used in fire extinguishers and for the dry cleaning of fabrics.

CARBORUNDUM. *See* ABRASIVE.

CARBOXYLIC ACID, any of a class of organic compounds containing one, two, or several carboxyl (—COOH) groups. The simplest is formic acid, while acetic acid (q.v.) is familiar in dilute form as vinegar. Straight-chain carboxylic acids are called fatty acids. Many of the carboxylic acids play important roles in the chemistry of organisms, and a number of them are major industrial chemicals.

CARBUNCLE, in medicine, localized inflammation of tissue under the skin caused by infection. A carbuncle is usually caused by the bacteria *Staphylococcus* and is larger and more serious than a boil that results from an inflammation beginning in an infected hair sac. As the carbuncle develops, the area affected becomes red and swells slightly. The subcutaneous tissue becomes hard, the color darkens, and several heads may develop and discharge plus. Tissue is destroyed and sloughs off, leaving a scar upon healing. Building up the general health and resistance of the patient is the principal treatment. Local treatment usually includes surgery and the use of antibiotics and antiseptics.

CARBURETOR. *See* AUTOMOBILE.

CARCASSONNE, city, S France, capital of Aude Department, on the Aude R. and the Canal du

The crenellated walls of the Cité (restored in 1855–79) once protected Carcassonne against the siege (1355) of Edward the Black Prince of England. French Cultural Services

Midi. It is divided into two sections, Ville Basse and the medieval walled community known as the Cité. The business of Carcassonne is concentrated in Ville Basse, which is an important center of trade in wine, grain, and fruit produced in the surrounding region and has clothing factories. Ville Basse also contains the Cathedral of Saint Michael and the Church of Saint Vincent (both mainly 13th cent.). The Cité contains some of the finest remains of medieval fortifications in Europe and is a popular tourist attraction. Set atop a hill on the left bank of the Aude R., the Cité includes ancient ramparts and towers, some parts dating from the 5th century, during the time of the Visigoths, and others from the 11th to the 13th century. In addition, a 12th-century castle and the Romanesque and Gothic Church of Saint Nazaire (11th–14th cent.) are located in the Cité.

The Cité was the site of a Roman town, which fell to the Visigoths in the 5th century. In the 8th century it came under Frankish rule. During the 13th-century crusade against the Albigenses, a religious sect holding a Manichaean world view, Carcassonne was captured and its inhabitants massacred by the Anglo-Norman soldier Simon de Montfort. Carcassonne became a possession of the French crown in 1247. Restoration of the Cité was begun in the 19th century by the architect Eugène Emmanuel Viollet-le-Duc. Pop. (1982) 42,450.

CARCINOGEN, any chemical, biological, or physical agent that can potentially be a cause of cancer (q.v.). The term is most commonly applied to chemicals introduced into the environment by human activity. Researchers label a substance a carcinogen if it causes a statistically significant increase in some form of neoplasm, or anomalous cell growth, when applied to a population of previously unexposed organisms. The modes of cancer initiation are still little understood, however, and efforts to establish the carcinogenic hazards of substances have aroused great controversy. The question of the usefulness of laboratory tests on animals in assessing human risks is particularly complex. The more recent development of short-term tests using cell cultures of microorganisms, however, is considered a major advance in carcinogen research.

Substances indicted as carcinogenic over the past few decades include the pesticides DDT, Kepone, and EDB; the synthetic hormone DES; the artificial sweetener cyclamate; and a wide range of other industrial and environmental substances. In the early 1980s, U.S. health officials began to place more emphasis on the dangers of cigarette smoking and unbalanced diets for the general public.

CARCINOMA. *See* CANCER.

CARDAMOM, aromatic seed of certain species of the family Zingiberaceae (*see* GINGER), particularly *Elettaria cardamomum,* native to India and southeastern Asia. The plant has large leaves and white flowers with blue stripes and yellow borders; it grows to about 3 m (about 10 ft) in height. The fruit is a small capsule that contains 8 to 16 brown seeds; the seeds are used as a spice.

CÁRDENAS, Lázaro (1895–1970), Mexican president (1934–40), born in Jiquilpán de Juárez, Michocán. Cárdenas rose from humble origins in the revolutionary turmoil of post-1910 Mexico, and in 1925 was made a brigadier general in the Mexican revolutionary army. He served as governor of his native state, Michoacán, from 1928 to 1932, and in the same period (1930) was chosen president of the National Revolutionary party. He was minister of the interior (1931) and minister of war and marine (1933) before being elected president of Mexico in 1934. During his administration the six-year plan for economic and social reform formulated by his party was put into action. Large tracts of privately owned land were divided and distributed among the peasants, and many industries were converted to worker cooperatives. In 1938 foreign-owned oil properties were nationalized. Although a conciliatory attitude was taken toward the Roman Catholic church, education was secularized. Cárdenas was one of the most popular presidents of Mexico, but under Mexican law he could not run for a second term. In 1942 he was made commander of all Mexican forces on the Pacific coast, and he also served as minister of defense (1942–45). Thereafter he lived in retirement.

CARDIFF, city, administrative center of South Glamorgan, capital of Wales, S Wales, on the Taff and Ely rivers, at their mouths on Bristol Channel. Cardiff is an important seaport and industrial center. Among its manufactures are steel, machinery, processed foods, metal products, textiles, and paper. Notable structures include the 11th-century Cardiff Castle, Llandaff Cathedral, and the 15th-century Church of Saint John the Baptist. Also of interest is the National Museum of Wales. Cardiff is the seat of University College, Cardiff (1883), the University of Wales Institute of Science and Technology (1866), and the Welsh National School of Medicine (1931). A Roman outpost was established on the site in about AD 75. Occupied by the Normans in the 11th century, the community became a possession of feudal lords. It remained a small town until the opening of the Glamorganshire Canal in 1794 made it an outlet for the mineral wealth of S Wales. The first docks were completed in 1839, and Cardiff eventually became the world's largest coal-shipping port, an activity that has since declined. During World War II the city suffered damage from German bombing. Until 1974 Cardiff was the county town of the former county of Glamorganshire. Pop. (1981) 273,856.

CARDIGAN, James Thomas Brudenell, 7th Earl of (1797–1868), British army officer, born in Hambleden, England, and educated at the University of Oxford. Cardigan was a member of the House of Commons from 1818 to 1829 and entered the army in 1824. He was forced to give up his first command in 1834, however, because of his dictatorial behavior toward a subordinate officer. In 1836 he was able to secure command of a unit later known as the 11th Hussars. As commander of a light cavalry brigade in the Crimean War, he led the famous Charge of the Six Hundred at the Battle of Balaklava on Oct. 25, 1854. The British brigade was virtually annihilated by the Russians. Cardigan survived the battle, was acclaimed a hero, and became a lieutenant general in 1861. The cardigan sweater is named for him.

CARDIGAN BAY, semicircular inlet of Saint George's Channel in the Irish Sea, W Wales. The bay is about 105 km (about 65 mi) long and about 56 km (about 35 mi) wide.

CARDIGANSHIRE, former county, W Wales; Cardigan was the county town. Cardiganshire consisted of a mountainous E section and a hilly coastal region. Relics dating from the Bronze Age and Roman ruins, including the remnants of a highway, have been found in the county. In 1284 part of the area was constituted as the shire of Ceredigion by Edward I; the county was enlarged during the reign of Henry VIII. Cardiganshire was noted for its lead mines in the 19th century. In 1974 it became part of the county of Dyfed (q.v.).

CARDINAL (Lat. *cardinalis,* "pivotal," principal," from *cardo,* "hinge"), highest dignitary in the Roman Catholic church after the pope, whose elector and councillor he is. Applied in the period following the councils of Nicaea to the clergy who were permanently attached to a cathedral church anywhere, the title was later restricted to particular members of the clergy in Rome. Gradually the priests permanently ruling the parish churches in Rome were called cardinal priests; the deacons permanently administering the charities of a particular region of the city were called cardinal deacons; and the bishops in charge of the suburban sees of Rome were called cardinal bishops. Until the late Middle Ages the term *cardinal* was used to designate prominent priests in important churches, such as those of Constantinople, Naples, and Milan.

The cardinals are appointed by the pope and constitute the Sacred College. The pope is not obliged to consult them, but does so as a matter of course. Their number has varied at different times; in 1586 it was fixed by Pope Sixtus V at 70, that is, 6 cardinal bishops, 50 cardinal priests, and 14 cardinal deacons. The pope, however, was not obliged to maintain this number, and there were generally from 10 to 15 vacancies. The cardinal bishops take their ecclesiastical names from the suburban sees mentioned above; the cardinal priests, the majority of whom are bishops throughout the world, are given titles taken from the churches of Rome; and the cardinal deacons are usually priests associated with the administrative offices of the Vatican. In 1958 Pope John XXIII abrogated the legislation that limited the number of cardinals to 70; Pope Paul VI followed John's tradition, so that, by the late 1960s, no limit was set on the number of cardinals at any given time. In 1988 the college included 160 cardinals, 10 of them from the U.S.

Precedence in the Sacred College is determined by the see held and by the date of consecration of the individual cardinal. Those consecrated earlier rank higher in the college. The dean of the Sacred College, a cardinal bishop, is elected to the post of dean, according to a ruling by Pope Paul VI in 1965. The first cardinal bishop has the right to consecrate the pope if the pope is not a bishop at the time of his installation. The first cardinal deacon is first deacon of the college and has the right to proclaim and install the new pope. The cardinal camerlengo (chamberlain) takes care of the temporal goods of the Holy See and rules the church during a papal vacancy.

The cardinals are chief members of the Sacred Congregations of the papal government. They meet in consistory, or assembly, over which the pope presides. Cardinals are limited in their duties according to age; like other high prelates, they are expected to retire at the age of 75 from administrative duties. At 80 they are no longer permitted to serve as papal electors. These restrictions were announced by Paul VI in 1970. As electors of the pope, they usually choose one of their own number for honor. They enjoy extraordinary privileges and honors and are addressed as "Eminence," usually either "His Eminence" or "Your Eminence," or "lord cardinal." They wear a distinctive scarlet dress and a red cap, or biretta, that is placed on their heads by the pope. The use of the galero, or large, tasseled, red hat, given to them in public consistory, was discarded by decree of the pope in 1969. Cardinals in charge of Sacred Congregations, tribunals, or offices enjoy an income from the papal treasury. Cardinals frequently act as the pope's representatives upon delicate missions; for the duration of such missions they are called *legati a latere.*

CARDINAL, a large songbird, *Richmondena cardinalis,* of the finch family, common throughout the southern U.S. The cardinal grows to a length of 20 cm (8 in). The general color of the male is red; the head is vermilion, with a small black portion around the base of the bill. The female cardinal is not as brightly colored as the male. The feathers of the crown are long and erected into a conical crest. The cardinal migrates northward in spring, but seldom farther than Massachusetts. Its loud, clear song, noted for its sweetness and variety, is heard chiefly in the mornings and evenings. The cardinal's nest is built in bushes and consists of twigs, rootlets, and strips of bark, lined with grasses and other finer material. The eggs are usually four in number, white or bluish, speckled and spotted with brown. Geographical races of this species range westward to southern California and Mexico, and related species are found in Mexico and Central America.

CARDINAL FLOWER. *See* LOBELIA.

CARDIOPULMONARY RESUSCITATION. *See* ARTIFICIAL RESPIRATION; FIRST AID.

CARDOZO, Benjamin Nathan (1870–1938), American jurist, born in New York City, and educated at Columbia University. In 1891 Cardozo was admitted to the bar and began to practice law in New York City. In 1914 he was elected justice of the New York Supreme Court. The following year Cardozo became associate justice of the New York Court of Appeals, and in 1927 he was appointed chief justice of that court. Five years later Cardozo succeeded Oliver Wendell Holmes as associate justice of the U.S. Supreme Court. Recognized as one of the most influential liberal judges of his time, Cardozo was famous for his clearly written, scholarly opinions and for his liberal interpretation of legal questions, particularly those dealing with public welfare. Cardozo upheld most of the New Deal measures advocated by the administration of President Franklin D. Roosevelt that came before the U.S. Supreme Court, notably the Social Security Act, for which he wrote the majority opinion. The writings of Cardozo include *The Nature of the Judicial Process* (1921), *The Growth of the Law* (1924), and *The Paradoxes of Legal Science* (1928).

CARDS AND CARD GAMES, sets of flat, usually rectangular pieces of pasteboard, cardboard, or plastic, generally ornamented with figures and numbers, used in playing various games of skill or chance. Playing cards began to be used in antiquity, perhaps originally for magical purposes and later as markers in games simulating battle maneuvers. Some scholars believe that cards originated in India as a derivative of the game of chess; other theories suggest that cards were first used in China or Egypt. From the Middle East they were, presumably, introduced into Europe by the Crusaders.

In China, one type of cards apparently was derived from paper money, another type from dominoes. In India, one of the best known sets is the *dasavatara*. This is a deck of ten suits, based upon the ten avatars, or incarnations of the god Vishnu: fish, tortoise, wild boar, lion, dwarf, ax, bow and arrow, thunderbolt, conch, and horse. Most Indian cards are round, of various sizes, and usually made of heavily lacquered cardboard, papier-mâché, or occasionally ivory. In Japan, two popular decks are the *hana fuda* ("flower game") and the *uta garuta* ("the game of 100 poets").

The first mentions of playing cards in Europe date from the 13th and 14th centuries, and the earliest known examples were usually hand-painted paper. The cost of a single deck was prohibitive; their use was therefore restricted to the aristocracy. In 1397, however, a decree issued in Paris forbade the playing of cards by working people on working days. This seems to indicate that cards were mass produced, probably by wood-block printing, before the invention of the printing press. During the 15th century wood-block cards were designed in Germany and exported in great numbers. With the advances in printing, card playing increased in popularity.

Suit Designs. Types of playing cards and their designs, or suit symbols, vary throughout the world. The oldest European cards are of 14th-century Italian design. The origin of the suit signs now used almost universally can be traced to French designs that, when introduced into England, were named hearts, spades, diamonds, and clubs.

The earliest existing printed European playing cards were made from wood blocks in 15th-century France.
U.S. Playing Card Co.

"Costume" decks, cards showing actual historical personages in the dress of this period, were made in France in the mid-19th century. This card represents the king of clubs. Stuart and Marilyn R. Kaplan Playing Card Collection

The Standard Deck. Of the many types of playing-card decks, one of the oldest is the tarot deck. Designed in Italy in the early 14th century for the game of tarot (q.v.), these cards are now best known as a fortune-telling medium. A tarot deck consists of 78 cards, 22 of which portray symbolic and allegorical objects or personages; the rest are numbered cards, from which evolved the 52-card decks that are used in England, France, the U.S., and several other countries.

In the standard deck, each of the 4 suits comprises 13 cards, consisting of 3 court, or face cards (king, queen, and jack, or—in England—knave), and cards numbered from ace to 10. In addition to these, one or two cards known as jokers. Jokers were introduced in the U.S. in 1872 and are derived from the tarot card known as the fool. Other changes in the standard deck have been few. The 52 cards are sometimes trimmed to 36 or 32 for the games of piquet, euchre, or bezique, or to 48 for games of the pinochle family. Double-headed court cards were created in France, in the early 19th century, to facilitate recognition of the cards being played. Indices, that is, the small suit symbols at opposite corners of cards, were added in the late 19th century so that a card hand could be held in a close fan with individual cards still distinguishable. Cards embossed in Braille are available, enabling the blind to play card games.

Nonstandard Decks. Nonstandard playing-card decks abounded in Europe from the 17th to the 19th century. In England, from about 1670 to about 1720, a series of historical playing cards were issued. They were engraved with intricate comic-strip drawings, each depicting a significant event relating to the title of the deck. About 15 such decks were designed, among them: "The Knavery of the Rump," satirizing Oliver Cromwell's Rump Parliament, "The Reign of Queen Anne," and "Marlborough's Victories." Many beautiful decks of cards were made in 18th- and 19th-century France. Of greatest interest are the "revolutionary" decks, which, instead of kings and queens, had cards representing "citizens," and the exquisitely hand-colored "costume cards," dating from the mid-19th century. The court cards of these latter decks represented actual people, dressed in the sumptuous costumes of the period.

Perhaps the most intriguing of all decks of cards, however, is the "transformation" deck. In the early 19th century, when no indices were yet used on cards, people would amuse themselves by trying to create drawings based on the pips, or suit symbols, on the cards. The term *transformation* refers to changing a plain card to a work of art. About 75 such decks were printed.

Card Collecting. Playing cards are the most widely used objects of diversion in the world; estimates suggest that more than three-quarters of all people play some type or types of card games. Also, old and unusual playing cards have become valuable collectibles; and playing-card collections are housed in many museums throughout the world.

Card Games. Hundreds of card games have been devised over the centuries, but relatively few have had lasting appeal. Such games as ombre, popular in the 17th and 18th centuries, survive only through their influence on modern games. Poker, for example, is based on several now-forgotten games.

Although no precise classification is possible, card games may be divided, for convenience, into five broad categories. The first group includes the trick-winning games, in which certain cards or an entire suit are trumps. Among these are the various forms of whist, bridge, and euchre. A second group comprises games in which the object is to own or win certain valuable counting cards and sometimes to show specific scoring combinations known as melds. Among such games are pinochle, bezique, and piquet. The nontrump game of casino and the game of hearts, in which the aim is to avoid the capture of counting cards, may also be included in this category.

The object of another group of games is to obtain a given score by matching, assembling, or discarding cards. Of these, the rummy games are the most widely played. Two of the most popular forms are gin and canasta. Related to rummy are the so-called stop games, such as fan tan, in which players may either match eligible cards to a table layout according to denomination, suit, or sequence or pass their turns if unable to do so. A similar idea of card disposal by matching plus rearranging underlies the varied forms of solitaire, as well as such children's games as authors and old maid.

Constituting a fourth category are the showdown games, in which players wager that they can show cards, or combinations of cards, out ranking those of their opponents. Poker is the best known of the showdown games. A final group, based on adding or matching numbers, includes such betting games as blackjack or twenty-one, baccarat and chemin de fer, and cribbage.

Popular card games are described in this encyclopedia under individual names. G.Ho.

For further information on this topic, see the Bibliography in volume 28, sections 773-74.

CARDUCCI, Giosuè (1835-1907), Italian poet, critic, and teacher, generally regarded as the greatest Italian poet of the late 19th century. He was born in Val di Castello, Tuscany, and educated at the University of Pisa. From 1860 to 1904 he was professor of Italian literature at the University of Bologna. Carducci was opposed to the papacy, the monarchy, and the romantic sentimentalism that dominated Italian literature at the time. He advocated a return to the pagan spirit in religion and a revival of the classical spirit and forms in literature. As a young man he frequently expressed his radical ideas in his poetry, but in his later years his writing became less polemical. He was the first to adapt successfully classical Latin meters to modern Italian verse.

In 1906 Carducci became the first Italian to receive the Nobel Prize for literature. Among his best works are *New Rhymes* (1861-87; trans. 1916), *Pagan Odes* (1877-89 trans. 1950), and *Lyrics and Rhythms* (1899; trans. 1942).

CARÊME, Marie Antoine (1784-1833), French master chef and writer on cookery. He rose from tavern apprentice to pastry cook in an elegant patisserie in Paris. About 1805 he became cook to the French statesman Talleyrand. Subsequently Carême was head chef in the households of the prince regent, later George IV of England; Emperor Alexander I of Russia; and the French banker, Baron James de Rothschild. It is believed that Carême's great skill in making the elaborate pastry constructions used as centerpieces at great banquets was due to the study and practice of architectural drawing. Among his writings—on food and its service as well as on pastry making—is *L'art de la cuisine française au XIXe siècle* (The Art of French Cuisine in the 19th Century, 1833-34). This five-volume work, completed by an associate after Carême's death, set the standards for French classic cuisine.

CAREW, Thomas (1595?-1645?), English poet, born probably in West Wickham, Kent, and educated at the University of Oxford. In 1630 he became a court official to Charles I, who presented him with an estate. Carew was the first of the so-called Cavalier poets. He was strongly influenced by both Ben Jonson and John Donne. He wrote numerous short songs and light love lyrics, many of which were set to music by English composers. The poems are notable for their sensuous imagery and polished beauty. Carew is also well known for a longer love poem, "The Rapture," a masque, and the poem "Elegy on the Death of Dr. Donne."

CARGO CULTS, religious movements arising from the impact of modern technology and mercantilism on developing cultures. Such movements appeared, for example, in 19th-century Melanesia and New Guinea when European trading stations and colonial administration became dominant. Possession of trade goods—cargo—came to typify prosperity. The traditional native cultures were weakened by the contact with Westerners, but they deliberately rejected or were unable to adopt Western culture as an alternative. Native groups developed around prophetic leaders, who promised a new age of blessings and salvation that would be heralded by the arrival of special cargoes of European goods. Tribal deities, culture heroes, or ancestors were invoked to drive the foreigners away, and various rituals were enacted to speed the arrival of the promised goods. World War II brought further cultural disruptions to the area, and new cults arose. After the war and the withdrawal of military personnel, some cults built landing strips, believing that planes would continue to arrive bringing cargo.

Typically, cult members do not associate the awaited cargo with the Western economic system that produces it and cannot understand why the goods do not arrive. Eventually, the leaders are discredited by the failure of their prophecies, and the groups disband.

Cargo cults have been explained in various ways. One explanation is that they are social movements that help people cope with the problem of culture contact and change (*see* ACCULTURATION). Because they express dissatisfaction with current cultural conditions, they are also explained as attempts to launch a redemptive process by which the social and moral order may be rebuilt. J.A.Sa.

CARIA, ancient country of southwestern Asia Minor (now part of Turkey), south of the Maeander (now Menderes) River, bordered on the south by the Aegean Sea. The Taurus Mountains extend into the interior region, and the irregular coastline has numerous deep inlets. The islands of Rhodes and Kos lie off the coast.

Ancient Greek and Roman historians recorded that the original inhabitants of this region were pushed inland by an influx of people called Carians. The Carians, who were notable as mercenary soldiers, had been driven from their native islands in the Aegean Sea by invading Greeks. The Greeks also established colonies along the coast of Caria, notably Cnidus and Halicarnassus. In the 6th century BC, Caria was incorporated into the kingdom of Lydia; subsequently, it became a Persian dominion, ruled by Carian kings who were subject to Cyrus the Great. Mausolus (d. 353? BC) was the best known of these monarchs; his widow built the Mausoleum at Halicarnassus, one of the Seven Wonders of the Ancient World. In the 4th century BC, Alexander the Great seized Caria. After his rule, the country became a part first of the Seleucid kingdom of Syria and later of the kingdom of Pergamum; in the 2d century BC, Pergamum was turned into the Roman province of Asia.

CARIB, tribe of native American Indians of the Cariban linguistic stock, occupying various regions of South and Central America. The Carib, who probably originated in the valley of the Orinoco River, were noted for their ferocity. The tribe practiced cannibalism (q.v.); in fact, the word *cannibal* is derived from the Spanish term for these Indians, *caníbales.* During the late 15th century the Carib inhabited most of the islands of the Lesser Antilles and the coast of what is now Venezuela, territories from which they had expelled the Arawak Indians.

Carib men valued exploits in combat above all else. They were not organized into a hierarchical structure under a chief, but fought as individual warriors and raided other peoples. Male captives were tortured and eaten; female captives became slave-wives.

The Carib were expert canoeists, and their fleets sometimes included 100 sail-fitted, dugout canoes. The Caribbean Sea is named after them. On land, they lived in small settlements, farmed and fished, and hunted game with blowguns and bows and arrows. Carib communities were generally made up of several matrilineal kin groups.

In the 17th century, when several European countries struggled for control of the Lesser Antilles, the Carib were all but eliminated. Groups remained only on the islands of Saint Vincent and Dominica. In 1796 the British government deported almost all of the 5000 remaining members of the tribe from St. Vincent to Roatan Island off the coast of Honduras. They spread over the neighboring mainland and today survive in Guatemala and on a reservation in Dominica.

See also AMERICAN INDIAN LANGUAGES; AMERICAN INDIANS.

CARIBBEAN SEA, arm of the Atlantic Ocean, partially enclosed on the N and E by the islands of the West Indies, and bounded on the S by South America and Panama, and on the W by Central America. The name of the sea is derived from the Carib (q.v.) Indians, who inhabited the area when Spanish explorers arrived there in the 15th century. The Caribbean is approximately 2415 km (approximately 1500 mi) long E and W and between about 640 and 1450 km (about 400 and 900 mi) wide. It has an area of about 1,942,500 sq km (about 750,000 sq mi). At the NW extremity it is connected with the Gulf of Mexico by the Yucatán Channel, a passage about 193 km (about 120 mi) wide between Cuba and the Yucatán Peninsula. The Windward Passage between Cuba and Haiti is a major shipping route between the U.S. and the Panama Canal. Many gulfs and bays indent the coastline of South America, notably the Gulf of Venezuela, which carries tidal waters to Lake Maracaibo in Venezuela. With a few exceptions the entire Caribbean Basin is more than 1830 m (more than 6000 ft) deep. Large areas of the sea exceed 3660 m (12,000 ft) in depth; the greatest depth measured thus far is Cayman Trench (7535 m/24,720 ft) between Jamaica and Cayman Islands. Navigation is open and clear, making the Caribbean a major trade route for Latin American countries. The main oceanic current in the Caribbean Sea is an extension of the North Equatorial and South Equatorial currents, which enter the sea at the SE extremity and flow in a generally NW direction. A popular resort area, the Caribbean Sea is noted for its mild tropical climate.

CARIBOO MOUNTAINS, rugged mountain range, E British Columbia, Canada. Situated W of the Rocky Mts., the Cariboo Mts. reach a maxi-

Barren Ground bull caribou, Rangifer tarandus
Charles J. Ott–National Audubon Society

mum elevation of 3444 m (11,299 ft) atop Mt. Sir Wilfrid Laurier. Tourism, lumbering, ranching and mining are the chief economic activities. The mountains contain the Thompson Ice Fields and Bowron Lake and Wells Gray provincial parks. A gold rush occurred near Barkerville in the 1860s.

CARIBOU, common name for a North American deer (q.v.) of the same species, *Rangifer tarandus,* family Cervidae, order Artiodactyla (*see* ARTIODACTYL), as the reindeer (q.v.) of Eurasia. Caribou range in height from 100 to 150 cm (40 to 60 in) at the shoulder and weigh from 90 to more than 300 kg (200 to more than 660 lb). Both sexes have antlers, but the female's are smaller and simpler. Two principal groups exist: the Barren Ground, or Arctic, caribou and the woodland caribou.

Barren Ground caribou are native to the tundra regions of northern Canada, Greenland, and Alaska. Historically, the Inuit (Eskimo) living in arctic regions have depended on these animals for survival, using every part of the body for food, implements, or clothing. The caribou usually live in small herds of cows and calves and a few bulls. Most of the older bulls stay in separate small bands except during rut and travel on the fringes of migrating herds. Breeding takes place in September and October, and the calves are born in May and June. These caribou have a gray or light brown summer coat and a white winter coat. In winter they gather in large herds and migrate south to warmer Canadian forests, sometimes traveling 1300 km (800 mi), then return north in springtime. The staple diet of caribou is lichens, but they also eat grasses, shrubs, tree shoots, and mushrooms. Plans for oil- and gas-pipeline construction in Alaska and Canada were altered, through environmentalist efforts, so as not to interfere with caribou migration.

Of less economic significance are the woodland caribou, which are darker and stockier and have heavier antlers than Barren Ground caribou. At one time they were common from Maine to Montana, but they have since been exterminated in most parts of the U.S.

CARICATURE, picture or other representation that exaggerates the particular physical or facial features, dress, or manners of an individual to produce a ludicrous effect. Caricature (Ital. *caricare,* "to overload," "exaggerate") may also be used to ridicule political, social, or religious situations and institutions, or actions by various groups or classes of a society. The latter types of caricature are usually done with satirical rather than humorous intent in order to encourage political or social change. The most common form of these political and social caricatures is the cartoon (q.v.).

Although, by extension, the term *caricature* also applies to exaggerations by means of verbal description, its use is generally restricted to pictorial representations.

Caricature in its modern sense originated at the close of the 16th century in the art school founded by the Carracci family in Bologna. For

Caricature of a British lord by William Hogarth.
Newark Public Library

The Legislative Body, *a caricature of the French national assembly by Honoré Daumier, the outstanding social caricaturist of the 19th century.*
National Gallery of Art, Washington

diversion, the students at this academy often drew pictures of visitors in the likeness of various animals or inanimate objects. The engraver Pier Leone Ghezzi (1674–1755), working in Rome, continued the Carracci tradition, making caricatures for tourists for a small fee. The caricatures done by these Italian artists were humorous portraits intended for private circulation; they were rarely satirical or malicious.

Caricature in England. Political caricatures intended for wide distribution originated in England about the mid-18th century. One of the first artists to caricature well-known persons was George Townshend (1724–1807), who had his caricatures printed on cards and distributed as handbills. The painter and engraver William Hogarth, perhaps the greatest of all English pictorial satirists, caricatured the absurdities of social customs and the corruption of morals in the Londoners of his day. Between 1761 and 1770 publications such as the *Town and Country Magazine,* the *Political Register,* and the *Universal Museum* offered artists a new vehicle for satirizing prominent personalities and political issues. Three of the most important of these caricaturists were the engraver Thomas Rowlandson, who ridiculed the ludicrous behavior of such types as the aristocrat and the pedant; the illustrator James Gillray, who comically pictured the public characters of his day with fantastic costumes and enormous heads; and the etcher George Cruikshank, who spread his satire among all classes and all institutions of English life.

In 1841 the humorous weekly magazine *Punch* was founded, and it soon became one of the best-known publications in the world for caricature. It was noted for its satirical thrusts at the royal family. Among the caricaturists who contributed to the magazine were George du Maurier, who satirized the fashionable social life of the middle and upper classes; John Leech (1817–64), who dwelt on the careers of prominent, contemporary statesmen; and Sir John Tenniel, whose cartoons chronicled the international events of the times. After 1868 the magazine *Vanity Fair* featured colored lithographic caricatures of prominent personalities, chiefly the work of Sir Leslie Ward (1851–1922), known as "Spy." In the late 19th and early 20th centuries, outstanding caricaturists were Sir Max Beerbohm, who specialized in social and literary personages, and David Low (1891–1963), who through his caricatures became one of the most influential political commentators of his time. Low created many political symbols, the most famous being Colonel Blimp, a symbol for British conservatism. Gerald Scarfe (1936-) was a leading political cartoonist in the late 20th century.

Caricature on the Continent. In France the art of political caricaturing also began to flourish in the early 18th century. Numerous books and magazines containing caricatures were published from the late 18th century through the 19th century, particularly during the revolutionary period. The French journalist Charles Philipon (1800-62) made the caricature an important part of French political life through his satirical magazines *La Caricature* (founded 1830), *Le Charivari* (1832), and *Le Journal pour Rire* (1848). The principal contributors were the artists Honoré Daumier, Gustave Doré, and Gavarni. Daumier, the most famous of the group, was thrown into prison for his scathing caricature of King Louis Philippe. Later influential French caricaturists were the artists Henri Toulouse-Lautrec, who caricatured theater and music hall habitués, and Jean Louis Forain (1852-1931), who was particularly noted for his attacks on the French legal system.

Elsewhere on the Continent other artists used the caricature as a vehicle for social criticism. The early 19th-century Spanish painter Francisco José de Goya bitterly satirized the religious, political, and social injustices of his age in a series of 80 etchings called *Caprichos* (1799). These caricatures, among the most powerful in the history of art, were thinly veiled caricatures of well-known personages and were confiscated by the government. The noted German painter George Grosz was another vehement social critic. His most famous collection of cartoons and caricatures, *Ecce homo* (Behold the Man, 1922), fiercely attacked the growing militarism in Germany following World War I.

Caricature in the U.S.. Perhaps the most important 19th-century American caricaturist was Thomas Nast. His work, the best of which appeared in *Harper's Weekly,* was a powerful weapon on the side of the North during the Civil War, and in the overthrow of the corrupt political group known as the Tweed Ring, which controlled the government of New York City from about 1869 to 1872. Nast also created the symbols for the Republican and Democratic parties, the elephant and the donkey. Other important American cartoonists of the century were Joseph Keppler (1838-94), who founded (1876) and edited the humorous weekly *Puck,* and his associate Bernhard Gillam (1856-96), both of whom attacked the corrupt practices of political bosses as well as the many wealthy industrialists.

In the 20th century cartoonists and caricaturists have continued to have a profound effect on American life. Some of the more effective cartoon campaigns were conducted by Rollin Kirby (1875-1952), who focused anti-Prohibitionist sentiment in his Mr. Bluenose figure; Bill Mauldin (1921-), who, in his cartoons during World War II, focused on the drudgery, rather than the glory, of war; and Clarence Daniel Batchelor (1888-1977), who used his cartoons to promote nationwide concern for public health and automobile safety. All of the above have won Pulitzer prizes for their work, as have the influential political cartoonists Daniel Robert Fitzpatrick (1891-1969), "Herblock" (Herbert Lawrence Block, 1909-), and Pat Oliphant (1935-). David Levine (1926-) is well known for witty caricatures of literary and political figures.

One of the most powerful outlets of American social satire in recent times has been *The New Yorker* magazine. Regular contributors have included the critics of café society and the idle rich, Peter Arno (1904-68) and Whitney Darrow, Jr. (1909-), and the satirists of suburbia, Helen Hokinson (c. 1900-49) and Gluyas Williams (1888-1982). Jules Feiffer (1929-) and Walt Kelly (1913-73) did caricature work in the comic strip form. The theatrical caricatures of Al Hirschfeld (1903-) were also well known. In Canada, 20th-century caricaturists of note included Len Norris (1913-), Duncan Macpherson (1924-), Edward Franklin (1921-), and Andrew Donato.

For further information on this topic, see the Bibliography in volume 28, section 693.

CARILLON, group of cast bells (23 or more) tuned to a chromatic musical scale of more than two octaves. The carillon is hung in a fixed position in a tower. It is played manually by a keyboard called a clavier, or automatically by a clockwork mechanism or electropneumatically. The lowest tones are produced by the largest bells, some of which weigh several tons; the highest tones are made by bells weighing as little as 4.5 to 9 kg (10 to 20 lb). When the carillon is played manually, the clapper of each bell is wired to the clavier keys; the bellmaster, or carillonneur, depresses the clavier keys with a closed hand, and the clapper strikes the inside of the bell. The essential differences between a chime and a carillon, both of which are constructed in the same way, are the number of bells and the method of tuning; the chime is tuned to the diatonic scale and has fewer than 23 bells.

The art of carillon playing is called campanology, and the best-known school is in Malines, Belgium, founded by Jef Denijn (1862-1941), the

Carillon in bell tower, Mechelen, Belgium.
Belgian Information Center

famous carillonneur. The art of casting bells and making large carillons was perfected in Europe between the 15th and 18th centuries, particularly in Belgium, the Netherlands, and France. The largest carillon in the world is the Rockefeller Memorial Carillon in Riverside Church, in New York City. It contains 74 bells, of which the deepest-tuned, weighing 20.5 tons, is the heaviest in existence.

The so-called electromechanical carillons are electronic devices made of tiny bars of bell metal that are struck by hammers operated by keyboards.

CARINTHIA (Ger. *Kärnten*) province, S Austria, bordered by the provinces of Tirol on the NW and E, Salzburg and Styria on the N, Yugoslavia on the SE, and Italy on the SW. The principal rivers are the Drau, which flows in a generally W to E direction, and the Gail, which flows generally E and then N to join the Drau near the town of Villach. The area W of the confluence of the rivers, known as Upper Carinthia, is in a mountainous section of the Alps and is the site of the Grossglockner 3797 m (12,457 ft), the highest peak in Austria. Mining of lead, zinc, iron, and lignite are important in the region, as are lumbering and the raising of cattle and sheep. The area E of the confluence of the Drau and the Gail is known as Lower Carinthia. This region is also mountainous, but it contains the fertile Drau Basin, in which wheat, rye, corn, and fruit are grown. The Wörthersee is a resort lake that attracts many tourists. The capital city of Klagenfurt and the town of Villach are the chief industrial centers, with plants for the manufacture of metals, chemicals, and textiles. Carinthia, originally a Roman possession, was made an independent duchy in 976. It fell to the Habsburg family in the 13th century and became an Austrian crown land in the 14th century. After World War I Carinthia lost some of its territory to Italy and Yugoslavia. The present province is sparsely populated. Slovenes predominate in the S section. Area, 9534 sq km (3681 sq mi); pop. (1981) 536,179.

CARISSIMI, Giacomo (1604?–74), Italian composer, born in Marino, near Rome. Carissimi began his career as a singer and organist. In 1627 he was appointed choirmaster in Assisi, and from about 1628 to 1674 he held that office in the Church of Sant' Apollinare in Rome. He was a pioneer in the development of the chamber cantata and the oratorio. His masterpiece was the oratorio *Jephtha.* As a teacher Carissimi influenced many Italian composers, notably Alessandro Scarlatti.

CARL XVI GUSTAF (1946–), king of Sweden (1973–), the grandson of King Gustav VI Adolph, whom he succeeded. During his reign the last vestiges of authority were stripped from the Swedish crown, leaving him a purely ceremonial figurehead. In 1976 he married a West German commoner, Silvia Sommerlath (1943–). The couple have three children: Crown Princess Victoria, born in 1977; Prince Carl, born in 1979; and Princess Madeleine, born in 1982.

CARLETON, Guy, 1st Baron Dorchester (1724–1808), British soldier and administrator, born in Strabane, Ireland. Carleton entered the British army in 1742 and went to Canada in 1758 to serve as an officer in the French and Indian War. After the war ended, he was appointed lieutenant governor of Lower Canada (now Québec Province) in 1766 and was appointed governor in 1768. He was also placed in command of all British troops in Canada during the American Revolution. Carleton defended Québec successfully against the American attack in December 1775. The next year, he drove the Americans out of Canada and defeated the American general Benedict Arnold in a battle on Lake Champlain. In 1777 Carleton was succeeded as commander in Canada by Gen. John Burgoyne, but five years later Carleton became commander in chief of British forces in America during the period of their evacuation. For his services, he was created Baron Dorchester and was commissioned governor of all British possessions in Canada in 1786.

CARLISLE, city, administrative center of Cumbria, N England, on the Eden R. The city, formed in 1974, includes the former county borough of Carlisle and a rolling rural area adjacent to the border of Scotland. The town of Carlisle is an important transportation center with manufactures that include textiles and food products. It also serves as a market for the surrounding agricultural region and is the site of important livestock auctions. Places of historical interest include Hadrian's Wall to the N of the town and the remains of the medieval Carlisle Castle. Among the principal buildings are the Carlisle Cathedral and Tullie House (1689), containing a museum and art gallery.

On the site of present-day Carlisle was the ancient Roman defense post of Luguvalium and the later British settlement of Caer Luel. Carlisle Castle, built in 1092, became a strategic English bulwark during the wars with the Scots in the following centuries. During the Middle Ages Carlisle was a thriving commercial and handicraft center. The modern textile industry dates from the late 18th century, and during the 19th century the city became an important railroad center. Until 1974 Carlisle was the county town of the former county of Cumberland. Pop. (1981) 100,692.

CARLISLE, borough, seat of Cumberland Co., S Pennsylvania, near Harrisburg; inc. 1751. It is a manufacturing and educational center, seat of Dickinson College, Dickinson School of Law (1834), and a U.S. Army war college. From 1879 to 1918 it was the site of the Carlisle Indian School. Manufactures include carpets, shoes, tires, and quartz crystals. The borough served (1794) as George Washington's headquarters during the Whiskey Rebellion and was later a stop on the Underground Railroad. It is named for Carlisle, England. Pop. (1970) 18,079; (1980) 18,314.

CARLISTS, members of a Royalist faction in 19th- and 20th-century Spain. Carlism originated in the 1830s among followers of Don Carlos de Borbon, count of Molina (1788-1855), brother of King Ferdinand VII. Invoking the Salic Law that excluded females from the throne, Don Carlos opposed the succession of Ferdinand's daughter, Isabella II, when her father died in 1833. His claim was supported by various traditionalists opposed to liberalism and parliamentary government. Carlists were most numerous in rural northern Spain, especially in Navarre. They tended to be strongly Roman Catholic, hostile to foreign ideas, and fervent champions of the *fueros,* the traditional liberties of the northern provinces. In the first Carlist war (1833-39) Ferdinand's widow, Maria Christina (1806-78), acting as regent for the infant Isabella, was supported by the liberal faction against the Carlists, who were forced to surrender in 1839. Don Carlos (known to his followers as King Charles V) went into exile, and in 1845 renounced his claim to the throne in favor of his son Carlos, count of Montemolín (1818-61). Carlos returned to Spain in 1860 and tried to organize a revolt but was captured. When he died the following year, his brother Juan (1822-87) assumed the leadership. Juan in turn gave up his rights in favor of his son Don Carlos, duke of Madrid (1848-1909), in 1867. Another defeat in the Carlist war of 1872-76, coupled with internal disputes, subsequently weakened the movement, but it revived during the Spanish civil war of 1936-39, when Navarrese Carlist volunteers (*requetés*) fought for Gen. Francisco Franco against the republic. Franco appointed many Carlists to important posts in his regime (1939-75).

On the death of Alfonso Carlos, duke of San Jaime (1849-1936), the last direct descendant of the original Carlist pretender, some Carlists transferred their allegiance to the family of deposed King Alfonso XIII, whose grandson, Juan Carlos I, ascended the throne in 1975. Others have remained adamant and still support the latest Carlist pretender, Prince Carlos Hugo of Bourbon-Parma (1930-). Although a 1978 visit by the prince to King Juan Carlos was taken by some as a tacit recognition of the king, the pretender still declined to make an explicit renunciation of his claim.

CARLOS I (1863-1908), king of Portugal (1889-1908), born in Lisbon, the son and successor of King Louis, of the royal house of Braganza. In 1891 Carlos concluded a treaty with Great Britain ending a long-standing dispute over the border between the Portuguese colony of Mozambique and British possessions in Africa. The treaty, however, was strongly opposed in Portugal. To curb the growing dissent, Carlos in 1906 gave the Portuguese statesman João Franco (1855-1929) virtual dictatorial powers. Franco's harsh measures, however, further increased the unrest, and resulted in the assassination of the king and his eldest son. A younger son succeeded Carlos as Manuel II.

CARLOS, Don, also called Carlos de Austria (1545-68), son of King Philip II of Spain. His father betrothed him to Princess Elizabeth of France (1545-68) but married her himself in 1559. During the revolt of the Netherlands against Spanish rule in 1567, Don Carlos apparently conspired against his father; as a result, Philip imprisoned him in 1568. When the prince died, later that year, Philip's enemies accused him of having murdered his son. Carlos's sad fate has inspired several dramatic works, including the tragedy *Don Carlos* (1787), by the German dramatist Johann Christoph Friedrich von Schiller, and the opera *Don Carlos* (1867), by the Italian composer Giuseppe Verdi.

CARLOVINGIAN. *See* CAROLINGIAN.

CARLOW, county, SE Republic of Ireland, in Leinster Province. The terrain is mostly level, but in the SE are barren mountains, the highest peak of which is Mt. Leinster (796 m/2610 ft). The great coalfield of Leinster is in the W part of the county. The chief rivers are the Barrow and the Slaney. Among the principal towns are the county seat of Carlow, Tullow, and Muinebeag. The most important industry is the raising of dairy cattle, sheep, and poultry. Chief articles of trade produced in the county are grains, beet sugar, flour, and dairy products. Area, 896 sq km (346 sq mi); pop. (1981) 39,820.

CARLSBAD, city, San Diego Co., SW California, on the Pacific Ocean; inc. 1952. The city's major industries include tourism, farming, and the manufacture of electronic equipment. Tomatoes and flowers are the principal crops of the area. Settled in the 1870s and called Frazier's Station, the community developed as a health resort because of local mineral springs with waters similar to those of the European spa of Karlsbad, or Carlsbad (now Karlovy Vary, Czechoslovakia). The settlement was renamed for the spa in 1883. Pop. (1970) 14,944; (1980) 35,490.

CARLSBAD, city, seat of Eddy Co., SE New Mexico, on the Pecos R.; inc. as a city 1918. Major industries of the area include the mining and refining of potash, irrigated farming and livestock raising, and tourism. The city has a junior college, and Carlsbad Caverns National Park is nearby. Settled about 1888, the community was originally called Eddy. It was renamed in 1899 for the European spa of Karlsbad, or Carlsbad (now Karlovy Vary, Czechoslovakia), because of the mineral springs in the area. Increased agricultural productivity resulted from the Carlsbad reclamation project, begun in the region in 1906. Pop. (1970) 21,297; (1980) 25,496.

CARLSBAD CAVERNS NATIONAL PARK, SE New Mexico, established as a national monument in 1923, as a national park in 1930. Located in the semiarid foothills of the Guadalupe Mts., the park is the site of Carlsbad Caverns, one of the largest subterranean labyrinths in the world. The caverns are believed to have been hollowed out, beginning about 60 million years ago, by the dissolving action of water on limestone. The first scientific exploration of the caverns was made in 1924 by a National Geographic Society party, but the full extent of the caverns is still not known.

About 60 km (about 37 mi) of connecting corridors and chambers have been explored, and the deepest known level is 335 m (1100 ft) below the earth's surface. The principal chamber, the Big Room, is the world's largest subterranean chamber; it is about 1220 m (about 4000 ft) long and about 190 m (about 625 ft) wide and reaches a height of 87 m (285 ft). Stalactites and stalagmites of various colors and sizes, ranging from massive to delicate, are found in the caverns' chambers, which include King's Palace, Green Lake Room, Papoose Room, and Queen's Chamber. Nearly 1 million bats inhabit the caverns, emerging nightly from May to October in search of insects. Area, 189.2 sq km (73.1 sq mi).

CARLSBAD DECREES, repressive measures drafted at a conference of German states in Carlsbad (now Karlovy Vary, Czechoslovakia) and enacted by the diet of the German Confederation in 1819. Proposed by Austrian foreign minister Klemens von Metternich to counteract the threat of revolution, they provided for uniform press censorship, abolition of liberal student organizations (*Burschenschaften*), state supervision of universities, and a federal commission to investigate subversive activities.

CARLSTADT. *See* KARLSTADT.

CARLYLE, Thomas (1795–1881), Scottish essayist and historian, who was an influential social critic. He was born in Ecclefechan on Dec. 4, 1795, and educated as a divinity student at the University of Edinburgh. After five years of study he abandoned the clergy in 1814 and spent the next four years teaching mathematics. Dissatisfied with teaching, Carlyle moved to Edinburgh in 1818, where, after studying law briefly, he became a tutor and wrote articles for the *Edinburgh Encyclopedia.* He also made an intensive study of German literature, publishing *Wilhelm Meister's Apprenticeship* (1824), a translation of the novel *Wilhelm Meisters Lehrjahre* (1796) by the German writer Johann von Goethe. Carlyle also wrote *Life of Schiller* (1825), which appeared first in serial form in 1823 and 1824 in the *London Magazine.* After a trip to Paris and London, he returned to Scotland and wrote for the *Edinburgh Review,* a literary periodical.

In 1826 Carlyle married Jane Baillie Welsh (1801–66), a writer, whom he had met in 1821. After 1828 the Carlyles lived on a farm in Craigenputtock, Scotland, where Carlyle wrote a philosophical satire, *Sartor Resartus* (The Tailor Retailored). The work, first published between 1833 and 1834 in *Fraser's Magazine,* is partly autobiographical. In the guise of a "philosophy of clothes," Carlyle comments on the falseness of material wealth; and in the form of a philosophical romance, he details the crises in his life and affirms his spiritual idealism. In the satire, Carlyle

Thomas Carlyle Granger Collection

emerged as a social critic deeply concerned with the living conditions of British workers. At the farm he also wrote some of his most distinguished essays, and he established a lifelong friendship with the American essayist Ralph Waldo Emerson. In 1834 Carlyle moved to the Chelsea section of London, where he soon became known as the Sage of Chelsea and was a member of a literary circle that included the essayists Leigh Hunt and John Stuart Mill.

In London Carlyle wrote *The French Revolution, A History* (2 vol., 1837), a historical study concentrating on the oppression of the poor, which was immediately successful. This was followed by a series of lectures, in one of which, published as *On Heroes, Hero-Worship, and the Heroic in History* (1841), he contended that world civilization had developed because of the activities of heroes. His hatred and fear of democracy and praise of feudal society were reflected in much of his subsequent writing, especially in *Chartism* (1839) and *Past and Present* (1843). His concept of history appeared in a number of his later works, notably in *Oliver Cromwell's Letters and Speeches, with Elucidations* (1845) and *History of Frederick II of Prussia, Called Frederick the Great* (10 vol., 1858–65), his most extensive work. After the death of his wife, he edited her letters; his autobiography, *Reminiscences,* was published in 1881. He died in London on Feb. 5, 1881.

CARMAGNOLE, an anonymous song and street dance popular during the Reign of Terror of the French Revolution. Reportedly brought into Paris from Marseille, the song became well known after the storming of the Tuileries, a royal palace, on Aug. 10, 1792. The carmagnole consisted originally of 13 two-line stanzas, each of which ended with a refrain praising the Revolution. New stanzas were added from time to time, and a street dance was improvised. The dance itself was a form of farandole, the ancient chain dance of France. The carmagnole was sung and danced at revolutionary gatherings, including festivals and executions. Carmagnole was also the name of an Italian peasant jacket worn by the French revolutionists.

CARMAN, (William) Bliss (1861–1929), Canadian poet, born in Fredericton, N.B., and educated at the universities of New Brunswick and Edinburgh and at Harvard University. After 1890 he did editorial work in New York City and Boston. Carman was a lyric poet; his poems were in praise of joy, love, and nature. His first book of poetry was *Low Tide on Grand Pré* (1893) and his last was *Wild Garden* (1929). His most famous poems were published in *Vagabondia* (3 vol., 1894–1901). In 1928 he received the Lorne Pierce Gold Medal of the Royal Society of Canada.

CARMARTHENSHIRE, former county, S Wales; Carmarthen was the county town. Carmarthenshire comprised a hilly, largely agricultural region. Coal mining was important in the SE. In the area are numerous relics of prehistoric habitation and Roman occupation. In 1974 Carmarthenshire became part of the new county of Dyfed (q.v.).

CARMEL *or* **CARMEL-BY-THE-SEA,** village, Monterey Co., W California, on Carmel Bay (an inlet of the Pacific Ocean); inc. 1916. With its scenic location, it is a tourist center and has been a retreat for writers and artists since its founding in 1904. Nearby is Mission San Carlos Borroneo (1771), burial place of Father Junípero Serra, who brought the mission to Carmel. The name of the village is taken from the bay, which was named in 1602 by an expedition of the Spanish explorer Sebastián Vizcaíno that included a group of Carmelite monks. Pop. (1970) 4525; (1980) 4707.

CARMEL, MOUNT, short mountan ridge, NW Israel. A peak of the ridge is also called Mt. Carmel (546 m/1791 ft). Mt. Carmel is famous for connections with biblical characters and events. The ridge is 21 km (13 mi) long and 5 to 13 km (3 to 8 mi) wide; it extends in a northwesterly direction from the Plain of Esdraelon, or Jezreel, to the Mediterranean Sea, near the port of Haifa. There, the ridge ends in a promontory that marks the S limit of the Bay of Acre. The highest point of the ridge is about 549 m (about 1800 ft) above sea level.

From early times Mt. Carmel was a holy place,

containing an altar for Jehovah long before the contest for allegiance of the children of Israel was fought out here (see 1 Kings 18) between the Hebrew prophet Elijah and the prophets of the divinity Baal. Mt. Carmel also was famed in literary composition for natural beauty (see Song 7:5; Isa. 35:2). According to religious tradition, it is one of the points of Palestine that especially demonstrates God's favor to the Israelites in bestowing upon them such a beautiful country (see Jer. 50:19; Mic. 7:14). The devastation of Mt. Carmel is, therefore, considered a sign of God's decided displeasure (see Isa. 33:9; Jer. 4:26; Amos 1:2; Nah. 1:4). In postbiblical times Carmel continued to be a holy site for many religions, serving finally as the site of a renowned monastery.

CARMELITES, popular name for members of the Order of Our Lady of Mount Carmel, a Roman Catholic religious order founded as a community of hermits in Palestine during the 12th century by the French hermit St. Berthold (fl. 1150–95). The original rule, written for them in 1209 by the Latin patriarch of Jerusalem, Albert of Vercelli (1149–1214), was severe, prescribing poverty, abstinence from meat, and solitude. It was approved in 1226 by Pope Honorius III (fl. 1188–1227).

After the Crusades, the Englishman St. Simon Stock (fl. 1200–65) reorganized the Carmelites as mendicant friars. Under him, a change of rule was made to facilitate a more active apostolate. Offshoot communities quickly sprang up in Cyprus, Messina, Marseille, and parts of England, where they were known as White Friars. During the 16th century two independent branches of the order were created: the Calced Carmelites, who were permitted to wear shoes and followed the mitigated rule of St. Simon Stock; and the Discalced Carmelites, who went without shoes as a sign of austerity and followed the reforms of the Spanish mystic St. John of the Cross. This reform endeavored to restore the spirit of the original rule of Albert of Vercelli. The main purpose of the order is contemplation, missionary work, and theology.

Among the several orders of Carmelite nuns, the best known is the Order of Discalced Carmelites, founded during the 16th century by the Spanish mystic St. Teresa of Ávila. The life of a Carmelite nun is completely contemplative, consisting of prayer, penance, hard work, and silence. The nuns are strictly enclosed, or cloistered; they never eat meat, and from the feast of the Exaltation of the Cross (September 14) until Easter, no milk, cheese, or eggs are allowed on Fridays and during Lent, except for the sick. The order has produced some of the greatest Roman Catholic mystics.

CARMICHAEL, unincorporated community, Sacramento Co., N California, on the American R. It is primarily a residential community. A botanical garden and the state governor's residence are here. The community is named for Daniel W. Carmichael (1867–1936), who developed the area about 1910. Pop. (1970) 37,625; (1980) 43,108.

CARMICHAEL, Hoagy, full name HOAGLAND HOWARD CARMICHAEL (1899–1981), American composer of popular music, born in Bloomington, Ind. He practiced law before turning to writing songs full time. Carmichael's most famous song, "Stardust" (1931), quickly became a standard among popular songs. Among his other well-known compositions are "Lazy Bones" and "I Get Along Without You Very Well."

CARMONA, António Oscar de Fragoso (1869–1951), president of Portugal (1926–51), who launched the 40-year dictatorial regime of António de Oliveira Salazar. He was one of three generals who overthrew the provisional government of Portugal in May 1926 and soon assumed full leadership as prime minister and provisional president. Suppressing popular revolts in Oporto and Lisbon in 1927, he subsequently outlawed political parties, and in 1928, as the sole candidate, he was elected president. As such, he appointed Salazar his finance minister (1928) and prime minister (1932). Carmona was reelected in 1935, 1942, and 1949, but after 1932 the country was controlled by Salazar.

CARNAC, village, NW France, in Morbihan Department, on the S coast of Brittany. Within the village and the surrounding area are thousands of megalithic monuments consisting of menhirs, dolmens, and tumuli. The monuments were arranged in three groups that archaeologists believe were joined at one time. The principal group lies NW of the village and has some 1100 monoliths of granite. They are arranged in 11 roughly parallel rows (about 1030 m/3380 ft long) and end in an arc, the extremities of which touch the outer horizontal rows. Although their origin and object remain a mystery, they are generally considered to have been associated with Druidism (q.v.). The Bossenno, about 1.6 km (about 1 mi) E of Carnac, is the site of numerous burial mounds and the remains of a Gallo-Roman villa. Pop. (1982) 3964.

CARNALLITE, greasy, milk-white or reddish mineral, an important source of potash compounds used in fertilizers. It is found in massive form in extensive deposits near Stassfurt, Germany; smaller deposits occur in Alsace, France, in Poland, and in Iran. Small amounts of carnallite are also found in the potassium deposits in Texas and New Mexico. This hydrous potassium-magnesium chloride, $KMgCl_3 \cdot 6H_2O$, crystallizes in the orthorhombic system. It is brittle and highly soluble in water.

CARNAP, Rudolf (1891-1970), prominent figure in the philosophical movement known as logical positivism or logical empiricism (*see* POSITIVISM).

Carnap was born on May 18, 1891, in Ronsdorf, Germany. Educated at the universities of Jena and Freiburg, he specialized in mathematics, physics, and philosophy. He particularly acknowledged the influence of the German mathematician Gottlob Frege in mathematics and the British philosophers Bertrand Russell and Ludwig Wittgenstein in philosophy. Carnap became a leading member of the Vienna Circle, a group of positivist scientists and philosophers. In 1935 he went to the U.S. to escape Nazism and joined the faculty of the University of Chicago. In 1954 he accepted a position at the University of California, Los Angeles. He died in Santa Monica, Calif., on Sept. 14, 1970.

Carnap interpreted philosophy as logical analysis. He was primarily concerned with the analysis of the language of science, because he judged the empirical statements of science to be the only factually meaningful ones. His early effort in *The Logical Structure of the World* (1928; trans. 1967) to reduce all knowledge claims to the language of sense data, his developing preference for language that described behavior (physicalistic language), his work on the syntax of scientific language in *The Logical Syntax of Language* (1934; trans. 1937), and his various treatments of the verifiability, testability, or confirmability of empirical statements are testimonies to his belief that the problems of philosophy are reducible to the problems of language.

Carnap's principle of tolerance, or the conventionality of language forms, emphasized freedom and variety in language construction. He was particularly interested in the construction of formal, logical systems. He also did significant work in the area of probability, distinguishing between statistical and logical probability in his work *Logical Foundations of Probability* (1950).

Carnap helped found and edit the journal *Erkenntnis* and the *International Encyclopedia of Unified Science.* R.M.B.

CARNARVON, George Edward Stanhope Molyneux Herbert, 5th Earl of (1866-1923), British Egyptologist, born near Newbury, and educated at Eton College and the University of Cambridge. He traveled widely as a young man, and in 1903 he went to Egypt for the first time. Four years later, he and the British archaeologist Howard Carter began excavations at the ancient city of Thebes. They gave an account of their findings in *Five Years' Exploration at Thebes* (1912). Their work was interrupted by World War I, but they returned to Egypt after the war. On Nov. 4, 1922, while digging in the Valley of the Kings, they discovered the tomb of King Tutankhamen of the 18th Dynasty. On Feb. 17, 1923, they opened the tomb, which contained a magnificent collection of Egyptian art, as well as the mummy of the boy king. Carnarvon died two months later.

CARNARVONSHIRE. *See* CAERNARVONSHIRE.

CARNATIC WARS, Anglo-French conflicts in India during the 18th century, so called because they were centered in the Carnatic, a region on the east coast of south India. The wars reflected the rivalry between the British and French trading companies in India and were really part of the wider Anglo-French wars of the 18th century. In the First Carnatic War, part of Europe's War of the Austrian Succession (1740-48), the French, led by Joseph François Dupleix, captured the British territory of Madras, but it was returned to the British by the peace treaty. The war demonstrated the superiority of European technology and discipline over larger native armies.

The Second Carnatic War (1751-54) was an unofficial war fought between the British East India Co. and the French Compagnie des Indes at a time when there was peace between the two powers in Europe. Its roots lay in Dupleix's skillful exploitation of the confused politics of the region to enhance French power through a series of native alliances. The daring of the East India Co.'s Robert Clive, who defeated the French-backed claimant to the throne of the Carnatic, ended the second phase of Anglo-French struggle in India as Dupleix was recalled to France in 1754.

The Third Carnatic War followed just two years later, in 1756, when the Seven Years' War broke out in Europe. This time the war passed beyond the limits of south India into the rich province of Bengal, where the English captured the French possession of Chandernagore in 1757. The most decisive battles of the war, however, were fought in the south. Here, the military balance tilted decisively in favor of Britain when the French capital of Pondicherry fell in 1761. The war ended in 1763 with the Peace of Paris, and so too ended the French pursuit of empire in India. A.P.K.

CARNATION. *See* PINK.

CARNAUBA PALM, common name for a species of palm tree, *Copernicia cerifera.* This slender tree grows to a height of 12 m (40 ft). It is found from Brazil to Argentina. The hard wood of this tree is used in making excellent veneers. The tree bears a sweet black fruit that is about the size of an olive and is edible either raw or cooked. Starch is obtained from the stems of the tree and sugar from the sap. The leaf fibers are made into cordage, mats, and hats.

A wax, also called carnauba, forms in scales on the lower surfaces of the leaves and is removed by shaking the dried harvested leaves. It is processed for use in lubricants, polishes, floor wax, plastics, and carbon paper. *See* PALM.

CARNEADES (214?-129 BC), Greek philosopher, born in Cyrene (now Shahat, Libya). He studied Stoicism in Athens and later founded the New, or Third, Academy, an extension of the Old Academy begun by Plato. In 155 BC Carneades was sent as a member of an embassy to Rome. While there he lectured on skepticism, asserting that knowlege is impossible and that truth has no criterion. The Roman statesman Cato the Elder, however, believed the philosophy was dangerous to the youth of Rome, and he forced the Roman Senate to banish Carneades.

CARNEGIE, Andrew (1835-1919), American industrialist and philanthropist, who, at the age of 33, when he had an annual income of $50,000, said, "Beyond this never earn, make no effort to increase fortune, but spend the surplus each year for benevolent purposes."

Andrew Carnegie Wide World Photos

Carnegie was born in Dunfermline, Scotland. He went to the U.S. in 1848 and soon began work as a bobbin boy in a cotton mill in Allegheny, Pa., for $1.20 per week. The following year he became a messenger in a Pittsburgh telegraph office and learned telegraphy. He was then employed by the Pennsylvania Railroad as the private secretary and telegrapher to the railroad official Thomas Alexander Scott (1823-81). Carnegie advanced by successive promotions until he was superintendent of the Pittsburgh division of the railroad. His financial interest in what is now the Pullman Co. laid the foundation of his fortune, and investments in oil lands near Oil City, Pa., increased his means. During the American Civil War he served in the War Department under Scott, who was in charge of military transportation and government telegraph service. After the war Carnegie left the railroad and formed a company to produce iron railroad bridges. He later founded a steel mill and was one of the earliest users of the Bessemer process of making steel in the U.S. Carnegie was extremely successful, acquiring a controlling interest in other large steel plants. By 1899, when he consolidated his interests in the Carnegie Steel Co., he controlled about 25 percent of the American iron and steel production. In 1901 he sold his company to the United States Steel Corp. for $250 million and retired.

Carnegie did not have a formal education, but as a youth working in Pennsylvania he developed a life-long interest in books and education. During his lifetime he gave more than $350 million to various educational, cultural, and peace institutions, many of which bear his name. His first public gift was in 1873 for baths in the town of his birth; his largest single gift was in 1911 for $125 million to establish the Carnegie Corporation of New York. He was a benefactor of Tuskegee Institute. He also endowed nearly 1700 libraries in the U.S. and Great Britain, and he donated funds for the construction of the Peace Palace at The Hague, Netherlands, for what is now the International Court of Justice of the UN. Carnegie was honored throughout the world during his lifetime.

CARNEGIE CORPORATION OF NEW YORK, American public trust, the largest of the philanthropic agencies founded by the industrialist Andrew Carnegie. The Carnegie Corporation was established in 1911 for "the advancement and diffusion of knowledge and understanding." Among its first efforts was the establishment of free public libraries throughout the English-speaking world; this program was terminated in 1917. Since then, grants have been made to colleges and universities, professional associations, and other educational organizations for specific programs in higher education and early childhood education, as well as certain aspects of elementary and secondary schooling. Notable grants awarded by the corporation include those for the improvement of education of blacks in the American South, for a study of the future of higher education in the U.S., and for the development of educational television.

CARNEGIE ENDOWMENT FOR INTERNATIONAL PEACE, private foundation established in 1910 by the philanthropist Andrew Carnegie for the purpose of abolishing war. Since World War II the Carnegie Endowment has concentrated on the development of international institutions, particularly the UN; it is also concerned with American foreign policy and with military, political, and economic issues. Headquarters is in Washington, D.C.

CARNEGIE FOUNDATION FOR THE ADVANCEMENT OF TEACHING, private foundation established in 1905 by the American philanthropist Andrew Carnegie to provide free pensions for American and Canadian college teachers. In 1918 the foundation established the Teachers Insurance and Annuity Association, a nonprofit company designed to provide those in the academic profession with retirement allowances and other insurance. Headquarters is in Princeton, N.J.

CARNEGIE INSTITUTE OF TECHNOLOGY. *See* CARNEGIE-MELLON UNIVERSITY.

CARNEGIE-MELLON UNIVERSITY, privately controlled institution of higher learning, in Pittsburgh, Pa., founded in 1900 by the American industrialist and philanthropist Andrew Carnegie. The university was originally named the Carnegie Technical Schools and became Carnegie Institute of Technology in 1912, when the institution received a state charter. The institute merged with Mellon Institute (founded 1913) on July 1, 1967. The colleges of the university are the Carnegie Institute of Technology, which offers programs in chemical, civil, electrical, mechanical, and metallurgical engineering; the Mellon College of Science, offering programs in biological sciences, chemistry, computer science, mathematics, and physics; the College of Fine Arts, with courses in drama, music, painting, design, sculpture, and architecture; the College of Humanities and Social Sciences, with courses in English, history, modern languages, psychology, and social studies; the College of Administration and Management Science; and graduate and research facilities. Research units include the Mellon Institute, the Software Engineering Institute, the Robotics Institute, the Center for Molecular Electronics, a metals research laboratory, a radiation chemistry laboratory, and institutes of environmental and transportation research. Bachelor's, master's, and doctoral degrees are conferred.

CARNELIAN, also cornelian, translucent form of the silica (SiO_2) mineral chalcedony, itself a variety of quartz. It has a hardness (q.v.) of 7 and a sp.gr. of 2.65 and ranges in color from yellow to a deep red. The finest specimens come from Brazil, India, and Arabia. Carnelian is cut and polished and used in jewelry. The blood-red varieties were greatly valued by the ancients, who produced beautiful engravings in carnelian and also used them for seals.

CARNIC ALPS, range of the Eastern Alps of Europe. Forming a part of the border between Italy and Austria, they extend from the frontiers of the Austrian province of Tirol and the Italian region of Veneto to the frontier of Carinthia. Hohe Warte, the highest peak of the Carnic Alps, rises 2780 m (9121 ft) above sea level.

CARNIOLA (Ger. *Krain*), region, NW Yugoslavia, in Slovenia, formerly a crown land and duchy of Austria. The mountainous region, with an area of about 9838 sq km (about 3800 sq mi), was settled by the Slovenes during the 6th century AD and was an Austrian duchy from the 14th century until 1849, when it became a crown land. In 1918 Carniola was partitioned between Yugoslavia and Italy. Nearly 80 percent was given to Yugoslavia. In 1947 the Italian portion passed to Yugoslavia. *See* SLOVENIA.

CARNIVORE, general term for any animal that subsists mainly on the flesh of other animals; more restrictedly, it refers to any member of the mammal order Carnivora. The carnivores are at the top of the food chains that make up the food web (q.v.) of the earth's life forms. They feed on herbivores, or planteaters, which in turn feed on the plants or dinoflagellates, at the bottom of the food chains, that absorb and store energy directly from the sun. Carnivores live mainly alone or in small groups and are not preyed upon except by other carnivores.

This general meaning of the term *carnivore* also applies more specifically to the Carnivora, except that some members of the order—many bears, for example—are omnivorous (eat both animals and plants) and may sometimes even have a largely vegetable diet. A widespread group, the Carnivora have teeth adapted for grasping and tearing, highly developed physical coordination and flexibility of behavior, and extended parent-offspring bonds. The order has been divided into two suborders: the Pinnipedia, with finlike feet, and the Fissipedia, with pawlike feet. The Pinnipedia are the sea lions and fur seals (family Otaridae); the true seals (Phocidae);

The leopard, a carnivore of Asia and Africa, uses its sharp, pointed teeth to tear the flesh of its prey. South African Tourist Corp.

and the walruses (Odobaenidae). The suborder Fissipedia has two superfamilies: Canoidea (dog, bear, raccoon, and weasel families); and Feloidea (cat, civet, and hyena families).

The jaws of the Carnivora are powerful and move only up and down on a transverse hinge with none of the rotary motion found in other animals. The teeth have been adapted for the feeding habits, so that in most carnivores each jaw contains six pointed cutting teeth; two strong, sharp, recurved canines; and molar teeth that have been developed into cutting blades. The number of molars varies among the different families. The cats have only a single vestige of molar in each jaw, whereas dogs retain more molars, which they use for bone crushing. The bears (Ursidae), except for the polar bear, are omnivorous, and their back molars show tubercles on the crowns, which improve their ability to grind vegetable matter. The digestive system of carnivores is much less complicated than that of herbivores because it does not have to break down the cellulose in plant matter.

For further information on this topic, see the Bibliography in volume 28, sections 440, 461–63, 475, 479–81.

CARNIVOROUS PLANTS. *See* INSECTIVOROUS PLANTS.

CARNOT, Lazare Nicolas Marguerite (1753–1823), French statesman and military engineer, born in Nolay, and prominent during the French Revolution. He became a member of the Legislative Assembly in 1791, of the National Convention in 1792, and of the Committee of Public Safety in 1793. Although never in full command, Carnot was the principal strategist of the victories of French troops in the battles of 1792–95. His aptitude for military tactics made him known as the Organizer of Victory.

During the complex events that followed the Reign of Terror and continued through the accession of Napoleon, Carnot moved in and out of France several times. He died in exile in Magdeburg (now in East Germany). Books written by Carnot include several on mathematical theory, but more important are his works on military tactics. *De la défense des places fortes* (On the Defense of Fortresses, 1810) is a classic study of fortification.

CARNOT, Marie François Sadi (1837–94), French statesman, born in Limoges, and educated at the École Polytechnique. He entered the civil service and later gained renown as an organizer of French resistance to the Germans in 1870 during the Franco-Prussian War. In 1871 he was made prefect of what is now the Seine-Maritime Department and was elected to the National Assembly. He served as minister of public works in 1880–81 and again in 1885 and was minister of finance from 1885 to 1886. The following year, he was elected the fourth president of the Third Republic. His tenure was marred by the scandal over construction of the Panama Canal and by the conspiracy trial of Gen. Georges Boulanger. Carnot was assassinated by an Italian anarchist.

CARNOT, Nicolas Léonard Sadi (1796–1832), French physicist and military engineer, son of Lazare Nicolas Marguerite Carnot, born in Paris, and educated at the École Polytechnique. In 1824 he described his conception of the perfect engine, the so-called Carnot engine, in which all available energy is utilized. He discovered that heat cannot pass from a colder to a warmer body, and that the efficiency of an engine depends upon the amount of heat it is able to utilize. This discovery, called Carnot's cycle, is the basis of the second law of thermodynamics.

CARNOTITE. *See* URANIUM; VANADIUM.

CARO, Anthony (1924–), English sculptor, whose large, powerful works are important examples of modern constructivist and minimal art. Strongly influenced by the American abstract sculptor David Smith during a trip to the U.S. in 1959, Caro abandoned traditional cast-metal sculpture in favor of a technique involving the construction of abstract works from rigid pieces of metal. His sculptures are large, often massive assemblages of sheet metal, industrial girders, piping, or pieces of steel, welded together. They are either allowed to rust naturally or are painted bright colors as, for example, *Midday* (1960, T. and P. Caro Collection, London). In a different mode, works such as *Riviera* (1974, private collection, Seattle) consist of several freestanding metal segments loosely grouped on a floor. As a teacher in London and the U.S., Caro strongly influenced younger sculptors.

CARO, Joseph ben Ephraim (1488–1575), talmudic scholar and codifier of Jewish law, born in Toledo, Spain. To escape religious persecution, his family fled in 1492 to Portugal and later to Turkey and Palestine. His notable works are *Bet Yoseph* (House of Joseph, 1550–59), a commentary on religious law, and the *Shulhan Arukh* (The Prepared Table, 1564–65), a compilation, mainly from talmudic and later sources, of Jewish civil and religious law. The code of the *Shulhan Arukh* was praised by many scholars and opposed by others. Orthodox Jews, however, accepted it as authoritative in religious matters. Caro (sometimes spelled Karo) belonged to the Cabalist circle at Safed, Palestine. N.N.G.

CAROB, common name for a tree, *Ceratonia siliqua,* of the family Leguminosae (*see* LEGUME), also called Saint-John's-bread or locust bean. It is about 15 m (50 ft) high and has dark, evergreen, pinnate leaves. The small, red flowers have no petals. The fruit is a brown, leathery pod about 10 to 30 cm (about 4 to 12 in) long and contains gummy pulp of an agreeable sweet taste, in which lie a number of seeds. The pods are edible and are often used for livestock feed. The seeds, which are remarkably uniform in size and weight, are thought to have been the original standard karat weight used by jewelers and goldsmiths. The carob is native to the Mediterranean area and is grown in other warm climates.

CAROL I, original name Karl Eitel Friedrich (1839–1914), King of Romania (1866–1914), born in Sigmaringen (now in West Germany), and educated in Dresden and Bonn. A prince of the house of Hohenzollern-Sigmaringen, he was elected (1866) prince of Romania, then a Turkish principality. During the Russo-Turkish War of 1877–78, Carol supported Russia and proclaimed the independence of Romania, which was recognized by the Treaty of Berlin (1878). Carol was crowned as the first king of Romania in 1881. He established a parliamentary form of government for the nation. During his reign, Romania took part in the Balkan Wars. Carol was succeeded by his nephew Ferdinand I.

CAROL II (1893–1953), king of Romania (1930–40). Son of Ferdinand I, Carol was born in Sinaia and became crown prince in 1914, when his father ascended the throne. His first marriage, to a commoner, was dissolved, and in 1921 he married a Greek princess. Four years later he left his wife, renounced his right to the throne, and went into exile in order to live with his mistress, Magda Lupescu (1896–1977). He returned in 1930 at the invitation of Prime Minister Iuliu Maniu (1873–1948) and was crowned king, replacing his young son, Michael (1921–), who had been placed on the throne under a regency in 1927. Despite opposition from the politicians, Lupescu joined him in 1931.

Following his authoritarian bent, Carol gave covert support to the Iron Guard, a Romanian Fascist movement, but later became alarmed by its growing power. He then (1938) established a royal dictatorship and had the Iron Guard leaders executed. At the outbreak of World War II, Carol tried to remain neutral, but in 1940 the Germans occupied Romania, and he was forced to abdicate. The rest of his life was spent in exile. He married Lupescu in 1947.

CAROL (Fr. *noël*), popular religious song, usually associated with Christmas, but also celebrating Easter and folk holidays, such as May Day. Carols, known throughout Europe, flourished in late medieval England. One of the earliest extant English carols is the "Boar's Head Carol," printed in 1521. Such songs consisted of an unharmonized melody that alternated verse and burden (refrain) tunes. They were probably related to the carole, a chain dance to verse-and-burden songs. Between 1350 and 1550, in a major outpouring of English art music, composers wrote sophisticated polyphonic (multipart) carols.

The carol subsequently had two lines of development. The popular carol merged with folk song and with the broadside songs sold on city streets. Modern folk carols include the "Cherry Tree Carol" and "I Saw Three Ships." Composed carols gained variety in form in the 17th century, while their texts began to center on Christmas. After a decline, the composed carol was revived about 1800 by religious reformers promoting devotional hymn singing. Their efforts gave rise to newly written carols such as "Hark, the Herald Angels Sing," by the Methodist clergyman Charles Wesley, and to translations of foreign carols, such as "Silent Night" (from German) and "O Come, All Ye Faithful" (from Latin).

CAROL CITY, unincorporated community, Dade Co., SE Florida. It is a residential suburb NW of Miami. Originally called Coral City, the community's name was altered to avoid confusion with nearby Coral Gables. Pop. (1970) 27,361; (1980) 47,349.

CAROLINE, privately owned American ship seized and destroyed by Canadian troops on the American side of the Niagara River off Grand Island, N.Y., on Dec. 29, 1837. The incident, in which one American was killed, occurred during a rebellion in Upper Canada (now Ontario Province) and threatened to cause war between the U.S. and Great Britain (at the time, Canada was a British colony). The steamer had been used by American sympathizers to carry supplies to a party of Canadian rebels on Navy Island, above Niagara Falls. In 1840 Great Britain asserted that the destruction of the *Caroline* was a legitimate act of war. The U.S., however, repeatedly demanded redress on the grounds that the Canadians had invaded U.S. territory in time of peace. The matter came to a crisis during the same year when a Canadian deputy sheriff visiting the U.S. boasted of participating in the affair and was tried for murder in a New York State court. In spite of the demand of the British ministry for his release, the trial continued; war between the two nations was prevented only by his acquittal. Peaceful relations between Great Britain and the U.S. were finally restored in 1842 with the signing of the Webster-Ashburton Treaty, in which Great Britain expressed regret for failing to make an immediate apology for the *Caroline* affair.

CAROLINE OF ANSBACH (1683–1737), queen consort of Great Britain and Ireland (1727–37) as wife of King George II, whom she married in 1705. She was the daughter of John Frederick, margrave of Brandenburg-Ansbach (1654–1686). In London, Caroline made her home the meeting place of noted literary figures. She acted as regent on several occasions during absences of her husband from England and aided the career of the British statesman Robert Walpole.

CAROLINE OF BRUNSWICK (1768–1821), queen consort of Great Britain as wife of King George IV. She was the daughter of Charles William Ferdinand, duke of Brunswick (1735–1806); her uncle King George III arranged her marriage to his son, George, then prince of Wales, in 1795. George, however, disliked her and, after the birth of their daughter, Charlotte Augusta (1796–1817), deserted her; from 1813 on, she lived much of the time in Italy. She returned to England in 1820, when George ascended the throne. Accused of adultery, she was tried by the House of Lords but drew such enthusiastic crowds at her public appearances that the trial was abandoned. Her husband, however, would not be reconciled with her, and she was forcibly prevented from attending his coronation in 1821. She died shortly afterward.

CAROLINE ISLANDS, archipelago, W Pacific Ocean, consisting of more than 600 islands, atolls, and islets. Formerly part of the U.S. Trust Territory of the Pacific Islands, the Carolines were divided administratively into Ponape, Yap, Truk, Kosrae, and Palau (Belau) districts. Agriculture and fishing are the main economic activities. Products include copra, tapioca, bonita and other fish, sugarcane, and handicrafts. Phosphates and bauxite are mined in the Palau district. Ruins on some of the islands indicate early settlement and possible contact with Chinese civilization. The islands were visited by Spanish navigators in the early 16th century, but were not colonized by Spain until the late 19th century. Sold to Germany in 1899, the islands came under Japanese mandate following Germany's defeat in World War I. During World War II some of the islands (notably Truk) were heavily bombarded by U.S. forces. In 1947 the islands were placed under UN trusteeship and administered by the U.S. (*see* PACIFIC ISLANDS, TRUST TERRITORY OF THE). In 1979 the Palau group (*see* PALAU ISLANDS) voted to become self-governing, and the rest of the islands became the Federated States of Micronesia (*see* MICRONESIA, FEDERATED STATES OF). Area, about 1165 sq km (about 450 sq mi); pop. (1980) 85,932.

CAROLINE MATILDA (1751–75), queen consort of Denmark (1766–71) as wife of King Christian VII (1749–1808). Born in London, the sister of King George III of Great Britain, she married her cousin Christian in 1766, shortly after he became king. King Christian, however, was insane, and Caroline Matilda formed a liaison with Count Johann Friedrich Struensee, the court physician and a brilliant statesman, who subsequently was created count and named minister of state. Sixteen months later, he was toppled by a palace

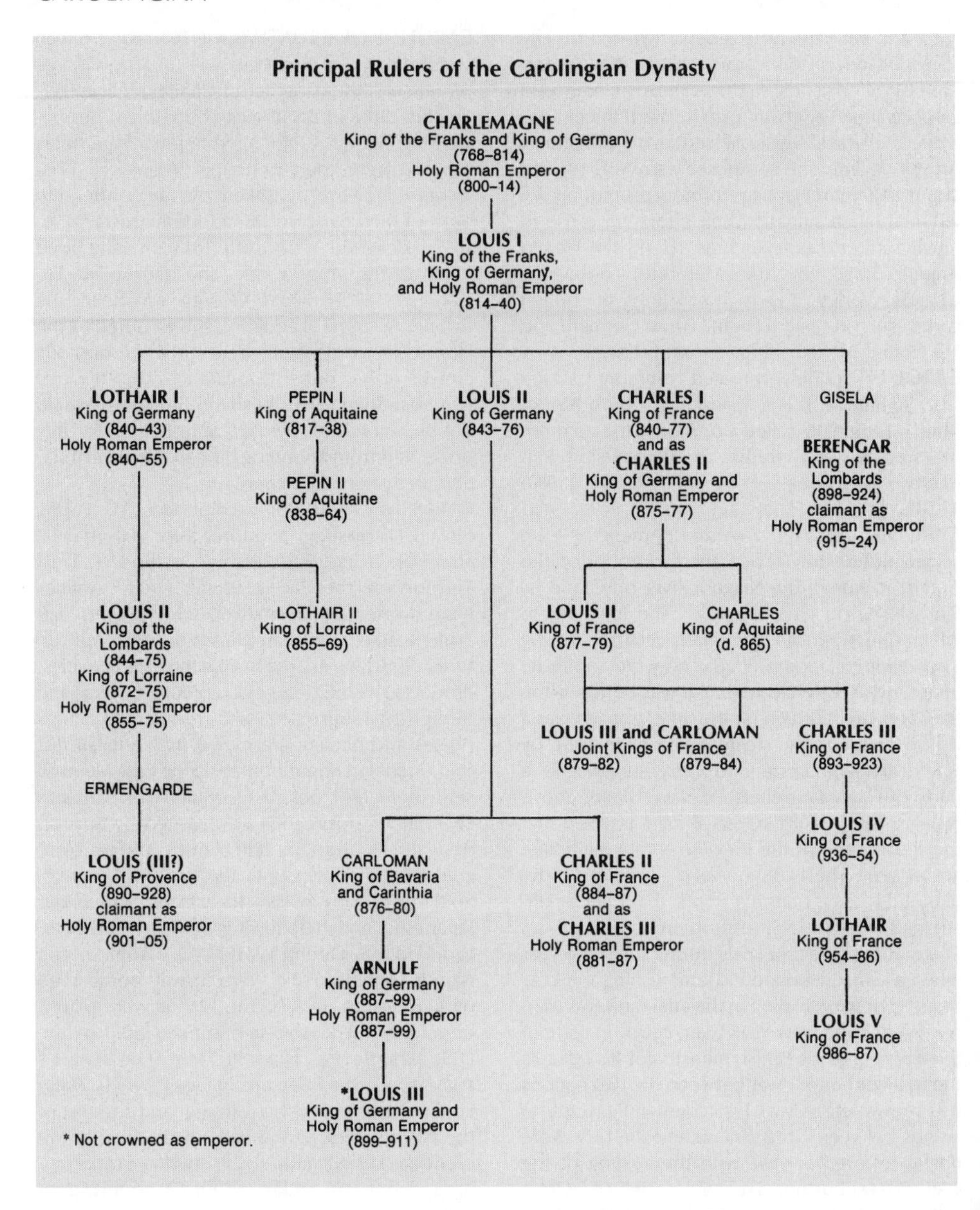

Principal Rulers of the Carolingian Dynasty

cabal, and their affair was made public. Struensee was eventually beheaded, and the queen was divorced from her husband. Imprisoned at first, Caroline Matilda was later freed and spent her last years in Celle (now in West Germany). Her son ruled later as King Frederick VI of Denmark and Norway.

CAROLINGIAN, sometimes called Carlovingian, second dynasty of Frankish kings. The family was descended from Pepin the Elder of Landen, a powerful landowner who served Clotaire II, the Merovingian king of the Franks, as mayor of the palace of Austrasia, the eastern part of the kingdom. Pepin's grandson, Pepin of Herstal, eventually succeeded to the mayor's position, and by 687 he had become the effective ruler of the entire Frankish kingdom, although the Merovingians nominally wielded the royal power. Pepin of Herstal was in turn succeeded by his illegitimate son, Charles Martel, and by two grandsons, Carloman (c. 715–54) and Pepin the Short. Carloman later abdicated, and in 751 Pepin the Short was crowned as the first Carolingian king of the Franks. This date is generally regarded as the be-

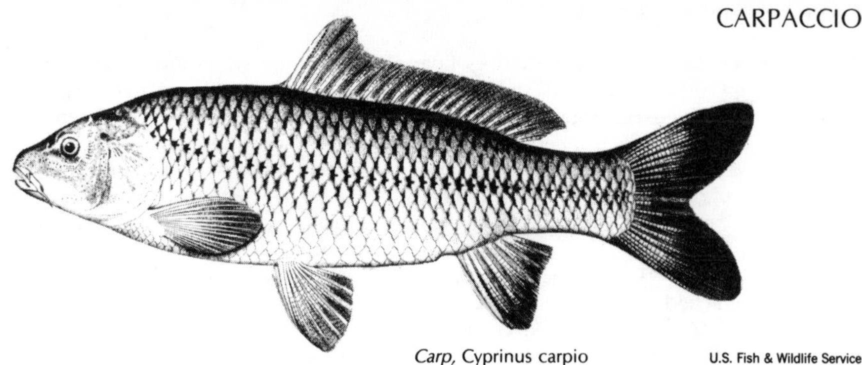

Carp, Cyprinus carpio U.S. Fish & Wildlife Service

ginning of the Carolingian dynasty. It is historically significant that Pepin was the first Frankish king whose coronation was sanctified by the church.

Pepin was succeeded by his two sons Carloman (751–71) and Charlemagne, who at first ruled the kingdom jointly. After 771 Charlemagne was sole ruler and vastly increased the kingdom. At its greatest extent, it included what is now France, West Germany, Austria, Switzerland, the Low Countries, and northern Italy. On Dec. 25, 800, Charlemagne was crowned the first emperor of the revived Western Roman Empire. The kingdom was inherited by Louis I; upon his death, it was divided among his three surviving sons. The kingdom was disturbed by civil war rising from questions of inheritance, and in 843 it was formally divided by the treaty of Verdun. Thereafter the power of the dynasty further declined. The German line, which also ruled the Holy Roman Empire, became extinct in 911 and was replaced by the Saxons; the French line held power until 987, when it was succeeded by the Capetians.

CAROLINGIAN ART AND ARCHITECTURE. *See* ARCHITECTURE; ROMANESQUE ART AND ARCHITECTURE.

CAROTENE. *See* PIGMENT.

CARP, common name for the freshwater fish that constitute the family Cyprinidae, order Cypriniformes, also known as the minnow (q.v.) family. The largest of the fish families, with about 2000 known species, it includes such familiar forms as the barbel, dace, goldfish, and roach (qq.v.). Cyprinids in general are characterized by a single, usually soft-rayed dorsal fin and by one to three rows of teeth in the throat but never in the jaw. Species more specifically known as carp are differentiated from most other cyprinids by a stiff spine at the leading edge of a long, 15-rayed dorsal fin, usually two pairs of barbels at the mouth corners, and three rows of throat teeth.

The cyprinid species called the common carp, *Cyprinus carpio,* apparently originated in ancient China, where many exotic varieties were bred. It was introduced into Europe in the 12th century and into the U.S. in the 1870s, and it now exists worldwide except for South America, Australia, and the island of Madagascar. In the wild, the olive-brown common carp comes in three forms: the leather carp, with almost no scales; the mirror carp, with a few large scales; and the scale carp, which is covered with scales. Adults generally weigh no more than 2.3 kg (5 lb), but specimens weighing more than 35 kg (more than 80 lb) have been recorded. The fish breed from May to July, and the females lay their eggs among water plants. They prefer relatively warm waters, especially shallow, mud-bottomed lakes. In the winter they become torpid, stop feeding, and stay near the bottom; in dry spells they may even burrow into the mud and survive for several weeks in that way.

Carp are prolific and breed rapidly, and they are bred and fished commercially in Asia, Europe, southern Africa, and, on a smaller scale, the U.S. As bottom feeders they stir up mud and uproot vegetation, often driving out other fish; on the other hand, they can survive in stagnant or polluted waters that most other fish do not inhabit.

CARPACCIO, Vittore (1455?–1526?), Italian painter, born in Venice. He was greatly influenced by the Venetian painters Gentile and Giovanni Bellini. Carpaccio executed four cycles of narrative paintings, of which only the first two are notable. The first, done between 1490 and 1495, was the cycle of nine large paintings, *Legend of Saint Ursula* (Academy of Fine Arts, Venice), considered his finest work. Especially important is the painting *Dream of St. Ursula.* The second cycle, painted 1502–07, consists of nine scenes that are mainly from the lives of St. George and St. Jerome (Scuola San Giorgio degli Schiavoni, Venice). The two best-known paintings of this cycle are *St. George Slaying the Dragon* and *St. Jerome in His Study.* Among Carpaccio's other paintings are *A Saint Reading* and *Virgin and Child* (both in the National Gallery of

Art, Washington, D.C.). Carpaccio was one of the most able and attractive painters of the early Renaissance in Venice. His pageant paintings illustrate in an incomparable manner the Venetian life of his day. Carpaccio's drawing is sometimes faulty; his use of color, however, is clear and harmonious, and he handles light and atmosphere with masterly effect.

CARPATHIAN MOUNTAINS, major mountain system of central and E Europe, extending about 1450 km (about 900 mi) in a great semicircle from Bratislava, Czechoslovakia, to the Iron Gate near Orşova, Romania. Both ends of the arc rest upon the Danube R. The Carpathians, varying between 32 and 257 km (20 and 160 mi) in width, are divided into smaller ranges, including the Little Carpathians, the White Carpathians, the High Tatra Range, the East Carpathians, and the Transylvanian Alps. The system, although extensive, is not high; the highest point, Gerlachovka Peak in Czechoslovakia, is 2654 m (8707 ft) above sea level. The system is broken by numerous passes that were used frequently by invading armies. Several major rivers, including the Dnestr and the Vistula, are formed in the Carpathians. Rich deposits of gold, silver, lead, iron ore, mercury, copper, petroleum, coal, and salt are found. Forests of oak, beech, fir, and pine cover the slopes from about 460 to 1830 m (about 1500 to 6000 ft), and bears, lynx, and wolves still inhabit remote forest areas.

CARPEAUX, Jean Baptiste (1836–1875), French sculptor, who was a leading exponent of romanticism. Inspired by the Renaissance Italians Michelangelo and Donatello, as well as by 18th-century rococo sculpture, he produced works outstanding for their animation and lifelike grace. His masterpiece, *La Danse* (1867–69, Paris Opéra), expresses joyful abandon with its gracefully intertwined figures, flowing draperies, and intense facial expressions.

CARPENTARIA, GULF OF, arm of the Arafura Sea, N Australia. The gulf is more than 644 km (more than 400 mi) wide and nearly 805 km (500 mi) long. It contains many islands, and the shores are generally low with extensive indentations on the W coast.

CARPENTER, John Alden (1876–1951), American composer, born in Park Ridge, Ill., and educated at Harvard University. He later studied with the British composer Sir Edward Elgar. Carpenter is best known for his ballet *Skyscrapers* (1926) and for his Concertino for Piano and Orchestra (1916).

CARPENTRY. *See* WOODWORKING.

CARPETBAGGERS, term of contempt applied by the people of the Southern states mainly to Northerners who came to the South during the Reconstruction period following the American Civil War. They were called carpetbaggers because they often carried their belongings in satchels made of carpet. Some were representatives of the Freedmen's Bureau and other Reconstruction agencies; some were humanitarians intent on aiding the blacks; and some were adventurers who hoped to benefit themselves by questionable means. Those carpetbaggers who were unscrupulous came to control the black vote and in some instances to establish dishonest governments. The carpetbaggers did serve to broaden black voting activity, to improve education, and to aid in the restoration of Southern cities and roads. The carpetbaggers generally cooperated with their Southern counterparts, called scalawags, and both groups were bitterly resented by most white Southerners. Secret terrorist societies such as the Ku Klux Klan were formed to terrorize the blacks and drive the carpetbaggers out. Today the term *carpetbagger* refers to roving opportunists or politicians.

CARPET BEETLE, common name for a beetle, *Anthrenus scrophulariae,* of the family Dermestidae, the larvae of which feed on carpets and various other materials of animal origin. The adult beetle, also called the buffalo carpet beetle, is oval in form, with black, red, and white markings on the back and white scales on the underside. The spindle-shaped larva has tufts of

Caricature of carpetbagger, 1872, by Thomas Nast.
Granger Collection

stiff bristles along the sides and at the ends of the body. The beetle eggs are deposited in cracks in the floor under the carpet; the developing larvae then feed on the carpet, often following the cracks and cutting long slits. A related species of the same family is *Attagenus piceus,* a black beetle, the larvae of which are more cylindrical and not so destructive.

CARPETING. *See* FLOORS AND FLOOR COVERINGS; RUGS AND CARPETS (in art).

CARPINI, Giovanni de Piano (c. 1180–1252), Italian Franciscan friar, historian, and the first European to record a visit to China, born near Perugia, Italy. One of the original followers of St. Francis of Assisi, he served for several years in minor clerical offices in Germany and Spain. In 1245 he was summoned by Pope Innocent IV to establish an embassy among the Mongols, who had invaded Europe several years before. The pope hoped to dissuade the Mongols from further attack by a personal appeal and to secure information about them. Carpini led the mission from Lyon, France, to Kiev (now in the USSR), then the outpost of Christianity, and to the Mongol imperial capital, Karakorum, Mongolia. There the legates witnessed the enthronement of Kuyuk (r. 1246–48). Several months later, the legation began the arduous journey back to Lyon. The mission failed to halt the Mongol invasions but is memorable for the account set down by Carpini, *Liber Tatarorum* (The Book of Tatars), which describes the customs, geography, history, and leading personages of the Mongols and the country between Kiev and Mongolia.

CARR, Emily (1871–1945), Canadian artist, who painted the Indian villages and forests of British Columbia. Influenced by impressionism, Fauvism, and cubism, she portrayed nature in a powerful style of her own. Paintings such as *Rushing Sea of Undergrowth* (1936) are characterized by intense colors and swirling forms based on the spiral. Carr wrote *Klee Wyck* (1941) and other books of sketches about Indian life.

CARRÀ, Carlo (1881–1966), Italian artist, who was a leader of both futurist and metaphysical painting. At first he tried to infuse the geometric structure and neutral palette of cubism with a futurist sense of movement. In the army he met Giorgio de Chirico, founder of *pittura metafisica* ("metaphysical painting") and adopted this new concept. In such works as *The Enchanted Room* (1917), he created an atmosphere of mystery and apprehension through exaggerated Renaissance perspective and ominous light. Later works were influenced by Giotto and Paul Cézanne.

CARRACCI, Annibale (1560–1609), Italian early baroque artist, whose reform of Mannerist ex-

Madonna with St. Luke and St. Catherine *(1592, Louvre, Paris), oil painting by Annibale Carracci.* Alinari

cesses (*see* MANNERISM) foreshadowed the emergence of high baroque art in Europe.

Annibale, born in Bologna on Nov. 3, 1560, was the most important member of an influential family of painters that included his elder brother Agostino (1557–1602) and their cousin Lodovico (1555–1619). They established (1585) the Accademia degli Incamminati, a painting school with the avowed purpose of reforming the art by retrieving the classical principles of the High Renaissance masters, as exemplified in the work of Michelangelo, Raphael, and Correggio. The academy attracted such promising young painters as Alessandro Algardi, Domenichino, and Guido Reni and made Bologna one of the most active and influential Italian art centers for over two decades. Annibale, with the design and execution of such noble fresco series as the lyrical *Romulus* cycle (1588–92), in Bologna's Palazzo Magnani, soon was recognized as the most gifted of the Carracci. Among his oil paintings of this period are *The Butcher's Shop* (c. 1583, Christ Church, Oxford, England) and *The Assumption*

(1587, Gemäldegalerie, Dresden).

Annibale was summoned to Rome in 1595 to decorate the state apartments of the Palazzo Farnese, the city's most splendid new private palace. He began his masterpiece, the magnificent illusionistic ceiling frescoes in the main reception room, the Galleria, in 1597. Against a painted architectural background representing stucco heroic nudes, bronze plaques, and carved marble decorations are set what appear to be 11 huge easel paintings in ornate frames, depicting in idealized human form scenes of the loves of the pagan gods, derived from the Roman poet Ovid's fables. Finished by 1604, the frescoes astounded Rome's artistic world. They were extravagantly praised by such baroque artists as the Italian master Gian Lorenzo Bernini and the Flemish painter Peter Paul Rubens; both freely acknowledged the powerful influence of the Galleria frescoes on the development of their own art.

Despite the urging of his devoted assistants, including his chosen artistic successor Domenichino, Annibale undertook few commissions after this monumental work. Outstanding are his serene landscape settings for Christ's Passion (Galleria Doria-Pamphili, Rome), which directly presage the neoclassical landscapes of the French painters Claude Lorrain and Nicolas Poussin. He contracted a form of paralysis in 1605, and died in Rome July 15, 1609.

CARRAGEENIN. *See* RED ALGAE.

CARRANZA, Venustiano (1859–1920), Mexican president (1914–20), who represented the conservative faction in the Mexican Revolution of the early 20th century. He was born in Cuatro Ciénagas, Coahuila, and educated in Mexico City. A supporter of Francisco I. Madero, whom he joined in 1911, he was named governor of his home state later that year, and after Madero's murder in 1913, he led the Constitutionalist forces that in 1914 overthrew Gen. Victoriano Huerta, Madero's assassin. He was then installed as provisional head of the new government. Two contenders for the presidency, Emiliano Zapata and Francisco (Pancho) Villa, mounted a mass movement against Carranza, and he was driven from Mexico City. In 1915, however, he won popular support by projecting far-reaching programs of social and agrarian reform. Two years later he was elected president of Mexico, following the adoption of a new constitution that mandated the projected reforms.

Carranza's regime was marked by a series of conflicts with foreign investors over its attempts to restrict foreign ownership of agricultural and other property and to establish national ownership of oil and mineral deposits. Carranza, however, did not fulfill his promises for reform, and Gen. Álvaro Obregón, a former ally, led a popular revolt. Carranza fled to the state of Puebla, where he was captured and killed.

CARREL, Alexis (1873–1944), French surgeon and Nobel laureate, known for his research on keeping animal organs alive outside the body. Born in Lyon and educated at the University of Lyon, Carrel came to the U.S. in 1905 and, except for service in the French army during World War I, remained in the U.S. until 1939. He worked at the Rockefeller Institute for Medical Research (now Rockefeller University) in New York City. He was awarded the 1912 Nobel Prize in physiology or medicine for his development in 1902 of a technique for suturing blood vessels. In the early 1930s, he and the American aviator Charles Lindbergh invented a mechanical heart capable of passing vital fluids through excised organs. Various animal tissues and organs were kept alive for many years in this fashion. After his return to France in 1939, Carrel worked during World War II for the pro-German French government at Vichy. He wrote *Man the Unknown* (1935), expounding his elitist philosophy, and collaborated with Lindbergh on *The Culture of Organs* (1938).

CARRERA, (José) Rafael (1814–65), Guatemalan revolutionist and dictator, born in Guatemala City. In 1837 he participated in the armed struggle against the regime of Francisco Morazán, president of the Central American Federation, which included present-day Guatemala, Honduras, El Salvador, Nicaragua, and Costa Rica. As leader of the insurgent forces, which included many Indians, he helped to destroy the union in 1839; in 1847 he proclaimed Guatemala a sovereign republic. From 1840 on, he was the virtual dictator of the nation, ruling with the support of conservative and clerical political groups until his death. During this period, he served as president on two occasions, from 1844 to 1848 and from 1851 until his death. He was involved in two wars (1850–53, 1863) with El Salvador; in the second, he deposed the president of that country and installed a regime sympathetic to his own policies.

CARRERA ANDRADE, Jorge (1903–), Ecuadorian poet and diplomat. He was born in Quito and is considered the greatest Ecuadorian writer and one of the foremost Spanish-language poets of the 20th century. He held diplomatic posts in Europe, South America, and Japan and served as Ecuadorian minister of foreign affairs. His travels had a marked influence on his poetry, which abounds in place-names and descriptions. Although some of his poems reflect his identification with social revolution, most of his poetry consists of metaphorical descriptions of places and objects and is noted for its sensitive, original imagery. Among Carrera's works are *Secret Country* (1922; trans. 1946), *Rol de la manzana* (Catalogue of the Apple, 1935), *La hora de las ventanas iluminadas* (Hour of the Lighted Windows, 1937); and *Edades poéticas* (Poetic Eras, 1958). A volume of *Selected Poems,* in English translation, appeared in 1972.

CARRIAGE, wheeled vehicle, specifically, a vehicle for carrying persons, designed to be drawn by one or more draft animals. Dating from earliest history, it is a development of the sledge, a platform on runners frequently depicted on ancient Egyptian monuments. The first wheels, solid disks cut from tree trunks, doubtless evolved from rollers that were placed under sledges to lessen friction (*see* WHEEL). By 1500 BC, horse-drawn, two-wheeled chariots for hunting and military purposes were being used by the Egyptians. The Assyrians, Greeks, and Romans also used this kind of chariot. The chariot of antiquity was the prototype of the cart.

The primitive form of the chariot (q.v.) was changed as it was adopted by different nations. Its wheels were enlarged, it was made to hold many persons, and finally four wheels were used. Little remained of the original chariot but the name. According to the Greek historian Herodotus, the Scythians used a four-wheeled vehicle, consisting of a platform on which a covering of basketwork and hides was placed.

During the Middle Ages carriages fell into disuse, mainly because of the ruinous condition of the old Roman roads. Travelers moved from place to place chiefly on horseback, on mule, or carried on litters. Goods were conveyed in huge panniers hung on the sides of strong draft animals. The use of carriages was revived gradually, however, at first by the nobility and later by wealthy burghers. One of the earliest vehicles to appear in medieval times was the whirlicote, a form of horse-drawn litter on wheels. Also developed in the Middle Ages was the carretta, a highly ornamented two-wheeled cart. The most important development of carriage making occurred possibly before the 16th century, when the first coach (q.v.) was made, probably in Hungary. Later, leather springs and small front wheels were introduced, a modification that made turns in a narrow space possible.

Carriages were not generally in use in England until long after they had become popular on the Continent. Although stagecoaches were first built during the reign of Queen Elizabeth I of England, and other changes in the art of carriage making occurred during the 17th and 18th centuries, the most significant developments in the field did not begin, in the British Isles, until the early part of the 19th century. Then, as a result of the work of the British engineer John Loudon McAdam and others, the highways of Great Britain were put into a condition that made vehicular travel pleasant. In 1804 a device was patented

Eighteenth-century carriage.

in Great Britain by which vehicles were hung upon elliptic springs, thus eliminating the heavy perch, or longitudinal wood or iron pole, that had always been used to connect the front and back wheels of four-wheeled carriages. With this invention modern methods of carriage construction began. The best known of the many types of carriages developed in the course of the 19th century include the phaeton, the brougham, the barouche, the chaise, the omnibus, and the hansom cab.

In the U.S. the manufacture of carriages and wagons was an important industry throughout the 18th and 19th centuries. Among the many types of horse-drawn vehicles produced during this period were the backboard, the surrey, and the Conestoga wagon (q.v.), the forerunner of the famed prairie schooner (q.v.). The buggy, mass produced between 1865 and 1910 in the U.S., became very important as a family conveyance before the introduction of the bicycle and the horseless carriage, or automobile, in the 1890s.

CARRIER WAVE, radio waves that can be used to carry modulated signals. Radiobroadcast signals are impressed on the carrier by frequency modulation (FM) or amplitude modulation (AM).

The carrier wave is usually kept at a fixed frequency by the transmitter and is detected in the receiver by a resonant circuit at the carrier frequency. A message is sent by changing the carrier wave's amplitude or its phase proportional to the desired transmission signal. If the amplitude is changed, amplitude modulation results, and a change of phase results in phase modulation, a form of frequency modulation.

CARRION FLOWER, common name for any plant of the genus *Stapelia,* of the family Asclepiadaceae (*see* MILKWEED). *Stapelia* are cactuslike desert herbs with flowers that have a putrid odor. The term is also used for *Smilax herbacea* of the lily family (Liliaceae), a greenbrier climbing vine with flowers that smell like carrion.

CARROLL, Charles, called Charles Carroll of Carrollton (1737–1832), American patriot, born in Annapolis, Md., and educated in Paris and London. Upon his return to America in 1764, his father presented him with the large estate known subsequently as Carrollton Manor. In 1775 he was elected to the Continental Congress, and in the following year he signed the Declaration of Independence. He was also a member of the commission, appointed by the Continental Congress, that visited Canada in 1776 in a vain effort to induce the Canadians to join the war against Great Britain. He resigned from the Continental Congress in 1778 to serve in the Maryland state Senate. He was one of the first U.S. senators from Maryland, serving from 1789 to 1792. Carroll was the last survivor of the 56 signers of the Declaration of Independence.

CARROLL, John (1735–1815), American Roman Catholic prelate, born in Upper Marlboro, Md., and educated at Saint-Omer's College and at Liège, Belgium. In 1771 he joined the Society of Jesus, or Jesuits, and taught at the College of Bruges, maintained by the order. He returned to America in 1774, following the suppression of the Jesuits by Pope Clement XIV. In 1776 he joined Benjamin Franklin, his cousin Charles Carroll, and Samuel Chase in a delegation to Montréal, unsuccessfully attempting to bring Canada into the American Revolution on the side of the colonists. In 1784 he was confirmed as head of the Roman Catholic missions in the U.S. by Pope Pius VI. In 1790 Carroll was consecrated bishop, the first American to hold that position. He founded Georgetown Academy (now Georgetown University) in 1789 and established several other colleges and seminaries. In 1808, when the diocese of Baltimore became an archdiocese, he was made archbishop.

CARROLL, Lewis, pseudonym of Charles Lutwidge Dodgson (1832–98), English author, mathematician, and logician, best known for his creation of the immortal fantasy *Alice in Wonderland.*

Carroll was born in Daresbury, Cheshire, on Jan. 27, 1832, and was educated at Rugby and at Christ Church College, University of Oxford.

An illustration by Sir John Tenniel for Lewis Carroll's Alice's Adventures in Wonderland. Bettmann Archive

From 1855 to 1881 he was a member of the faculty of mathematics at Oxford. He was the author of several mathematical treatises, including *Euclid and His Modern Rivals* (1879). In 1865 he published under his pseudonym *Alice's Adventures in Wonderland.* Its sequel, *Through the Looking-Glass and What Alice Found There,* appeared in 1872. These were followed by *Phantasmagoria and Other Poems* (1869), *The Hunting of the Snark* (1876), and a novel, *Sylvie and Bruno* (2 vol., 1889–93). He died at Guildford, Surrey, on Jan. 14, 1898.

Always a friend of children, particularly little girls, Carroll wrote thousands of letters to them, delightful flights of fantasy, many illustrated with little sketches. They have been collected and published as *The Letters of Lewis Carroll* (2 vol., 1979) by Morton N. Cohen (1921–) and Roger L. Green (1918–). Carroll gained an additional measure of fame as an amateur photographer. Most of his camera portraits were of children in various costumes and poses, including nude studies; he also did portraits of adults, including the actress Ellen Terry and the poets Alfred Lord Tennyson and Dante Gabriel Rossetti. Apparently because his posing of children was criticized, he abandoned photography in 1880.

The *Alice* stories, which have made the name Lewis Carroll famous throughout the world, and have been translated into many languages, were originally written in 1862 for Alice Liddell (d. 1934), a daughter of Henry George Liddell (1811–98), dean of Christ Church College. On publication, the works, illustrated by the English cartoonist Sir John Tenniel, became immediately popular as books for children. Their subsequent appeal to adults is based upon the ingenious mixture of fantasy and realism, gentle satire, absurdity, and logic. The names and sayings of the characters, such as the March Hare, the Mad Hatter, the Cheshire Cat, and the White Knight, have become part of everyday speech.

CARROLLTON, city, Collin, Dallas, and Denton counties, N Texas, on the Elm Fork of the Trinity R., a residential and commercial suburb of Dallas; inc. 1913. The community, settled in 1846, is named either for Carrollton, Ill., or for John and George Carroll, pioneers from Carrollton, Md. Pop. (1970) 13,855; (1980) 40,591.

CARROT, plant, *Daucus carota,* of the family Umbelliferae (*see* PARSLEY), native to Eurasia and northern Africa and widely distributed throughout the North Temperate Zone; the name is also applied to the root of this plant. The wild variety, popularly known as Queen Anne's lace, has a tough, woody root, unsuitable for food. The cultivated variety (var. *sativa*) is the popular table vegetable. It is a biennial. During the first season of its growth it forms a rosette of finely divided leaves and stores a surplus of food in its root, which thus becomes large and fleshy. First-season carrots are harvested for food. If left in the ground for a second season, a terminal bud in the center lengthens, at the expense of the food stored in the root, into a bristly branched stem 91 to 152 cm (36 to 60 in) high; this stem bears a nestlike umbel of white or pinkish flowers, the central flower of each umbelet often being purple. The fruit consists of two one-seeded nutlets, each of which has four rows of radiating spines, which cause the ripe seeds to cling to animals and thus to be dispersed to new locations.

Popular varieties among cultivated carrots are the Oxheart, the Chantenay, the Danvers Half-Long, and the Danvers Long. Large-rooted late types are used for stock feeding and are relished by farm animals. Carotene is the orange coloring matter of the root, a prolific source of provitamin A. In the U.S., California and Texas are the foremost carrot-producing states.

CARSON, city, Los Angeles Co., SW California, a commercial center near Los Angeles; inc. 1868. Refined petroleum, rubber products, toys, paper and metal containers, plywood, chemicals, photographic supplies, and steel are manufactured. California State University at Dominguez Hills (1960) is here. A land grant for the Carson area was issued to Juan José Dominguez (1736–1809) in 1782, and the community is named for George H. Carson (1829–1901), who married one of Dominguez's descendants. Oil was discovered here in 1923. Pop. (1970) 71,150; (1980) 81,221.

CARSON, river, rising on the E slope of the Sierra Nevada in E California, and flowing generally NE for 274 km (170 mi) into Nevada. Its several distributaries empty into the arid Carson Sink, a saline basin, and, to the S, into Carson Lake, which is periodically dry. Before the construction (1915) of the Lahontan Dam on the lower course, high waters in late spring would flood the Carson Sink, forming marshlands.

CARSON, Kit, real name CHRISTOPHER CARSON (1809–68), American hunter, trapper, and scout, born in Madison Co., Ky. When he was an infant his parents moved to Howard Co., Mo., where he later became an apprentice to a saddler. He ran away from home in 1826 to accompany a party of hunters to Santa Fe, N.Mex., and thereafter devoted himself almost entirely to hunting and trapping and making trips to California in 1829 and to the Rocky Mountains in 1830. From 1832 to 1840 he was employed as hunter for the garrison at Bent's Fort, Colo. Between 1842 and 1846 he accompanied the American explorer

Kit Carson Brown Brothers

John Charles Frémont on expeditions, serving as a guide in Frémont's expedition to California. Carson served in the Mexican War in 1846 and 1847, playing an important part in the conquest of California. In 1854 he was appointed Indian agent for the Ute and Apache at Taos, N.Mex. During the American Civil War he helped organize New Mexican infantry volunteers, and in 1865 he was brevetted brigadier general. The Kit Carson legend developed in the 1860s and '70s when Carson was popularized in dime novels.

CARSON, Rachel Louise (1907-64), American marine biologist and the author of widely read books on ecological themes. Born in Springdale, Pa., and educated at the former Pennsylvania College for Women and Johns Hopkins University, she taught zoology at the University of Maryland from 1931 to 1936. She was aquatic biologist at the U.S. Bureau of Fisheries and its successor, the Fish and Wildlife Service, from 1936 to 1952. Her books on the sea, *Under the Sea Wind* (1941), *The Sea Around Us* (1951), for which she was awarded the 1952 National Book Award in nonfiction, and *The Edge of the Sea* (1955), are praised for beauty of language as well as scientific accuracy. In *Silent Spring* (1962), she questioned the use of chemical pesticides and was responsible for arousing worldwide concern for the preservation of the environment.

CARSON CITY, city, capital of Nevada, in Eagle Valley, in the W part of the state, near Reno and Lake Tahoe; inc. 1875. The major economic factor is tourism, with visitors attracted by gaming casinos and the numerous Old West ghost towns and abandoned gold and silver mines of the region. Many persons also are employed by the state government. Points of interest in Carson City include the State Capitol (1870s); the Governor's Mansion; the Nevada State Museum (housed in the old U.S. branch mint building), featuring a full-scale model of a mine and displays on Nevada history; and homes from the 19th century.

Settled as a trading post in 1851 on land inhabited by Washo and Paiute Indians, the community was platted in 1858 and named for the frontiersman Kit Carson. In 1861 Carson City became the capital of Nevada Territory, and it was retained as the seat of government when Nevada entered the Union as a state in 1864. The growth of Carson City was stimulated by the discovery (1850s) and subsequent working of the great silver deposits in the nearby Comstock Lode, and until significant mining operations in the area were ended about 1950 the city served as a transportation and processing center for silver ore. A U.S. branch mint here struck the famous Carson City silver dollar before being closed in 1893. In 1969 Carson City and surrounding Ormsby Co. were consolidated into a single municipal unit. Pop. (1970) 15,468; (1980) 32,022.

CARTAGENA, city and seaport, N Colombia, capital of Bolívar Department, on the Caribbean Sea. The city is on an island formed by a shallow extension of the harbor, one of the best in N South America. Cartagena is connected by a causeway with the mainland. The older part of the city contains two old forts and is surrounded by a wall 12 m (40 ft) thick in places, constructed in Spanish colonial times. Among the notable buildings of the city are the cathedral, the Jesuit church of San Juan de Dios, and the palace that was the headquarters of the Spanish Inquisition in South America. The site of the University of Cartagena (1827), Cartagena also is the terminus of an oil pipeline extending about 600 km (about 375 mi) into the interior of Colombia. The principal exports are oil and petroleum products and coffee. Other exports include tobacco, cattle and cattle products, fine woods, and precious stones. Chocolate and candles are among the products manufactured here.

Founded in 1533 by the Spanish, the city rapidly became a thriving commercial port, later referred to as the Queen of the Indies. Pirates sacked the city in 1544. In the first half of the early 17th century the city was second to Mexico City in commercial importance in the New World. Nationalist revolutionists, led by Simón Bolívar, in 1815 took the city from the Spanish, lost it the same year, and recaptured it in 1821. Pop. (1982 est.) 470,000.

CARTAGENA (anc. *Carthago Nova*), city and seaport, S Spain, in Murcia Province, on the Mediterranean Sea, near the city of Murcia. Lead, iron, copper, zinc, and sulfur are mined in the surrounding region. The principal exports of Cartagena are metallic ores, hydraulically compressed esparto grass, olive oil, wine, and fried fruits; imports include machinery, coal, coke, lumber, and codfish. Smelters are the principal industrial establishments in the city. Others include glass works and factories for the manufacture of esparto-grass fabrics. Cartagena is encircled by mountains and is a principal naval base of Spain. Its fortifications include forts and other military and naval installations. The city contains the remains of old walls, a castle probably constructed in Carthaginian times, and a church that was formerly a 13th-century cathedral. Cartagena is on a site selected, about 243 BC, by the Carthaginian general Hasdrubal. When captured by the Roman general Publius Cornelius Scipio Africanus in 209 BC, the city was a flourishing port exporting gold and silver mined in the surrounding region. Sacked by the Goths in AD 425, Cartagena was restored and improved by the Moors during their occupation of Spain. A possession of the kings of Aragón from 1269, it was later included in the kingdom of Spain. It served as a naval base for the Republicans in the Spanish civil war (1936–39). Pop. (1985 prelim.) 530,000.

CARTAGO, city, central Costa Rica, capital of Cartago Province, near San José. It is on the plateau of San José, about 1500 m (about 4930 ft) above sea level, at the base of Irazú, a volcano 3432 m (11,260 ft) above sea level. Hot mineral springs are in the suburb of Bella Vista. Cartago is a center for trade in coffee produced in the volcanic soil of the surrounding region. Founded in 1563 by the Spanish conquistador Juan Vásquez de Coronado (1525?–65), the town subsequently became an important commercial center with an estimated population of more than 35,000. Until 1823 Cartago was the seat of government in Costa Rica. The town was several times severely damaged by earthquakes, the most destructive being that of 1841. Pop. (1979 est.) 25,300.

CARTE, Richard D'Oyly. *See* D'OYLY CARTE, RICHARD.

CARTEL, formal or informal agreement among business firms designed to reduce or suppress competition in a particular market. Cartels control production and distribution. The main activities in which they engage are fixing prices, limiting available supplies, dividing the market, and pooling profits. Today the term *cartel* is usually applied to arrangements that regulate competition in international commerce. Similar national collaborations are known as trusts.

History. Cartels originated in Germany during the 1870s, coinciding with the growth of that

A view of the marketplace in Cartagena, Colombia, with a portion of the city's skyline in the background.
Luis Villota

country's economy. Their successful operation is thought to be partially responsible for German aggression, which led to two world wars. During World War I the government of Germany utilized domestic cartels to produce armaments and other war materials. In the next two decades German firms continued to combine to control production. One of the most important was I. G. Farbenindustrie, which produced chemicals and dyestuffs. By the start of World War II almost all German industry was controlled by cartels, supervised and encouraged by the government.

Basic economic beliefs in the U.S. have long been opposed to group monopolies. In general, domestic cartels are considered in restraint of trade and are illegal, and participation of firms in international cartels is not sanctioned.

Support and Opposition. Defenders have claimed that cartels stabilize markets, reduce costs of production, eliminate high tariffs, distribute profits equitably, and benefit the consumer. Those who object to cartels point out that prices are higher and output is lower when firms do not engage in competition. Today their disadvantages are considered to outweigh their advantages; legal barriers often restrict development of new cartels. Some do exist, however, notably in the oil industry and the diamond trade.

See BUSINESS; MONOPOLY.

CARTER, Elliott Cook, Jr. (1908-), American composer, who expanded the twelve-tone method of composition to include serialization not only of pitch but also of rhythm, harmony, and timbre (tone color). Born in New York City, he studied with the American composer Walter Piston, the British composer Gustav Holst, and the influential French teacher Nadia Boulanger. Carter taught music at Columbia and Yale universities. In his first and second string quartets (1951, 1959) he used progressions of rhythms in a system he called "metric modulation." The Russian-born composer Igor Stravinsky called Carter's Double Concerto for Harpsichord and Piano (1961) the first true American masterpiece. His later works include Brass Quintet (1974) and *A Mirror on Which to Dwell* (1978), a song cycle based on the work of the American poet Elizabeth Bishop.

CARTER, Howard (1873-1939), British archaeologist and Egyptologist, born in London. From 1891 to 1899 he served in Egypt on the staff of the Archaeological Survey of Egypt. In 1892 he assisted the British Egyptologist Sir Flinders Petrie in the excavation at Tell el-Amarna, Egypt. Carter also served as inspector in chief of the antiquities department of the Egyptian government. Among the discoveries he made in Egypt were the tombs of the pharaoh Thutmose IV and Queen Hatshepsut. In 1922 Carter and the British Egyptologist George Herbert, 5th earl of Carnarvon, made one of the greatest archaeological finds of the 20th century. In the Valley of the Tombs of the Kings in Luxor, Egypt, they discovered the tomb of Tutankhamen, a pharaoh who reigned in the 14th century BC. The tomb, which was untouched, held a great collection of treasures, which are now on display in the Egyptian Museum in Cairo. The treasures of Tutankhamen were exhibited during 1972 at the British Museum in London; from 1976 to 1979 a similar exhibition was shown at six museums in the U.S.

Howard Carter precedes an assistant carrying a statue found in 1922 in the tomb of the pharaoh Tutankhamen, said to be a likeness of his young queen, Ankhes-en-Amen. UPI

CARTER, Jimmy, full name JAMES EARL CARTER, JR. (1924-), 39th president of the U.S. (1977-81), the first from the Deep South since Andrew Jackson, and an outsider to traditional party politics.

Carter was born in Plains, Ga., on Oct. 1, 1924. In 1927 his family moved to the tiny settlement of Archery, just outside Plains, where he lived until he was 17 years old. He graduated from high school in 1941, then spent a year at Georgia Southwestern College and another at Georgia Institute of Technology.

Early Career. Carter began a military career in June 1943 by enrolling in the U.S. Naval Academy. By 1946 he was serving as a commissioned officer, and in that same year he married Rosalynn Smith (1927-). In 1948 he entered submarine school, subsequently serving as the junior officer on four submarines. He was accepted into the navy's prototype nuclear submarine training program in 1952 and remained there for 11 months. On his father's death he left the navy to take over the family's peanut business in Plains.

From 1953 to 1962 Carter was a prominent businessman and active citizen, known as a liberal on racial matters. In 1962 he was elected to the state senate and was reelected in 1964. He campaigned unsuccessfully for the Georgia governorship in 1966, and at this time he had a religious experience, becoming a "born-again" Christian. He won the governorship in 1970 and headed a politically moderate administration, representative of the New South.

Before his gubernatorial term ended, Carter had decided to run for the presidency. After intense primary battles, he surmounted the liabilities of being unknown, from the Deep South, and having no national constituency, gaining (1976) the Democratic party's nomination on the first ballot. Carter and his vice-presidential running mate, Senator Walter F. Mondale, defeated President Gerald R. Ford and Senator Robert Dole (1923-) with an electoral vote of 297 to 241. Carter received 40,800,000 popular votes to Ford's 39,100,000.

Presidency. One of Carter's most difficult challenges was to combat rising inflation; another, to institute an energy program that would decrease U.S. dependence on foreign oil. Inflation reached a high of 20 percent a year in 1980, but when the government raised interest rates in an attempt to bring it down, unemployment became a serious problem. The economy eventually became the thorniest issue of his reelection campaign. Carter did, however, secure passage of a comprehensive energy program that was supportive of private energy development.

In matters of defense, Carter advocated increased spending, favoring a cruise missile system. He endorsed a strong North Atlantic Treaty Organization but opposed its use of neutron bombs. He secured passage of a new Panama Canal treaty and concluded a Strategic Arms Limitation Talks (SALT II) Treaty.

President Jimmy Carter — The White House

Carter initiated a foreign policy based on respect for human rights. Critics charged that he applied the policy unevenly, leading to a deterioration in relations with the Soviet Union. He retaliated for Soviet intervention in Afghanistan by instigating an international boycott of the 1980 Olympic Games in Moscow.

Carter's greatest triumph came in 1978, when he provided the framework for an Egyptian-Israeli peace treaty that was signed in 1979. His greatest frustration was his inability, until the day he left office, to free the more than 50 U.S. hostages who had been taken by the revolutionary regime of Iran late in 1979.

Although Carter's popularity declined sharply during his term, he successfully campaigned for renomination in 1980, fighting off a strong challenge from Senator Edward M. Kennedy. In the election, however, Carter and Mondale were overwhelmingly defeated by Republicans Ronald Reagan and George Bush. In January 1981 Carter retired to his native Georgia. D.M.Ja.

For further information on this person, see the section Biographies in the Bibliography in volume 28.

CARTERET, Sir George (c. 1610-80), English naval officer and colonial proprietor, born on the island of Jersey, in the Channel Islands. He joined the navy as a boy and rose through the ranks, becoming comptroller of the English navy in 1639. During the English Revolution, he fought for the Royalists and was rewarded for his services by being made lieutenant governor of Jersey. In 1651 he was forced to surrender the island to the Commonwealth, and later joined other English exiles in the French navy. Returning to England after the restoration of King Charles II in 1660, Carteret held several important offices, including that of treasurer of the navy (1661-67), which he relinquished when discrepancies were found in his accounts. He took an active interest in the colonization of America. In 1663 he became one of the original proprietors of Carolina; in 1664 he and John, Lord Berkeley (d. 1678), were made lords proprietors and were granted the territory that is now the state of New Jersey. The name New Jersey was given to the colony in honor of Carteret's administration of the island of Jersey. In 1676 the colony was divided into West Jersey and East Jersey; Carteret became sole proprietor of East Jersey.

CARTERET, John, 1st Earl Granville (1690-1763), British statesman and diplomat, great-grandson of Sir George Carteret, born in Bath, England, and educated at the University of Oxford. He succeeded to the title of Baron Carteret in 1695 and took his seat in the House of Lords in 1711. Carteret was appointed ambassador to Sweden in 1719, secretary of state in 1721, and lord lieutenant of Ireland in 1724. From 1730 to 1742, he led the opposition in the House of Lords to the government of Sir Robert Walpole. When Walpole's government fell in 1742, Carteret again became secretary of state. In this office, which he held for two years, he was the most influential member of the cabinet. From 1751 to 1763, Carteret served as lord president of the Privy Council.

CARTERET, Philip (1639–82), English colonial governor in America, born on the island of Jersey in the Channel Islands. He was the first colonial governor of New Jersey, having been appointed in 1664 by the lords proprietors, one of whom was his fourth cousin, Sir George Carteret. Philip Carteret arrived at New Jersey in 1665 and founded Elizabethtown (now Elizabeth). He tried to attract emigrants from the New England colonies by publicizing among them the liberal concessions granted by the proprietors of New Jersey. Except in 1673 and 1674, when the western part of New Jersey was held by the Dutch, he was governor of the entire colony until it was divided into East Jersey and West Jersey in 1676. From 1676 until his death, he was governor of East Jersey. The early part of his administration was marked by conflicts with Sir Edmund Andros, governor of New York, who claimed that New Jersey belonged under his jurisdiction.

CARTESIANISM. *See* DESCARTES, RENÉ.

CARTHAGE (Lat. *Carthago*) great city of antiquity, on the northern coast of Africa, near modern Tunis, Tunisia. Dido was the legendary founder and queen of Carthage; the city was probably established as a trading post toward the end of the 9th century BC by Phoenicians. The earliest artifacts unearthed by archaeologists at the site date from 800 BC. The city was known to its Punic or Phoenician inhabitants as the "new city," probably to distinguish it from Utica, the "old city." Built on a peninsula jutting into the Gulf of Tunis, Carthage had two splendid harbors, connected by a canal. Above the harbors on a hill was the Byrsa, a walled fortress.

Extension of Empire. By the subjugation of the Libyan tribes and by the annexation of older Phoenician colonies, Carthage in the 6th century BC controlled the entire North African coast from the Atlantic Ocean to the western border of Egypt, as well as Sardinia, Malta, the Balearic Islands, and part of Sicily. A Carthaginian admiral, Hanno, made a voyage along the Atlantic coast of North Africa. The maritime power of the Carthaginians enabled them to extend their settlements and conquests, forming a scattered empire devoted to commerce. Among the commercial enterprises were the mining of silver and lead; the manufacture of beds and bedding; a lumber industry in the Atlas Mountains; the production of simple, cheap pottery, jewelry, and glassware for trade; and the export of wild animals from African jungles, of fruits and nuts, and of ivory and gold.

Carthage produced little art. Most of the work of the Carthaginians was imitative of Egyptian, Greek, and Phoenician originals. In literature only a few technical works appeared. Thus, little is known of the everyday life of Carthage, its government, or its language. Religion in Carthage involved human sacrifice to the principal gods, Baal and Tanit, the equivalent of the Phoenician goddess Astarte. The Greek gods Demeter and Persephone and the Roman goddess Juno were adapted to later religious patterns of the Carthaginians.

Carthage engaged in war almost continually with Greece and with Rome for 150 years. Wars with Greece, beginning in 409 BC, concerned the control of Sicily, which lay only about 160 km (about 100 mi) from Carthage and formed a natural bridge between North Africa and Italy. Carthage first encountered defeat in Sicily in 480 BC, when the Carthaginian general Hamilcar (fl. 5th cent. BC) commanded a force that hoped to expand Carthaginian influence throughout Sicily, but was defeated by Gelon, the tyrant (ruler) of Syracuse. Further Carthaginian attempts to conquer Sicily were thwarted by armies under the command of the Syracusan tyrants Dionysius the Younger, Dionysius the Elder, Agathocles, and Pyrrhus, king of Epirus. After their final defeat in 276 BC, the Carthaginians continued to hold territory in Sicily; 12 years later the first of the Punic Wars against Rome began.

Punic Wars. The First Punic War (264–241 BC) brought to the fore the Carthaginian general Hamilcar Barca. Defeated in Sicily, Hamilcar invaded Spain. His conquests in southern Spain were completed by his son-in-law Hasdrubal and by his son Hannibal. Carthage ceded its holdings in Sicily to Rome after the final Roman victory at the Aegates Islands. During the Second Punic War (218–201 BC), Hannibal marched eastward along the northern shore of the Mediterranean from Spain and finally crossed the Alps into Italy. Hannibal's final defeat, however, resulted in the loss of Spain and various island possessions of Carthage. In the Third Punic War (149–146 BC), the Romans under Publius Cornelius Scipio Aemelianus Africanus Numantinus destroyed the

Ruins of public baths from the Roman period, on the site of ancient Carthage. Trans World Airlines

city of Carthage. In a final gesture of contempt, the Romans spread salt over the ruins. The victors thus fulfilled the wish of the Roman statesman Cato the Elder.

Occupancy of the site was forbidden for 25 years. In 122 BC a new city, Colonia Junonia, was founded; it lasted only 30 years. In 46 BC Julius Caesar visited the site and proclaimed that a city should be built there. His wishes were fulfilled by the Roman emperor Augustus, in 29 BC, when a city called Colonia Julia Carthago was founded. This new city flourished until, according to some historians, it was second only to Rome in prosperity and administrative importance. Roman Carthage also became a center of Christianity, being the seat of a bishop from late in the 2d century. St. Cyprian was bishop there in 248; Tertullian, a Christian ecclesiastical writer, lived and worked in Carthage in the 3d century; and St. Augustine was bishop of nearby Hippo in the early 5th century.

Carthage was fortifed against barbarian attack in 425. In 439 the Vandal king Gaiseric subjugated the city. It remained the Vandal capital until 533, when the Byzantine general Belisarius captured the city, renaming it Colonia Justiniana Carthago in honor of the Byzantine emperor Justinian I. In 697 the city was seized by the Arabs, and in 698 it was again destroyed. A great deal of archaeological activity was carried on at the site, particularly in the late 19th century, uncovering early Punic artifacts and Roman, Byzantine, and Vandal buildings. Today Carthage is a wealthy suburb of Tunis.

For further information on this topic, see the Bibliography in volume 28, sections 886–87, 892.

CARTHUSIANS, monastic order founded by St. Bruno, who in 1084 retired with six companions to the solitude of the valley of Chartreuse, near Grenoble. There they lived as hermits, wearing rude clothing and eating vegetables and coarse bread. After 1170, when the order received papal approbation, it expanded rapidly. It dates from 1180 in England, where the name Chartreuse Houses was corrupted into Charter Houses. The order is now conducted under the rules approved in 1682 by Pope Innocent XI.

The Carthusians were divided into two classes, fathers (*patres*) and lay brothers (*conversi*). Each father occupied a separate cell, with a bed of straw, a pillow, a woolen coverlet, and the tools for manual labor or for writing. Monks left their cells only on festivals and on days of the funeral of a brother of the order. Three times a week they fasted on bread, water, and salt, and several long fasts were observed during the year. Meat was forbidden at all times, and so was wine, unless it was mixed with water. Unbroken silence was enforced except on rare occasions.

These austerities were continued, with little modification, by the modern Carthusians. The order at one time counted 16 provinces and boasted the most magnificent convents in the world, including La Grande Chartreuse, in France, now a museum consisting chiefly of 17th-century buildings, and the Certosa di Palva near Milan, in Italy. The church of the Certosa di Palva was begun in 1396 and expanded during the 15th and 16th centuries; it is a national monument.

The order of Carthusian nuns was founded at Salette, on the Rhône, in France, about 1229. They followed the rules of the Carthusian monks. When the monasteries in England were suppressed under King Henry VIII in the 16th century, nine Carthusian monasteries were active in the country. Today only one remains, at Steyning, near Brighton. One Carthusian monastery is located in the U.S., in Arlington, Vt.

CARTIER, Sir George Étienne (1814–73), Canadian statesman, born in Saint-Antoine, Lower Canada (now Québec Province). After practicing law for a short time, Cartier took part in the rebellion of 1837–38 and fled the country to avoid arrest, but, after public feeling began to subside, he returned and resumed his law practice. In 1848 he was elected to the Canadian legislative assembly and soon became a leader of the French-Canadians. He was secretary of Lower Canada from 1855 to 1857, when he became provincial attorney general. Between 1858 and 1862 he shared the office of prime minister with Sir John Alexander Macdonald. In this office, Cartier favored the plan to federate Lower Canada and Upper Canada (now Ontario Province) with the other British colonies in North America; the plan resulted in the establishment of the Dominion of Canada in 1867. Cartier joined Macdonald's first dominion cabinet as minister of militia and defense (1867–73). He was influential in getting approval from the Canadian parliament for the initial charter of the Canadian Pacific Railway.

Jacques Cartier

CARTIER, Jacques (1491–1557), French explorer and mariner, discoverer of the Saint Lawrence River, born in Saint-Malo. Selected by King Francis I of France to lead an expedition to discover the Northwest Passage to China, he departed from St.-Malo with two ships in April 1534. He sighted Newfoundland after 20 days, and sailing through Belle Isle Strait, between Newfoundland and Labrador, he proceeded southward along the western coast of Newfoundland and rounded the entire Gulf of Saint Lawrence. On this voyage he saw Prince Edward Island and the New Brunswick mainland, sailed into Chaleur Bay, which he named, landed on the Gaspé Peninsula, and crossed the St. Lawrence River estuary. Much of the French claim to Canada is based on Cartier's explorations.

Again sailing on orders from King Francis in 1535, Cartier crossed Belle Isle for the second time and then sailed up the St. Lawrence River, which he named on this occasion, as far as the Indian village of Stadacona, where modern Québec stands. He later proceeded up the river to the Indian village of Hochelaga and climbed the hill behind the village to observe the Ottawa River and Lachine Rapids. Cartier called the hill Mont Réal (Mount Royal), from which the name of the city of Montréal is derived. After spending the winter in Stadacona, Cartier sailed for France on a course south of Newfoundland, and for the first time passed through what is now called Cabot Strait.

Beginning his third voyage in 1541, Cartier again sailed up the St. Lawrence, this time as far as Lachine Rapids. His purpose was to establish a colony in Canada, but the mission was not successful. He returned to France the following year. He settled in St.-Malo and wrote an account of his expeditions that was published in 1545.

CARTIER-BRESSON, Henri (1908–), French photographer, born in Chanteloup, and educated at the Lycée Condorcet in Paris. Originally interested in painting, he took up photography in 1930. Since 1931 Cartier-Bresson has traveled widely, and the many photographs made on his

The photographic originality of Henri Cartier-Bresson is epitomized in this picture of Alberto Giacometti, taken in Paris in 1963. Museum of Modern Art trips have been published and frequently exhibited. He excels in composition without cropping his negatives, and he has a unique ability to capture a fleeting moment in time.

During World War II, Cartier-Bresson spent 35 months in German prison camps. After three attempts, he escaped and made his way to Paris, where he set up photography groups for the Underground. In 1945 he directed the documentary film *Le retour* (The Return) for the U.S. Office of War Information. Two years later he had a one-man exhibition of his photographs at the Museum of Modern Art in New York City. In 1955 he was invited to become the first photographer to exhibit at the Louvre in Paris. Among the published collections of his photographs are *The Decisive Moment* (1952), *The World of Henri Cartier-Bresson* (1968), and *Henri Cartier-Bresson* (1980).

CARTILAGE, or gristle, fibrous connective tissue found in humans and animals that have backbones. *See* BONE; CONNECTIVE TISSUE; SKELETON.

CARTOGRAPHY. *See* MAP.

CARTOON, in the fine arts, design drawn on paper or pasteboard as a model for a work to be executed in fresco, mosaic, tapestry, or other media. The cartoon (Ital. *cartone,* "pasteboard") allows the artist to make alterations in the design

The Virgin and Child with St. John the Baptist and St. Anne, *a cartoon, or preliminary drawing, by Leonardo da Vinci. The final version did not include the figure of John the Baptist.* UPI

The first American cartoon, published (1754) by Benjamin Franklin in his Pennsylvania Gazette. Granger Collection

before the projected work is begun. A cartoon is the same size as the projected work. The design is transferred to the plaster or other permanent surface in one of two ways: either by rubbing the back with charcoal and chalk and then tracing the design on the front with a hard point, or by pouncing charcoal dust through pinpricks along the design. In tapestry weaving, the color cartoon is placed under the warp threads for a low-warp loom; for a high-warp loom it is placed behind the weaver, who works from mirrors.

A cartoon may be a line drawing or a finished chiaroscuro study. The cartoons drawn by Raphael, Leonardo, Andrea Mantegna, and other great masters of the Renaissance as guides for almost all their works are often as interesting artistically as the completed frescoes and panels.

A pictorial sketch, usually humorous or satirical, published in a magazine or newspaper, is also called a cartoon.

See CARICATURE; COMICS.

For further information on this topic, see the Bibliography in volume 28, section 693.

CARTWRIGHT, Edmund (1743–1823), British inventor, born in Nottinghamshire, England, and educated at the University of Oxford. After spending several years as a country clergyman, he visited the cotton-spinning mills of the British inventor Sir Richard Arkwright in Derbyshire and became interested in new methods of weaving. The result was Cartwright's invention of a power loom (1785), upon which he subsequently made major improvements. The introduction of the power loom was vehemently opposed by those whose jobs were replaced, and a mill at Manchester equipped with his looms was burned down. Cartwright took out a patent for a wool-combing machine (1789) and secured patents for various other machines. In 1797 he patented a steam engine fueled by alcohol. He also assisted the American inventor Robert Fulton in his steamboat experiments. But Cartwright's patents yielded him little return, and in 1809 the British government, in consideration of his inventions, granted him £10,000. He retired to a farm in Kent and spent the rest of his life inventing improvements for farm machinery. Meanwhile the power loom became one of the machines that made the Industrial Revolution possible.

CARTWRIGHT, John (1740–1824), British politician and pamphleteer, born in Marnham, England. He entered the navy at the age of 18 and rose rapidly as an officer. At the outbreak of the American Revolution, however, he espoused the cause of the colonies and declined to fight against them. He devoted himself instead to political writing, urging such reforms as universal male suffrage, the secret ballot, annual parliaments, the improvement of national defenses, the freedom of Spain and Greece from foreign rule, and other causes. In 1820 he was indicted for sedition and fined £100. He became known as the Father of Reform.

CARUSO, Enrico (1873–1921), Italian dramatic tenor, born in Naples. He made his debut in Naples in 1894. His first great success was in Milan in 1898 when he created the role of Loris in *Fedora* by the Italian composer Umberto Giordano (1867–1948). Engagements followed in Saint Petersburg (now Leningrad), Monte Carlo, London, Rome, and Lisbon. In 1903 he made his debut at the Metropolitan Opera House in New York City in *Rigoletto* by the Italian composer Giuseppe Verdi. His repertoire included more than 40 operas (chiefly Italian). He created roles in *Adriana Lecouvreur* by the Italian composer Francesco Cilea (1886–1950) and *The Girl of the Golden West* by the Italian composer Giacomo Puccini. He is especially remembered for the role of Canio in *I Pagliacci* by the Italian composer Ruggero Leoncavallo. From his first appearance, Caruso became the chief attraction of the Metropolitan Opera House, his voice being one of extraordinary beauty and power. One of the first singers to make phonograph records, Caruso became universally famous by means of the new medium. Several of his recordings were successively reissued in new formats and remain available today. His position as the greatest living dramatic tenor was unchallenged to the end of his life. Caruso's last appearance was at the Metropolitan Opera House on Dec. 24, 1920.

CARVER, George Washington (1864–1943), American educator and an outstanding innovator in the agricultural sciences. Carver was born of slave parents near Diamond, Mo. He left the farm where he was born when he was about ten years old and eventually settled in Minneapolis, Kans., where he worked his way through high school.

Following his graduation in 1894 from Iowa State College of Agriculture and Mechanic Arts (now Iowa State University), Carver joined the college faculty and continued his studies, specializing in bacteriological laboratory work in

George Washington Carver in his laboratory. UPI

systematic botany. In 1896 he became director of the Department of Agricultural Research at Tuskegee Normal and Industrial Institute (now Tuskegee Institute), where he began an exhaustive series of experiments with peanuts. Carver developed several hundred industrial uses for peanuts, sweet potatoes, and soybeans and developed a new type of cotton known as Carver's hybrid. His discoveries induced southern farmers to raise other crops in addition to cotton. He also taught methods of soil improvement.

In recognition of his accomplishments, Carver was awarded the Spingarn Medal in 1923 by the National Association for the Advancement of Colored People. In 1935 he was appointed collaborator in the Division of Plant Mycology and Disease Survey of the Bureau of Plant Industry of the U.S. Department of Agriculture. In 1940 he donated all his savings to the establishment of the George Washington Carver Foundation at Tuskegee for research in natural science. Carver died at Tuskegee, on Jan. 5, 1943. His birthplace was established as the George Washington Carver National Monument in 1951.

For further information on this person, see the section Biographies in the Bibliography in volume 28.

CARVER, John (1576–1621), Pilgrim leader and the first governor of Plymouth Colony, born probably in Nottinghamshire, England. Carver was a wealthy London merchant, but he left England and went to Leiden, Netherlands, in 1607 or 1608 because of religious persecution. In 1617 he became the agent for the Pilgrims in securing a charter and financial support for the establishment of a colony in America. He chartered the *Mayflower* and, with 101 other colonists, set sail from Plymouth, England, in September 1620. He signed the Mayflower Compact on Nov. 11, 1620, and on the same day was elected to a one-year term as governor. He was probably instrumental in choosing Plymouth as the site for settlement and in making the treaty of alliance with Chief Massasoit of the Wampanoag tribe in 1621. Shortly after being reelected governor, he died of a stroke.

CARVING. *See* IVORY CARVING; JADE CARVING; SCULPTURE; WOOD CARVING.

CARY, (Arthur) Joyce Lunel (1888–1957), Anglo-Irish novelist and poet, born in Londonderry, Northern Ireland, and educated at the University of Oxford. He was a public administrator in Africa for two years. Ill health and injuries forced Cary to retire in 1920 to Oxford, where he began his writing career. *Aissa Saved* (1932) concerns the conversion of an African girl to Christianity. Cary is best known for a trilogy that includes

Joyce Cary Harper & Row Publishers, Inc.

Herself Surprised (1941), *To Be a Pilgrim* (1942), and *The Horse's Mouth* (1944), later made into a film. These three works were acclaimed for their well-developed plots and credible characterization of an artist. Literary critics have noted Cary's superb skill in producing high comic effect.

CARYATID. *See* GREEK ART AND ARCHITECTURE.

CASABIANCA, Louis de (1755?–98), French naval officer, born in Bastia, Corsica. He fought against the British in the American Revolution, serving under the French admiral Comte François de Grasse at the siege of Yorktown, Va. In 1792 he was a member of the National Convention in France. He commanded the *Orient,* flagship of the fleet that transported Napoleon Bonaparte and his army to Egypt in 1798. In the Battle of the Nile, the commander of the fleet, Vice Admiral François Brueys d'Aigalliers (1753–98), was killed, and Casabianca assumed command. Although he was seriously wounded and the *Orient* was in flames, he remained at his post. His son, ten years old, refused to leave him, and both were lost with the vessel. The story of their death is recounted in the poem *Casabianca* (1829) by the British poet Felicia Hemans (1739–1835).

CASABLANCA, largest city and chief seaport of W Morocco, on the Atlantic Ocean, near Rabat. Casablanca is one of the leading commercial cities of North Africa. It is served by railroads, highways, and an international airport and has one of the largest artificial harbors in the world; most of the foreign trade of Morocco passes through the city. Cereals, leather, wool, and phosphates are the chief exports. Casablanca also is the country's chief industrial center. The leading industries are fishing, fish canning, sawmilling, and the manufacture of furniture, construction materials, glass, and tobacco products. Hassan II University (1976) is here.

In medieval times Casablanca was a prosperous town known as Anfa. It was destroyed by the Portuguese in 1468 and rebuilt by them in 1515. Following a severe earthquake in 1755, the city was again rebuilt. In 1907 Casablanca was occupied by the French. Under French administration it grew rapidly, and the modern city was built around the old Moorish city.

During World War II, Casablanca was one of the three major landing places in the invasion of North Africa by Allied forces. The city was the site of the Casablanca Conference (January 1943) between U.S. President Franklin D. Roosevelt and British Prime Minister Winston Churchill, at which both leaders pledged that their countries would fight until the Axis powers surrendered unconditionally.

The withdrawal of the French in 1956, after Morocco became independent, caused Casablanca severe economic hardship. A thriving tourist trade and increased industry have restored prosperity to the city. Pop. (1982 prelim., greater city) 2,436,664.

CASA GRANDE NATIONAL MONUMENT, S central Arizona, established in 1918. The monument contains the prehistoric ruins of an Indian people, known today as the Hohokam, who came to the Gila Valley about AD 700 and built villages and an extensive irrigation system for farming. They were joined in the 14th century by the Pueblo Indians. The principal building, Casa Grande, was a watchtower and is the best-preserved structure of its age and type in the U.S. Its walls, of caliche blocks (a cement composed of lime, earth, and pebbles), still stand at their original height of four stories. In addition to Casa Grande are ruins of several Hohokam villages. The ruins were discovered by the Jesuit missionary Eusebio Kino in 1694, at which time they had been abandoned for more than two centuries. Area, 1.9 sq km (0.7 sq mi).

CASALS, Pablo (1876–1973), Spanish cellist, conductor, composer, pianist, and humanitarian, who was one of the most influential musicians of the 20th century.

Casals, who was originally named Pau Carlos Salvador Defillo de Casals, was born in Vendrell, on Dec. 29, 1876. He received his first musical instruction from his father; later he studied at the Madrid Conservatory. After making his debut as a cello soloist at the Concerts Lamoureux in Paris in 1898, he toured Europe, the U.S., and South America. He revolutionized the role of the cello by the virtuosity of his technique and his indisputable musicality. He was particularly noted for his interpretation of the suites for unaccompanied cello of Johann Sebastian Bach. With the French pianist Alfred Cortot and the French violinist Jacques Thibaud (1880–1953), Casals formed a noted chamber music trio. In 1919 he founded the Orquesta Pau Casals in Barcelona, which, with Casals as conductor, became an important cultural organization in Catalonia until 1936, when the Spanish civil war interrupted its activities. After the overthrow of the Republican government in Spain, Casals took up residence in France. In 1950 he organized the first annual music festival in Prades, France, commemorating Bach. In 1956 he moved to San Juan, Puerto Rico; the annual Casals Festival originated there in 1957. Casals died at Rio Piedras, Puerto Rico, Oct. 22, 1973.

To promote world peace, Casals composed the oratorio *El pesebre* (The Manger, 1960), which he conducted throughout the world. His reminiscences are contained in *Conversations with Casals* (recorded by José María Corredor, 1955). His reflections on his life were published as *Joys and Sorrows* (1970).

Pablo Casals with his wife, Marta.

CASANOVA, Giovanni Giacomo, Chevalier de Seingalt (1725–98), Italian adventurer, born in Venice. His parents, who were actors, intended him for the priesthood, but when he was 16 years old, he was expelled from a seminary for misconduct. Thereafter, Casanova was in turn a secretary, a soldier in the Venetian army, a preacher, an alchemist, a gambler, a violinist, a lottery director, and a spy. In addition, he was constantly involved in political and amatory intrigues. In 1755 the Venetian authorities imprisoned him for impiety and practicing magic, but he made a sensational escape the following year. He traveled throughout Europe, winning the confidence or friendship of many important people and gaining a reputation for his wit and charm with women. He was a favorite in the court of Louis XV, king of France, and was a lover of the Marquise de Pompadour. In 1785 Casanova retired to the castle of a friend to write his memoirs, which were published posthumously (12 vol., abridged version 1826–38; unabridged ed. 1960). The work recounts his adventures and love affairs and has historical value because it gives an account of the personages and customs of the period.

CASBAH (Arab. *qasabah,* "fortress"), in N Africa, refers to an old section of a town. Originally designating a Moorish fortress in such a quarter, the term is now suggestive of narrow streets, nightlife, and mystery. The best-known casbah is that in Algiers.

CASCA, Publius Servilius (d. about 42 BC), Roman politician, one of the assassins of Julius Caesar. According to the Greek biographer Plutarch, Casca was the one who struck the first blow, stabbing Caesar in the back. He probably committed suicide after the Battle of Phillipi.

CASCADE RANGE, lofty mountain range of the northwestern U.S. and SW Canada, about 1130 km (about 700 mi) long. The N continuation of the Sierra Nevada, the range extends from N California through Oregon and Washington into British Columbia, Canada. In the U.S. the Cascades lie from about 160 to 240 km (about 100 to 150 mi) inland from the Pacific Ocean.

The Cascades form an important climatic divide, with the W slope receiving abundant precipitation but the E slopes very little. As a result, the W part of the range is heavily wooded and the E section is covered mainly by grass and scrub plants. In the Cascades are many lakes and several large rivers that are harnessed for hydroelectric power. The name of the range is taken from the great cascades of the Columbia R.

Mt. Shuksan (about 2755 m/9038 ft), a peak of the Cascade Range in the state of Washington.
Harvey Lloyd–Peter Arnold, Inc.

The highest point in the Cascades is Mt. Rainier (4392 m/14,410 ft), in Washington. Other lofty peaks include Mt. Shasta (4317 m/14,162 ft) and Lassen Peak (3187 m/10,457 ft), an active volcano, in California; Mt. Hood (3424 m/11,233 ft) and Mt. Jefferson (3199 m/10,495 ft), in Oregon; and Mt. Adams (3751 m/12,307 ft) and Mt. Baker (3285 m/10,778 ft), in Washington. The British Columbia section has elevations reaching about 2440 m (about 8000 ft). Mt. Saint Helens (2549 m/8364 ft), in Washington, erupted in 1980 and 1982.

The Cascade Range has had a complicated geologic history. It was formed toward the close of the Pliocene epoch, but later was altered considerably by volcanic action and glaciation. Today the range affords varied opportunities for outdoor recreation, and it has several large parks.

For further information on this topic, see the Bibliography in volume 28, section 867.

CASCARA SAGRADA, (Sp., "sacred bark"), aromatic bark of the cascara, *Rhamnus purshiana,* a tall shrub also called bearberry or California buckthorn, of the family Rhamnaceae. Various ingredients in the bark give it therapeutic properties. Fluid extracts of cascara sagrada are used as mild purgatives and intestinal tonics.

CASCO BAY, inlet of the Atlantic Ocean, SW Maine, extending about 19 km (about 12 mi) inland. The city of Portland is on the W shore of Casco Bay. Many of the more than 200 small islands in the bay are popular as summer resorts.

CASE HARDENING, any of several processes for hardening the surfaces of steel products in order to make them more resistant to abrasion and wear, while leaving the interior soft and therefore more resistant to strain and impact. Case hardening is important in the manufacture of gears, axles, and other machine parts subject to much mechanical wear. The hardening may be accomplished by dissolving carbon into the surface, called carburizing, or by adding nitrogen, called cyaniding or nitriding. Steel may be carburized by being embedded in glowing charcoal, from which it absorbs carbon, in a furnace at a temperature of 800° to 900° C (1470° to 1652° F) for periods varying from several hours to several days. The steel is then suddenly immersed in cold water. In another process articles are case hardened by being heated to redness in powdered potassium cyanide, which decomposes and liberates carbon. The carbon dissolves into the steel to a depth usually of 0.3 to 3 mm (0 to 0.10 in), depending on the length of treatment.

CASEIN, group of proteins precipitated when milk is mildly acidified. Casein constitutes about 80% of the total proteins in cow's milk and about 3% of its weight. It is the chief ingredient in cheese. When dried, it is a white, amorphous powder without taste or odor. Casein dissolves slightly in water, extensively in alkalies or strong acids.

When added to milk the enzyme rennin produces a precipitate of proteins different from the material precipitated by acids, and the resulting product is known by a modified name, paracasein. This variety of casein is preferred for making a plastic, through the reaction of the casein with formaldehyde, that goes into the manufacture of buttons and other small objects. Casein is also used as a food supplement and as an adhesive, a constituent of water paints, and a finishing material for paper and textiles.

CASE INSTITUTE OF TECHNOLOGY. *See* CASE WESTERN RESERVE UNIVERSITY.

CASELLA, Alfredo (1883–1947), Italian composer, pianist, conductor, and teacher, known for his encouragement of 20th-century music. A child prodigy, Casella studied at the Paris Conservatoire. Although he knew the French composers Maurice Ravel and Claude Debussy and studied with the French composer Gabriel Fauré, Casella was influenced more by German romanticism than by these impressionist composers. His later works are in a neoclassical style; compositions such as his *Scarlattiana* (1927) use contrapuntal techniques with a contemporary harmonic idiom. He founded the Società Nazionale di Musica and the review *Ars Nova* as forums for new music. His most famous work is his ballet *La Giara* (The Jar, 1924).

CASEMENT, Sir Roger David (1864–1916), Irish revolutionist, born in Sandycove, near Dublin. After holding consular posts in the British foreign service in several parts of Africa between 1892 and 1903, Casement returned to England to present to the foreign office the results of his two-year study of the inhuman treatment of the native population in Congo Free State, then the personal holding of Leopold II, king of the Belgians. World opinion was aroused by Casement's report, with its detailed, eyewitness accounts of atrocities, and the Belgian king was eventually forced to relinquish his personal sovereignty over the Congo.

Plagued by ill health, and disdaining the posts offered by the foreign office, Casement remained in the British Isles for almost three years. During this time he seriously considered resigning but could not afford to do so. Finally, in 1906, he accepted a post in Brazil, where he served as consul in various cities for the next years.

In 1910–11, he again investigated and exposed conditions of brutal exploitation, this time of the

Indians of Brazil. For these services he was knighted in 1911. As a result of his findings (published by Parliament in 1912) the British company he accused was dissolved in 1913.

Casement retired from consular service and in 1913 returned to Ireland. A dedicated Irish nationalist, he took an active part in the movement for Irish independence. He sought help for the Irish cause, first in America and then, after World War I broke out, in Germany, where he remained until 1916. In March 1916, the Germans agreed to send 20,000 rifles to Ireland to help the Easter Rebellion, an uprising of Irish patriots. The British intercepted the arms and captured Casement after he landed from a German submarine in Ireland three days before the Easter Rebellion on April 24. Imprisoned in the Tower of London, he was convicted of high treason and hanged. The Irish consider Casement a martyr patriot; his remains were obtained from England in 1965 and reburied in Ireland.

CASERTA, town, S Italy, capital of Caserta Province, in Campania Region, near Naples. A railroad junction and agricultural center, it has industries producing explosives and soap. The modern town, Caserta, grew up around a huge 18th-century palace. The old town, Caserta Vecchia, founded in the 9th century, is NE of Caserta. During World War II, Caserta served as a Mediterranean headquarters of the Allied forces, and the surrender of the German forces in Italy was signed here on April 29, 1945. Pop. (est.) 51,600.

CASE WESTERN RESERVE UNIVERSITY, privately controlled institution of higher learning, in Cleveland, Ohio. The university comprises two formerly separate institutions, Western Reserve University and Case Institute of Technology. The latter was founded in Cleveland in 1880 and named for its endower, Leonard Case (1820–80). Until 1947 its name was Case School of Applied Science. Western Reserve University was founded in 1826 in Hudson, Ohio, as Western Reserve College for men. In 1882 it was renamed Adelbert College of Western Reserve University and moved to Cleveland. It was incorporated as Western Reserve University in 1884. Women were admitted in 1888, with the founding of Flora Stone Mather College.

In July 1967, Case Institute of Technology and Western Reserve University federated to become Case Western Reserve University. The university has two undergraduate colleges: Western Reserve College, offering programs in the arts and sciences, and the College of Case Institute of Technology, offering programs in engineering, the sciences, and management. Other divisions of the university are the schools of medicine, dentistry, law, library science, social sciences, business and management, the Frances Payne Bolton School of Nursing, and the School of Graduate Studies. The bachelor's, master's, doctor's, and initial and advanced professional degrees are conferred.

Twig of the cashew-nut tree, Anacardium occidentale.

The university libraries include several noted collections, among them the Scherer collection in Germanic literature and philology and the Kirtland collection in natural history.

CASEWORM. *See* CADDIS FLY.

CASGRAIN, Henri Raymond (1831–1904), French-Canadian historian, born in Rivière-Ouelle, Québec Province. Casgrain was ordained a Roman Catholic priest in 1856. During his early career he founded two literary periodicals and was an influential member of a group of intellectuals known as the École de Québec. Compelled to give up his parochial duties in 1870 because of ill health, Casgrain devoted himself to writing. His main interest was French-Canadian history, and he wrote prolifically about the life and customs of Canadian pioneers. His master work was *Montcalm et Lévis* (2 vol., 1891). In 1889 he was elected president of the Royal Society of Canada, of which he was a charter member.

CASHEW, tropical evergreen tree, *Anacardium occidentale,* native to the Americas but now widely cultivated in Asia (especially India) and Africa for its edible nuts and other products. Cashew is also the common name for the family to which the tree belongs, Anacardiaceae, which also includes poison ivy, poison oak, and poison sumac (q.v.), the mango, the pistachio (qq.v.), and the smoke tree. The cashew grows as high as 12 m (40 ft) and has leathery, oval leaves. The fragrant, reddish flowers grow in clusters, and the pear-shaped fruits, called cashew apples, are reddish or yellowish. At the end of each fruit is a kidney-shaped ovary, the nut, with a hard double shell. Between the shells is a caustic, black oil that has to be removed by a difficult roasting process; the oil is used in the plastics and varnish industries. Another roasting removes the second shell, freeing the nut. The trunk of the tree yields a milky gum also used to make varnish. The sour fruits can be eaten after processing and are used in making condiments.

CASHMERE, fine, soft, light wool from the undercoat of the Kashmir goat, originally raised in central and southwestern Asia, especially in Kashmir; also the fabric made from the wool of the Kashmir goat. The term is sometimes applied to fabrics that contain other fibers in addition to cashmere wool. Cashmere yarns spun in Scotland, among the softest and most luxurious of all woolens, are used primarily for knitting sweaters and shawls and for weaving paisley shawls.

CASH REGISTER, machine that records the amount of a sale as the transaction is made. Payment is placed in a cash drawer that is part of the machine and that opens only when the sale is registered. The first practical cash register was invented by James Ritty (1836–1918), of Dayton, Ohio, who secured his patent in 1879. When a sale was registered on his machine, the amount of the sale appeared on a large dial on the front of the machine. The sale was also recorded within the cash register as a series of holes punched on a roll of paper tape. At the end of the day, the merchant totaled the sales by adding up the rows of punched holes.

Cash register invented by James Ritty.
National Cash Register Co.

Today, a cash register not only performs these

In the newest cash register system, shown here in operation, an optical scanning device reads a special light-reflecting code printed on each item and automatically records the correct price. NCR Corp. Photo functions but it also (1) calculates the total sale when a customer purchases several items, (2) maintains a printed record of each sale and the department in which it was made, (3) records whether the sale was paid for by cash or is to be charged, and (4) prints the details of the sale on a sales check, which is given to the customer as a receipt. Running totals of sales by each department are also printed on the paper tape. Cash registers can also record automatically the information embossed on charge account plates as part of the sales information. Cash registers used in supermarkets not only perform the functions described above but they also automatically calculate the sales tax on taxable items as they are recorded and add the tax to the sales total; some models can also calculate change.

Special printed numbers that can be "read" by a computer have been developed for the cash register. The tape is placed on an optical device that converts the printed numbers into electrical impulses that are fed into the computer. The computer then processes the sales information automatically.

CASIMIR I, called The Restorer (1016–58), duke of Poland (1038–58). Son of Poland's King Mieszko II, Casimir succeeded his father in 1034 but was deposed by a rebellion of the nobles in 1037. The following year he returned to power as duke of Poland with the support of Holy Roman Emperor Conrad II, whom he then recognized as his overlord. Allying himself with Yaroslav the Wise, ruler of the Russian state of Kiev, he subjected the Polish tribes to his rule and drove the Czechs from Silesia. His successor, Boleslav I, reassumed the royal title.

CASIMIR II, called The Just (1138–94), duke of Poland (1177–94). Casimir was one of the four sons of Boleslav III, duke of Poland, among whom the country was divided on their father's death. Although he was the youngest of the four, he eventually established his seniority over the others, expelling his older brother Mieszko from Kraków, the principal duchy, in 1177. In 1180 the Polish nobility and clergy granted sovereignty over Poland to him and his descendants.

CASIMIR III, called The Great (1309–70), king of Poland (1333–70). The son of Władysław I, who had ended two centuries of national disunity, Casimir continued his father's work, making Poland a major power in eastern Europe. He began his reign by making peace with the Teutonic Knights and King John of Bohemia. To the knights he relinquished eastern Pomerania and Chelmno in exchange for the territories of Kujavia and Dobryzn; in 1343 they agreed to pay him tribute. To John of Bohemia he ceded Silesia and Mazovia, and in return John renounced his claim to the Polish throne. Allied with his nephew, King Louis of Hungary, Casimir later fought an indecisive war with Bohemia (1346); he regained control of Mazovia in 1350 and (again with the aid of Hungary) defeated the Lithuanians in 1353. At home he developed commerce, encouraged Jewish immigration to Poland, and so improved the condition of the peasants that he became known as the Peasants' King. He codified the laws of the kingdom in 1347, and in 1364, founded the University of Kraków. Casimir was the last king of the Piast dynasty; having no sons, he was succeeded by Louis of Hungary.

CASIMIR IV (1427–92), king of Poland (1447–92) and grand duke of Lithuania, third ruler of the Jagiełłon dynasty. A younger son of King Władysław II, Casimir succeeded his brother Władysław III. Unpopular in Poland, where he was thought to be too favorable to Lithuanians, he courted the support of the lower nobility by giving them the right to refuse taxation. He fought a long war against the Teutonic Knights, winning a great victory over them at Zarnowiec (Puck) in 1462. Four years later, by the second treaty of Torun (Thorn), he regained from the knights the extensive territory on the Baltic coast that became known as West Prussia; the order also acknowledged him as its overlord in East Prussia. From 1485 to 1489 Casimir aided his vassal, Prince Stephen of Moldavia, in his struggle against the Ottoman Turks. Casimir's son Władysław was elected king of Bohemia in 1471 and of Hungary in 1490.

CASINO, popular family card game that originated in Italy in the 19th century. Casino is played with a 52-card deck by two, three, or four participants, but is best played with two hands or four in partnerships. Points are scored by taking in the ten of diamonds, called "big casino," counted as 2 points; the two of spades, called "little casino," 1 point; aces, 1 each; the majority of cards, 3; and the majority of spades, 1. The winner is the player or side scoring highest after all cards have been played once, or the player or side scoring 21 points.

The dealer in casino is the player with the low cut. On the first deal each player, including the dealer, receives two cards, and two cards are also placed faceup on the table. A second round is dealt in similar fashion, thus giving each player and the table four cards, and play begins. This process is repeated in subsequent deals, except that no more cards are dealt to the table.

Play begins with the nondealer in the two-handed game, or the player to the left of the dealer in a three-handed or partnership contest.

Players in turn may make one of the following plays. (*a*) *Take in.* If a player has a card of the same rank as one or more on the table, he or she may show it and take in such cards. An alternate play is to take in table cards whose spot values add up to the value of a card shown from the hand. (*b*) *Build.* A build is made by adding one hand card to one or more on the table, putting them into a single pile faceup, and announcing their total point value. A player must have a card in hand to match this total, except that in the partnership game he or she can add to a build initiated by the partner. A build may not be taken in until a later turn. Picture cards, which have no numerical value, may not be built. (*c*) *Continue building.* A player may form new builds and add them to any already made. (*d*) *Change the point value of a single build.* This is done by adding a card from the hand and announcing the new point value of the build. (*e*) *Trail.* A player may place a card faceup on the table instead of taking in or building.

Players may take in any build, whether formed by them or not. They must take in their own build at the next turn unless they choose to make further builds, take in a card or combination of cards, or take in the build of an opponent. They may not trail with their own build waiting. In the final deal of a deck any cards remaining on the table go to the last player to take in cards.

CASINO, Monte. *See* MONTE CASSINO.

CASLON, William (1692–1766), English typefounder, born in Cradley, Worcestershire. He began his career in London as an engraver of firearms and later became a tool cutter in a book bindery. Subsequently, he established a typefoundry and developed a remarkably legible type, notable for the simplicity of its design and for its readability.

This is a sample of Caslon type.

The outstanding printers of the period in both Europe and the U.S. were supplied by Caslon's foundry. In 1776 the American Declaration of Independence was printed in Caslon type. The type diminished in popularity in the early 19th century, but about 1845 printers again began to use it widely.

CASPER, city, seat of Natrona Co., central Wyoming, on the North Platte R.; inc. as a city 1917. Casper is an important petroleum-producing and -refining center and the commercial focus of a vast ranching area. Nearby deposits of natural gas, coal, and uranium also are exploited. A community college is here. The site of the city was the river crossing of the Oregon, California, and Overland trails. A Mormon ferry was established here in 1847, and a bridge was completed in 1859. The first oil well was drilled in 1883, and the first refinery was erected in 1895. The city's name is derived from Fort Caspar (built 1861; now restored), which is named for Lt. Caspar Collins, who was killed by Indians in 1865. A clerk's spelling error accounts for the city's present name. Pop. (1970) 39,361; (1980) 51,016.

CASPIAN SEA (anc. *Caspium Mare* or *Hyrcanium Mare*), landlocked saltwater lake, the largest inland body of water in the world, located on the boundary between Europe and Asia. The Caspian Sea is bordered by the USSR on all sides except on the S, which is bounded by Iran. It extends about 1210 km (about 750 mi) in a N and S direction and from about 210 to 436 km (about 130 to 271 mi) in an E and W direction. It has an area of 370,998 sq km (143,243 sq mi). The coastline is irregular, with large gulfs on the E such as Krasnovodsk Gulf and the very shallow Kara-Bogaz-Gol, which acts as an evaporation basin and is the site of a major chemical plant that extracts salts from the deposits.

The Caspian Sea has a mean depth of about 170 m (about 550 ft) and is deepest in the S. Its level varies from year to year but averages about 28 m (92 ft) below sea level. In the 1960s and '70s the level fell substantially, partly because of water withdrawals from tributary rivers for irrigation and other purposes. In 1980 the Soviet Union completed a dike across the mouth of Kara-Bogaz-Gol to reduce water loss, creating a lake that was expected to last for several years. Instead, the gulf dried up completely by 1983. In the meantime, the level of the Caspian Sea began rising again, apparently as part of a long-term environmental cycle that is not yet fully understood. As a result, an aqueduct had to be built to restore water flow into Kara-Bogaz-Gol.

The S and SW shorelines of the Caspian Sea are bordered by the Elburz and Greater Caucasus mountain ranges. The sea has numerous tributaries, notably the Volga, Ural, and Emba rivers, all of which flow into it from the N. Other tributaries include the Gorgan (Gurgan) and Atrek rivers, flowing from the E, and the Kura R., flowing from the W. The sea has no outlet. The Caspian Sea is linked to the Baltic, White, and Black seas by an extensive network of inland waterways, the chief of which is the Volga R. These waterways provide an outlet to N Europe for the oil fields of Baku on the Apsheron Peninsula. The Caspian Sea also contains highly productive fisheries, yielding valuable catches of sturgeon (chief source of caviar), salmon, perch, herring, and carp. Animal life in the Caspian Sea includes tortoises, porpoises, and seals.

Navigation is frequently dangerous because of violent SE storms, and during the winter months the N parts of the Caspian Sea are closed by ice. The chief ports are Krasnovodsk, Baku, and Makhachkala, all in the USSR.

CASS, Lewis (1782–1866), American statesman, born in Exeter, N.H., and educated at Phillips Exeter Academy. Cass studied law privately in Ohio and was admitted to the bar in 1802. He was elected to the Ohio legislature in 1806. When the War of 1812 with Great Britain broke out, he entered the U.S. Army and rose rapidly to the rank of brigadier general. From 1813 to 1831, he was governor of the Michigan Territory, and in 1831 he became secretary of war in the cabinet of President Andrew Jackson. He resigned the post in 1836 to serve as the U.S. minister to France. Cass was elected to the U.S. Senate, serving from 1845 to 1848, when he was the unsuccessful Democratic presidential candidate; he was defeated by the Whig candidate, Gen. Zachary Taylor. He again served in the Senate from 1849 to 1857, when he was appointed secretary of state under President James Buchanan. Cass resigned from the cabinet in 1860, when the president refused to reinforce Fort Sumter in Charleston, S.C.

CASSANDRA, in Greek mythology, daughter of King Priam and Queen Hecuba of Troy. The god Apollo, who loved Cassandra, granted her the gift of prophecy, but when she refused to return his love, Apollo made the gift useless by decreeing that no one would believe her predictions. Cassandra warned the Trojans of many dangers, including the wooden horse by which the Greeks entered the city, but she was dismissed as a madwoman. After the fall of Troy, she was dragged from her sanctuary in the temple of the goddess Athena by Ajax the Lesser and brought to the Greek camp. When the spoils were divided, Cassandra was awarded to King Agamemnon as his slave and mistress. Cassandra warned him that he would be killed if he returned to Greece; again she was not believed. Upon their arrival in Mycenae she and Agamemnon were murdered by Clytemnestra, queen of Mycenae and wife of Agamemnon.

CASSATT, Mary (1844–1926), American painter and etcher, who lived and worked in France as an important member of the impressionist group.

Cassatt was born on May 22, 1844, in Allegheny City, Pa. In 1861 she began to study painting at the Pennsylvania Academy of the Fine Arts in Philadelphia, but proclaimed her independence by leaving in 1866 to paint in France. By 1872, after study in the major museums of Europe, her style began to mature, and she settled in Paris. There her work attracted the attention of the French painter Edgar Degas, who invited her to exhibit with his fellow impressionists. One of the works she showed was *The Cup of Tea* (1879, Metropolitan Museum, New York City), a portrait of her sister Lydia (1838?–83) in luminescent pinks. Beginning in 1882 Cassatt's style took a new turn. Influenced, like Degas, by Japanese woodcuts, she began to emphasize line over mass and experimented with asymmetric composition—as in *The Boating Party* (1893, National Gallery, Washington, D.C.)—and informal, natural gestures and positionings. Portrayals of mothers

Located on the western shore of the Caspian Sea, Baku is a major Caspian port city and the capital of the Azerbaijan SSR. Vance Henry–Taurus Photos

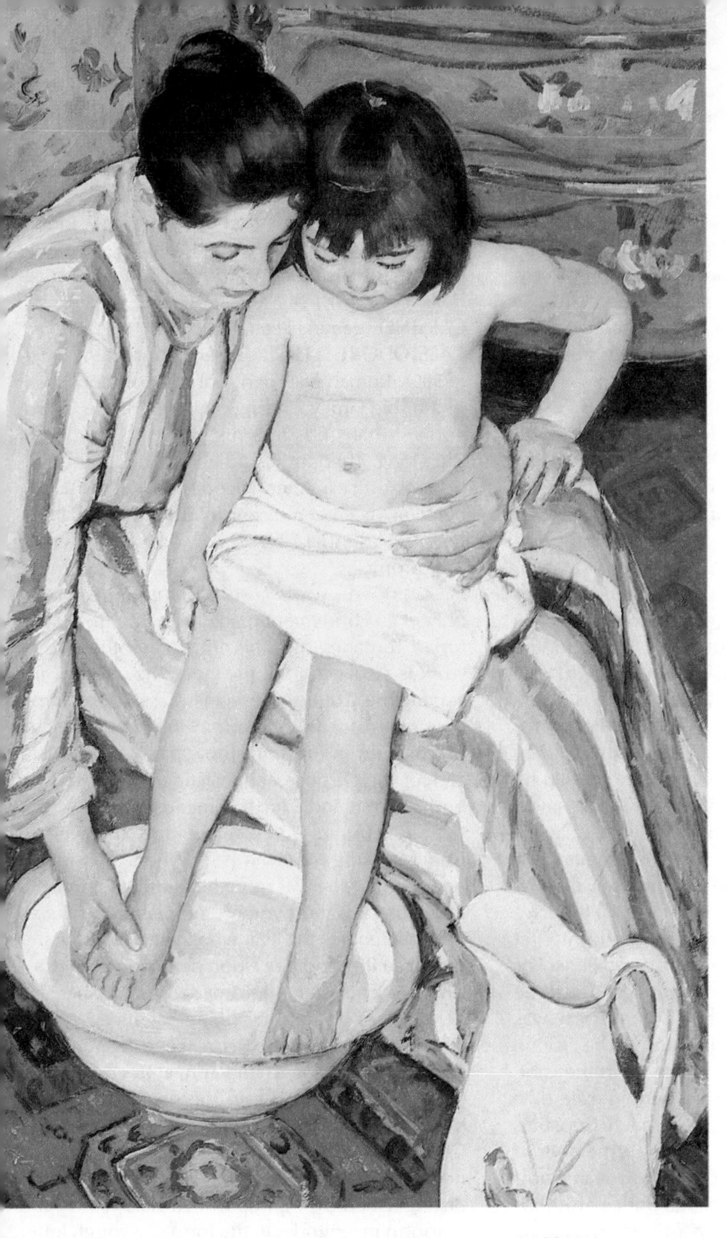

La toilette *(The Bath, 1892) exemplifies Casatt's sensitive studies of women and children. The loose painting technique shows the influence of French impressionism; the oblique, downward-focused perspective was inspired by Japanese woodcuts.*

Art Institute of Chicago–Scala–Editorial Photocolor Archives

and children in intimate relationship and domestic settings became her theme. Her portraits were not commissioned; instead, she used members of her own family as subjects.

France awarded Cassatt the Legion of Honor in 1904; although she had been instrumental in advising the first American collectors of impressionist works, recognition came more slowly in the U.S. With loss of sight she was no longer able to paint after 1914; she died June 14, 1926, at her country house near Paris.

For further information on this person, see the section Biographies in the Bibliography in volume 28.

CASSAVA, common name for any of several plants of the genus *Manihot,* of the family Euphorbiaceae (*see* SPURGE), native to tropical regions in the Americas. Cassava is the West Indian name and is used in the U.S.; manioc, or mandioc, is the Brazilian name; and juca, or yucca, is used in other parts of South America. The plant grows in a bushy form, up to 2.4 m (8 ft) high, with greenish-yellow flowers. The roots are up to 8 cm (3 in) thick and 91 cm (36 in) long.

Two varieties of cassava are of economic value, the bitter, or poisonous, (*M. esculenta*) and the sweet, or nonpoisonous, (*M. dulcis*). Because the volatile poison can be destroyed by heat, both varieties yield a wholesome food. Cassava is the chief source of tapioca, and in South America a sauce and an intoxicating beverage are prepared from the juice. The root in powder form is used to prepare farinha, a meal used to make thin cakes sometimes called cassava bread. The starch of cassava yields a product called Brazilian arrowroot. In Florida, where sweet cassava is grown, the roots are eaten as food, fed to stock, or used in the manufacture of starch and glucose.

CASSEL. *See* KASSEL.

CASSIAN, John, also called Johannes Eremita or Johannes Massiliensis (360–435), early Christian monk and theologian. After spending perhaps 15 years among the ascetics of the Egyptian deserts, he studied in Constantinople with St. John Chrysostom, by whom he was ordained a deacon. About 415, by now a priest, he settled in Marseille (in what is now southern France), where he founded the monasteries of Saints Peter and Victor, for men, and St. Savior, for women, and brought Eastern monasticism to the West. Cassian was one of the first of the Semi-Pelagians, who rejected the view of the Latin Father St. Augustine that humankind generally is damned by the sin of Adam and that some souls are saved purely through the grace of God, which cannot be earned. He also opposed the Augustinian concept of moral choice in attaining salvation.

CASSIN, René (1887–1976), French jurist and Nobel laureate, born in Bayonne, and educated at the universities of Aix-en-Provence and Paris. For more than 40 years Cassin combined the three careers of jurist, diplomat, and educator. He was a member of the French delegation to the League of Nations from 1921 to 1938, served in the cabinet of the Free French government-in-exile during World War II, joined the French Constitutional Council in 1960, and became a member in 1959 and president in 1965 of the European Court of Human Rights. Cassin was the principal author of the Universal Declaration of Human Rights, which was adopted by the UN General Assembly in 1948; he also served as president of the UN Human Rights Commission from 1954 to 1956. He was a founder of the UN Educational, Scientific, and Cultural Organization. Cassin was awarded the Grand Cross of the French Legion of Honor. He received the 1968 Nobel Peace Prize for his role in fostering the UN declaration on human rights.

CASSINO, town, central Italy, in Latium Region, on the Rapido R. An agricultural center, Cassino lies at the foot of a hill crowned by the Benedictine monastery of Monte Cassino. Peace between Holy Roman Emperor Frederick II and Pope Gregory IX was signed here in 1230. In 1943, during World War II, the Germans attempted to block the Allied advance to Rome by using both the town and the abbey as key defense points. When the Germans surrendered in 1944, the air and artillery bombing had reduced the town and the abbey to rubble. Both have since been rebuilt. Pop. (est.) 14,700.

CASSINO (game). *See* CASINO.

CASSIODORUS, Flavius Magnus Aurelius (c. 490–c. 585), Roman historian, born in southern Italy, of a noble family. During the reign of the Ostrogoths in Italy, Cassiodorus became secretary to their king, Theodoric, and held several other important offices. After Theodoric's death in 526, he acted as chief minister to Theodoric's daughter, Amalasuntha (498–535), who succeeded to the throne.

Cassiodorus wrote *History of the Goths,* extant only in an abridgment made by the medieval historian Jordanes (fl. 6th cent.). His other major work is a collection of the letters he wrote while serving the Gothic sovereigns. Cassiodorus is remembered for founding (c. 550) the monastery of Vivarium in Bruttium (now part of Apulia, Italy) for the purpose of translating and preserving both ancient and Christian manuscripts.

CASSIOPEIA, in Greek mythology, the wife of Cephus, king of Ethiopia. When Cassiopeia boasted that she was more beautiful than the Nereids, these water nymphs complained to Poseidon, the god of the sea, who sent a sea monster to ravage the land. Poseidon demanded that Cassiopeia's daughter Andromeda be punished for her mother's vanity by being sacrificed to the monster, but the girl was rescued by the hero Perseus. According to tradition, at her death Cassiopeia was changed into the constellation that bears her name.

CASSIOPEIA, in astronomy, constellation of the northern heavens, near the celestial pole. It is distinguished by a group of five stars, of second to fourth magnitude, in the form of a rough letter W. The brightest supernova on record appeared in the constellation in 1572 and was observed by the Danish astronomer Tycho Brahe. Brighter than the planet Venus, for about 16 months Cassiopeia was visible to the naked eye even at noon. The constellation is named for the mythological Ethiopian queen Cassiopeia, the mother of Andromeda.

CASSIRER, Ernst (1874–1945), German philosopher and educator, born in Breslau (now Wrocław, Poland), and educated at the universities of Berlin, Leipzig, Munich, Heidelberg, and Marburg. Cassirer became professor of philosophy at Hamburg University in 1919 and taught there until he was ousted in 1933, when Hitler came to power. Subsequently Cassirer lectured at the universities of Oxford and Göteborg, became visiting professor at Yale University in 1941, and joined the faculty of Columbia University in 1944. A great admirer of the philosophy of the German philosopher Immanuel Kant, Cassirer was a leader of the so-called Marburg Neo-Kantian school of philosophy. His works deal mainly with the theory of knowledge, the history of epistemology, and the philosophy of science. He also revised and annotated Kant's writings. Cassirer's works include *The Problem of Knowledge* (3 vol., 1906-20) and *The Philosophy of Symbolic Forms* (3 vol., 1923-29).

CASSITERITE, also tinstone, mineral consisting of tin dioxide (SnO_2). It forms crystals in the tetragonal system (*see* CRYSTAL) and has a hardness (q.v.) of 6 to 7 and a sp.gr. of 7. Usually dark brown to black, it has a dull adamantine luster. Cassiterite is the only commercially important ore of tin. It has been mined in Cornwall, England, since ancient times, but the principal sources today are Bolivia, the Malay Peninsula, Indonesia, Nigeria, and the Republic of the Congo.

CASSIUS, Dio. *See* DIO CASSIUS.

CASSIUS LONGINUS, Gaius (d. 42 BC), Roman general and one of the assassins of Julius Caesar. Cassius distinguished himself in the war against the Parthians (53-51 BC). In 49 BC, he fought against Caesar in a civil war as fleet commander under the Roman general and statesman Pompey the Great. Although pardoned by Caesar, who made him a legate, Cassius subsequently became one of the leaders of the conspiracy against Caesar and participated in Caesar's assassination. Subsequently, he raised an army to fight against Caesar's commander in chief, Mark Antony, and later against the Triumvirate, the three men who ruled Rome after Caesar's assassination. With his fellow conspirator, the Roman politician Marcus Junius Brutus, Cassius besieged his foes at Philippi in Macedonia but was defeated in battle. Cassius committed suicide so that he would not be captured. Parts of his life are presented in the play *Julius Caesar* by Shakespeare.

CASSIVELLAUNUS (fl. 1st cent. BC), ancient British tribal chieftain. He ruled the Catuvellauni in the region just north of London. In 54 BC he opposed the second invasion of Britain by Julius Caesar, but was compelled to pay tribute and give hostages to the Romans after Caesar captured his stronghold on the site of the modern town of Wheathampstead.

CASSOWARY, common name for a genus, *Casuarius,* of flightless, running birds of the family Casuariidae, closely related to the true ostrich,

Double-wattled cassowary, Casuarius casuarius
Kenneth W. Fink–Bruce Coleman, Inc.

and more closely to the emu. Cassowaries are found mainly in Queensland, Australia, in New Guinea, and in Ceram, Indonesia. About 65 cm (about 5 ft) high, it resembles the ostrich but has a shorter neck. The loose, hairlike feathers are brownish-black. The head and neck are bare and brilliantly colored in red, blue, and yellow. On top of the head is a large, bony, helmetlike crest. Two species have wattles hanging from the chin. The cassowary can run up to 48 km/hr (30 mph) and, when attacked, can kick forward lethally with sharp claws, or strike with the rigid barbs of its degenerate wings. Cassowaries live in pairs in wooded districts. The three to six eggs laid by the female are incubated mainly by the male cassowary and are of greenish color; they are thinner in shell than those of the ostrich.

CASTAGNO, Andrea del. *See* ANDREA DEL CASTAGNO.

CASTANETS, in music, percussion instrument consisting of a pair of hollow shells of hardwood, ivory, or composition material loosely bound together by a cord. The cord is generally fastened around the first finger and thumb of the performer's hand. When the other fingers strike the two castanets together, a hollow, clicking sound is produced. Used chiefly with Spanish music to accent the rhythm of the piece being performed, castanets are also played by female performers of Spanish dances, who usually hold one instrument in each hand. Wood and ivory instruments similar to castanets were used in ancient times, but the modern term is derived from the Spanish word for "chestnut" (*castaño*), from which castanets were commonly made.

CASTE, term applied to one of the many hereditary classes established among the Hindus on the Indian subcontinent. Sometimes the term is also used in a general sense to refer to any society that has a rigid class structure. The word *caste* was first used by 16th-century Portuguese traders; it is derived from the Portuguese *casta,* denoting family strain, breed, or race. The Sanskrit word is *jati.* The Sanskrit term *varna* denotes a group of *jati,* or the system of caste.

The traditional caste system of India developed more than 3000 years ago when Aryan-speaking nomadic groups migrated from the north to India about 1500 BC. The Aryan priests, according to the ancient sacred literature of India, divided society into a basic caste system. Sometime between 200 BC and AD 100, the *Manu Smriti,* or *Law of Manu,* was written. In it the Aryan priest-lawmakers created the four great hereditary divisions of society still surviving today, placing their own priestly class at the head of this caste system with the title of earthly gods, or Brahmans. Next in order of rank were the warriors, the Kshatriyas. Then came the Vaisyas, the farmers and merchants. The fourth of the original castes was the Sudras, the laborers, born to be servants to the other three castes, especially the Brahman. Far lower than the Sudras—in fact, entirely outside the social order and limited to doing the most menial tasks—were those persons of no caste, the Untouchables. These were the Dravidians, the original aboriginal inhabitants of India, to whose ranks from time to time were added the pariahs, or outcasts, persons expelled for religious or social sins from the classes into which they had been born. Thus created by the priests, the caste system was made a part of Hindu religious law, rendered secure by the claim of divine revelation.

The characteristics of an Indian caste include rigid, hereditary membership in the caste into which one is born; the practice of marrying only members of the same caste; restrictions on the choice of occupation and on personal contact with members of other castes; and the acceptance of each individual of a fixed place in society. The caste system has been perpetuated by the Hindu idea of karma. According to this religious belief, all people are reincarnated on earth, at which time they have a chance to be born into another, higher caste, but only if they have been obedient to the rules of their caste in their previous life on earth. In this way karma has discouraged people from attempting to rise to a higher caste or to cross caste lines for social relations of any kind.

The four original castes have been subdivided again and again over many centuries, until today it is impossible to tell their exact number. Estimates range from 2000 to 3000 different castes established by Brahmanical law throughout India, each region having its own distinct groups defined by craft and fixed by custom.

The complexities of the system have constituted a serious obstacle to civil progress in India. The trend today is toward the dissolution of the artificial barriers between the castes. The stringency of the caste system of the Hindus was broken down greatly during the period of British rule in India. The obligation of the son to follow the calling of his father is no longer binding; men of low castes have risen to high ranks and positions of power; and excommunication, or the loss of caste, is not as serious as it may once have been. In addition, the caste system was from time to time burst from within by ecclesiastical schisms, most notably the rise of Buddhism, itself a reaction from, and protest against, the intolerable bondage of the caste system.

In recent years considerable strides toward eradicating unjust social and economic aspects of the caste system as practiced in India have been made through educational and reform movements. The great leader in this endeavor was Mohandas Gandhi. The drafted constitution of India, which was published a few days after the assassination of Gandhi in January 1948, stated in a special clause under the heading "human rights": "Untouchability is abolished and its practice in any form is forbidden."

CASTEL GANDOLFO, town, central Italy, in Latium Region, on Lake Albano, near Rome. The town is the site of a papal residence, Castel Gandolfo, a palace constructed in the 17th century, and of the Church of Saint Thomas of Villanova. The Vatican observatory also is here. Much of the town is part of the independent papal state of Vatican City. Pop. (est.) 3000.

CASTELO BRANCO, Camilo (1825-90), Portuguese writer, born in Lisbon. Orphaned when very young, he led a dissolute life for a number of years. He took minor orders, but, tiring of religious life, resumed his secular existence and devoted himself to writing. In 1885 he was made viscount of Correia-Botelho in recognition of his work. A few years later, after his health failed and he became blind, he committed suicide.

Although Castelo Branco wrote about 100 volumes of poetry, plays, critical writing, and novels, his significance as a writer rests almost entirely on his 58 novels. These portray the social and domestic life of his time, in which idealization of some of his characters was intermingled with savage ridicule of such characters as members of the commercial middle class. His style was remarkable for the brilliant use of Portuguese.

His novels include *Onde está a felicidade?* (Where Is Happiness? 1856); *O que fazem as mulheres* (What Women Do, 1858); *Amor de perdiçã* (Love of Perdition, 1862), considered his most beautiful work; and *A brasileira de Prazins* (The Brazilian Girl from Prazens, 1882).

CASTIGLIONE, Baldassare, Conte (1478-1529), Italian diplomat and writer, born in Casatico, near Mantua. Throughout his life he held a number of posts in the great courts of Italy and Spain, and it was upon his observations of courtly life that he based the work for which he is best known, *The Book of the Courtier* (1528; trans. 1561). Written in the form of a dialogue, it is a treatise on the accomplishments and code of behavior essential for the ideal courtier. Translated into many languages, the book became a primer of aristocratic manners, influencing Renaissance nobility and writers throughout Europe, including, notably, the English courtier-poet Sir Philip

Conte Baldassare Castiglione New York Public Library

Sidney. Apart from its importance as a book of etiquette, *The Courtier* is a firsthand source of 16th-century social and intellectual history.

Castiglione also wrote pastoral and courtly poetry in Italian and Latin, including the verse drama *Tirsi* (1506).

CASTILE (Span. *Castilla*), former kingdom in Spain, comprising Old Castile and New Castile. It extended from the Bay of Biscay on the north to Andalusia on the south and included most of the central portion of the Spanish Peninsula. In 1833 Old Castile, which made up the northern half of the kingdom, was divided into the provinces of Palencia, Valladolid, Ávila, Segovia, Soria, Burgos, Logroño, and Santander. New Castile was divided into the provinces of Madrid, Toledo, Guadalajara, Cuidad Real, and Cuenca. Receiving its name because of the large number of its frontier castles, Old Castile was under the suzerainty of the kings of Asturias and León from the 8th century to 1035, when Ferdinand I established a unified kingdom. In 1058 Ferdinand initiated the first of a long series of wars against the Moors, beginning the conquest of New Castile. Despite internal strife, the kingdom was further expanded in the following centuries, and in 1479, as a result of the marriage of Ferdinand V of Castile and Isabella I, it was united with Aragón. The united kingdom subsequently became the kingdom of Spain.

CASTILLA, Ramón (1797-1867), Peruvian general and statesman, who twice (1845-51, 1855-62) held office as the country's president. He was born in Tarapacá Province (now in Chile); as a youth, he served in the Spanish army, but in 1822 he joined the liberation force of José de San Martín. After independence had been secured, he was appointed prefect of his native province in 1824 and chief of staff in 1830. In 1837 he joined the Peruvians who marched against Santa Cruz; he was made minister of war under President Agustín Gamarra (1785-1841). In 1841 Castilla was one of the leaders of the Peruvian force that invaded Bolivia, and in 1845 he was elected president of Peru. When his successor, José Rufino Echenique (1808-79), became unpopular, Castilla started a revolution, overcame Echenique, and became, in 1855, sole ruler of the country. One of his most important reforms was the abolition of slavery; another was the abolition of tribute paid by the Indians to the great landed proprietors. In 1858 he was reelected president, and in 1860 he proclaimed a new constitution that remained in force until 1920. In 1862 he resigned and lived in retirement until he became president of the Peruvian senate in 1865.

CASTILLO DE SAN MARCOS NATIONAL MONUMENT. *See* NATIONAL PARK SERVICE (table).

CASTING. *See* FOUNDING.

CAST IRON. *See* IRON; IRON AND STEEL MANUFACTURE.

CASTLE (Lat. *castellum,* "small fortified place"), fortified residence of a feudal lord or monarch. Derived from the walled cities of ancient Rome and the fortified palaces of Byzantium, the castle became virtually ubiquitous in western Europe during the wars of the late Middle Ages.

At first the castle consisted of a simple wooden structure on top of a mound, surrounded by a ditch. If a lord's domains were flat, he constructed an artificial mound, or motte. As medieval siegecraft developed, a wall or series of

The ruined walls and keep of Château Gaillard, built by Richard I the Lionhearted in the late 12th century, stand guard over the Seine at Les Andelys in Normandy, France.
P. Belzaux-Rapho–Photo Researchers, Inc.

The 12th-century turreted castle of Carcassonne, an ancient fortified town in southern France, was protected by the town's crenellated walls and hilltop site. It was heavily restored in the 19th century. Walter S. Clark

walls or palisades was raised around the motte and at a distance from it; the open area within these walls became known as the bailey. By the 11th century the motte-and-bailey form of castle was widely prevalent. Outer walls gradually became thicker and were topped with wide battlemented parapets.

The next step in the development of the castle was the addition by the Normans of a towering masonry keep, or donjon, within the bailey. The keep, often some 12 to 15 m (some 40 to 50 ft) high, had thick walls and small windows. The White Tower within the Tower of London is an example of a Norman keep. Wide, deep moats replaced the crude ditches; ideally filled with water but often dry, these moats were crossed by drawbridges that could be raised from within the castle. At the castle end of the drawbridge was an opening in the wall, containing a portcullis, a thick, iron-plated wooden door that could be

Warwick Castle, in Warwick, England, stands on an island in a river. Incorporating a 10th-century fortification, it was rebuilt in the 14th century and became a mansion in the 17th century. British Tourist Authority

Kronborg Castle (16th cent.) in Elsinore, Denmark, built in the Renaissance style, ensured the collection of tolls from passing ships. Shakespeare's Hamlet, *set in Elsinore, is sometimes performed here.* Danish Tourist Board

raised to clear the entrance. Within the Norman keep were private apartments, a well for water, and everything else necessary to sustain the inhabitants of the castle through a long siege. At first the keep was rectangular; later, it was learned that a round keep was easier to defend. In the 13th century the castle became increasingly sophisticated. Living and administrative quarters were moved from the keep into new buildings raised within the bailey. The keep, made smaller and stronger, became the final defensive position within a series of battlements.

A castle was often built on the edge of an impregnable cliff, ideally at a bend in the river where it could command a view of the surrounding countryside. The Château Gaillard, built by Richard I, King of England, in Les Andelys, France, is an example of a strategically located castle. The use of gunpowder in projectiles brought to an end the impregnability of the medieval castle. After 1500 the construction of castles was no longer feasible, and *castle* became a term for an imposing residence. *See also* FORTIFICATION AND SIEGE WARFARE.

For further information on this topic, see the Bibliography in volume 28, sections 277, 896–97.

CASTLE, Vernon (1887–1918), *and* **Irene** (1893–1969), husband-and-wife team of exhibition ballroom dancers. He was born in Norwich, England; she, in New Rochelle, N.Y. After their marriage in 1911 they developed and popularized a new style of social dancing and they were immensely popular performers until his death in World War I. Among the dances they performed were the turkey trot, the Maxixe, and the one-step or Castle walk (*see* FOX-TROT). Together they wrote *Modern Dancing* (1914); Irene Castle wrote *My Memories of Vernon Castle* (1918) and collaborated with the American writers Bob and Wanda Duncan on *Castles in the Air* (1958).

CASTLE CLINTON NATIONAL MONUMENT. *See* NATIONAL PARK SERVICE (table).

CASTLEREAGH, Robert Stewart, Viscount (1769–1822), British statesman, born in county Down, Ireland, and educated at the University of Cambridge. In 1790 he entered the Irish parliament as a Whig, but he joined the Tory party when he entered the British House of Commons in 1795. A year later he was created Viscount Castlereagh, a courtesy title. As chief secretary for Ireland from 1799, he energetically supported the attempt of the British Prime Minister William Pitt the Younger to bring about the political union of Ireland with Great Britain. Pitt's proposed legislation, known as the Act of Union, was carried in the Irish parliament in 1800, largely through Castlereagh's skill in bribing parliamentary members. Soon after the act became law (Jan. 1, 1801), Castlereagh resigned from office because of the opposition of King George III to the passing of a Catholic emancipation act, which Castlereagh had hoped would follow the Act of Union.

Castlereagh was a member of the House of Commons from 1801 until his death, serving as leader from 1812. As secretary of state for the war and colonial department during most of the period from 1805 to 1809, he helped plan British campaigns in the Napoleonic Wars.

From 1812, as foreign secretary in the Tory cabinet of Robert Banks Jenkinson (1770–1828), 2d earl of Liverpool, Castlereagh played a leading part in the coalition of nations against Napoleon, keeping it united during the critical campaigns of 1813–14. He represented Great Britain at the Congress of Vienna (1814–15), which redrew the map of Europe after the Napoleonic Wars. At the Congress of Aix-la-Chapelle (1818), he resisted Russian attempts to draw Britain into a European league to oppose revolution.

In 1822, suffering from depression and fearful that he was about to be exposed as a homosexual, Castlereagh committed suicide.

CASTOR, star, α Geminorum, of magnitude 1.6, the fainter star of the zodiacal constellation Gemini, or the Twins. In 1719 it was discovered to be a visual binary star, with components of magnitudes 2.8 and 2.0 separated by 6 sec of arc and revolving around each other in about 350 years. Each of these components has been found to be a spectroscopic binary. In addition, a faint companion, separated from the other two by 72 sec of arc, has been discovered. This star is also a spectroscopic binary, the two components of which revolve around each other in about one day. Hence, the entire system of the star Castor contains at least six stars. Its distance is about 45 light-years from the earth.

CASTOR BEAN, common name for the species *Ricinus communis,* of the family Euphorbiaceae (*see* SPURGE). Native to tropical Africa, where it grows to 12 m (40 ft) or more, it is widely planted in temperate areas as an annual ornamental for its large, lobed, fanlike leaves. It rarely exceeds 4.5 m (15 ft) in height in cooler climates. The bean-shaped seeds contain an oil that is the castor oil (q.v.) of commerce, and in Brazil, India, and Thailand the plant is an important crop. The orange flowers are without petals and are clustered in long panicles; the fruit is covered with soft, orange-brown spines. All parts of the plant are poisonous to humans and animals; the seeds are extremely poisonous.

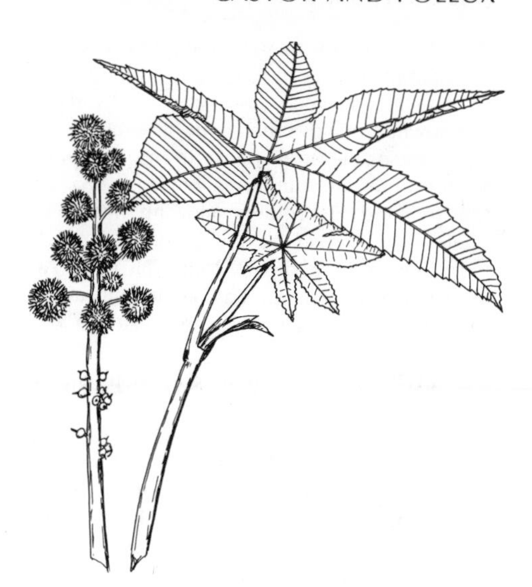

Castor bean, Ricinus communis

CASTOR OIL, colorless or yellow to yellowish-brown, thick, oily liquid obtained from the seeds of the castor-bean plant. Although it has a disagreeable taste, it is practically odorless. It is insoluble in water, but soluble in organic solvents. The medicinal oil is prepared from husked seeds. Unhusked seeds, the source of industrial castor oil, yield from 45 to 55 percent oil. The oil is pressed from the seeds, purified, and then bleached.

In addition to its use as a simple purgative, castor oil is used as a plasticizer in nitrocellulose compositions, in cosmetics, and in insulation products. It is also used in the manufacture of waterproof lacquers and paints.

CASTOR AND POLLUX, in Greek and Roman mythology, the twin sons of Leda, wife of the Spartan king Tyndareus. They were the brothers of Clytemnestra, queen of Mycenae, and Helen of Troy. Although both boys were known as the Dioscuri, or Sons of Zeus, in most accounts only Pollux was held to be immortal, having been conceived when Zeus appeared to Leda in the form of a swan. Castor, his fraternal twin, was considered the mortal son of Tyndareus. Both were worshiped as deities in the Roman world, however, and were regarded as the special protectors of sailors and warriors. Living just before the Trojan War, the brothers took part in many of the famous events of the day, including the Calydonian boar hunt, the expedition of the Argonauts, and the rescue of their sister Helen when she was carried off by the Greek hero Theseus. Throughout their adventures the brothers were inseparable, and when Castor was slain by Idas, a cattle owner, in a dispute about his oxen, Pollux was inconsolable. In response to his prayers for death for himself or immortality for his brother, Zeus reunited the brothers, allowing them to be together always, half the time in the underworld and half with the gods on Mount Olympus. According to a later legend, Castor and Pollux were transformed by Zeus into the constellation Gemini, or The Twins.

CASTRATION, removal of the gonads in humans or animals. With the advent of newer, less drastic methods of sterilization, this procedure is no longer used as a means of family planning. Castration has been employed medically to combat some forms of cancer, but this use also is declining. At one time it was used as a means of eugenics. In China and the Middle East, selected male children were castrated to serve as guards of womens' quarters or as chamberlains, but this practice ceased in the 20th century (*see* EUNUCH). In Europe in the 16th and 17th centuries, boys with fine voices were sometimes castrated to sing in church choirs as castratos because of the Roman Catholic ban on female singers (*see* SINGING); this practice has also ceased.

In animal husbandry, castration of male animals is called gelding and castration of females is called spaying. It is used for such purposes as selective breeding, increased docility, and, for pet cats and dogs, simple sterility.

CASTRIES, city, capital of Saint Lucia, in the West Indies. It is a seaport situated on a nearly landlocked harbor in the NW part of the island of St. Lucia. Major exports include bananas, sugarcane, limes, cacao, coconuts, and rum. The city also has a substantial tourist industry. Nearby are Vigie Airport and Morne Fortune, a hill that affords a good view of the area. Founded by the French in 1650, Castries changed hands several times before coming under definitive British control in 1814. Much of the city was destroyed by fire in 1948. It became the capital of independent St. Lucia in 1979. Pop. (1984 est.) 50,700.

CASTRO, Cipriano (1858–1924), Venezuelan military leader and dictator, born near San Antonio, Táchira State. In 1899 Castro led an insurrection, captured Caracas, and became president of Venezuela. One of the most corrupt dictators in South American history, Castro was also a libertine. His administration was marked by insurrections and by disputes with foreign countries over his attempts to confiscate foreign property and over Venezuelan foreign debt. These quarrels with European creditor nations took place between 1902 and 1907, and Venezuela was brought close to bankruptcy. In 1908, during Castro's absence in Europe, his lieutenant and friend, Vice-President Juan Vicente Gómez, declared him deposed and had himself elected president. Castro lived in exile for the rest of his life, mostly in Puerto Rico.

CASTRO, Fidel (1927–), Cuban prime minister (1959–76) and president (1976–), whose revolutionary regime made Cuba one of the leading nations of Latin America and of the Third World.

Castro was born in Mayari on Aug. 13, 1927. He received a degree in law from the University of Havana in 1950. After Fulgencio Batista seized control of the Cuban government in 1952, Castro became the leader of an underground, antigovernment faction. In 1953 he was jailed for having led the July 26th uprising against Batista. Released in 1955, he went into exile. In 1956 he returned to Cuba and led a rebellion from the Sierra Maestra region of Oriente Province. His rebel forces, known as the 26th of July movement, won steadily increasing popular support. Batista fled from the country on Jan. 1, 1959, and Castro assumed power. He became premier of Cuba on February 16.

At first Castro seemed to be a moderate leftist, but once in power he became increasingly radical, executing and imprisoning thousands of political opponents, nationalizing industry, collectivizing agriculture, and establishing a one-party socialist state that drove large numbers of middle- and upper-class Cubans into exile. He was especially hostile to the U.S., which had been friendly to Batista and had frequently intervened in Cuban affairs. The U.S. in turn was angered by Castro's seizure of American-owned companies and backed an unsuccessful attempt by Cuban exiles to overthrow him in 1961 (*see* BAY OF PIGS INVASION).

In the early 1960s Castro openly embraced communism and formed close ties with the Soviet bloc, relying increasingly on Soviet economic and military aid. The bearded, cigar-smoking Cuban leader, invariably dressed in army fatigue uniform, soon became a familiar figure to millions of people all over the world. Offering the Cuban revolution as an example to other developing countries, he gave active support to revolutionary movements in Latin America and, during the 1970s, in Africa as well. Despite his alliance with the USSR, he joined the Nonaligned Nations movement, acting as its chairman from 1979 to 1982. *See also* CUBA.

For further information on this person, see the section Biographies in the Bibliography in volume 28, and section 1131.

In the driver's seat, Fidel Castro is interviewed by Barbara Walters, a newscaster and reporter, for a 1977 television special.

CASTRO, Inés de (d. 1355), Spanish noblewoman, descended from the Castilian line, whose unhappy fate has been the subject of tragedies and poems. After 1340, Inés lived with her cousin Constantia (d. 1345), who was later the wife of Dom Pedro (1320–67), son of Alfonso IV, king of Portugal. After the death of Constantia, Dom Pedro secretly married Inés. Alfonso feared that this union might affect the claim to the throne of his grandson, Constantia's son, and he therefore had Inés executed. Dom Pedro declared civil war against Alfonso, but they were soon reconciled. According to legend, when Pedro became king (as Pedro I) he established the legality of his marriage with Inés and had her body exhumed and placed on the throne.

CASTRO, João de (1500–48), Portuguese naval officer and explorer, born in Lisbon. As a youth he distinguished himself in a number of campaigns against the Moors of Tangier and Tunis. In 1543, when he returned from an expedition to the Red Sea, he was appointed commander of a fleet to clear the European seas of pirates. Castro was sent in 1545 to Portuguese India, where he overthrew the king of Gujurat and relieved the beleaguered town of Diu. He subsequently completed the subjugation of Malacca and prepared the way for the invasion of Sri Lanka. In 1547 he was made viceroy of Portuguese India.

CASTRO, Rosalía de (1837–85), Spanish poet, born in Santiago de Compostela. She revived the language of her native Galicia (in northwestern Spain), introducing new poetical meters. *Cantares gallegos* (Galician Songs, 1863), depicting the life and recalling the lore of the area, has a lyrical folk song quality. A later collection of verse, *Follas novas* (1880), is much more personal, concerned with loneliness and fear of death, and the anguish of suppressed desires. De Castro also wrote in Castilian, using it in the somber *Beside the River Sar* (1884; trans. 1937). Primarily a poet, she produced several novels, one of the best known of which is *La hija del mar* (The Daughter of the Sea, 1859).

CASTRO VALLEY, unincorporated urban community, Alameda Co., W California, near the city of Oakland and San Francisco Bay. It is mainly residential. The site was part of a Mexican land grant made in the early 1840s to Guillermo Castro (b. 1810), hence the community's name. Pop. (1970) 44,760; (1980) 44,011.

CASTRO Y BELLVÍS, Guillén de (1569–1631), Spanish dramatist, born in Valencia of a distinguished family. He enjoyed the friendship of many celebrated and powerful personages and was a captain in the military forces of Valencia. Like his friend the renowned Spanish dramatist Lope de Vega, Castro was a well-known playwright of the Golden Age of Spanish literature. Castro's most celebrated play is *The Youthful Deeds of the Cid* (1618; trans. 1969), from which the French dramatist Pierre Corneille derived his masterpiece *Le Cid.* Most of the approximately 50 dramas written by Castro deal with the legendary deeds of El Cid.

CASUISTRY, a method of resolving questions of conscience by applying moral principles or laws to concrete cases. Although the case method is used in many professional schools as diverse as law and business administration, the term *casuistry* is usually restricted to the realm of ethics or moral theology. Casuistry has been used as a teaching vehicle by religions and philosophies seeking to inculcate a moral code, most notably in Confucianism, Stoicism, Talmudic Judaism, Islam, and Christianity. Christ resorted to it in dealing with the Pharisees (see Matt. 12:9-14) but also condemned its abuse (see Mark 7:1-13). St. Augustine's two treatises on lying (c. 400) exemplify the casuistic form. He took up such questions as whether good intention excuses one from guilt and whether it is wrong to tell a lie in jest or as a figure of speech. The Scholastics, however—especially the Italian philosopher St. Thomas Aquinas—approached moral theology in a more speculative and metaphysical fashion.

The 16th century marked the high point in casuistic practice for both Roman Catholics and Protestants. The Cambridge Puritan preacher William Perkins (1558-1602), in *The Whole Treatise of the Cases of Conscience,* presented the first sustained treatment of casuistry in English. A period of decadence followed in the 17th century. Some Roman Catholic authors in particular, concentrating on the mere avoidance of sin, tended to present a minimalistic ethics. The rise of Jansenism (q.v.) and the bitter debate over the use of probabilism in reaching moral decisions provoked the French philosopher Blaise Pascal to write *Lettres provinciales* (1656), in which he attacked the Jesuits for the lax morality evidenced in their casuistry. The more balanced approach of the Italian theologian St. Alphonsus Liguori reestablished the usefulness of the method.

Since the late 1940s an increasing reaction against the too formal or overjuridical approach to morality has resulted in an approach known as "situation ethics." According to this position, moral decisions and the circumstances evoking them are unique and unrepeatable; therefore, it is impossible to apply universal laws or principles, and all casuistry is thus eliminated. J.E.L.

CAT. *See* CAT, DOMESTIC; CAT FAMILY.

CAT, DOMESTIC, small, mainly carnivorous animal, *Felis catus,* member of the family Felidae (*see* CAT FAMILY), popular as a household pet, and valuable for killing mice and rats. Like other members of the family, the domestic cat has retractile claws; keen hearing and smell; remarkable night vision; and a compact, muscular, and highly supple body. About 36 varieties, or breeds, of *F. catus* are recognized internationally; they are divided into two main groups, the shorthaired and the long-haired cats. As a household pet the cat is second in popularity only to the dog. Affectionate but reserved, the cat is more independent than the dog, possesses an excellent memory, and exhibits considerable aptitude

The American, or domestic, shorthair cat is the most common modern breed. Shown here is the calico type, named for its many-colored coat.
Alice Su

The popular Siamese cat is a slim animal with a long body, very lithe and muscular. Shown here is the dark-faced seal point variety. Creszentia

for learning by observation and experience. Its homing instinct is proverbial, as is its cleanliness. The life span of the cat is about 15 years. The gestation period is about 63 days, and the litter averages from two to five offspring. Kittens begin to be weaned about eight weeks after birth.

Origin of Species. Most authorities believe that the short-haired breeds are derived from the Caffre cat, *F. libyca,* a species of African wildcat domesticated by the ancient Egyptians perhaps as early as 2500 BC and transported by the Crusaders to Europe, where it interbred with the indigenous smaller wildcats. According to some authorities, the long-haired breeds may have sprung from the Asian wildcat, *F. manul.*

Over the centuries cats have remained virtually the same in size, weighing approximately 3.6 kg (about 8 lb) when full-grown, and have preserved their instinct for solitary hunting. Tabby markings (either stripes or blotches) that occur frequently in all breeds and even appear underlying solid-colored coats, are also believed to be descended from remote ancestors.

Modern Breeds. The first long-haired cats in Europe were seen in the 16th century. Often popularly called Persian or Angora cats (*see* PERSIAN), they have been specially bred to produce several other breeds and color varieties for about the past hundred years. Today these are the most popular in the cat fancy (a term referring to the breeding and judging of pedigreed cats). Included among the longhairs are the long-haired Siamese, known as the Balinese; the Himalayan (q.v.), which is Persian in appearance but carries the Siamese color pattern; the Birman, the sacred cat of Burma; the Somali, a long-haired Abyssinian; the Maine coon cat (q.v.); the Cymric, a tailless cat derived from the short-haired Manx (q.v.); and the Turkish Angora. A more recent long-hair breed is the Ragdoll, not recognized by all cat associations, but so named because of its ability to relax so completely it resembles a rag doll. It is large and has a mild disposition.

Short-haired cats, a much larger category, include the Abyssinian (q.v., which greatly resembles the sacred cat of Egypt, discussed below), Burmese (q.v.), British Shorthair, American Shorthair, American Wirehair, Bombay, Chartreux, Cornish Rex, Colorpoint Shorthair, Devon Rex, Egyptian Mau, Exotic Shorthair, Havana Brown, Japanese Bobtail, Javanese, Korat, Oriental Shorthair, Russian Blue (q.v.), Scottish Fold, Singapura, Tonkinese, and the most popular of all short-hair breeds, Siamese (q.v.). Hairless cats, the Sphynx, which are rarely seen, are said to have been treasured pets of the Aztecs.

Genetic mutations perpetuated by selective breeding have produced such variants as the tailless Manx, the Scottish Fold with its ears carried close to the head, and the Rex with its kinky coat and curled whiskers.

THE CARE OF CATS

Cats are known for their ability to fend for themselves in the wild, but household pets, dependent on human beings for care and feeding, require considerable attention. Educational materials on the care of cats and responsible cat ownership are usually available through local humane societies.

Diseases in Cats. Regular checkups for cats by a veterinarian should be the first consideration of cat owners. Diseases contracted by cats include pneumonia, rabies (q.v.), skin ailments, worms, and feline enteritis. The last named, a highly contagious, often fatal disease, is now controlled by inoculations that are started while kittens are being weaned.

General Care. In addition to veterinary supervision, domestic cats require general attention from their owners. A balanced daily diet, such as provided by commercial cat foods, and a regular supply of fresh water are essential for good health and longevity. Regular cleaning of litter pans is also necessary for the animals' comfort and health. Cats' nails need frequent trimming; to prevent damage to furniture, animals that live indoors without access to trees should be provided with a scratching post. Cats also use trees to rub out dead hair from their coats; if they are allowed to lick themselves clean, especially during the semiannual shedding periods, hairballs may form in their stomachs. Indoor cats must therefore be brushed and combed a few times each week.

Fresh air and exercise are also necessary for domestic cats. Cats that do not get outdoors on their own should be leash-trained at an early age. Car training, in a protective carrying case or crate, is recommended for cats travelling with the family. Outdoor cats must be protected from traffic, poisoning, and injury from other animals.

Every year hundreds of thousands of unwanted cats and kittens are destroyed because homes cannot be found for them. Cats that have not been altered (that is, surgically treated to make them incapable of breeding) should not be allowed outdoors unless confined to an enclosure.

SHOWING AND JUDGING CATS

The showing of pedigreed cats requires considerable time and expense; judging calls for much knowledge and experience. Purebred cats are judged according to requirements for size, color, and conformation contained in a standard of perfection for each breed set by various cat associations that monitor cat clubs and shows.

Cat Shows. An ever-increasing number of local, regional, and national cat shows are held throughout the year in the U.S., with hundreds of cats competing for awards and best-of-breed and best-of-show titles.

Cat Associations. At present in the U.S. about six cat associations select cat show judges, schedule shows, and register pedigreed cats and kittens. These associations also award championships and ensure correct show procedures. The largest of these groups is the Cat Fanciers Association, Inc., with headquarters in Ocean, N.J.; as many as 80,000 animals are registered with them each year. Cat clubs and breeders choose which association they wish to join and by whose breed standards and rules they wish to abide.

CAT LORE

Cats have figured in the history of all nations, are the subject of much superstition and legend, and are a favorite subject of artists and writers.

History and Legend. Because of their extraordinary ability to keep down the rodent population in the grain fields along the Nile, cats became objects of worship when Egypt was known as the granary of the world. The Egyptian cat goddess Bast, or Bastet, depicted as having the body of a woman and the head of a cat, was the goddess of love and fertility as well. Egyptian cats were also used for sport by their owners. Attached to leashes, these animals hunted birds for the family table; a boomerang flung by the master brought the birds down and the cats, unleashed, would retrieve them. Because they were economically useful and were believed to ensure many children for a family, cats were so revered that they were mummified and buried either with their owners or in special cemeteries.

Despite Egyptian laws that forbade the removal of the sacred cats, Phoenician sailors smuggled them out of the country. Cats were traded along with other treasure from the Middle East and in antiquity could be found throughout the Mediterranean area. Archaeological evidence indicates that the Romans were the first to bring cats to the British Isles.

The value of cats as predators was recognized and appreciated in Europe in the middle of the 14th century, when the rat-borne Black Death, or plague, struck. Generally, however, during the Middle Ages cats were feared and hated. Because of their nocturnal habits, they were believed to consort with the devil. This association with witchcraft has been responsible for untold cruelties to cats down through the centuries. The Renaissance was, in contrast, the golden age for cats. Almost everyone had one, from members of royal families and their staffs to the peasantry.

The first domestic felines to arrive in North America were those that came over with the colonists and were employed to keep the rodent population under control in the settlers' fields, barns, and homes. Cats are said to have played an important part in keeping rats out of the California gold mines.

While cats served many practical purposes in Europe and America, in countries such as Siam and China they continued to be worshiped as deities. In India, although not worshiped, cats often played an important part in religious or occult ceremonies. In South America the Incas revered sacred cats, representations of which can be seen in pre-Columbian Peruvian artifacts.

Cats in Art and Literature. The earliest representations of the domestic cat were Egyptian tomb paintings and sculpture. By the 5th century BC images of cats appeared on Greek coins, and later they were depicted in Roman mosaics and paintings and on earthenware, coins, and shields. The 8th-century Irish manuscript of the Gospels, the *Book of Kells,* has a representation of cats and kittens in one of its illuminations. Later artists, such as Leonardo da Vinci and his German contemporary Albrecht Dürer, are among the many who included cats in their works.

Although the Old Testament makes no men-tion of cats, the Babylonian Talmud tells of their admirable qualities and encourages the breeding of cats "to help keep the houses clean." Memorable literary cats include the British writer Rudyard Kipling's "Cat That Walked by Himself" (one of the *Just So Stories,* 1902), the delightful cats of *Old Possum's Book of Practical Cats* (1939) by the Anglo-American poet T. S. Eliot, and the Cheshire Cat, joint creation of the English writer Lewis Carroll and the illustrator Sir John Tenniel in the children's classic *Alice's Adventures in Wonderland* (1865). In addition to the classics, comic-strip and animated-cartoon cats continue to delight ailurophiles (lovers of cats) of all ages.

Jo.B.

For further information on this topic, see the Bibliography in volume 28, sections 594-95, 598.

CATACOMBS, network of subterranean chambers and galleries used for burial purposes by peoples of the ancient Mediterranean world, especially the early Christians. By far the most important group are outside Rome. The word *catacomb* is probably derived from the Latin *ad catacumbas,* meaning "at the hollows," a phrase that referred to the chambers at a hollow south of Rome. The Romans at first buried their dead in family catacombs, which were excavated outside the city walls and protected by law, but later Romans preferred cremation. The Christians continued the practice of interring the dead in catacombs, which they called *koimetaria,* or "sleeping places," to suggest that, for a Christian, death was merely sleep before resurrection. By the 3d century the catacombs were administered by the church.

In its simplest form, a catacomb consisted of several underground galleries and chambers in a rectangular or grid plan. *Loculi* (recesses) were

An arcosolium (an arched cell that held a sarcophagus) in the catacombs southeast of Rome, beneath the Via Latina. Wall paintings depict the legend of Hercules and Alcestis.
Scala–Editorial Photocolor Archives

cut in the walls, one above another, to receive the bodies of from one to four family members. Persons of distinction were buried in stone coffins or carved sarcophagi placed in arched niches. The tombs of martyrs, usually in separate chambers, served as altars. As Christianity gained converts and burials multiplied, the catacombs were expanded into honeycombs of galleries. When one level was no longer sufficient, staircases were dug and a second, third, fourth, or even fifth level of galleries was excavated below. Many of the catacombs of prominent Christians were decorated with wall paintings depicting Christian symbols, such as the fish, lamb, and anchor, or with biblical scenes. Similar motifs were carved on tombs.

During times of persecution, the catacombs became places of refuge because burial places were sacrosanct by law. When churches above ground were destroyed by imperial order, worshipers met in the catacomb chapels. In the middle of the 3d century, as mobs and officials began to violate the catacombs, Christians destroyed the old entrances and made secret ones.

The persecution of the Christians came to an end with the conversion of the Roman emperor Constantine in the 4th century. Soon after, Pope Damasus I began a monumental restoration of the catacombs. By the 5th century, however, all burials were transferred to surface cemeteries connected with churches. The catacombs, especially the tombs of martyrs, became places of pilgrimage. In the unsettled period when Rome suffered waves of barbarian invaders, the catacombs were filled in to prevent desecration, their entrances sealed, and the remains of the martyrs transported to places of safety. From the 16th century, abandoned catacombs were gradually restored by the Roman Catholic church.

See also CRYPT; EARLY CHRISTIAN ART AND ARCHITECTURE; MAUSOLEUM.

CATALAN LANGUAGE, language that originated in Catalonia, a region in northeastern Spain. Catalan is spoken, in Spain, in the provinces of Gerona, Lérida, Barcelona, Tarragona, Castellón, Valencia, Alicante, and the Balearic Islands; in France, in nearly the whole of the Pyrénées-Orientales; and in parts of Cuba and Argentina.

The Catalan language is a Romance language. For years some philologists held that it was merely a dialectal offshoot of Provençal and that during the Middle Ages it had raised itself for a time to the dignity of a literary language. Subsequent research led other scholars to claim the complete independence of Catalan as a language. Ranged in the group of Hispanic languages, Catalan has a character as distinctive as that of Castilian, Portuguese, and Galician. Among the characteristics of Catalan are the following: A number of perfect participles are formed from the perfect stem instead of from the infinitive stem; the pronunciation of *b* and *v* has not merged; the voiced sound of intervocalic *s* has persisted; in unaccented final vowels, *a* is retained and other vowels are dropped; the Latin *au* is changed to *o* as in Castilian; final dentals are vocalized, which is held to be the essential characteristic of classic Catalan; noun declensions are totally absent; and the original pronunciation of the Latin *ū* is retained in cases in which French and Provençal use *ü*.

CATALAN LITERATURE, literature of Catalonia, a region in northeastern Spain. Under the influence of the splendor of the literary courts of independent Provençal potentates, the first Catalan poets adopted the verse forms of the troubadours of Provence and Toulouse. The 15th century was the Golden Age of Catalan poetry. During this period the language used in poetry as well as prose showed an increasing devotion to purely Catalan forms until it became an entirely native product. The greatest among the brilliant poets of this period was Ausías March (c. 1397–1460), a Valencian. The subsequent decline of Catalan poetry was caused not by a lessening of the genius of Catalan poets, but by the loss of independence of Aragón to Castile and the triumphant rise and spread of Castilian. A Catalan, Juan Boscán Almogáver (1493–1542), inaugurated in Castilian the use of Italian poetic forms.

Few important prose works were produced in Catalan before the end of the 13th century. The 15th-century chivalric novel *Tirant lo Blanc,* written by Joanot Martorell (1415?–80?), was translated into English in 1984. A humorous, ironic, yet compassionate account of the adventures of an imaginary knight, it gives vivid descriptions of the life of the time. Catalan writers produced very little other notable literature until the 19th-century renaissance. A major writer during the early years of this period was Buenaventura Carlos Ariba (1798–1862), whose *Oda a la patria,* written in 1833, is one of the best poems in modern Catalan. Other Catalan writers attained celebrity, including Mosén Jacinto Verdaguer (1845–1902), author of two epics; and Ángel Guimerá (1847–1924), poet and dramatist. Among important Catalan writers of the 20th century are the novelists Narcís Oller (1846–1930), Joaquim Ruyra (1858–1939), and Prudenci Bertrana (1867–1941) and the poets Joan Maragall (1860–1911) and Carles Riba Bracóns (1893–1959). Under the regime (1939–75) of the Spanish dictator Francisco Franco, all traces of Catalan autonomy were temporarily abolished; the use of the Catalan language has since revived, however.

CATALEPSY, nervous condition characterized by loss of voluntary motion and by a plastic rigidity of the muscles. The cataleptic state may occur as a symptom in epilepsy, narcolepsy, or schizophrenia and occasionally in hysteria (*see* MENTAL DISORDERS). Although circulation, respiration, digestion, and similar organic functions continue, they may be so reduced as to be almost imperceptible. In such cases catalepsy may resemble death, but ordinary tests are sufficient to distinguish it, even though sensibility to pain or heat may be lost.

CATALINA. *See* SANTA CATALINA.

CATALONIA (Span. *Cataluña*), region, NE Spain, comprising the provinces of Tarragona, Lérida, Barcelona, and Gerona. The shape of an inverted triangle, Catalonia is bounded on the N by the Pyrenees Mts., on the W by the region of Aragón, and on the E by the Mediterranean Sea. It is bisected by the Sierra Llena mountain range, which extends from the SW to the NE. Most of the territory is wooded and contains few meadows and little pastureland. Among the principal rivers are the Ebro, the Llobregat, and the Ter, which drain into the Mediterranean. The principal cities include the ports of Tarragona and Barcelona.

Corn, wheat, rye, flax, and licorice are cultivated; pigs, goats, and sheep are raised; and almonds, chestnuts, walnuts, figs, oranges, and grapes are grown in Catalonia. Among the main industries are fishing, wine making, the manufacture of cotton textiles, and potash mining.

Catalonia was an early possession of the Romans, who lost it to the Goths and Alans about 470 BC. The Moors conquered the region in AD 712, but were expelled 76 years later by Spaniards allied with Charlemagne. Frankish counts subsequently ruled Catalonia and made it an independent domain. In 1137 it was united with the kingdom of Aragón and later was included in the kingdom of Spain. The French held it as a possession from 1640 to 1659, from 1694 to 1697, and again from 1808 to 1813.

French influence in Catalonia contributed to the development of a distinct Catalan culture. In the 19th century a movement for cultural and governmental autonomy developed in Catalonia. In 1932, following the overthrow of King Alfonso XIII in the Spanish revolution of 1930–31, Catalonia was granted the right to have its own pres-

The Eastern (or Mediterranean) Pyrenees, the rocky foothills of which are seen here, form the northern boundary of the region of Catalonia. S. C. Bisserot–Bruce Coleman, Inc.

The village of Salardu in the mountainous province of Lérida in Catalonia.
Spanish National Tourist Office

ident and parliament, within the framework of the Spanish republic. In the Spanish civil war (1936–39), Catalonia supported the Republican cause against the counterrevolution led by Gen. Francisco Franco. Franco was victorious, and under his regime (1939–75) the autonomy of Catalonia was ended. In 1977, however, the Spanish government granted the Catalan provinces limited autonomy and permitted the reestablishment of the Generalitat, Catalonia's historical governing body, both legislature and executive council; its members are elected for 4-year terms.

Area, 31,930 sq km (12,328 sq mi); pop. (1981) 5,958,208.

For further information on this topic, see the Bibliography in volume 28, section 968.

CATALPA, common name of a tree, *Catalpa bignonioides,* of the family Bignoniaceae (*see* BIGNONIA). Native to the southern U.S., it is cultivated widely as an ornamental shade tree, growing to 12 m (40 ft) tall. It has silver-gray bark; widely spread branches; and large, pale green, heart-shaped leaves. The flowers are white, tinged and dotted with violet or purple. They are succeeded by long, beanlike pods, called Indian beans, that sometimes hang on the limbs all winter. The seeds are winged. Catalpa wood is light and fine and useful in cabinetwork.

CATALYSIS, alteration of the speed of a chemical reaction, through the presence of an additional substance, known as a catalyst, that remains chemically unchanged by the reaction. Enzymes (*see* ENZYME), which are among the most powerful catalysts, play an essential role in living organisms, where they accelerate reactions that otherwise would require temperatures that would destroy most of the organic matter.

A catalyst in a solution with—or in the same phase as—the reactants is called a homogeneous catalyst. The catalyst combines with one of the reactants to form an intermediate compound that reacts more readily with the other reactant. The catalyst, however, does not influence the equilibrium of the reaction, because the decomposition of the products into the reactants is speeded up to a similar degree. An example of homogeneous catalysis is the formation of sulfur trioxide by the reaction of sulfur dioxide with oxygen, in which nitric oxide serves as a catalyst. The reaction temporarily forms the intermediate compound nitrogen dioxide, which then reacts with oxygen to form sulfur oxide. The same amount of nitric oxide exists at the end as at the start of the reaction.

A catalyst that is in a separate phase from the reactants is said to be a heterogeneous, or contact, catalyst. Contact catalysts are materials with the capability of adsorbing (*see* ADSORPTION) molecules of gases or liquids onto their surfaces. An example of heterogeneous catalysis is the use of finely divided platinum to catalyze the reaction of carbon monoxide with oxygen to form carbon dioxide. This reaction is used in catalytic converters mounted in automobiles to eliminate carbon monoxide from the exhaust gases.

Some substances, called promoters, do not

have catalytic ability by themselves but increase the effectiveness of a catalyst. For example, if alumina is added to finely divided iron, it increases the ability of the iron to catalyze the formation of ammonia from a mixture of nitrogen and hydrogen. Materials that reduce the effectiveness of a catalyst, on the other hand, are referred to as poisons. Lead compounds reduce the ability of platinum to act as a catalyst; therefore, an automobile equipped with a catalytic converter for emission control must be fueled with unleaded gasoline.

Catalysts are of major importance in today's industrial world. It has been estimated that about 20 percent of the U.S. gross national product is generated through the use of catalytic processes. One current area of active research in catalysis is that of enzymes. Natural enzymes have long been used by a few industries, but fewer than 20 such enzymes are presently available in industrial amounts. Biotechnologists are seeking ways in which to expand this resource and also to develop semisynthetic enzymes for highly specific tasks.

CATALYTIC CONVERTER, device incorporated into an automobile's exhaust system to reduce the pollutants in the exhaust gases to environmentally harmless levels. Most converters are designed to pass the exhaust gases through a mass of small beads coated with palladium and platinum, which act as catalysts—in combination with an air pump and the heat of the gases, themselves—in converting such pollutants as carbon monoxide and various hydrocarbons to carbon dioxide and water. Lead-free gasoline must be used with such catalytic converters, or else the beads would become lead-coated and cease to function. Some converters deal with nitrogen oxide pollutants as well, yielding nitrogen gas.

A three-bowed catamaran, built for Johns Hopkins University as an oceanographic research vessel. UPI

CATAMARAN, name applied to any craft having twin hulls. Originally it denoted a form of sailing and paddling raft employed on the coasts of India. In a catamaran two similar or identical hulls are joined parallel to each other at some distance apart by beams or a platform. Such craft were highly developed in the Hawaiian, Marquesas, and Tuamotu islands and Tahiti. Some of these craft had hulls of unequal length.

The double hull probably was employed occasionally in ancient and medieval Europe to transport cargoes too heavy for the capacity of a single small hull. At least four sailing double-hull craft were built in England during the reign of King Charles II. A few double-hull gunboats were built in England at the end of the 18th century, and during the next century many double-hull pleasure craft, gunboats, and steamers were constructed and tested. The first U.S. Navy steam-propelled man-of-war, the USS *Demologos,* which was designed by the American inventor Robert Fulton, appears to have been a double-hull vessel. In both the U.S. and Europe during the 19th century, experiments were made with catamaran steamers up to 91 m (300 ft) in length. Power catamarans were found useful as ferries, dumping scows, research vessels, and river snag boats, as well as for salvage work.

In recent years the sailing catamaran has again become popular. In general, modern catamarans have returned to the original rigid-platform connection of the hulls (as opposed to the Herreshoff design, developed in 1876, in which the hulls could pitch independently). The advantage of the catamaran is that great stability can be combined with lightness and low water resistance. In general, however, all catamarans require large turning circles for their size. The sailing catamaran is, therefore, often slow in tacking. Structurally, large catamarans of the rigid-platform type are subject to very great strains in rough water, and some of the craft have broken up in heavy seas. The planing catamaran, which can skim on top of the water, has been developed to a limited degree in both power and sailing forms. The planing type requires rather large power to be effective. In recent years a triple-hull craft, called a trimaran (q.v.) has also been developed. H.I.C.

CATANIA, city in Italy, capital of Catania Province, on the E coast of Sicily, at the base of Mt. Etna. It is a major seaport and a commercial and manufacturing center. In the city are flour mills, sugar refineries, sulfur refineries, and asphalt and chemical factories. Catania contains numerous architectural remains of ancient times, including the ruins of Greek and Roman theaters and Roman aqueducts and baths. Also here are a cathedral (founded 11th cent.) and Ursino Castle (13th cent.). The University of Catania (1443), the first university established in Sicily, is here.

Catania, founded as a Greek colony in the 8th century BC, was captured by the Romans in 263 BC, during the First Punic War. It was plundered by the Normans in the late 11th century. It has suffered many earthquakes and volcanic eruptions and was severely damaged by bombing in World War II. Pop. (1983 est.) 382,800.

CATANZARO, city, S Italy, capital of Catanzaro Province and Calabria Region, near the Ionian Sea. The city is an important rail junction and a center of trade in wheat, oil, and wine. Founded in the 10th century, Catanzaro was famous in the 17th century for the silks, velvet, and damask produced here. Pop. (est.) 52,000.

CATAPULT, any of various engines of war used in ancient and medieval times to discharge javelins, darts, rocks, and other missiles. The larger kinds were mounted on a strong wooden platform; the trigger or projector of a gigantic crossbow was drawn back by ropes and held by a catch. Another type of catapult employed the principle of torsion to hurl heavy stones or objects over walls and across moats, cords being twisted by winches to pull back the propelling mechanism. Smaller hand-carried catapults were also used. *See* FORTIFICATION AND SIEGE WARFARE.

In modern naval warfare, airplanes are catapulted from the decks of aircraft carriers along a runner or track. The plane is propelled off the runner at flying speed by means of an explosive charge or by hydraulic or steam pressure.

CATARACT, in medicine, opaque condition of the lens of the eye or of its capsule. Its position behind the pupil readily distinguishes it from opacities of the cornea. Cataract may affect the lens alone (lenticular), or the front or back of the capsule of the lens (capsular), or both lens and capsule (capsulolenticular). Cataract is painless and unaccompanied by inflammation. It causes blindness by obstructing passage of light, but the patient can distinguish light from darkness.

Traumatic cataract results from a perforating wound of the capsule of the lens. The entire lens becomes opaque, and a portion usually remains so; but at times, unless inflammation of other portions follows, the cloudiness entirely disappears. Congenital cataract is due to imperfect development or to inflammation. Juvenile cataract may be hereditary. The lens is soft and white in both congenital and juvenile cataracts. Both are treated by "needling," an operation in which a needlelike knife or a laser beam is used to cut and break up the lens. The injured lens tissue is then absorbed by the body.

Senile cataract, the most important form, usually occurs in persons over 50 and generally involves both eyes. Beginning in the form of dark streaks extending from the periphery toward the center of the lens, or as spots in any portion, it eventually makes the entire lens opaque. As the fluid of the lens is absorbed, the lens becomes easily separated from its capsule and is considered mature, or "ripe" for operation. Later, if not extracted, the lens undergoes degenerative changes, or liquefies, and the capsule becomes thickened and opaque, making the results of operation less satisfactory. The only method of relieving senile cataract is extraction of the lens. Special glasses worn after the operation restore partial sight. Recently, scientists have developed an artificial lens that is implanted in the eye after operation and restores sight to many patients.

CATASTROPHE THEORY, term for an attempt to develop a more satisfactory mathematical modeling system for dealing with sharply discontinuous natural events than can be provided by differential calculus. One such physical "catastrophe," for example, would be the sudden yielding of metal to strain. Catastrophe theory was first presented in 1968 by the French mathematician René Thom (1923-), and it attracted many researchers in the 1970s. Intended to be useful for discontinuous events in the biological and social sciences, the theory has since been criticized as impractical.

CATAVI MASSACRE, violent confrontation on Dec. 21, 1942, between Bolivian soldiers on the one hand and tin miners and their families on the other at the Catavi mining camp north of Uncía. The clash was the result of unionization efforts by the miners to alleviate poor living and working conditions in the mining camps, which included unsanitary housing, inadequate medical care, low wages, and hazardous labor conditions. These attempts to unionize were met with implacable opposition by the government. A strike called by the workers in late 1942 culminated shortly before Christmas in a demonstration by unarmed strikers and their families. Facing a contingent of troops, they were ordered to disperse.

When the order was ignored, the soldiers fired. Hundreds of miners were killed, as well as many women and children. In the spate of international indignation that followed, some improvements were made in the camps.

CATBIRD, common name for an American songbird, *Dumetella carolinensis,* of the family Mimidae (*see* MOCKINGBIRD). The catbird is about 25 cm (about 10 in) long and is slate gray except for a black crown and tail and a chestnut-colored region under the tail. The name refers to the mewing call of the bird, but, like its relatives, the catbird can engage in ornate song and mimicry of other birds; it is therefore often called the gray mockingbird. Ranging as far north as southern Canada in the summer, the catbird winters in the Gulf states and in Mexico.

CATEAU-CAMBRÉSIS, TREATY OF, peace treaty between Henry II of France and Philip II of Spain and Philip's ally, England, signed in the town of Cateau-Cambrésis (now Le Cateau), France, on April 3, 1559. By the terms of the treaty, France returned most of the territories in the Low Countries and Italy, which it had taken from Spain, but retained the bishoprics of Toul, Verdun, and Metz. The treaty reaffirmed control by Spain over the greater part of the Italian Peninsula and England's surrender of Calais to France.

CATECHISM, a manual of Christian doctrine drawn up in the form of questions and answers, especially one for religious instruction. The first such manual was compiled by the English scholar Alcuin in the 8th century and was followed in the next 100 years by many others, among them those of Notker Labeo (952?-1022), monk of the Abbey of Saint Gall, in Switzerland, and of the German monk Otfried of Weissenburg (800?-80?) in Alsace. At an early period in the history of the Reformation, catechisms became important because of Martin Luther's insistence on the religious instruction of children. After Luther published his primer of religion, *A Brief Explanation of the Ten Commandments, the Creed, and the Lord's Prayer* (1520), several catechisms were prepared by leading Protestant theologians. Luther's visitation of the Saxon churches in 1528 led to preparation of his Larger and Smaller Catechisms (1529). The Reformed churches also published catechisms. The most noteworthy are the Geneva and Heidelberg catechisms, and those of the German theologian Johannes Oecolampadius, in Basel in 1526, and of the Swiss reformer Heinrich Bullinger, in Zürich in 1555. The Geneva Catechisms, Larger and Smaller, were the work of the French Protestant theologian John Calvin. The Smaller was published in French in 1536; the Larger appeared in French in 1541 or 1542, was translated into various languages, and became an acknowledged standard of the Reformed churches.

The Heidelberg, or Palatinate, Catechism was compiled in Heidelberg by the German theologians Caspar Olevianus (1536-87) and Zacharias Ursinus (1534-83), at the request of the Elector Frederick III (1515-76) of the Palatinate. It was published in 1563 and has been translated into all the languages of Europe. It is the standard of the Dutch and German Reformed churches of America. The Protestant religious doctrines of the Socinians are embodied in the greater and smaller Racovian Catechisms (Raków, Poland, 1605). Besides a catechism of 1660, in the form of a conversation between father and son, said to have been written by the English founder of the Society of Friends, George Fox, the Quakers have that of the Scottish writer Robert Barclay, which appeared in 1673.

In the Roman Catholic church, the first official catechism, prepared by the Council of Trent and published in 1566, was known as the *Roman Catechism,* or the *Catechism of Pius V.* It was not a textbook, but a compendium of doctrine for the guidance of pastors and teachers. Catechisms for popular use were prepared by the German Jesuit Peter Canisius and published in 1555-58. In the U.S., a committee of American bishops of the Third Plenary Council of Baltimore, Md., published the Baltimore Catechism in 1885.

The catechism of the Church of England in the smaller form, published in the Book of Common Prayer, is in two parts. The first contains and explains the Baptismal Covenant, the Creed, the Ten Commandments, and the Lord's Prayer; and the second explains the two sacraments, baptism and the Eucharist. The catechism was originally published in the reign of King Edward VI, was condemned as heretical in the reign of Queen Mary I and underwent several modifications from 1549 to 1661. The first part of the catechism, once known as the Shorter Catechism, at the Hampton Court Conference (1604) was considered too short. Accordingly, at the suggestion of King James I, the explanation of the two sacraments that now form the second part of the church catechism was added.

The Larger and Shorter Catechisms, which, with the Westminster Confession of Faith, are the standard catechisms of the Presbyterian churches throughout the countries of the former British Empire and the U.S., were compiled by the Assembly of Divines at Westminster (1645-52). In July 1648, the General Assembly of the Church of Scotland adopted both the Larger and Shorter Catechisms.

Emphasis on the use of a catechism, particularly its memorization by rote, has diminished in recent years.

CATEGORICAL IMPERATIVE, term coined by the German philosopher Immanuel Kant to designate what he considered an absolute moral law in which reason was inherent. "So act," he wrote, "that the moral of thy doing shall, at thy will, become universal law." In Kant's view the categorical imperative was an injunction, to be obeyed as a moral duty, regardless of an individual's impulses, to produce a humanitarian society based on reason, and thus created by free will.

CATERPILLAR, larval stage of butterflies and moths, members of the order Lepidoptera, and corresponding in this special order to the grub, maggot, or larva phase in the life history of other insects. The caterpillar develops like any other larva from the segmented egg and differentiating embryo and undergoes several moltings, or ecdyses. It later falls into a quiescent pupa stage, and the pupa is usually sheathed in a silken cocoon. It may be fixed or free, suspended by one thread or more to leaf or branch, or hidden underground. *See* BUTTERFLIES AND MOTHS.

Comparatively few caterpillars reach maturity. Many are destroyed by weather, by birds, reptiles, and other animals, and by insect pests of the families Ichneumonidae, such as the ichneumon fly; Tachinariae, such as the tachina fly; and Carabidae, such as the caterpillar hunter. The ichneumon flies pierce the caterpillars and make them receptacles for their eggs and the edible cradles of their larvae.

CATERPILLAR HUNTER, common name for a predatory beetle of the genus *Calosoma,* of the family Carabidae (*see* GROUND BEETLE). It is a large, brightly colored, nocturnal beetle. Several species prey on caterpillars and earthworms. *C. scrutator* is a common American species, and *C. sycophanta* was imported into the U.S. in large numbers to combat the brown-tail moth.

CAT FAMILY, common name for the Felidae, an almost exclusively meat-eating family of mammals of the order Carnivora (*see* CARNIVORE) that are superbly adapted for their typically predatory life. All members of the family are closely similar in having a lithe and agile soft-furred body, acute vision and hearing, and claws and teeth that are highly adapted for grasping and tearing. The seven genera, containing 36 species, are found in all parts of the world except Antarctica, Australia, and a few Oceanic islands. The tiger, lion, jaguar, and leopard, the so-called big cats, constitute the

Caterpillar, or larval stage, of a Baltimore butterfly, Euphydras phaeton. J. Shaw–Bruce Coleman, Inc.

genus *Panthera* (formerly *Leo*). The clouded leopard is the sole species in the genus *Neofelis,* as is the snow leopard of the genus *Uncia.* Two species of the cheetah, *Acinonyx jubatus* and *A. rex,* make up the genus *Acinonyx.* Nine species of the Felidae family occur in the western hemisphere, of which the best known are the puma, cougar, or mountain lion, *Felis concolor;* the lynx, *Lynx canadensis;* the bobcat, *Lynx rufus;* the ocelot, *F. pardalis;* and the jaguar, *P. onca.*

Cats as a family have characteristically short faces and small, broad skulls. The ears are erect and readily rotate to pick up sound or to signal intention; they range in shape from round to pointed. The strong jaws do almost no grinding; food is cut and chopped with a tooth formation in the upper and lower jaws of six incisors, two canines, four or six premolars, and two molars. The molar is modified to a formidable shearing tooth, or carnassial, and three incisors. The tongue is covered with sharp, backward-slanted projections, or papillae, which help to clean the flesh from the bones of animal prey. The paws are well padded; the forefeet have five toes and the hindfeet have four. All cats are digitigrade, that is, they walk on the toes with the back part of the foot raised. The claws are long, sharp, and, with the sole exception of the cheetah, completely retractile, that is, they can be drawn in so that the paw can be used without scratching or ripping. Cats have certain characteristic traits such as sharpening the claws and washing the face with the front paws.

Most cats hunt in dim light. They either stalk their prey or lie in wait and spring upon their quarry unexpectedly. They generally hunt alone or in family parties, relying mostly on their sight and hearing. Their sense of smell is also keen but is usually employed in the examination of the kill. The pupils of the eyes, which contract to vertical slits during the daytime, become rounded and greatly expanded in the dark.

Species of cat that live in cold regions are covered with long, soft fur. The male is usually longer and heavier than the female but otherwise has about the same coloring and build. All cats except the lion are thought to be monogamous. Offspring are usually two to three in number in the larger species and may be up to five in the smaller. See individual articles on the cats named. *See also* CAT, DOMESTIC.

For further information on this topic, see the Bibliography in volume 28, sections 440, 461–63, 475, 480, 598.

CATFISH, common name for fish of the order Siluriformes, or Nematognathi, of the superorder Otophysi, or Ostariophysi. The order contains 25 to 31 families and about 2000 species, of which some 1200 are South American. Two families, the Ariidae and the Plotosidae, are primarily marine. All other families inhabit fresh water. Catfishes are mostly nocturnal scavengers, living near the bottom in shallow waters.

The name catfish is derived from the feelers, or barbels, that extend from each side of the upper jaw of the fish and, in some species, from the lower jaw also, suggesting the whiskers of a cat. The dorsal and pectoral fins are often edged with sharp spines, in some cases poisonous, which are used as weapons and can inflict severe wounds. Members of two primitive catfish families in South America are covered with bony plates. A European species, the sheatfish or wels, *Silurus glanis,* of the family Siluridae, is the largest catfish, reportedly reaching a weight of 290 kg (650 lb) and a length of almost 4 m (13 ft).

Of the numerous species of North American catfish, of the family Ictaluridae, the bullhead, *Ictalurus nebulosus,* is commonly fished for eating. Of greatest commercial importance are catfish of the genus *Ictalurus* in the Mississippi River valley and the Gulf states, some of which weigh as much as 70 kg (150 lb). The species *I. furcatus,* the blue catfish, or chucklehead, and *I. punctatus,* the channel cat, the flesh of which is esteemed as equal to that of black bass, form the major part of the catch.

The blind catfish, *Gronias nigrilabris,* found in caverns in eastern Pennsylvania, has atrophied eyes, and the electric catfish of the Nile River and tropical central Africa, *Malapterurus electricus,* is capable of giving an electric shock (*see* ELECTRIC FISH). Another odd catfish, the so-called walking catfish, *Clarias batrachus,* was discovered in 1968 near Boca Raton, Fla. This species was originally imported from eastern India and Southeast Asia by tropical-fish dealers. Its maximum length is 56 cm (22 in). In "walking" to areas of deeper water in dry spells, this catfish moves by a slithering motion combined with a thrashing of its tail. In addition, a stout spine in each pectoral fin digs into the ground to help balance and propel the fish. In order for the fish to breathe air, the rear part of each gill has evolved into a form of lung. K.A.C.

CATGUT, tough, membranous cord made from the intestines of certain animals. It is used primarily for surgical sutures, strings of musical instruments, and tennis racket strings. Because the intestines of hogs, horses, and sheep are used for the cord, the name *catgut* is a misnomer of uncertain origin. The intestines are first cleaned, scraped, and cured and then dried and polished before being woven into cords.

CATHARI (Gr. *katharos,* "pure"), name assumed by many widely diffused heretical Christian sects of the Middle Ages. The Cathari were characterized by a rigid asceticism and by a dualistic theology based on the belief that the universe comprised two conflicting worlds, the spiritual world created by God and the material world created by Satan. Their views were based on the religious doctrine of Manichaeism (q.v).

Under the general name of Cathari were included the Novatians, a sect originating in the 3d century that advocated the denial of church membership to "fallen" Christians. The Paulicians were a kindred sect; they had been transported to the region of Thrace in southeastern Europe in the 9th century and united with the Bogomils. In the second half of the 12th century the Cathari were in great strength in Bulgaria, Albania, and Slavonia. They divided into two branches, distinguished as the Albanenses (absolute dualists) and the Garatenses (moderate dualists). In Italy the heresy appeared in the 11th and 12th centuries. The Milanese adherents of the heresy were known as Patarini (or Patarines), from Pataria, a street in Milan frequented by rag gatherers. The Patarine movement assumed some importance in the 11th century as a reform movement, emphasizing action by laypeople against a corrupt clergy.

The Cathari reached their greatest numbers in southern France; here they were called Albigenses (q.v.) or Poblicants, the latter term being a corruption of Paulicians, with whom they were confused. By the late 14th century, however, the Cathari had all but disappeared. Their decline was caused, for the most part, by a rise in the popularity of mendicant orders. The only extant Catharist writing is a short ritual in the Romance language of the 13th-century troubadours.

CATHARSIS, in psychology, term used to describe the therapeutic release of emotions that cause tension or anxiety. In their early work on hysteria, Sigmund Freud and Josef Breuer (1842-1925) used hypnosis as a means of treatment. Under hypnosis some patients were able to relate and reexperience repressed conflicts or emotion-producing incidents. Bringing these experiences to the surface generally enabled the patients to release tensions and reduce the symptoms of their illness. Freud referred to this as "cathartic therapy." He later achieved this effect without hypnosis by using free association with his patients.

The process of catharsis always involves bringing repressed emotions to a conscious level. Talking about disturbing feelings and events may bring superficial relief, but only catharsis through some form of therapy can lead to a long-lasting elimination of the symptoms.

CATHEDRAL, the principal church of a diocese. *See* CHURCH.

CATHER, Willa Sibert (1873-1947), one of America's foremost novelists, whose carefully crafted prose conveys vivid pictures of the American landscape and the people it molded.

Cather was born Dec. 7, 1873, near Winchester, Va. When she was about 10 years old her family moved to Red Cloud, Nebr., which is the setting for a number of her best-known novels and short stories. Educated at the University of Nebraska, Cather was a newspaperwoman and teacher in Pittsburgh before coming to New York City in 1906 to work as an editor on *McClure's Magazine.*

From her college years on Cather had written short stories and poetry; her first published book was a collection of verse, *April Twilights* (1903); her first prose was a group of stories, *The Troll Garden* (1905). Not until 1913, however, after having resigned from *McClure's,* did Cather devote herself solely to writing. Her earliest novels, *O Pioneers!* (1913), *The Song of the Lark* (1915), and *My Ántonia* (1918), depict the resolute, dignified life of immigrant farm families on the Great Plains, in contrast to that of the native-born town dwellers. Cather also used the prairie setting in her next two novels, *One of Ours* (1922), which won a Pulitzer Prize for fiction in 1923, and *A Lost Lady* (1923). In these her theme is the contrast between encroaching urbanization and the achievements of the pioneers. In *Death Comes for the Archbishop* (1927), considered by some critics her greatest novel, she deals with the missionary experiences of a Roman Catholic bishop among the Indians of New Mexico. Several trips through the Southwest provided the stimulus for this work, as well as for sections of *The Professor's House* (1925) and *The Song of the Lark.* As early as 1909, however, in her haunting short story "The Enchanted Bluff," the mesas and the ancient people who had dwelt there had captured Cather's imagination. In *Shadows on the Rock* (1931) she went further afield to describe French Roman Catholic life in 17th-century Québec. *Sapphira and the Slave Girl,* her last novel and her only book set in the South, the land of her forebears, was published in 1940. Cather died on April 24, 1947, in New York City.

CATHERINE I, real name MARTA SKAVRONSKAYA (1682?-1727), empress of Russia (1725-27). Of peasant origin, she was born in Jakobstadt (now Jēkabpils, Latvian SSR) but was early orphaned and reared by a pastor in Marienburg (now Malbork, Poland). When the Russians captured Marienburg in 1702, she was taken prisoner by the Russian commander, who sold her to Prince Aleksandr Menshikov (1673-1729), a close adviser of Peter the Great. She soon became Peter's mistress and most influential counselor. Peter, who had divorced his first wife in 1699, married Catherine in 1712. After his son Alexis (1690-1718) died, Peter issued an *ukaz* ("imperial order") declaring his right to name his own successor; he died in 1725 without doing so. Catherine, however, had been crowned empress-consort in 1724, and on Peter's death she was proclaimed his successor; the claims of Alexis's son (later Peter III) were bypassed. Shrewd and courageous, Catherine defended Peter's advisers against his rages, and in her own reign she established, and concentrated power in, the supreme privy council. Two of her eight children by Peter survived, Anna (mother of Peter III) and Elizabeth Petrovna (empress 1741-62).

CATHERINE OF ALEXANDRIA, Saint (d. early 4th cent.), Christian virgin and martyr, whose historical actuality is doubtful. Although she was a popular early martyr, she is not mentioned before the 10th century, and little is known about her. According to legend, she was extremely learned even as a child. In Alexandria she rebuked the Roman emperor Maxentius (r. 306-12) for his persecution of Christians and converted the philosophers he had ordered to debate with her. Maxentius condemned her to be broken on the wheel, but, by a miracle, the wheel collapsed. She was subsequently beheaded. Her traditional feast day, November 25, was dropped from the Roman Catholic calendar in 1969.

CATHERINE OF ARAGÓN (1485-1536), queen consort of England (1509-33), the first wife of King Henry VIII and the daughter of Ferdinand V and Isabella I, king and queen of Aragón and Castile. Catherine was born in Alcalá de Henares, Spain. She occupies a prominent place in history, because the question of her marriage to Henry was a factor in the Reformation in England. Henry's father, King Henry VII, hoped to form a binding alliance with Spain when he negotiated the marriage of Catherine and his son Arthur, prince of Wales (1486-1502). She went to England in 1501 and was married in November, but Arthur died in April 1502. A few months later Henry VII arranged a second marriage for Catherine with his second son Henry, then 12 years old. A papal dispensation enabling Henry to marry the widow of his brother was obtained in 1503. Henry succeeded to the throne in April 1509 and in June he married Catherine.

Although the marriage was, on the whole, fairly successful, the pro-Spanish sympathies of Catherine brought some difficulties during the periods of French alliance. Catherine bore Henry six children, only one of whom, a daughter, later Queen Mary I, survived.

In 1527 Henry tried to annul his marriage to Catherine so that he could marry Anne Boleyn, who he hoped would give him a male heir to the throne. The pope refused to make a decision on the proposed annulment, and in 1533 Henry was married to Anne by the archbishop of Canterbury. In 1534 the pope finally declared that the first marriage was valid, thus bringing about the alienation of Henry VIII from the Roman Catholic church. Catherine did not quit the kingdom, but was thereafter closely guarded. During this time she displayed heroic courage and steadfastly refused to sign away her rights and those of Mary.

For further information on this person, see the section Biographies in the Bibliography in volume 28.

CATHERINE DE MÉDICIS (1519-89), queen of France (1547-59) and mother of the last three Valois kings of France. She was a major force in French politics during the 30 years of Roman Catholic-Huguenot wars and an instigator of the St. Bartholomew's Day Massacre.

Catherine was born on April 13, 1519, in Florence, Italy, the daughter of the Florentine ruler Lorenzo de' Medici, called Lorenzo the Magnificent. In 1533 she married the duc d'Orléans, who became king of France in 1547 as Henry II. She had little power during the reign of her husband and that of her first son, Francis II, but on Francis's death in 1560 the government fell entirely into her hands. She ruled as regent for her second son, Charles IX, until he reached his majority in 1563, and she continued to dominate him for the duration of his reign.

Political Role. In her determination to preserve royal power at any cost, Catherine devoted her energies to maintaining a balance between the Protestant group known as the Huguenots, led by the French military leader Gaspard de Coligny, and the Roman Catholics, led by the powerful house of Guise. During the religious civil wars that began in 1562, Catherine, a Roman Catholic, usually supported the Catholics; sometimes, however, political expediency led her to switch her support to the Huguenots. Her political manipulations also affected the personal affairs of her family. In 1560 she arranged for her daughter, Elizabeth of Valois (1545-68), to become the third wife of the powerful Roman Catholic king of Spain, Philip II. In 1572 Catherine found it propitious to marry another daughter, Margaret of Valois, to the Protestant king Henry of Navarre, who later became Henry IV,

Catherine de Médicis, in an 18th-century French copper engraving. Granger Collection

king of France. Later in 1572 she found the growing Huguenot influence over her son Charles, the French king, frightening; accordingly, she instigated the assassination of the Protestant leader Coligny and the death of 50,000 other Huguenots in the St. Bartholomew's Day Massacre (1572). After the death of Charles in 1574 and the accession to the throne of her third son as Henry III, Catherine's power declined. She died in Blois, France, on Jan. 5, 1589.

Art Patron. Apart from her political role, Catherine was a patron of the arts. Her interest in architecture was demonstrated in the building of a new wing of the Louvre Museum, in initiating construction of the Tuileries gardens, and in building the château of Monceau. Her personal library, containing numerous rare manuscripts, was renowned in Renaissance France.

CATHERINE THE GREAT (1729–96), empress of Russia (1762–96), the second of that name, who continued the process of Westernization begun by Peter the Great and made Russia a European power.

Originally named Sophie Fredericke Auguste von Anhalt-Zerbst, Catherine was born in Stettin (now Szczecin, Poland) on May 2, 1729, the daughter of a minor German prince. In 1745, she married Grand Duke Peter of Holstein, heir to the Russian throne. The marriage was an unhappy one, but the intelligent and ambitious Catherine soon managed to build up a circle of supporters in Saint Petersburg (now Leningrad). In 1754 she gave birth to a son, the future emperor Paul (d. 1801). Her husband succeeded to the throne as Peter III in 1761. Erratic, unstable, and contemptuous of his Russian subjects, he soon alienated several important groups in Russian society. On July 9, 1762, following a pattern well established in 18th-century Russia, the Imperial Guards overthrew him and placed Catherine on the throne in his stead.

Catherine and the Enlightenment. Catherine was well acquainted with the literature of the French Enlightenment, which was an important influence in her own political thinking. She corresponded extensively with Voltaire and Denis Diderot, gave financial support to them and a number of other French writers, and played host to Diderot at her court in 1773. Although this activity was partly aimed at creating a favorable image in Western Europe, she was probably sincere in her interest and her hope to apply some of the ideas of the Enlightenment to rationalize and reform the administration of the Russian Empire. Despite her interest in legal reform, however, the commission she appointed for that purpose in 1767 failed to accomplish its goals. Among Catherine's more benevolent achievements were the foundation of the first Russian schools for girls and of a medical college to provide health care for her subjects.

In the early years of her reign, Catherine sought to win the support of the Russian gentry, and, in particular, of a small group of nobles. She

Catherine the Great

confirmed Peter III's emancipation of the gentry from compulsory military service, granted them many other privileges, and showered her supporters with titles, offices, state lands, and serfs to work their fields. Thus, despite a professed abhorrence for serfdom, she did much to expand that institution by transferring state-owned serfs to private landowners, extending serfdom to newly acquired territories, and greatly increasing the legal control of the gentry over their serfs.

Later Conservatism. Peasant unrest culminated in a great revolt (1773-75), led by the cossack Yemelyan Pugachov (1726-75), that raged over much of the Volga River Basin and the Urals before it was finally crushed by military force. The revolt marked a turn toward a more reactionary internal policy. The cossack army was disbanded, and other cossacks were granted special privileges in an effort to transform them into loyal supporters of the autocracy. In 1775 a major reform of provincial administration was undertaken in an effort to ensure better control of the empire. A major reform of urban administration was also promulgated. The French Revolution increased Catherine's hostility toward liberal ideas. Several outspoken critics of serfdom such as Nikolay I. Novikov (1744-1818) and Aleksandr N. Radishchev (1749-1802), were imprisoned, and Catherine seems to have been planning to join a European coalition against France when she died on Nov. 17, 1796, in St. Petersburg.

Under Catherine, the territory of the Russian Empire was greatly expanded. As a result of two wars against the Ottoman Empire (1768-74 and 1787-91) and the annexation of the Crimea (1783), Russia gained control of the northern coast of the Black Sea. Russian control over Poland-Lithuania was also greatly extended, culminating in the annexation of large tracts of territory in the three partitions of Poland (1772, 1793, 1795).

Character of the Reign. One characteristic of Catherine's reign was the important role played by her lovers, or favorites. Ten men occupied this semiofficial position, and at least two, Grigory Orlov (1734-83) and Grigory Potemkin, were important in formulating foreign and domestic policy. Although assessments of Catherine vary, she undoubtedly played a key role in the development of Russia as a modern state. R.H.S.

For further information on this person, see the section Biographies in the Bibliography in volume 28.

CATHERINE OF SIENA, Saint (1347-80), Dominican nun (tertiary), mystic, and Doctor of the Church, who played a significant role in the public affairs of her day.

Originally named Caterina Benincasa, she was born in Siena, Italy, on March 25, 1347, to a family of modest means. She probably learned to read at an early age but could not write until she was an adult. Even as a child she claimed to have visions and lived austerely. At the age of 16, she joined the Third Order of St. Dominic in Siena, where she became noted for her gift of contemplation and her devotion to the poor. She soon began to dictate letters on spiritual matters that won her even more admiration. In 1374 Raymond of Capua (c. 1330-99), future master general of the Dominican order, became her spiritual director and was from then on closely associated with all her activities.

In 1376 Catherine journeyed to Avignon to plead with Pope Gregory XI on behalf of Florence, then at war with the papacy. Although she failed in this mission, she convinced the pope to return to Rome and end the Avignonese exile of the popes. Catherine returned to contemplation and works of mercy in Siena and simultaneously tried to promote peace in Italy and a crusade to recover the Holy Land, long one of her favorite projects. Deeply distressed by the Great Schism (*see* SCHISM, GREAT), which broke out in 1378, she went to Rome in November to rally support for Pope Urban VI and work for unity. She died there on April 29, 1380; her body is buried in the Church of Saint Maria sopra Minerva. She was canonized by Pope Pius II in 1461 and made a Doctor of the Church in 1970; her feast day is April 29. J.W.O.

CATHERINE OF VALOIS (1401-37), queen consort of England (1420-22), wife of Henry V, king of England, and daughter of Charles VI, king of France, born in Paris. When she was 12 years old, Henry V renewed the negotiations begun by his father for a marriage with Catherine. Henry demanded a large dowry and the French regions of Aquitaine and Normandy. The proposition was rejected, and in 1415 Henry invaded France and forced compliance with his terms. When he married Catherine in Troyes, France, in June 1420, he received the provinces claimed, the regency of France during the life of Charles, and the right to succeed to the French throne after Charles's death. In February 1421 Catherine was crowned at Westminster Abbey, and in December she bore a son, later King Henry VI. After the death of Henry V in 1422, Catherine's union with the Welsh squire Owen Tudor produced four children. One of her sons, Edmund Tudor, earl of Richmond (1430?-56), married Margaret Beaufort; their son became Henry VII, the first Tudor king of England.

CATHODE. *See* ELECTRODE.

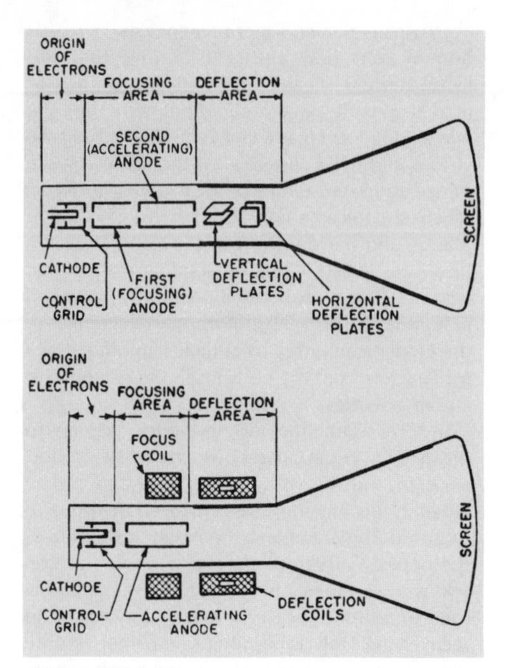

Diagrams of two types of cathode-ray tubes used in electronic systems. General Electric Co.

CATHODE RAY, a high-speed electron emitted by the negative electrode of a vacuum tube when an electric current is passed through it. Cathode rays were first generated by means of the Crookes tube, an invention of the British physicist Sir William Crookes. While conducting research, the German physicist Wilhelm Roentgen in 1895 accidentally discovered that cathode rays striking a metal target produce X rays. Cathode rays can be deflected and focused by magnetic fields. These properties are utilized in the electron microscope, in the cathode-ray oscilloscope, and in the image tube of a television receiver. *See* ELECTRON; ELECTRONICS; TELEVISION.

CATHODE-RAY TUBE, an electron tube, or evacuated glass container, having at one end a cathode, or negative electrode, and a device called an electron gun that projects a beam of electrons against a luminescent screen at the opposite end of the tube. A bright spot of light appears wherever the electrons strike the screen. Cathode-ray tubes, or CRTs, are used as picture tubes in television receivers and as visual display screens in radar-receiving equipment, computer installations, and oscilloscopes (*see* COMPUTER; OSCILLOSCOPE; RADAR; TELEVISION).

Electrons are emitted from a heated cathode in the electron gun. A series of grids having a positive potential with respect to the cathode accelerate the electrons as they pass. The electrons next pass through a series of doughnut-shaped anodes that focus the stream of electrons so that they strike the luminescent screen as a fine point. Between the electron gun and the screen are either two sets of electric deflecting plates or two sets of magnetic deflecting rings. Electric deflecting plates are used in small CRTs, whereas magnetic deflecting rings are used in large CRTs in which a large deflection is required, as in television tubes.

In CRTs containing electric deflecting plates, a horizontal pair of plates controls the up-and-down motion of the electron beam, and a vertical pair controls the left-to-right motion of the beam. In each pair of plates, one plate has a negative charge of electricity, and the other plate has a positive charge. If the charges are equal in value, the beam will strike the center of the luminescent screen. If the charges are unequal, the electron beam will be deflected. The amount of deflection depends on the voltage applied to the plates. As the signal applied to the horizontal plates varies, so will the spot of light on the face of the tube, which will move up or down in response to the changes in voltage. If the voltage of the vertical plates is varied, the beam of electrons can be made to sweep horizontally across the face of the tube.

Magnetic deflecting rings work in an analogous manner, except that the electron beam is deflected by variations in the strength of the magnetic fields through which the beam must pass.

CATHOLIC CHURCH. The term *catholic* (Gr. *katholikos,* "universal," from *katholou,* "in general") was first used in the letter of St. Ignatius of Antioch to the Smyrnaeans (about AD 110). The term was later used by Clement of Alexandria in his *Stromata* (Miscellanies). The technical use of the word seems to have been established by the beginning of the 3d century. The formal principle of the Catholic church was expressed by the French theologian Vincent of Lérins as follows: "That which has been believed everywhere, always, and by all. This is what is truly and properly catholic."

CATHOLIC EMANCIPATION ACT, statute of the British Parliament, passed in 1829, enabling Roman Catholics in Great Britain and Ireland to vote and hold many public offices. The act superseded earlier anti-Catholic laws, some of which dated from the time of King Henry VIII in the 16th century. The gradual granting of British liberties to Catholics began in 1778, when Catholics were permitted to buy and inherit land if they swore loyalty to the king. A second relief measure, sponsored by Prime Minister William Pitt the Younger, was passed in 1791. This law granted Catholics the right to serve in the military, practice law, worship, and organize religious schools. Irish Catholics, who had been given wider freedoms in the 1790s, were subjected to the British restrictions when Ireland was united with Great Britain in 1801. Catholic agitation led to the formation of the Roman Catholic Association (1823) by the Irish statesman Daniel O'Connell and finally to passage of the Roman Catholic Relief Bill, better known as the Catholic Emancipation Act, in April 1829. The act, introduced by the home secretary, Sir Robert Peel, through the efforts of O'Connell, provided for Catholics' admission to Parliament. Certain disabilities still existed, however, some of which lingered until 1926. In 1910, language offensive to Roman Catholics was removed from the British coronation ceremonies.

CATHOLIC UNIVERSITY OF AMERICA, institution of higher learning, in Washington, D.C., and affiliated with the Roman Catholic church. The university was chartered by Congress and opened for instruction in 1889. The board of trustees comprises 30 members, of whom at least 15 must be lay, together with some U.S. cardinals in an ex officio capacity. Among the various divisions of the university are the undergraduate and graduate colleges of arts and sciences, the school of education, engineering and architecture, law, music, philosophy, religious studies, social service, and nursing. The degrees of bachelor, master, and doctor are conferred. Numerous residence and study halls are maintained by various Roman Catholic religious orders for their student members.

CATILINE, full name LUCIUS SERGIUS CATILINA (108?–62 BC), Roman political leader and conspirator. He was a partisan of Lucius Sulla, whom he succeeded as quaestor, or judge, in 77 BC. Catiline was also praetor, or magistrate, in 68 and governor of the province of Africa in the following year. Shortly thereafter he was falsely accused of misconduct and was thus prevented from becoming a candidate for consul, or chief magistrate. Catiline was acquitted of the charges, and in 63 he again ran for consul against the statesman and orator Marcus Cicero. Losing again to Cicero, Catiline hatched a plot to seize power by armed insurrection. Cicero, informed of the conspiracy, exposed it, delivering his famous first oration against Catiline: *Quousque tandem abutere, Catilina, patientia nostra?* ("How long now, Catiline, will you abuse our patience?"). After a second oration, in which Cicero was able to present tangible evidence of the plot, Catiline and his coconspirators were proclaimed public enemies. He was killed in battle near Pistoia in central Italy.

CATLIN, George (1796–1872), American painter and writer, born in Wilkes-Barre, Pa., whose art was self-taught. Eager to preserve a record of vanishing types and customs of the American Indians, Catlin traveled for years in North and South America, painting and sketching hundreds of portraits and scenes. He stimulated popular interest in Indian culture by publicly exhibiting his work and by presenting groups of Indians to audiences in the U.S. and Europe. Most of his paintings are in the Smithsonian Institution, Washington, D.C. The American Museum of Natural History in New York City owns about 700 of his sketches. Catlin also wrote and illustrated *Manners, Customs, and Conditions of the North American Indians* (2 vol., 1841), *Catlin's North American Indian Portfolio* (1844), and *My Life Among the Indians* (1867). His work is a valuable source of historical information.

CATNIP, common name for a hardy perennial herb, *Nepeta cataria,* of the family Labiatae (*see* MINT). Native to Europe, it has become a common weed in North America. The sharp fragrance of the plant is attractive and exciting to cats, which enjoy eating catnip.

Catnip, Nepeta cataria

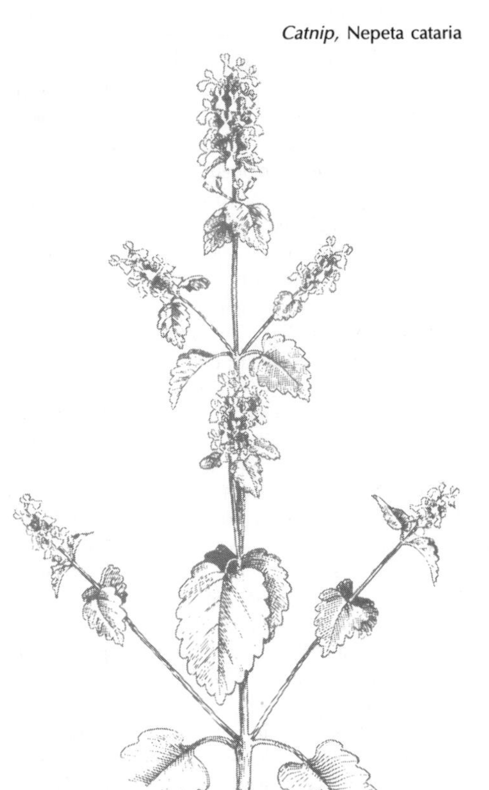

CATOCTIN MOUNTAIN, E spur of the Blue Ridge, central Maryland. It extends some 60 km (some 37 mi) in a generally N-S direction. Its elevation decreases from a maximum of about 580 m (about 1900 ft) in the N to about 150 m (about 500 ft) in the S. The ridge, which is forested, is the site of Catoctin Mountain Park, which includes the presidential retreat, Camp David.

CATO THE ELDER, full name MARCUS PORCIUS CATO (234-149 BC), Roman statesman and writer. Born on a farm in Tusculum (near modern Frascati), he remained interested in agriculture and the simple life typical of Roman landholders of early Republican times. He distinguished himself while still young as an enemy of Greek culture, which he believed enervated the Romans. Cato served as a quaestor in 204 BC, as aedile in 199, as praetor in 198, and as consul in 195. He also served in the army, winning the honor of a triumph for his victories in Spain. His chief renown, however, came from his activities as censor in 184. He campaigned against the immorality and luxury of Roman life and used the privileges of his office to weed out of the Senate all he considered unworthy, either because of their extravagance or their departure from his own conception of virtuous Roman character. In 157 he was sent to Africa on a mission of arbitration between the Carthaginians and Numidian tribesmen. During this visit he became obsessed with the idea that the city of Carthage, which both repelled him because of its luxury and wealth and aroused his native xenophobia, was a menace to Rome. Until his death he concluded every speech, regardless of the subject, with the words: *Delenda est Carthago* ("Carthage must be destroyed"). In the year of his death, largely due to his influence, war between Carthage and Rome, the Third Punic War, began, resulting three years later in the complete destruction of Carthage. Cato is also remembered as the first to write a prose history of Rome, *Origines.* Only small portions of the work are extant. His *De Agri Cultura,* a treatise on farming, is the oldest surviving prose work in Latin.

CATONSVILLE. *See* BALTIMORE COUNTY.

CATO THE YOUNGER, full name MARCUS PORCIUS CATO (95-46 BC), Roman statesman, the great-grandson of Cato the Elder, born in Rome. His conduct in his first important public office, that of quaestor in 65 BC, gave him a reputation for frugality and honesty. An ardent opponent of the triumvirate, Cato resisted Pompey the Great when the latter returned from his victories in the East to demand land for his veterans, a step that had become the means of building a personal following. In 60 he also opposed the candidacy of Julius Caesar for the consulship. Cato's influence was so great that the leaders comprising the First Triumvirate, Pompey, Caesar, and Marcus Crassus, sent him on a two-year mission to Cyprus to remove him from active politics. During the civil war between Caesar and Pompey in 49, Cato sided with Pompey. He attempted unsuccessfully to defend Sicily against Caesar's forces and maintained a hopeless defense in the city of Utica, in Africa, after which he committed suicide rather than surrender to Caesar. His writings, except for a letter to the statesman and orator Marcus Cicero, have not survived; however, his reputation as an incorruptible citizen became legendary in the writings of contemporaneous and later Romans. Cato was the father-in-law of Marcus Brutus.

CATS, Jacob (1577-1660), Dutch poet and statesman, born in Brouwershaven, Zeeland, and educated as a lawyer. In 1602 he married a woman of wealth and was able to retire to a farm in Zeeland, where he spent his time in farming and writing poetry. In 1627 and 1631 he was sent by the government of Holland on missions to England. He served from 1636 to 1651 as grand pensionary of Holland, the highest office of the province. He was the author of many books of poetry that, although relatively unknown elsewhere, were so popular in the Netherlands for about 200 years, he was given the name Father Cats. His autobiography, *Eighty-two Years of My Life,* was published posthumously in 1734.

CAT, *or* **CT, SCANNER.** *See* X RAY.

CAT'S-EYE, gem-quality chrysoberyl, that when cut *en cabochon,* that is, in an oval, rounded form, shows a light-colored line that changes position as the gem is turned, giving the stone a resemblance to the eye of a cat. This property, known as chatoyance, is related to asterism and is caused by a parallel arrangement of fine fibers of some foreign substance, such as amianthus, or of minute hollow tubules similarly arranged.

CATSKILL MOUNTAINS, low mountain group, SE New York, forming part of the Appalachian Mts., near the Hudson R. The highest peak is Slide Mt., 1274 m (4180 ft) above sea level. The region is drained by the headstreams of the Delaware R. and has several reservoirs owned by New York City. The Catskills are well wooded and contain many lakes and streams for fishing and swimming. Picturesque features of the area include many deep gorges and waterfalls. The summer climate is cool, and the area is noted as a vacation ground. The large Catskill Forest Preserve is here. The American writer Washington Irving used the region as the locale of his novel *Rip Van Winkle.*

Carrie Chapman Catt UPI

CATT, Carrie Chapman (1859–1947), American woman suffrage leader, born in Ripon, Wis., and educated at the State College of Iowa. After serving as teacher and principal in the schools of Mason City, Iowa, she became in the 1890s an organizer and lecturer for the woman suffrage movement. She was president of the National American Woman Suffrage Association from 1900 to 1904 and of the International Woman Suffrage Alliance, which she helped to organize, from 1904 to 1923. She was reelected president of the national association in 1915, retaining this post until her death. Catt's campaign achieved success in 1920, when all American women won the right to vote. In the same year she participated in founding the National League of Women Voters. In the 1920s and '30s, Catt was active in the cause of international peace, serving as head of the National Committee on the Cause and Cure of War from 1925 to 1932.

CATTAIL, common name for a tall perennial herb of the genus *Typha,* of the family Typhaceae. It is characterized by a creeping rootstock, long, flat leaves, flowers in dense cylindrical terminal spikes, and brown, cylindrical fruit with a velvety surface. The plant grows in freshwater swamps, in both temperate and tropical climates, and is occasionally cultivated along pond borders and in bog gardens. It grows and spreads rapidly when sufficient water is present in the soil. The most common species, *T. latifolia,* grows to about 1 to 2 m (about 5 to 9 ft) high. Another species widely distributed throughout the northern hemisphere, *T. augustifolia,* grows to a height of 3 m (10 ft), and *T. domingensis,* of California, Texas, Mexico, and Argentina, attains a height of about 5 m (about 18 ft) and an inflorescence of 1 m (3 ft). The leaves are often used for making chair seats, mats, and baskets. The cattail family is in the order Typhales, class Angiospermae (*see* ANGIOSPERM).

CATTEGAT. *See* KATTEGAT.

CATTLE, common term for the domesticated herbivorous mammals that constitute the genus *Bos,* of the family Bovidae (q.v.), and that are of great importance to humans because of the meat, milk, leather, glue, gelatin, and other items of commerce they yield. Modern cattle are divided into two species: *B. taurus,* which originated in Europe and includes most modern breeds of dairy and beef cattle, and *B. indicus,* which originated in India and is characterized by a hump at the withers. The latter are now widespread in Africa and Asia, with lesser numbers imported to North America (primarily in the southern U.S.), Central America, and northern and central South America.

The general characteristics of cattle can be provided through their classification. They belong to the order Artiodactyla (even-toed, hoofed mammals) and the suborder Ruminantia (four-compartmented stomachs and a decreased number of teeth, with the upper incisors missing). Like others of the family Bovidae, they have paired, hollow, unbranched horns that do not shed. Other Bovidae that are so closely related to true cattle that they can still interbreed include the anoa, bison, gaur, Indian and African buffalo, and yak.

Domestication and Modern Breeds. European cattle probably are descended from the wild cattle, *B. primigenius,* of Europe and were first domesticated in southeastern Europe about 8500 years ago. The zebu, or Brahman, cattle, *B. indicus,* were domesticated in southern Asia about the same time or a little later. Early records indicate that cattle were used for draft, milk, sacrifice, and, in some instances, for meat and sport. Some of these early uses have continued in modified forms into the present, such as in bullfighting, as in sacrificing animals for religious purposes, and as in considering cows sacred.

The concept and formulation of modern breeds of cattle began in the midregions of England, in northern Europe, and on the Channel Islands during the mid-1800s, and most modern

Brahman bulls, or zebu Florida State News Bureau

breeds were formed in the latter half of that century. Cattle with similar characteristics, however, were present in these areas even before the concept of breeds became dominant. Today about 274 important recognized breeds exist, and many other varieties and types that could be described have not attained breed status. Thus, new breeds continue to evolve, such as the Brangus, Santa Gertrudis, Charbray, Beef Master, and Braford.

Dairy Cattle. Dairy cattle are those breeds that have been developed primarily to produce milk. The achievements of careful breeding have been remarkable. For example, in the U.S. in recent years, the average dairy cow produced nearly 5200 kg (11,500 lb) of milk and 190 kg (420 lb) of butterfat during a lactation period of 305 days in which it was milked twice daily. Individual high-performance cows could produce more than four times this average amount.

In North America the major breeds of dairy cattle are the Holstein-Friesian, Ayrshire, Brown Swiss, Guernsey, and Jersey. The ancestors of these animals were imported from Europe, where similar cattle exist today. The Holstein-Friesian came from Holland and adjacent areas, the Ayrshire from Scotland, the Jersey and the Guernsey from the Channel Islands off the coast of England, and the Brown Swiss from Switzerland. Among the major dairy breeds of *B. indicus* found primarily in India are the Gir, Hariana, Red Sindhi, Sahiwal, and Tharparker.

The major breeds show distinctive characteris-

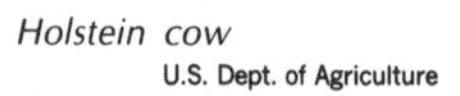

Holstein cow
U.S. Dept. of Agriculture

tics that may be used for identification. The Holstein-Friesian is the largest; a mature cow weighs at least 675 kg (1500 lb). It is followed in size by the Brown Swiss, Ayrshire, and Guernsey. The Jersey is the smallest, with mature cows weighing 450 kg (1000 lb). Breeds also differ in color. The Holstein is black and white, although some animals may be red and white; the Brown Swiss varies from a very light grayish-brown to dark brown; and the Ayrshire can be red, brown, or mahogany with white. The Guernsey is fawn, with white markings and a yellow skin, and the Jersey may vary from a light gray to a very dark fawn, usually solid in color but sometimes with white spots. Breeds also differ with respect to volume of milk produced and milk composition. Holstein-Friesians produce the largest volume, averaging 6300 kg (14,000 lb), followed by the Brown Swiss, Ayrshire, Guernsey, and Jersey. Milk from the Jersey contains the highest concentration of fat (5 percent), however, followed by that of the Guernsey, Brown Swiss, Ayrshire, and the Holstein (3.61 percent). *See also* DAIRY FARMING.

Beef Cattle. Beef cattle have been bred and selected primarily for the production of meat, and many breeds have been developed or adapted for special conditions. The major breeds of registered beef cattle in North America, listed in order of numbers, are Angus, Hereford, Polled Hereford, Charolais, Shorthorn, Santa Gertrudis, Brahman, Brangus, and Red Angus. In recent years, several "exotic" breeds also have been imported, including the Simmental, Gelbvieh, Fleckvieh, Limousin, Maine-Anjou, and Chianina. These later arrivals have been used primarily for crossing with the major American breeds to increase the size and milking ability of the crossbred offspring for commercial production.

Hereford cow U.S. Dept. of Agriculture

Herefords are characterized by a red coat color and a white face. Polled Herefords have the same characteristics, but they are hornless (polled). Angus are solid black in color and are polled; the Charolais are white or cream-colored; and the Shorthorn may be red, white, or roan (a mixture of red and white). The Brahman is usually white in color with a dark skin, large droopy ears, and a large dewlap. The Santa Gertrudis was developed in Texas from crossbreeding the Brahman and Shorthorn breeds, followed by selection and inbreeding to fix characteristics. These cattle were selected and adapted to the arid region where they originated and have been used successfully in other areas with similar climatic conditions.

The recent importation and crossbreeding with the "exotic" breeds may result in the establishment of new breeds in North America in the near future. The various breeds of beef cattle also differ in mature size, growth rate, gestation length, and birth weight. Limited data indicate, however, that strains within the breeds may differ as much as the different breeds in many of these characteristics. *See also* MEAT-PACKING INDUSTRY.

Dual-Purpose Breeds. Dual-purpose breeds are breeds that have been selected for both meat and milk production. They include the Milking Shorthorn, Red Dane, Red Polled, and Pinzgauer. Many of the animals classified as either dairy or beef breed, particularly those of continental Europe, could alternatively be classified as dual-purpose breeds.

Distribution. Cattle are widely distributed throughout the world. The total world cattle population in the mid-1980s was estimated to be nearly 1.3 billion head, with about 30 percent in Asia, 20 percent in South America, 14 percent in Africa, 13 percent in North America, and 10 percent in Europe. The leading countries are, in decreasing order, India, Brazil, the USSR (9 percent of the world total), China, and Argentina. Beef cattle used for breeding in the U.S. are estimated at about 34 million head, and the leading states are Texas, Missouri, Oklahoma, Nebraska, Kansas, Montana, South Dakota, Iowa, Florida, and Tennessee. Dairy cattle in the U.S. is estimated to be 11.2 million head; the leading states are Wisconsin, California, New York, Minnesota, Pennsylvania, Michigan, Ohio, Iowa, and Texas.

See also ANIMAL HUSBANDRY; BRANDING; DISEASES OF ANIMALS. P.T.C.

For further information on this topic, see the Bibliography in volume 28, sections 594, 596.

CATTON, Bruce (1899–1978), Pulitzer Prize-winning American historian, born in Petoskey, Mich. He attended Oberlin College. Early in his career as a journalist he worked in Cleveland, Ohio;

Boston; and Washington, D.C. From 1942 to 1948 he held various posts with the World War II Production Board and the U.S. Department of Commerce. In 1954 he became an editor of *American Heritage,* a magazine on Americana, and in 1959 was named senior editor of the American Heritage Publishing Co. He wrote more than a dozen evocative, scholarly books on the American Civil War, including *Mr. Lincoln's Army* (1951), *Glory Road* (1952), and *Grant Takes Command* (1969). For *A Stillness at Appomattox* (1953), Catton was awarded both the 1954 Pulitzer Prize in history and the 1954 National Book Award in history and biography.

CATULLUS, full name GAIUS VALERIUS CATULLUS (84?-54? BC), Roman poet, often considered the greatest writer of Latin lyric verse.

It is thought that Catullus was born in Verona and went to Rome about 62 BC, where he became the leader of a group of young poets who emulated the verse forms of the Greek poets of Alexandria, Egypt.

Among the most famous of Catullus's works are the so-called Lesbia poems, which variously express deep passion and devotion and hatred and scorn for a mysterious lady, identified only as Lesbia. Scholars conjecture that Lesbia was in reality Clodia, a beautiful but unscrupulous woman who had been unfaithful to the young poet. Although the focus is on Lesbia, many of the poems express self-doubt, self-criticism, and self-pity. Whatever the exact facts of the affair may be, critics generally agree that the Lesbia poems rank among the most intense and effective expressions of passion in Roman literature. Interspersed with the Lesbia poems are epigrammatic verses attacking his rivals and enemies.

Emotionally distraught after his break with Clodia about 57 BC, Catullus apparently took a long journey to the Roman provinces in Asia Minor. His popular ode with the line *frater ave atque vale* ("brother, hail and farewell") was inspired by a visit to his brother's grave at the site of Troy. Upon his return (c. 56 BC), Catullus wrote his longest poem, on the marriage of Peleus and Thetis. Toward the end of his life he wrote direct, personal attacks on Julius Caesar and his political associates. He is thought to have died young, perhaps at the age of 30.

Catullus's influence is seen not only in the love poetry of later Latin poets, such as Ovid and Horace, but also in the marriage odes of English poets of the Renaissance, such as Robert Herrick, Ben Jonson, and Edmund Spenser.

CATULUS, Gaius Lutatius (fl. 3d cent. BC), Roman soldier and statesman. He became a consul in 242 BC and the following year commanded the Roman fleet that defeated a Carthaginian armada off the Aegates Islands (now Egadi Islands) near Sicily, thus ending the First Punic War.

CATULUS, Quintus Lutatius (150?-87 BC), Roman statesman. In 102 BC he became a consul with Gaius Marius; the following year, the two of them conquered and destroyed the Cimbri, a Teutonic people. In 88, however, Catulus supported Lucius Sulla in the civil war against Marius. Catulus was proscribed by Marius in 87 and committed suicide or was killed.

CATULUS, Quintus Lutatius (c. 120-61? BC), Roman statesman, the son of Quintus Lutatius Catulus. He became a consul in 78 BC and the following year supported Pompey the Great in suppressing the armed uprising of Marcus Aemilius Lepidus (c. 121-77 BC). In 63 he accused Julius Caesar of sharing in Catiline's conspiracy to seize power in Rome by armed rebellion, and Caesar in turn charged Catulus with embezzling state funds. Caesar later dropped his accusation, and the charges against Caesar were not pressed.

CAUCA, river of Colombia, chief tributary of the Magdalena R. Rising in W Colombia, it flows in a northerly direction through the Andes Mts., forming many waterfalls and becoming navigable at Cáceres. The Cauca R. joins the Magdalena near Mompós, after a course of about 965 km (about 600 mi).

CAUCASIA, region of the USSR, in the extreme SE part of Europe, between the Black and Caspian seas, and divided into two parts by the Caucasus Mts. The portion to the N, known as the Caucasus (formerly Ciscaucasia), is characterized physically by gently sloping plains ending in low, marshy steppes. Lying within the Russian SFSR, it contains the autonomous republics of Chechen-Ingush, Kabardin-Balkar, North Ossetian, and Dagestan and the autonomous oblasts of Karachay-Cherkess and Adygey. From the late 1920s until World War II, the Karachay-Cherkess Autonomous Oblast was divided into separate Karachay and Cherkess autonomous regions. The present autonomous oblast was established in 1957. The S and larger portion of Caucasia (Transcaucasia) is physically characterized by a rugged terrain, with chains of mountains (the Little Caucasus) running parallel to the central range of the Caucasus Mts. This region consists of the Georgian SSR, Armenian SSR, and Azerbaijan SSR.

Caucasia is noted for fertile lands, mineral deposits, and, in modern times, oil fields. Although Russian attempts to conquer the rich region, containing independent tribes ruled by their own princes, began early in the 18th century, the warlike Georgians, Circassians, and other Caucasian mountain peoples withstood Russian dominattion until 1865. Russian rule was marked by great severity and the repression of the native peoples. After the collapse of czarist Russia in World War I, the S section of Caucasia became independent republics. In 1921 they became the Transcaucasian SFSR, one of the four original union republics of the USSR. They separated again in 1936, however, becoming union republics in their own right. Caucasia was subjected to mass purges and executions under the Soviets; in 1943 almost all the Chechen-Ingush, Karachay, and Balkar peoples were deported in large groups to Siberia.

The people of Caucasia are largely Muslim, with the exception of the Georgians and Armenians, who are Christian. The predominant ethnic strains are, in the N, Japhetic, Turco-Tatar, and Iranian; and, in the S, Japhetic and Turco-Tatar. Because some anthropologists have maintained that the Caucasus was the cradle of the white race, the word Caucasian has come to designate any white person (*see* CAUCASIAN RACE).

Farming, livestock raising, and mining are the principal industries in Caucasia. Azerbaijan, Chechen-Ingush, and Adygey are noted particularly for the production of oil (at Baku, Groznyy, and Maykop, respectively). For further information on Caucasia see the various political units and divisions under separate headings. Total area of Caucasia, about 399,506 sq km (about 154,250 sq mi). Pop. (1983 est.) 19,693,000.

CAUCASIAN LANGUAGES, geographical group of about 24 languages spoken in the Caucasus region of the USSR (*see* CAUCASIA). They are usually classified into three groups: Northwestern, or Abkhazo-Adyghian; Northeastern or Dagestanian (possibly of common ancestry with the Northwestern group); and Southern or Kartvelian, the leading member of which is Georgian, the language of the Georgian SSR and neighboring areas. Caucasian languages tend to be agglutinative in type and show some inflection, but the three groups vary strikingly in their grammar and word formation. In general these languages are characterized by combinations of consonants, especially of gutturals and sibilants, that are difficult to pronounce. *See also* GEORGIAN LITERATURE.

CAUCASIAN RACE, term sometimes applied to a broad, vague racial subdivision of *Homo sapiens* with a predominance of light skin color, and higher percentages of light-colored eyes and hair than are found in other segments of the population. The designation Caucasian was first used in the 19th and early 20th centuries by scholars who believed that this division of humankind originated in the Caucasus Mountain region, near the Caspian Sea. Caucasians are now more commonly known as the white race.

The center of the white population is usually thought of as Europe and the Americas, although the spread into North and South America began only a few centuries ago. Hundreds of millions of people in India and the Middle East, however, are most frequently classified as "Caucasoid" peoples, in areas where distinctions are not clear between white and nonwhite populations.

In North America confusion is mounting over the designation white or Caucasian. Many people, including Puerto Ricans and Mexican-Americans, are now being identified as "Hispanic" rather than white in various social counts of American populations such as the U.S. Census. Increasingly, the term *white* is becoming a residual category, denoting that part of the population not covered by the following classifications: blacks, Hispanics, East Asians, native Americans, Pacific Islanders, and other "socioracial" subdivisions.

See also RACES, CLASSIFICATION OF. P.J.P.

CAUCASUS MOUNTAINS (Russ. *Kavkaz*), mountain range, SE European USSR, considered a boundary between Europe and Asia. The range extends for about 1200 km (about 750 mi) from the Apsheron Peninsula on the SW shore of the Caspian Sea to the mouth of the Kuban R. on the NE shore of the Black Sea. The W region is drained by the Kuban R. and the E portion by the Kura R. Of the two principal chains within the

Mt. Kazbek, one of the many lofty peaks in the Caucasus Mts. Ewing Galloway

Caucasus, the most northerly range has a number of peaks higher than about 4570 m (15,000 ft) above sea level. Mt. Elbrus, which has an altitude of 5642 m (18,510 ft), is the highest peak in Europe. Other notable peaks include Dykh-Tau, 5198 m (17,054 ft); Koshtan-Tau, 5145 m (16,880 ft); and Kazbek, 5047 m (16,558 ft). The highest peaks of the W chain are about 3660 m (12,000 ft) above sea level. Geologically, the Caucasus Mts. belong to a system that extends from SE Europe into Asia. The mountains are composed of granite and crystalline rock. Some volcanic formations and many glaciers are found throughout the range.

The uplifting of the N chain was begun during the Jurassic period. The W chain dates from the Tertiary period. Of the few practicable routes through the range, one of the most important is a Georgian military highway from Ordzhonikidze, in the North Ossetian ASSR, on the N side, to Tbilisi, in the Georgian SSR, on the S side. The chief minerals of the Caucasus Mts. are coal, copper, lead, manganese, and oil.

CAUCHY, Augustin Louis (1789-1857), French mathematician, born in Paris, and educated at the École Polytechnique. Cauchy was appointed professor simultaneously at the École Polytechnique, the University of Paris, and the Collège de France. In 1848 he was made professor of mathematical astronomy at the University of Paris.

Cauchy verified the existence of recurrent elliptic functions, gave the first impetus to the general theory of functions, and laid the foundation for the modern treatment of the convergence of infinite series. He perfected the method of integration of linear differential equations (*see* CALCULUS), invented the calculus of residues, and in general was one of the leaders of the 19th century in infusing vigor into analysis. He also gave his attention to the propagation of light and the theory of elasticity.

CAUCUS, closed meeting of members of a political party or faction for the purpose of making decisions expected to be binding on the party or faction as a whole. The word is of uncertain origin. Its first significant usage was in connection with an 18th-century political organization in Boston, the Caucus Club, which was influential in local elections. Between 1800 and 1824 candidates for the presidency of the U.S. were regularly chosen by meetings, or caucuses, of the members of Congress belonging to the respective political parties. Subsequently these candidates were selected by conventions, but congressional caucuses have continued to function for the purpose of deciding the official party position on matters of importance before the legislature. Similar political caucuses in many state and local legislative bodies have continued to meet, although their function of selecting candidates has been superseded by direct primaries. In other organizations in which factions may exist, such as clubs or trade unions, a meeting of the members of a faction to formulate policy or choose candidates for office is often called a caucus. In Great Britain the term designates a partisan organization that would be called a "political machine" in the U.S., or refers to the system of forming or maintaining such an organization.

CAULFIELD, residential city, SE Australia, in Victoria State, in the Melbourne metropolitan area. It is the site of Caulfield Race Course. Pop. (est.) 81,900.

CAULIFLOWER, common name for *Brassica oleracea capitata,* a variety of the cabbage species, of the family Cruciferae (*see* MUSTARD). Only the deformed inflorescence, or head, of the cauliflower is used for food. It is less hardy than broccoli, another related plant, and the cauliflowers that are reared in August for the purpose of supplying the first crop of the following summer need to be protected in cold frames during winter. To produce cauliflower of first-rate quality the ground must be rich and well cultivated.

CAUSALITY, in philosophy, relationship of a cause to its effect. Aristotle enumerated four different kinds of causes: the material, the formal, the efficient, and the final. The material cause is what anything is made of, for example, brass or marble is the material cause of a given statue. The formal cause is the form, type, or pattern according to which anything is made; thus, the style of architecture would be the formal cause of a house. The efficient cause is the immediate power acting to produce the work, such as the manual energy of the laborers. The final cause is the end or motive for the sake of which the work is produced, that is, the pleasure of the owner. The principles that Aristotle outlined formed the basis of the modern scientific concept that specific stimuli will produce standard results under controlled conditions. Other Greek philosophers, particularly the skeptic Sextus Empiricus (c. 200-50), attacked the principles of causality.

Rival Notions. In early modern philosophy, Aristotle's laws of causality were again challenged, resulting in two rival notions of cause. The French philosopher and mathematician René Descartes and his school made cause identical with substance. The physical scientists often had a mechanical view of causality, reducing cause to a motion or change followed by other motion or change with a mathematical equality between measures of motion. The British philosopher David Hume carried to a logical conclusion the contention of Sextus Empiricus that causality is not a real relation, but a fiction of the mind. To account for the origin of this fiction Hume used the doctrine of association.

Hume's explanation of cause led the German philosopher Immanuel Kant to posit cause as a fundamental category of understanding. Kant held that the only knowable objective world is the product of a synthetic activity of the mind. He accepted Hume's skeptical result as far as it concerned itself with the world of things-in-themselves. Dissatisfied, however, with the concept that experience is only a succession of perceptions without any discoverable relationship or coherence, Kant decided that causality is one of the principles of coherence obtaining in the world of phenomena, and that it is universally present there because thought, as part of its contribution to the nature of that world, always puts it there.

The British philosopher John Stuart Mill took up the problem at this point. He denied the fundamental postulate of Kant's transcendentalism, namely, that thought is responsible for the order of this world. Mill sought to justify belief in universal causation on empiricist principles; for him, a proposition is meaningful only if it describes what can be experienced.

Modern Directions. Along with the method of empiricism as the source of all knowledge goes a definition of cause that is widely accepted today. The cause of any event is a preceding event without which the event in question would not have occurred. This is a mechanistic view of causality popular in scientific circles. All the previous events would constitute the complete cause.

Many philosophers deny the ultimate reality, or at least the fundamental validity, of the causal relation. Thus, the American philosopher Josiah Royce maintained that the category of serial order, of which the category of cause is a particular case, is itself subordinate to the ultimate category of purpose. The French philosopher Henri Bergson maintained that ultimate reality or life is not bound by exact causal sequences. It is a process of growth in which the unpredictable, and therefore the uncaused, constantly occurs. No exact repetition happens in real time; and where there is no repetition, there is no cause, for cause means the antecedent that repeatedly is followed by the same consequence.

For further information on this topic, see the Bibliography in volume 28, section 25.

CAUSSES, region of limestone plateaus, called *causses* (Fr. *chaux,* "lime, limestone"), in south-central France, constituting part of the Lot, Aveyron, Lozère, and Tarn-et-Garonne departments. The plateaus are separated by deeply eroded river valleys. Causses is sparsely populated and is principally a sheep-raising area. The region dates from the Jurassic period, and it has underground streams, stalactite caverns, and sinkholes.

CAUSTIC CHEMICALS, chemicals that can destroy or severely damage the flesh on contact. Such chemicals include various inorganic and organic acids and bases. The most familiar chemicals called caustics are sodium hydroxide (caustic soda, or lye) and potassium hydroxide (caustic potash). Other chemicals are also caustics, for example, silver nitrate, which has been used as an antibacterial agent and for treating warts. *See also* ALKALIES; POTASSIUM; SODIUM.

CAUTO, longest river of Cuba. It rises in the Sierra Maestra in the extreme SE part of the island and flows NW and then W into the Gulf of Guacanayabo. Nearly 241 km (nearly 150 mi) long, it is navigable for about 120 km (about 75 mi).

CAUVERY, also Kaveri, river, S India, about 764 km (about 475 mi) long, rising in the Western Ghats mountains. It flows SE across Karnataka and Tamil Nadu states, entering the Bay of Bengal through two principal mouths. Although of no value for commercial navigation, the Cauvery is highly important for irrigation purposes, chiefly in its Tanjore delta region, where there are extensive irrigation works. In Karnataka the falls of the river are utilized for the generation of electric power. The river is sacred to the Hindus, who call it Dakshini Ganga, the Ganges of the South.

CAVAFY, Constantine (Gr. Konstantínos Pétrou Kaváfis) (1863–1933), one of the leading 20th-century Greek poets. He was born in Alexandria, Egypt, where he spent most of his life. A ruthless self-critic who was often troubled by his own unorthodoxy, Cavafy published little during his lifetime. He rejected the traditional values of Christianity, the heterosexual ethic, nationalism, and patriotism. Cavafy developed an individualistic style, mixing stilted, artificial literary language with the Greek vernacular. His verses often superimpose events from Hellenistic and Byzantine history on contemporary affairs, as in two of his best-known poems, "The God Abandons Antony" and "Ithaca," both written in 1911.

Cavafy's works became known to English readers through references in E. M. Forster's study of Alexandria, *Pharos and Pharillon* (1923), and in Lawrence Durrell's *Alexandria Quartet* (1957–60). *The Complete Poems of Cavafy* (1961), translated by Rae Dalven (1904–), with an introduction by W. H. Auden, established Cavafy's reputation and ensured his influence on Western literature.

CAVALCANTI, Guido (1250?–1300), Italian poet, born in Florence. During the civil war in Florence between the political parties known as the Guelphs and Ghibellines, Cavalcanti became the head of the Ghibellines. In 1266 the Ghibellines were exiled to Sarzana, in northwestern Italy; Cavalcanti contracted malaria there and died soon after his return to Florence. The author of many sonnets expressing idealistic love, Cavalcanti was the most important Florentine poet before Dante, his friend and admirer. Translations of many of Cavalcanti's sonnets, originally published as *Canzone d'amore* (Song of Love), were included in *Dante and His Circle* (1874) by the English poet and painter Dante Gabriel Rossetti.

CAVALIER (Fr., from Lat. *caballus,* "a nag"), term meaning originally a horseman and later a mounted knight. By extension the word acquired the meanings "gallant" and "haughty." During the English Revolution in the 17th century, the term Cavaliers was applied as a nickname to the partisans of King Charles I, in opposition to the Roundheads, or Parliamentarians.

CAVALIER, Jean (1681–1740), French soldier and leader of the Camisards, born near Anduze and brought up in the Huguenot (Protestant) faith. When threatened with persecution for his religious beliefs, he fled to Geneva. He returned to France in 1702 and led the Camisard revolt in the Cévennes Mountains of Languedoc, defeating the forces of King Louis XIV in a number of engagements. In 1704 Cavalier abandoned the struggle for religious freedom in exchange for a commission as a colonel in the French army and a yearly pension from the king. He was disavowed by all but a handful of his followers, found no favor at the French court, and went to England. In 1706 he fought for the English in Spain and later settled in Dublin. In 1738 he was appointed lieutenant governor of the island of Jersey. He wrote *Memoirs of the Wars of the Cévennes Under Col. Cavalier* (1726).

CAVALIER POETS, group of 17-century English lyric poets, associated with the Royalists, who were the followers of Charles I at the time of the English Civil War. Three of them—Thomas Carew, Sir John Suckling, and Richard Lovelace—were attached to the court of Charles, and one, Robert Herrick, was a clergyman. The term *Cavalier lyrics* is often applied to the poetry of these authors and to that of some of their contemporaries, such as John Cleveland (1613–58). Generally marked by brevity, correct and polished form, and restrained emotion, these poems deal with loyalty, beauty, and love. Their philosophy is often cynical and hedonistic.

CAVALLINI, Pietro (c. 1250–c. 1330), one of the most important Italian painters of his day. Born in Rome, he was one of the first painters to break away from the austere and rigid Byzantine style by attempting to render space in a naturalistic three-dimensional manner that was a precursor of actual perspective. He influenced the lifelike style of the famous Florentine painter Giotto. His works include mosaics in Santa Maria in Trastevere and frescoes in Santa Cecilia, both in Rome.

Persian cavalry of the period of the Mughal emperor Akbar, late 16th and early 17th centuries.

Metropolitan Museum of Art–Gift of Alexander Smith Cochran

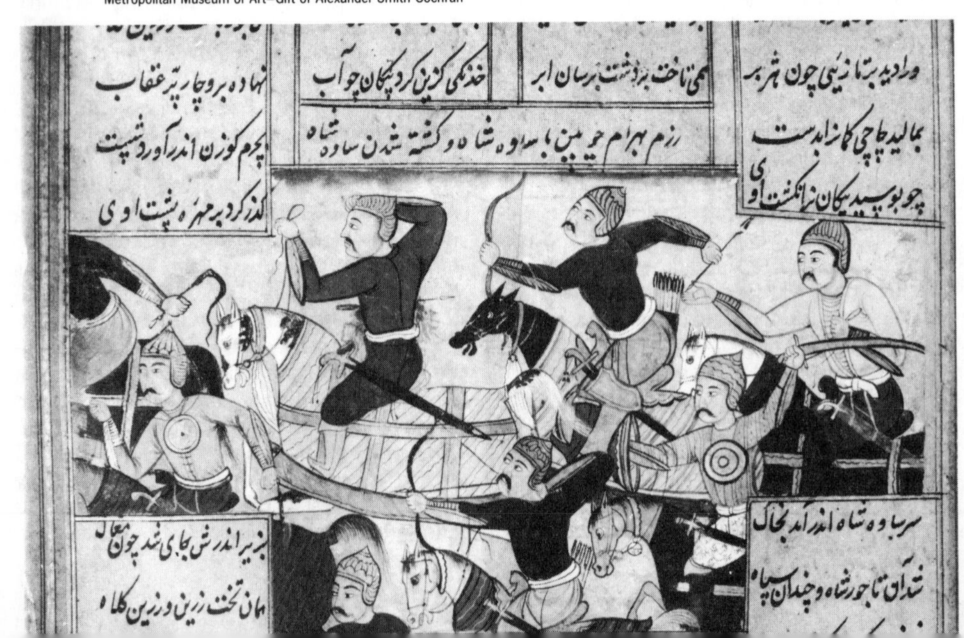

Cavalry Charge on the Southern Plains, *an oil painting by Frederic Remington.*
Metropolitan Museum of Art–Gift of several gentlemen

CAVALRY, mounted soldiers trained to fight on horseback, as distinguished from mounted infantrymen, who use horses for rapid transportation between engagements, but fight on foot. Throughout history cavalry troops were valued for their speed and mobility, and were used for reconnaissance, delaying actions, raiding parties, and pursuit and harassment of enemy troops. In modern armies cavalry and mounted infantry have been largely replaced by armored cavalry, in which soldiers use tanks, armored cars, helicopters, and other mechanized equipment.

The earliest known cavalry consisted mainly of horse-drawn chariots, which seemingly antedated mounted soldiery. The wheels of some war chariots were fitted with sharp scythe blades designed to cut a wide swathe through enemy ranks. Although cavalry units were employed by the Assyrians, Babylonians, and other ancient peoples, the first regular cavalry, consisting of trained mounted troops, was probably created by the Egyptian pharoah Ramses II. With the rise of the Persian Empire in the 6th century BC, cavalry developed into a fully effective operational force.

Among the ancient Greeks the development of cavalry was hindered for centuries by a lack of horses. In Macedonia, however, where horses were plentiful, the military leader Philip II of Macedon and his son, Alexander the Great, developed a formidable striking force by adding cavalry wings to the heavy infantry formation known as the phalanx. Later the Carthaginians, the Romans, and the Gothic barbarians who conquered Rome in the 5th century AD used similar cavalry wings with devastating effect.

The earliest cavalry weapons were the lance, the javelin, and other weapons thrown by hand; the sword; and the bow and arrow. Until about AD 300 troops rode without saddles, but they often were protected by leather armor and helmets of metal or leather. During the Middle Ages warfare was dominated by mounted knights wearing metal armor and wielding the iron-tipped lance and the two-edged sword. Probably the greatest cavalry genius in history was the Mongol warrior Genghis Khan, whose mounted hordes conquered much of Asia and Russia during the 13th century. Tightly coordinated and disciplined, his armies used the smoke screen and such novel devices as signal flags and signal lanterns.

With the advent of gunpowder and armor-piercing bullets early in the 14th century, cavalry organization and strategy were profoundly modified. The era of disorganized clashes between heavily armored knights came to an end. Mounted troops gradually were forged into disciplined units armed with swords and hand-held firearms. Firearms also enhanced the importance of the infantry. Under Napoleon, mounted troops became an elite military force, although the infantry did most of the fighting. Napoleon was the first general to employ cavalry simultaneously to conceal his main troop movements and to reconnoiter the front. In Russia the Cossacks became famous for their daring and skill as cavalrymen.

The emergence of the repeating rifle in the latter half of the 19th century was the most serious blow to the importance of cavalry. Charging cavalrymen were easy prey for infantry troops armed with automatic weapons. Among the last major conflicts in which horse cavalry figured prominently were the American Civil War (1861–65), the Austro-Prussian War (1866), and the South African War (1899–1902). Horse cavalry was used only to a limited extent during World War I. Between World Wars I and II the cavalry in most armies was transformed into armored cavalry units. The few horse cavalry units remaining in the U.S. Army after World War II were absorbed in 1946 into the armored forces.

CAVAN, county, N Republic of Ireland, in the province of Ulster, bordering on Northern Ireland, about midway between the Atlantic Ocean and the Irish Sea. Except for the mountainous NW section, the terrain is generally undulating, with many bogs and lakes. The principal river is the Erne. Small-scale farming is the chief activity of the county, where oats, potatoes, and flax are the primary crops. Stock farming is conducted in the highlands. Industrial activity consists of whiskey distilling and linen bleaching. The administrative center of the county is Cavan. Area, 1891 sq km (730 sq mi); pop. (1981) 53,855.

CAVE, chamber of varying size and shape beneath the surface of the earth or in the side of a hill, cliff, or mountain. Many caves have large openings to the surface.

Formation of Caves. Naturally formed caves evolve in various ways, mainly as a result of the solvent action of water and compounds in it. Known technically as caves of solution, such chambers are most common in limestone formations, particularly in regions that have ample rainfall. The surface water in such regions contains carbon dioxide and humid acids derived from the organic constituents of the soil. Attacking the soluble limestone, this acidic water dissolves and carries the limestone away in solution. Over long periods of time, such action results in the formation of subterranean chambers. The depth of such chambers depends on the depth of the water table (*see* WATER). If after several unusually wet years the water table is rising, old cave chambers become flooded and new ones begin forming at higher levels. Likewise, during a long dry spell, chambers will begin forming at lower levels, closer to the declining water table. Over thousands of years, fluctuations such as these produce multi-level cave systems, as in Mammoth Cave National Park (q.v.), where a subterranean stream flows through the lowest level. Underground rivers erode and transport sediments and rock fragments in a manner analogous to that of surface streams. If such action has been predominant, the cave is said to have been formed by mechanical abrasion.

Other types of caves include the sea cave, which is formed by wave action against seaside cliffs; lava caves, which form under lava flows; and ice caves, which form in glaciers and icebergs. River action forms still another type of cave, commonly with a very large opening that gives it the appearance of a natural amphitheater. A river entrenched in a steep-walled canyon most actively erodes that portion of the canyon wall against which the current is strongest, as at a bend or in a meander. By erosion, solution, and quarrying, the river excavates a large quantity of rock, forming a large undercut area in the side of the canyon. With the passage of time the riverbed is lowered, and eventually the cave is left high in the side of the canyon. Such rock shelters were used extensively in what is now the southwestern U.S. by the prehistoric American Indians known as Cliff Dwellers, who built their homes within them (*see* CLIFF DWELLER).

Finally, aeolian, or wind, action is partly responsible for the formation of small caves that are confined mostly to desert or semidesert regions. The action of windblown sand is one of several forces involved in the formation of these grottoes and caves in rock ledges and cliffs.

Cave Detection. The presence of caves in limestone regions may be detected by means of clues provided by the topography of the land. In such a region the roofs of large caverns may collapse and leave depressions and troughs at the surface of the ground. Natural bridges, another phenomenon of cave regions, may remain after the collapse of a tunnel bearing an underground stream. The Natural Bridge in Virginia is a classic example of this type of formation. In the phenomenon known as disappearing streams, which is a common feature in areas underlain by caves, whole watercourses may vanish down sinks, or sinkholes, leading to the underground caverns. The sinks are indicative of caves below. Because of the capture of the surface waters by the subterranean drainage system, some cave regions have a rather dry, dusty, poorly vegetated appearance. Such regions are said to have a karst topography, a name derived from a famous cave

Empress Grotto in Orient Cave, New South Wales, Australia. Australian News & Information Bureau

region along the Adriatic Sea in Italy and Yugoslavia. Steep-walled sinks called cenotes, found in Yucatán, Mexico, constituted a chief source of water for the Mayan Indians.

Interesting Features. Caves range in size from small hillside openings to vast interconnected subterranean systems of many chambers and galleries. Some cave systems extend for miles underground and may have many outlets.

Natural air conditioning occurs in large caverns if the temperature varies only a few degrees yearly, and the caves are more or less constantly ventilated with fresh air. These conditions are, in part, the result of complex meteorological phenomena, mainly variations in barometric pressure.

Caves formed by abrasion commonly consist of myriads of winding tunnels and former underground waterways that show many features analogous to those of surface streams, such as deposits of sand and gravel. Abrasion-formed caves normally lack the weird formations found in caves of solution.

In caves of solution, the dissolved lime carbonate is often precipitated in such a fashion as to form grotesque deposits. The best-known structures are the stalactites, which hang like icicles from the roofs of caves, and the stalagmites, which extend upward from the cavern floors (*see* STALACTITE AND STALAGMITE). If the two growths meet and join, a pillar forms, helping to support the roof. Less well-known forms of carbonate deposition include flowstone and dripstone. Depending on dissolved mineral impurities brought into the cave by the groundwaters, the formations vary in color from alabaster white to hues of dusky red and brown. The dripstone formations may be exceedingly thin and translucent. Among rare formations is the helictite, a twisted, flowerlike variety of stalactite. Many cave formations are rather delicate and easily broken, and some of the best examples have been damaged or removed by unscrupulous cave explorers and visitors to public caves.

Many formations in commercial caves have been given fanciful names, such as "Rock of Ages" and "Temple of the Sun" in Carlsbad Caverns and "Martha Washington's Statue" and "Fatman's Misery" in Mammoth Cave. Frequently recurring names include "Japanese Temple," "Frozen Waterfall," "King's Bed Chamber," and "Great Hall."

A practice in many large caves, particularly those administered by the U.S. National Park Service, is to illuminate the more spectacular formations for the benefit of sightseers. Many public caverns have miles of lighted trails, with stairways and adequate safety guards near areas considered dangerous. In some caves visitors can take all-day hiking tours.

Cave Life. Through evolutionary processes some plants and animals have become specially adapted to living in caves. As a rule, these organisms are confined to the area near the entrance, but some species penetrate to the darkest reaches of the cave. Properly, cave life may be divided into those forms living exclusively in caves and those that live in caves part of the time but forage in the open. The cave cricket and some cave fish are examples of animals modified for continuous life in caves. Although such species are blind, as is usual among animal forms completely adapted to cave life, their organs of touch are highly developed. Animals that live completely in caves commonly have as their diet the edible matter, such as microorganisms and decaying organic material, carried into the caves by streams.

Limestone formation in Boyden Caves, Fresno, Calif.
Fresno County Chamber of Commerce

Bats exemplify animals that utilize caves for resting and hibernating purposes but forage in the open for their food. Rich deposits of guano, or bat droppings, have accumulated over the centuries in caves where bats congregate. Such detritus deposits support a variety of insects and simpler organisms. The guano is sometimes marketed as fertilizer. The number of bats inhabiting a large cave may be astoundingly large. For example, hundreds of thousands of the animals can be observed in the evening flight of bats from Carlsbad Caverns.

Because lack of sunlight precludes green-plant growth, fungi is the only form of plant life that can grow in caves. Groundwaters containing dissolved organic substances frequently provide nutrients for the fungi.

In past ages people often took shelter in caves, notably in western Europe, the Mediterranean regions, China, southern Africa, and Chile. These early cave inhabitants popularly have been called cavemen, but the term is misleading, for it implies that a race of people at one time dwelt exclusively in caves. Actually, during the Ice Age, people, like other animals, sought refuge in caves from time to time. Many artifacts of Paleolithic and Neolithic peoples have been found in refuse heaps near the entrances of caves. Primitive paintings have been found on the walls of some caves, notably in France and Spain. Modern critics acclaim the artistic beauty of these paintings, attributed to the Cro-Magnon, a race of the late Paleolithic period. *See* CAVE DWELLERS.

Speleology. The science of cave study is termed *speleology.* A subdivision of geology, speleology has furthered knowledge in mineralogy, hydrodynamics, archaeology, biology, and many other formal disciplines. Speleologists use many special contrivances and methods in exploring caves. One technique is the use of dye stains to reveal the outlets of complicated underground-stream systems. Use of special shoes, safety helmets, flexible ladders and cables, and dependable lamps enables present-day speleologists to explore the recesses of large caves much more thoroughly than was formerly possible. Cave explorers occasionally stay underground for days, mapping and studying an extensive area.

For further information on this topic, see the Bibliography in volume 28, sections 417, 428.

CAVE ART. *See* PALEOLITHIC ART.

CAVEAT EMPTOR (Lat., "let the buyer beware"), principle applied in early common law that the buyer of defective goods could not hold the seller legally responsible. The theory of the early common law was based on the assumption that the buyer was able to examine the goods for any obvious defects, and that if the goods had latent defects of which the seller was unaware the buyer should bear the loss. Under modern law, however, the rule of caveat emptor does not apply to the sale of goods. The rule instead is that the seller is deemed to make an implied warranty that the goods are reasonably fit for the purpose intended by the buyer. Goods that are defective may be sold without legal liability if the fact is brought to the attention of the buyer. The rule of caveat emptor is sometimes used in modern law in reference to a real estate sale in which the seller does not specifically state that the title to the real estate is clear. In such sales, which usually are conducted under supervision of a court in bankruptcy or mortgage foreclosure, or in other judicial proceedings, the buyer takes the risk of acquiring a defective title.

CAVE DWELLERS, term used to designate ancient people who occupied caves in various parts of the world. Cave dwellers date generally from that part of the Stone Age (q.v.) called the Paleolithic, which started, according to some authorities, about 2 million years ago. Caves are natural shelters, offering shade and protection from wind, rain, and snow. As archaeological sites, caves are easy to locate and often provide conditions that encourage the preservation of normally perishable materials, such as bone. As a result, the archaeological exploration of caves has contributed significantly to the reconstruction of the human past.

Cro-Magnon cave dwellers left impressive paintings on the walls of caves in southern France (mural by Robert Knight). American Museum of Natural History

CAVE DWELLERS

Wherever caves were available, prehistoric nomadic hunters and gatherers incorporated them into the yearly cycle of seasonal camps. Most of their activities took place around campfires at the cave mouth, and some caves contain stone walls and pavements providing additional protection from winds and dampness. Hunting, particularly of reindeer, horse, red deer, and bison, was important; many caves are situated on valley slopes providing views of animal migration routes.

The Variety of Artifacts. Artifacts have been found in caves in France, Spain, Belgium, Germany, Italy, and Great Britain. The association of these remains with the bones of extinct animals, such as the cave bear and saber-toothed tiger, indicates the great antiquity of many of the cave deposits. A variety of stone and bone points discovered in excavated caves documents the importance of spears until the bow and arrow appeared in the late Paleolithic era. Other common tools included stone scrapers for working hides and wood, burins for engraving, and knives for butchering and cutting. Throughout the Paleolithic period such tools became increasingly diverse and well made. Bone needles, barbed harpoons, and spear-throwers were made and decorated with carved designs. Evidence of bone pendants and shell necklaces also exists. Among the caves that have yielded relics of early humans are the Cro-Magnon and Vallonnet in France.

Wall paintings and engravings have been found in more than 200 caves, largely in Spain and France, dating from 25,000 to 10,000 years ago. Frequently found deep inside the caves, the paintings depict animals, geometric signs, and occasional human figures. In the cave of La Colombière in France, a remarkable series of sketches engraved on bone and smoothed stones was unearthed in 1913. In caves such as Altamira in Spain and Lascaux in France, multicolored animal figures were drawn using mineral pigments mixed with animal fats. Some of the paintings adorn walls of large chambers suitable for ritual gatherings; others are found in narrow passages accessible only to individuals. Hunting and fertility seem to have been important artistic themes. The ritual gatherings themselves promoted communication and intermarriage among the normally scattered small groups.

On every continent, prehistoric foragers made use of caves. Chinese caves contain some of the earliest evidence of human use of fire, approximately 400,000 years ago. In the Zhoukoudian (Chou-k'ou-tien) Cave near Peking, remains of bones and tools of *Homo erectus* (Peking Man) have been discovered. In the Shanidar Cave in Iraq, 50,000-year-old Neanderthal skeletons were unearthed in 1957. Ancient pollen buried with them has been interpreted as evidence that these cave dwellers had developed funeral rituals. In the western deserts of North America, caves have been located that contain plant foods, woven sandals, and baskets, representing the desert culture of 9000 years ago. Early inhabitants of Australia, the Middle East, and the Peruvian Andes have also left remains in caves.

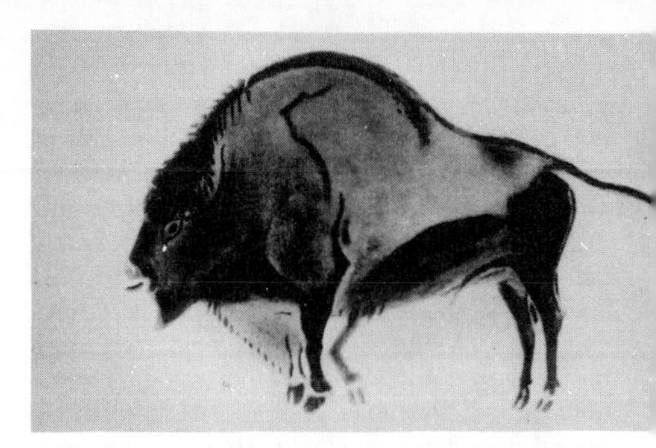

Prehistoric painting in Altamira Cave, near Santillana, Spain.

Gradually people learned to grow food, rather than forage for it. This was the beginning of the Neolithic age, which, although ending in western Europe some 4500 years ago, continued elsewhere in the world until modern times. Once agriculture became important, people established villages of permanent houses and found new uses for caves, mainly as hunting and herding campsites and for ceremonial activities. In Europe, Asia, and Africa caves continued to be used as shelters by nomadic groups.

Preservation in Caves. In dry caves, preservation is often excellent, due to moistureless air and limited bacterial activity. Organic remains such as charred wood, nutshells, plant fibers, and bones sometimes are found intact. In wet caves, artifacts and other remains often are found encrusted with, or buried beneath, calcareous deposits of dripstone. The collected evidence of human habitation on the cave floor was often buried under rockfalls from the ceilings of caverns. Intentional burials have also been found in a number of cave sites.

Because of the unusual preservative nature of caves and the great age of many of the remains found in them, the fallacious belief has arisen that a race of cave people existed. Actually, most cave sites represent small, seasonal camps. Because prehistoric people spent much of the year in open-air camps, the caves contain the remains of only part of a group's total activities. Also, the cultural remains outside caves were subject to greater decay. Thus, the archaeological record of remote times is better seen in cave deposits.

Caves have been systematically excavated during the past one hundred years. Since they often contain the remains of repeated occupations, caves can document changing cultures. For example, the economic transition from food collecting to agriculture is demonstrated by finds in highland Mexico and in Southeast Asia. Some caves in the Old World continued to be inhabited even after the close of the Stone Age; relics from the Bronze and Iron ages have been found in cave deposits. On occasion, material dating from the time of the Roman Empire has been recovered. The famous Dead Sea Scrolls (q.v.), discovered in 1947, were preserved in caves.

See also ARCHAEOLOGY. M.J.

For further information on this topic, see the Bibliography in volume 28, sections 436, 877–78.

CAVELL, Edith Louisa (1865–1915), British nurse, born in Swardeston, England. After studying nursing in London, she was invited in 1907 to become matron of a large training center for nurses in Brussels. In 1914, at the outbreak of World War I, this school became a Red Cross hospital, and she attended many wounded German and Allied soldiers there. On Aug. 5, 1915, during the German occupation of Brussels, she was arrested by the Germans for having sheltered 200 British, French, and Belgian soldiers in her house and for having helped them to escape from Belgium. Unsuccessful appeals for postponement of her execution were made by the American and Spanish ministers to Germany; she was shot by a firing squad on Oct. 12, 1915. The execution aroused widespread indignation. Vast multitudes attended her memorial service at Westminster Abbey, and a commemorative statue was erected in Saint Martin's Place, Trafalgar Square, London.

CAVENDISH, Henry (1731–1810), British physicist and chemist, born of British parents in Nice, France, and educated at Peterhouse College, University of Cambridge. His earliest experiments involved the specific heats of substances. In 1766 he discovered the properties of the element hydrogen and determined its specific gravity. His most celebrated work was the discovery of the composition of water; he stated that "water consists of dephlogisticated air (oxygen) united with phlogiston (hydrogen)." By what is now known as the Cavendish experiment, he determined that the density of the earth was 5.45 times as great as the density of water, a calculation very close to the 5.5268 established by modern techniques. Cavendish also determined the density of the atmosphere and made important investigations of electrical currents.

CAVENDISH, Thomas (c. 1560–c. 1592), English navigator and buccaneer, the third circumnavigator of the globe. Cavendish sought to retrace the exploits (1557–80) of the English navigator Sir Francis Drake. Setting out in 1586, he founded Port Desire (now Puerto Deseado, Argentina), sailed through the Straits of Magellan, and plundered Spanish settlements and ships as far north as California. The voyage was completed in 2 years, 50 days. Cavendish died while attempting a second circumnavigation.

CAVIAR. *See* STURGEON.

CAVITE, city and seaport, N Philippines, in Cavite Province, on Luzon Island, on Manila Bay, near Manila. The city has a fine harbor and is encircled by walls. The principal articles of trade include corn, rice, sugar, coffee, cacao, copra, and Manila hemp. On a narrow neck of land extending E into the bay are the remains of fortifications dating from Spanish colonial times and a U.S. naval facility. Under Spanish rule Cavite was a naval base and following its capture by the American admiral George Dewey in 1898, in the Spanish-American War, it became the principal base of the U.S. Asian Fleet. The Japanese captured Cavite in December 1941, in World War II, and held it until 1945. Pop. (1980 prelim.) 87,813.

CAVITY. *See* TEETH.

CAVOUR, Camillo Benso, Conte di (1810–61), Sardinian statesman and chief architect of Italy's unification.

Cavour was born in Turin, Piedmont, then part of the kingdom of Sardinia, on Aug. 10, 1810. From 1826 to 1831 he was a lieutenant of engineers in the Sardinian army. After resigning his commission, he became interested in politics, and in 1847 he helped to found the newspaper *Il Risorgimento* (The Resurgence), a nationalist journal that advocated expelling the Austrians from Sardinia and unifying all of Italy under a Sardinian constitutional monarchy. In 1848 Cavour became a member of the Sardinian chamber of deputies. During the ministry of the Marchese d'Azeglio (1798–1866), Cavour served in important cabinet positions, and in 1852 he became prime minister. He improved internal conditions in Sardinia and conducted the foreign affairs of the country with the aim of unifying the Italian Peninsula. He allied Sardinia with Great Britain and France in the Crimean War (1854–56) against Russia. In 1858 he made an alliance with Napoleon III against Austria. The following year Cavour maneuvered Austria into a war against Sardinia and France, expecting by a victory to drive the Austrians from Lombardy and Venetia, which they controlled. Although France and Sardinia were victorious, Napoleon III made peace with Austria in July 1859 without consulting Cavour. By the terms of the Treaty of Zürich in November 1859, Austria retained Venetia and ceded most of Lombardy to France. France in turn transferred the Lombardy cities of Peschiera and Mantua to Sardinia. When Victor Emmanuel II, king of Sardinia, accepted these peace terms, which left Austria powerful in northern Italy, Cavour resigned as prime minister.

In August and September 1859, the people of Parma, Modena, Romagna, and Tuscany voted for annexation to Sardinia. Cavour became prime minister again in early 1860, and, as the price of Napoleon III's consent to the annexations, ceded Nice and Savoy to France (Treaty of Turin, March 1860). In September 1860, Cavour sent Sardinian troops to aid Giuseppe Garibaldi in the conquest of the kingdom of the Two Sicilies. As a result of Cavour's intervention, Sicily voted (Oct. 21 and Oct. 22, 1860) for union with Sardinia. Cavour was also instrumental in bringing about the proclamation of the kingdom of Italy on March 17, 1861, and the proclamation of Victor Emmanuel II as the first king. Cavour's diplomacy, which prepared the way for the unification of Italy in 1870, earned him the reputation of being one of the most skillful European statesmen of the 19th century. He died in Turin on June 6, 1861.

CAVY, common name for several genera of rodents native to South America, including the common guinea pig (q.v.), *Cavia,* of the forest cavies. Other genera include the savannah cavies, *Galea;* rock cavies, *Kerodon;* and Patagonian cavies, or maras, *Dolichotis* and *Pediolagus.* The first three genera all generally resemble guinea pigs, with coat and color variations. The Patagonian cavies look more like short-eared rabbits and measure up to 80 cm (30 in) long. All cavies have three digits on their hind feet and four on their forefeet. Most of them are nocturnal plant-eaters that dig burrows and live in large groups.

CAWNPORE. *See* KANPUR.

CAXTON, William (1422?–91), first English printer, born probably in Tenterden, Kent. In 1441 Caxton moved to Bruges, Flanders (now part of Belgium), where he opened his own textile business, and about 1471 he moved to Cologne, Germany, where he learned the art of printing. At this time Caxton was also translating into English a popular French romance, which he printed in Bruges as *The Recuyell of the Historyes of Troye* (c. 1474). It is famous as the first book printed in English. Returning to England in 1476, Caxton set up a printing press at Westminster Abbey. His first publication there was an indulgence, which was distributed in December 1476. During his career Caxton printed nearly 100 publications, about 20 of which he also translated from French and Dutch. Among the more notable books from his press are *The Canterbury Tales* and *Troilus and Criseyde* by the English poet Goeffrey Chaucer and *Confessio Amantis* by the English poet John Gower. Caxton also wrote prefaces and epilogues to many of the works he published, notably the preface to the prose epic *Le Morte d'Arthur* by Sir Thomas Malory. In this, as in all his original writing, he displayed a lively, humorous style that considerably influenced 15th-century English literature. Fewer than 40 of his publications are extant, in single copies or in fragments.

William Caxton (from a woodcut); under the portrait are his initials and trademark. Granger Collection

CAYAMBE, extinct volcano of the Andes Mts., N Ecuador, almost directly at the equator. Covered with perpetual snow, it has an elevation of 5790 m (18,996 ft) above sea level.

CAYENNE, city, port, and capital of French Guiana, N French Guiana, on Cayenne Island, at the mouth of the Cayenne R. The leading port of French Guiana, it has steamboat service to other coastal points and is included in the itinerary of an air-transport system. The harbor is shallow, and large ships are handled nearby. The chief exports include bananas, gold, rum, hides, spices, fish glue, and various kinds of timber. Among the imports are grain, flour, wines, clothing, glass, hardware, cotton and silk goods, and tobacco. The first French settlement at Cayenne was established early in the 17th century. It was occupied by the Dutch from 1654 to 1664, when the French reestablished their control. Following another period of Dutch occupation, beginning in 1667, the French acquired permanent control of the town early in the 18th century. A French penal colony was established in Cayenne in the 1850s. In 1946, the French government abandoned the practice of transporting prisoners to the colony. Devil's Island, another former French penal colony, is nearby. Pop. (1982) 38,135.

CAYES. *See* Les Cayes.

CAYEY, town, in Cayey Municipality, SW Puerto Rico, in the Sierra de Cayey. Situated in a tobacco-growing region, Cayey is known for the manufacture of cigars. Clothing also is produced, and the town has a substantial tourist industry. Henry Barracks, a U.S. military facility, is nearby. The community was founded as Cayey de Muesas by the Spanish in 1774. Pop. (1970) 21,562; (1980) 23,305.

CAYLEY, Arthur (1821–95), British mathematician, whose most important contribution to mathematics is the theory of algebraic invariants. He was born in Richmond, Surrey, England, and educated at King's College and Trinity College, University of Cambridge. While devoting himself early in his career to the study and practice of law, he made some of his most brilliant mathematical discoveries. In 1863 he became professor of pure mathematics at Cambridge. His work on four-dimensional geometry provided 20th-century physicists, notably Albert Einstein, with the mathematical framework for developing theories of relativity.

CAYMAN ISLANDS, British dependency in the Caribbean Sea. It comprises three islands, Grand Cayman, located NW of Jamaica, and Little Cayman and Cayman Brac, located about 130 km (about 80 mi) NE of Grand Cayman. The islands are generally low-lying and of coral formation. Tourism and international banking form the backbone of the economy. Fishing, shipbuilding, turtle raising, and crop farming are locally important. The leading exports include turtle shells, green turtles, lobster, finfish, and fish for aquariums. The capital is George Town, on Grand Cayman. Discovered in 1503 by Christopher Columbus, who named them Las Tortugas (Span., "turtles"), the Cayman Islands were colonized about 1734 by British settlers from Jamaica. The islands remained a dependency of Jamaica until 1959, when they became a self-governing member of the Federation of the West Indies. In 1962 they became a British dependency again. Area, about 262 sq km (about 101 sq mi); pop. (1980 est.) 17,300.

CAYUGA (Iroquoian, "the place where locusts were taken out"), one of the original five tribes of the Iroquois, or Five Nations. Although their home in colonial times was on Cayuga Lake, in New York state, when the American Revolution broke out many members of the tribe took the side of the British and moved to Canada. The Cayuga who remained in America were absorbed into other Iroquois tribes. Now the Cayuga live chiefly in the Six Nations Reserve in Ontario.

CAYUSE, North American Indian tribe that formerly occupied the Blue Mountain region of northeastern Oregon and sections of Washington. During a severe smallpox epidemic in 1847 many members of the tribe died. The remnants of the tribe now live on the Umatilla Reservation, Ore., where they have largely intermarried with other Indian tribes. The Cayuse were probably the first North American Indians to domesticate the bronco, which in the northwestern U.S. is often called the Indian pony, or cayuse.

CB RADIO. *See* Citizens Band Radio.

CEAUŞESCU, Nicolae (1918–   ), president of Romania (1967–   ). Born in Scorniceşti, he joined (1933) the Union of Communist Youth and was imprisoned (1936; 1940) for his political activities. While in prison, he became the protégé of Gheorghe Gheorghiu-Dej (1901–65), the Romanian Communist leader. After World War II, Ceauşescu served in several governmental and party posts, becoming a member of the ruling Politburo in 1955. When Gheorghiu-Dej died, he became first secretary of the party and the effective ruler of Romania; in 1967 he became president of the country as well. Ceauşescu promoted industrialization and pursued a foreign policy relatively independent of the Soviet Union, while keeping domestic political opponents firmly in line. During the late 1980s he rejected the political and economic reforms introduced in the USSR and other East European countries.

CEBU, also Cebu City, city, central Philippines, capital of Cebu Province, on Cebu Island. The city is connected with other points on the island by rail and has an excellent harbor. Shipping is a chief industry and consists mainly of trade with other Philippine ports. Among other industries in the city are the manufacture of processed food, textiles, and chemicals. Cebu has an 18th-century cathedral and several universities, including the University of San Carlos (1595). One of the oldest settlements in the Philippines, Cebu was first visited by a European on April 7, 1521, when the Portuguese navigator Ferdinand Magellan landed here. Spanish conquerors made it their capital from 1565 to 1571. Pop. (1980) 490,281.

CEBU, island and province, central Philippines, between Bohol and Leyte islands on the E and the island of Negros on the W. The province includes also several small islands adjacent to Cebu, which is about 217 km (about 135 mi) long and about 32 km (about 20 mi) across at its greatest width. The terrain is mountainous, with an extreme elevation of about 670 m (about 2200 ft). Its fertile soil yields valuable crops of tobacco, sugar, cotton, coffee, hemp, and rice. Principal industries include coal mining and the manufacture of wines, cloth, pottery, and refined sugar. The administrative center of the province is the city of Cebu. Area of island, 4421 sq km (1707 sq mi); of province, 4864 sq km (1878 sq mi). Pop. of province (1980 prelim.) 1,234,009.

CECCHETTI, Enrico (1850–1928), Italian dancer and teacher. Born in Rome, he was the son of two dancers and danced professionally as a child. In 1879 he made his adult debut at La Scala in Milan, Italy. His brilliant technique led in 1890 to his appointment as ballet master of the Imperial Theaters in Saint Petersburg (now Leningrad); there he made striking improvements in technical standards. In 1910–13 he was ballet master to the Diaghilev Ballets Russes. Cecchetti opened his own school in London in 1918, returning to Milan in 1925. Cecchetti was one of the most gifted teachers in ballet history. His many famous pupils included the Russian ballerina Anna Pavlova (with whom he toured in 1913–18), the Russian-born choreographer Léonide Massine, and the Russian dancer Vaslav Nijinsky.

CECIL, Edgar Algernon Robert, 1st Viscount Cecil of Chelwood (1864–1958), British statesman and Nobel laureate, son of the 3d marquess of Salisbury. Cecil was born in London and educated at University College, University of Oxford. He was elected to Parliament in 1906 as a Conservative, and during World War I he held several ministerial positions. At the 1919 Paris Peace Conference, he helped draft the covenant of the League of Nations. An ardent believer in disarmament, he resigned as Lord Privy Seal from the cabinet of Prime Minister Stanley Baldwin in 1927 when the government failed to support compromise measures at the Geneva Naval Conference. Cecil was awarded the Nobel Peace Prize in 1937.

CECIL, Robert. *See* SALISBURY, ROBERT CECIL, 1ST EARL OF.

CECIL, William. *See* BURGHLEY, WILLIAM CECIL, 1ST BARON.

CECILIA, Saint (d. 230?), Christian martyr. According to tradition she was betrothed to a youth named Valerian, whom she converted to Christianity, and the two were martyred for refusing to honor the Roman gods. She is said to have been thrown into a boiling bath but to have escaped unharmed. The executioner attempted to behead her in three strokes, but he failed, and she lived three days longer. In 821 her remains were interred in a crypt in the Basilica of Saint Cecilia in Rome. Since legend speaks of her singing to God in her heart, she came to be regarded as the patron of music. The English poets Geoffrey Chaucer, John Dryden, and Alexander Pope have celebrated St. Cecilia in literature, and she has been the subject of many paintings. Her feast day is November 22.

CECROPIA MOTH, common name for a large American silkworm moth, *Samia cecropia,* of the family Saturniidae. Cecropia, the largest moth native to the eastern U.S., has a wingspread of 15 to 18 cm (6 to 7 in). The reddish-brown wings are bordered with red, white, and gray markings with an outlined white crescent-shaped mark in the center. In the larva stage, the moth is about 10 cm (about 4 in) long, bluish-green, and covered with rows of blue, yellow, and coral-red tubercles, or knoblike projections. The larvae feed on, and eventually destroy, the foliage of many forest and fruit trees.

CECROPS, in Greek mythology, the founder of Athens and of Greek civilization. Reputed to have sprung half man, half serpent from the soil, he became the first king of Attica, which he divided into 12 communities. He established marriage and property laws, introduced bloodless sacrifice and burial of the dead, and invented writing. During his 50-year rule he arbitrated a dispute over possession of Athens between Athena and Poseidon, awarding it to Athena.

CEDAR, common name for the genus *Cedrus,* three or four species of large trees native to

Cedar of Lebanon, Cedrus libani, *a true cedar belonging to the pine family.* Brooklyn Botanic Garden

White cedar, Chamaecyparis thyoides, *a member of the cypress family.* U.S. Forest Service

mountainous areas of North Africa and Asia. Cedar trees belong to the family Pinaceae (*see* PINE), the members of which have needlelike leaves and, like all conifers, bear their seeds on scales clustered into cones. They differ from other members of the family in their evergreen four-angled leaves borne on short side-branches. The genus produces fragrant, durable, red-colored wood used in construction and cabinetry. Although no true cedars are native to North America, they are planted as ornamentals in milder areas, and various horticultural varieties, based on growth form and leaf color, exist.

The best-known cedar is the cedar of Lebanon *(C. lebani),* mentioned often in the Old Testament; the First Temple of Solomon was built of this wood (see 1 Kings 5:6). It is native to Asia Minor, and today only a few original groves remain, although they contain some trees of great age. Trees may reach 30 m (100 ft) in height and produce spreading branches that split off from the main trunk, unlike most conifers, which have a single dominant trunk. The dark to bright green leaves are about 2.5 cm (about 1 in) long, and the upright cones are about 10 cm (4 in) long. The Cyprus cedar (*C. brevifolia*), usually considered only a variety of the cedar of Lebanon, occurs on the island of Cyprus in the Mediterranean. The Atlas cedar (*C. atlantica*) is closely related to the cedar of Lebanon and occurs in the Atlas Mountains of North Africa. The remaining cedar, deodar (*C. deodara*), occurs in the Himalaya and is an important timber tree in India. Unlike the other species, which have horizontal branches and cones flat at the apex, the deodar has pendulous branches and rounded cones.

The name cedar is also applied to other conifer trees with fragrant wood, especially members of the family Cupressaceae (*see* CYPRESS). The well-known white cedar (*Chamaecyparis thujoides*) grows in swamps of the eastern U.S. and reaches a height of 24 m (80 ft). The genus *Thuja,* an arborvitae (q.v.), is also called cedar; western cedar (*T. plicata*) and eastern white cedar (*T. occidentalis*) are both important timber trees in the U.S. Southern red cedar (*Juniperus virginiana*), widespread in the eastern U.S., is a juniper (q.v.). The flowering plant genus *Cedrela,* a tropical American mahogany (q.v.), is known as Spanish or West Indian cedar.

CEDAR, river rising in SE Minnesota and flowing across Iowa. It empties into the Iowa R. at Columbus Junction, near where the Iowa R. joins the Mississippi. The Cedar R. is about 483 km (about 300 mi) long and drains a beautiful and fertile region. The chief cities along its course are Cedar Rapids, Vinton, and Waterloo, Iowa.

CEDAR BREAKS NATIONAL MONUMENT. *See* NATIONAL PARK SERVICE (table).

CEDAR CREEK, BATTLE OF, important military engagement of the American Civil War, fought on Oct. 19, 1864, near Cedar Creek, a tributary of the Shenandoah River, in Shenandoah Co., Va. The action began when a Confederate force of about 18,000 men under Gen. Jubal A. Early made a surprise attack on contingents, totaling about 31,000 troops, of the Army of the Shenandoah, commanded by the Union general Philip H. Sheridan. Early's forces struck at dawn under the cover of fog and darkness, overrunning the Union positions, and by midday they had succeeded in advancing as far as Middletown, Va. Meanwhile, Sheridan, who had been absent from the front on official business, rejoined his army after a fast ride from Winchester, Va., and assumed command. Late in the afternoon he ordered a general counter-offensive, which broke through the Confederate lines. Early's army retreated in panic, pursued by Sheridan's cavalry across Cedar Creek to Woodstock, Va. Union casualties were 644 killed, 3430 wounded, and 1591 missing; Confederate casualties were about 320 killed, 1540 wounded, and 1050 missing. As a result of their defeat at Cedar Creek, the Confederate forces made no further attempts to strike the North through the Shenandoah Valley. Sheridan's famous ride from Winchester and its aftermath, one of the most dramatic episodes of the Civil War, are the theme of "Sheridan's Ride," by the American poet Thomas Read (1822–72).

CEDAR FALLS, city, Black Hawk Co., NE Iowa, at falls on the Cedar R. (hence its name); settled 1845, inc. 1853. It is a residential suburb of Waterloo and the seat of the University of Northern Iowa (1876). Manufactures include pumps, farm equipment, and processed food. A state park adjoins the city. During the mid-19th century, the town grew as a lumber- and grain-milling center. Pop. (1970) 29,597; (1980) 36,322.

CEDAR MOUNTAIN, BATTLE OF, indecisive military engagement of the American Civil War, fought on Aug. 9, 1862, near a hill called Cedar Mountain, in Culpeper Co., Va.

A Union force led by Gen. John Pope (1822–92), commander of the Army of Virginia, met an advancing Confederate army of about 24,000, commanded by Gen. Stonewall Jackson. Pope sent Gen. Nathaniel Banks (1816–94) to meet Jackson with a force of about 8000, about half the size of the Confederate force that was engaged in the battle. After furious fighting, Banks's troops, pursued by Jackson's forces, withdrew toward the town of Culpeper. The Union army received reinforcements, however, and counterattacked, checking Jackson's advance. On August 11 the Confederate army fell back toward Gordonsville, Va. Jackson's losses were 1338 killed and wounded; Pope's included 1759 killed and wounded and 594 missing.

CEDAR RAPIDS, city, seat of Linn Co., E Iowa, at rapids on the Cedar R. (hence its name); inc. as a city 1856. It is the processing and distributing hub of a rich agricultural area, where corn, soybeans, and livestock are raised. Manufactures here include navigation equipment, construction machinery, electrical goods, and processed food. Coe College (1851), Mount Mercy College (1928), and a community college are here. The site was settled in 1837, and the community was platted in 1842. Cedar Rapids became a railroad terminus in 1859 and grew as a gateway for westward migration. Pop. (1970) 110,642; (1980) 110,243.

CEDAR WAXWING. *See* WAXWING.

CEIBA, common and generic name of a large genus of trees of the bombax family, Bombacaceae, which attain a height of 40 m (130 ft) or more. They have palmate leaves and large, bell-shaped flowers. Their thick, woody seed capsules contain a kind of fiber that resembles cotton.

The ceiba tree, kapok tree, or silk-cotton tree, *Ceiba pentandra,* is widely cultivated in tropical regions for its fiber, known as kapok (q.v.). Because of its shortness, elasticity, and brittleness, the fiber cannot be spun like cotton but is used in various ways in upholstery and in making floss. Because of its lightness and water-repellent properties, kapok has been used in large quantities in life preservers and as stuffing and insulation. The principal supplies of kapok come from the island of Java. The seeds of the tree also yield kapok oil, used in making soap. The soft, spongy wood of the African variety, which is called bentang, is used for making canoes. The round seeds, the size of peas, are eaten on the Indonesian island of Celebes.

CEILING, overhead surface of a room, opposite the floor. Usually the term refers to a flat, beamed, or curved surface that conceals the underside of the roof or the floor above, but it may also refer generally to the exposed underside.

In ancient Egyptian temples the underside of the flat stone roof was generally painted blue with yellow stars, bands of hieroglyphs, and emblems of the heavens. In Greek temples the pitched timber roof was sometimes left uncovered and sometimes hidden by a coffered (deeply paneled) ceiling, often decoratively painted. Roman ceilings were similar but also included flat ceilings of planks and plaster as well as vaulted and domed ceilings of brick, concrete, or stone, such as the coffered dome of the Pantheon in Rome.

In the Middle Ages, churches and important secular buildings usually had pitched roofs, left open to show the structural timbers or, later, covered by barrel, groined, or rib vaulting in stone. Some ceilings were flat and made of boards, plaster, or coffering, and others incorporated structural beams. Many ceilings were painted in all-over patterns or with biblical scenes. In the Renaissance, most roof structures were hidden behind flat or domed ceilings, which might be richly ornamented. Some had carved and gilded coffering or molding, often framing paintings by great masters such as Titian and Veronese, as in the Doges' Palace in Venice. Others had elaborate carved or molded plaster decoration sometimes extending into pendants, as in 16th- and 17th-century English country houses.

Ceilings in the 18th century were sometimes coved, or curved into the walls where a right angle ordinarily would be. Decoration in paint and plaster was generally more delicate in rococo or neoclassical buildings. Ceilings in the 19th century repeated older styles or in less pretentious

A view of the coffered ceiling in the Doge's Palace, Venice. Alinari

buildings used such new materials as pressed tin. In the more austerely functional buildings of the 20th century, ceilings, of plaster or acoustical tile, tended to be flat and unadorned. Frequently they hid elaborate heating, plumbing, air-conditioning, and electrical systems. In many public buildings, however, architects, such as the American Louis I. Kahn and the Italian Pier Luigi Nervi, revealed both structural members and mechanical equipment as part of the architectural design.

In the Islamic world great mosques and palaces usually had vaulted or domed ceilings, which were often decorated with mosaic, painted Koranic inscriptions, or carved stalactite (honeycomblike) ornament. Simpler buildings had flat ceilings of beams and plaster or flat or concave ceilings or *artesonado* work—delicate coffering richly painted and gilded. Indian temples were often domed and decorated with rich stone or stucco carving. In Chinese and Japanese temples the roof beams, supported on elaborately carved painted wooden brackets, were revealed.

CELA, Camilo José (1916–), noted Spanish writer of fiction, poetry, and travel accounts. Born in El Padrón, Cela attended the University of Madrid, and also served in Gen. Francisco Franco's army during the Spanish civil war. His career and literary interests were deeply affected by his early acceptance and later rejection of Franco's dictatorial rule. His style of brutal realism, known as *tremendista,* was apparent in his first novel, *The Family of Pascal Duarte* (1941; trans. 1947). Other novels include *The Hive* (1951; trans. 1953), depicting life in a cheap Madrid cafe, and the bizarre *Mrs. Caldwell Speaks to Her Son* (1953; trans. 1968). In 1956 Cela founded the influential Spanish literary magazine *Papeles de Son Armadáns* and served thereafter as its editor.

CELADON. *See* POTTERY.

CELEBES *or* **SULAWESI,** island, E Indonesia, and one of the larger islands of the Malay Archipelago, situated E of Borneo and W of the Moluccas. It consists mainly of four peninsulas, separated by deep gulfs, two of the peninsulas extending southward and two northeastward. This singular conformation gives the island a coastline of about 5630 km (about 3500 mi). The surface reaches one of its highest elevations in Mt. Lompobatang, an extinct volcano in the S part of the island 2871 m (9419 ft) high. A number of active volcanoes are also found in the E end of the N peninsula, but most of the volcanoes have reached the latent stage. The largest river is the Sadang, which is navigable by small boats.

The climate is tropical, but somewhat modified by the elevation and the proximity of the sea. Among the animals peculiar to the island are the tailless baboon; the babiroussa, with upper canines curved backward and nearly touching the forehead; the marsupial cuscus; and the sapiutan or wild cow. The forests include oak, teak, palm, cedar, upas trees, and bamboo. Cloves, nutmeg, spices, tropical fruits, corn, rice, tobacco, and sugar are raised. The coffee crop is not large, but is of superior quality. The minerals include gold, copper, tin, sulfur, salt, and diamonds and other precious stones. Among the chief items of trade are coffee, spices, copra, coconuts, and trepang, an edible sea slug.

The Portuguese first discovered and named the island in 1512, but from about 1607 the Dutch gradually obtained supremacy, although it was not until well into the 19th century that every district was under their control. Under the Dutch the island formed an important province of the Netherlands East Indies, consisting of the Celebes government in the S part of the island and the Manado residency in the N. The capital of the Celebes government and chief port of the island was Makassar (now Ujung Pandang), situated on Makassar Peninsula, on the Strait of Makassar. The seat of the residency was in Manado, at the end of the Manado Peninsula on the Celebes Sea. During World War II, the Japanese held the island from 1942 until 1945. In 1946 Celebes Island was included in the autonomous state of East Indonesia, a part of the new United States of Indonesia (now Republic of Indonesia). Area, about 189,070 sq km (about 73,000 sq mi), pop. (1980) 10,409,533.

CELERY, common name for a biennial herb, *Apium graveolens,* of the family Umbelliferae (*see* PARSLEY), a native of Europe but now widely grown throughout the world. The stalks, about 30 to 76 cm (about 12 to 30 in) high in cultivated varieties, are eaten, raw or cooked, as a vegetable or salad. When allowed to grow naturally, the stalks are greenish in color and slightly bitter in taste. They are often blanched during the last stages of their growth by preventing access of sunlight except to the leaves; this process removes the color and the bitter taste, but also some of the vitamins. If allowed to grow a second year, celery sends up flower stalks about 61 to 91 cm (about 24 to 36 in) tall with small white flowers in umbels. The dried fruit of celery is used as a condiment alone under the name of celery seed or ground and mixed with salt under the name of celery salt. Celery seed is also used in pharmacy, as a sedative or to disguise the flavor of other drugs.

Celery is subject to attack by several blights, by the tarnished plant bug (*Lygus pratensis*), and by the larva of the black swallowtail butterfly. In the U.S., celery crops are grown principally in California and Florida.

CELESTA. *See* GLOCKENSPIEL.

CELESTIAL MECHANICS. *See* ORBIT.

CELESTIAL NAVIGATION. *See* NAVIGATION.

CELESTIAL SPHERE, imaginary sphere of the heavens, with the earth at its center. The sphere forms the basis for the coordinate systems used in assigning positions to objects observed in the sky. It is also used for designating time intervals and for navigation.

The equatorial system of coordinates establishes a grid in the celestial sphere that is based on the earth's equator and poles, projected outwards to intersect with the sphere. Because the earth is moving around the sun, the appearance of celestial objects such as stars changes on the sphere from day to day. Thus one particular moment of the year is assigned as the time when the celestial grid is established. This moment is the vernal equinox, when the sun's disk passes directly above the equator and marks the beginning of spring in the northern hemisphere (*see* ECLIPTIC). Celestial latitude is called declination, and celestial longitude is called right ascension in this equatorial system. Right ascension is measured from the zero-hour circle established by the vernal equinox. The yearly path traced by the sun across the celestial sphere forms a great circle, called the ecliptic, on the sphere. A coordinate system that establishes a grid on the celestial sphere using the ecliptic rather than the equator as its reference plane is also sometimes employed, as are other systems.

The apparent daily movement of the celestial sphere about the earth, caused by the earth's own rotation, is actually about four minutes shorter than the mean solar day. *See* DAY.

CELESTINE I, Saint (d. 432), pope (422–32). Born in the Roman Campagna, he was archdeacon of the Roman church before his election to the papacy. Recorded details of his pontificate deal mainly with the controversy over Nestorianism (q.v.), the heretical doctrine that Christ was two distinct persons inseparably united. After the Council of Ephesus (431) defined that Christ was one person in two natures, human and divine, Celestine excommunicated Nestorius, patriarch of Constantinople and instigator of the controversy. He also sent St. Germain of Auxerre (378–448) to Britain to convert the adherents of Pelagianism (q.v.). Celestine's traditional feast day is April 6.

CELESTINE V, Saint (c. 1215–96), pope (1294), who after five months resigned from the papacy because of incompetence.

Born Pietro da Morrone in Isernia, Italy, Celestine became a Benedictine monk at the age of 17. Inclining to a life of solitude, however, he retired to the Abruzzi Mountains. There he attracted many followers who became the nucleus of a religious order of hermits. Known later as Celestines, the order was a branch of the Benedictines; it survived until 1785, when its last monastery was closed.

Celestine was living as a hermit when he was elected pope on July 5, 1294. Recognized for his holiness, he was chosen as a compromise candidate after a two-year deadlock among the cardinals over a successor to Nicholas IV (1227–92). Naive and administratively inexperienced, he allowed King Charles II of Naples to dictate church policy. Soon, however, he realized his inability to govern the church and voluntarily resigned his office on December 13 of his election year. To prevent Celestine's followers from going into schism, Boniface VIII, Celestine's successor, held him prisoner in the castle of Monte Fumone until his death. He was canonized in 1313. His traditional feast day is May 19.

CELESTINE III (c. 1106–98), pope (1191–98). Born Giacinto Bobo, of noble Roman ancestry, he served the papal court as cardinal deacon for 47 years. Elected pope at the age of 85, he was ordained priest the day before his installation. The day following his installation he crowned the German king Henry VI as Holy Roman emperor. A learned theologian, skilled diplomat, and good administrator, Celestine was a central figure in the long struggle between the Holy Roman Empire and the papacy.

CELESTITE, mineral variety of strontium sulfate, $SrSO_4$, which is one of the principal sources of the element strontium (q.v.). Widely distributed, it is found in whitish orthorhombic crystals (*see* CRYSTAL) with a hardness (q.v.) of 3 to 3.5 and a sp.gr. of 4. Although celestite is found in several localities in the U.S., little is produced domestically.

CELIBACY, the state of being ummarried, with abstinence from sexual activity. Considered a form of asceticism (q.v.), it has been practiced in many religious traditions: in ancient Judaism, by the Essenes; and in Buddhism, Jainism, and Hinduism, by the members of monastic groups.

In Christianity, celibacy has been practiced by monks and nuns in both the Western and Eastern churches. In the Eastern church, parish clergy are permitted to marry before ordination, but bishops are selected from among the unmarried clergy. In the Roman Catholic church, celibacy is required of all clergy in the Latin Rite. The church holds that this practice is sanctioned, although not required, by the New Testament, basing this claim upon what it avers to have been the constant tradition of the church and upon several biblical texts (notably, 1 Cor. 7:6–7, 25; Matt. 19:12). The principles upon which the law of celibacy is founded are (1) that the clergy may serve God with more freedom and with undivided heart; and (2) that, being called to serve Jesus Christ, they may embrace the holier life of self-restraint. This statement does not imply, it is said, that matrimony is not a holy state, but simply that celibacy is a state of greater perfection.

Having no doctrinal bearing in the Roman Catholic church, celibacy is regarded as a purely disciplinary law. A dispensation from the obligation of celibacy has occasionally been granted to ecclesiastics under exceptional circumstances, for instance, to provide an heir for a noble family in danger of extinction.

The celibacy of the clergy was rejected by the Protestant reformers, Martin Luther setting the example to his followers by marrying a former nun. Both the marriage of ministers and the abolition of monastic vows became common features of those bodies that withdrew their allegiance from the Roman Catholic church. According to the articles of religion of the Church of England, "bishops, priests, and deacons are not commanded by God's law, either to vow the estate of single life, or to abstain from marriage; therefore it is lawful for them, as for all other Christian men, to marry at their own discretion, as they shall judge the same to serve better to godliness."

The history of priestly celibacy has been a stormy one since it became law for the clergy of the Latin Rite in the 6th century. Although Pope Paul VI, in his encyclical of June 24, 1967, reaffirmed the traditional position, the requirement of priestly celibacy remains a much-disputed ecclesiastical question.

CÉLINE, Louis Ferdinand, pseudonym of LOUIS FERDINAND DESTOUCHES (1894–1961), French novelist and physician. Born in Courbevoie, a Paris suburb, he studied medicine and from 1924 to 1928 traveled widely as a physician and medical researcher. Back in France, he joined the staff of a state clinic in Clichy, working mainly as a physician to the poor. His nihilistic first novel, *Journey to the End of the Night* (1932; trans. 1934) was followed by a similar work, *Death on the Installment Plan* (1936; trans. 1938), and *Guignol's Band* (1944; trans. 1954). Celine's savagely misanthropic outlook, combined with his anti-Semitic writings of the late 1930s, caused him to be accused of collaboration with the Nazis, although he was a pacifist. As a result, Celine fled to Germany in 1944. Finally exonerated by the French government, he returned to France in 1950. His experiences in exile are recorded fictionally in *Castle to Castle* (1957; trans. 1968) and two later works. His writings continue to be valued for their stylistic innovations and absurdist outlook.

CELL, the fundamental structural unit of all living organisms. Some cells are complete organisms, such as the unicellular bacteria and protozoa; others, such as nerve, liver, and muscle cells, are specialized components of multicellular organisms. Cells range in size from the smallest bacterialike mycoplasmas, which are 0.1 micron in diameter, to the egg yolks of ostriches, which are about 8 cm (about 3 in) in diameter. Although they may differ widely in appearance and function, all cells have a surrounding membrane and an internal, water-rich substance called the cytoplasm, the composition of which differs significantly from the external environment of the cell. Within the cell is genetic material, deoxyribonucleic acid (DNA), containing coded instructions for the behavior and reproduction of the cell and also the chemical machinery for the translation of these instructions into the manufacture of proteins (*see* GENETICS). Viruses are not considered cells because they lack this translation machinery; they must parasitize cells in order to translate their own genetic code and reproduce themselves.

Cells are of two distinctly different types, procaryotes and eucaryotes; thus, the living world is divided into two broad categories (*see* CLASSIFICATION). The DNA of procaryotes is a single molecule in direct contact with the cell cytoplasm, whereas the DNA of eucaryotes is much greater in amount and diversity and is contained within a nucleus separated from the cell cytoplasm by a membranous nuclear envelope. Many eucaryotic cells are further divided into compartments by internal membranes in addition to the nuclear envelope, whereas procaryotic cells never contain completely internal membranes. The procaryotes include the mycoplasmas, bacteria, and blue-green algae. The eucaryotes comprise all plant and animal cells. In general, plant cells differ from animal cells in that they have a rigid cell wall exterior to the plasma membrane; a large vacuole, or fluid-filled pouch; and chloroplasts that convert light energy to chemical energy for the synthesis of glucose.

STRUCTURE AND FUNCTION

Cells are composed primarily of oxygen, hydrogen, carbon, and nitrogen, the elements that make up the majority of organic compounds. The most important organic compounds in a cell are proteins, nucleic acids, lipids, and polysaccharides (carbohydrates). The "solid" structures of the cell are complex combinations of these large molecules. Water makes up 60 to 65 percent of the cell, because water is a favorable environment for biochemical reactions.

All cells are dynamic at some stage of their life cycle, in the sense that they use energy to perform a variety of cell functions: movement, growth, maintenance and repair of cell structure, reproduction of the cell, and manufacture of specialized cell products such as enzymes and hormones. These functions are also the result of interactions of organic molecules.

Plasma Membrane. The plasma membrane (PM), a continuous double layer of phospholipid molecules 75 to 100 angstroms thick, constitutes the boundary between the cell and its external environment. In addition to lipids, the PM has protein components (polypeptides) that are associated with either the outer or inner surfaces of its layers or are buried within them. The structure as a whole is selectively permeable, or semipermeable; that is, it permits the exchange of water and selected atoms and molecules between the cell exterior and interior. This is vital to the cell because while the PM helps maintain high local concentrations of organic molecules within the cell, it also allows interaction between the cell and its external environment.

The PM mediates such interactions in various ways. The exchange of mineral ions and small nutrient molecules is controlled by PM proteins that act as pumps, carriers, and channels. The PM also participates in the exchange of larger molecules through phagocytosis, the engulfing of large food particles; endocytosis, the intake of fluids and membrane components; and exocytosis, the expulsion of cell products or cell waste. (The PM of some cells, such as those of the human intestine, is convoluted to enhance the surface area for these exchanges.) In addition, the PM contains receptors that selectively receive nerve and hormone signals and transmit them to the interior of the cell. Finally, direct cell-to-cell interactions can occur through specialized regions of the PM known as junctions. Organs such as the skin and the small intestine consist of cells held together by tight junctions and local thickenings, or desmosomes, which constitute another type of junction. Cells can communicate electrically through a third type of junction, called a gap junction, that consists of tiny protein "tunnels" between two cells, through which tiny "message" molecules and ions may be passed. When the PMs of two cells are continuous, an actual bridge of cytoplasm forms between them; in plants these bridges are called plasmodesmata.

Cells Walls. Exterior to the PM of most plant cells and bacteria is a cell wall, a cell product made largely of complex polysaccharides. In higher plants the polysaccharide is cellulose. The presence of a cell wall makes these cells rigid and sturdy, but it poses special problems for the transport of substances into and out of the cell.

Cytoplasm. The cytoplasm is the water-rich matrix within a cell that contains and surrounds the other cellular contents. It is more like a viscous gel than a watery solution, but it liquefies when shaken or stirred. Such gel-to-sol transitions are thought by some cell biologists to play a role in the movement of a cell's components from place to place within the cell. Rapid movement of cell components is called either streaming or cyclosis, depending on whether it occurs linearly or circularly.

Through an electron microscope the cytoplasmic gel appears as a three-dimensional lattice of slender, protein-rich strands in a continuous water-rich phase. Because the latticework is reminiscent of the internal structure of spongy bone, which is composed of many struts, or trabeculae, it is called the microtrabecular lattice (MTL). The MTL appears to interconnect and support the other "solid" structures of the cell. The composition and function of the MTL are as yet still unknown, but it is thought to control the spatial arrangement of cell components within the cytoplasm.

Cytoskeleton. The so-called cytoskeleton influences the shape of the cell in much the same way tent poles determine the shape of a tent. Without the cytoskeleton a cell tends to become spherical. The cytoskeleton probably gives direction to the movement of components within the cytoplasm as well and participates in movement of the cell itself. The cytoskeleton is composed of three main filament types: the microtubules, microfilaments, and intermediate-sized filaments that are supported and distributed within the

This drawing of a typical animal cell is cut away to reveal the complex array of interior structures. All material entering or leaving the cell must pass through its outer membrane. From Helena Curtis: *Biology*, Third Edition, Worth Publishers, Inc., New York, 1979.

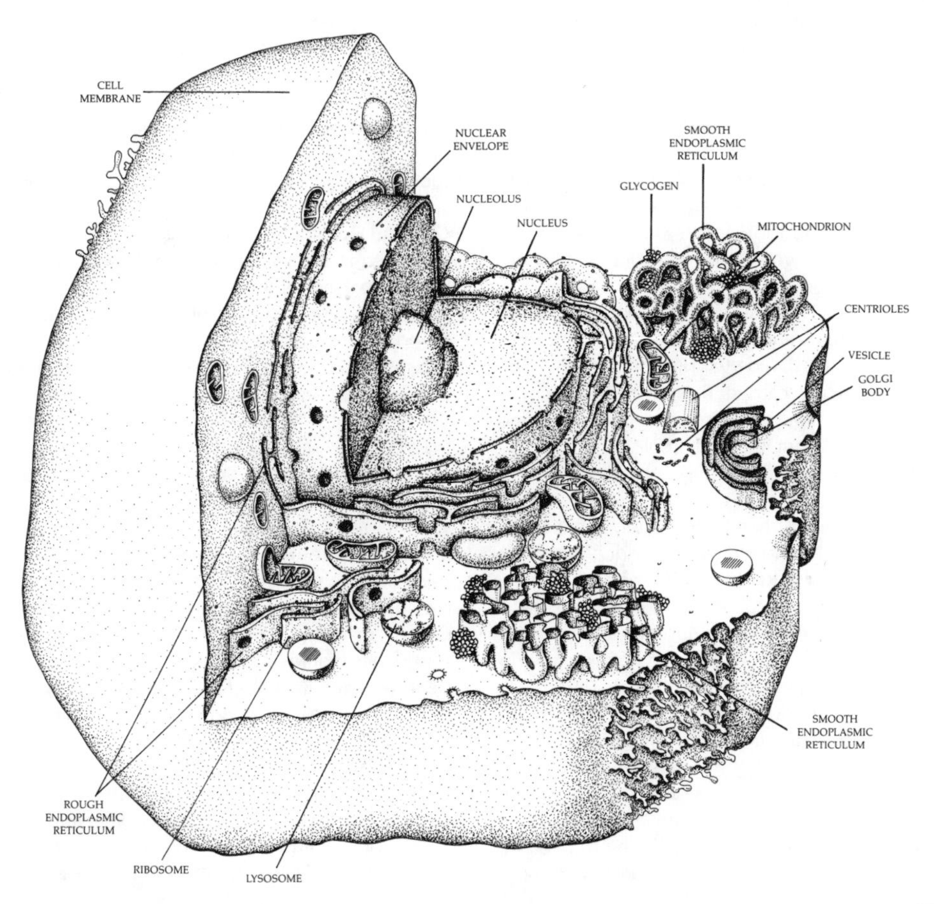

MTL. Microtubules are long rigid cylinders that act as the bones of the cell. They also may act as tracks along which intracellular components are transported. The walls of the cylinders are composed of two proteins, alpha- and beta-tubulin. Microfilaments are composed of actin, a major protein of muscle. They often occur in long bundles called stress fibers and may act as the muscles of the cell. The intermediate-sized filaments are a heterogeneous class of proteins whose function is largely unknown.

Nucleus. The membrane-bounded structures contained within the cytoplasm of eucaryotes are referred to as organelles. The nucleus is the most easily recognizable of these. DNA, combined with protein, is organized inside the nucleus into structural units called chromosomes, which usually occur in identical pairs. The DNA in each chromosome is a single, very long, highly coiled molecule subdivided into functional subunits called genes. Genes contain the coded instructions for the assembly of polypeptides and larger proteins. Together the chromosomes contain all the information needed to build an identical functioning copy of the cell.

The nucleus is surrounded by an envelope of two concentric membranes. Interaction between the nuclear contents and the surrounding cytoplasm is permitted through holes, called nuclear pores, in this envelope. The nucleus also contains a specialized region, the nucleolus, where nucleoprotein particles are assembled. These particles migrate through the nuclear pores into the cytoplasm, where they are modified to become ribosomes.

Ribosomes. Ribosomes are the "factories" where the instructions encoded in the DNA of the nucleus are translated to make proteins. The instructions are carried from the DNA to the ribosomes by long nucleic-acid molecules called messenger ribonucleic acids (RNAs).

Endoplasmic Reticulum (ER). Among the other membranous structures within the eucaryotic cell are extensive membrane systems that make up the smooth and the rough endoplasmic reticulum (SER and RER). The SER often takes the form of branching tubes. (In skeletal muscle it acts as a reservoir for calcium ions and is called the sacroplasmic reticulum.) The RER is made up of sheetlike flattened sacs, which often are stacked one on top of the other; the term *rough* refers to the numerous ribosomes that dot the cytoplasmic surfaces of the sacs. The RER is one of the sites of protein synthesis in the cytoplasm. Proteins are synthesized on the cytoplasmic surface and pass through the membrane to become sequestered within the sacs. These packaged proteins are destined for secretion to the outside of the cell. Other proteins, synthesized on ribosomes that are not attached to membranes, are not secreted and remain as structural proteins or metabolic enzymes.

Golgi Apparatus. Similar in appearance to and perhaps continuous with the ER is a region of smooth, stacked membranous sacs known as the Golgi apparatus. Cell biologists think that the apparatus modifies proteins, after they are synthesized and packaged on the RER, by linking them with sugars or other molecules.

Lysosomes. Lysosomes are membrane-bounded bags, or vesicles, containing digestive enzymes. Their normal function is digestion of complex nutrients and broken-down organelles. In disease fighting, the lysosomes of white blood cells aid in the digestion of engulfed bacteria and other foreign or toxic materials.

Mitochondria and Chloroplasts (Plastids). Mitochondria are the powerhouses of the animal cell, where the products of the enzymatic breakdown, or metabolism, of nutrients such as glucose are converted into energy in the form of the molecule adenosine triphosphate (ATP). This process uses up oxygen and is called aerobic respiration. Plants possess, in addition to mitochondria, similar organelles called chloroplasts. Each chloroplast contains the green pigment chlorophyll, which is used to convert light energy from the sun into ATP. This process is called photosynthesis (q.v.).

Cilia and Flagella. Some cells have flexible, whiplike external appendages called cilia and flagella, which are used for locomotion and for capturing food. Cilia are 3 to 10 microns long and are found on protozoa as well as in human oviducts and respiratory tracts. In the respiratory tract they sweep large particles up the trachea and prevent them from passing into the lungs. Flagella, which may be ten times as long, are found on some protozoa and unicellular plants, and they are used for locomotion by the sperm of higher organisms. Eucaryotic cilia and flagella are composed of microtubules covered by a membrane sheath. Procaryotic flagella are more slender and are composed of the protein flagellin. They propel the cell by rotating like the propeller of a ship rather than by a whipping motion.

Centrioles and Basal Bodies. All animal and some plant cells contain a pair of centrioles, which are cylindrical structures composed of short microtubules. They are surrounded by a cloud of fuzzy material, the exact function of which is unknown. Centrioles control the arrangement of microtubules in the cell cytoskeleton. Basal bodies, which are similar, are structures that anchor

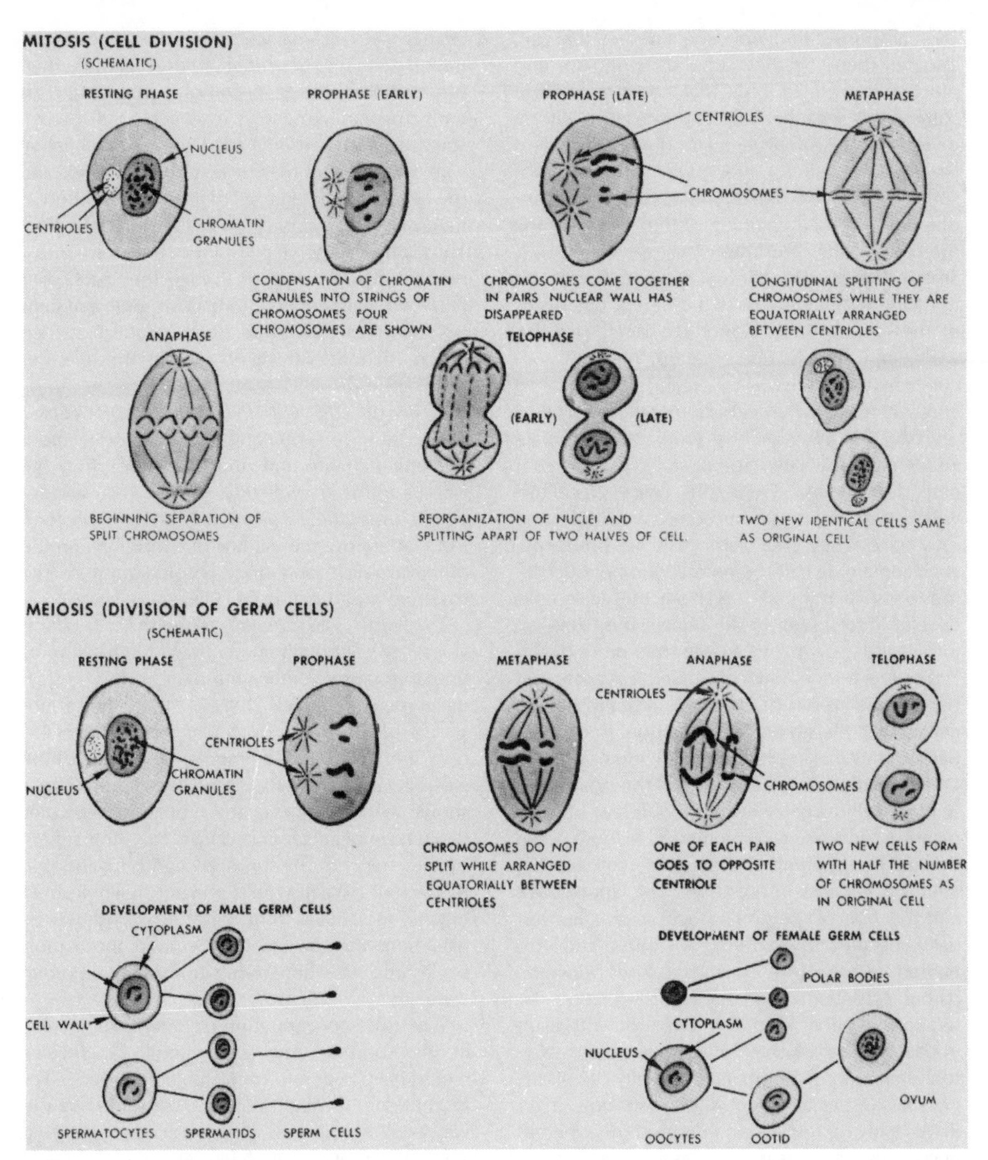

Two types of cell division. Mitosis (top) is the process by which tissues increase in size. Cell parts organize themselves in a pattern that distributes chromosomes and other material equally so that each new cell is identical to the original cell. Meiosis (above), the process by which germ cells divide, differs from mitosis in that each new cell contains only half the chromosomes from the original cell. The normal number of chromosomes is restored through fertilization.

TODAY'S HEALTH, published by the American Medical Association

cilia and flagella within the cytoplasm, just inside the plasma membrane. Centrioles and basal bodies both contain DNA and apparently can duplicate themselves independently of duplication of the entire cell.

DIVISION, REPRODUCTION, AND DIFFERENTIATION

All cells are the products of the division of preexisting cells. Simple cell division, or asexual reproduction, normally results in the production of two identical daughter cells, each containing a set of chromosomes identical with those of the parent cell. Before the onset of division, a cell grows to roughly twice its original size. In doing so it duplicates its DNA, so that each chromosome is doubled. During division the duplicate sets are physically separated, following longitudinal splitting of each double chromosome, and are transported into opposite sides of the cell. The cell then constricts around its equator and pinches in two. In cells that contain chromosomes, the separation of chromosomes during division (mitosis) requires an oblong scaffold of parallel microtubules, along which the chromosomes are moved. This scaffold, called the spindle, forms at the beginning of mitosis under the direction of the centrioles.

Sexual Reproduction. Sexual reproduction is the mingling of the DNA of two different organisms of the same species to produce a cell, or cells, with a new combination of genes. When this occurs between single-celled organisms, it is called conjugation. In multicellular organisms, sexual reproduction requires the production of male and female germ cells (sperm and eggs) by a process called meiosis. During this process a cell divides twice; but its chromosomes are duplicated only once. Thus, four germ cells are produced, each containing half the normal number of chromosomes. In the male organism the germ cells develop into sperm; in the female they develop into eggs. A sperm and an egg then unite (fertilization) to form a new cell, called a zygote, that has a complete set of chromosomes and has received half its genetic information from each parent, thus making it a new individual.

Differentiation. Differentiation is the process by which a cell daughter becomes different from its parent in appearance or function, or both, even though both parent and daughter cell contain identical genetic information. The appearance and function of identical daughter cells are initially specified by two kinds of information inherited by each in equal measure from the parent: cytoplasmic and nuclear information. Alterations in either kind of information will result in daughter cells being unlike their parents. Cytoplasmic information consists chiefly of cell organelles (especially centrioles) and messenger RNAs ready for translation into proteins, whereas nuclear information is contained in the genetic code. Changes in cytoplasmic information generally are the result of unequal divisions that produce an asymmetrical distribution of cytoplasmic organelles and messenger RNAs between daughter cells. Changes in nuclear information involve restriction of the use of some portion of the cell's genes, because genes can be turned on or off by the cell in response to cellular environmental signals. The behavior of a cell at any given time in differentiation largely depends on which subset of genes is turned on.

Differentiation primarily occurs through activation and deactivation of genes in a programmed succession to produce orchestrated changes in cell characteristics. During differentiation certain genes often are irreversibly turned off, and the change becomes permanent. This limits the variety of ways in which a cell can respond to an environmental signal, as well as the variety of signals to which it can respond, and the cell is channeled toward its ultimate differentiated fate. This process is called determination. Thus, a human nerve cell cannot transform into a human muscle cell even though they each contain identical genetic information. Aging of cells is sometimes viewed as a continuation of their differentiation, with death seen as the final determination.

ORIGIN OF LIFE AND EVOLUTION OF CELLS

Scientists have formulated many theories about the origin of life and how it evolved into the various forms known today. These ideas are deduced from the evidence of the fossil record, from laboratory simulations of conditions on the primeval earth, and from consideration of the structure and function of cells.

The earth was created more than 3 billion years ago, although more than 2 billion years probably passed before life as it is now known developed. Scientists believe that the atmosphere of the young earth was mostly water vapor, methane, and ammonia, with very little gaseous oxygen. Laboratory simulations have shown that all major classes of organic molecules could have been generated from this atmosphere by the energy of the sun or by lightning and that the lack of oxygen would prevent newly formed organic molecules from being broken down by oxidation. Rain would have carried these molecules into lakes and oceans to form a primordial soup.

When the concentration of organic molecules in this soup became high enough, molecules would have begun to form stable aggregates. For example, lipids might coalesce into droplets the way cooking oil does in water, thus generating simple membranes and trapping other organic molecules in the interior of the droplet. Randomly formed aggregations that could harness energy to grow and reproduce themselves would eventually far outnumber other combinations. DNA may have been an essential component of the self-reproducing aggregates; it and RNA are the only organic molecules able to duplicate themselves. These supramolecular aggregations would have been extremely lifelike and with some refinements would have resembled primitive procaryotes. This concept of the origin of life, however, does not explain the development of the genetic code and the precise interdependence between the code and protein synthesis.

The relative absence of oxygen from the atmosphere of the young earth meant that no ozone layer existed to screen out ultraviolet radiation and no oxygen was available for aerobic respiration. Therefore, the first cells were probably photosynthetic and used ultraviolet light. Because photosynthesis generates oxygen, the oxygen content of the atmosphere gradually increased. As a result, cells that could use this oxygen to generate energy, and photosynthetic cells that could use light other than ultraviolet, eventually became predominant.

Eucaryotes may have evolved from procaryotes. This idea comes from speculation about the origin of mitochondria and chloroplasts. These organelles may be the degenerate descendants of aerobic and photosynthetic procaryotes that were engulfed by larger procaryotes but remained alive within them (endosymbiosis). Over the years the host cell became dependent on the endosymbionts for energy (ATP), while they in turn became dependent on the host for most other cell functions. The fact that mitochondria and chloroplasts are surrounded by two membranes, as if they had originally entered the cell by phagocytosis, supports this theory. In addition, these organelles contain their own DNA and ribosomes, which resemble the DNA and ribosomes of bacteria more than those of eucaryotes. It is possible that other eucaryotic organelles originated similarly.

HISTORY

Cells were first described in 1665 by the English scientist Robert Hooke, who studied the dead cells of cork with a crude microscope. Living cells were first described in detail in the 1670s by the Dutch scientist Anton van Leeuwenhoek. These early descriptions were not improved on until the early 19th century, when better-quality microscope lenses were developed. In 1839 the German botanist Matthias Schleiden and the German zoologist Theodor Schwann formulated the basic cell theory of today. Struck by the underlying similarity between plant and animal cells, they stated that all living organisms consist of cells and cell products. Thus, a whole organism could be understood through the study of its cellular parts. In 1858 the German pathologist Rudolf Virchow's theory, that all cells come from preexisting cells, led to the development of ideas about cell division and cell differentiation.

The development in the late 19th century of techniques for staining cell parts enabled scientists to detect tiny cell structures that were not actually seen in detail until the advent of the electron microscope in the 1940s. The development of various advanced optical techniques in the 20th century also increased the detection power of the light microscope for observations of living cells.

The study of cells (cytology) is not limited to describing structures (morphology). A central concept in modern cytology is that each structure has a function that may be understood as a series of biochemical reactions. The understanding of these functions has been greatly aided by the development of cell fractionation techniques, using an ultracentrifuge to separate specific intracellular structures from the rest of the cell. Another technique is tissue culture, by which specific kinds of cells can be isolated and grown for study. K.R.P. & K.L-P.

For further information on this topic, see the Bibliography in volume 28, sections 438–39, 443–44.

CELL, ELECTRIC. *See* BATTERY.

CELLINI, Benvenuto (1500–71), Florentine sculptor and engraver, who became one of the foremost goldsmiths of the Italian Renaissance, executing exquisitely crafted coins, jewelry, vases, and ornaments.

Born in Florence, on Nov. 3, 1500, Cellini was apprenticed to a goldsmith at the age of 15. When he was 16, his fiery temper and continual dueling and brawling caused him to be exiled to Siena. Later, in Rome, he was Michelangelo's pupil for a short while.

Among Cellini's most famous patrons were Pope Clement VII, Pope Paul III, Francis I of France, and the Florentine noble Cosimo I de' Medici. Francis I invited him to Paris in 1540, where he modeled the bronze reliefs of the *Nymph of Fontainebleau* (Louvre, Paris). He also executed an elaborate gold saltcellar for Francis (1539–43, Kunsthistorisches Museum, Vienna). Compelled to leave in 1545 because of his quarrels with the king's mistress and his eccentricities, Cellini returned to Florence. There, under the patronage of Cosimo de' Medici, he executed many fine works in metal, among them a bronze portrait bust of Cosimo and the colossal bronze statue *Perseus and Medusa* (1545–54, Loggia dei Lanzi, Florence). He died in Florence, on Feb. 13, 1571.

Cellini is also noted for his autobiography, written between 1538 and 1562, the standard English version of which was published in 1960. An embellished account of Cellini's escapades, adventures, and intrigues, this text provides a valuable portrait of daily, political, social, and ecclesiastical life in the 16th century.

CELLO *or* **VIOLONCELLO,** large, low-pitched musical instrument of the violin family, held between the performer's knees. It has four strings tuned C G d a (C = two C's below middle C; a = the A below middle C). Its range extends over more than four octaves. The earliest surviving cellos are two from the 1560s by the Italian violinmaker Andrea Amati. Until the late 18th century the cello was primarily a supporting instrument, playing bass lines and adding fullness to musical textures. During the baroque era unaccompanied cello suites were composed (1720?) by the German composer Johann Sebastian Bach, as were cello concertos by Antonio Vivaldi and Luigi Boccherini, the Italian composers. In the 19th century, works for the cello included concertos by Johannes Brahms and the Czech composer Antonín Dvořák. In the 20th century, composers such as the Russians Sergey Prokofiev and Dmitry Shostakovich further explored its solo capabilities. The most prominent 20th-century cellist was the Spanish-born Pablo Casals. Other leading soloists are the Russian-born Gregor Piatigorsky and Mstislav Rostropovich. *See also* VIOLIN. J.V.

CELLOPHANE, originally a trade name and now a common name for a flexible, transparent film made of regenerated cellulose and used principally as a wrapping material. Cellophane is produced by dissolving wood pulp or other cellulose material in an alkali with carbon disulfide, neutralizing the alkaline solvent with an acid, extruding the precipitate into a sheet, impregnating it with glycerine, and then drying and cutting the sheets to the desired size. Cellophane was invented about 1910 by the Swiss chemist Jacques Brandenberger (1873?–1954), who in 1912 invented the first machines for large-scale production and established a factory near Paris.

CELLULAR RADIO, mobile radiotelephone system, in use in several major cities of the world, that was given its first U.S. test in Chicago in 1978 and has since been adopted in other urban areas. The system, a miniature version of large radio networks, is named for the unit "cells" into which it divides an area. Each cell has a radius of about 1.5 to 2.4 km (1 to 2.5 mi) and is equipped with a radio transmitter that employs its own range of radio frequencies. The same range can be repeated several times across a large city as long as the cells using them are not neighbors. As a mobile radiophone moves through this pattern of cells, its user's calls—made as on regular telephones—are switched from one cell to the next by a computerized system. The Federal Communications Commission licenses a telephone and a radiocommunications company to serve a given area as competitors.

CELLULOID, originally the trade name and now the common name of a synthetic plastic made by mixing pyroxylin, or cellulose nitrate, with pigments and fillers in a solution of camphor in alcohol. When heated, the substance is pliable or plastic and can be molded into a variety of shapes. Upon drying and cooling, the material becomes hard. In the U.S. celluloid was invented by John Hyatt (1837–1920), who was trying to win a $10,000 award for finding a substitute for ivory in making billiard balls. Hyatt failed to win the prize, but he received a patent for his discovery in 1870. The patent was disputed by the British inventor of Xylonite, a similiar product.

Celluloid is transparent and colorless and in paste form can be colored or rolled or molded into specific shapes. Some of its advantages are that it is inexpensive and durable, takes a high polish, does not warp or discolor, and is not affected by moisture. It is, however, highly flammable, and although modifications in manufacture have reduced the dangers of fire, it has been largely superseded by other materials. Celluloid is used in making combs, brushes, and buttons.

CELLULOSE (Lat. *cellula,* "little cell"), complex carbohydrate (q.v.), the chief constituent of the cell wall of all plant cells. In plants, cellulose is normally combined with woody, fatty, or gummy substances. With some exceptions among insects, true cellulose is not found in animal tissues. Microorganisms in the digestive tracts of herbivorous animals break down the cellulose into products that can then be absorbed. Cellulose is insoluble in all ordinary solvents and may be readily separated from the other constituents of plants. Depending on its concentration, sulfuric acid acts on cellulose to produce glucose, soluble starch, or amyloid; the last is a form of starch used for the coating of parchment paper. When cellulose is treated with an alkali and then exposed to the fumes of carbon disulfide, the solution yields films and threads. Rayon and cellophane (qq.v.) are cellulose regenerated from such solutions. Cellulose acetates are spun into fine filaments for the manufacture of some fabrics and are also used for photographic safety film, as a substitute for glass, for the manufacture of safety glass, and as a molding material. Cellulose ethers are used in paper sizings, adhesives, soaps, and synthetic resins.

With mixtures of nitric and sulfuric acids, cellulose forms a series of flammable and explosive compounds known as cellulose nitrates, or nitrocelluloses. Pyroxylin, also called collodion cotton, is a nitrate used in various lacquers and plastics; another, collodion, is used in medicine, photography, and the manufacture of artificial leather and some lacquers. A third nitrate, guncotton, is a high explosive.

CELSIUS, Anders (1701–44), Swedish astronomer, who invented (1742) the centigrade, or Celsius, thermometer. As professor of astronomy at Uppsala University (1730–44), he built the observatory there in 1740, serving as its director. In 1733 his collection of 316 observations of the aurora borealis was published. In 1737 he took part in the French expedition sent to measure one degree of meridian in the polar regions.

CELSIUS TEMPERATURE SCALE. *See* HEAT; TEMPERATURE.

CELSUS, Aulus Cornelius (fl. 1st cent. AD), Roman writer. He wrote an encyclopedia on the subjects of medicine, rhetoric, history, philosophy, warfare, and agriculture. Part of this work, the eight books on medicine, *De medicina* (Of Medicine), were translated into English in 1756; three are still in print. The books were largely based on the ideas of the Greek physician Hippocrates.

CELTIC LANGUAGES, subfamily of the Indo-European family of languages. Geographically and historically, this subfamily is divided into a Continental group (now extinct) and an Insular group. On linguistic grounds the Insular languages fall into two groups: the Brythonic (or British), including Breton, Cornish, and Welsh; and the Goidelic (or Gaelic), including Irish, Scottish Gaelic (or Erse), and Manx. Until the 5th century, Continental Celtic languages, among them, Gaulish, were spoken throughout western Europe, but little information survives about them. Only the Brythonic and Goidelic groups survive, limited to the British Isles, Brittany, and some North and South American communities.

The characteristic of Celtic languages that most conspicuously distinguishes them from other Indo-European linguistic groups is their loss of the original Indo-European sound *p.* Thus, a Latin, Greek, and Sanskrit word containing an initial or medial *p* will appear in the Celtic language family without it (for example, Lat. *porcus,* Goidelic *orc*). The Goidelic and Brythonic groups of Celtic languages differ in that Goidelic preserves the velar element of the Indo-European labiovelar *qu* sound (later written *c*), whereas Brythonic renders this sound as *p.* Thus Irish *cūig* or *coo-ig* (or *cuig*), "five" corresponds to Welsh *pump.*

The rules of pronunciation in all the Celtic languages are extremely complicated; the spelling generally does not correspond to the pronunciation, and initial consonants change according to the final sound of the preceding word. For example, in Irish, *fuil* is "blood," but "our blood" is *ar bhfuil.* In Welsh *tad* ("a father") becomes *fy nhad* for "my father," *ei thad* for "her father," and *i dad* for "his father."

All modern Celtic languages use the Roman alphabet. They have only two genders, feminine and masculine; adjectives usually follow nouns. Like some non-Indo-European languages they use verbal nouns instead of present participles, always begin sentences with the verb, and express agency by means of the impersonal passive.

Breton. The Breton language is spoken today in various dialects in Brittany; most Breton speakers also speak French. Developed between the 4th and 6th centuries by Welsh and Cornish exiles fleeing invaders, it differs from the Welsh and Cornish of their homelands in its use of nasals and loanwords from the French.

Cornish. Once the language of Cornwall, Cornish has been extinct since the late 18th century, despite recent efforts to revive it. It survives only in a few proper names and certain words in the English dialect spoken in Cornwall.

Welsh. Welsh, called Cymraeg or Cymric (from *Cymru,* "Wales") by its speakers, is the native language of Wales and the most flourishing of the Celtic languages. It is spoken in Wales (where the majority of its users also speak English) and in some communities in the U.S. and Argentina. Organizations such as the Society for the Welsh Language have saved the language from dying out and are working to assure its official status along with English. Several schools in Wales now use Welsh as the medium of instruction, and television and radio broadcasts are made in the language.

Like Breton, Welsh has discarded case endings for nouns; verbs, however, are elaborately inflected. The alternation of consonants, called mutation, plays a role, as in all Celtic languages. Welsh spelling is phonemic, representing unambiguously the pertinent sounds. In most cases Welsh speakers will know how to pronounce a word they have never seen before. The letter *w* can represent either a consonant or a vowel, however, and y stands for two vowel sounds. The consonant *f* has the sound of English *v; ff* of *f; dd* of *th,* as in *then;* and *th* of *th,* as in thin. Popular attempts to describe pronunciation of double *l* (*ll*) all fail. It is a voiceless lateral fricative, and facile comparison to English *thl* is invalid. Welsh words are accented on the next to last syllable and have a characteristic intonation.

Scholars recognize three periods of Welsh: Old (800–1100), Middle (1100–1500), and Modern (from 1500). Old Welsh survives only in isolated words and names, plus a few lines of verse. Welsh has borrowed words throughout all these periods from Latin, Anglo-Saxon, Norman French, and extensively from English, but it still has a large native vocabulary of Celtic origin.

Forty dialects have been identified in Wales. Standard Welsh has both a Northern and Southern variety.

Irish. Irish, or Irish Gaelic, is the oldest of the Goidelic group of Celtic languages. Ancient written examples exist in the ogham inscriptions, on about 370 gravestones scattered through southwestern Ireland and Wales. Dating from the 5th to the 8th century, the inscriptions consist almost entirely of proper names. Irish can be grouped into four periods: Old (c. 800–1000), Early or Early Middle (1200–1500), Middle (1200–1500), and Modern (from 1500). Originally a highly inflected language, Irish retains essentially two noun cases, nominative and genitive, with the dative surviving in the singular of feminine nouns; the language has only two verb tenses in the indicative mood. It is chiefly spoken in the western and southwestern parts of the Republic of Ireland, where it is an official language, and to some extent in Northern Ireland. In the past century, the number of Irish-speaking persons has declined from 50 percent of the population of Ireland to less than 20 percent.

Scottish Gaelic. A form of Gaelic was brought to Scotland by Irish invaders about the 5th century, where it replaced an older Brythonic language. By the 15th century, with the accretion of Norse and English loanwords, the Scottish branch differed significantly enough from the Irish to warrant definition as a separate language.

The alphabet of Irish and Scottish Gaelic is identical, consisting of 18 letters. Scottish Gaelic employs four cases of nouns: nominative, genitive, dative, and vocative. Like Irish, the accent is on the initial syllable.

Scottish Gaelic exists in two main dialects, Northern and Southern, roughly geographically determined by a line up the Firth of Lorne to the town of Ballachulish and then across to the Grampian Mountains, which it follows. The Southern dialect is more akin to Irish than is the Northern, and is more inflected. The main difference is the change of the *é* sound, which is *eu* in Northern dialect and *ia* in Southern. Thus, the word for "grass" is pronounced *feur* in Northern and *fiar* in Southern. Scottish Gaelic also has a few thousand speakers in Nova Scotia.

Manx. The language of the Isle of Man is classed as a dialect of Scottish Gaelic, with strong Norse influence. It began to decline in the 19th century, and in the early 20th century it became virtually extinct. The first written records are of the 17th century, and Manx literature, apart from ballads and carols, is negligible.

CELTIC LITERATURE, literature of the Celts (q.v.), written in the various Celtic languages (q.v.): Breton, Cornish, Gaelic (which includes Irish and Scottish Gaelic), Manx, and Welsh. See separate articles on these literatures.

CELTS, a people who dominated much of western and central Europe in the 1st millennium BC, giving their language, customs, and religion to the other peoples of that area.

History. The earliest archaeological evidence associated with the Celts places them in what is now France and western Germany in the late Bronze Age, around 1200 BC. In the early Iron Age, they are associated with the Halstatt culture (8th–6th cent. BC), named for an archaeological site in Upper Austria. They probably began to settle in the British Isles during this period. Be-

This bronze mirror, known as the Desborough Mirror, was found in 1908 at Desborough, Northamptonshire, England. An excellent example of the delicate, graceful Celtic style, it was made early in the 1st century AD. The reverse side is richly decorated with a flowing, sinuous abstract design.
British Museum

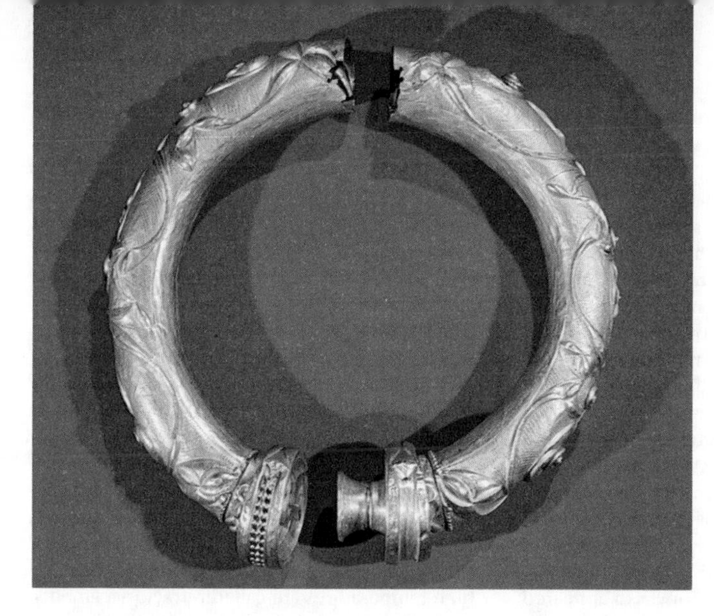

The Broighter Collar, also called a torc, from county Derry, Ireland. This 1st-century work illustrates the delicacy and careful attention to detail of Celtic art.
National Museum of Ireland

tween the 5th and 1st centuries BC, their influence extended from what is now Spain to the shores of the Black Sea. This later Iron Age phase is called La Tène, after a site in Switzerland.

The word Celt is derived from Keltoi, the name given to these people by Herodotus and other Greek writers. To the Romans, the Continental Celts were known as Galli, or Gauls; those in Britain were called Britanni.

In the 4th century BC, the Celts invaded the Greco-Roman world, conquering northern Italy Macedonia, and Thessaly. They plundered Rome in 390, sacked Delphi in 279, and penetrated Asia Minor, where they were known as Galatians. The "Cisalpine Gauls" of northern Italy were conquered by the Romans in the 2d century BC; Transalpine Gaul (modern France and the Rhineland) was subdued by Julius Caesar in the 1st century BC, and most of Britain came under Roman rule in the 1st century AD. In the same period, the Celts of central Europe were dominated by the Germanic peoples. In medieval and modern times the Celtic tradition and languages survived in Brittany (in western France), Wales, the Scottish Highlands, and Ireland.

Way of Life. The various Celtic tribes were bound together by common speech, customs, and religion, rather than by any well-defined central governments. The absence of political unity contributed substantially to the extinction of their way of life, making them vulnerable to their enemies. Their economy was pastoral and agricultural, and they had no real urban life. Each tribe was headed by a king and was divided by class into Druids (priests), warrior nobles, and commoners (*see* DRUIDISM). The nobles fought on foot with swords and spears and were fond of feasting and drinking. Celtic mythology, which included earth gods, various woodland spirits, and sun deities, was particularly rich in elfin demons and tutelaries, beings that still pervade the lore of peoples of Celtic ancestry.

Celtic Christianity. The Christian faith was well established in Celtic Britain by the 4th century AD, but in the 5th century the Saxons and other Germanic peoples invaded the country, driving most of the Celtic Christians into Wales and Cornwall. At the same time, St. Patrick and other British missionaries founded a new church in Ireland, which then became the center of Celtic Christianity. The Irish church developed a distinctive organization in which bishops were subordinate to the abbots of monasteries (*see* COLUMBA, SAINT). The Irish monks, devoted to learning as well as religion, did much to preserve a knowledge of ancient Roman literature in early medieval Europe. Between the late 6th and the early 8th centuries, Irish missionaries were active in Christianizing the Germanic peoples that had conquered the Western Roman Empire, and they founded numerous monasteries in present-day France, Germany, Switzerland, and Italy. Celtic Christianity in Ireland was weakened by the Viking invasions of the 9th and 10th centuries, and by the 12th century its characteristic institutions, which were incompatible with those of the dominant Roman church, had largely disappeared from Europe.

Art. Celtic art is considered the first great contribution to European art made by non-Mediterranean peoples. Its roots go back to the artisans of the Urnfield culture and the Hallstatt culture (8th–6th cent. BC) at the beginning of the Iron Age. It flowered in the period of the La Tène culture. Although Celtic art was influenced by ancient Persian, Greek, Etruscan, and Roman art and by that of the nomads of the Eurasian steppes, it developed distinctive characteristics. These are evident in its major artifacts—weapons, vessels, and jewelry in bronze, gold, and occasionally silver. Many of these objects were made for chieftains in southern Germany and France and were recovered from their tombs.

The Celtic style is marked by a preference for stylized plant motifs, usually of Greek origin, and fantastic animals, derived from the Scythians and other steppe peoples; the human figure plays a secondary role. Other favorite motifs are elliptical curves and opposing curves, spirals, and chevrons, also derived from steppe art. These elements were combined in dynamic yet balanced, intricate geometrical patterns carried out in relief, engraving, or red, yellow, blue, and green champlevé enamel on shields, swords, sheaths, helmets, bowls, and jewelry. They also appeared on painted pottery cinerary urns, food vessels, incense bowls, and drinking cups. Examples of Celtic art include *torcs,* or neck rings, with the two open ends ornamented with animal heads; the silver repoussé Gundestorp cauldron (c. 100 BC, National Museum, Copenhagen); a bronze lozenge-shaped shield with circular medallions and small enamel circles (1st cent. BC–1st cent. AD); and a bronze mirror with enameled decoration (1st cent. BC) (both British Museum, London). Also surviving are roughly carved stone monuments and wooden objects.

During the period of Roman domination of Western Europe in and after the 1st century BC, the art of Celtic peoples on the Continent gradually lost its distinctive style. The Celts of Ireland continued to work with traditional motifs, but, as Christianity took hold, they combined them with Christian motifs and employed their skills in the service of the church. Their carved stone crosses; intricate metal chalices, bells, and reliquaries; and magnificently illuminated liturgical books may more properly be considered Irish art (q.v.).

For further information on this topic, see the Bibliography in volume 28, sections 884, 893.

CEMENT, any material that hardens and becomes strongly adhesive after application in plastic form. The term *cement* is often used interchangeably with *glue* and *adhesive* (*see* ADHESIVE); in engineering and building construction the term usually refers to a finely powdered, manufactured substance consisting of gypsum plaster or portland cement that hardens and adheres after being mixed with water.

Cements are used for various purposes, such as binding sand and gravel together with portland cement to form concrete (q.v.), for uniting the surfaces of various materials, or for coating surfaces to protect them from chemical attack. Cements are made in a wide variety of compositions for a wide variety of uses. They may be named for the principal constituents, such as calcareous cement, which contains silica, and epoxy cement, which contains epoxy resins (*see* RESINS); for the materials they join, such as glass or vinyl cement; for the object to which they are applied, such as boiler cement, or for their characteristic property, such as hydraulic cement, which hardens underwater, or acid-resisting cement, or quick-setting cement. Cements used in construction are sometimes named for their commonly reported place of origin, like Roman cement, or for their resemblance to other materials, such as portland cement, which produces a concrete resembling the Portland stone used for building in England. Cements that resist high temperatures are called refractory cements.

Cements set, or harden, by the evaporation of the plasticizing liquid such as water, alcohol, or oil, by internal chemical change, by hydration, or by the growth of interlacing sets of crystals. Other cements harden as they react with the oxygen or carbon dioxide in the atmosphere.

Portland Cement. Typical portland cements are mixtures of tricalcium silicate ($3CaO \cdot SiO_2$), tricalcium aluminate ($3CaO \cdot Al_2O_3$), and dicalcium silicate ($2CaO \cdot SiO_2$), in varying proportions, together with small amounts of magnesium and iron compounds. Gypsum is often added to slow the hardening process.

These active compounds in cement are unstable, and when water is added they rearrange their structure. The initial hardening of the cement is caused by the hydration of tricalcium silicate, which forms jellylike hydrated silica and calcium hydroxide. These substances ultimately crystallize and bind together the particles of sand or stone, which are always included in a mortar or concrete mixture, into a hard mass. Tricalcium aluminate acts in the same way to produce the initial set, but does not contribute to the ultimate hardening of the mixture. The hydration of dicalcium silicate proceeds similarly but far more slowly, hardening gradually over a period of years. The process of hydration and setting of a cement mixture is known as curing; during this period heat is evolved.

Portland cement is manufactured from lime-bearing materials, usually limestone, together with clays, shales, or blast-furnace slag containing alumina and silica, in the approximate proportions of 60 percent lime, 19 percent silica, and 8 percent alumina, 5 percent iron, 5 percent magnesia, and 3 percent sulfur trioxide. Some rocks, called cement rocks, are naturally composed of

Steps in the manufacture of portland cement. Above: In huge kilns, rotating at about one turn per minute, raw materials are burned into clinkers. Below: After cooling, the clinkers are conveyed to grinders, where they are ground into fine powder. Portland Cement Assn.

these elements in approximately suitable proportions and can be made into cement without the use of large quantities of other raw materials. In general, however, cement plants rely on mixed materials.

In the manufacture of cement the raw materials are ground together, the mixture is heated until it fuses into a clinker, and the clinker is ground into a fine powder. The heating is usually accomplished in rotary kilns more than 150 m (500 ft) long and 3.7 m (12 ft) or more in diameter. The kilns are slightly tilted from the horizontal, and the raw material is introduced at the upper end, either in the form of a dry rock powder or as a wet paste composed of ground-up rock and water. As the charge progresses down through the kiln, it is dried and heated by the hot gases from a flame at the lower end. As it comes nearer the flame, carbon dioxide is driven off, and in the area of the flame itself the charge is fused at temperatures between 1540° and 1600° C (2800° and 2900° F). The material takes approximately 6 hours to pass from one end of the kiln to the other. After it leaves the kiln, the clinker is cooled quickly and ground, and then conveyed by a blower to packing machinery or storage silos. The amount thus produced is so fine in texture that 90 percent or more of its particles will pass through a sieve with 6200 openings per sq cm (40,000 per sq in).

In a modern kiln, 45 kg (about 100 lb) of raw material will make 27 to 30 kg (about 59 to 66 lb) of cement. The weight lost is largely carbon dioxide and water. Kilns usually burn coal in the form of powder and consume about 450 g (about 1 lb) of coal for about every 900 g (about 2 lb) of cement produced. Oil and gas are also used.

A number of tests are used to check the quality of the cement. A common one is to use a mortar specimen of one part cement and three parts of sand and measure its tensile strength after a week in air and underwater. A good cement will show a tensile strength of 19.4 kg per sq cm (275 lb per sq in) under these conditions.

Special Cements. By varying the percentage of its normal components or adding others, portland cement can be given various desirable characteristics, such as rapid hardening, low heat during hydration and resistance to alkalis. Rapid-hardening cements, sometimes called high-early-strength cements, are made by increasing the proportion of tricalcium silicate or by finer grinding, so that up to 99.5 percent will pass through a screen with 16,370 openings per sq cm (105,625

Finished cement is stored in silos, from which it can then be loaded into trucks or into railroad cars.
Portland Cement Assn.

per sq in). Some of these cements will harden as much in a day as ordinary cement does in a month. They have the disadvantage, however, of producing much heat during hydration, which makes them unsuitable for large structures where such heat may cause cracks. Special low-heat cements, which usually have a large proportion of dicalcium silicate, are generally used for massive pourings. Where concrete work must be exposed to alkaline conditions, which attack concretes made with ordinary portland cement, resistant cements with a low aluminum content are generally employed. Cements for use under salt water may contain as much as 5 percent iron oxide, and those with as much as 40 percent aluminum oxide are used to resist the action of sulfate-bearing waters.

Production. It was not until the 20th century that the U.S. produced portland cement in any great quantity. In 1910, 13 million metric tons were manufactured. After 1910 production rose steadily until 1928, when 30 million metric tons were made. Production dropped sharply in the early 1930s, then began to rise again. In the mid-1980s the U.S. cement industry annually produced about 70 million metric tons.

History. Although various types of mineral-based hydraulic cement are of ancient origin, hydraulic cements have been used only since the middle of the 18th century. The term *portland cement* was first used in 1824 by Joseph Aspdin (1799–1855), a British cement maker, because of the resemblance between concrete made from his cement and Portland stone, which was much used in building in England. The first modern portland cement, made from lime and clay or shale materials heated until they formed cinders (called clinkers in the industry) and then ground, was produced in England in 1845. At that time cements were usually made in upright kilns where the raw materials were spread between layers of coke, which was then burned. The first rotary kilns were introduced about 1880. Portland cement is now almost universally used for structural concrete.

CENCI, Beatrice (1577–99), Italian noblewoman, called the "beautiful parricide." She was the daughter of Francesco Cenci (1549–98), a wealthy and cruel Roman nobleman. According to legend, after his second marriage he imprisoned her and made incestuous advances until circumstances enabled him to gratify his lust. She sought the help of her relatives and, with her stepmother and her brother, conspired to murder Francesco on Sept. 9, 1598. During the lengthy trial, in which the conspirators were charged with murder, Beatrice persisted in declaring her innocence. All three, however, were condemned and beheaded in 1599. The story has inspired many works of art, from Guido Reni's 17th-century portrait and Percy Bysshe Shelley's tragedy *The Cenci* (1819) to the modern opera *Beatrix Cenci* (1971) by Alberto Ginastera.

CENIS, MONT (Ital. *Moncenisio*), pass in the Alps, on the border between France and Italy. The pass reaches an elevation of about 2088 m (about 6850 ft) above sea level. A road was constructed between 1803 and 1810 by order of Napoleon. A tunnel, completed in 1871, is about 13 km (about 8 mi) long and connects Turin, Italy, with Chambéry, France.

CENOZOIC ERA, last of the five major eras of geologic time, beginning about 65 million years ago and extending through the present. It follows the Cretaceous period of the Mesozoic era and is subdivided into the Tertiary period and the Quaternary period. Features of Tertiary times are considered in articles under the names of the various shorter time periods (epochs) making up the Tertiary period; in order, from earliest to latest, these are the Paleocene, Eocene, Oligocene, Miocene, and Pliocene. For discussions of the last two, the Pleistocene, and the Recent epochs, *see* QUATERNARY PERIOD.

The Cenozoic, shortest of the geologic eras, is that period during which the modern world, with its characteristic geographical features and its animals and plants, came into being.

CENSORSHIP, supervision and control of the information and ideas that are circulated among the people within a society. In modern times, censorship refers to the examination of books, periodicals, plays, films, television and radio programs, news reports, and other communication media for the purpose of altering or suppressing parts thought to be objectionable or offensive. The objectionable material may be considered immoral or obscene, heretical or blasphemous, seditious or treasonable, or injurious to the national security. Thus, the rationale for censorship is that it is necessary for the protection of three basic social institutions: the family, the church, and the state.

Until recently, censorship was firmly established in various institutional forms in even the most advanced democratic societies. By the mid-20th century a revolutionary change in social attitudes and societal controls weakened the existence and strength of censorship in many democracies; however, all forms of censorship have not been universally eliminated. Today many persons, including some civil libertarians, object to the "new permissiveness" in the arts and mass media; they claim it debases the public taste, corrupts all sense of decency and civility, and even undermines civilization.

In nondemocratic societies censorship is a dominant and all-pervasive force, felt on all levels of artistic, intellectual, religious, political, public, and personal life. Hardly any act, expression, or relationship is exempt from official surveillance and accountability.

Although the Universal Declaration of Human Rights, adopted by the UN General Assembly in 1948, says nothing explicitly about the right of freedom from censorship, certain articles, if strictly observed, would tend to mitigate the rigor of censorship in nondemocratic countries. Among such provisions are those that prohibit interference with a person's home, family, privacy, or correspondence, and those that provide for the right to freedom of thought, conscience, religion, opinion, and expression without interference. Thus, the worldwide struggle for human rights often involves problems of censorship as well as the fate of those dissidents who are its victims.

EARLY HISTORY

Censorship and the ideology supporting it go back to ancient times. Every society has had customs, taboos, or laws by which speech, play, dress, religious observance, and sexual expression were regulated.

Greek Censorship. In Athens, where democracy first flourished, Socrates preferred to sacrifice his life rather than accept censorship of his teachings. Charged with the worship of strange gods and with the corruption of the youth he taught, Socrates defended free discussion as a supreme public service. He was thus the first person to formulate a philosophy of intellectual freedom. Ironically, his disciple Plato was the first philosopher to formulate a rationale for intellectual, religious, and artistic censorship.

Plato believed that art should be subservient to morality; art that could not be used to inculcate moral principles should be banned. In the ideal state outlined in *The Republic,* censors would prohibit mothers and nurses from relating tales considered bad or evil; and in his *Laws* Plato proposed that wrong beliefs about God or the hereafter be treated as crimes and that formal machinery be set up to suppress heresy.

In the 5th century BC, the Athenian philosopher Anaxagoras was punished for impiety; Protagoras, another leading philosopher, was charged with blasphemy, and his books were burned. These instances of repression and persecution in Athens were not truly typical of Greek democracy, for usually the freedom to speak openly in private or in the assembly was respected.

Roman Censorship. In Rome the general attitude was that only persons in authority, particularly members of the Senate, enjoyed the privilege of speaking freely. Public prosecution and punishment, supported by popular approval, occurred frequently. The Roman poets Ovid and Juvenal were both banished. Authors of seditious or scurrilous utterances or writings were punished. The emperor Caligula, for example, ordered an offending writer to be burned alive, and Nero deported his critics and burned their books.

The far-flung Roman Empire could not have lasted for some four centuries if it had not maintained a policy of toleration toward the many religions and cults of the diverse nations and races it ruled. The only demand made was that Roman citizens, as a political act, worship the imperial person or image; beyond that, all citizens were free to worship their own gods and to observe their own rites and rituals. To Jews and early Christians, however, emperor or image worship was idolatry, and they refused to obey. They were persecuted and frequently martyred for their religious beliefs.

CHURCH CENSORSHIP

In AD 313 the Roman emperor Constantine decreed toleration of Christianity. Twenty years later, Constantine set the pattern of religious censorship that was to be followed for centuries by ordering the burning of all books by the Greek theologian Arius.

Roman Catholic Censorship. After the emperor Theodosius made Christianity the established religion of the empire, the Roman government and the church began to persecute both pagans and Christian heretics who deviated from orthodox doctrine or practice. The pope was recognized as the final authority in church doctrine and government, and the secular state used force to compel obedience to his decisions. Books or sermons that were opposed to orthodox faith or morals were prohibited, and their authors were punished. The first catalog of forbidden books was issued by Pope Gelasius in 496. Individual heretical books were subsequently forbidden by special papal edicts. Censorship in this period was concerned primarily with suppressing heresy (q.v.). For the purpose of punishing all such manifestations, Pope Gregory IX instituted the Inquisition (q.v.) in 1233. For almost 500 years the Inquisition remained an influential agency of religious censorship.

The invention of printing in the 15th century made prepublication censorship possible. In 1487 Pope Innocent VIII (1432–92) introduced such censorship. Printers were required to submit all manuscripts to church authorities, and a work could be printed only after it had been approved. Pope Paul III in 1542 established the Universal Roman Inquisition, or Congregation of the Holy Office, one of whose duties was to examine and condemn heretical or immoral works. In 1559 Pope Paul IV first issued the Index of Forbidden Books (q.v.), which was supplemented by his successors. Approximately 5000 books were ultimately listed in the Index, and the last edition was issued in 1948. Pope Paul VI in 1965 made substantial reforms, changed the name of the Holy Office to the Congregation for the Doctrine of the Faith, and abolished the position of censor. It was announced that the Index would not be renewed, that the penalty of excommunication would no longer have the force of law, but that the Congregation for the Doctrine of the Faith would occasionally publish lists of books that were not recommended for reading by Roman Catholics.

Protestant Censorship. The Protestant Reformation did not itself erect a change in the practice of censorship. Its leaders—among them John Calvin, John Knox, and Martin Luther—claimed liberty of conscience and toleration only for themselves and their followers. When in power, they too attempted to suppress all deviation from their own brands of orthodoxy; they persecuted Protestant heretics and Roman Catholics.

In England King Henry VIII supplanted the pope as head of the Church of England. The Act of Supremacy (1534) vested in the king power to declare and punish heresies. He persecuted both papists and reformers, and he burned copies of the English translation of the New Testament.

Henry VIII established a licensing system that resembled the prepublication censorship of Pope Innocent VIII. It required printers to submit all manuscripts to church authorities for their approval prior to publication. This licensing system continued in England until 1695. The English poet John Milton protested against such censorship in his classic essay *Areopagitica* (1644). Many English people associated licensing by church censors with ecclesiastical supervision, the Inquisition, and restraints on religion, education, and intellectual pursuits.

CENSORSHIP IN THE MODERN WORLD

The 18th century marks the beginning of the modern period, with its emphasis on toleration and liberty—a beginning that reflects the influence of the Age of Enlightenment and the American and French revolutions (*see* ENLIGHTENMENT, AGE OF). Although the new spirit of liberty was first felt in the area of religious belief, it rapidly affected political life, science, and literature. The U.S., France, and England set the pattern and the pace. The Declaration of Independence (1776), the U.S. Constitution (1787) with its Bill of Rights (1789–91), and the French Declaration of the Rights of Man and of the Citizen (1789) became models for the modern world. In England Roman Catholics were freed of all disabilities in 1829; Jews achieved the same freedom in 1858.

Religious Toleration. In modern democratic countries, certain basic constitutional principles are generally accepted: A person's religious beliefs and forms of worship are matters of strictly private conscience, into which no government act or official may intrude; no religious requirements may be stipulated for any public office or benefit; and the state and religion are independent of each other. Although these principles do not resolve all problems, and perplexing questions must be faced continually, the principles have established peaceful relations between the government and religious systems in truly democratic societies. The situation is quite different in Communist countries such as the USSR, where religion is not at all, or only grudgingly, recognized, and atheism is the established ideology. Another exception is the kind of theocracy (q.v.) established in Iran after the 1979 revolution with the institution of an Islamic republic.

XCIII.

THE

New-York Weekly JOURNAL

Containing the freſheſt Advices, Foreign, and Domeſtick.

MUNDAY Auguſt 18th, 1735.

To my Subſcribers and Benefactors.

Gentlemen ;

I Think my ſelf in Duty bound to to make publick Acknowledgment for the many Favours received at your Hands, which I do in this Manner return you my hearty Thanks for. I very ſoon intend to print my Tryal at Length, that the World may ſee how unjuſt my Sufferings have been, ſo will only at this Time give this ſhort Account of it.

On *Munday* the 4*th* Inſtant my Tryal for Printing Parts of my Journal *No.* 13. and 23. came on, in the Supreme Court of this Province, before the moſt numerous Auditory of People, I may with Juſtice ſay, that ever were ſeen in that Place at once ; my Jury ſworn were,

1 *Harmanus Rutgers*,
2 *Stanley Holms*,
3 *Edward Man*,
4 *John Bell*,
5 *Samuel Weaver*,
6 *Andrew Marſchalk*,
7 *Egbert Van Borſen*,
8 *Thomas Hunt*,
9 *Benjamin Hildrith*,
10 *Abraham Kiteltaſs*,
11 *John Goelet*,
12 *Hercules Wendover*,

John Chambers, Eſq; had been appointed the Term before by the Court as my Council, in the Place of *James Alexander* and *William Smith*, who were then ſilenced on my Account, and to Mr. *Chambers*'s Aſſiſtance came *Andrew Hamilton*, Eſq; of *Philadelphia* Barreſter at Law ; when Mr Attorney offered the Information and the Proofs, Mr. *Hamilton* told him, he would acknowledge my Printing and Publiſhing the Papers in the Information, and ſave him the Trouble of that Proof, and offered to prove the Facts of thoſe Papers true, and had Witneſſes ready to prove every Fact ; he long inſiſted on the Liberty of Making Proof thereof, but was over-ruled therein. Mr. Attorney offered no Proofs of my Papers being *falſe*, *malicious* and *ſeditious*, as they were charged to be, but inſiſted that they were Lybels tho' true. There were many Arguments and Authorities on this point, and the Court were of Opinion with Mr. Attorney on that Head : But the Jury having taken the Information out with them, they returned in about Ten Minutes, and found me *Not Guilty* ; upon which there were immediately three Hurra's of many Hundreds of People in the preſence of the Court, before the Verdict was returned. The next Morning my Diſcharge was moved for and granted, and ſufficient was ſub-

The tradition of a free press in America dates from the trial of the colonial newspaperman John Peter Zenger on charges of libeling public officials. His acquittal is celebrated in the Aug. 18, 1735, issue of the New-York Weekly Journal, *of which Zenger was editor. Zenger based his defense on his right to print the truth no matter how unflattering it might be.* Granger Collection

Government Censorship. In England religious conflict bred general intolerance, which resulted in censorship that embraced political as well as religious expression. At a time when religion dominated society, every aspect of life was necessarily subject to official control. In 1662, for instance, a licensing act created a surveyor of the press who had power to investigate and suppress unauthorized publications. The Toleration Act and the Bill of Rights in 1689 dealt with important personal liberties but said nothing about freedom from censorship. To publish an unfavorable opinion of the government was still a "seditious libel." As the 18th century began, however, English newspapers became more numerous, books on a greater variety of subjects were published, and arbitrary censorship was slowly reduced. Freedom of the press came about gradually as a result of judicial decisions and popular opposition to political oppression.

Except for a brief period in France after the Revolution of 1789, political censorship continued to flourish in continental Europe until the rise of republican governments in the mid-19th century. In the 1930s a new wave of political censorship swept Europe, especially in the totalitarian regimes of Germany, Italy, and Spain. Since the end of World War II, however, political censorship has diminished in Western nations.

State censorship remains severe in the Soviet Union and other countries where political opposition is suppressed by permitting the existence of only one party. One-party nations determine directly the ideas and information to be published, circulated, and taught. When publishers, authors, or broadcasters are adjudged to have trespassed the political or moral boundaries set by law or administrative edict, they may be arbitrarily punished by fines, imprisonment, confiscation of their publication, prohibition of future publications, or closing of the medium of communication.

A reliable survey of freedom in the world in the mid-1970s disclosed that only one in five persons lives in freedom—that is, in countries where individuals enjoy political rights to bring about changes in government peacefully, and where they enjoy freedom of speech and the press and free access to other mass communications. Measured by these standards, only some 40 nations, with about 800 million people—notably in North America and Western Europe, as well as in Japan, Israel, Australia, and New Zealand—could be said to be free. Partial freedom was found in 53 nations with 1.5 billion people. Almost 2 billion

BOSTON

A 1929 cartoon by Rollin Kirby satirized the reading material acceptable to those censors who had made the phrase "banned in Boston" famous throughout the country. Granger Collection people in 65 nations lived under dictatorships or other forms of government that denied citizens most political and civil rights.

Much attention has been focused on censorship in the USSR and other Communist countries. Exiles from the Soviet Union have disclosed the severe persecution to which they were subjected. Among such exiles have been literary personalities and scientists, such as Aleksandr I. Solzhenitsyn, who was awarded the Nobel Prize for literature in 1970, and Andrey D. Sakharov, who won the Nobel Peace Prize in 1975. Their world recognition and acclaim did not prevent the Soviet government from attempting to suppress their work and persecute them.

The Communist countries have not, however, been the only ones to impose control over thought and expression in modern times. In the mid-1970s India imposed strict censorship as part of an alleged state of emergency, while Argentina virtually suspended the importation of all foreign publications. Even in democratic France, the government started criminal proceedings in 1980 against the newspaper *Le Monde* for publishing five articles in the preceding three years that allegedly cast discredit on French courts. These are only a few examples of the censorship currently imposed on people in nations around the world.

CENSORSHIP IN THE U.S.

When the American colonists drafted laws before 1776, they borrowed from English precedents regarding personal rights and liberties but went far beyond Great Britain in the fields of freedom of religion, speech, press, and assembly. After the American Revolution and the adoption of the U.S. Constitution, these freedoms were guaranteed in the Bill of Rights, the first ten amendments to the Constitution.

Protection from Censorship. The 1st Amendment, in broad terms, forbids Congress from enacting laws that would regulate speech or press before publication or punish after publication. At various times many states passed laws in contra-

A Nazi youth group collects books for a mass book burning in 1933. All books censored or proscribed by the government were destroyed. UPI

diction to the freedoms guaranteed in the 1st Amendment. For example, in the pre-American Civil War period abolitionist literature against slavery was outlawed in the South. In the 1920s, the U.S. Supreme Court ruled that the guarantee of liberty in the due process clause of the 14th Amendment (adopted in 1868) makes the 1st Amendment applicable also to the states. The Supreme Court has held that although all previous restraint on publication is unconstitutional, exceptional circumstances may justify such restraint—in wartime, for instance, publication of the number, location, or sailing dates of troops may be prohibited.

Public officials and all official acts, including the existence of government itself, may be openly criticized and attacked by speech or publication, provided only that the words used are not of such a nature and are not used in such circumstances "as to create a clear and present danger that they will bring about the substantive evils that Congress [or the state] has a right to prevent." The classic example is that a person has no right to shout "Fire!" in a crowded theater when there is no fire. Thus, a person addressing an angry mob has no right to urge them on to riot, which would be a clear and present danger to the peace and security of the community. Cases in which a court was persuaded that such a danger had been proved beyond a reasonable doubt, however, have been extremely rare.

In 1971 the Supreme Court considered the sensational Pentagon Papers case. A 47-volume official classified report on U.S. policy in Vietnam came into the possession of Daniel Ellsberg (1931-   ), a former federal official. The *New York Times* and several other leading newspapers began publishing parts of the report. The government asked for an injunction to stop publication. In considering the case, the Court said that any prior restraint on publication comes before the courts with a heavy presumption that it is unconstitutional, and that the government must prove that the restraint is justified. The Court, by a 6-3 vote, refused to bar the newspapers from reprinting the report.

Less dramatic expressions of a spirit of censorship have tended to persist. In some state or local communities textbook commissions or school boards have exerted pressure on authors and publishers to omit from or include in school texts certain materials relating to various sensitive areas such as evolution, the biblical account of creation, discussions of religious or racial groups, and expressions that are allegedly sexist. Some groups have attempted to pressure public and school libraries to prevent circulation of books and periodicals they consider morally or otherwise offensive. In the past, serious censorship problems were presented by the operations of the U.S. Post Office and the Customs Bureau, which refused to allow certain books and other materials to be brought into the country or sent through the mails. Since the early 1970s, however, court decisions, congressional legislation, and administrative regulations have resolved the great majority of these problems, at least for the present.

Censorship of Obscenity. Until about the mid-20th century government policies provided for the strict suppression of obscene publications. The test, as developed in Great Britain and substantially followed in the U.S., was whether the publication "tended . . . to deprave and corrupt those whose minds are open to such immoral influences." The law was invoked against works of recognized merit as well as against pornographic publications. Successful prosecutions were common, as were seizures of books by post office, customs, and police officials.

The beginning of a new legal approach may be traced to the action of the federal courts in the 1930s, when they held that the Irish author James Joyce's *Ulysses* was not obscene and could be freely passed through customs. The courts ruled that the use of "dirty words" in "a sincere and honest book" did not make the book "dirty." Since the 1950s many obscenity cases—involving books, magazines, and films—have been brought before the Supreme Court. In the cases during the 1970s the Court ruled that laws against obscenity must be limited "to works which, taken as a whole, appeal to the prurient interest in sex; which portray sexual conduct in a patently offensive way; and which, taken as a whole, do not have serious literary, artistic, political, or scientific value." The Court has further held that obscenity should be determined by applying "contemporary community standards" rather than national standards.

Private Action. One U.S. industry, the film industry, has for many years practiced a form of self-censorship. In the 1920s, responding to public demands for strong controls, the Motion Picture Association of America imposed on its constituents a Production Act; compliance with its standards gave a movie a seal of approval. A system of film classification was begun in 1968 (rev. in 1970) by the industry. Under the system, films are given ratings as follows: PG (parental guidance advised), R (restricted—persons under the age of 17 not admitted unless accompanied by parent or adult guardian), and X (persons under the age of 18 not admitted).

For the television and radio industries the Federal Communications Commission (FCC) has generally promulgated vague rules about program content containing an implied threat that a license can be revoked for repeated poor judgment involving program content. In 1987, however, the FCC responded to public complaints by adopting measures to restrict the use of explicit language about sex and bodily functions from the broadcasting media. Another code, designed by the National Association of Broadcasters, is voluntarily adhered to by station operators. The major networks also have their own self-regulating system. The Columbia Broadcasting System (CBS), for example, has a staff of people who review scripts and watch everything that is aired on CBS-TV, including commercials; every contract with a producer provides that the project is subject to approval under this system.

In the U.S. many different private groups attempt to influence government agencies, businesses, libraries, radio and television broadcasters, newspapers, and other communications media to suppress material that they consider objectionable. Religious, ethnic, and racial groups have tried to prevent plays, movies, and television programs from being presented because of elements they deem offensive.

One private group, the American Civil Liberties Union (q.v.), promotes the open flow of all types of information in the belief that individuals should have free access and opportunities for the exercise of their personal discretion and that no group should limit the availability of the resources from which such choices are made.

CURRENT PROBLEMS AND TRENDS

In the 20th century, as in all previous history, freedom from censorship has been the exception in the world. The rule has been, and continues to be, repression, suppression, and oppression. It may, however, be considered a sign of political and social progress that, everywhere in the world, at least lip-service is paid to the ideal of liberty, and that no country brazenly admits that it is committed to a policy of religious, intellectual, artistic, or political censorship. This is apparent in the many covenants and declarations that have been passed in support of freedom and human rights; these include the UN Charter (1945), the UN Declaration of Human Rights (1948), the UN Covenants on Civil and Political Rights (1966) and on Economic, Social, and Cultural Rights (1966), the European Convention on Human Rights (1953), the Helsinki Final Act (1975), and the American (Western Hemisphere) Convention on Human Rights (1978).

For additional information on individuals mentioned, see biographies of those whose names are not followed by dates. M.R.K.

For further information on this topic, see the Bibliography in volume 28, sections 156, 256–57, 311.

CENSUS (Lat. *censere,* "to assess"), term primarily referring to the official and periodical counting of the people of a country or section of a country; also, the printed record of such a counting. In actual usage the term is applied to the collection of information on the size and characteristics of population, as well as on the number and characteristics of dwelling units, various business enterprises, and governmental agencies.

HISTORY

The earliest known census enumerations were conducted for purposes of levying taxes or for military conscription. Clay tablet fragments from ancient Babylon indicate that a census was taken there as early as 3800 BC to estimate forthcoming tax revenues. The ancient Chinese, Hebrews, Egyptians, and Greeks also are known to have conducted censuses. Not until the Romans began a count of their empire's inhabitants, however, did enumerations take place at regular intervals. The Roman censuses, designed for both taxation and military conscription, were the responsibility of local censors. In addition to registering the population and collecting taxes, the censor was also in charge of maintaining public morals.

With the dominance of the feudal system in the Middle Ages, information on taxation and personnel for military conscription became unnecessary. Not until the 17th century did a nation again attempt an accurate count of its population. Sweden has been cited as the forerunner in the collection of information on its inhabitants. Its churches were required by law to keep continuous records of births, deaths, and marriages occurring among all people residing within the parish boundaries. Such vital statistics registrations are still maintained in Scandinavia, Finland, the Netherlands, and Belgium.

The first true census in modern times, however, was taken in the colony of New France (now Québec), where the enumeration of individuals began in 1665. The rise of democratic governments resulted in a new feature of the census process: The 1790 census of the U.S. was the first to be made public upon tabulation of the gathered information.

During the 19th century and the first half of the 20th century, the practice of census taking spread throughout the world. International organizations, such as the UN, have encouraged all countries to adopt uniform standards in taking their censuses. Decennial censuses are now taken by many countries throughout the world. According to the UN, about 120 countries conducted censuses between 1980 and 1984.

THE U.S. CENSUS

The first census enumeration in the U.S. began on the first Monday in August 1790, under the authority of Secretary of State Thomas Jefferson. Seventeen U.S. marshals hired as many assistants as was deemed necessary to travel through the countryside soliciting answers to six questions: the name of the head of the household; the number of free white males 16 years of age and older; the number of free white males under 16 years of age; the number of free white females; the number of other free persons; and the number of slaves.

When the first U.S. census was taken, maps of the new nation were scarce, town and country boundaries were vague or unknown, and many untrusting citizens were uncooperative. Eighteen months after the enumeration began, the work was completed. Final tallying revealed a population of slightly less than 4 million inhabitants in the 16 states and the Southwest Territory, which later became Tennessee and part of Mississippi.

The 19th Century. For the next 50 years, the census questions remained basically unchanged, with only the introduction in 1830 of a printed census form modifying the data-gathering process. In 1840 the government expanded the scope of census information, introducing censuses of agriculture and mineral industries. The number of questions asked then increased rapidly, and by 1860 six separate census questionnaires posed 142 different questions covering population, health, mortality, literacy, occupation, income, agriculture, manufactures, mining, fishing, commerce, banking, insurance, transportation, schools, libraries, newspapers, crime, taxes, and religion. Hand tallying led to many errors, but no attempt was made to verify the data. In 1880, with 50 million residents in the 38 states and 9 territories, Congress created a temporary civilian census office headed by an appointed official known as the superintendent of the census.

The invention in the 1880s of the punch-card system of tabulation (*see* COMPUTER) resulted in two major advances in data handling. First, vast quantities of data could be processed in record time; second, information could be cross-tabulated, yielding the number of instances in which two or more characteristics were present.

In 1902, Congress established the Bureau of the Census as a permanent organization within the Department of the Interior, with responsibility for the decennial census and for interim censuses and surveys. The bureau was transferred to the jurisdiction of the Department of Commerce and Labor in 1903, and then to the separate Commerce Department in 1913.

The 20th Century. The New Deal programs of the 1930s and the subsequent wartime emergency made unprecedented demands for accurate, up-to-date information on the population. To meet these needs, the Census Bureau developed sampling techniques, statistically selecting a small number of individuals to represent the whole

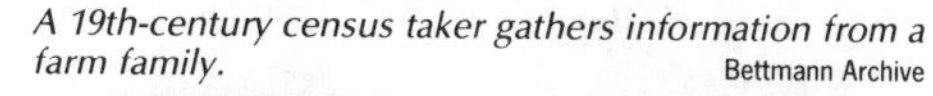

A 19th-century census taker gathers information from a farm family. Bettmann Archive

population. Sampling has enabled the Census Bureau to provide a wide range of useful, reliable information on a regular and continuing basis.

The volume of information collected, however, continued to exceed the bureau's mechanical capacity to process it. In April 1951 the first computer for nonmilitary use began tabulating data from the 1950 census.

In addition to the census of population and housing, the bureau also issues a battery of other enumerations. In those years ending in the numbers two and seven, it conducts censuses of agriculture, manufacturing, construction, retail trade, wholesale trade, service industries, transportation, mineral industries, and governments.

The Census Today. With growing governmental involvement in the lives of the citizens, the Census Bureau has taken on an expanded role. The bureau is required by the U.S. Constitution to report the state population counts to the president by January 1 of the year following the census for the purposes of apportioning seats in the House of Representatives. Population totals for all counties, cities, and certain recognized political and statistical subdivisions are submitted to each state legislature one year after census day. Court rulings on the one-person, one-vote principle have led state and local governments to use this information for drawing legislative and other district boundaries.

Uses of the Census. In addition to operations mandated by law, the Census Bureau has developed an extensive program of consulting the users of its statistics. Advisory committees meeting at conferences and workshops discuss methods of handling census materials so that the statistics are appropriate for most data users.

Census data directly influence decisions on matters of national and local importance such as education, employment, transportation, military-personnel potential, business cycles, health-care needs, parks, natural resources, energy, and international relations. By comparing successive censuses, demographers can extrapolate population trends and predict future patterns of settlement, population age structure, and population growth. Examining the age structure in a given community, for example, assists local planners in deciding whether to build elementary schools or housing for the elderly.

The 1980 census gathered additional information about racial and ethnic origin, national energy usage, and journey-to-work patterns. It also provided more statistical information about geographic areas than any previous census. These findings were necessary for planning and managing programs at all levels of government.

Response to the census is required by law—specifically, Title 13, United States Code. By this same law, the information obtained is kept strictly confidential. Data collected from individuals can be used for statistical purposes only, not for taxation, investigation, or regulation. The law also requires that published data be in such a form that it is impossible to identify an individual or a single business establishment. It stipulates that no one other than sworn officers and employees may have access to individual information, and each census employee signs an affidavit to uphold that law. Identifiable census data are not subject to the Freedom of Information Act.

Collection of Data. The 20th Decennial Census of Population and Housing officially began on April 1, 1980. Data were subsequently compiled for 3200 counties; 20,000 incorporated towns, cities, and villages; 45,000 census tracts; and 2.5 million city blocks.

Every household in the U.S. received a census questionnaire in the mail on or about March 28, 1980, and was asked to answer the questions contained therein. Approximately four out of five households were asked to answer the 19 questions on the short version of the form. The remaining households responded to a longer version with 46 additional questions. About 90 percent of the households were to mail back their completed questionnaires on April 1. The remaining 10 percent, primarily those in sparsely settled areas, were instructed to keep their completed questionnaires until census takers came in person to pick them up.

Tabulation of Data. A temporary work force of approximately 275,000 persons was hired to check the returned census forms, visit households from which questionnaires had not been returned, and perform a wide range of clerical tasks. The questionnaires were checked for completeness in one of the 12 regional offices, and they were then shipped to major processing centers in Indiana, Louisiana, and California. After processing through high-speed microfilming equipment, the data were transmitted electronically to computers at Census Bureau headquarters in Suitland, Md. Tabulation of the data yielded 300,000 pages of statistics, which were made available to the public in printed form, on microfilm, and on computer tape. Personal data, such as name, address, and marital status, had been promptly separated from the rest of the forms and sent to the Personal Census Service Branch in Pittsburg, Kans. Such data can be obtained when proof of age or residence is needed.

Accuracy of the Census. Because many public programs are funded according to population, and because congressional representation is based on the number of residents, state and local authorities are particularly concerned with obtaining an accurate census count. A number of cities instituted court challenges against the population totals reported for their communities following the 1980 census—the first time such lawsuits were permitted.

A technique employed by the bureau to increase the accuracy of the population count is the precensus canvass. Census workers check addresses of private homes and other residences to ensure that all households will receive questionnaires. This check is very important in new housing areas or where individual structures have been subdivided into multiple-dwelling units since the previous census.

The majority of residents who were not included in the census count appeared to be undocumented aliens and those living in the inner cities of metropolitan areas. The former group often failed to complete the questionnaire for fear of reprisals from immigration authorities. Such anxiety was unfounded, however; no record exists of any individual charged with illegal residency on the basis of a census reply. For those living in inner cities, the possible interception of the census questionnaire by an apartment building owner stopped some respondents from completing the census form. It had been hoped that the language barrier would be broken for some by providing census forms in Spanish for the first time. Additionally, efforts were made through mass media to convey the importance of responding to the census. *See also* POPULATION.

BUREAU OF THE CENSUS

For further information on this topic, see the Bibliography in volume 28, sections 167-68.

CENTAURS, in Greek mythology, a race of monsters believed to have inhabited the mountain regions of Thessaly and Arcadia. They were usually represented as human down to the waist, with the lower torso and legs of a horse. The centaurs were characterized by savageness and violence; they were known for their drunkenness and lust and were often portrayed as followers of Dionysus, the god of wine. The centaurs were driven from Thessaly when, in a drunken frenzy, they attempted to abduct the bride of the king of the Lapiths from her wedding feast. The centaur Chiron, noted for his goodness and wisdom, was an exception among them. Several Greek heroes, including Achilles and Jason, were educated by him.

CENTAURUS, constellation of stars, the Centaur, located in the southern celestial hemisphere, and visible chiefly south of the equator. The brightest star in this constellation, Alpha Centauri, is also the third brightest star in the sky. It is about 4.3 light-years from the earth and is the closest visible star to the earth's solar system. The star is actually a double star, with a third star, Proxima Centauri, revolving around the other two.

CENTER OF GRAVITY, for any three-dimensional body or system, that point where the body's weight, or mass, may be considered to be located. The center of gravity of a uniform sphere, for example, is the center of the sphere. The center of gravity of an irregular object, however, may lie outside the object. When an object is in free motion, the center of gravity describes a smooth curve around which the rest of the object, or system, may rotate in a complex manner.

CENTERS FOR DISEASE CONTROL (CDC), agency of the U.S. Public Health Service, with headquarters and main laboratories in Atlanta, Ga. The CDC conducts research into the origin and occurrence of diseases and develops methods for their control and prevention. It also develops immunization services, together with state and local agencies; provides public health information; and aids in the training of health workers. Among its divisions are the Center for Environmental Health and the National Institute for Occupational Safety. The CDC conducts international programs as well. The agency had its origin in the U.S. antimalaria office of World War II and was established as the Communicable Disease Center in 1946; it gained its present title in 1970. Recent accomplishments of the agency include identification of the causes of toxic shock syndrome and of Legionnaires' disease (qq.v.).

CENTIGRADE. *See* HEAT; TEMPERATURE.

CENTIMETER-GRAM-SECOND SYSTEM. *See* CGS SYSTEM.

CENTIPEDE, common name for the members of the class Chilopoda of the phylum Arthropoda (*see* ARTHROPOD), which also includes crustaceans, insects, and spiders. The centipedes are long, segmented animals with jointed appendages and a poisonous "bite."

Characteristics. The centipede body is divided into well-marked segments, the number of which varies from 12 to more than 100. The head, which is covered by a flat shield above, bears a pair of antennae, usually of considerable length and consisting of from 12 to more than 100 joints; a pair of small, strong, toothed, and bristly mandibles; and a pair of underjaws, usually with palps. The first body segment bears a modified pair of legs, the strong joints of which terminate in a sharp claw into which a poison gland opens, for seizing and killing prey. The two legs on each of the other segments are usually seven-jointed, sometimes bearing spurs and glands, and generally clawed.

The relatively large brain is connected with a ventral chain of ganglia. Compound eyes occur in one family, and simple eyes or none at all in many. The feelers, certain bristles, and portions of the skin are also sensory. The heart is a chambered dorsal vessel. Tracheae, or air tubes, open on the sides of the body. Most centipedes are 2.5 to 5 cm (1 to 2 in) long, but some tropical species grow to 30 cm (12 in).

Centipedes are nocturnal and remain under stones or wood during the day. They are all carnivorous. *Scolopendra* bears live young; the others lay eggs.

Classification. Of the four principal families, the family Scutigeridae, to which the common house centipede belongs, includes forms with compound eyes, long feelers, 8 shields along the back, and 15 pairs of very long legs. Lithobiidae have simple eyes, 15 pairs of legs, antennae measuring a third or more of the body length, and 15 dorsal shields. The Scolopendridae have more than 20 pairs of legs; short, many-jointed antennae; and simple eyes or none at all. The poisonous bite of some of the larger forms is dangerous to humans. The Geophilidae are long, wormlike centipedes, of sluggish habit, with 31 to 173 pairs of legs, short feelers, and no eyes. Well-developed spinning glands are seen in this family, and their secretion cements together ova and spermatozoa.

For further information on this topic, see the Bibliography in volume 28, section 464.

CENTRAL, region, central Scotland; Stirling is the administrative center. The region was created in 1975, merging the former county of Clackmannan with parts of Stirlingshire, West Lothian, and Perth (qq.v). Its S portion, including the Forth Valley, is an industrial area; a petroleum refinery is in the port of Grangemouth. To the N is the wooded valley of The Trossachs. Area, 2621 sq km (1012 sq mi); pop. (1981) 373,078.

CENTRAL AFRICAN REPUBLIC, formerly (1976–79) CENTRAL AFRICAN EMPIRE, republic, central Africa, bordered on the N by Chad, on the E by Sudan, on the S by Zaire and the People's Republic of the Congo, and on the W by Cameroon. The landlocked nation has an area of 622,984 sq km (240,535 sq mi).

LAND AND RESOURCES

The Central African Republic is situated on the N edge of the Congo Basin. Most of the land is a plateau that ranges in elevation from about 610 to 790 m (about 2000 to 2600 ft). Two ranges of hills in the N and NE rise to maximum heights of about 1400 m (about 4600 ft). Most of the country has a savanna vegetation—a grassland interspersed with trees. Open grassland is found in the extreme N, and a dense rain forest covers the major part of the SW area. The country is drained by the Shari (Chari) R. in the N and the Ubangi (a tributary of the Congo R.) in the S.

Climate. The climate of the Central African Republic is hot and humid; the average annual temperature is about 26° C (about 79° F). Tornadoes and floods are common at the onset of the rainy season, which lasts from June to November. Annual rainfall varies from about 1780 mm (about 70 in) in the Ubangi R. valley to about 760 mm (about 30 in) in the semiarid NE and E.

Natural Resources. The mineral resources of this primarily agricultural country are relatively undeveloped. Diamonds are the dominant exploited mineral. Deposits of uranium exist, as well as iron ore, gold, lime, zinc, copper, and tin. Commercially valuable trees include the sapele mahogany and the obeche. Almost every animal of the African Tropics is found in the country.

POPULATION

The four main ethnic groups of the Central African Republic are the Mandjia-Baya, the Banda, the Mbaka, and the Azande. More than half the population inhabits small villages, living and working according to traditional customs.

Population Characteristics. The population of the Central African Republic was determined by the census of 1975 to be 2,054,610; in 1985 the population was officially estimated at 2,608,000. The average population density (1985) was about 4 persons per sq km (about 11 per sq mi). Most of the population is concentrated in the W half of the country. The capital and chief city is Bangui (pop., 1981 est., 387,100).

Religion and Language. Christians make up about 85% of the total population and Muslims a bit less than 5%. The remainder of the population follows traditional religions. French is the official language. Numerous African languages are spoken; Sango, a trade language, is common.

Education. About three-fourths of the eligible children of the Central African Republic receive primary education. Secondary and higher education facilities are limited. Only about 40% of the population is literate. In the early 1980s about 291,400 pupils annually attended primary schools, and about 54,100 students were enrolled in secondary and teacher-training institutions. The country's one university, the University of Bangui (1969), has an enrollment of about 2000 students.

ECONOMY

The Central African Republic is one of the most underdeveloped areas in Africa. Growth of the

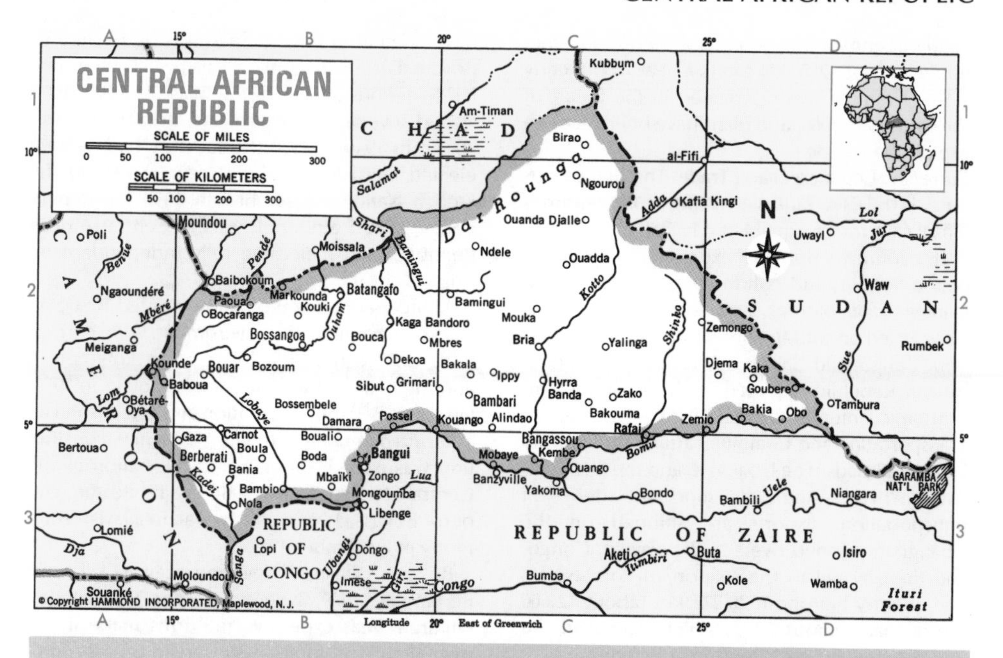

INDEX TO MAP OF CENTRAL AFRICAN REPUBLIC

Cities and Towns

Place	Key
Alindao	C 2
Bakala	C 2
Bakia	D 2
Bakouma	C 2
Bambari	C 2
Bambio	B 3
Bamingui	C 2
Bangassou	C 3
Bangui (cap.)	B 3
Bania	B 3
Batangafo	B 2
Berberati	B 3
Birao	C 1
Bocaranga	B 2
Bossangoa	B 2
Bossembele	B 2
Bouali	B 3
Bouar	B 2
Bouca	B 2
Boula	B 3
Bria	C 2
Carnot	B 3
Damara	B 2
Dekoa	B 2
Djema	D 2
Gaza	B 3
Goubere	D 2
Grimari	B 2
Kaga Bandoro	B 2
Kaka	D 2
Kembe	C 3
Kouango	C 2
Kouki	B 2
Kounde	A 2
Markounda	B 2
Mbaïki	B 3
Mbres	B 2
Mobaye	C 3
Mongoumba	B 3
Mouka	C 2
Ngourou	C 2
Ouadda	C 2
Ouanda Djalle	C 2
Ouango	C 3
Paoua	B 2
Possel	B 2
Rafai	C 2
Sibut	B 2
Zako	C 2
Zemio	C 2
Zemongo	D 2

Other Features

Feature	Key
Aouk, Bahr (river)	C 2
Bamingui (river)	B 2
Bomu (river)	C 3
Kadei (river)	B 3
Kotto (river)	C 2
Lobaye (river)	B 2
Ouham (river)	B 2
Pende (river)	B 2
Sanga (river)	B 3
Shari (river)	B 2
Shinko (river)	C 2
Ubangi (river)	B 3

export economy is hindered by the difficulty of transporting goods to a seaport. About 85% of the population earns its livelihood by farming. The agricultural output is fairly evenly balanced between subsistence and export crops. The principal sources of revenue are diamonds, coffee, cotton, and timber exports. The annual national budget in the mid-1980s showed revenues at $93.3 million and expenditures at $90.8 million.

Agriculture and Forestry. About 3% of the total land area is suitable for crops. Basic food crops include cassava, plantains, corn, peanuts, sweet potatoes, and millet. In order to increase the wage-earning power of the peasant farmer, the government has organized agricultural cooperatives, placing primary emphasis on introducing new crops that are expected to produce a higher income. The cultivation of tobacco, sesame, and rice is encouraged by the government. The most important cash crop is coffee, formerly grown mostly on European-owned plantations, but now produced largely on smaller African-owned farms. The annual coffee crop in the mid-1980s totaled about 15,000 metric tons. Cotton, the second ranking cash crop, is widely grown.

Exploitation of forest reserves was slow to develop but has increased in importance, and by the mid-1980s some 3.2 million cu m (about 113 million cu ft) of roundwood were produced. About 80% of the wood is used as fuel.

Manufacturing and Mining. Manufacturing activity in the Central African Republic is very limited. Products include cottonseed, peanut, and sesame oils; textiles; leather goods; tobacco products; soap; flour; bricks; and paint. The annual output of electricity is about 68 million kwh, approximately 95% of which is generated in hydroelectric installations. Diamonds account for nearly all the country's mineral output. Production was about 295,000 carats a year in the early 1980s. Uranium was discovered in the E part of the country in 1966, and plans have been made to exploit the reserves.

Currency, Commerce, and Trade. The unit of currency is the CFA franc, consisting of 100 centimes (302.8 CFA francs equal U.S.$1; 1987).

The country's principal exports are diamonds, coffee, timber, and cotton. France is by far the leading trade partner, and some commerce is also carried on with the nearby nations of Cameroon, Congo, and Gabon, with which the Central African Republic is joined in the Customs and Economic Union of Central Africa.

Transportation and Communication. The country has no railroads. The Ubangi R. and the Shari and Logone river systems are important arteries of transportation. Exports are shipped on the Ubangi and Congo rivers to Brazzaville, Congo, and then by rail to the seaport of Point-Noire. The country has about 20,275 km (about 12,600 mi) of roads, about 2% of which are paved. An international airport is located at Bangui.

One daily newspaper and several other periodicals are published in Bangui. The single radio-broadcasting station is government owned and provides programs in French, English, and Sango. Television broadcasting began in 1974. In the early 1980s, about 135,000 radio receivers, 1200 television sets, and 2700 telephones were in use.

GOVERNMENT

In 1979 the Central African Empire was ended, and a republic was reestablished. A new constitution was approved in February 1981. According to this constitution, executive authority is held by the president and the Council of Ministers, which the president heads; the president is popularly elected to a 6-year term. Legislative authority is held by a National Assembly, the members of which are popularly elected to 5-year terms. Following a coup in September 1981, the constitution was suspended and a ruling military committee was installed. A new constitution calling for a single-party republic was approved by referendum in November 1986.

HISTORY

Most of the ethnic groups inhabiting the present-day Central African Republic entered the region in the 19th century to escape Fulani armies or to avoid slave traders operating in the Congo River Basin and modern Sudan. In the 1880s the French annexed the area, and in 1894 it was organized as the territory of Ubangi-Shari. In 1910 the dependency became part of the Federation of French Equatorial Africa. Under the French, economic development in Ubangi-Shari was dominated by private European concessionaires. This system led to serious abuses of the black Africans, who staged several violent protests, notably in 1928–30. From 1946 to 1958 the territory had its own elected legislature and was represented in the French National Assembly. In 1958 the dependency gained autonomy as the Central African Republic, and it became fully independent on Aug. 13, 1960.

At independence the nation was led by David Dacko. Charging his government with corruption, Col. Jean Bédel Bokassa, Dacko's cousin and the head of the army, seized power in 1966. He abrogated the constitution and established an authoritarian regime. In late 1976 a new constitution was issued, reorganizing the nation as the Central African Empire. Bokassa became Emperor Bokassa I; he was crowned in a lavish ceremony in December 1977.

Bokassa's despotic regime began to fall apart in January 1979, when an order that schoolchildren wear expensive uniforms made in his own factory prompted widespread protest demonstrations. The army was called in, and many children were put in prison, where they were then massacred by the imperial guard. A committee of African judges later concluded that Bokassa had personally participated in the killings. In September 1979 he was overthrown in a French-backed coup led by former president Dacko, who then resumed power. Dacko was confirmed in office by the electorate in March 1981, but was deposed six months later in a coup led by the commander in chief of the army, Gen. André Kolingba (1936–). Bokassa returned to the Central African Republic in October 1986 and was tried and convicted for ordering the murders of political opponents while he was in power. In November Kolingba was confirmed by popular referendum for a six-year term as head of state.

For further information on this topic, see the Bibliography in volume 28, sections 1009, 1012.

CENTRAL AMERICA, a region of the western hemisphere, made up of a long, tapering isthmus that forms a bridge between North and South America. Central America, which is defined by geographers as part of North America, has an area of about 523,000 sq km (about 201,930 sq mi) and includes the countries of Guatemala, Belize, El Salvador, Honduras, Nicaragua, Costa Rica, and Panama. The region has a population of approximately 22.7 million (1980 UN est.).

THE NATURAL ENVIRONMENT

In strictly geological terms, Central America begins at the narrow Isthmus of Tehuantepec, in S Mexico. That narrow section divides the volcanic

A view of farmland near Cartago, Costa Rica. In the uplands of Central America a year-round temperate climate is conducive to producing three crops annually.
Carlos Sanuvo–Bruce Coleman, Inc.

rocks to the NW from the folded and faulted structures of Central America. The southernmost geological limit of Central America is the Atrato R. valley, in Colombia, South America, just E of the Panama border.

Geologic History. Central America, a particularly unstable region of the earth's crust, is on the western edge of the Caribbean plate (*see* PLATE TECTONICS). Subduction of oceanic crust beneath this edge, beginning in the Miocene epoch (q.v.), about 25 million years ago, has lifted the land from the sea. In the earliest stage, a peninsula and archipelago formed. Later, about 3 million years ago, the scattered islands coalesced to form a true land bridge, or isthmus, linking North and South America.

Keeping pace with subduction and uplift have been volcanic eruptions—Central America has at least 14 active volcanoes—and frequent earthquakes. In this century alone, Managua, the capital of Nicaragua, has twice been destroyed by earthquakes. The most recent, in 1972, took 10,000 lives. Volcanic activity has produced a landscape dotted with majestic cones built from eruptions of ash and lava, and beautiful lakes formed in collapsed volcanic craters (calderas).

Physiographic Regions. For the most part Central America is a rugged, mountainous area, with 109 large volcanoes, some more than 4000 m (13,120 ft) high; Volcán Tajumulco, in Guatemala, is the highest at 4220 m (13,845 ft). Central America is one of the most active volcanic zones in the western hemisphere. The land surface slopes up rather abruptly from a narrow coastal plain along the Pacific Ocean to the mountain crests and then descends more gradually to a broader plain along the Caribbean Sea. Two major interoceanic passes cut through the highlands of Central America, one in Nicaragua (from the mouth of the San Juan R. to Lake Nicaragua) and the other in Panama (along the route of the Panama Canal). The Pacific coastline is about 2830 km (about 1760 mi) long, and the Caribbean coastline is approximately 2740 km (approximately 1700 mi) long. Several groups of small islands lie off the Caribbean coast, and some of them, such as the Islas de la Bahía in the Gulf of Honduras, are inhabited.

Rivers and Lakes. The longest rivers of Central America flow to the Caribbean, and many small streams drain into the Pacific. Longer rivers include the Motagua of Guatemala; the Ulúa, Aguán, and Patuca of Honduras; the Coco, which forms part of the Honduras-Nicaragua boundary; the Río Grande and Escondido of Nicaragua; and the San Juan, which forms a section of the Nicaragua-Costa Rica border. Some of the rivers flowing to the Caribbean are navigable by small craft, but the streams flowing to the Pacific are too steep or too shallow for navigation.

Central America has three large lakes—Lakes Nicaragua and Managua in Nicaragua and Gatun Lake in Panama. Part of the Panama Canal, a great commercial waterway between the Atlantic and the Pacific, is in Gatun Lake.

Climate. Temperatures in Central America, which is situated between the tropic of Cancer and the equator, vary principally according to altitude rather than latitude. Three main temperature zones are discernible. The *tierra caliente* ("hot country"), which extends from sea level to an altitude of about 915 m (about 3000 ft), has average yearly temperatures of 24° C (75° F) or more; the *tierra templada* ("temperate country"), from about 915 to 1830 m (about 3000 to 6000 ft), has a mean annual temperature of 18.3° to 24° C (65° to 75° F); and the *tierra fría* ("cold country"), from about 1830 to 3050 m (about 6000 to 10,000 ft), has average yearly temperatures of 12.8° to 18.3° C (55° to 65° F).

The Caribbean coast and E mountain slopes generally receive twice as much annual precipitation as the Pacific coast and W mountain slopes. The relative dryness of the Pacific slope is due to the presence of cold stable air caused by the cold California Current. This current, much like the Peru, or Humboldt, Current along the Peruvian coast, chills the air, thus preventing it from absorbing much water vapor and reducing the possibilities for precipitation. In contrast, the effects of the warm water of the Caribbean Sea allow the air to absorb abundant moisture, which is then carried by the prevailing easterly winds. Much condensation and rainfall occur as the winds flow up and over the high slopes of Central America. Rainfall is greatest along the Mosquito Coast of easternmost Nicaragua—San Juan del Norte receives about 6350 mm (about 250 in) of rain per year.

Vegetation. Central America has a great variety of plants, and the vegetation is similar to that of North and South America. The lowland rain forest of the Caribbean and Pacific coasts resembles the selva, or tropical rain forest, of South America. This is especially true below an elevation of about 1000 m (about 3280 ft), with large numbers of palms, tree ferns, lianas, and epiphytes (air plants) reflecting the high rainfall and humidity of the region. Vegetation at altitudes of about 1000 to 1600 m (about 3280 to 5250 ft) shows ties with North America. The pine and oak forests of these highlands are like those of the Mexican highlands. High-altitude regions of Guatemala contain grasses like those of Mexico and the U.S., and at about 3100 m (about 10,170 ft) in Costa Rica are tall grasses similar to those growing above the tree line in the Andes Mts. of South America.

Animal Life. Most of the animal life of Central America is similar to that of South America, but some animals have ties with North America. The marley and opossum have links with South America, as do the jaguar, ocelot, jaguarundi, and margay, which are members of the cat family. In contrast, the puma, gray fox, and coyote are of North American origin. The armadillo, anteater, and sloth have ties to the S, deer to the N. The large manatee, an aquatic plant eater, survives in the isolated lagoons of E Central America. Other food sources are the large green turtle and the iguana. Central America provides a habitat for numerous snakes such as the boa constrictor and the bushmaster. Parrots, the quetzal, toucans, and fish are common; notable are the landlocked sharks of Lake Nicaragua.

Mineral Resources. The minerals of Central America were an early lure for European settlers. Gold and silver are in Honduras and the highlands of Nicaragua. In addition, Honduras has significant deposits of lead, zinc, copper, and low-grade iron ore, and Nicaragua has large deposits of natural gas offshore in the Pacific. Large nickel deposits are in the vicinity of Izabal in Guatemala, and the country also has substantial reserves of petroleum, including those near Chinajá. Costa Rica contains much bauxite around Boruca. Panama has considerable deposits of copper.

THE PEOPLE

Most of the inhabitants of Central America live on the Pacific side of the isthmus, where they occupy both lowland and highland environments. The rainy, forested Caribbean slope and coast are sparsely settled.

Ethnography. A substantial majority of the people of Central America are Indians or mestizos

Indian weavers fashion shawls, mats, and wall hangings in Guatemala. Handicrafts such as these are among the few surviving expressions of the ancient Indian heritage.
Norman Myers–Bruce Coleman, Inc.

(persons of mixed heritage, chiefly of Spanish and Indian descent). Along the narrow Caribbean coast blacks and mulattos (people of mixed white and black-African backgrounds) predominate. About half of the people of Belize are of black-African or partly black-African ancestry. The great majority of Costa Ricans are of unmixed Spanish background, and approximately 90% of the inhabitants of El Salvador and Honduras are of mixed Spanish and Indian descent. About 45% of Guatemalans are Indians, and mestizos make up most of the rest of the country's population. More than 60% of Nicaragua's and Panama's inhabitants are mestizos. Panama has a sizable black minority. In general, the Indian element is less apparent in the S countries of Nicaragua, Costa Rica, and Panama.

Demography. The population of Central America is concentrated in districts of dense settlement, separated by areas of sparse habitation. Population densities reach more than 385 people per sq km (more than 1000 per sq mi) in parts of the Meseta Central of Costa Rica, but vast areas of E Honduras and Nicaragua have fewer than 4 persons per sq km (fewer than 10 per sq mi). The rate of population increase in much of Central America is high; during 1975-79 Nicaragua had an annual growth rate of 5.2%; Guatemala, 3.7%; Panama and Belize, 3.1%; and Costa Rica, 2.7%. The population increase is principally the result of continuing high birthrates and falling death rates. By the year 2000 it is estimated that Central America will have 40 million inhabitants. To escape overcrowded areas some people have moved to the region's relatively empty Caribbean coast and to the U.S.

Most of the people of Central America are defined as rural. In the 1970s only about one-third of the inhabitants of El Salvador, Guatemala, and Honduras were considered urban, whereas about half the people of Nicaragua and Panama were so defined. In each country except Belize the national capital is the largest city; the biggest urban center of Belize is Belize City.

Language and Religion. Spanish is the official language of all Central American countries except Belize, where English is the language of government. Many highland Indians use traditional languages, and some also speak Spanish as well. Roman Catholicism is by far the dominant religion of Central America.

Cultural Activity. Cultural patterns in Central America are based largely on the heritage of the Maya and other Indians and of the Spanish colonial period. Considerable change has occurred in the region's cities, however, where the mass media and modern cultural institutions have much influence. The countries of Central America have established many educational facilities, but a comparatively large proportion of the children do not attend school. Although the great majority of people aged 15 and over in Costa Rica and Panama are literate, more than one-third of the persons of like age in El Salvador, Guatemala, Honduras, and Nicaragua cannot read or write.

PATTERNS OF ECONOMIC DEVELOPMENT

In the early 1980s the countries of Central America had relatively undeveloped economies in which agriculture was the most important sector. Manufacturing largely involved processing raw materials. The annual per capita income was low.

Agriculture. Farming is by far the leading economic activity in Central America. The principal cash crops, such as coffee, bananas, sugarcane, cacao, rubber, and coconuts, are typically produced on large landholdings, and a substantial proportion are exported, mainly to the U.S. and Europe. Food for local consumption is raised mainly on small farms; most of it is consumed by the farm families, and relatively little is marketed. The chief subsistence food commodities are corn, beans, bananas, manioc, rice, and poultry. Cattle are raised on big ranches located mainly in

Coffee pickers unload ripe coffee berries on a plantation in Costa Rica. Coffee is a prime upland agricultural commodity in Central America.

Nicholas DeVore III–Bruce Coleman, Inc.

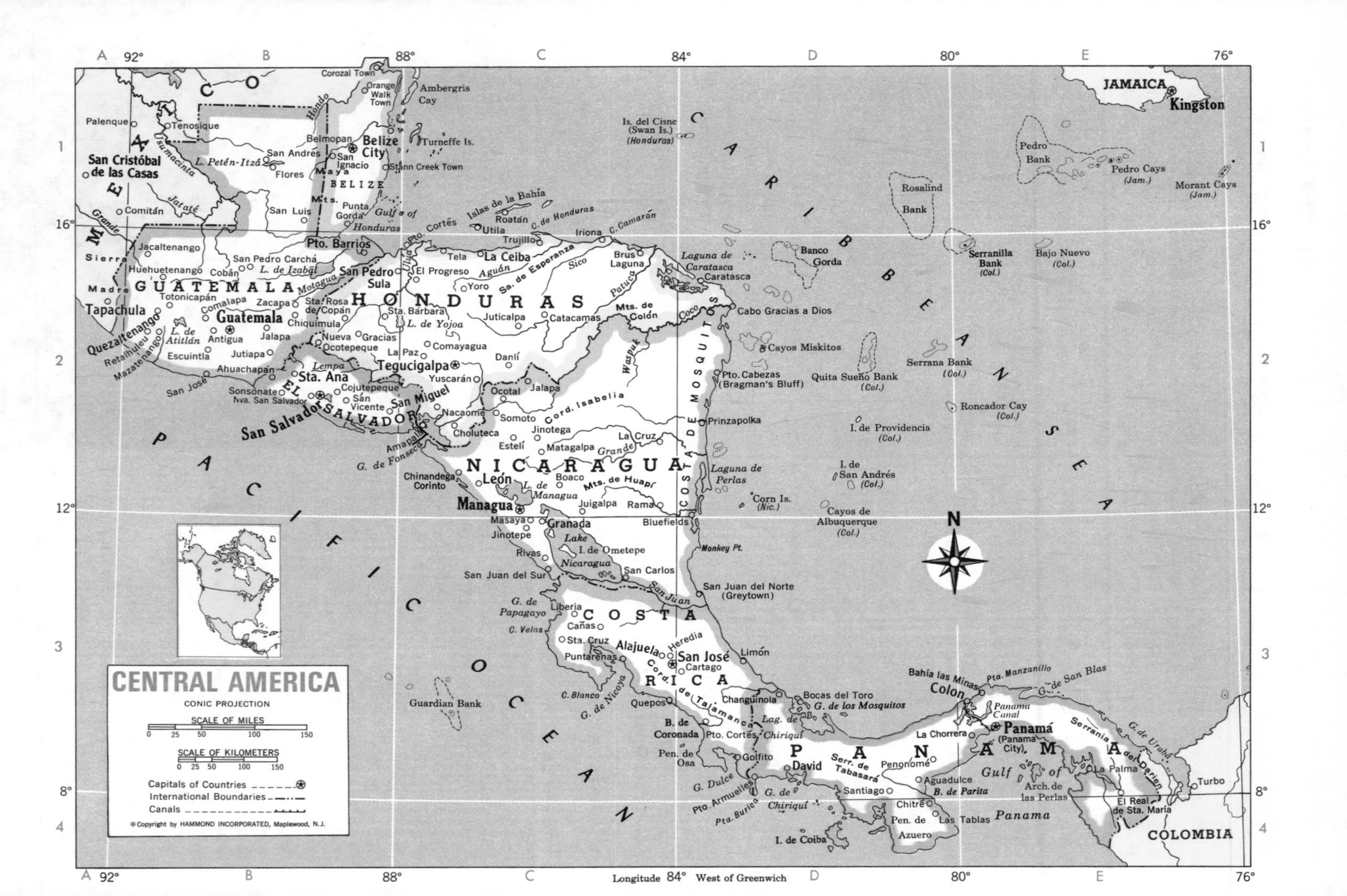

CENTRAL AMERICA
CONIC PROJECTION
SCALE OF MILES
0 25 50 100 150
SCALE OF KILOMETERS
0 25 50 100 150
Capitals of Countries
International Boundaries
Canals
© Copyright by HAMMOND INCORPORATED, Maplewood, N.J.
Longitude 84° West of Greenwich
MEXICO
Palenque
Tenosique
Usumacinta
San Cristóbal de las Casas
Comitán
Jataté
Grande
Sierra Madre
Tapachula
GUATEMALA
Guatemala
Jacaltenango
Huehuetenango
Totonicapán
Quezaltenango
Retalhuleu
Mazatenango
L. de Atitlán
Antigua
Escuintla
Comalapa
Cobán
San Pedro Carchá
L. de Izabal
Zacapa
Chiquimula
Jalapa
Jutiapa
Flores
L. Petén-Itzá
San Andrés
San Luis
Pto. Barrios
Motagua
BELIZE
Belize City
Belmopan
San Ignacio
Maya Mts.
Punta Gorda
Stann Creek Town
Orange Walk Town
Corozal Town
Hondo
Ambergris Cay
Turneffe Is.
Gulf of Honduras
EL SALVADOR
San Salvador
Sta. Ana
Sonsonate
Nva. San Salvador
Ahuachapán
Cojutepeque
San Vicente
San Miguel
Lempa
HONDURAS
Tegucigalpa
San Pedro Sula
La Ceiba
Tela
El Progreso
Pto. Cortés
Ulúa
Utila
Roatán
Islas de la Bahía
Trujillo
Iriona
C. Camarón
C. de Honduras
Aguán
Sa. de Esperanza
Sico
Brus Laguna
Patuca
Coco
Mts. de Colón
Yoro
Juticalpa
Catacamas
Comayagua
Sta. Bárbara
L. de Yojoa
Sta. Rosa de Copán
Gracias
Nueva Ocotepeque
La Paz
Danlí
Yuscarán
Nacaome
Choluteca
Amapala
G. de Fonseca
Laguna de Caratasca
Caratasca
Cabo Gracias a Dios
NICARAGUA
Managua
León
Chinandega
Corinto
L. de Managua
Masaya
Granada
Jinotepe
Rivas
San Juan del Sur
Lake Nicaragua
I. de Ometepe
San Carlos
San Juan
Boaco
Juigalpa
Matagalpa
Jinotega
Estelí
Somoto
Ocotal
Jalapa
Cord. Isabelia
Mts. de Huapí
Grande
La Cruz
Waspuk
Rama
Bluefields
Monkey Pt.
San Juan del Norte (Greytown)
Laguna de Perlas
Prinzapolka
Pto. Cabezas (Bragman's Bluff)
COSTA DE MOSQUITOS
COSTA RICA
San José
Alajuela
Heredia
Cartago
Cord. de Talamanca
Puntarenas
Liberia
Cañas
Sta. Cruz
G. de Papagayo
C. Velas
C. Blanco
G. de Nicoya
Quepos
B. de Coronada
Pen. de Osa
Pto. Cortés
Golfito
G. Dulce
Limón
PANAMA
Panamá (Panama City)
Colon
Panama Canal
Bahía las Minas
Pta. Manzanillo
G. de San Blas
Serranía del Darien
G. de Urabá
La Chorrera
Penonomé
Aguadulce
B. de Parita
Santiago
Chitré
Las Tablas
Pen. de Azuero
Serr. de Tabasará
David
Changuinola
Bocas del Toro
G. de los Mosquitos
Lag. de Chiriquí
G. de Chiriquí
Pto. Armuelles
Pta. Burica
I. de Coiba
Gulf of Panama
Arch. de las Perlas
La Palma
El Real de Sta. María
Turbo
COLOMBIA
JAMAICA
Kingston
Pedro Bank
Pedro Cays (Jam.)
Morant Cays (Jam.)
Rosalind Bank
Serranilla Bank (Col.)
Bajo Nuevo (Col.)
Banco Gorda
Is. del Cisne (Swan Is.) (Honduras)
Cayos Miskitos
Serrana Bank (Col.)
Quita Sueño Bank (Col.)
Roncador Cay (Col.)
I. de Providencia (Col.)
I. de San Andrés (Col.)
Corn Is. (Nic.)
Cayos de Albuquerque (Col.)
CARIBBEAN SEA
PACIFIC OCEAN
Guardian Bank
N

INDEX TO MAP OF CENTRAL AMERICA

the drier regions of W Central America. Modern farming methods are used on the large landholdings, but the small farmers generally use relatively simple techniques that hold down productivity.

Forestry and Fishing. Almost half of Central America is forested. The early years of European activity in Belize, for example, revolved around the extraction of dyewoods, and later mahogany, chicle, and pine timber were produced. British timber companies also cut mahogany and cedar along the greater Caribbean coast. In the early 1980s forestry was a relatively unimportant aspect of the Central American economy. Pine was the main wood harvested, and some hardwoods, such as cedar, mahogany, and rosewood, also were cut.

Fishing too is a comparatively minor economic activity in Central America. Shrimp and spiny lobster, caught off the coasts of Belize, El Salvador, and Panama, are mostly exported to the U.S. Since the mid-1960s Panama has developed a fish-meal and fish-oil industry. Central America has a low rate of per capita fish consumption.

Mining. The mineral output of Central America is small. El Salvador, Honduras, and Nicaragua produce limited quantities of silver, gold, lead, copper, and antimony. In the early 1980s Guatemala was beginning to exploit its petroleum deposits.

Manufacturing. Most of the manufacturing plants of Central America process raw materials of the region such as sugarcane, coffee, cotton, timber, and fish. In addition, since the 1950s a concerted attempt has been made to reduce the need to import basic fabricated articles. Thus, factories making paint, detergents, tires, paper and cardboard articles, fertilizer, and insecticide have been established in the major urban areas.

Most manufacturing establishments in Central America employ less than 100 people, and many involve only a handful of workers. Large-scale manufacturing is hindered by the region's lack of energy sources, its undeveloped transportation systems, and its small markets.

Energy. About half of the electricity of Central America is generated by the hydroelectric installations, and most of the rest is produced in plants using petroleum products. A small amount is generated in wood-burning facilities.

Transportation. The mountains of Central America present a major obstacle to overland transport, and the only surface transportation artery linking all the countries of the region is a section of the Pan-American Highway. Railroads connect the Caribbean and Pacific coasts in Guatemala, Costa Rica, and Panama. Inland water transportation is of little economic importance, but Central America has several important seaports, such as Santo Tomás de Castilla and San José in Guatemala; Puerto Cortés in Honduras; Acajutla in El Salvador; Corinto in Nicaragua; Limón in Costa Rica; and Bahía las Minas in Panama. The Panama Canal is a major shipping link between the Atlantic and Pacific oceans. A crude-petroleum pipeline across W Panama was completed in 1982. Airlines provide transportation among the big cities of Central America and serve some remote mountain communities.

Foreign Trade. About two-thirds of Central America's intercontinental trade is with the U.S. Almost all the rest is with Western Europe, Canada, Mexico, and countries of South America. Central America's principal imports are manufactured goods, such as motor vehicles, farm machines, textiles, electrical equipment, processed food, chemicals, and pharmaceuticals. The main Central American exports are basic commodities, which include bananas, coffee, cacao, meat, chicle, cotton, mahogany, balsa, hides and skins, and rubber.

Trade among the countries of Central America has increased substantially since the 1960s, and such commerce was estimated to total about $950 million per year in the late 1970s. The Central American Common Market, established under a treaty signed in 1960, has reduced barriers to trade among the region's countries as well as establishing a common external tariff on many goods. One of its institutions, the Central American Bank for Economic Integration, makes loans to finance development projects. K.E.W.

CHIEF POLITICAL DIVISIONS OF CENTRAL AMERICA

Political Unit	Political Status
Belize	Independent country
Costa Rica	Republic
El Salvador	Republic
Guatemala	Republic
Honduras	Republic
Nicaragua	Republic
Panama	Republic

HISTORY

The region between Mexico and Colombia supported a large pre-Columbian population, the most important of whom were the Maya (q.v.). The Maya civilization originated in the highlands of Guatemala during the 1st millennium BC and reached its greatest flowering between AD 300 and 900 in autonomous city-states in northern Guatemala, Honduras, Belize, and Mexico's Yucatan Peninsula. Maya unity was cultural rather than political, but the civilization's influence was widespread. Maya artistic and scientific achievements surpassed those of contemporary Europeans. After 900, however, the Maya civilization declined, and the people were conquered by Toltec invaders from Mexico.

Numerous, if less civilized, peoples inhabited the remainder of the isthmus and traded with both South and North American tribes, making ancient Central America an archaeological bridge between the Americas. The population of the isthmus on the eve of the Spanish conquest may have been as large as 6 million, a figure not again achieved until the 20th century.

The Colonial Period. Christopher Columbus established Spain's claim to Central America in 1502, when he sailed along its coast from the Gulf of Honduras to Panama. His reports of great wealth beyond the mountains that ran the length of the heavily populated isthmus stimulated Spanish conquest, which was launched from Hispaniola under the administration of his son Diego Colón (c. 1480–1526). The charismatic Vasco Núñez de Balboa founded (1510) Spain's first truly productive colony in America at Darién and went on to discover (1513) the Pacific Ocean. His successor, Pedrarias Dávila, who ordered Balboa's death in 1517, extended the colony considerably, founding (1519) Panamá City, from which

Sculptured clay vase from Guatemala, a typical art form of the Mayan Indians.
Museum of the American Indian–Heye Foundation

Man's collar of beadwork of the Guaymi Indians, one of the important indigenous peoples of Panama.
Museum of the American Indian–Heye Foundation

he initiated the subjugation of Nicaragua and Honduras. The subsequent conquest of Central America became a bloody struggle among Spaniards representing interests in Panama, Hispaniola, and Mexico. Eventually, Pedro de Alvarado, the loyal lieutenant of the conqueror of Mexico, Hernán Cortés, consolidated control over most of the isthmus. The conquerors killed vast numbers of Indians, but even more died from devastating epidemics of smallpox, plague, dysentery, and syphilis, introduced by the Europeans. The Spanish enslaved or reduced to serfdom those who remained, establishing an agricultural society based on institutions they had brought from Spain. Indian customs and traditions survived, however, because most of the relatively few Spaniards remained in the towns and cities.

Colonial Central America was divided into two jurisdictions. The kingdom of Guatemala extended from Chiapas (present-day Mexico's southernmost state) through Costa Rica. Although nominally part of the viceroyalty of New Spain, it was relatively autonomous. Its capital city, Antigua, became a center for bureaucrats, clerics, and the landholding and commercial elite of the colony. The rest of Central America (all of what is present-day Panama), with its important transit route, became attached to New Granada (modern Colombia) in the viceroyalty of Peru.

Ruins of an ancient Mayan temple at Tikal, Guatemala. The Mayan civilization flourished in Guatemala, British Honduras, and southern Mexico before the Spanish conquest.
Ronald F. Thomas–Bruce Coleman, Inc.

Spanish decline during the 17th century permitted increased autonomy for the colonial elite that, with the cooperation of church and state, dominated the oppressed Indian and mestizo (mixed Spanish-Indian heritage) working class. In the 18th century Spain's Bourbon kings, trying to regenerate the empire, inaugurated reforms that promoted new economic activity, but also challenged the longtime accommodation between the landholding elite and the bureaucracy.

Federation. The Creole elite in the kingdom of Guatemala followed Mexico's lead and severed its allegiance to Spain in 1821. The area then became part of Agustín de Iturbide's Mexican Empire, but when Iturbide's conservative government fell in 1823, liberals seized control, declared independence from Mexico, and formed the United Provinces of Central America. Chiapas, however, remained with Mexico, and Panama joined Simón Bolívar's Gran Colombia.

The United Provinces embarked on an ambitious but unrealistic program of republican reform and economic development, rejecting the Spanish heritage. Intense regionalism, political intrigue among the elite, and civil war resulted. In 1834 the liberals moved the capital from Guatemala to San Salvador, but their policies still faced bitter opposition and rebellion from conservative members of the elite and the rural masses. After the Guatemalan peasant leader Rafael Carrera defeated the federal president Francisco Morazán, in 1840, the federation disintegrated. Guatemala, Honduras, El Salvador, Nicaragua, and Costa Rica emerged as independent, conservative republics.

The Central American Republics. England, by this time, had replaced Spain as the dominant external force in the region. The British settlement at Belize had grown from a buccaneering and logging camp in the 17th century to become the principal port of Central America's foreign trade. British influence extended along the Caribbean coast as far as Panama, and in 1862, Belize officially became a British colony (British Honduras). U.S. interest, however, rivaled British after 1849, for the isthmus offered the quickest routes to the gold mines of California. The Clayton-Bulwer Treaty (q.v.) of 1850 resolved some areas of this Anglo-American conflict, but in 1855 William Walker, a U.S. soldier of fortune, invaded Nicaragua with an army of followers. A united Central American conservative army drove him out with British assistance in 1857. Meanwhile, the completion of the Panama Railway in 1855 caused Central American commerce to shift dramatically away from Belize to the more accessible Pacific coast ports, and British influence receded thereafter.

After 1870 liberal dictatorship arose which, in the name of order and progress, promoted the development of coffee as the region's main export; at the expense of a more diversified agriculture, banana cultivation, mostly controlled by foreign interests, also became important. After 1900, the U.S.-based United Fruit Co. was a major force in Central America's economy. Developing railroads, shipping, and other subsidiary interests, the company was known as the "Octopus" among resentful Central Americans. U.S. investment and government became the dominant force on the isthmus, beginning with the establishment of Panamanian independence in 1903. The U.S. helped form the Central American Court of Justice, but U.S. military occupation of Nicaragua from 1911 to 1933 undermined its effectiveness.

Economic growth in the 20th century produced new middle classes that began to challenge the continued rule of traditional elites. Beginning in Costa Rica, reformist and revolutionary parties had emerged in every country by the middle of the century.

Nicaraguan Pres. Daniel Ortega meets with U.S. Secretary of State George Shultz in Montevideo, Uruguay, in 1985. Shown here are (from left) Ortega, unidentified man, Shultz, and U.S. ambassador Larry Shlauderman.
UPI/Bettmann Newsphotos

Yaks are driven to new pastures in the Altai Mts. of the Kirgiz SSR. The animal is raised for its fur, meat, and milk. UPI

The Central American Common Market provided a basis for cooperation and interstate trade in the 1960s, but the region did not become integrated. By the 1980s, Central American countries had a variety of economies and governments. Hostility between the U.S. and Nicaragua and perceived Soviet influence posed major questions on hemisphere stability, and armed conflict proliferated between governments and revolutionaries of the right and the left. R.L.W.

For further information on this topic, see the Bibliography in volume 28, sections 117, 665, 1105, 1118, 1120–21, 1124–30.

CENTRAL ASIAN USSR, also Soviet Central Asia, region, W Central Asia. It extends from the Caspian Sea on the W to China on the E; the N boundary is coextensive with the N border of Kazakh SSR; the S boundary is formed by Iran and Afghanistan. Administratively the region comprises the following Soviet republics: Kazakh, Kirgiz, Tadzhik, Turkmen, and Uzbek. Russian domination of the area dates from the second half of the 19th century, before which much of the territory was ruled by the khanates of Bukhara, Khiva, and Kokand. The term Central Asia is sometimes used to denote the inclusion of adjacent portions of China, Mongolia, Afghanistan, Iran, and the Himalayan lands.

For further information on this topic, see the Bibliography in volume 28, section 981.

CENTRAL INTELLIGENCE AGENCY (CIA), agency of the Executive Office of the President of the U.S., created in 1947, together with the National Security Council (q.v.). The CIA is America's first permanent peacetime intelligence agency responsible for keeping the government informed of foreign actions affecting the nation's interests. It was established by the National Security Act of 1947 and is charged with coordinating all U.S. intelligence activities, as well as such functions and duties related to intelligence as directed by the National Security Council. A director and deputy director of the agency are appointed by the president with the consent of the Senate.

History. The CIA's original mission was primarily intelligence gathering, but after Communist takeovers in Eastern Europe and mainland China, the National Security Council directed that the agency engage in political, covert psychological, paramilitary, and economic operations. U.S. participation in the Korean War (1950–53) placed additional requirements on the CIA to support the combat forces.

The first major CIA reorganization occurred between 1950 and 1953. An Office of National Estimates was given the mission of projecting future developments. Overseas operations were placed in one directorate; another directorate encompassed all intelligence production; and a third included all support activities. In the period from 1953 to 1961 the CIA was at the height of its cold war activities, carrying out continuous foreign intelligence, counterintelligence, political action, and propaganda operations. In late 1961 the CIA was reorganized to put more emphasis on science, technology, and internal management. The agency was heavily committed in the war in Southeast Asia. In 1963 an Office of National Intelligence Programs Evaluation was established to coordinate community activities; this was replaced in 1972 by an Intelligence Community Staff.

Activities. The activities of the CIA are many and varied. Clandestine collection of vital information that cannot be obtained by any overt means requires recruiting agents who can obtain the needed intelligence without detection. Intelligence reports from all sources are reviewed by analysts who produce studies ranging from basic surveys to estimates of future developments. Current intelligence of major importance is detailed in daily, weekly, or monthly bulletins. Periodic projections of the future course of action of key nations are presented as national intelligence estimates.

The CIA is also responsible for counterespionage activities. Its mission is to prevent the placement of foreign agents in sensitive U.S. agencies; domestically this work is handled in cooperation with the Federal Bureau of Investigation (q.v.).

Selective use of covert political operations have ranged from subsidizing friendly foreign politicians, parties, or pressure groups to providing assistance in combating subversion. Paramilitary operations support certain exile forces with training and equipment; one example was the CIA's support of Cuban exiles before and during the Bay of Pigs invasion of Cuba (*see* BAY OF PIGS INVASION).

Modern technology has increased the capabilities of intelligence collection. In the 1960s a U-2 aircraft introduced a new era of aerial photography; this was quickly followed by transmissions from space satellites. Similarly, underseas intelligence work was advanced by a vessel capable of raising a submarine from great depths.

Controversy and Investigations. All clandestine activities are considered abhorrent by some people. Many, however, recognize secret intelligence collection necessary to protect national security. Generally, people support covert political activities in times of crisis.

The role of the CIA director as the principal U.S. intelligence officer and coordinator of activities of the other agencies has often been in dispute. Over the years frequent proposals have been made to divest the head of the CIA of the coordinating role and assign that function to a member of the White House staff.

The CIA has been investigated a number of times by various task force groups, one of which in 1949 recommended major reorganization of CIA operations. Following the Bay of Pigs invasion in 1961, President John F. Kennedy appointed a group to analyze the failure.

In 1975 the CIA came under extensive congressional and White House examination. It was found that the agency had been engaged in "unlawful" domestic spying activities and had been implicated in assassination attempts abroad. As a result of these investigations, permanent congressional committees were established to oversee CIA operations. By 1980 these committees had exclusive jurisdiction over review of CIA activities.

By 1986, however, the agency was involved in a new controversy concerning the secret sale of arms to Iran and the disbursement of monies from the sale to the rebels (known as the contras) fighting the government of Nicaragua. The late CIA director William J. Casey (1913–87), among others, was suspected of being implicated in the arms scandal. L.B.K.

For further information on this topic, see the Bibliography in volume 28, sections 203, 269.

CENTRAL NERVOUS SYSTEM. *See* NERVOUS SYSTEM.

CENTRAL POWERS, name of a coalition during World War I comprising the German and Austro-Hungarian empires and, by extension, their allies, Bulgaria and Turkey. Originally, the term referred to the geographical position of Germany and Austria-Hungary in Europe.

CENTRAL TREATY ORGANIZATION (CENTO), mutual defense and security organization that functioned between 1959 and 1979. It evolved from the earlier Middle East Treaty Organization (METO), which in turn had succeeded the Baghdad Pact of 1955. The purpose of the organization was to provide joint defense against possible aggressors and to encourage the economic and scientific development of the member nations: Iran, Pakistan, Turkey, and Great Britain. The name CENTO was adopted in 1959 after Iraq, originally a cosigner, withdrew from the Baghdad Pact; CENTO referred to a central area between regions included in the North Atlantic Treaty Organization, to which Turkey belongs, and the now defunct Southeast Asia Treaty Organization, of which Pakistan was a member. Although not an official member of CENTO, the U.S. actively supported the organization. Its headquarters, originally established at Baghdad, was moved to Ankara, Turkey, after the pro-Western Iraqi government was overthrown in 1958.

Following the Islamic revolution in Iran in 1979, the new Iranian regime announced its intention to withdraw from CENTO. Shortly afterward, Pakistan also quit the organization, arguing that Iran's withdrawal had deprived it of any meaning. This rendered CENTO defunct.

CENTRAL VALLEY, also Great Valley, in central California, comprising the valleys of the Sacramento R. (in the N) and the San Joaquin R. (in the S). The valley, which is more than 640 km (more than 400 mi) long, is almost totally enclosed by mountains and is one of the most productive agricultural regions in the U.S. Massive irrigation projects transfer water from the humid N half to the drier S half.

CENTRIFUGAL FORCE, an apparent force associated with an object moving on a curved path. This concept is best illustrated by considering the forces acting on a system consisting of a ball swung in a circle and at a constant speed at the end of a string. According to Newton's first law of motion, a moving object will travel in a straight path unless acted on by a force. The force exerted on the ball by the string acts to pull the ball toward the center of its circular path and has the net effect of keeping the ball on a circular path. This force is called the centripetal, or center-seeking, force. The magnitude of the force (F) is expressed by the formula

$$F = \frac{mv^2}{r}$$

where m is the mass of the object, v its velocity, and r the radius of its path. Other examples of this force are the gravitational force, which keeps satellites in orbit around parent bodies, and the electrical force, which keeps electrons in orbit around atomic nuclei.

Newton's third law of motion states that for every action there is an equal and opposite reaction. The centripetal force exerted on the ball by the string must therefore be balanced by a force equal in magnitude but opposite in direction. This force is exerted by the string on the hand of the person swinging the string and is known as the centrifugal, or center-fleeing, force.

CENTRIFUGE, mechanical device using the principle of centrifugal force to separate substances of different densities. A common centrifuge is a container that is spun rapidly. The only limit to the centifugal force is the strength of the metal of which the device is made. Centrifugal forces may be thousands of times as great as the force of gravity.

Centrifuges may be used for rapid separation of substances that would normally separate slowly under the influence of gravity. For example, the draining of water from a wet solid may be accelerated by spinning the solid. This principle is used in the spin cycle of an ordinary automatic washing machine. The first successful centrifuge, a cream separator, was invented in 1883 by the Swedish engineer Carl de Laval (1845-1913). Since then numerous other applications of centrifugation have been made. (For the separation of isotopes, *see* ISOTOPE; for the separation of blood cells from whole blood, *see* BLOOD; and for the separation of sugar from syrup, *see* SUGAR.)

The smaller the diameter of a centrifuge, the greater the forces and accelerations exerted on the contents and the more rapidly it may be spun without breaking. The most powerful centrifuges, known as ultracentrifuges, are long, narrow tubes rotated at enormous speeds. The ultracentrifuge was developed about 1920 by the Swedish chemist Theodor Svedberg (1884-1971) and improved by the American physicist Jesse Beams (1898-1977).

The rotor, the spinning part of the centrifuge, in the Beams ultracentrifuge is magnetically suspended in a vacuum and electrically driven. Friction is thus reduced to a negligible amount; for example, if a 2-mm ($\frac{1}{16}$-in) rotor is spinning in a vacuum of 1/400,000,000 atmospheric pressure at 100,000 revolutions/sec and the driving force is turned off, it will lose only 100 revolutions/sec in an hour.

CENTURION, officer commanding a century in the ancient Roman army. A century was made up of 100 men, and 60 centuries constituted a legion. Within each Roman legion, centurions held degrees of rank; the senior centurion took part in councils of war. Centurions were chosen from among veteran soldiers by the six tribunes in command of a legion. Although they were of plebeian origin, their military counterparts today would be commissioned rather than noncommissioned officers.

CENTURY PLANT. *See* AGAVE.

CEPHALIC INDEX, basic measure of the shape of the skull, used by anthropometrists in classifying dimensions and proportions characteristic of various human groupings and various prehistorical humans and prehumans. It expresses the width of the skull as a percentage of the length from front to back. When measurements are made directly on a skull, the percentage is known as the cranial index. Craniologists distinguish three basic classifications of skulls based on cranial and cephalic indexes: dolichocephalic (long skulls), with widths of less than 75 percent of the length; mesocephalic (medium skulls), with indexes of 75 to 80; and brachycephalic (broad skulls), with indexes of more than 80 percent.

Indexes derived from proportions of other parts of the human body or skeleton are also used for the same purposes as the cephalic index.

CEPHALONIA. *See* KEFALLINÍA.

CEPHALOPOD, common name for actively predatory marine mollusks (*see* MOLLUSK), constituting the invertebrate class Cephalopoda and including the squid, octopus, and nautilus (qq.v). The word *cephalopod* means "head footed," and the animals are so named because the arms sur-

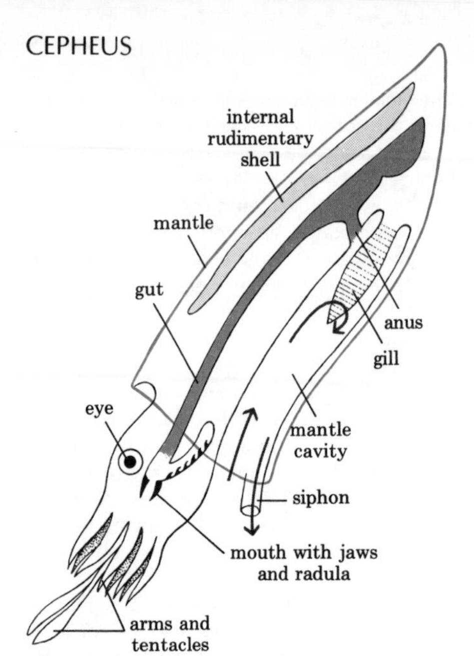

Structure of a typical cephalopod, the squid, shows that only a rudimentary shell is present.

From Helena Curtis; *Biology* Third Edition, Worth Publishers, Inc., New York, 1979.

round the mouth. Cephalopods are advanced animals in terms of structure and physiology, and their level of behavior is equal to that of fish. Ecologically successful, they are among the more common predators in the sea; in turn they are eaten by many other animals, including humans. Giant squid, which can weigh as much as 2000 kg (4400 lb), are the largest of all invertebrates. About 650 species of cephalopod are known.

The class is an ancient one, first appearing in the fossil record during the Cambrian period, about 600 million years ago. Primitive cephalopods, like other mollusks, had large external shells, but these were gradually reduced as the animals grew faster and more active. The remaining primitive cephalopod, the nautilus, retains many archaic traits, such as an external shell with gas-filled chambers that aid flotation. The front of the nautiloid body protrudes from the opening of the shell and bears many suckerless arms. Below the head is a mantle cavity with four gills; a funnel around its opening ejects water to provide weak jet propulsion. The eyes lack lenses, and the nervous system is fairly simple. Prey is grasped with the tentacles and can be bitten with the mouth's sharp beak.

More advanced cephalopods are exemplified by the squid and cuttlefish (q.v.), in which the shell is reduced and covered by tissue; the squid has a thin, horny, internal shell called a pen. The two-gilled mantle cavity is surrounded by muscles and provides much more effective jet propulsion, which is aided by fins. The squid has ten sucker-bearing arms, one pair of which is longer than the rest. The eyes are comparable in structure to the human eye, and the brain and nervous system are fairly complex. The octopus and its allies are even more modified. The shell is entirely absent, and the animal has only eight arms. Most octopuses are bottom dwellers, and a few attain a large size.

Digestion in cephalopods is rapid, and the circulatory and reproductive systems are complicated. The animals avoid predators mainly through flight or concealment, including an ability to change colors for camouflage, and some cephalopods eject a black secretion, called ink, to confuse predators. The sexes are separate; some species engage in complex mating displays. Cephalopod embryos develop in egg masses that are often cared for by the female.

Two cephalopod orders exist. Tetrabranchia, with four gills, includes the nautilus and many fossil forms. Dibranchia, with two gills, contains the ten-armed Decapoda (squid and cuttlefish) and the eight-armed Octopoda. M.T.G.

For further information on this topic, see the Bibliography in volume 28, sections 464–65.

CEPHEUS, northern constellation, located near the north celestial pole. Alderamin, the brightest star of the constellation, is of the third magnitude. More important, however, is the fainter Delta Cephei, which is a star of the class known as Cepheid variables.

CERAM, island, E Indonesia, one of the Molucca Islands, in the province of Maluku, between the Ceram Sea on the N and the Banda Sea on the S. It lies between New Guinea on the E and Buru on the W. Ceram is about 350 km (about 216 mi) long from W to E, is mountainous, and has jungles containing ironwood trees and sago palms. Many rivers of the island drain to the Ceram Sea and are dry part of the year. The climate is tropical, hot and humid, with heavy rains in the wet season. Earthquakes sometimes occur. The greater part of the interior is unexplored. A majority of the population lives along the coasts. The principal towns, Amahai and Tehoru on the S coast, Bula on the E coast, Wahai on the N coast, and Piru on the W coast, are ports of call.

The people along the coast are principally Malay emigrants from the islands of Celebes, Java, and Ternate and are engaged mainly in fishing and as workers on plantations devoted to the cultivation of coconuts, spices, rice, corn, sugarcane, and tobacco. They are also employed in the production of sago flour and cajuput oil. Trade is partly controlled by Chinese merchants;

copra is the principal export. The prevailing religions of Ceram are Islam and Christianity. The people of the interior, descendants of intermarriages between Malayans and Papuans, live mostly by hunting and fishing and observe traditional religious rites. Under Dutch rule, which began in the mid-17th century, Ceram was included, for administrative purposes, in the residency of Amboina. In 1946, following the uprising of the Indonesians against Dutch rule, Ceram became a part of the self-governing state of East Indonesia. Area, 17,148 sq km (6621 sq mi); pop. (est.) 158,600.

CERAMICS (Gr. *keramos,* "potter's clay"), originally the art of making pottery (q.v.), now a general term for the science of manufacturing articles prepared from pliable, earthy materials that are made rigid by high-temperature treatment. Ceramics now includes the manufacture of earthenware, porcelain, bricks, and some kinds of tile and stoneware. Ceramic products are used not only for artistic objects and tableware, but also for such utilitarian items as sewer pipe and the walls of buildings. Ceramic insulators with a wide range of electrical properties have increasingly replaced conventional manufacturing materials. The electrical properties of a recently discovered family of copper-oxide-based ceramics allow them to become superconductive at temperatures much higher than those at which metals display this phenomenon (*see* SUPERCONDUCTIVITY). In nuclear reactors, the radioactive fuel is composed of a ceramic compound of uranium oxide, and in space technology, ceramic materials and cermets (strong, highly heat-resistant alloys, typically made by mixing, pressing, and then baking an oxide or carbide with a powdered metal) are used to make nose cones, the heat-shield tiles on the space shuttle, and many other components.

See also CLAY.

Ceramic plate made in Pennsylvania in the 19th century. National Gallery of Art

CERBERUS, in Greek mythology, a three-headed, dragon-tailed god that guarded the entrance to the lower world. The monster permitted all spirits to enter Hades, but would allow none to leave. Only a few heroes ever escaped Cerberus's guard; the great musician Orpheus charmed it with his lyre, and the Greek hero Hercules captured it bare-handed and brought it for a short time from the underworld to the regions above. In Roman mythology both the beautiful maiden Psyche and the Trojan prince Aeneas were able to pacify Cerberus with a honey cake and thus continue their journey through the underworld. Cerberus is sometimes pictured with a mane of snakes wrapped around its body.

CERCEAU, du, family of French architects and designers, who worked for the kings of France. The name du Cerceau (Fr., "hoop") was derived from a circle used as a sign over their workshop.

Jacques Androuet du Cerceau the Elder (c. 1520–c. 1584), studied classical Roman architecture on a trip to Italy in the 1530s. Although he designed several buildings (not extant) for Charles IX, he is known primarily for his influential books of engravings. His *Plus excellents bastiments de France* (2 vol., 1576, 1579) depicts many notable 16th-century mansions that no longer exist. In other works he introduced to France a fantastically ornamented version of Italian Renaissance style in architecture, ironwork, and furniture.

Baptiste Androuet du Cerceau (1544–1602), elder son of Jacques the Elder, was architect in charge of the Louvre. He also designed the Pont Neuf across the Seine and supervised all the royal buildings in Paris.

Jacques Androuet du Cerceau the Younger (c. 1550–1614), younger son of Jacques the Elder, assisted Baptiste on the Louvre.

Jean Androuet du Cerceau (c. 1585–c. 1649), son of Baptiste, was an architect to Louis XIII, for whom he built the horseshoe stair at Fontainebleau. He also designed the Hôtel de Sully (1624–29) and other private mansions in Paris.

CEREALS, various species of the family Gramineae (*see* GRASSES), cultivated for their seed, which is used as food. The name is derived from Ceres, the Roman goddess of grains and agriculture. Although the cereals proper do not belong to any particular tribe of the grasses, the use of particular species as bread plants seems to have been determined chiefly by the superior size of the seed or by the ease of procuring it in sufficient quantity and of freeing it from its inedible covering. The most extensively cultivated grains

Five of the most widely grown cereals. Left to right: wheat, oats, rye, barley, rice.

are wheat (*Triticum*), barley (*Hordeum*), rye (*Secale*), oats (*Avena*), rice (*Oryza*), corn or maize (*Zea*), different kinds of millet (*Setatia, Eleusine, Panicum,* and *Pennisetum*), and the grain sorghums known as durra or Guinea corn (*Sorghum* or *Andropogon*). These have all been cultivated since ancient times. Maize is the only grain that originated in America; the others were developed in Europe, Asia, and Africa.

CEREBRAL HEMORRHAGE. *See* STROKE.

CEREBRAL PALSY, inclusive term for various nonprogressive disorders, resulting from brain damage, of motor function in young children. The cause of most cases of cerebral palsy is unknown. Damage to the brain could occur before, during, or shortly after birth. Prenatal causes might include developmental defects, inherited metabolic errors, maternal infections, irradiation, asphyxia, harmful drugs taken by the mother, and toxemia of pregnancy. Natal factors could include trauma in delivery; anoxia, or oxygen deficiency; and prematurity. In the postnatal period possible injurious factors include trauma, anoxia, infections, cerebral vascular lesions, and Rh incompatibility.

The symptoms and signs of cerebral palsy depend upon the distribution and severity of the changes in the brain. On this basis, five groups are recognized: (1) spastic diplegia, with exaggeration of voluntary movements; (2) hemiplegic cerebral palsy, with half of the body affected; (3) spastic quadriplegia, with choreoathetosis, or uncontrollable movement; (4) atheotic cerebral palsy, with uncontrolled movements of the affected muscles; and (5) ataxic cerebral palsy, in which balance is disturbed. These categories commonly overlap because of multiple symptoms. Moreover, defects in vision and speech and convulsive seizures may be present. About 30 percent or more of children having cerebral palsy are mentally retarded.

The variable manifestations and the lack of specific clinical classification make it difficult to obtain definitive data on incidence of the disease. Some authorities find the rate to be about 6 per 1000 births, and the prevalence among children aged five to nine years to be 600 per 100,000. In many cases, evidence of brain damage may not be apparent until several months after birth. In instances where defects are less severe, the disorder may not be recognized for some years.

The chief goals in treating cerebral palsy are the improvement of symptoms and the teaching of the patient to compensate for the disability. Usually the full extent of damage cannot be fully appraised until about the second year. When damage is relatively severe, physical therapy when indicated, and in some cases, orthopedic surgery, may be useful. Patients with seizure can be treated with appropriate drugs. A.T.Mi.

CEREBROSPINAL MENINGITIS. *See* MENINGITIS.

CERES, in Roman mythology, the goddess of agriculture. She and her daughter Proserpine were the counterparts of the Greek goddesses Demeter and Persephone. The Greek belief that her joy at being reunited with her daughter each spring caused the earth to bring forth an abundance of fruits and grains was introduced into Rome in the 5th century BC, and her cult became extremely popular, especially with the plebeians. The word *cereal* is derived from her name. Her chief festival, the Cerealia, was celebrated from April 12 to 19.

CERES. *See* ASTEROID.

CEREUS, genus of plants of the family Cactaceae (*see* CACTUS), including a large but undetermined number of species. The genus is found in the southern U.S., Mexico, South America, and the West Indies. Many species are common in cultivation, some of them under the name of night-blooming cereus. Some of the most popular are *Cereus nycticalus, C. triangularis,* and *C. grandiflorus.* The best-known species in the U.S. is the saguaro, or giant cactus, *C. giganteus,* which commonly occurs in Arizona and adjacent Sonora State, Mexico. This plant grows to 15 m (50 ft) high. Young plants consist of a single trunk, but older plants may have 20 or more upturned branches. The night-blooming cereus of the desert, *C. gregaii,* is well known for its very large white, fragrant flowers, nearly all of which bloom at night. In several different recent classifications, *Cereus* is divided into as many as ten genera.

A night-blooming cereus, Cereus undulatus
Robert C. Hermes–National Audubon Society

A physician gently examines and evaluates the condition of a young cerebral palsy victim. United Cerebral Palsy

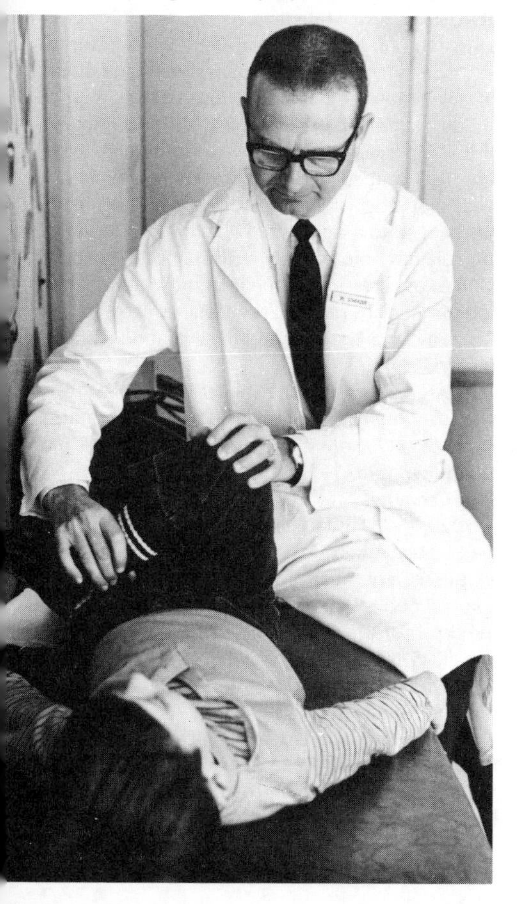

CERINTHUS (fl. about AD 100), Christian heretic, considered a Gnostic by modern scholars. He had a number of followers in Asia Minor. He preached that the world was created by a subordinate deity, called a demiurge, or by angels, one of whom gave the Ten Commandments to Moses. Cerinthus also asserted that Jesus Christ was the natural son of Mary and Joseph. He taught that the spirit of God, called Christ, descended upon Jesus at his baptism and enabled him to work miracles and to proclaim the unknown Father, but that the spirit of Christ left Jesus before the Passion and the resurrection.

CERIUM, metallic element, symbol Ce, in group IIIb of the periodic table (*see* PERIODIC LAW); at.no. 58, at.wt. 140.12. Cerium was discovered independently in 1804 by the Swedish chemist Baron Jöns Jakob Berzelius and by the German chemist Martin Heinrich Klaproth; the pure metallic element was not isolated until 1875.

Cerium is the most abundant of the rare earth elements (q.v.); it is more abundant in the crust of the earth than the more familiar metals zinc, lead, and tin. It occurs with the other rare earth metals in monazite sand and samarskite in the Ural Mountains of the USSR, in Norway, Brazil, and the U.S. (North Carolina). It also occurs in the minerals cerite, found in Sweden, and allanite, found in Greenland and New York State. Cerium is the only one of the rare earth metals that can be easily separated from the others.

Cerium melts at 795° C (1463° F), boils at about 3470° C (about 6280° F), and has a sp.gr. of 6.77.

Metallic cerium is found chiefly in an alloy with iron that composes the flints used in cigarette lighters. Ceric oxide was formerly employed in the manufacture of gas mantles. Compounds of cerium are employed in small quantities in the manufacture of glass, ceramics, arc-lamp electrodes, and photoelectric cells. Cerous nitrate has been used medicinally in the treatment of seasickness and chronic vomiting. Ceric sulfate is employed in analytic-chemistry laboratories as an oxidizing agent.

CERNĂUŢI. *See* CHERNOVTSY.

CERRITO, Fanny, real name FRANCESCA CERRITO (1817-1909), Italian ballerina, one of the most brilliant, vivacious dancers and one of the few female choreographers of the 19th century. Born in Naples, she studied under the celebrated Italian teacher Carlo Blasis (1797-1878) and the noted French choreographers Jules Perrot and Arthur Saint-Léon (1821-70; her favorite partner and, from 1845 to 1851, her husband). She was famous for her roles in *Pas de quatre* (1845), *Ondine* (1843), and *Gemma* (1854, her choreography).

CERRITOS, city, Los Angeles Co., SW California, on the San Gabriel R., near Los Angeles; inc. 1956. Manufactures include furniture, carpets, aerospace equipment, and recreational vehicles. Formerly an agricultural center, the community was known as Dairy Valley until 1967. The city then was renamed Cerritos (Span., "little hills") after a ranch established here in the 1780s. Cerritos Community College is located here. Pop. (1970) 15,856; (1980) 52,756.

CERRO DE PASCO, town, central Peru, capital of Pasco Department, about 4265 m (about 14,000 ft) above sea level. It is connected by rail with Lima. The town was once noted as one of the world's richest silver-mining centers but is more important now for the mining of copper, which began here in the early 20th century under the management of the Cerro de Pasco Corp., a U.S.-controlled firm. Gold, lead, zinc, and bismuth are also mined at Cerro de Pasco; the valuable silver deposits were exhausted by the Spanish. Copper is smelted in one of the largest metallurgical plants in the world, in La Oroya, S of Cerro de Pasco. The city has been relocated a short distance from its original site. Pop. (est.) 47,200.

CERTIORARI, in common law, writ or written command issued by a superior court to a lower court, or to a public officer or public board, having judicial authority that requires the record of the proceedings in a lower court to be sent to the superior court for review. The higher court studies the record while the case is still pending and decides whether or not the inferior court is acting in accordance with the law. Superior courts may use the writ in either criminal or civil cases to ensure speedier justice. They do not judge the proceedings according to their merits; they review only the legal aspects of the case, such as whether the lower court has jurisdiction to try the case. On the basis of its findings, the superior court may remove the action or proceedings to a higher court for trial.

CERUSSITE, also white lead ore, mineral ($PbCO_3$) consisting of lead carbonate. In a pure form cerussite is colorless and transparent, but it is usually yellow or grayish because of various impurities. It has a hardness of 3 to 3.5 and a sp.gr. of 6.5 and crystallizes in the orthorhombic system. It is formed by the alteration of galena or lead sulfide, which, as it oxidizes to sulfate, may be changed to a carbonate by action of solutions of calcium bicarbonate. The most famous sources of cerussite are the lead mines of Siberia and the Altai Territory, various places in Sweden, Germany, and England, and in several regions of the U.S.

CERVANTES SAAVEDRA, Miguel de (1547-1616), Spanish writer of the Golden Age, whose satiric novel *Don Quixote* is one of the masterpieces of world literature.

Life. Cervantes was born in Alcalá de Henares, Sept. 29, 1547. His father was an indigent surgeon with a large family. In 1568, when Cervantes was a student, a number of his poems appeared in a volume published in Madrid to commemorate the death of the Spanish queen Elizabeth of Valois (1545-68). In 1569 he went to Rome, where in the following year he entered the service of Cardinal Giulio Acquaviva (1546-74). Soon afterward Cervantes joined a Spanish regiment in Naples. He fought in 1571 against the Turks in the naval battle in Lepanto, in which he lost the use of his left hand. While returning to Spain in 1575, Cervantes was captured by Barbary pirates. He was taken to Algeria as a slave and held there

Miguel de Cervantes Saavedra

for ransom. During the next five years he made several heroic but unsuccessful attempts to escape, and he was finally ransomed in 1580 by his family and friends.

Returning to Spain at the age of 33, Cervantes, despite his wartime service and Algerian adventure, was unable to obtain employment with a noble family, the usual reward for veterans who had distinguished themselves. Deciding to become a writer, he turned out poems and plays at a prodigious rate between 1582 and 1585; few of these are extant. His pastoral novel *La Galatea* (1585) gained him a reputation, but the proceeds from its sale were insufficient to support him. Cervantes then took government jobs, first furnishing goods to the fleet of the Armada and later collecting taxes. The government imprisoned him several times because he failed to give a satisfactory explanation of his tax-collecting activities.

While in prison Cervantes conceived the idea for a story about a madman who imagines himself a knight-errant performing the splendid feats described in medieval tales of chivalry. The first part was issued under the title *The History of the Valorous and Wittie Knight-Errant Don Quixote of the Mancha* (1605; trans. 1612). It became such an immediate success that within two weeks after publication three pirated editions appeared in Madrid. Partly because of the pirating and partly because of his lack of financial acumen, Cervantes never gained substantial wealth from the enormous success of the work.

His *Novelas ejemplares* (Exemplary Novels, 1613), a collection of 12 short stories, includes romances in the Italian style, descriptions of criminal life in Seville, and sketches of unusual events and characters. One of these stories, "El coloquio de los perros" (The Talking Dogs), is particularly renowned for its satirical prose style. The second part of *Don Quixote* was published in 1615. Cervantes completed the fantastic allegorical novel *Persiles y Sigismunda* (1617) four days before he died in Madrid on April 23, 1616.

Don Quixote. Cervantes's most important work, called in full *The History of Don Quixote de la Mancha,* is generally regarded as the first modern novel. It is a brilliant satire, not only of the chivalric romances of the Middle Ages and early Renaissance but also of the sentimental and pastoral novels popular in Cervantes's own time.

The principal character of the novel is Don Quixote, an elderly village gentleman of modest means. An avid reader of old-fashioned tales of chivalry, he becomes obsessed with the idea of reintroducing the practice of knight-errantry into the world. In Part I Don Quixote equips himself with arms and armor and rides forth on Rosinante, a broken-down horse, to challenge evil wherever he may find it. He is accompanied by the loyal and shrewd, but credulous, peasant Sancho Panza, who serves him as squire.

In his deranged state, Don Quixote sets himself the task of defending orphans, protecting maidens and widows, befriending the helpless, serving the causes of truth and beauty, and reestablishing justice. His adventures and skirmishes are often grotesquely inappropriate to the situation; for example, he attacks a windmill, thinking it a giant, and a flock of sheep, thinking it an army. The obstinacy of his illusions never permits him to heed the warnings of Sancho Panza, whose attitude is as realistic as that of his master is idealistic. The philosophical perception of the novel lies in the suggested balance of their contrasting views.

In Part II the contrast between the romanticism of Don Quixote and the practical wisdom of Sancho Panza is less striking. Don Quixote becomes a trifle more reasonable, and Sancho Panza begins to understand rather dimly the illusions of his master. In the end Don Quixote returns to his village and abandons knighthood. He realizes the error of his ways, declaring that "in the nests of yesteryear there are no birds today," falls ill, and dies. Critics generally agree that Part II of *Don Quixote* is superior because of its compact organization.

Don Quixote has had a tremendous influence on the development of prose fiction; it has been translated into all modern languages and has appeared in some 700 editions. The first publication in English was in a translation by Thomas Shelton (Pt. I, 1612; Pt. II, 1620). It has been the subject of a variety of works in other fields of art, including operas by the Italian composer Giovanni Paisiello, the French Jules Massenet, and the Spanish Manuel de Falla; a tone poem by the German composer Richard Strauss; a German film (1933) directed by G. W. Pabst (1885-1967) and a Soviet film (1957) directed by Grigori Kozintzev (1905-73); a ballet (1965) by George Balanchine; and an American musical, *Man of La Mancha* (1965), by Mitch Leigh (1928-). The theme also inspired the 19th-century French artists Honoré Daumier and Gustave Doré. E.F.

For further information on this person, see the section Biographies in the Bibliography in volume 28.

CÉSAIRE, Aimé (1913-), French West Indian poet and political leader, born in Basse-Pointe, Martinique, and educated at the Sorbonne and the École Normale Supérieure, Paris. Césaire was discovered by the surrealist poet and critic André Breton, who wrote the preface to the 1942 edition of *Return to My Native Land* (1939; trans. 1968), in which Césaire explores what he calls *négritude,* black culture as a valid and independent entity. His verse, although influenced by surrealism, remains impassioned and clear. His later books of poetry include *Les armes miraculeuses* (Miraculous Weapons, 1946) and *Ferrements* (Ironwork, 1959).

CESALPINO, Andrea, in Latin, Andreas Caesalpinus (1519-1603), Italian botanist and physician, born in Arezzo, Tuscany, and educated at the University of Pisa. He became director of the botanical garden and professor of materia medica (the science dealing with the preparation of drugs) at that university in 1555. In 1592 he became physician to Pope Clement VIII in Rome. Cesalpino theorized on the circulation of the blood in the human body, thereby anticipating the discoveries of the English anatomist William Harvey. Among Cesalpino's written works are 16 short books entitled *De Plantis* (Of Plants, 1583), the first classification of plants according to the characteristics of their fruits and seeds. The work formed, in part, the basis of the classification system established by the Swedish botanist Carolus Linnaeus.

CESAREAN SECTION, surgical removal of the fetus through incisions in the abdominal wall and the uterus. This operation has been practiced since ancient times on dead and, probably, dying mothers to save the life of the fetus. According to tradition, Julius Caesar was born by this method, hence its name. Roman law, however, restricted the operation to women who died before childbirth, and as Caesar's mother lived long after he was born, the tradition is probably false. The first authenticated case of a cesarean section on a living woman occurred in 1610. Because of the high mortality risk, this operation did not become widespread until the end of the 19th century, when increased use of antiseptics and advances in surgical techniques made it less dangerous.

In present-day obstetrics a cesarean section is scheduled for those cases in which the size of the birth canal is too small to allow the fetus to pass. The operation is used also in cases of abnormal developments during delivery, such as hemorrhage or tumors in the mother or difficult positioning of the fetus. The number of cesarean deliveries increased during the 1970s until they accounted for almost one in every five births. Then new evidence indicated that not all these operations were needed. For instance, it was believed that a woman who had had one cesarean delivery always needed to have subsequent children this way or her scars would rupture, but this proved not to be an important risk. Because even a modern surgical delivery carries a threefold higher risk of death for the mother, obstetricians are being encouraged to decrease the number of cesarean births. *See* PREGNANCY AND CHILDBIRTH.

CESIUM, element, symbol Cs, one of the alkali metals (q.v.) in group Ia of the periodic table (*see* PERIODIC LAW); at.no. 55, at.wt. 132.91. This white, soft element was discovered in 1860 by Robert Wilhelm Bunsen and Gustav Robert Kirchhoff through the use of a spectroscope (*see* SPECTRUM).

The natural source yielding the greatest quantity of cesium is the rare mineral pollux (or pollucite). Ores of this mineral found on the island of Elba contain 34 percent of cesium oxide; American ores of pollux, found in Maine and South Dakota, contain 13 percent of the oxide. Cesium also occurs in lepidolite, carnallite, and certain feldspars. It is extracted by separating the cesium compound from the mineral, transforming the compound thus obtained into the cyanide, and electrolysis of the fused cyanide. Cesium may also be obtained by heating its hydroxides or carbonates with magnesium or aluminum and by heating its chlorides with calcium. Commercial cesium usually contains rubidium, with which it usually occurs and which resembles it so closely that no effort is made to separate them. Cesium melts at 28.5° C (83.3° F), boils at 705° C (1301° F), and has a sp.gr. of 1.87.

Like potassium, cesium oxidizes readily when exposed to air and is thus used to remove residual oxygen from radio vacuum tubes. Because of its property of emitting electrons when exposed to light, it is used in the photosensitive surface of the cathode of the photoelectric cell. The radioactive isotope cesium-137, which is produced by nuclear fission, is a useful by-product of atomic-energy plants. Cesium-137 emits more energy than radium and is employed in medical and industrial research. *See* ISOTOPIC TRACER.

ČESKÉ BUDĚJOVICE (Ger. *Budweis*), city and river port, SW Czechoslovakia, in Jihočeský Region, on the Vltava R. It is a rail junction and the trade center of S Bohemia. Among its principal articles of commerce are lignite, iron ore, and other raw materials produced in the surrounding region and a variety of products manufactured in the city, including beer, porcelain, earthenware, and lead pencils. Founded in the 13th century, the city became an episcopal see in the 18th century. Among the city's notable buildings are the Gothic Church of Saint Mary, the bishop's palace, and the town hall. Pop. (1980 est.) 89,400.

CETACEA. *See* WHALE.

CETUS, also the Whale, equatorial constellation lying to the south of Aries, the Ram. The two brightest stars are normally Beta Ceti, a second-magnitude star also called Deneb Kaitos (Arab., "tail of the whale"), and Alpha Ceti, a third-magnitude star also called Menkar (Arab., "nose"). The most remarkable star is Omicron Ceti, called Mira (New Lat., fr. Lat. *Mirus,* "wonderful"), a variable star first discovered in 1596. It usually varies in brightness from the ninth to the third magnitude over a period of about 11 months. Occasionally it reaches a brightness of second magnitude. Mira is one of the largest stars known, with a diameter of about 354 million km (about 220 million mi), slightly larger than the diameter of the orbit of the earth. The constellation is named after the sea monster of Greek mythology sent by the god Neptune to destroy Andromeda, but killed by Perseus.

CEULEMANS, Raymond (1938-), Belgian billiard master, regarded as the greatest all-around player in history. A world-class performer in straight billiards, cushion caroms, and all forms of balkline, he has been, since 1962, almost invincible in three-cushion billiards. In 1980 in Buenos Aires he won his 16th world tournament out of the last 17 held. His most impressive record is his 1.678 points per inning scoring average in the 1978 world tournament in Las Vegas, Nev. In all forms of carom billiards (he does not play pocket games), Ceulemans has won more than 100 European and world titles.

CEUTA, city and seaport, an exclave of Spain in NW Africa, on the Strait of Gibraltar, bordered also by Morocco. For administrative purposes Ceuta is governed as part of Cádiz Province in Spain. The city is on a headland consisting of seven peaks, at the end of a narrow isthmus. The highest of these peaks, Jebel Musa, thought to be the ancient Abila, is one of the two Pillars of Hercules (q.v.).

A military and penal station, Ceuta is on the site of a Carthaginian settlement on which a Roman colony was later built. The Vandals took it from the Romans and lost it to Byzantium. It later became successively a possession of the Visigoths and of the Arabs. The latter called it Sebta or Cibta, from which the modern name is derived. Ceuta became an important center for the manufacture of brassware and for trade in slaves, gold, and ivory under later Berber and Spanish-Moorish rulers. The Portuguese captured the city in 1415 and the Spaniards in 1580. Moors laid siege to it unsuccessfully several times, one siege lasting from 1694 to 1720. Pop. (1981) 70,864.

CÉVENNES, mountain range, S France, forming an arc from NE to SW, and marking the SE limit of the large plateau region of central France called the Massif Central. The Cévennes form the watershed between the river systems of the Rhône and the Saône on the E and those of the Garonne and the Loire on the W. The Cévennes proper have a length of about 64 km (about 40 mi). The highest peak of the range is Mont Mézenc (elevation 1754 m/5755 ft), and the average height is from 910 to 1220 m (about 3000 to 4000 ft). The chief industries in the mountain area are raising sheep, mining coal, and cultivating olives and other fruit. The mountains were the scenes of the persecutions of religious groups, including the Albigenses and the Waldenses in the Middle Ages and the Camisards in the 17th century.

CEYLON. *See* SRI LANKA.

CÉZANNE, Paul (1839-1906), French painter, often called the father of modern art, who strove to develop an ideal synthesis of naturalistic representation, personal expression, and abstract pictorial order.

Among the artists of his time, Cézanne perhaps has had the most profound effect on the art of the 20th century. He was the greatest single influence on both the French artist Henri Matisse, who admired his color, and the Spanish artist Pablo Picasso, who developed Cézanne's planar compositional structure into the cubist style. During the greater part of his own lifetime, however, Cézanne was largely ignored, and he worked in isolation. He mistrusted critics, had few friends, and, until 1895, exhibited only occasionally. He was alienated even from his family, who found his behavior peculiar and failed to appreciate his revolutionary art.

Still Life on a Bureau, *one of the numerous still lifes created by Paul Cézanne that reflect his artistic development and changes of style.*

Early Life and Work. Cézanne was born in the southern French town of Aix-en-Provence, Jan. 19, 1839, the son of a wealthy banker. His boyhood companion was Émile Zola, who later gained fame as a novelist and man of letters. As did Zola, Cézanne developed artistic interests at an early age, much to the dismay of his father. In 1862, after a number of bitter family disputes, the aspiring artist was given a small allowance and sent to study art in Paris, where Zola had already gone. From the start he was drawn to the more radical elements of the Parisian art world. He especially admired the romantic painter Eugène Delacroix and, among the younger masters, Gustave Courbet and the notorious Édouard Manet, who exhibited realist paintings that were shocking in both style and subject matter to most of their contemporaries.

Influence of the Impressionists. Many of Cézanne's early works were painted in dark tones applied with heavy, fluid pigment, suggesting the moody, romantic expressionism of previous generations. Just as Zola pursued his interest in the realist novel, however, Cézanne also gradually developed a commitment to the representation of contemporary life, painting the world he observed without concern for thematic idealization or stylistic affectation. The most significant influence on the work of his early maturity proved to be Camille Pissarro, an older but as yet unrecognized painter who lived with his large family in a rural area outside Paris. Pissarro not only provided the moral encouragement that the insecure Cézanne required, but he also introduced him to the new impressionist technique (*see* IMPRESSIONISM) for rendering outdoor light. Along with the painters Claude Monet, Auguste Renoir, and a few others, Pissarro had developed a painting style that involved working outdoors (*en plein air*) rapidly and on a reduced scale, employing small touches of pure color, generally without the use of preparatory sketches or linear outlines. In such a manner Pissarro and the others hoped to capture the most transient natural effects as well as their own passing emotional states as the artists stood before nature. Under Pissarro's tutelage, and within a very short time during 1872–73, Cézanne shifted from dark tones to bright hues and began to concentrate on scenes of farmland and rural villages.

Return to Aix. Although he seemed less technically accomplished than the other impressionists, Cézanne was accepted by the group and exhibited with them in 1874 and 1877. In general the impressionists did not have much commercial success, and Cézanne's works received the harshest critical commentary. He drifted away from many of his Parisian contacts during the late 1870s and '80s and spent much of his time in his native Aix. After 1882, he did not work closely again with Pissarro. In 1886, Cézanne became embittered over what he took to be thinly disguised references to his own failures in one of Zola's novels. As a result he broke off relations with his oldest supporter. In the same year, he inherited his father's wealth and finally, at the age of 47, became financially independent, but socially he remained quite isolated.

Cézanne's Use of Color. This isolation and Cézanne's concentration and singleness of purpose may account for the remarkable development he sustained during the 1880s and '90s. In this period he continued to paint studies from nature in brilliant impressionist colors, but he gradually simplified his application of the paint to the point where he seemed able to define volumetric forms with juxtaposed strokes of pure color. Critics eventually argued that Cézanne had discovered a means of rendering both nature's light and nature's form with a single application of color. He seemed to be reintroducing a formal structure that the impressionists had abandoned, without sacrificing the sense of brilliant illumination they had achieved. Cézanne himself spoke of "modulating" with color rather than "modeling" with dark and light. By this he meant that he would replace an artificial convention of representation (modeling) with a more expressive system (modulating) that was closer still to nature, or, as the artist himself said, "parallel to nature." For Cézanne, the answer to all the technical problems of impressionism lay in a use of color both more orderly and more expressive than that of his fellow impressionists.

Cézanne's goal was, in his own mind, never fully attained. He left most of his works unfinished and destroyed many others. He complained of his failure at rendering the human figure, and indeed the great figural works of his last years—such as the *Large Bathers* (c. 1899-1906, Museum of Art, Philadelphia)—reveal curious distortions that seem to have been dictated by the rigor of the system of color modulation he imposed on his own representations. The succeeding generation of painters, however, eventually came to be receptive to nearly all of Cézanne's idiosyncrasies. Cézanne's heirs felt that the naturalistic painting of impressionism had become formularized, and a new and original style, however difficult it might be, was needed to return a sense of sincerity and commitment to modern art.

Significance of Cézanne's Work. For many years Cézanne was known only to his old impressionist colleagues and to a few younger radical postimpressionist artists, including the Dutch painter Vincent van Gogh and the French painter Paul Gauguin. In 1895, however, Ambroise Vollard (1865-1939), an ambitious Paris art dealer, arranged a show of Cézanne's works and over the next few years promoted them successfully. By 1904, Cézanne was featured in a major official exhibition, and by the time of his death (in Aix on Oct. 22, 1906) he had attained the status of a legendary figure. During his last years many younger artists traveled to Aix to observe him at work and to receive any words of wisdom he might offer. Both his style and his theory remained mysterious and cryptic; he seemed to some a naive primitive, while to others he was a sophisticated master of technical procedure. The intensity of his color, coupled with the apparent rigor of his compositional organization, signaled to most that, despite the artist's own frequent despair, he had synthesized the basic expressive and representational elements of painting in a highly original manner.

See also MODERN ART AND ARCHITECTURE; PAINTING; POSTIMPRESSIONISM. R.Sh.

For further information on this person, see the section Biographies in the Bibliography in volume 28.

CGS SYSTEM, also centimeter-gram-second system (usually written "cgs system"), a metric system based on the centimeter (c) for length, the gram (g) for mass, and the second (s) for time. It is derived from the meter-kilogram-second (or mks) system but uses certain special designations such as the dyne (for force) and the erg (for energy). It has generally been employed where small quantities are encountered, as in physics and chemistry.

See also INTERNATIONAL SYSTEM OF UNITS; METRIC SYSTEM; WEIGHTS AND MEASURES.

CHABRIER, (Alexis) Emmanuel (1841-94), French composer, born in Ambert, Puy-de-Dôme. Largely self-educated as a musician, Chabrier was for 18 years a civil servant in the French government before retiring to devote himself to musical composition. His works are characterized by rich color, vivacity, humor, and strongly marked rhythm. Among his compositions are the operas *Gwendoline* (1886) and *Le roi malgré lui* (King in Spite of Himself, 1887) and the orchestral pieces *España* (1883) and *Joyeuse marche* (1888). He also composed choral works and music for piano and for voice and piano. Chabrier's style and unconventional harmonies influenced such French composers as Maurice Ravel and Erik Satie.

CHACABUCO, BATTLE OF, first major battle of the Chilean War of Independence against Spain, fought on Feb. 12, 1817. Having spent two years organizing the invasion of Chile from neighboring Argentina, in January 1817 José de San Martín led his Army of the Andes (some 3500 men) across the forbidding 3660 m (12,000 ft) passes of the Andean Mountains separating the two countries. They were met by a royalist force of 1500 under Spanish command in the hills of Chacabuco at the entrance to the valley leading to the city of Santiago. An initial charge by San Martín's chief aide, Bernardo O'Higgins, was repulsed by the royalists, who then counterattacked. Eventually, however, San Martín's forces caused the royalists to withdraw with heavy losses. On the 14th San Martín captured Santiago.

CHA-CHA. *See* Popular and Social Dance.

CHACO. *See* Gran Chaco.

CHACO CULTURE NATIONAL HISTORICAL PARK, NW New Mexico, proclaimed a national monument in 1907, redesignated as a national historical park in 1980. The site is distinguished by the archaeological remains of the Anasazi Indian culture (AD 900–1275). Thirteen major ruins and more than 300 smaller sites, among the finest ancient structures in the U.S., are found here. Two important features of these ruins are the extensive irrigation system and the road network, some of it still visible.

The largest and best-preserved site is Pueblo Bonito, the ruins of a 10th-century, five-story building estimated to have contained 800 rooms with more than 30 kivas, or ceremonial chambers (bowl-shaped depressions hollowed out of the earth and covered with conical roofs of wood and adobe). An extended drought forced the abandonment of Chaco Canyon in the late 13th century. Area, 137.5 sq km (53.1 sq mi).

CHACONNE, a dance and a musical form, both in slow triple meter. The dance emerged about 1600 in Latin America and Spain as a humorous, risqué solo or couple dance. By the 1700s it had become a solemn figure dance for a double line of couples and was popular at the French court. Some writers define the musical form as variations on a ground bass, or constantly repeated bass phrase; others define it as continuous variations on a series of harmonies. The term *passacaglia* (q.v.) was also used for similar pieces; the distinction is ambiguous. French composers such as François Couperin used the term *chaconne en rondeau* for harpsichord pieces that are in the form A B A C A D . . . A.

CHACO WAR (1932–35), conflict between Bolivia and Paraguay over the Chaco, a sparsely populated region to which both countries laid claim. Beginning in 1906, Bolivia began constructing small forts in the Chaco, inching progressively farther into what Paraguay considered its territory. Paraguay then countered with its own forts and in the 1920s encouraged settlements in the area by Canadian Mennonites to bolster its claims.

Full-scale warfare broke out in 1932. The larger and better-trained Bolivian army initially held the advantage, but the Bolivians, used to a mountain climate, found it difficult to operate in the hot and humid conditions of the Chaco lowlands. Superior tactics and knowledge of the terrain, combined with fierce fighting, enabled the Paraguayans to gain control of most of the area by 1935. A truce was agreed upon and a final treaty was signed in 1938, giving Paraguay three-fourths of the region and Bolivia the rest. About 50,000 Bolivians and 35,000 Paraguayans died in the war.

CHAD, LAKE, lake, central Africa, at the junction of Chad, Cameroon, Nigeria, and Niger, about 250 m (about 820 ft) above sea level. Lake Chad is fed principally by the Shari (Chari) and Logone rivers. Although the lake has no visible outlet, it is steadily decreasing in size because of evaporation and underground seepage. In the rainy season the area of the lake is as great as 25,900 sq km (10,000 sq mi), but in the dry season it shrinks to as little as 10,360 sq km (4000 sq mi). In open water the depth of the lake varies from about 1 m (about 3 ft) in the NW to more than 6 m (20 ft) in the S. The numerous islands lying along the E shore of the lake are inhabited. The first Europeans to visit the lake were a party of British explorers in 1823.

CHAD, REPUBLIC OF, republic in N central Africa. Chad is bounded on the N by Libya; on the E by Sudan; on the S by the Central African Republic; and on the W by Cameroon, Nigeria, and Niger. The landlocked country has an area of 1,284,000 sq km (495,755 sq mi).

LAND AND RESOURCES

Chad's terrain is dominated by the low-lying Lake Chad Basin (elevation about 250 m/820 ft), which rises gradually to mountains and plateaus on the N, E, and S. In the E heights of more than 910 m (more than 3000 ft) are attained in the Ennedi and Wadai plateaus. The greatest elevations are reached in the Tibesti Massif in the N, with a maximum height of 3415 m (11,204 ft) at Emi Koussi. The N half of the republic lies in the Sahara. The only important rivers, the Logone and Shari (Chari), are located in the SW and flow into Lake Chad. The lake doubles in size during the rainy season.

Climate. The N portion of Chad is hot and arid. The central section has three seasons: hot from March to July; rainy from July to October, with rainfall averaging from about 250 to 750 mm (about 10 to 30 in); and cool during the remaining months. The S section has similar seasons but receives about 1145 mm (about 45 in) of rain in the same four months.

Natural Resources. Although only about 3% of Chad's land is under cultivation, the agricultural resources are of primary importance. Indigenous crops, as well as those recently introduced, yield important food products. Extensive fish resources in Lake Chad and the Shari R. are also of vital importance. Natron (sodium carbonate) is

Using a primitive hoe, a Buduma woman prepares the soil for planting. The Buduma cultivate corn, okra, beans, and other crops. Jacques Jangoux

mined. Deposits of petroleum near Lake Chad and uranium in the N have been discovered but remain unexploited.

POPULATION

The population of Chad consists of numerous ethnic groups. Arab peoples are important in the N and E, and black-African peoples dominate in the S.

Population Characteristics. The population may be divided into two main groups: a Muslim population in the N and E portions of the country and the non-Muslims of black-African origin in the S regions. The Muslim population includes both nomadic Arabs and sedentary non-Arab peoples. The largest group among the non-Muslims is the Sara tribe. Chad culture draws most heavily on the ethnic heritage of its black peoples, but Islamic and French influences are much in evidence. The population (1986 est.) of Chad was 5,139,000. The overall population density was about 4 per sq km (about 10 per sq mi). About 75% of the people live in rural areas. Most of the population is concentrated in the S.

Political Divisions and Principal Cities. Chad is divided into 14 prefectures. N'Djamena (formerly Fort-Lamy), with a population (1986 est.) of 511,700, is the capital and largest city. Other cities, with estimated populations (1986), are Sarh, formerly Fort-Archambault (100,000), Moundou (90,000), and Abéché (71,000).

Language and Religion. The official language of Chad is French, but Arabic and numerous African languages are spoken. Chadic languages, especially Hausa, are spoken in the Lake Chad area. Muslims make up about 45% of the population. About 33% of the people are Christians. Traditional religions are adhered to by 23% of the population.

Education. In the early 1980s Chad had a literacy rate of about 18%. Yearly school attendance was estimated at 288,500 elementary and 43,000 secondary students. During this period about 800 schools existed, including the country's one university, the University of Chad (1971), which had about 1370 students.

ECONOMY

The economy of Chad is based largely on subsistance agriculture; more than 80% of the labor force is engaged in farming and animal husbandry. In the mid-1980s national budget figures showed revenues of about $56 million and expenditures of some $68 million.

The currency is the CFA franc, consisting of 100 centimes (302.8 CFA francs equal U.S.$1; 1987). In the mid-1980s yearly imports exceeded $128 million, and exports were about $110 million.

Fishing is a major occupation of the people who live on Lake Chad. The canoes, known as kadei *among the Buduma, are made of papyrus stalks. Paddles, like the one lying across the forward part of this boat, are used to propel the craft on the lake; poling is more common in shallower waters. Commonest in the catch of this fisherman, who is shown holding his net, is the tilapia, an excellent food fish.*
Jacques Jangoux

Agriculture. Cotton is the only important cash crop of Chad and accounts for more than 90% of all exports. Production in the early 1980s was about 40,000 metric tons of lint cotton annually. The rice crop is becoming increasingly important. Millet, potatoes, squash, beans, peanuts, and other vegetables are grown for local consumption. Livestock raising is important in the central region and in areas of the N. Livestock estimates in the mid-1980s were about 3.4 million head of cattle, 2.2 million sheep, 2 million goats, 421,000 camels, and 150,000 horses. About one-third of the land is used for grazing.
Industries. The processing of cotton and cottonseed oil and the manufacturing of peanut oil are major industries in Chad. Modern meat-packing plants have been established in N'Djamena and Sarh. The fishing industry furnishes fresh, dried, and smoked fish for domestic use and export. Natron is the only exploited mineral. Forestry is important in the S. The yearly output of electricity in the mid-1980s was about 65 million kwh.
Transportation and Communications. Of a road network of some 40,000 km (about 24,850 mi), less than 1% is paved. Chad has no railroads. The main airport at N'Djamena can accommodate large jets, and about 40 other airports accommodate smaller craft. The one radio station, in N'Djamena, is government owned and broadcasts programs in French, Arabic, and several African languages.

GOVERNMENT

A transitional government was established in Chad in 1979 following a period of civil war. Executive and legislative powers were vested in a council of ministers headed by a president. Political conditions in the country were very unsettled in the early and mid-1980s. Military aid from France helped stabilize the central government in the face of a Libyan-backed insurgency.

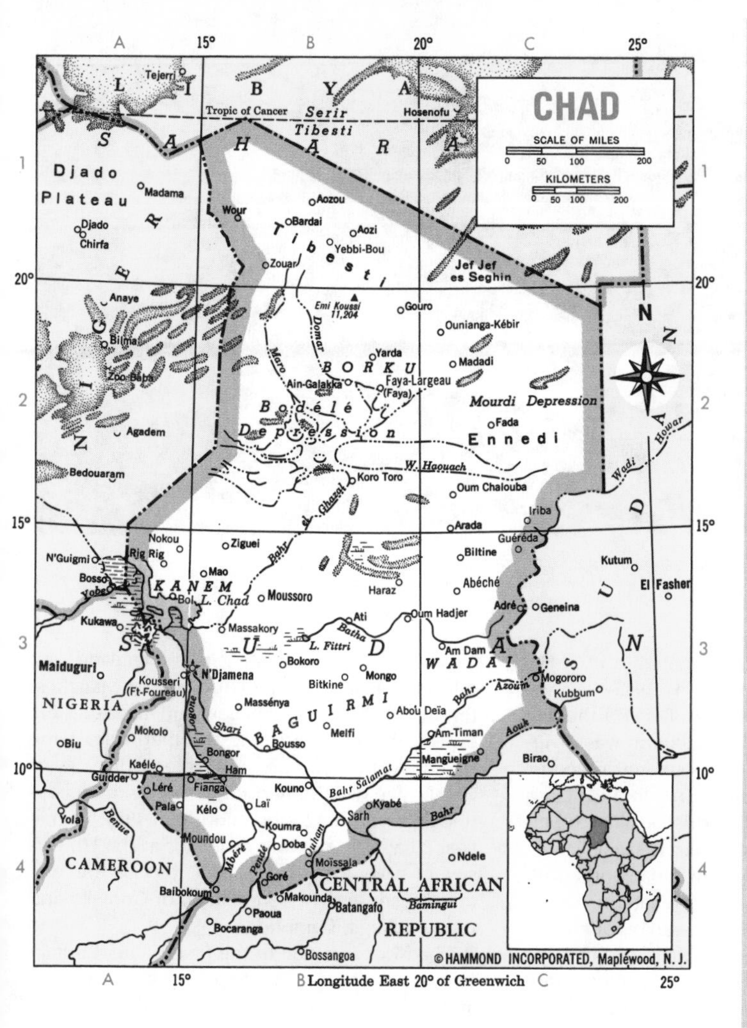

INDEX TO MAP OF CHAD

Cities and Towns

Name	Grid
Abéché	C 3
Abou Deïa	B 3
Adré	C 3
Am Timan	C 3
Ati	B 3
Baibokoum	B 4
Biltine	C 3
Bitkine	B 3
Bokoro	B 3
Bol	A 3
Bongor	B 3
Bousso	B 3
Doba	B 4
Faya-Largeau	B 2
Fianga	B 4
Kélo	B 4
Koumra	B 4
Kyabé	B 4
Laï	B 4
Léré	A 4
Mao	B 3
Massakory	B 3
Moïssala	B 4
Mongo	B 3
Moundou	B 4
Moussoro	B 3
N'Djamena (cap.)	B 3
Oum Hadjer	C 3
Pala	A 4
Sarh	B 4

Other Features

Name	Grid
Aouk, Bahr (river)	C 3
Azoum, Bahr (dry river)	C 3
Batha (river)	B 3
Chad (lake)	B 3
Emi Koussi (mt.)	B 2
Ennedi (plat.)	C 2
Fittri (lake)	B 3
Ghazal, Bahr el (dry river)	B 2
Kanem (reg.)	A 3
Logone (river)	B 3
Mbéré (river)	B 4
Ouham (river)	B 4
Pendé (river)	B 4
Sahara (desert)	B 1
Salamat, Bahr (river)	B 4
Shari (river)	B 3
Tibesti (mts.)	B 1
Wadai (reg.)	C 3

HISTORY

Cave paintings indicate that Chad was a fertile and populous country in ancient times. By the 9th century AD, the kingdom of Kanem was established in what is now western Chad, with its capital at Njimi, near Mao. Its rulers adopted Islam in the 11th century. Kanem was subjected to neighboring Bornu in the 16th century, and in the succeeding period the chief powers were the sultanates of Baguirmi and Wadai in the south. The export of slaves to North Africa was an important sector of the economy of these states. In the late 19th century the area was subdued by the Sudanese conqueror Rabah Zubayr (d. 1900), and it was taken over by the French on his death. In 1910 Chad became a part of the French Equatorial Federation, with headquarters in Brazzaville, Congo, about 2400 km (about 1500 mi) away. The change to colonial status resulted in little interference in the way of life of the indigenous peoples and little development beyond the establishment of cotton plantations in the south. In 1960 Chad, like its neighbors in the French community, became independent. Desperately poor, the governments of President François Tombalbaye (1918–75), a southerner, were supported by French aid. The dissatisfaction of northern Muslims first surfaced in 1963 and forced some changes in the Bantu-dominated one-party government. This, however, was not enough to satisfy them, and in 1969 Muslim guerrillas began to operate in the north. With support from neighboring Libya, their attacks escalated during the following years. Despite military aid from France, Tombalbaye's situation was made totally untenable by the drought of

N'Djamena, the capital of Chad, is at the confluence of the Shari and Logone rivers.
Michel Hunt–French Embassy Press & Information Division

the early 1970s. He was assassinated in 1975. His successor, Gen. Félix Malloum (1932–), was not able to end the civil strife. By 1979 the war had engulfed the south, Malloum was overthrown, and a northerner, Goukouni Oueddei (1944–), emerged as president. In 1980 Libya intervened to support Oueddei against rebels under former defense minister Hissène Habré (1943–), who was backed by Sudan and Egypt. After the Libyan forces withdrew late in 1981 at Oueddei's request, Habré renewed his offensive, and his troops captured N'Djamena, in June 1982. In 1983 the ousted Oueddei formed a rival government in the north. In the continued civil strife, Oueddei had the backing of Libyan troops, while France sent troops and supplies to aid Habré. H.A.G.

For further information on this topic, see the Bibliography in volume 28, sections 131, 1009, 1012.

CHADWICK, Florence (1918–), American swimmer, born in San Diego, Calif. On Aug. 8, 1950, she swam the English Channel from France to England in a record 13 hr 20 min. She swam from England to France on Sept. 11, 1951, in 16 hr 19 min, becoming the first woman to swim the channel in both directions. On Oct. 12, 1955, she swam from England to France in 13 hr 55 min, a world record for the southward crossing.

CHADWICK, Sir James (1891–1974), British physicist and Nobel laureate, who is best known for his discovery in 1932 of one of the fundamental particles of matter, the neutron, a discovery that led directly to nuclear fission and the atomic bomb. He was born in Manchester, England, and educated at the Victoria University of Manchester. In 1909 he met and began working under the British physicist Lord Ernest Rutherford. At the end of World War I he went to the University of Cambridge with Rutherford, with whom he continued a fruitful collaboration until 1935. In that year Chadwick became professor at the University of Liverpool. From 1948 to 1958 he was master, and from 1959 a fellow, of Gonville and Caius College, Cambridge.

Chadwick was one of the first in Great Britain to stress the possibility of the development of an atomic bomb and was the chief scientist associated with the British atomic bomb effort. He spent much of his time from 1943 to 1945 in the U.S., principally at the Los Alamos Scientific Laboratory at Los Alamos, N. Mex. A fellow of the Royal Society, Chadwick received the 1935 Nobel Prize in physics and was knighted in 1945.

CHAERONEA, ancient town of Boeotia, Greece, now named Chaironeia. It was the site of the disastrous defeat of the Athenians and Thebans by King Philip II of Macedonia and his son Alexander the Great in 338 BC. This defeat was a prelude to the Macedonian domination of Greece. A well-preserved Greek theater has been unearthed on the site, and a restored statue of a huge lion, which the Thebans erected to honor soldiers lost in the battle, also stands here. The Greek essayist and biographer Plutarch was a native of Chaeronea.

CHAETOGNATHA. *See* ARROWWORM.